This is the first biography of one of the wealthiest and most influential bishops of medieval Europe, who for a period of more than thirty years exercised a degree of power over the thirteenth-century Plantagenet court second only to that of the king.

The career of Peter des Roches and the activities of his fellow aliens – examined here in detail for the first time – are fundamental to an understanding of the process by which England and France developed as two separate kingdoms. As a politician, des Roches cast a shadow across the reigns of both John and Henry III. His biography encompasses the first detailed narrative yet attempted of English political history in the early 1230s and of the civil war of 1233–4: a period which, as the author argues, has been much misunderstood. In the process it sheds new light on such hotly debated issues as the role of aliens in English politics, the reception of Magna Carta, the loss of Normandy, and the constitutional and administrative developments of the reign of Henry III.

Cambridge Studies in Medieval Life and Thought

PETER DES ROCHES

Cambridge Studies in Medieval Life and Thought
Fourth Series

General Editor:

D. E. LUSCOMBE
Professor of Medieval History, University of Sheffield

Advisory Editors:

R. B. DOBSON
Professor of Medieval History, University of Cambridge, and Fellow of Christ's College

ROSAMOND MCKITTERICK
Reader in Early European History, University of Cambridge, and Fellow of Newnham College

The series Cambridge Studies in Medieval Life and Thought was inaugurated by G. G. Coulton in 1921. Professor D. E. Luscombe now acts as General Editor of the Fourth Series, with Professor R. B. Dobson and Dr Rosamond McKitterick as Advisory Editors. The series brings together outstanding work by medieval scholars over a wide range of human endeavour extending from political economy to the history of ideas.

For a list of titles in the series, see end of book.

PETER DES ROCHES

An alien in English politics, 1205–1238

NICHOLAS VINCENT
Canterbury, Christ Church College

CAMBRIDGE
UNIVERSITY PRESS

Published by the Press Syndicate of the University of Cambridge
The Pitt Building, Trumpington Street, Cambridge CB2 1RP
40 West 20th Street, New York, NY 10011–4211, USA
10 Stamford Road, Oakleigh, Melbourne 3166, Australia

First published 1996

Printed in Great Britain at the University Press, Cambridge

A catalogue record for this book is available from the British Library

Library of Congress cataloguing in publication data

Vincent, Nicholas.
Peter des Roches: an alien in English politics, 1205–1238 /
Nicholas Vincent.
p.   cm. – (Cambridge studies in medieval life and thought; 4th ser., 31)
Includes bibliographical references and index.
ISBN 0 521 55254 0
1. Des Roches, Peter, d. 1238.   2. Great Britain – History – Henry
III, 1216–1272 – Biography.   3. Catholic Church – England – Winchester –
Bishops – Biography.   4. Great Britain – Politics and
government – 1216–1272.   5. Great Britain – History – John, 1199–1216 –
Biography.   6. French – England – Winchester – Biography.   7. Poitou
(France) – Biography. I. Series.
DA228.D47V56 1996
942.03′4 – dc20   95–17649   CIP

ISBN 0 521 55254 0 hardback

For my parents

CONTENTS

Contents

Contents

MAPS

ACKNOWLEDGEMENTS

This study has been in the writing for the best part of ten years. In the beginning it was intended to deal only with the diocesan career of Peter des Roches. But my plans soon changed. St Paul saw the light on the road to Damascus. In my case, the setting was less exotic: a commuter train from Charing Cross, late at night, travelling home to my parents' house in Kent. It was then, for the first time, that I began to question what little I knew of des Roches' family and his supposed connection to Poitou. Since then, bishop Peter has lived with me on a more or less daily basis, for a year in Gstaad (an improbable setting for a cleric, though not perhaps for such a cleric as Peter des Roches), three years at Stonesfield Manor and more recently at Peterhouse.

At a comparatively late stage I became aware that I was not the first historian to attempt a biography of des Roches. James P. Barefield, in his unpublished doctoral thesis of 1967, provides a detailed survey of the bishop's administrative activities to 1216, indeed a far more detailed survey than anything attempted here. His is an excellent piece of work that by rights should have been published many years ago. However, given that he enjoyed only limited access to the French and to the manuscript sources, and given that the present study adopts a very different approach, I trust that Dr Barefield will forgive me for trespassing upon territory which he may continue to regard as his own.

For the rest, so many people have assisted me over the years that not all of them can be mentioned here by name. For whatever merit this study may possess I am obliged to my supervisor, John Maddicott, and my undergraduate tutor, Henry Mayr-Harting. They, together with David Carpenter, David Crouch, Barrie Dobson and Sir James Holt read the complete biography in typescript and provided invaluable encouragement, criticism and advice. Michael Clanchy read the chapters on the 1230s and persuaded me to make numerous changes. For help with particular problems and for commentary on individual chapters I am indebted to Paul Brand, Christopher Brooke, Fred

Acknowledgements

Cazel, Maurice Cowling, David Crook, William Davies, Taavi Davies, the Eastwood family, Peter Gallup, Diana Greenway, Sebastian Guinness, Michael Holmes, Clive Knowles, Simon Lloyd, Madame Laurent of the Bibliothèque Municipale at Tours, Roger Lovatt, Marcel M. Mille, Falko Neininger, Daniel Power, J. O. Prestwich, Nigel Ramsay, Sean Ramsden, Huw Ridgeway, Jane Sayers, Robert Stacey, Timothy Toulmin and Brian Wormald. Financial support was provided by the British Academy, the Leverhulme Foundation and more recently by the Master and Fellows of Peterhouse, who by electing me to a research fellowship rescued me from impending bankruptcy. Cambiz Alikhani and Jeremy Barnes extended unlimited hospitality in London, as did Robert Ferguson in Winchester and Robert Oresko, Nicholas Growse and Juliet Tyson in Paris. Jonathon Bayntun transported me to various unlikely destinations. My parents are most to be thanked. Little did they know where it would lead when they bought me my first books, the Ladybird stories of William the Conqueror and Richard the Lionheart.

December 1993

ABBREVIATIONS

Unless otherwise specified, all references are to unpublished manuscripts in the Public Record Office, London.

Acta	*English Episcopal Acta IX: Winchester 1205–1238*, ed. N. Vincent (Oxford 1994)
Acta Guala	*Acta of the Legate Guala 1216–1218*, ed. N. Vincent, Canterbury and York Society (forthcoming)
Acta Langton	*Acta Stephani Langton Cantuariensis Archiepiscopi AD 1207–1228*, ed. K. Major, Canterbury and York Society I (1950)
Add.	Additional
AM	*Annales Monastici*, ed. H. R. Luard, 5 vols., Rolls Series (London 1864–9)
BF	*Liber Feodorum. The Book of Fees commonly called Testa de Nevill*, 3 vols. (London 1920–31)
BIHR	*Bulletin of the Institute of Historical Research*
BL	British Library
Bodl.	Bodleian Library Oxford
Bouquet, *Recueil*	*Recueil des Historiens des Gaules et de la France*, ed. M. Bouquet and others, 24 vols. (Paris 1734–1904)
Cal. Chart. R.	*Calendar of the Charter Rolls*, 6 vols. (London 1903–27)
Cal. Inq. Misc.	*Calendar of Miscellaneous Inquisitions I: Henry III and Edward I* (London 1916)
CAR	*Cartae Antiquae Rolls*, ed. L. Landon and J. Conway Davies, 2 vols., Pipe Roll Society, new series xvii, xxxiii (1939–60)
Ch.	Charter
Cheney, *Innocent III*	C. R. Cheney, *Pope Innocent III and England* (Stuttgart 1976)

CIPM	*Calendar of Inquisitions Post Mortem*, 19 vols. (London 1904–92)
Cl.R.	*Close Rolls of the Reign of Henry III*, 14 vols. (London 1902–38)
Coggeshall	*Radulphi de Coggeshall Chronicon Anglicanum*, ed. J. Stevenson, Rolls Series (London 1875)
Cole, *Documents*	*Documents illustrative of English History in the Thirteenth and Fourteenth Centuries*, ed. H. Cole (London 1844)
CP	*The Complete Peerage*, ed. G. E. Cockayne, revised by V. Gibbs, H. E. Doubleday, Lord Howard de Walden and G. H. White, 12 vols. in 13 (London 1910–57)
CRR	*Curia Regis Rolls of the Reigns of Richard I, John and Henry III preserved in the Public Record Office*, 17 vols. (London 1922–90)
C & S	*Councils and Synods with other documents relating to the English Church II: 1205–1313*, ed. F. M. Powicke and C. R. Cheney, 2 vols. (Oxford 1964)
CUL	Cambridge University Library
DBM	*Documents of the Baronial Movement of Reform and Rebellion 1258–1267*, ed. R. F. Treharne and I. J. Sanders (Oxford 1973)
DD	*Diplomatic Documents preserved in the Public Record Office 1101–1272*, ed. P. Chaplais (London 1964)
EHR	*English Historical Review*
E. Rot. Fin.	*Excerpta e Rotulis Finium in Turri Londinensi Asservatis . . . AD 1216–72*, ed. C. Roberts, 2 vols. (London 1835–6)
f.	folio
Fasti	John Le Neve, *Fasti Ecclesiae Anglicanae 1066–1300*, rev. edn D. E. Greenway, 4 vols. (London 1968–)
Flores Hist.	*Flores Historiarum*, ed. H. R. Luard, 3 vols., Rolls Series (London 1890)
Foedera	*Foedera, Conventiones, Litterae et cujuscunque generis Acta Publica*, ed. T. Rymer, new edn vol. i part 1, ed. A. Clark and F. Holbrooke (London 1816)

Foreign Accounts	Roll of Divers accounts for the early years of the Reign of Henry III, ed. F. A. Cazel Jr, Pipe Roll Society, new series xliv (1982)
Hist. de Maréchal	L'Histoire de Guillaume le Maréchal, ed. P. Meyer, 3 vols., Société de l'Histoire de France (Paris 1891–1901)
Hist. des Ducs	Histoire des Ducs de Normandie et des Rois d'Angleterre, ed. F. Michel, Société de l'Histoire de France (Paris 1840)
HMC	Historical Manuscripts Commission
HMC Wells	Calendar of the Manuscripts of the Dean and Chapter of Wells Vol. I, Historical Manuscripts Commission (London 1907)
HRO	Winchester, Hampshire Record Office
Letters of Innocent III	The Letters of Pope Innocent III (1198–1216) concerning England and Wales, ed. C. R. Cheney and M. G. Cheney (Oxford 1967)
m.	membrane
Memoranda Rolls 1231–3	Memoranda Rolls 16–17 Henry III, ed. R. Allen Brown (London 1991)
MGHS	Monumenta Germaniae Historica: Scriptores
Migne, *PL*	Patrologiae cursus completus: series Latina, ed. J.-P. Migne, 221 vols. (Paris 1841–64)
Misae Roll 11 John	Misae Roll 11 John in Rotuli de Liberate ac de Misis et Praestitis, ed. T. Duffus Hardy (London 1844)
Misae Roll 14 John	Misae Roll 14 John in Documents illustrative of English History in the Thirteenth and Fourteenth Centuries, ed. H. Cole (London 1844)
ms(s).	manuscript(s)
Ms. 7DR	Winchester, Hampshire Record Office ms. Eccl.II 159271 (Pipe Roll of the Bishopric of Winchester for the year 7 Des Roches, Michaelmas 1211–12)
Ms. 9DR	Winchester, Hampshire Record Office ms. Eccl.II 159272 (Pipe Roll of the Bishopric of Winchester for the year 9 Des Roches, Michaelmas 1213–14)
Ms. 11DR	Winchester, Hampshire Record Office ms. Eccl.II 159273 (Pipe Roll of the Bishopric of

Winchester for the year 11 Des Roches, Michaelmas 1215–16)

Ms. 13DR   Winchester, Hampshire Record Office ms. Eccl.II 159274 (Pipe Roll of the Bishopric of Winchester for the year 13 Des Roches, Michaelmas 1217–18)

Ms. 14DR   Winchester, Hampshire Record Office ms. Eccl.II 159275 (Pipe Roll of the Bishopric of Winchester for the year 14 Des Roches, Michaelmas 1218–19)

Ms. 15DR   Winchester, Hampshire Record Office ms. Eccl.II 159276 (Pipe Roll of the Bishopric of Winchester for the year 15 Des Roches, Michaelmas 1219–20)

Ms. 16DR   Winchester, Hampshire Record Office ms. Eccl.II 159277 (Pipe Roll of the Bishopric of Winchester for the year 16 Des Roches, Michaelmas 1220–1)

Ms. 19DR   Winchester, Hampshire Record Office ms. Eccl.II 159278 (Pipe Roll of the Bishopric of Winchester for the year 19 Des Roches, Michaelmas 1223–4)

Ms. 20DR   Winchester, Hampshire Record Office ms. Eccl.II 159279 (Pipe Roll of the Bishopric of Winchester for the year 20 Des Roches, Michaelmas 1224–5)

Ms. 21DR   Winchester, Hampshire Record Office ms. Eccl.II 159280 (Pipe Roll of the Bishopric of Winchester for the year 21 Des Roches, Michaelmas 1225–6)

Ms. 22DR   Winchester, Hampshire Record Office ms. Eccl.II 159281 (Pipe Roll of the Bishopric of Winchester for the year 22 Des Roches, Michaelmas 1226–7)

Ms. 27DR   Winchester, Hampshire Record Office ms. Eccl.II 159282 (Pipe Roll of the Bishopric of Winchester for the year 27 Des Roches, Michaelmas 1231–2)

Ms. 28DR   Winchester, Hampshire Record Office ms. Eccl.II 159283 (Pipe Roll of the Bishopric of

	Winchester for the year 28 Des Roches, Michaelmas 1232–3)
Ms. 31DR	Winchester, Hampshire Record Office ms. Eccl.II 159284 (Pipe Roll of the Bishopric of Winchester for the year 31 Des Roches, Michaelmas 1235–6)
Ms. 32DR	Winchester, Hampshire Record Office ms. Eccl.II 159285 (Pipe Roll of the Bishopric of Winchester for the year 32 Des Roches, Michaelmas 1236–7)
MSAO	Mémoires de la Société des Antiquaires de l'Ouest
MSAT	Mémoires de la Société Archéologique de Touraine
Paris, CM	Matthaei Parisiensis, Monachi Sancti Albani, Chronica Majora, ed. H. R. Luard, 7 vols., Rolls Series (London 1872–83)
Paris, Hist. Ang. Min.	Matthaei Parisiensis Historia Anglorum, ed. F. Madden, 3 vols., Rolls Series (London 1866–9)
Pat. R.	Patent Rolls, 2 vols. (London 1901–3)
PBA	Proceedings of the British Academy
PR	Pipe Roll
PR4DR	The Pipe Roll of the Bishopric of Winchester 1208–9, ed. H. Hall (London 1903)
PR6DR	The Pipe Roll of the Bishopric of Winchester 1210–11, ed. N. R. Holt (Manchester 1964)
PRS	Pipe Roll Society
Prynne, Records	W. Prynne, The Third Tome of an Exact Chronological Vindication . . . of the Supreme Ecclesiastical Jurisdiction of our . . . English Kings (London 1668)
Reg. Antiq. Lincoln	The Registrum Antiquissimum of the Cathedral Church of Lincoln, ed. C. W. Foster and K. Major, 12 vols., Lincoln Record Society xxvii–xxix, xxxii, xxxiv, xli–xlii, xlvi, li, lxii, lxvii–lxviii (1931–73)
Reg. Greg. IX	Les Registres de Gregoire IX, ed. L. Auvray, 4 vols. (Paris 1896–1955)
Reg. Pontissara	Registrum Johannis de Pontissara, episcopi Wintoniensis, AD MCCLXXXII–MCCCIV, ed.

	C. Deedes, 2 vols., Canterbury and York Society xix, xxx (London 1915–24)
Reg. St Osmund	*The Register of St Osmund*, ed. W. H. Rich Jones, 2 vols., Rolls Series (London 1883–4)
RL	*Royal and other Historical Letters illustrative of the Reign of Henry III*, ed. W. W. Shirley, 2 vols., Rolls Series (London 1862–6)
RLC	*Rotuli Litterarum Clausarum in Turri Londinensi asservati*, ed. T. Duffus Hardy, 2 vols. (London 1833–4)
RLP	*Rotuli Litterarum Patentium in Turri Londinensi asservati*, ed. T. Duffus Hardy (London 1835)
RO	Record Office
Rot. Chart.	*Rotuli Chartarum in Turri Londinensi asservati*, ed. T. Duffus Hardy (London 1837)
Rot. Hugh Welles	*Rotuli Hugonis de Welles Episcopi Lincolniensis* AD *MCCIX–MCCXXXV*, ed. W. P. W. Phillimore and F. N. Davis, 3 vols., Canterbury and York Society i, iii, iv (London 1907–9)
Rot. Lib.	*Rotuli de Liberate ac de Misis et Praestitis*, ed. T. Duffus Hardy (London 1844)
Rot. Norm.	*Rotuli Normanniae in Turri Londinensi asservati*, ed. T. Duffus Hardy (London 1835)
Rot. Ob.	*Rotuli de Oblatis et Finibus in Turri Londinensi asservati*, ed. T. Duffus Hardy (London 1835)
RS	Rolls Series
SAHP	*Société des Archives Historiques de Poitou*
Tax. Eccl.	*Taxatio Ecclesiastica Angliae et Walliae, auctoritate Papae Nicholai IV, circa 1291*, ed. S. Ayscough and J. Caley (London 1802)
TRHS	*Transactions of the Royal Historical Society*
VCH	*Victoria History of the Counties of England*, ed. H. A. Doubleday and others (London 1900–)
Wendover, *Flores*	*Rogeri de Wendover Chronica sive Flores Historiarum*, ed. H. O. Coxe, 5 vols., English Historical Society (London 1841–4)

INTRODUCTION

This is a book about politics, power and national identity, as reflected in the life of one particular man. For a period of more than thirty years Peter des Roches exercised an influence over the politics of the Plantagenet court greater, arguably, than that of anyone else save King John. His influence will bear comparison to that of Robert Walpole over the Hanoverian court, or of cardinal Richelieu over the Bourbon kings of France. Amongst des Roches' contemporaries, only one other courtier, Hubert de Burgh, commanded the same magnitude of authority, and in Hubert's case, this was an authority restricted to a far narrower span of years.[1] Yet, whereas de Burgh has formed the subject of at least one full-scale study, and whereas many books have been written on the lives of King John and his son, King Henry III, there has to date been no attempt to present a detailed biography of Peter des Roches.

In part, this omission reflects the nature of the sources. Des Roches, so far as we know, was not commemorated by any contemporary biographer in the way that Thomas Becket inspired a host of writers, or William Marshal the epic *Histoire de Guillaume le Maréchal*. He was neither a saint, nor a scholar. Beyond a highly formal series of diocesan statutes, and a collection of one hundred or so charters issued in his capacity as bishop of Winchester, he left behind no corpus of writings – nothing to compare to the letter collections of politician bishops such as Arnulf of Lisieux and Gilbert Foliot, or to the literary output of the scholars Stephen Langton and Robert Grosseteste. As a result, des Roches' biographer is forced to adopt very different methods from those that have been employed so ably by the various modern writers on William Marshal, Langton or Grosseteste. Added to this, Peter des Roches was a Frenchman, whose family origins and whose circle of alien familiars play a crucial part in any assessment of his

---

[1] For a useful comparison between the careers of des Roches and de Burgh, see F. A. Cazel, 'Intertwined careers: Hubert de Burgh and Peter des Roches', *The Haskins Society Journal I*, ed. R. B. Patterson (Woodbridge 1989), pp. 173–81.

career. Historians of thirteenth-century England have been understandably reluctant to embark upon a study that necessitates almost as wide a reading in the sources from France as it does in those from England. For all of these reasons, the present study is the first to attempt a rounded portrait of bishop Peter, although it is not the very first to provide a detailed study of his administrative activities, an accolade that belongs to James P. Barefield and his survey of the bishop's career to 1216.[2]

In the absence of any contemporary biography, and without a collection of theological or literary works to serve as guide, we are forced to fall back upon the many thousands of references to des Roches, scattered across the writings of medieval chroniclers, the records of central and local government, and the charter collections of England and France. Here the source material is both massive in its extent and disappointingly narrow in its scope. It tells us a great deal about des Roches as landowner, financier and politician. Amongst the chroniclers, most report the suspicions entertained against the bishop and his associates as a result of their alien birth. By collecting the bishop's surviving letters and charters, we can go some way towards reconstructing his activities as diocesan and his role as a patron of the religious. The records of the royal exchequer and chancery, which survive in ever greater numbers after 1200, enable us to say a great deal about des Roches' administrative and political activities at court. Above all, the series of account rolls for the see of Winchester, the so-called Winchester pipe rolls, probably initiated by des Roches, provides a wealth of previously unexploited material, relating to the bishop's network of political associates and allies, the provisioning of his household, the names of his clerks, bailiffs and officials. Yet even here, the emphasis is chiefly upon the manorial economy, with only vague hints as to the destination of the enormous sums released in cash each year to the bishop's exchequer.[3] Of the more human side of Peter des Roches, we know very little. The bishop was a prolific founder of monasteries, and apparently a man of considerable artistic taste, the patron of scholars and poets. He commissioned the building of nearly a dozen abbeys, priories and hospitals. The Winchester pipe rolls reveal his love of luxury, his fondness for wine, spices, jewels and gold, and perhaps above all his devotion to hunting. The expenses of

[2] J. P. Barefield, 'The king's bishop: the career of Peter des Roches in the royal administration 1197–1216', unpublished Ph.D. thesis, Johns Hopkins University (Maryland 1967).

[3] N. Vincent, 'The origins of the Winchester Pipe Rolls', *Archives* 21 (1994), pp. 25–42.

hounds, hawks and huntsmen are a constant theme. During his years as bishop several new hunting parks were created on the episcopal estates. Des Roches himself is to be found in 1224, hunting wild pigs in the park at Taunton, and a decade later arranging for the importation of rabbits from Normandy, to stock a new warren.[4] The chronicle of Lanercost claims that he took more delight in the sufferings of wild animals than he did in the salvation of men's souls.[5]

Courtier bishops were expected to be men of imposing physical appearance. A shapely leg was certainly no disadvantage to the ambitious, whilst the squat, the lame and the downright ugly might find themselves passed over in their pursuit of a bishopric, precisely because of their lack of good looks. In des Roches' case, we know little of his outward appearance, save for a highly formalized image on his seal, and a tomb effigy, whose attribution is far from certain, showing a man who would have stood six feet tall from shoes to mitre, fat-cheeked, purse-lipped, long and broad of neck, perhaps rather corpulent and narrow-shouldered, with a peculiar fringe of beard shaved clean below the mouth.[6] Of his psychological make-up we know even less. Even the names of his father and mother remain obscure, whilst we can only guess at his date of birth, probably at some time in the 1160s or early 1170s. Just as a bishop was expected to be handsome, so in general he was required to possess the virtues of grace, elegance and good breeding, At court, wit and polished manners were valued at least as highly as a pious devotion to duty. In this respect, although blessed with great native intelligence, des Roches seems to have been considered something of a rough diamond. Contemporaries were swift to pounce upon his name, Peter des Roches, literally 'Stone of the Rocks' or 'Rocky Stones', to conjure up an image of the man as harsh and unyielding. To the monks of Winchester he is said to have been 'hard as rocks' (*durus ut rupes*), whilst in the 1230s, King Henry III was warned to beware of des Roches and so to steer between the rocks and the stones, the

---

[4] Mss. 19DR, m. 11; 32DR, m. 11d, and see *English Episcopal Acta IX: Winchester 1205–1238*, ed. N. Vincent (Oxford 1994), nos. 191, 251, 283, 322, 343.

[5] *Chronicon de Lanercost*, ed. J. Stevenson, Maitland Club (Edinburgh 1839), p. 23.

[6] For the effigy, see *Winchester Cathedral: Nine Hundred Years 1093–1993*, ed. J. Crook (Chichester 1993), pp. 102–3, 120n. For the seal, see *Acta*, pp. lx–lxi and plate iv. The roll of the justices in eyre for Hampshire in 1235 carries a very crude drawing of a mitred figure, presumably to be identified as Peter des Roches, next to the entry for the bishop's liberty on the Isle of Wight; JUST1/775, m. 21d. In general, for the qualities expected of courtier bishops, see C. S. Jaeger, 'The courtier bishop in "Vitae" from the tenth to the twelfth century', *Speculum* 58 (1983), pp. 291–325, esp. pp. 298–300.

petrae and the *rupes*.[7] More flatteringly, a poem commissioned by the bishop, before his departure for crusade in 1227, refers to Peter as the rock from which the walls of Jerusalem might be refashioned, whilst the canons of Titchfield, one of the houses founded by des Roches, could describe their establishment as being made 'on a firm rock', *super firmam petram*.[8] To some extent, Peter des Roches lived up to his name. Certainly, contemporaries portrayed him as one of the 'hard men' at the Plantagenet court. Roger of Wendover numbered him amongst the evil councillors, the *consiliarios iniquissimos*, of King John.[9] In some intentionally malicious accounts, he is credited with having fathered a son.[10] Several writers refer to his prowess as a soldier. As Matthew Paris puts it, in youth Peter was better versed in how to lay siege to a castle than in preaching the gospels. In contemporary satire, des Roches became 'the warrior of Winchester, up at the Exchequer, good at finance, slack at the Gospels'.[11] Even at the height of his triumph, at the battle of Lincoln in 1217, the chroniclers mingle respect for his military prowess with a suggestion that he was involved in the seamier professional side of army life: the command of the king's highly unrespectable crossbowmen.[12]

Not surprisingly, to a more recent generation of historians, des Roches has appeared to be a warrior and financier first and foremost, a bishop in little more than name. As one critic writes, 'To Winchester diocese belongs the discredit of having the only bishop who abetted the king in his evil ways, and who, as a foreigner, counselled John to resist the national will ... Bishop Peter's gross neglect of his spiritual obligations brought upon him, even in those lax days, not only the stern rebuke of his metropolitan, but a singularly severe censure from the Roman pontiff.'[13] From the seventeenth century onwards, historians have tended to judge him harshly.[14] To David Hume, the father of British political history, des Roches 'was

7   *AM*, i (Tewkesbury), p. 110; Paris, *CM*, iii, pp. 244–5.
8   *The Shorter Latin Poems of Master Henry of Avranches relating to England*, ed. J. Cox Russell and J. P. Heironimus, Medieval Academy of America Studies and Documents no. 1 (Cambridge, Mass. 1935), pp. 125–6; *Acta*, no. 67.
9   Paris, *CM*, ii, pp. 532–3.
10 For the probably unfounded allegation that Peter de Rivallis was des Roches' son, see below p. 293.
11 Below p. 57.
12 Below pp. 138–9.
13 J. C. Cox, writing in the *VCH Hampshire*, ii, p. 14.
14 See, for example, *A Short View of the long life and Raigne of Henry the Third, king of England presented to King James 1627*, rep. B. T. J. (Newcastle upon Tyne 1817), pp. 5–6, where Peter is presented as 'an ill man, but gracious with the King ... corrupt and ambitious'.

no less distinguished by his arbitrary principles and violent conduct than by his courage and ability', a judgement echoed by Stubbs, for whom 'Bishop Peter was cunning as well as violent'.[15] And yet, as I have tried to demonstrate elsewhere, in an extended study of the bishop's episcopal administration, it would be wrong to dismiss des Roches as an out-and-out secularist, uninterested in matters spiritual or in the good government of his diocese.[16]

Des Roches' career as diocesan lies beyond the confines of this study, which is devoted to his life in politics. Nonetheless, in essence, he appears to have been a conscientious and extremely competent pastor. Prolonged absences from his diocese forced him to delegate the day-to-day running of the see to suffragan bishops drawn from the Celtic fringe, to the archdeacons, many of whom were des Roches' own kinsmen, and above all to an officer known as the bishop's official, a dignity introduced to the see of Winchester under des Roches, and filled in succession by at least four men, all of whom appear to have been scholars or canon lawyers of no mean ability. His household at Winchester contained a large number of men styling themselves *magister*, some of whom are well known from other sources, as authors, book collectors, scholars or patrons of the arts. As for the bishop himself, although in some respects he may have lagged behind the vanguard of ecclesiastical reform, it would be entirely wrong to regard him as a protector of the old abuses against an up-and-coming generation of enthusiastic promoters of reform. It is true that he may have been lax in his endowment of vicarages. There is no evidence that he conducted visitations of the monastic houses of his see, or that he laid any great stress upon the ordination of the parish clergy to the priesthood. Compared to bishops such as Richard Poer at Salisbury, or Alexander of Stainsby at Coventry, he was commissioned only rarely as a papal judge delegate. Nonetheless, the diocesan legislation that he issued for the see of Winchester contains many of the new measures then being implemented elsewhere in the English church. In several respects, such as the licensing of preachers, the employment of friars and other clergy to hear confessions, the prohibition of rowdy drinking contests, the restriction of business transacted on the Sabbath, it is possible to show that des Roches' legislation was not mere window-dressing, but achieved practical implementation.

---

[15] D. Hume, *The History of England from the Invasion of Julius Caesar to the Revolution in 1688*, new edn in 8 vols. (London 1778), ii, pp. 160–1; W. Stubbs, *The Constitutional History of England*, 3 vols. (Oxford 1873–8), ii, p. 48.

[16] See the introduction to *Acta*, *passim*.

Branded a secularist by his critics, des Roches and his chancery clerks appear to have gone out of their way to dispel this reputation, resorting to direct scriptural quotation in the bishop's charters in a way that may well be unique amongst the churchmen of his day. The *arengas*, or solemn preambles to his charters, rehearse whole passages of the gospels and the Epistles of St Paul, besides tags from writers such as St Jerome and St Gregory the Great, in what may well amount to a deliberate display of pious learning. Most striking of all, des Roches was a patron of the religious orders on a scale otherwise unprecedented at the courts of either King John or Henry III. In all, he founded, or assisted in the foundation of, nearly a dozen abbeys, priories, friaries and hospitals. His greatest enthusiasm appears to have been reserved for the orders of Prémontré and Cîteaux, for whom he established houses at Halesowen, Titchfield, Netley, and at La Clarté Dieu in France. However, he did not neglect the needs of the new urban communities, helping to establish hospitals at Portsmouth and Southwark, introducing the Dominican friars to Winchester, and assisting in the refoundation of yet another hospital, at Acre, during his time on crusade. He is to be ranked as one of the leading 'building-bishops' of his day. At Winchester, he not only continued the work on the cathedral Lady Chapel begun by his predecessor, but did much to foster the cult of the cathedral's Anglo-Saxon saints, Birinus, Swithun and Aethelwold.[17] There is an irony to this, since in popular legend des Roches has been presented as the very embodiment of alien, French influence at the English court. It is the nature of this alien influence and of the workings of the bishop's circle of alien familiars, that provides the present study with one of its two principal themes.

Beginning with the thirteenth century chroniclers, des Roches has been described, quite correctly, as the central figure amongst a group of aliens at the courts of King John and Henry III. Although, as we shall see, the chroniclers misrepresent the precise geographical origins of many of these 'aliens', including those of des Roches, they were undoubtedly right to point to the political significance of des Roches and his fellow Frenchmen. To the English chroniclers, and above all to the two great historians who wrote at St Albans Abbey, Roger of Wendover and Matthew Paris, the 'aliens' were by definition a baleful influence upon the court. The very word 'alien', literally 'a stranger', was invested with a whole series of pejorative meanings, derived in no

---

[17]   Below pp. 81, 244–7.

small part from the Vulgate translation of the Bible, and in particular from such books as Deuteronomy, Jeremiah and Maccabees, where 'alien' is a term associated with the worship of strange gods, and the subjection of the people of Israel to the yoke of foreign rule. Supported by the vast material resources of the see of Winchester, des Roches served as an important patron of aliens both at court and within his own episcopal establishment. His household functioned as a magnet, attracting Frenchmen, both laymen and clerks, from across the Channel. Such men were to have a decisive influence upon the course of English politics. In 1215, 1224, and again between 1232 and 1234, they were to be involved in major political crises in which 'the aliens' appear to have been opposed and ultimately defeated by the native English baronage. And yet, as I hope to demonstrate, the opposition to des Roches and his alien supporters represents more than an outburst of crude xenophobia. As Huw Ridgeway has observed, in writing of the alien courtiers of the 1240s and 1250s, contemporaries were capable of drawing sophisticated distinctions between the various non-English outsiders gathered together at the court of Henry III, between the natives of Savoy, Poitou, Gascony, Normandy and the other provinces of France. Various of these aliens were attacked with a crudely Francophobic rhetoric, but in reality such attacks took place within the context of subtle political rivalry at court, between the aliens themselves as much as between aliens and Englishmen.[18] As most historians now recognize, it would be entirely wrong to write of thirteenth-century England in the language of nineteenth-century nationalism. Between 1066 and 1204 England was governed as part of a cross-Channel, Anglo-French lordship. Thereafter, it was to take many years, arguably several centuries, for the patterns of this cross-Channel lordship to break down. It is one of the principal fascinations of des Roches' career, that it enables us to observe the opening stages of this collapse. Even by the time of des Roches' death in 1238, the situation was by no means resolved. England was not yet an insular nation state. There were many at court, above all the king himself, who continued to press for the reconquest of the lands lost to France in 1204 and for the greater consolidation of Plantagenet lordship over Gascony and Poitou. Such

[18] H. Ridgeway, 'King Henry III and the "aliens"', in *Thirteenth Century England II*, ed. P. R. Coss and S. D. Lloyd (Woodbridge 1988), pp. 81–92; 'Foreign favourites and Henry III's problems of patronage, 1247–1258', *EHR* 104 (1989), pp. 590–610; and see more recently, D. A. Carpenter, 'King Henry III's statute against aliens: July 1263', *EHR* 107 (1992), pp. 925–44.

reconquest and consolidation served, at least to begin with, as a guiding principle behind the style of government favoured by the alien, Peter des Roches.

Amongst modern historians, no one has written of these matters with greater sensitivity than Michael Clanchy. It is Clanchy's contention that under John and Henry III, a new style of 'Poitevin Government' came to be adopted at the Plantagenet court, replacing the 'Angevin Kingship' of Henry II, described in a classic study by J. E. A. Jolliffe. To Clanchy, it is Peter des Roches and his kinsman, Peter de Rivallis, who served as the principal protagonists of 'Poitevin Government' into the 1230s. The present study will suggest significant revisions to Clanchy's thesis, arguing for a far greater degree of continuity between the lordship of Henry II and that of Henry III. Neither des Roches nor de Rivallis was a Poitevin by birth. The aliens they sponsored at court were drawn from Normandy and Brittany, from Anjou, Maine and from their own native Touraine, the heartlands of the old Plantagenet dominion lost in 1204, not principally from Poitou. To this extent, I find it impossible to accept the argument that des Roches was the sponsor of a new style of 'Poitevin Government'. On the contrary, he was in many ways a reactionary who looked back to the heyday of twelfth-century Plantagenet lordship. Nonetheless, for all that a closer investigation may require amendments to the picture painted by Clanchy, the basic pattern that he traces remains unchanged. Amongst historians, he is one of the few to appreciate the full significance attached to France and the ideas of cross-Channel lordship by both John and Henry III. But for a desire to reconquer the lands lost in 1204, and but for the belief that such reconquest was feasible, indeed that it was all but inevitable, the course of English political history would have taken a very different direction. Had John not embarked upon his Poitevin expedition in 1214, or had Henry III not devoted vast financial resources to the support of alliances in Britanny and Poitou after 1230, it is improbable that the political crises of 1215 or of 1232–4 would ever have come into being. In this way, there might have been no Magna Carta, no civil war in 1215 or 1233, and none of the significant changes in English government brought about, at least in part, in reaction to the policies espoused by Peter des Roches.

This in turn carries us on to the second main preoccupation of this book: the role of des Roches in the government of England. Although we may be inadequately supplied with information about des Roches the man, des Roches the king's minister is to be found at work wherever we turn in the Chancery and Exchequer records between 1200 and 1238. As a baron of the Exchequer, as a leading figure within the *camera regis*, as *de facto* chancellor in 1213, Justiciar and regent in 1214–15, guardian of the infant Henry III after 1216, and as *eminence grise* behind the regime that held power between 1232 and 1234, his influence is stamped across a very broad canvas. Clearly he was a skilful financier, administrator and diplomat. But competence alone would not have sufficed to keep him in power. Above all else, he was a courtier of genius, working amongst the intrigues and suspicions that attend royal courts at all times in history, capable of securing and maintaining the confidence of the king. When outsiders required admittance to royal favour, when difficult decisions had to be made, when the king required counsel, it was des Roches who was called upon to act as mediator, hatchet-man or adviser. To this extent, the biographer's task is made all the more difficult, since often it is impossible to distinguish the decisions that were made by des Roches alone, or the policies that he himself espoused, from those decisions and policies in which he merely reflected the temper and interests of the king. Government was not the work of faceless bureaucrats or administrative departments, but an expression of the king's own will. No courtier was autonomous, not even such an influential courtier as des Roches. All served the king. All, to a greater or lesser extent, were dependent upon royal favour. No one was invulnerable from intrigue or the loss of the king's support.

From his first appearance at court through to 1216, des Roches functioned as one of the closest advisers, indeed to all intents and purposes as one of the closest friends of King John. So far as we can establish, he enthusiastically endorsed the king's style of government, even to the extent of remaining at court, at the risk of ecclesiastical censure, throughout the five years of papal Interdict, when virtually every other bishop went into exile abroad. As a royal counsellor, he must take at least some of the responsibility for the harshness of John's government, for the stringent levying of taxes and scutages, for the exploitation of the English Jewry and the estates of exiled churchmen, for the denial and sale of justice. As Justiciar and regent during the king's expedition to Poitou in 1214, he was to be blamed for much of the rancour that invaded relations between John and the English baronage. Thereafter, he appears to have done his best to ensure that the settlement agreed at Runnymede, embodied in Magna Carta, was stifled at birth. It would seem that in his appreciation of royal power, he looked back to the halcyon days before 1215, when the king's will, the royal *vis* and *voluntas*, held absolute sway. This is all the more significant given that it was to des Roches that John entrusted the upbringing of the future King Henry III. Henry appears to have been in the bishop's care from at least 1212, from the age of only five or six. His education remained the bishop's charge even after John's death, so that from 1216 until at least 1221, it was des Roches who enjoyed day-to-day custody of the king and a correspondingly exalted place in the ruling minority council. The significance of this for the future development of the reign can hardly be exaggerated. Much of Henry's character; his affection for the memory of his father; his taste for luxury; his patronage of building and the arts; his piety; his attachment to the idea of reconquest in France; even perhaps his petulance and his exalted conception of the responsibilities and powers of kingship, may well have been moulded under instruction from des Roches. The bishop cast a very long shadow. Yet, meanwhile, his relations with the other members of the minority council had deteriorated to such an extent, undermined by his personal profiteering and by his support for a volatile and mistrusted group of fellow aliens, that in 1221 he was supplanted by the Englishman, Hubert de Burgh, as the king's personal guardian. Three years later, with the backing of the English bishops, de Burgh was able to eject des Roches and his fellow aliens from court.

For the first time in his career, des Roches found himself excluded from the king's inner counsels. Instead, he sought consolation in adventures overseas, participating in the crusade of the emperor Frederick II. Here, as during the Interdict of John's reign, he risked papal and ecclesiastical censure through his support for a secular ruler against the pope. Des Roches may well have looked upon the emperor Frederick as the very model of sovereignty; rich and powerful, determined to get his own way regardless of the cost, disdainful of the carping of critics in church or state, bolstered by a conception of kingship in which the king enjoyed absolute supremacy. Certainly, when the bishop returned to England in 1231 he was to be criticized for looking with too much longing upon the emperor's style of government.

Thus far, des Roches' biography can be written as but one aspect of a wider history whose basic pattern has been described elsewhere, most recently and most ably in the works of J. C. Holt on the reign of King John, and David Carpenter on the minority of Henry III. But at this point, for the years 1231–4, the biographer is forced to broaden his approach, painting in not only the figure of des Roches, but the wider background to the development of court politics. The years in question witnessed momentous events: the fall of Hubert de Burgh and the return of Peter des Roches to a leading place in government; a series of changes in financial administration; the pouring of vast sums of money into alliances with Brittany and Poitou; the rejection of many of the policies of de Burgh, over-turning the landed settlement put in place since 1224, in the process challenging the very basis of tenure by royal charter; and at the end of all this a civil war, as significant in its way as the better-known wars of 1215–17 and 1264–5. In 1234 des Roches was to be brought low by a coalition between the church and the English baronage, headed by the earl of Pembroke, Richard Marshal. And yet the bishop's regime of 1232–4 has never before been studied in any detail. Historians, including David Hume, Stubbs, and more recently Sir Maurice Powicke, have been content to rely upon the accounts provided by the chronicler Roger of Wendover. As a result, not even the basic chronology of the period has been established with any accuracy. Much misunderstanding has grown up around the nature of the financial experiments attempted by des Roches, and over the part played by aliens in the bishop's regime. Just as it would be inconceivable to write a biography of Peter des Roches that excluded his activities after 1231, in many ways the most crucial phase of his career, so it is impossible to attempt a history of the regime of 1232–4 without taking into account the bishop's previous experience in government. The policies that des Roches espoused after 1232 appear to represent a quite deliberate harking back to the reign of King John. For a brief few years, ended by the bishop's fall in 1234, King Henry III was to be accused of acting in much the same way that his father had acted before 1215, governing by arbitrary royal will, overturning royal charters, denying many of the liberties guaranteed to his subjects by Magna Carta. Powicke entitled his chapter on these events 'Henry III's lesson in kingship'; an apt description, since it was through the failure of the regime of 1232–4, and through the concerted resistance from church and baronage that this regime inspired, that Henry was to be persuaded to adopt very different methods from those of his father for the next twenty years of his reign. Magna Carta had been issued as long ago as 1215, and Henry III came of age in the late 1220s, but it is arguable that not until 1234 and the removal of des Roches from power, did the full implications of the Charter become apparent. Not until then did the king take over the reins of government, previously held on his behalf by the veterans Hubert de Burgh and Peter des Roches, the one-time servants of his father.

For all of these reasons, the present study can be divided into two complimentary but distinct sections: a biography of Peter des Roches to 1231, concentrating upon the bishop's circle of alien patronage, his work as administrator, courtier and crusader; and a second section, providing a detailed treatment of the regime that held power between 1232 and 1234, with a brief coda carrying des Roches to his death in 1238. Given the nature of the material, such a division is unavoidable, though perhaps to be regretted. Between 1232 and 1234, des Roches himself becomes little more than a brooding presence in the wings, overshadowed by his circle of friends and associates and by the personalities who opposed him, most notably by Richard Marshal. Contemporaries agreed that it was des Roches who after 1232 controlled the course of English politics. From 1233 hardly a single royal charter was issued that he did not witness. The king was very rarely out of his sight, and yet in writing of these events we are faced more than ever with the difficulty of distinguishing between the initiatives sponsored by des Roches himself, and those that were the responsibility of the king. It was Henry III who ordered the seizure of estates, who repudiated various of his own charters, who promoted and deposed officials. Albeit that the king might never have acted in this way but for the advice and guidance of des Roches, it was nonetheless Henry who ruled. To this extent, the biography of des Roches becomes only one aspect of a history of the king and his court.

Various suggestions have been made as to how this treatment might be altered. J. C. Holt, for example, suggested that I play down the role of des Roches after 1231, John Maddicott that I lend it even greater emphasis. Michael Clanchy suggested that I should write two separate books, on Peter des Roches, and on court politics in the 1230s. To Clanchy my portrait of King Henry III appears inconsistent, at one and the same time crediting him with a taste for greater personal authority, and yet allowing for his subservience to the policies urged on him by des Roches. Here I must beg to disagree. As Henry was to demonstrate time and time again after 1234, a high conception of his own personal dignity and power could go hand in hand with subservience on a day-to-day basis to whichever group of courtiers succeeded in persuading the king of its competence to govern in his name. Henry was to become notorious for the way in which he veered between the advice offered by various leading ministers; before 1234 by des Roches and Hubert de Burgh; later by such men as Richard of Cornwall, Thomas of Savoy, William de Raleigh, Simon de Montfort and William de Valence. In every case, Henry patronized and depended upon the advice of a chief minister, only to reject him at a later stage amidst acrimony and mutual recriminations. Dependence and petulance, government on the advice of others, and the exercise of the royal will, go hand in hand throughout the reign. In my treatment of the relations between Henry and des Roches, only David Carpenter expressed himself entirely satisfied with the balance that I strike. To him, as to all the others who have offered comment, particularly Michael Clanchy, I am indebted for many corrections in point of detail and emphasis. The responsibility for dividing the present study as I have done, remains entirely my own. The shoddy workman blames his tools, and the shoddy historian his sources. The sources for the life of Peter des Roches are richer than those for most twelfth-century kings, and yet I would suggest that they leave the biographer no choice but to attempt a detailed narrative of the events of 1232–4, without entirely resolving the question of who governed England during those years, des Roches or the king.

In this way, the present study is based around two chief preoccupations: the question of alien influence at the Plantagenet court, and the question of government and lordship, placing particular emphasis upon the events of the early 1230s. Perhaps, given the lack of more personal detail, any biography of des Roches is bound to degenerate into a mere 'life and times'. And yet, by the end, I hope to achieve something considerably more than a combination of narrative and life story. By examining the career of Peter des Roches, I believe that it is possible to obtain a far clearer understanding of why the breach that occurred in 1204 between England and the Plantagenet lands in France was never healed. At the same time, it may become easier to comprehend the significance of many of the changes brought about in royal government after 1215. Above all, I hope that an entire group of courtiers – not just des Roches, but all the many aliens who accompanied him into exile after 1204 – may at long last receive the attention that they so richly deserve. To date, historians have looked at des Roches and the aliens through the distorting lenses fashioned in the 1230s by the chroniclers, Roger of Wendover and Matthew Paris. The time has come to dust off the telescope and to take a closer look.

Chapter 1

AN ALIEN ABROAD

Peter des Roches was a Frenchman. Amidst the many accounts of his career one question looms larger than any other. From his first appearance in England under King John until his death in 1238, he was to be dogged by outcry against 'the aliens'. In 1214, it was said that his patronage and importation of aliens caused uproar and spurred on rebellion amongst the native English baronage. In 1221, he was accused of plotting together with his fellow aliens to deliver England into the hands of the French king Philip Augustus. Three years later, in 1224, he was removed from office amidst a concerted upsurge of anti-alien rhetoric. Finally, in the 1230s, his political rehabilitation was to be followed, according to the chroniclers, by the virtual subjection of England to the natives of Poitou; as one recent commentator puts it, part of a movement at the courts of King John and Henry III away from Angevin to Poitevin kingship, 'widen[ing] the circle at court to include the king's vassals south of the Loire'.[1] In 1234, this so-called Poitevin government was to collapse amidst native outcry against 'the aliens'.

In all of this, one assumption has remained constant and unchallenged; that des Roches was a Poitevin, a native of Poitou, sprung from a region of France south of the river Loire; a province annexed to the Angevin dominion by Henry II's marriage to Eleanor of Aquitaine, remaining under Plantagenet control, albeit a limited degree of control, until its conquest by the Capetians in the 1220s.[2] In terms of modern scholarship, the tradition that des Roches was a Poitevin goes back at least as far as the seventeenth century.[3] A

[1]   M. T. Clanchy, *England and its Rulers 1066–1272; Foreign Lordship and National Identity* (Oxford 1983), pp. 181–5, 219.
[2]   The one dissenter from the theory that des Roches was a Poitevin is J. P. Barefield, 'The king's bishop: the career of Peter des Roches in the royal administration 1197–1216', Ph.D. thesis, Johns Hopkins University (Maryland 1967), pp. 1–2, 232–4, who pre-empts several of the findings outlined below.
[3]   F. Godwin, *De Praesulibus Angliae Commentarius* (London 1616), p. 274, derived from Matthew Paris.

statement to this effect in Wright's edition of *Political Songs* (1839) fired the enthusiasm of Monsieur Lecointre-Dupont, a local Poitevin historian, who saw in des Roches a distinguished fellow countryman.[4] Lecointre-Dupont's short biography of 1868 has served as the basis of all subsequent accounts.[5] In turn it was taken as a starting point by Sir Maurice Powicke and by Kate Norgate.[6] Miss Norgate made the natural move of consulting a map, lighting upon the village of Roches-Prémarie-Andillé eight miles south of Poitiers, as des Roches' likely birthplace. Her only evidence here was the place-name Roches, and the fact that Roches-Prémarie boasted a fourteenth-century *donjon*.[7] But Poitou is a remarkably rugged province. Roches-Prémarie is one of perhaps two dozen Poitevin settlements which incorporate the name Roches and itself is an especially unpromising choice, controlled not as Miss Norgate supposed by a knightly dynasty but by the abbots of Montierneuf.[8]

Norgate deserves credit as the first commentator to attempt to pin down des Roches to a particular location in France. Like Wright and Lecointre-Dupont before her it was not without good reason that she looked to Poitou. There are statements in various of the chronicles that suggest Peter des Roches was a Poitevin, though not such categorical statements as at first sight they might appear. Neither Wendover nor the *Chronica Majora* of Matthew Paris states that des Roches was a Poitevin, although both associate him, during the 1230s, with the importation of Poitevins to England. The Margam

---

4 *The Political Songs of England, from the Reign of John to Edward II*, ed. J. T. Wright, Camden Society, 1st series vi (1839), p. 10; M. Lecointre-Dupont, 'Pierre des Roches, trésorier de Saint-Hilaire de Poitiers, évêque de Winchester', *Mémoires de la Société des Antiquaires de l'Ouest* (henceforth *MSAO*), series 1, xxxii pt. 1 (1868), pp. 3–16.

5 W. E. Rhodes, 'Peter des Roches', *Dictionary of National Biography*, ed. L. Stephen et al., reissued in 21 vols. (London 1908–9), xv, pp. 938–42 *sub* 'Peter'. The privately printed pamphlet by M. de Havilland, *Peter de Rupibus or Peter des Roches, Bishop of Winchester 1205–1238, Crusader and Benefactor* (Winchester 1936) relies almost exclusively on Rhodes. For other independent accounts of des Roches' career, see F. West, *The Justiciarship in England 1066–1232* (Cambridge 1966), pp. 178–211; E. Robo, *Mediaeval Farnham, Everyday Life in an Episcopal Manor* (Farnham 1935), pp. 70–82. Barefield, 'The king's bishop', provides an exhaustive investigation of des Roches' role in government to 1216. Montagu Burrows, *The Family of Brocas of Beaurepaire and Roche Court* (London 1886), pp. 107–10, 321–35, makes no investigation of the French sources, but traces the descent of des Roches' family in England, and prints a family tree (p. 323).

6 F. M. Powicke, *Henry III and the Lord Edward*, 2 vols. (Oxford 1947), i, pp. 75, 84–5, 123–4.

7 K. Norgate, *The Minority of Henry III* (London 1912), pp. 117–18, which in turn forms the basis of Clanchy's remarks, in *England and its Rulers*, pp. 183–4.

8 M. de Chergé, 'Mémoire historique sur l'abbaye de Montierneuf de Poitiers', *MSAO*, xi (1844), pp. 173, 192.

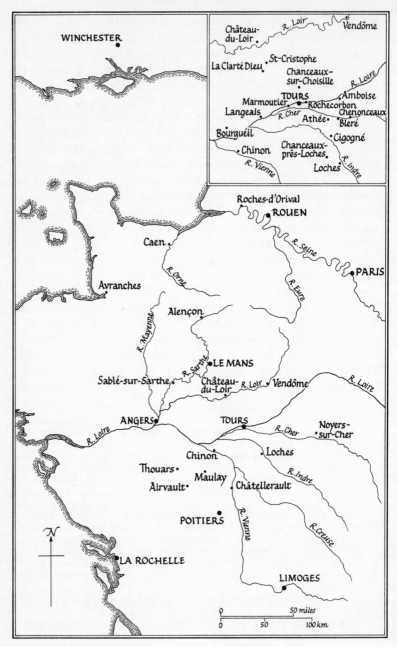

Map 1   North-western France and the Touraine

annals claim that he was archdeacon of Poitiers at the time of his election to Winchester in 1204; a claim which is unsubstantiated.[9] Wendover and Paris do state unequivocally that des Roches' kinsman Peter de Rivallis was *genere et natione Pictavensem*.[10] Only the later recension of Paris in the Westminster *Flores* describes des Roches himself as *natione Pictavensis*.[11]

Beyond the chronicles there is other evidence to link des Roches to Poitou, superficially overwhelming. Firstly and most significantly, between 1200 and 1205 he is credited with the title *thesaurius Pictavis* or *Pictavensis*, covering his office as treasurer of the collegiate church of St Hilaire at Poitiers, and perhaps too, a subsidiary role within the financial administration of Poitou.[12] Des Roches' kinsman Peter de Rivallis appears after 1230 with the title *capicerius Pictavis*, generally translated into English as treasurer of Poitou, in which office Powicke and others have suggested that he succeeded des Roches at St Hilaire.[13] In fact the *capicerius* was a subordinate official, independent of the treasurer.[14] *Capicerii* are to be found in several Poitevin churches, at least three in Poitiers alone.[15] There is no indication as to which of these churches de Rivallis was attached, but he certainly did not succeed des Roches as treasurer of St Hilaire.

There can be no doubt that des Roches enjoyed a lifelong connection with Poitou. He was involved in diplomatic initiatives to leading Poitevins.[16] As bishop of Winchester he was to employ several Poitevin clerks in his episcopal household, such as Walter de Montmorillon, whose services were shared between des Roches,

---

9 *AM*, i, p. 27, also found in Bodl. ms. Rawlinson B150 (Anonymous Brut), f. 47r. The succession of archdeacons at Poitiers is unclear between 1199 and 1216 when the office was held by a man named William; *Documents pour l'histoire de l'Eglise de St Hilaire de Poitiers*, ed. L. Rédet, 2 vols., *MSAO*, xiv, xix (Poitiers/Paris 1848, 1857), i, p. 216, and for William, see below pp. 115, 126–7 and nn. 68–9.

10 Paris, *CM*, iii, p. 220.

11 *Flores Hist.*, ii, p. 129.

12 See *Rot. Norm.*, p. 34 for his first recorded appearance with the title, 19 Dec. 1200. He still held the title after becoming elect of Winchester in Jan. 1205; *RLP*, p. 49. For the office itself, see M. de Longuemar, 'Essai historique sur l'église collégiale de Saint-Hilaire le Grand de Poitiers', *MSAO*, xxiii (Poitiers/Paris 1857), pp. 95, 327–37. For the possibility that there was an independent, royal treasury or exchequer for Poitou, see *Rot. Norm.*, p. 28; F. M. Powicke, *The Loss of Normandy 1189–1204*, 2nd edn (Manchester 1960), p. 31.

13 Powicke, *Henry III*, pp. 84–5, whence Clanchy, *England and its Rulers*, pp. 183–4.

14 de Longuemar, 'Essai historique', pp. 90, 135.

15 *Documents pour l'histoire de St Hilaire de Poitiers*, ed. Rédet, i, pp. 98, 122, 130, 156, 288. The title appears to have been known in England as in the name Agnes *filia Roberti capicerii* (*c*.1230); BL ms. Cotton Claudius B iii (York Minster cartulary), f. 13v.

16 Below pp. 66–7, 163–4.

King John and the Poitevin magnate Hugh de Lusignan; or Master John of Limoges, who witnesses several of the bishop's charters and served as des Roches' envoy to Rome.[17] In 1219 Hugh de Lusignan complained of the poaching of one of his clerks by the bishop's kinsman, Peter de Rivallis.[18]

But the fact that des Roches held office at Poitiers before 1204, and that he maintained contact with numerous Poitevins, no more makes him a Poitevin than his office as bishop of Winchester implies that he was a native of Hampshire. To take a local example, Richard of Ilchester, a Somerset man, served in the 1160s as both archdeacon and treasurer of Poitiers prior to his promotion to Winchester.[19] His contemporary John des Bellesmains, bishop of Poitiers, was likewise a native born Englishman.[20] As for the evidence of des Roches' Poitevin contacts, it is clear that the Poitevin contingent in his household was outnumbered by men from other parts of France. His activities as diplomat inevitably involved contact with Poitou, but in the same way they gave rise to contacts with the rest of France, with Rome, the Empire and even with Denmark and Hungary.

Turning from conjecture to hard fact, there is nothing to link des Roches to a particular place or a particular family in Poitou. In Poitou there are a multitude of locations named Roches, giving rise to various toponyms. However, with only a handful of exceptions, Peter des Roches and the kinsmen he brought with him to England appear with the family name *de Rupibus*, a form unknown in Poitou. The fact is that des Roches came not from Poitou but from the Touraine, a province of the old Plantagenet dominion lying north of the river Loire. There is evidence both circumstantial and specific to support this conclusion: first the circumstantial.

The English chroniclers tell us nothing of des Roches' family save for the fact that in his youth he had entered the service of King Richard, being better versed in how to lay siege to a castle than in preaching the gospel.[21] When he first appears at Richard's

---

[17]   For Montmorillon, see *RLC*, i, pp. 204b, 208b; SC1/1/127; Ms. 7DR, mm. 2d, 5d, 7, 8. For John of Limoges, see *Acta*, appendix 4 no. 33.

[18]   *DD*, nos. 128–9.

[19]   C. Duggan, 'Richard of Ilchester, royal servant and bishop', *TRHS*, 5th series 16 (1966), p. 2; *Radulfi de Diceto Opera Historica*, ed. W. Stubbs, 2 vols. (RS 1876), i, p. 319; de Longuemar, 'Essai historique', p. 330.

[20]   M. P. Boissonnade, 'Administrateurs laïques et ecclésiastiques Anglo-Normands en Poitou à l'époque d'Henri II Plantagenet (1152–1189)', *Bulletin de la Société des Antiquaires de l'Ouest*, 3rd series v (1922), pp. 170–84; *Fasti*, ed. Greenway, i, pp. 15, 69.

[21]   Wendover, *Flores*, iii, p. 181; iv, pp. 19, 327.

court in April 1197, it is at Tours not in Poitou, and thereafter his activities in royal service place him in the Touraine, Anjou, Maine and Normandy.[22] By June 1198 he is found witnessing as a member of the king's chamber.[23] Although never titular chamber clerk, he clearly enjoyed great *de facto* authority, witnessing and warranting a large number of royal writs. In 1200 he crossed with the new king's household to England, and was involved thereafter in a wide variety of royal schemes in northern France; the payment of crossbowmen at Les Andelys, negotiations of a truce on the Norman march, the custody of hostages and the payment of ransoms, pointing up the close association between the chamber and military operations.[24]

In 1200 he was appointed treasurer of St Hilaire, but for the rest, the rewards and promotions he received lay entirely outside Poitou. His earliest known preferment was as prior of the collegiate church of Loches in the Touraine.[25] In the following year he received the bailiwick of *Corneyus* in lieu of benefices worth 50 livres angevin, and a further 100 livres angevin in rents or benefices of the next vacancy in an unspecified church.[26] In May 1201 he was given custody of land in Anjou and in January 1203 the chapter of St Martin's Angers was instructed to elect him as dean, although his appointment may have

---

[22] *The Itinerary of King Richard I,* ed. L. Landon (PRS 1935), p. 117; *Lambeth Charters,* ed. D. Owen (London 1968), p. 127; *Rot. Norm.,* pp. 34–131 *passim; Rot. Lib.,* pp. 6–106 *passim; Rot. Chart.,* pp. 10b, 34, 57, 58, 86b, 109b; *Rot. Ob.,* pp. 108, 200, 204–5, 229; *RLC,* i, pp. 1–18 *passim; RLP,* pp. 1–48b *passim.*

[23] *Recueil de Documents concernant la commune et la ville de Poitiers,* ed. E. Audouin, *SAHP* xliv (1923), p. 44, calendared incorrectly by Landon, *The Itinerary of King Richard I,* p. 130.

[24] *Miscellaneous Records of the Norman Exchequer 1199–1204,* ed. S. R. Packard, Smith College Studies in History xii nos. 1–4 (Northampton Mass. 1926–7), p. 10; *Foedera,* p. 87; *Rot. Norm.,* pp. 47, 52, 55, 62, 65, 69, 87–9, 95; *RLP,* pp. 1b, 12, 22, 23; Powicke, *The Loss of Normandy,* p. 156n.; J. E. A. Jolliffe, 'The chamber and the castle treasures under King John', *Studies in Medieval History presented to F. M. Powicke,* ed. R. W. Hunt et al. (Oxford 1948), pp. 117–42.

[25] *Rot. Chart.,* p. 10b, which implies appointment prior to July 1199. An earlier prior of Loches, Thomas de Baccio, had played a prominent role in Plantagenet administration, serving as notary to count Geoffrey, and being credited in some accounts with a role in writing the *Gesta* of the counts of Anjou; *Recueil des Actes de Henri II,* ed. L. Delisle and E. Berger, 4 vols. (Paris 1909–27), i, p. 465; Paris, Bibliothèque Nationale ms. Touraine Anjou 12 part 1 ff. 233r–35v. Des Roches' absenteeism as prior and his demand for a share in the college's revenues which the canons considered excessive, resulted in a settlement of 1208, in which the respective rights of prior and canons were reassessed; Paris, Bibliothèque Nationale ms. Touraine-Anjou 12 part 1 f.235r no. 6150.

[26] *Rot. Chart.,* pp. 34, 57.

proved ineffective.[27] In February of the same year there was a further grant of land in Anjou.[28] Finally, in March 1203, he was entrusted with the revenues of the Abbey of St Martin's Troarn near Caen, during a vacancy.[29] By contrast he is found in Poitou on only two, or possibly three, occasions before 1205.[30]

For nearly twenty years the monks of La Couture at Le Mans were involved in a dispute over their English estates. In 1203 des Roches served as their proctor before the bishop of Lincoln, and the dispute was eventually settled in 1218 by des Roches' episcopal official and the prior of St Swithun's Winchester.[31] At some time before 1221, des Roches appears to have written to the pope in support of the neighbouring convent of St Pierre-de-la-Cour at Le Mans, and as late as 1232, he was appointed papal judge delegate over the English property of yet another Angevin convent, that of St Nicholas Angers.[32] Once again these contacts are all focussed upon the Plantagenet heartland, north of Poitou.

As to more definite evidence: in 1205 des Roches' bid for the see of Winchester was supported by letters to the pope from the archbishop of Tours, testifying to Peter's legitimate birth and orders.[33] A Poitevin would have looked not to Tours but to the metropolitan archbishop of Bordeaux. At the very end of his life, des Roches endowed a variety of obits, all to be celebrated in England save for a grant of 2 livres a year to the canons of the cathedral church of Tours.[34] His will also financed the foundation of two Cistercian houses: the first at Netley in Hampshire for which des Roches had already negotiated the purchase of land from the cathedral chapters of Le Mans, Angers, and from the monks of La Croix-St-Leufroy in Normandy. The second was to be established at La Clarté-Dieu in the Touraine.[35] For

---

[27]   *Rot. Lib.*, p. 11; *RLP*, p. 22b. On 15 Jan. des Roches warranted a royal writ ordering the seneschal of Normandy to give all the Norman land of the dean of Angers to Ernulf de Maudes; *Rot. Norm.*, p. 68.

[28]   *Rot. Norm.*, p. 77.

[29]   *RLP*, p. 27.

[30]   *Foedera*, p. 86; *RLP*, pp. 6, 7b, 12.

[31]   *Cartulaire des Abbayes de Saint-Pierre de la Couture et de Saint-Pierre de Solesmes*, ed. P. d'Albert Duc de Chaulnes (Le Mans 1881), pp. 144, 192–4.

[32]   *Acta* no. 121; BL ms. Add. 35296 (Spalding cartulary), ff. 13r–14r.

[33]   Migne, *PL*, ccxv, col. 672.

[34]   *Martyrologe Obituaire de l'Eglise Métropolitaine de Tours*, ed. J. J. Bourassé, *MSAT* xviii (1865), p. 44: 3 Ides June *Obiit Petrus, quondam episcopus Vintiniensis, qui dedit canonicis et clericis qui suo anniversario interfuerunt quadraginta solidos Turonenses annuatim.*

[35]   For Netley see C. A. F. Meekings, 'The early years of Netley Abbey', *Journal of Ecclesiastical History*, 30 (1979), pp. 1–37, reprinted in Meekings, *Studies in Thirteenth Century Justice and Administration* (London 1981), ch. xvii, esp. pp. 5–6; *Acta*, no. 25.

this latter foundation the bishop's executors passed on money to the abbots of L'Epau and Le Loroux. It has previously been regarded as mere accident that the resulting foundation should have been sited in the Touraine, twelve miles from the town of Château-du-Loir, centre of a major dynasty bearing the name *de Rupibus*, three miles from Bonlieu, a Cistercian monastery founded twenty years earlier by a member of this dynasty, and within the parish of St-Cristophe where the same *de Rupibus* family held land.[36]

Finally, and most telling of all, the poet Henry of Avranches, a member of the bishop's circle for many years, addressed the following lines to his patron in a poem des Roches had commissioned on the life of St Birinus:

Four men supply you (Peter des Roches) with a great protection; one of your native homeland, the other three of your episcopal office. Birinus, Swithun and Aethelwold provide Winchester with an example of the pontiff, St Martin gives such an example to the native (*alumnus*) of Tours.

Had the bishop been a Poitevin, as has previously been assumed, one must suppose him to have been thoroughly mystified by the lines just quoted.[37]

To return to the evidence of La Clarté Dieu: the *de Rupibus* dynasty amidst whose estates it was sited was the same dynasty which gave rise

[36] See Meekings, *Studies*, pp. 1–2; *Gallia Christiana in Provincias Ecclesiasticas distributa*, 16 vols. (Paris 1715–1865), xiv, pp. 327–31, printing evidences to be found in Paris, Bibliothèque Nationale ms. Latin 17129 (Gaignières transcripts), pp. 271–6; P. Robert, 'L'abbaye de La Clarté Dieu', *Bulletin trimestriel de la Société Archéologique de la Touraine*, 38 (1976), pp. 665–6; *Cartulaire de Château-du-Loir*, ed. E. Vallée, Archives Historiques du Maine vi (Le Mans 1905), pp. 83–4; F. de Maussabré, 'Genealogie historique', *Compte Rendu des Travaux de la Société du Département de l'Indre à Paris*, year 3 (Paris 1853–6), pp. 148–9; *Histoire Réligeuse de la Touraine*, ed. G.-R. Oury (Tours 1975), pp. 99–100. The earliest charters of La Clarté Dieu are today assembled as Tours, Archives Départementales de l'Indre-et-Loire H148. None of them, the earliest being dated October 1239, throws any direct light upon des Roches or his family, although in 1245 a *P. de Rupp'*, knight, sold the abbey all his rights in the *castellania* of St-Cristophe for 130 livres of the money of Tours. He might possibly be identified with Peter de Rupibus, kinsman of the bishop of Winchester, for whom see *Acta*, appendix 4, no. 44. A namesake held land at Langeais near Tours in 1247; Bouquet, *Recueil*, xxiv part 1, p. 208 no. 1371.

[37] *The Shorter Latin Poems of Master Henry of Avranches relating to England*, ed. J. Cox Russell and J. P. Heironimus, Medieval Academy of America studies and documents no. 1 (Cambridge, Mass. 1935), p. 25 lines 20–4: *Grande patrocinium prebent tibi quatuor, unus/ natalis patrie, tres pontificalis honoris./ Birinus, Suithinus, Adelwoldusque ducatum/ pontifici dant Wintonie, Martinus alumpno/ Turonie*, also printed in D. Townsend, 'The Vita Sancti Birini of Henry of Avranches (BHL 1364)', *Analecta Bollandiana*, cxii (1994), p. 317. Despite these lines, the editors of the poem continue to describe des Roches as a Poitevin; Russell and Heironimus, pp. 123–4, 129; Townsend, p. 336.

to William des Roches or *de Rupibus*, famous as seneschal of Anjou and the Touraine.[38] There is no satisfactory modern study of William des Roches.[39] The only detailed account of his career, published by Gaston Dubois between 1869 and 1873, missed many important details but is probably correct in suggesting that he was born *c.*1155 and that, despite an earlier marriage to a woman named Philippa, the turning point in his life came around 1190 with his second marriage to Margaret, heiress of Sablé in Maine. With the death of his father-in-law in 1196, this transformed William from a minor knight, holding land in Château-du-Loir, into one of the leading magnates in Maine and Anjou.[40] Dubois wrote his account before the publication of two chronicles which throw light on William's early years: the *Histoire de Guillaume le Maréchal*, which mentions him as one of those who loyally stood by Henry II during his last days at Le Mans, and the *Itinerarium Regis Ricardi*, which shows him to have been an active participant in the Third Crusade, conducting negotiations with Saladin in 1192, and being one of those permitted to enter Jerusalem that September.[41] William is best known for his changes of side after 1199, in which he first supported Arthur of Brittany, defected to John in 1201, but finally broke with the king when the latter refused to honour a promise to give him custody of Arthur. In the course of

---

[38] Various commentators have suggested that Peter and William were kinsmen, without mustering any evidence to that effect; West, *The Justiciarship*, p. 179; Burrows, *The Family of Brocas*, p. 108; S. Painter, *King John* (Baltimore 1949), p. 62.

[39] The best short account is by J. W. Baldwin, *The Government of Philip Augustus: Foundations of French Royal Power in the Middle Ages* (Berkeley 1986), pp. 233–7. G. Dubois, 'Recherches sur la vie de Guillaume des Roches', *Bibliothèque de l'Ecole des Chartes*, in 3 parts, vols. xxx (1869), pp. 378–424, xxxii (1871), pp. 88–146, and xxxiv (1873), pp. 503–41, covers the ground in exhaustive but by no means lucid detail. The *Cartulaire de Château-du-Loir*, ed. Vallée, contains a useful collection of documents on William's lands from a variety of sources, as does G. Menage, *Histoire de Sablé*, part 1 (Paris 1683), pp. 361–71, whose bk vii (pp. 191–211) comprises a genealogical note on des Roches. See also B. de Broussilon, *La Maison de Craon 1050–1480*, 2 vols. (Paris 1893), i, pp. 132–51.

[40] Dubois, 'Guillaume des Roches' (1869), i, pp. 378–87: his father-in-law, Robert de Sablé was grand master of the Temple and commanded part of the fleet on the Third Crusade.

[41] *Hist. de Maréchal*, ed. Meyer, lines 8817–18. William made a donation on behalf of Henry II and Richard I, *charissimorum dominorum meorum*, to the canons of Gâtines; *Cartulaire de Château-du-Loir*, ed. Vallée, pp. 86–7. For his activities on crusade, see *Chronicles and Memorials of the Reign of Richard I*, ed. W. Stubbs, 2 vols. (RS 1864–5), i, pp. 218, 432–4. He did not command one of the troops entering Jerusalem, as claimed by Landon, *Itinerary of Richard I*, p. 69, but by falling asleep on a mission to the Saracens very nearly brought about panic in the Christian army. In June 1193 he helped negotiate a truce between England and France; *Chronica Rogeri de Hovedene*, ed. W. Stubbs, 4 vols. (RS 1868–71), iii, pp. 217–20.

these activities, he made a considerable impact on the balance between Capetian and Angevin forces, and in the process consolidated his own position as hereditary seneschal of Anjou, a title first conferred on him by the hard-pressed Arthur in 1199, but subsequently confirmed by both Philip Augustus and John in their anxiety to win his support.[42]

Dubois made no attempt to trace the origins of William's family. A late source states that his parents were named Baldwin de Rupibus and Alice, daughter of the viscount of Châtellerault (dep. Vienne), and that William himself was born in Poitou.[43] His father and grandfather, Baldwin and Herbert de Rupibus, both held land at Château-du-Loir early in the twelfth century.[44] In all probability their family was an offshoot of the *de Rupibus* dynasty of Rochecorbon near Tours, with which they shared the same coat of arms, marked with a bar in the case of William des Roches, implying descent from a junior line.[45] Amongst the land held by William at Château-du-Loir was the wood of Bois-Corbon, presumably associated with Corbon, the founder of the *de Rupibus* lordship at Rochecorbon.[46] Corbon himself rose to prominence in the tenth century, and numbered amongst his descendants Hardouin de Rupibus, archbishop of Tours *c.*960–80, and Robert de Rupibus, governor of Amboise and a participant in the First Crusade.[47] Robert's marriage to the heiress of the lordship of

---

[42] See the awards by Arthur and Philip Augustus, *Catalogue des Actes de Philippe-Auguste*, ed. L. Delisle (Paris 1856), nos. 562, 752, 848–9, 859, and by John in *Rot. Chart.*, p. 72. In general, see Baldwin, *Government of Philip Augustus*, p. 234; Powicke, *The Loss of Normandy*, pp. 132–4, 138, 151–4, 285; W. L. Warren, *King John* (London 1961), pp. 53–4, 77–81; J. Boussard, *Le Comté d'Anjou sous Henri Plantagenêt et ses fils (1151–1204)* (Paris 1938), pp. 92ff.

[43] *Chronique de Parcé*, ed. H. de Berranger, Archives Départementales de la Sarthe Inventaires et Documents (Le Mans 1953), pp. 18–19. For the viscounts of Châtellerault, related to the great noble houses of Lusignan and Aquitaine and hence, via Eleanor of Aquitaine to the Plantagenet royal family, see S. Painter, 'The houses of Lusignan and Châtellerault, 1150–1250', *Speculum*, 30 (1955), pp. 374–84, rep. in Painter, *Feudalism and Liberty*, ed. F. A. Cazel (Baltimore 1961), pp. 73–89, esp. pp. 82–6, which incidentally demonstrates that Hugh, dean of St Hilaire Poitiers at the time Peter des Roches was treasurer, was himself a member of the comital family of Châtellerault.

[44] *Cartulaire de Château-du-Loir*, ed. Vallée, pp. 40–1, 43, 86.

[45] For the family, see F. de Maussabré, 'Genealogie historique', pp. 132–62, esp. pp. 157–8, a generally reliable account but without references. See also P. D. Abbott, *Provinces, Pays and Seigneuries of France* (Canberra 1981), p. 160, and the rather confused account by Menage, *Histoire de Sablé*, pp. 203–4, 261, 323–4. For the heraldic evidence see Maussabré, 'Genealogie historique', pp. 146–7, 157–8. Examples of William's seal and arms are reproduced by Broussilon, *La Maison de Craon*, i, pp. 136–8; *Cartulaire de la Couture*, ed. P. d'Albert, pp. 154–5.

[46] *Cartulaire de Château-du-Loir*, ed. Vallée, p. 87 no. 123, and Index *sub* Bois-Corbon.

[47] Maussabré, 'Genealogie historique', pp. 132–41.

Brenne led his son Robert II (d. after 1179), to assume the title *de Brenne*, which replaces *de Rupibus* as the family name from *c.*1160, by which time the *de Rupibus* line was already established separately at Château-du-Loir. Thus William des Roches originally sprang from a Tourangeau dynasty, and by his marriage to Margaret of Sablé acquired an extensive lordship further north in Maine.[48] His nephew Baldwin des Roches remained established at Château-du-Loir, where he was succeeded by a man named Geoffrey de Rupibus around the year 1215.[49]

William followed his cousins of Rochecorbon in patronizing a number of religious houses including Marmoutier where Hugh de Rupibus, brother of William de Brenne, lord of Rochecorbon, was abbot *c.*1210–27.[50] The appointment of William des Roches as hereditary seneschal of Anjou in 1199, and later as seneschal of Maine and Touraine, seems to have represented a recognition of the power that he had gained with his inheritance at Sablé rather than any dynastic claim to the seneschalship, not previously considered a hereditary office.[51] Nevertheless, the vice-regal authority he enjoyed between 1199 and his death in 1222 ensured that his two daughters obtained brilliant marriages: Clemencia was married to Thibault VI, count of Blois, and later to Geoffrey V de Châteaudun; Jeanne des Roches was married to Amaury I de Craon, whose heirs were later to

48 Maussabré, 'Genealogie historique', pp. 142–7. He also possessed rights in La Rochelle from the 1190s: *RLP*, pp. 6, 13b. Other branches of the de Rupibus family appear to have been established at Noyers in the eleventh century; *Cartulaire de l'abbaye de Noyers*, ed. C. Chevalier, *MSAT*, xxii (Tours 1872), pp. 270, 300, 313–14, 335, 430, 533, descended from Alexander de Rupibus, for whom see Maussabré, 'Genealogie historique', pp. 140–1.

49 *Cartulaire de Château-du-Loir*, ed. Vallée, pp. 79–80, 92–3, 95–7. Baldwin's father may have been the Geoffrey de Rupibus to whom Philip Augustus gave charge of the fortress of *Brandinellum* in 1202/3 (*Recueil de Chroniques de Touraine*, ed. A. Salmon (Tours 1854), p. 148), who witnessed a grant by William des Roches *c.*1208 (*Liber Controversiarum Sancti Vincentii Cenomannensis*, ed. A. Chédeville, Institut de Recherches Historiques de Rennes (Paris 1968), pp. 332–3 no. 321) and who was captured and ransomed by King John in 1203 along with Peter, a clerk of William des Roches, following the fall of Tours to the English; *RLP*, pp. 23, 24, 25. This may be the same Geoffrey de Rupibus on whose behalf Peter des Roches received arrears of wages in 1202; *Rot. Norm.*, p. 47. For the heir of Baldwin de Rupibus, named Geoffrey, see *Catalogue des Actes de Philippe-Auguste*, ed. Delisle, no. 1576; *Cartulaire de l'abbaye cardinale de la Trinité de Vendôme*, ed. C. Metais, Société Archéologique du Vendômois, 6 vols. in 5 (Paris/Chartres 1893–1904), ii, p. 38.

50 *Gallia Christiana*, xiv, pp. 211, 224; J. A. Meffre, 'Tablette chronologique de l'histoire de l'abbaye de Marmoutier', *MSAT* xvii, p. 567; Dubois, 'Guillaume des Roches', part 1, p. 380, part 2, p. 128.

51 Baldwin, *Government of Philip Augustus*, p. 234.

acquire the lordship of Rochecorbon, thereby eclipsing the dynasty from which William des Roches originally sprang.[52]

In the course of his career, William showed himself to be an enthusiastic patron of the religious orders, particularly of the Cistercians at La Boissière, Le Loroux (*Oratorium*), Fontaine-Daniel, Perseigne, St Mary Champagné and Bonlieu, where in 1219 he established a Cistercian nunnery, a few miles from his presumed birthplace at Château-du-Loir.[53] He also refounded the Premonstratensian house of Le Perray-Neuf, originally established by his father-in-law, Robert de Sablé.[54] A leading participant in the Third Crusade, and closely related to the family of Rochecorbon which included at least two members of the army which had captured Jerusalem in 1099, William went on to join the crusade against the Albigensians.[55] He died in 1222 and was buried at Bonlieu.[56]

Beyond the near certainty of their kinship it is impossible to determine the exact relation between William and Peter des Roches; they may have been brothers but more likely cousins or uncle and nephew. Peter's nephew Geoffrey des Roches, introduced to estates in Hampshire after 1224, used a similar device on his seal, a lion, to that borne by the de Brenne family of Rochecorbon, William's cousins.[57] Peter was to show himself an enthusiastic patron of the Cistercian and Premonstratensian orders most favoured by William, and like William he was to become an enthusiastic crusader, in 1229 being one of the first to enter Jerusalem since William's crusade of the 1190s.

There is an extraordinary irony to the fact that the leading ministers of John and Philip Augustus should have been close kin. In the train of William des Roches, Peter might have gone on to achieve high office under the Capetians. Hence perhaps the suspicion with which he was regarded by certain circles in England, particularly for a period

---

[52] See the authorities cited above and Menage, *Histoire de Sablé*, pp. 261, 323–4; Maussabré, 'Genealogie historique', pp. 154–7.

[53] The foundation charter of Bonlieu is printed by Menage, *Histoire de Sablé*, pp. 364–5. See also *Gallia Christiana*, xiv, pp. 518, 520, 530, 538–40; *Cartulaire de la Couture*, ed. d'Albert, p. 204; *Cartulaire de l'abbaye Cistercienne de Fontaine-Daniel*, ed. A. Grosse-Duperon and E. Gouvrion (Mayenne 1896), p. 76; *Cartulaire de Château-du-Loir*, ed. Vallée, pp. 5, 52, 79–80, 94.

[54] *Gallia Christiana*, xiv, p. 735; *Cartulaire de Château-du-Loir*, pp. 82–3.

[55] *Catalogue des Actes de Philippe-Auguste,* ed. Delisle, no. 1885.

[56] *Cartulaire de Château-du-Loir*, ed. Vallée, pp. 102–4; Menage, *Histoire de Sablé*, p. 366.

[57] *Acta*, appendix 4 no. 43. W. K. Ryland Bedford, *The Blazon of Episcopacy* (Oxford 1897), pp. 121, 125 gives Peter des Roches' arms as three roaches, clearly a fabrication based on the English homonym Roches/roach. However, the arms assigned there to William de Raleigh, des Roches' successor as bishop, a bend lozengy argent, are identical to those of William des Roches and the de Rupibus family of Rochecorbon.

during the minority of Henry III, when William des Roches was
forging dynastic alliances on behalf of the Capetians in Poitou.[58] His
family background points up the significance of Peter's decision in
1204 to join King John in exile. Peter was not a nobody with nothing
to lose, but a very real victim of the Plantagenet defeat.

Nonetheless, even if it be admitted that Peter des Roches was a
Tourangeau rather than a Poitevin, sprung from the same dynasty as
William des Roches, is this really to prove anything of significance?
Poitou and the Touraine lie only a finger's breadth apart on the map.
The various provinces of medieval France were not divided one from
another like modern nation states. The natives of Normandy, Anjou,
Poitou and the Touraine, all spoke the same French language, and
shared the same basic administrative structure imposed by the Plantagenets. Regional accents and variations in legal custom should not be
exalted to the status of some great divide, separating Normandy from
Anjou or Poitou from the Touraine. And yet, our discovery that des
Roches was a Tourangeau, rather than a Poitevin, is not without
significance. To begin with, it has fundamental implications for the
history of alien politics in England, indeed for the whole ingenious
idea recently canvassed that King John and Henry III should be
accounted the authors of a new style of 'Poitevin Kingship'.[59] If des
Roches, supposedly the chief representative of this new order, was
not himself a Poitevin, then who else amongst those aliens taken by
Powicke, Clanchy and others to be representative of Poitevin
influence in England actually sprang from Poitou?

To take three of the most prominent 'Poitevins': Peter de Maulay
was presumably a native of Maulay, between Loudun and Richelieu,
on the borders between Poitou and the Touraine, a region which
unlike the rest of Poitou effectively passed out of Plantagenet control
in 1204.[60] The Meaux chronicler states that he was *de partibus
Turonensibus et Pictavensibus*, a phrase which aptly describes the frontier

---

[58] Below p. 204.
[59] For the idea of Poitevin kingship, see Clanchy, *England and its Rulers*, pp. 181ff.
[60] *Hist. des Ducs*, p. 180 implies that de Maulay was of relatively humble birth. *Chronica
Monasterii de Melsa ab anno 1150 usque ad annum 1406*, ed. E. A. Bond, 3 vols. (RS
1866–8), i, pp. 105–6 states that after 1204 he relinquished his inheritance in France to a
younger brother named Aimery, who may conceivably be identified with namesakes
holding land at Quinçay in 1237 and 1259, and at La Rochelle in 1218; *Documents de
St Hilaire de Poitiers*, ed. Rédet, i, p. 243; *Cartulaire du Temple de La Rochelle (1139–1268)*,
ed. M. de Richmond, Archives Historiques de la Saintonge et de l'Aunis, i (1874),
p. 43 no. xv; Poitiers, Archives Départementales de la Vienne 1H16 liasse 12 no. 1, a
grant by Aimery de Maulay knight and Eustachia his wife to St Benoit de Quinçay,
1259.

region in which he was born.[61] Engelard de Cigogné, another of the supposed Poitevins, was self-evidently nothing of the sort but a native of Cigogné in the Touraine, part of a wider family network, all of them Tourangeaux, centred on King John's alien captain, Girard d'Athée, and including the clans of Chanceaux and Mark prohibited by name in Magna Carta clause 50.[62]

The third of the great 'Poitevins', des Roches' kinsman Peter de Rivallis, was undoubtedly an office-holder in Poitou and is described as a Poitevin by Matthew Paris. But office-holding is no sure indicator of birth. In his earliest appearances Peter bears the name *de Orivallis* or *Aurival*', dropped after *c*.1220 in favour of *de Rivallis*, rendered into English–French translation in the entirely nonsensical form 'des Rivaux', perhaps, bizarrely, by analogy with the Yorkshire abbey of Rievaulx (*Rievall*'). Orivallis and Rivallis are probably toponyms. There are several Poitevin place-names from which they might be derived, for example Orival or Airvault. At the same time, with no more than the place-name evidence to work from, it is tempting to look to Roches d'Orival (*Aurivall*') near Rouen in Normandy, an important seat of government under Richard I and John, suggesting that Peter was of Norman birth, fathered by one of Peter des Roches' various kinsmen known to have been active in Normandy in the late twelfth century.[63] For the rest he presumably shared des Roches' Tourangeau ancestry and descent.

There is no certain proof that any of the supposed great 'Poitevins' active in England during the 1220s and 1230s was actually a native of

---

61 *Chronica de Melsa*, ed. Bond, i, pp. 105–6.

62 For Girard d'Athée and his kin, see H. Lambron de Lignim, 'Girard d'Athée', *Touraine: Mélanges Historiques*, no. 2 (Tours 1855); A. Salmon, 'Nouveaux documents sur Girard d'Athée', *MSAT* xiii (1862), pp. 193–213; J. C. Holt, 'Philip Mark and the shrievalty of Nottinghamshire and Derbyshire in the early thirteenth century', *Transactions of the Thoroton Society of Nottinghamshire* lvi (1952), pp. 8–24; *Pleas of the Crown for the County of Gloucester*, ed. F. W. Maitland (London 1884), pp. xiii–xv. Holt's discussion of Philip Mark and his family background should be supplemented by the information that the family of Marques, knights holding land in Chenonceaux and Bléré near Athée, occurs frequently in local records of the thirteenth century. The earliest member of the family to be recorded may be the Robert Marques who in 1194 witnesses a grant by the lord of Amboise; Tours, Bibliothèque Municipale ms. 1324 (Transcripts for Fontaines-les-Blanches) nos. 32–3, 35. Thereafter the family made considerable grants of land to the priory of Montoussan, of the order of Grandmont. The family still held Chenonceaux in the fifteenth century; Tours, Archives Départementales de l'Indre-et-Loire mss. G48; G1066; H253; H373; H480; H513, and especially H710.

63 For example, the nephew captured at Caen in 1204, exchanged for a son of Richard de Fontenai, an important man in Norman affairs which suggests that des Roches' nephew was considered a valuable prisoner by the French; *RLP*, p. 45b. In general, see *Acta*, appendix 4 no. 41.

Poitou. Why then do the chroniclers dub them Poitevins? It is unlikely to have been through ignorance. Both Wendover and Matthew Paris were capable on occasion of distinguishing between the various provinces under Plantagenet lordship. It may have been through association; several of the men in question had seen service in Poitou. At the height of his influence in the 1230s, Peter de Rivallis was witness to a host of royal letters in which he was accorded his title as *capicerius* of Poitiers. There may also have been deliberate, abusive intent to the chroniclers' misattribution.

There is an analogy here in the popular use of the term Cahorsin, applied by Matthew Paris and others to cover all Christian usurers, not merely those native to Cahors.[64] By the 1230s Poitou and Poitevin had become bywords for duplicity and for the senseless waste of resources. The notorious Poitevin scutage of 1214, the expeditions to Poitou in 1206, 1214, 1225–7 and 1230, all had involved vast expense grudgingly borne, their failure ascribed to the disloyalty of the Poitevins themselves. Disloyalty was especially the attribute of the Lusignan counts of La Marche. From the murder of Patrick earl of Salisbury in the mid twelfth century, through to the collapse of Henry III's government in the 1260s, the Lusignans were the blight of Plantagenet policy abroad. It is no exaggeration to state that the terms Poitevin or Lusignan had become synonymous with everything that was untrustworthy, tainted, wasteful and bad. Small wonder, then, that the term 'Poitevin' should have been applied, abusively, to the likes of des Roches and those other aliens disapproved of by the English chroniclers.

Des Roches was a Tourangeau not a Poitevin. What implications does this have for his outlook and aspirations after 1204? What distinguished the natives of the Touraine from those of Poitou or from the Anglo-Norman baronage, many of whom shared des Roches' exile in England? The answer to these questions lies in the nature of the landed settlement of the Plantagenet dominions, both before and after 1204. To begin with Poitou: Poitou was not lost in 1204 but lingered on under Plantagenet influence for at least another twenty years. No irrevocable choice was demanded from the Poitevin baronage in 1204, between retaining their family lands and attachments in France or sacrificing them to join King John in exile. Indeed for the Poitevins, the loosening of Plantagenet control over northern

---

64 N. Denholm-Young, 'The merchants of Cahors', in Denholm-Young, *Collected Papers* (Cardiff 1969), pp. 290–7; R. W. Southern, *Robert Grosseteste: The Growth of an English Mind in Medieval Europe* (Oxford 1986), pp. 66–7 n. 7.

France brought distinct advantages. More than ever before, they were in a position to play off the Plantagenets against the Capetians and so to occupy the centre ground relatively free from foreign control.

If Poitevins were unpopular in England, then exactly the same could be said of the English, or more accurately of Plantagenet administration, in Poitou. Henry II had been known there as 'the king of the north'.[65] The English abbot of L'Etoile, subject to constant harassment by his Poitevin neighbours, lamented that they were using him to vent all their aggression towards the English: 'Oh, if only I'd not been born an Englishman, or that once exiled here, I never had to see another English face';[66] sentiments that chime all too well with those of many a latter-day expatriate. After 1204 the Poitevins became effectively their own masters. The regularity with which such magnates as the counts of La Marche or Thouars veered between half-hearted support for Philip Augustus and grudging allegiance to King John is testimony both to the eagerness with which they were courted by both sides, and to their own intelligence in appreciating that a victory for neither France nor the Plantagenets was nonetheless a victory for Poitou. What to the English seemed the appalling duplicity of the Lusignans, effectively sabotaging every attempt after 1204 to reconquer the lost Plantagenet domain, must from the standpoint of the Lusignans have seemed not so much duplicity as sound common sense.

By contrast, for a Tourangeau such as des Roches, or even for a man such as Peter de Maulay, sprung from lands which in 1204 effectively passed into Capetian control, the events of 1204 were nothing short of a catastrophe. Such men were called upon to chose between their careers in Plantagenet service, or their lands in France. By contrast to the tenurial links established after 1066 between England and Normandy, Henry II and his sons had made little attempt to bind their dominion together by the creation of cross-Channel Anglo-Angevin or Anglo-Tourangeau lordships. Many of the Normans who went into exile with King John already possessed estates in England and were accepted by their English peers with relative ease. Henceforth native resentment against 'the aliens' was not so much francophobic in character; rather, it was directed principally against those Angevin and Poitevin favourites for whom the Plantagenets were forced to establish wholly new landed settlements.

John received one major compensation for the loss of Normandy:

[65] Boissonnade, 'Administrateurs laïques', pp. 156–90.
[66] Migne, *PL*, cxciv, col. 1896.

the rich haul of *Terre Normannorum*, honours and estates in England
confiscated from those families which chose to remain behind in
Normandy, arguably the single greatest influx of land to the crown
between 1066 and the dissolution of the monasteries. Surprisingly
little has been written on this subject.[67] In general, as with the royal
demesne after 1066 or the monastic estates of the sixteenth century,
the bonanza of 1204 was to be swiftly dissipated, used to reward those
who had accompanied the king into exile. In the majority of cases
such rewards were reserved for the Normans themselves. Sometimes
this was done in such a way as to retain the confiscated English lands
in the hands of the same family which had previously controlled them
from Normandy. For example, Coleby, Lincs. and the English lands
of the barony of Graville, forfeited by William Malet as an adherent of
Philip Augustus, were granted to a kinsman and namesake who
remained loyal to King John. The English lands of the barony of
Orlande passed from their Norman holder to a kinsman by marriage,
Matthew fitz Herbert.[68] Similar patterns can be observed with parts of
the honours of Tillières, Tracy and Vieux-Pont.[69] Alternatively,
major Norman escheats in England were snatched up by families
bearing no immediate relation to the previous holders, but which had
nonetheless forfeited important estates in Normandy by adherence to
John. In this way the earls of Chester and Warenne suffered losses in
Normandy which to some extent were compensated by awards of
Terre Normannorum in England.[70]

It has been argued that the seizure of their English estates was
instrumental in persuading many Norman knights to abandon John
for Philip Augustus. Certainly, the fact that both John and Philip
insisted that Norman and Anglo-Norman landholders opt firmly,
either for England or France, made the rupture of 1204 all the more
difficult to heal.[71] And yet, in the actual distribution of the Norman
estates confiscated in England, there was considerable common sense.
To begin with, the Anglo-Norman loyalists were compensated for
their adherence to John. In the longer term this may have dampened
their enthusiasm for reconquest overseas. Had they been less well
provided for, it is possible that they might have shown greater

---

[67] The only general study remains that by Powicke, *The Loss of Normandy*, pp. 286–90,
328–58.
[68] *Ibid.*, pp. 341–2, 349.
[69] *Ibid.*, pp. 353–8.
[70] *Ibid.*, pp. 296–7, 340, 351.
[71] See, for example, the remarks of R. Jouet, *Et la Normandie devint Française* (Paris 1983),
pp. 69–77.

eagerness to recapture their lost Norman estates. However, in 1204, John's principal concern lay in attracting as many of the Anglo-Norman baronage to England as he possibly could. The easiest way to achieve this was for the king to offer such men the lands of knights and barons who had remained behind in Normandy. Furthermore, by distributing the confiscated lands amongst the loyalist Anglo-Normans, John appeared to ensure a relatively smooth transition, by exchange and family partition, as soon as Normandy was reconquered; an event that was widely believed to be inevitable. There are few better illustrations of the gradual abandonment of hopes of reconquest than the way in which later grants of *Terre Normannorum* were made to Englishmen who had not themselves suffered forfeiture in Normandy. In effect this was to supply a powerful disincentive against reconquest, since reconquest would necessarily involve the reseizure of Norman escheats in England with no very attractive prospect of compensation for the Englishmen who currently held them.

The whole subject of the Norman lands richly deserves further investigation. For the moment we need only observe that, whereas the Anglo-Norman baronage seem to have been adequately if not fully compensated for their losses after 1204, precious little land was left over for John's non-Norman supporters from Anjou, the Touraine or Poitou. No wonder that so few non-Normans accompanied the king into exile. Those that did were spurred on by a variety of motives. Some may have been hopelessly compromised by their previous service to the Plantagenets. Peter de Maulay, for example, appears to have been implicated in the murder of Arthur of Brittany.[72] Yet de Maulay was one of only a tiny few of John's alien followers who had been in any way significant as a landholder in France. For the most part, landholders stayed with their lands. The principal contingent of Angevin loyalists was made up of relatively landless men, whose allegiance lay not to their estates, but to the purse strings of King John, and for whom exile involved relatively few material losses. Girard d'Athée, for example, and his kinsmen, Engelard de Cigogné and the various brothers Chanceaux, appear to have sprung from servile origins.[73] The term *sequela* applied to them in Magna Carta is deliberately disparaging, normally reserved for serfs, or even for a brood of animals.

Alien clerks were more easily attracted to England than laymen.

[72] Below p. 70.
[73] *Oeuvres de Rigord et de Guillaume le Breton*, ed. H. F. Delaborde, 2 vols. (Paris 1882–5), ii, p. 226.

Des Roches appears to have been accompanied into exile by a large number of clerical supporters: the Poitevin Master Peter Russinol; William de Saint-Maixent, from near Le Mans, and des Roches' fellow Tourangeaux Peter de Rivallis, Denis de Bourgueil, John de Chinon and Bartholomew des Roches.[74] For them the break of 1204 was cushioned by the prospect of ecclesiastical preferment in England. Des Roches himself positively flourished in exile, rewarded for his loyalty in 1204 by the richest prize the king could offer, the vastly wealthy see of Winchester.

From the moment of their arrival in England, John's aliens were isolated. Few of them had any previous administrative experience there and fewer still owned land. The odds were already stacked against their assimilation into English society. Indeed the very *raison d'être* for their exile, at least as far as King John was concerned, was that they should behave differently and serve different interests from the king's English subjects; above all, that they should share his ambition of reconquest in France and therefore maintain their contacts with the lost Plantagenet domain. From the outset the aliens formed a distinct, interdependent group which at times of crisis could all too easily be transformed into faction.

At least to begin with, most aliens were entirely dependent upon court patronage and temporary promotion to local custodies, counties and escheats reversible at will. Des Roches by contrast was guaranteed lifelong tenure of his see. It is hardly surprising that, supported by the vast territorial resources of the bishopric of Winchester, he came to assume a position within the circle of alien patronage second only to that occupied by the king. The links between des Roches and his fellow aliens had been forged in some cases even before his election as bishop. Later, many other Frenchmen were to find haven in his household.

Peter de Maulay was to become one of the bishop's closest associates, making regular appearances as the bishop's guest at Taunton, Fareham and elsewhere.[75] In 1212 des Roches personally arranged securities on his behalf, and two years later presided over his installation as a major landholder in Yorkshire.[76] For the rest of their lives their political fortunes were to be inextricably linked. A William de Maulay is found in des Roches' household between 1207 and

---

[74] *Acta*, appendix 4, nos. 7, 14–15, 18, 35.
[75] *PR6DR*, p. 65; Mss. 7DR, mm. 7d-8; 11DR, m. 9; 13DR, mm. 1, 12, 12d, 13; 14DR, m. 8.
[76] *Rot. Chart.*, pp. 191–191b, and see below pp. 70, 112.

1214.[77] With the men proscribed by name in Magna Carta clause 50, des Roches' links were, if anything, even closer. At some time after becoming bishop, he witnessed a private charter of Girard d'Athée in favour of the canons of St Maurice at Tours, and, following Girard's capture by the French, he witnessed the arrangements for his ransom to be met by King John.[78] Girard's kinsmen, Engelard de Cigogné, Andrew, Guy and Peter de Chanceaux, were installed on the royal manor of Hurstbourne Tarrant, within the see of Winchester.[79] A close-knit group, all make regular appearances as guests on the Winchester estates.[80] Both Andrew and Peter de Chanceaux were to combine service under Engelard during his time as constable of Windsor with positions within des Roches' own household.[81] Peter served first in the bishop's butlery and later as keeper of his seal. After 1227 he accompanied des Roches on crusade.[82] Andrew de Chanceaux joined the many knights in des Roches' pay, at one time helping to tallage the bishop's estates.[83] Before September 1213, des Roches witnessed two private charters of Aimery de Chanceaux relating to land in Hampshire. His fellow witnesses included Girard d'Athée, Engelard, Guy, Andrew and Peter de Chanceaux.[84] Aimery appears to have served in the bishop's garrison at Farnham castle during the civil war of 1215–17.[85] As with Peter de Maulay, the

---

[77] *PR6DR*, pp. 35, 42; Mss. 7DR, mm. 2, 5, 8; 9DR, m. 3; *PR17John*, p. 86.

[78] *RLP*, p. 65; Lambron de Lignim, 'Girard d'Athée', p. 8, taken from a lost cartulary of St Maurice Tours. Another copy from the lost ms. provides a fuller witness list; P(eter) bishop of Winchester, Master Richard de Marsh, Master Gilbert de Aquila, Andrew *cancellarius* canon of Tours, John de Novo Vico, Engelard de Cigogné, Peter de Champmarle, Hemericus (alias Aimery) de Chanceaux, Girard the younger, Gyon (alias Guy) de Chanceaux, Peter de Chanceaux, Geoffrey de Martigny, Maceus de Martigny, Hemericus de Martigny; Paris, Bibliothèque Nationale ms. nouv. acq. Lat. 1183, p. 322. There are several places named Chanceaux in the Touraine. Note, however, that in 1200 Robert de Brenne, lord of Rochecorbon (*Rupibus*) enjoyed proprietary rights over the priory of Chanceaux-sur-Choisille, which might suggest even closer personal links between Peter des Roches and his Chanceaux protégés; *Chartes de Saint-Julien de Tours (1002–1300)*, ed. L.-J. Denis, Archives Historiques du Maine xii (Le Mans 1912–13), pp. 156–8 no. 131.

[79] *RLC*, i, p. 79b.

[80] See for example *PR4DR*, p. 17; Mss.7DR, m. 8d; 11DR, m. 2d.

[81] For their service under Engelard, see Cole, *Documents*, p. 236; *Hist. des Ducs*, p. 181; *PR 12 John*, pp. 143–4; *RLP*, p. 135; *E. Rot. Fin.*, i, p. 73; *CRR*, xiv, no. 487; E368/4, m. 4.

[82] *Acta*, appendix 4, no. 19.

[83] Mss.14DR, mm. 7, 7d, 8, 10d, 11; 15DR, m. 2; 16DR, mm. 1, 2, 4d, 5, 6d, 9–11; 21DR, mm. 1d, 5d, 9d.

[84] Winchester College Muniments mss. 15237–8.

[85] Ms.13DR, mm. 13d–14d.

association between des Roches, Engelard de Cigogné and the Chanceaux family was to persist long into the 1230s.

As an exile, anxious to find favour in England, des Roches might deliberately have severed his ties to France and to his fellow Frenchmen. In the 1250s, it appears that this was very much the strategy adopted by Henry III's step-brother, the Poitevin William de Valence, who surrounded himself with Englishmen rather than Poitevins.[86] Yet an examination of des Roches' episcopal establishment shows that perhaps as much as half of his inner household was made up of aliens. To begin with, the majority of these men were des Roches' fellow Tourangeaux, their numbers swollen after 1214 by the importation of at least half a dozen of the bishop's nephews: Peter de Rivallis, Bartholomew des Roches archdeacon of Winchester, Luke des Roches archdeacon of Surrey who retired after the bishop's death to his posthumous foundation at La Clarté-Dieu in the Touraine, and Hugh des Roches, head of the episcopal exchequer after 1227 and appointed archdeacon of Winchester in succession to Bartholomew. Hugh's brother Aimery was promoted rector of Preston by the king, but seems to have spent much of his time abroad. Another brother, Geoffrey des Roches, was married to a Hampshire heiress and founded a minor local dynasty, the Roches of Fareham. Like Geoffrey, the bishop's namesake Peter de Rupibus was also a knight, briefly retained in the king's household.[87]

The fact that such men congregated around him, complements the traditional presentation of des Roches as a figure isolated from the very outset by alien birth. Yet this is to oversimplify. At the time of his election to Winchester in 1205, aliens filled the vast majority of English sees: eight Frenchmen and one Italian, set against only four Englishmen of whom Giles de Briouze might best be styled Anglo-Norman.[88] This was a remarkably cosmopolitan

---

86 H. Ridgeway, 'William de Valence and his "Familiares", 1247–72', *Historical Research* 65 (1992), pp. 239–57.

87 *Acta*, appendix 4 nos. 7, 10, 13, 41–4.

88 The Frenchmen were William de St Mère Eglise (London, Norman), Philip of Poitiers (Durham, Poitevin), William de Blois (Lincoln), Eustace (Ely, former archdeacon of Evreux, Normandy), Mauger (Worcester, former archdeacon of Evreux, Normandy), Savaric (Bath, Burgundian), Gilbert Glanville (Rochester, former archdeacon of Lisieux, Normandy), Geoffrey Plantagenet (York, Angevin). The Italian, Bernard of Ragusa, held Carlisle, though he was probably never consecrated bishop; C. R. Cheney, *Innocent III*, pp. 74–5. For most see *Dictionary of National Biography* under name, and D. S. Spear, 'The Norman empire and the secular clergy 1066–1204', *Journal of British Studies*, 21 (1982), pp. 1–10.

bench, even by the standards of the late twelfth century. Nevertheless it is important to remember that des Roches' foreign birth was very much the rule rather than the exception amongst John's bishops. There can be few better illustrations of the change in attitudes towards aliens in England than a comparison between the episcopate at the start of des Roches' career, and that which held office during his regime of 1232–4. Of the latter, not one bishop save des Roches, can definitely be assigned a birthplace outside England.[89] Less than a generation later, in the baronial revolt of 1258–65, alien bishops were to be entirely banished, whilst St Bonaventure was to refuse the archdiocese of York for fear of the hatred his appointment might excite.[90]

Within this contracting network of patronage it is hardly surprising that des Roches came to assume an ever more important but at the same time an ever more isolated position. In some cases it is possible to observe a direct transferral of service from the older generation of alien bishops to des Roches. For example, he was to acquire at least three men from the household of Philip de Poitiers, bishop of Durham: the English scholar Master John of London, the Norman clerk Robert de Clinchamps and the Tourangeau knight Andrew de Chanceaux.[91] In other cases it was a question of men gravitating to des Roches direct from France. As the years went by and various of the older members of his household either died or returned to France, the bishop made no attempt to break with his past by replacing such losses with native born Englishmen.[92] On the contrary he continued to provide a haven for aliens increasingly at sea in an ever more hostile England.

Lucien Musset has shown how after 1204, Philip Augustus reserved offices within the newly conquered Normandy for his own Capetian adherents. As late as the 1230s, the Norman *Querimoniae*

---

[89] Of the Englishmen Richard Poer, Hugh of Lincoln and Jocelin of Wells had been exiles in France during the Interdict 1209–13. Poer had undoubtedly studied at Paris as perhaps had Henry of Sandford (Rochester) and Alexander of Stainsby (Coventry). The origins of Walter Mauclerk (Carlisle) are obscure, although he was possibly a Norman (below p. 324 n. 53). Despite his name William de Blois (Worcester) sprang from a family long settled in England.

[90] Aymer de Valence (Winchester, Poitevin), and the Savoyards, Boniface of Savoy (Canterbury) and Peter de Aigueblanche (Hereford) were all forced into exile. For St Bonaventure, see *AM*, iv (Wykes), p. 184.

[91] *Acta*, pp. xxxix–xl, appendix 4 nos.1, 17.

[92] For des Roches' clerks returning to France, see the examples of Walter de Montmorillon and William de Saint-Maixent; SC1/1/197; *Pat. R. 1216–25*, pp. 206, 252, 291, 351; *RLP*, p. 67; *Rot. Chart.*, p. 199b.

provide the names of clerks and others who had only recently fled Normandy for England, in search of the favours denied them in their native homeland.[93] From his earliest years, des Roches gave employment to several Normans besides a host of men with Anglo-Norman names who may well have been exiles after 1204: Roger Wacelin, des Roches' steward, a native of Barfleur; another of the episcopal stewards William de Batilly; clerks such as Robert de Clinchamps, Geoffrey de Caux and Master Robert de Pavilly.[94] After 1215 their numbers swelled rather than diminished. The office of bishop's official was filled successively by Normans, albeit by Normans with strong English connections: master William de St Mère-Eglise and Master Humphrey de Millières.[95] Master Humphrey appears alongside another of the bishop's alien protégés, master Nicholas de Vienne, as joint attorney of the bishop of Avranches in England.[96] The poet, Master Henry of Avranches, was patronized by des Roches for much of the 1220s. Nor was it merely in his episcopal household that the bishop strove to preserve the links between England and northern France. He is to be found active in the rehabilitation or introduction to court of several Norman landholders who late in the day decided to break with the Normandy of Philip Augustus, to reclaim their family lands in England.[97]

All of this suggests that the aliens did indeed form an identifiable, isolated group abroad in England. But what advantages did the king hope to gain by allowing such a group to flourish? Firstly, their very isolation ensured that the aliens looked to the royal court for protection and favour. They were likely to remain loyal to the king in times of crisis, hence their installation as constables and sheriffs in the provinces, where after 1215 they were to prove the king's most steadfast supporters against the rebellious native baronage. Secondly, they were useful to the king as go-betweens with France and as staunch enthusiasts for Plantagenet reconquest overseas. At a time when the English were coming increasingly to

---

93 L. Musset, 'Quelques problèmes posés par l'annexation de la Normandie au Domaine Royal Français', in *La France de Philippe-Auguste: Le Temps des Mutations*, ed. R. H. Bautier (Paris 1982), pp. 291–309. For a more general study of the conquest, over-inclined to stress the inevitability of Normandy's acceptance of French rule, see Jouet, *Et la Normandie devint Française*, esp. ch. iv, pp. 62–108.
94 *Acta*, appendix 4 nos. 17, 22, 25, 29. For Pavilly, see *ibid.*, nos. 11, 21, 32, 34.
95 *Ibid.*, appendix 4 nos. 3–4.
96 *Ibid.*, appendix 4 no. 36.
97 Below pp. 162–3.

resent the heavy impositions, in tax and military service, required to launch such reconquest, no group had more to gain and less to lose from a reassertion of Plantagenet control in France than the aliens. As for their role as go-betweens, no one better illustrates this function of John's alien patronage than des Roches, involved in virtually every diplomatic initiative to France in the thirty years after 1204.

Unfortunately for the aliens themselves, the very fidelity and cosmopolitanism that earned them gratitude and reward from the crown were the selfsame factors that served to heighten their unpopularity in England. Much has been written of the growing xenophobia of thirteenth-century England. Yet 'xenophobia' is a misleading term. Outbursts of anti-alien feeling were the result not so much of indiscriminate hatred of foreigners, as of a highly politicized, highly selective attack upon particular aliens in a particular set of political circumstances. Whether in local administration, as with the likes of Peter de Maulay or Girard d'Athée, or in the central offices of state occupied by des Roches, it was inevitable that John's aliens would come into competition with the native baronage in pursuit of offices and perquisites. As outsiders, they shared in the odium expressed towards *parvenus* in every age; as Frenchmen they were particularly vulnerable to attacks, politically rather than racially motivated, which picked upon their foreign birth and their cosmopolitanism as the most convenient stick with which to beat them.

Those who played upon such sentiments for political gain – Stephen Langton, who in 1224 warned against the alien wiles of Fawkes de Bréauté, Hubert de Burgh, who in 1221 exposed a mythical alien plot supposedly led by des Roches, and Richard Marshal, who in the 1230s accused des Roches of being in league with foreign powers against the true-born English – were themselves hardly the most insular of John Bulls. Langton was a Paris-educated cardinal whose exclusion from the see of Canterbury by King John had been justified on the grounds that he was too much a Parisian, too much a creature of the Capetians.[98] Hubert de Burgh had spent most of the first twenty years of his career abroad, as ambassador to Portugal and as seneschal of Poitou. Richard Marshal was more French than English, lord of Longueville and Orbec before his unexpected accession to the earldom of Pembroke, and by a splendid

---

[98] For Langton and his French connections, see N. Vincent, 'Master Simon Langton, King John and the court of France' (forthcoming).

irony married to a Breton heiress, Gervasia de Dinan, a kinswoman of William des Roches and hence of Richard's arch-rival, Peter des Roches, bishop of Winchester.[99]

King John regarded his aliens as a vital link to his lost continental domain. At least to begin with, the evidence suggests that the aliens themselves were willing and eager to serve the king in his strategy of reconquest. And yet, here too, we must tread with caution. Loyalty to the king was to bring the aliens rich rewards. To begin with, they were granted only temporary custodies and pensions. Over the course of time, however, they received more permanent settlements: heiresses and land. Peter de Maulay, for example, was married to a rich heiress, who brought him wide estates in Yorkshire. Roger Wacelin, des Roches' Norman steward, received a landed settlement from the bishop and married into the local Sussex gentry. Fawkes de Bréauté married the widowed countess of Devon.[100] Of the aliens singled out for attack in Magna Carta clause 50, at least three – Philip Mark, Andrew de Chanceaux and Guy de Chanceaux – went on to acquire English landholdings in fee. The first generation of exiles after 1204 might continue to support the king in his drive for reconquest in France. Yet the very fact that this support was rewarded with grants of English land, meant that within twenty or thirty years they and their children, often the children of mixed, Anglo-French marriages, began to look upon England, not France, as their home. Various of the marriages arranged between aliens and English heiresses appear to have given rise to genuine ties of affection. Peter de Maulay was to endow a chantry at Meaux in Yorkshire for his English wife.[101] The widow of Geoffrey des Roches, the bishop's nephew, bestowed land on the religious for the soul of her late husband, as did Sussanah de Chanceaux, the alien wife of the Englishman, Walter de Baskerville.[102] Short of some very rigid policy of apartheid or discrimination, within a generation or two, immigrants have a natural tendency to assume the outlook and manners of their adopted country. In thirteenth-century England, despite an initial period of tension, the

---

99 For Richard's French background, see *CP*, ix, pp. 368–71, esp. p. 370n. For the association between William des Roches and Juhel de Mayenne, see Dubois, 'Guillaume des Roches', xxx (1869), pp. 384, 398; *ibid.*, xxxii (1871), pp. 90, 118. Juhel, one-time husband of Gervaisa de Dinan, was uncle to William's wife.

100 For Wacelin and his family, see *Acta*, appendix 4 no. 25.

101 *Chronica de Melsa*, i, p. 106; *Cal. Chart. R. 1226–57*, pp. 233–4. He also confirmed the possessions of the priory of Eskdale, founded as a daughter house of Grandmont by Robert of Thurnham and Isabella; Limoges, Archives Départementales de Haute-Vienne ms. I Sem 82 (List of Benefactors of Grandmont) f. 122r–v.

102 *Acta*, appendix 4 no. 43; Hereford Cathedral Library ms. Muniments no. 868.

pressures towards assimilation were hard to resist. Some at least of the aliens were to flourish in exile. Peter de Maulay, Andrew and Guy de Chanceaux may still have been outsiders at the time of their deaths, but their sons were to become indistinguishable from the old Anglo-Norman gentry. Within another generation, Hugh and Thomas de Chanceaux, the grandsons of aliens specifically attacked in Magna Carta, were both to be accused of participating in the anti-alien, English baronial rebellion of 1264–5.[103]

Even Peter des Roches, the greatest of John's alien ministers, was not immune from this process. At Winchester he was to prove an enthusiastic patron of that most English of traditions, the cult of the Anglo-Saxon saints. Ironically, our clearest indication of his own French birthplace is to be found in the poem he commissioned on the life of the Saxon St Birinus.[104] Thirty years after the loss of Normandy, and in light of the failure of either King John or Henry III to achieve any dramatic reassertion of lordship on the continent, it is arguable that des Roches, like his fellow aliens, had come to accept that the old Plantagenet dominion was vanished for ever. The outsiders of 1204 became slowly inured to their exile from France. Des Roches endowed a posthumous religious foundation close to his birthplace in the Touraine, but it was in Winchester cathedral, close to the shrine of the English St Swithun, that he chose to be buried. Peter de Maulay buried his wife at the Yorkshire abbey of Meaux; Philip Mark was buried at Lenton priory; Giles, the son of Andrew de Chanceaux, in front of the high altar of Newenham abbey in Devon.[105] By the 1230s, such men had acquired more land and status in England than they had ever possessed in France. Though they may have continued to dream of a Plantagenet reconquest, it was no longer the overwhelming obsession that it once had been.

But in 1204 these developments were still many years in the future. By no means all of the aliens were to survive their first twenty years of exile in a hostile realm. Save at moments of political crisis, by no

---

[103] Hugh de Chanceaux was the grandson of Guy (alias Gioni de Chanceaux), holding at Upton in Northamptonshire. His lands were granted away after the battle of Evesham in 1265, although his innocence was later admitted by the king. Thomas de Chanceaux was a son of the alien Aimery de Chanceaux, who in turn may well have been the son or possibly the brother of the Andrew de Chanceaux proscribed in Magna Carta. He appears to have abandoned the rebels prior to Evesham; *CPR 1258–66*, pp. 500, 586; JUST1/618, m. 23, references which I owe to Clive Knowles.

[104] For des Roches and the Saxon saints, see below pp. 243–7.

[105] For de Maulay, see *CP*, viii, pp. 557–8. For Mark, see Holt, 'Philip Mark', pp. 23–4. For Giles de Chanceaux, see Bodl. ms. Top. Devon d5 (Newenham cartulary), ff. 97v–99v; BL ms. Arundel 17 (Newenham register), ff. 39v, 59r.

means all of them worked closely together as a coherent, political faction. The relations between des Roches, Peter de Maulay, Girard d'Athée and the various members of the family Chanceaux were very close. But with others, Fawkes de Bréauté, for example, or the Poitevin earl of Aumale, the bishop's contacts were restricted to times of war and political upheaval. Whilst the English chroniclers might seek to identify an alien faction at court, largely in order to pillory it, the aliens themselves remained a heterogeneous collection of men, by no means always united in mutual self-defence. We should be wary of exaggerating the solidarity or cohesion of what was in reality a diverse collection of individuals, each of them out for his own personal advantage. Nonetheless, in describing the aliens in generic terms, with des Roches portrayed as the central figure in an alien group at court, the chroniclers wrote with a fair degree of truth. There is a parallel here to the chroniclers' use of the term 'Northerners' to describe the rebel barons of 1215, as J. C. Holt puts it 'the first use in English history of a party-political label'.[106] As with the Northerners, there is no evidence that des Roches and his associates would ever have described themselves as 'Aliens'. Both labels, Alien and Northerner, were catch-all terms, applied by the chroniclers with abusive intent. Even so, for all the differences that distinguished one alien from another, *en masse*, like the Northerners, the Aliens shared far more in common with one another than they ever did with those from outside their circle. In consequence, in 1215, 1224 and again during the 1230s, at moments of particular crisis, they were capable of concerted action, operating together as an identifiable group.

As England broke free from the patterns of patronage established under Henry II and his Angevin successors, so des Roches came to meet a shortage felt more and more keenly: a shortage of protection and material support for those aliens who had made common cause with the Plantagenet kings. The bishop deliberately encouraged aliens in his household and at court. As the pool of patronage dried up around them, so des Roches' circle came to include Normans, Bretons, Poitevins, Angevins and Tourangeaux. It was a richly cosmopolitan group. Peter de Maulay, born on the Marches between Poitou and the Touraine, was reputed to be the murderer of an Angevin prince of Brittany, and was eventually married to a Yorkshire heiress whose father had served as seneschal of Poitou and Gascony; Andrew de Chanceaux, a landless Tourangeau, married his sister into

---

[106] J. C. Holt, *The Northerners*, 2nd edn (Oxford 1992), p. xv.

the Anglo-Norman gentry of Herefordshire and himself financed an obituary celebration at Tours for a Poitevin bishop of Durham.[107]

It was the very cosmopolitanism of these men rather than any narrow allegiance to a particular region of France, that after 1204 made them such isolated and such mistrusted figures in England. In patronizing them and in striving to maintain links with Normandy, with Anjou, the Touraine and Poitou, des Roches was not acting out of sectarian interest or homesick sentiment. Rather, he was performing one of the principal functions for which King John had first promoted him. Not to create some new style of 'Poitevin Kingship', but to keep alive an idea that was already half-a-century old by 1204; the idea of a Plantagenet dominion stretching from the Cheviots to the Pyrenees; keeping it alive as an idea long after it had ceased to have any practical reality, in the hope that one day John's dominion might be restored.

---

[107] For the obit, see *Martyrologe-Obituaire de Tours*, ed. J. J. Bourassé, p. 37, where the date of the death of *Philippus P. episcopus D.* accords with that of Philip de Poitiers, bishop of Durham. For the marriage of Andrew's sister Sussanah, see *Rot. Ob.*, pp. 512–13; *RLC*, i, p. 162.

Chapter 2

THE REIGN OF KING JOHN

In the five years after 1197, Peter des Roches had established himself in a prominent position amongst the clerks of the royal chamber. He enjoyed the confidence of King John, by whom he had been promoted to various churches in Anjou, Poitou and the Touraine. Altogether, his career seemed launched on a steady course. But appearances were deceptive. The Plantagenet dominion over north and western France, established a mere fifty years before, was coming increasingly under strain. Since the mid-1190s, much of Normandy had been plunged into near constant warfare between the Plantagenets and the Capetian kings of France. By employing mercenaries within what had once been areas of relative peace, away from the Franco-Norman frontier, John forfeited much of the sympathy that his family had previously commanded amongst the Norman baronage. At the same time, employing his titular claim to overlordship within most of the Plantagenet lands, the French king, Philip Augustus, was able further to undermine the relations between John and his subjects in France. The death of King Richard I in 1199 enabled Philip to exploit the dispute over the Plantagenet succession that erupted between John and his nephew, Arthur of Brittany. Added to this, by his skilful management of the Capetian demesne, Philip was by 1200 a richer king than John, better able to meet the costs of war. In 1202 John scored a notable military breakthrough at Mirebeau. Arthur was taken prisoner. But John's success was short-lived. Within a matter of months Arthur was dead, in all likelihood murdered by John, or at John's direct command: an act of brutality that was to shatter John's fragile reputation throughout the Plantagenet lands. Philip Augustus prepared an army of invasion, claiming to act as overlord, offering good government, an end to war, and justice against King John. One by one, John's supporters defected to the French.[1] Unable to meet the cost of his army, deserted by many

---

[1] For the general outline of events, see F. M. Powicke, *The Loss of Normandy*, esp. ch. vi; J. C. Holt, 'The end of the Anglo-Norman realm', *PBA* (1975), pp. 223–65. For France and its financial superiority, see J. W. Baldwin, 'La Décennie Décisive: les

of his leading men, bewildered and furious, in the winter of 1203 John fled to England. Peter des Roches fled with him.[2]

The revolt that had broken out in John's continental lands was by no means the first to threaten the Anglo-Norman realm with dismemberment: similar risings had been suppressed as recently as 1199 and 1202. For much of the reign of Henry I, and again during the 1140s, England and Normandy had been separated from one another by dynastic rivalries. Des Roches can have had little idea that he was to spend the remainder of his life as an exile. Yet the fall of Château Gaillard in May 1204 was followed by the total collapse of Plantagenet power in Normandy, Anjou, Maine and the Touraine.[3] Only the distant provinces of Aquitaine, those furthest removed from the fighting of the previous ten years, resisted the French invasion. Whereas on previous occasions, England and France had been severed, temporarily, by allegiance to rival members of the same Norman or Plantagenet ruling family, now for the first time the French lands were seized by their titular overlord, Philip Augustus. Landholders were required to declare their loyalties: either to do homage to Philip, in which case they would forfeit their lands in England, or to follow John and so abandon their lands in France. Over the next decade John was to devote vast resources to the recovery of his continental domain, and until at least the 1230s, there were many on both sides of the Channel who continued to hope for a Plantagenet reconquest. But the division of homage and land-holding, forced through in the aftermath of the Capetian invasion, had already loaded the dice heavily in favour of the French.

Why did the breach of 1204 prove permanent? This a question that many historians have pondered, and to which no simple answer has been forthcoming. To begin with, it is important to bear in mind that the Angevin lands before 1204 need to be seen, not as one united territorial empire, but as a conglomeration of lordships brought into existence through time and chance. The Anglo-Norman realm had existed since the Conquest of 1066, but elsewhere, Angevin dominion was of much more recent creation, combining the lands inherited by

---

années 1190–1203 dans la règne de Philippe Auguste', *Revue Historique*, 26 (1981), pp. 311–37; J. C. Holt, 'The loss of Normandy and royal finance', in *War and Government in the Middle Ages: Essays in Honour of J. O. Prestwich*, ed. J. Gillingham and J. C. Holt (Woodbridge 1984), pp. 92–105.

2   He is found at St Mère-Eglise on 23 November 1203, and next at Marlborough on 5 January 1204; *Rot. Norm.*, p. 113; *Rot. Ob.*, p. 108. For the king's flight see Powicke, *The Loss of Normandy*, pp. 166–9.

3   For the collapse of 1204, see Powicke, *The Loss of Normandy*, pp. 251–60.

Henry II from his predecessors as counts of Anjou, with the vast assembly of rights, customs and territorial lordships acquired at Henry's marriage to Eleanor of Aquitaine. From the 1150s through to 1204, a single king had ruled over all of these territories, but Angevin rule south of the river Loire was of a very different nature from Angevin rule in England, Normandy or Anjou itself. South of the Loire, and away from such outposts of ducal power as Saintes, Poitiers, Bordeaux and later Bayonne, Henry II and his sons appear to have exercised only the most vague of dominions. To judge from the charters that survive in France, Henry himself issued only a tiny handful of privileges to benefactors south of Poitiers. Even during the 1170s and 1180s, when Richard I was established as count of Poitiers and duke of Aquitaine, south of Poitiers the count/duke appears to have been restricted to the collection of tolls and *impôts*, and the issuing of a relatively small number of letters of protection and privilege for towns and monasteries, for the most part situated on strategic rivers such as the Garonne and the Adour.[4] The count/duke was above all a warrior, engaged in near constant warfare against his rebellious and over-mighty vassals. Indeed, it is striking testimony of this, that Richard I met his death in 1199, making war against the rebellious barons of the Limousin.[5] Whereas elsewhere in their dominion, even by the year 1200, the Angevins possessed an extensive and lucrative demesne, in Aquitaine and in particular in Gascony, their landholding appears to have been very small, indeed in Gascony south of the Garonne, almost non-existent. In Aquitaine, save for the actual periods when Henry II or Richard were in residence, Angevin lordship appears to have impinged relatively little upon the authority exercised by local magnates, ecclesiastical and secular. Hence, perhaps, the fact that in 1204 the great men of Aquitaine and Poitou failed to make any decisive break with their Angevin overlord.[6] For them, it

---

4   Remarks based upon an extended survey of southern French archives conducted in 1994, leading to the collection of some 50 charters of Richard as count/duke, and a mere half-dozen of Henry II. In a forthcoming article, I intend to deal with the implications of these discoveries at much greater length than is possible here.

5   In general, see J. Gillingham, *Richard the Lionheart*, 2nd edn (London 1989), esp. ch. 5; J. Gillingham, 'The unromantic death of Richard I', in Gillingham, *Richard Coeur de Lion: Kingship, Chivalry and War in the Twelfth Century* (London 1994), pp. 155–80.

6   Note, however, the invasion of Gascony launched in 1204 by Alfonso of Castile, who claimed the province as dower from his wife Eleanor, a daughter of Henry II; Gillingham, *Richard Coeur de Lion*, pp. 70–1, 124–5. The offer of Gascony at the time of Alfonso's marriage in 1170, and the similar offer made in 1190 as dower to Berengaria of Navarre at the time of her marriage to Richard I, suggest the extent to which the Angevins regarded Gascony as a peripheral, and ultimately expendable part of their dominion.

must have seemed far better to be ruled by the distant and, for the moment, seemingly unwarlike King John, than risk being swallowed up within the burgeoning lordship of the kings of France. Elsewhere, however, the picture was very different.

North of the Loire, men had good cause to complain of the oppressive nature of Angevin rule. Not only did the Plantagenets control an extensive network of demesne, towns and castles, but their authority exercised through the law courts and assizes, their collection of customs and dues via local officials, and their demand for military service and scutage, placed a constant drain upon the resources of their Norman and Angevin subjects. On the surface, even as late as 1200, the Plantagenets were as well entrenched in Normandy as they had been at any time since the conquest of the duchy by Geoffrey of Anjou fifty years before. As dukes of Normandy, Henry II and his sons appeared to be powerful, wealthy and respected. Rebellion and private warfare were as rare in Normandy as they were common south of the Loire. Yet the effects of fifty years of rivalry between the Plantagenets and the kings of France had encouraged discontent amongst the Norman baronage. As merely one part of the Angevin dominion, Normandy had ceased to command that absolute priority in the thinking and affections of Henry II and his sons, that it had enjoyed under the first three Anglo-Norman kings.[7] Added to this, amongst the Norman aristocracy, and particularly amongst their lesser knights and vassals, a fundamental breach had already been opened up, between those who held land in England and those who were chiefly resident in Normandy. As David Crouch has suggested, by 1200, save amongst the very highest levels of the old Anglo-Norman aristocracy, there seem to have been relatively few families which had not in some way divided into Norman and English branches. Many landholders continued to hold estates on both sides of the Channel, but of these, only a handful can have been in any doubt as to where their fundamental interests lay, in England or in Normandy. The possession of one or two manors in England was simply not enough to encourage such men as the lords of Gisors or Evreux to regard themselves as Anglo-Normans as opposed to Normans pure and simple. By the same token, of the many lesser families settled in England which could claim descent from an ancestor born in Normandy, the vast majority by 1200 had unloaded their Norman

---

[7] A theme stressed by D. Bates, 'The rise and fall of Normandy, c.911–1204', in *England and Normandy in the Middle Ages*, ed. D. Bates and A. Curry (London 1994), pp. 19–35.

patrimony upon a brother or a cousin.[8] Hence the relative speed with which, after 1204, such pre-existing divisions hardened into a permanent rift between England and Normandy. Finally, and perhaps most significantly, we should remember that in 1204 Normandy was lost by one king and conquered by another. King John it was who lost his continental lands. His failure here has been ascribed to any number of factors, from his relative financial weakness faced with the growing wealth of France, to sheer incompetence and inactivity. By the same token, the victor of 1204, Philip Augustus, has been portrayed as a strategist and financier of genius.

Personal factors undoubtedly played a part in the events of 1204. In 1200 John had married Isabella of Angoulême, no doubt hoping at long last to stamp Plantagenet authority upon a crucial frontier region, the Angoumois, separating Poitou from Bordeaux. In fact, however, far from consolidating his lordship over Poitou, John's marriage sparked off rebellion by the Poitevin aristocracy, led by Isabella's previous fiancé, Hugh de Lusignan. In turn, it was this rebellion, which first allowed the French king to intervene in the guise of overlord, to claim the forfeiture of John's continental lands. The subsequent imprisonment and murder of his nephew and rival, Arthur, appears to have been one of the chief causes of rebellion against John amongst the nobility of Anjou and the Plantagenet heartlands. John's marriage, and his treatment of Arthur were both major factors in the *débâcle* which ensued.[9] Arguably, however, John's policy was undone not so much by his own mistakes as by a series of long-standing fault-lines running through the Plantagenet dominion: the looseness of the ties that bound the Angevin dominions north and south of the Loire; the failure of Henry II and his sons to create Anglo-Angevin or Anglo-Poitevin cross-Channel lordships to rival those that had once bound together England and Normandy; the gradual weakening even of this Anglo-Norman connection amongst

---

[8] D. Crouch, 'Normans and Anglo-Normans: a divided aristocracy?', in *England and Normandy in the Middle Ages*, ed. Bates and Curry, pp. 51–67. For Normandy itself, the forthcoming work of Daniel Power will provide essential corrections to Powicke, demonstrating the complexity of Angevin-Capetian loyalties along the Norman frontier. For the moment, see D. J. Power, 'The Norman frontier in the 12th and early 13th centuries', unpublished Ph.D. thesis (Cambridge 1994); 'Between the Angevin and Capetian courts: John de Rouvray and the knights of the Pays de Bray, 1185–1214', in *Studies in Anglo-Norman Prosopography*, ed. K. Keats-Rohan (Woodbridge, forthcoming 1996).

[9] For the most keenly argued attempt to place personal responsibility upon the shoulders of King John, see Gillingham, *Richard Coeur de Lion*, pp. 66–76, 193–200.

barons and knights; on the French side, the fact that the Capetians were recognized not only as overlords to the Plantagenets, but, in some senses, as heirs to the idea of a united realm of France that had existed under Charlemagne and the Carolingians, and the gradual upsurge in Capetian finances brought about by the expansion in Philip Augustus' power over Amiens and the Vermandois at the end of the twelfth century.[10] All of these must be accounted factors in a complicated story: a story that cannot be reduced to a simple matter of the personal strengths and weaknesses of particular kings. By some of his Angevin and Norman subjects, King John may well have been regarded as incompetent, perhaps even as a tyrant. Others, however – amongst them the Tourangeau clerk Peter des Roches – must have viewed the events of 1204 as merely a temporary set-back for the Angevin cause. Why else would des Roches and many of his fellow Frenchmen have joined the king in exile? Time was to prove that he had backed the losing side, but for the moment, Peter des Roches can have had little idea that he was destined for a life as an alien abroad in England.

THE WINCHESTER ELECTION

By the end of his first year in exile des Roches had been rewarded with a rich haul of benefices and estates. He may already have held the living of Dartford by gift of the monks of Rochester.[11] As early as

---

[10] For Philip's use of the images of Charlemagne and a unified French nationhood, see Baldwin, *Philip Augustus*, pp. 362–74. In all of this, Philip's claim to act as patron of the French church, and of certain archbishoprics and bishoprics even within the Plantagenet lands, helped to keep alive some sense of a united French as opposed to a specifically Capetian church. The Capetians claimed regalian right over the archbishopric of Bourges, a see which asserted primacy over all of the churches of Aquitaine, and over the archbishopric of Tours; hence the attempts by Henry II to have Dol recognized as a metropolitan see at the head of the churches of Brittany, independent of Capetian controlled Tours, reviving a dispute that stretched back to the ninth century; Baldwin, *Philip Augustus*, pp. 69, 360; G. Conklin, 'Les Capétiens et l'affaire de Dol de Bretagne, 1179–1194', *Revue d'Histoire de l'Eglise de France*, 78 (1992), pp. 241–63; J. M. H. Smith, 'The "archbishopric" of Dol and the ecclesiastical politics of ninth-century Brittany', *Studies in Church History*, 18 (1982), pp. 69–70; D. Walker, 'Crown and episcopacy under the Normans and Angevins', *Anglo-Norman Studies*, v, ed. R. Allen Brown (Woodbridge 1983), pp. 228–31. See also Q. Griffiths, 'The Capetian kings and St Martin of Tours', *Studies in Medieval and Renaissance History*, 19 (1987), pp. 83–125, esp. pp. 98–9, for the way in which Philip Augustus commanded an outpost of church patronage via not only the archbishopric but the collegiate church of St Martin at Tours.

[11] E. Hasted, *The History and Topographical Survey of the County of Kent*, 4 vols. (Canterbury 1778–99), ii, p. 327, which cites no authority for the statement that des Roches was appointed rector of Dartford during the reign of Henry II, at the king's wish.

November 1202, he had acquired a prebend at Lincoln and was later appointed the cathedral's precentor.[12] Following the loss of Normandy he was granted the churches of Cave, Halesowen, and Kirby Misperton, a perpetual vicarage at Bamburgh, as well as lands confiscated from the countess of Perche, and from Aimery de Harcourt.[13] In April 1204 he was awarded the right to dispose of prebends and rents as he saw fit during a vacancy at Chichester.[14] Since a similar award preceded his election to Winchester later that same year, it is possible that the king considered promoting him bishop of Chichester. But Chichester was by no means a wealthy see. An astute pluralist such as des Roches faced a considerable reduction in income if not in status by accepting election to any but the richer bishoprics.[15] Des Roches' living of Bamburgh was alone worth as much as the see of Lichfield and more than those of Rochester and Carlisle combined.[16]

Winchester, which fell vacant in September 1204, was a desirable prize by any standard. The richest English diocese, it offered its incumbent a gross manorial income approaching £3,000 a year, besides control over some seventy knights' fees, three castles and thirty manors scattered across southern England, including the immensely valuable manor of Taunton, alone worth more than the average lay barony.[17] In addition, the bishops of Winchester exerted spiritual authority over the counties of Hampshire and Surrey, and as

[12]   *RLP*, pp. 20, 43, 49b; Migne, *PL*, ccxv, cols. 671–2; *Fasti*, ed. Greenway, iii, p. 114.
[13]   *RLP*, pp. 40b, 43, 47b, 49–49b; *Rot. Norm.*, p. 131; *Letters of Innocent III*, nos. 642, 719; Cheney, *Innocent III*, pp. 86–7.
[14]   *RLP*, p. 40.
[15]   Des Roches' predecessor at Winchester, Godfrey de Lucy, had refused the see of Exeter on these grounds in 1186. Aymer de Valence may deliberately have remained bishop-elect of Winchester in the 1250s, avoiding consecration to ensure that he continued to enjoy his other ecclesiastical revenues; *Gesta Regis Henrici Secundi*, ed. W. Stubbs, 2 vols. (RS 1867), i, p. 346; Paris, *CM*, v, pp. 224, 240–1.
[16]   For the relative values of the English bishoprics see the vacancy receipts listed in M. Howell, *Regalian Right in Medieval England* (London 1963), pp. 34–5, appendix 1. The Rochester receipts went to Canterbury during vacancies but can be gauged from a complaint by bishop Lawrence in 1256 that he had less than £40 p.a.; Strood, Medway Area Archives Office, ms. D. & C. Rochester L2; Register 3 (Registrum Temporalium), ff. 76v–77r. Carlisle's poverty ensured the vacancy of the see for much of the twelfth century. For the rectory of Bamburgh, valued at *c.*£230 with a further portion in the church of £30, see *Tax. Eccl.*, p. 317. The value of des Roches' vicarage there is unrecorded, although of the entire revenues of the church he was expected to pay only 40m a year to the rector.
[17]   For the manorial income, see J. Z. Titow, 'Land and population on the bishop of Winchester's estates 1209–1350', Cambridge Ph. D. thesis (1962), p. 68a. For the average barony, see S. Painter, *Studies in the History of the English Feudal Barony* (Baltimore 1943), ch. vii, pp. 170–90.

recently as the 1140s had aspired to metropolitan status.[18] Winchester, the ancient capital of Wessex, itself retained much of the economic prosperity it had enjoyed in earlier centuries. The Winchester fairs were commercial centres of international significance.[19] The city boasted a favourite royal residence where both of John's legitimate sons were to be born. The king rarely passed a year without visiting the numerous royal castles and manors that lay within the diocese, indeed he had chosen to be buried at his nearby foundation of Beaulieu.[20]

Within a fortnight of the death of bishop Godfrey de Lucy, des Roches was granted control over episcopal patronage. By prolonging the vacancy at Winchester, John might have obtained a much needed boost to royal finances in the lead up to his projected reconquest of Normandy. Henry III was to extract over £17,000 in regalian issues from Winchester after des Roches' death.[21] Instead, in 1204 John sought a speedy election suggesting that he valued des Roches sufficiently highly to sacrifice an opportunity for considerable financial profit. It may also have been that prompt action was required to prevent the election of a less desirable candidate.

The monks of St Swithun's who held the right to elect were a far more tractable body than many another monastic chapter. Unlike their counterparts at Canterbury they had never sought to promote to the bishopric from amongst their own number, nor is there any parallel at Winchester to the struggles between bishops and monks that had recently disturbed other monastic cathedrals such as Coventry or Norwich. Des Roches was to keep his convent on a tight rein, but his relations with the Winchester monks were generally harmonious. It is instructive that when, in 1238, Henry III sought to persuade them to elect another alien curialist, William de Valence, the monks of St Swithun's responded not by nominating a figure from outside the royal court but by electing the chancellor, Ralph de Neville, and when that failed, the chief justice *coram rege*, William de Raleigh.[22] Only in 1261, after the disastrous episcopacy of the Poitevin, Aymer de Valence, did they seek to assert their independence by nominating

---

[18] A. Saltman, *Theobald Archbishop of Canterbury* (London 1956), pp. 21–2.

[19] D. Keene, *Survey of Medieval Winchester*, Winchester Studies II, 2 vols. (Oxford 1985), pp. 102–3; J. Z. Titow, 'The decline of the fair of St Giles Winchester in the thirteenth and fourteenth centuries', *Nottingham Medieval Studies*, 31 (1987), pp. 58–75.

[20] *Radulphi de Coggeshall Chronicon Anglicanum*, ed. J. Stevenson (RS 1875), p. 109.

[21] Howell, *Regalian Right*, p. 229. For John's need for money see intro. to *PR7John*, pp. xxv–xxvi.

[22] Powicke, *Henry III*, pp. 270–3.

a succession of monk bishops.[23] Courtier bishops were by no means despised in the thirteenth century. On the contrary, by electing a bishop who enjoyed the confidence of the king, a monastic community could hope to reap many incidental benefits.

In 1204 the monks acted according to form. Early in November, the prior and twelve of his convent were ordered to meet archbishop Hubert Walter and Peter des Roches, to receive instructions on the election.[24] By late January, des Roches had resigned his church at Halesowen, and he makes his first appearance as bishop-elect on 5 February 1205.[25] But, unfortunately for the king, this was not the only election to take place. The archdeacons of Winchester and Surrey also claimed a part in choosing their bishop, acting together with a minority of the monks to elect Master Richard Poer, dean of Salisbury. Early in 1205 proctors of both parties were active in Rome, and on 9 March, the pope ordered that archbishop Hubert, and the bishops of Ely and London admonish the king to permit another, and this time, free election.[26] Des Roches and his monastic supporters, headed by the prior Stephen de Lucy, may already have set out for the papal curia. The king loaned them large sums of money to prosecute their cause.[27]

Des Roches' opponent, Richard Poer, was in many ways an admirable candidate: a student of Langton at Paris and an ardent reformer under his brother, bishop Herbert Poer of Salisbury, he was untainted by the distinctly secular reputation that must have clung to des Roches.[28] It is therefore all the more ironic that his candidature for Winchester laid him open to a charge of nicolaitism, since there can be no doubt that he was the son of a previous incumbent of the see.[29] His father, Richard of Ilchester, bishop of Winchester (1173–88), had granted land to Richard and Herbert Poer in Hampshire, Winchester and London, at least some of which appears to have

---

23 *Fasti*, ed. Greenway, ii, pp. 86–7.
24 *RLP*, p. 48b. On 1 Jan. the archdeacon of Winchester was instructed to induct one of des Roches' clerks to benefices in the city suburbs; *RLP*, p. 49b.
25 *RLP*, pp. 49–49b; *RLC*, i, pp. 18b, 19. On 7 Feb. he was sent to the archbishop who was asked to confirm the election: *RLP*, p. 49b.
26 The dispute is noticed by the Osney annalist: *AM*, iv, p. 51, and in papal letters of June 1205: Migne, *PL*, ccxv, cols. 671–3; *Letters of Innocent III*, no. 631. The only modern accounts are by Painter, *King John*, pp. 159–60, and Cheney, *Innocent III* , pp. 144–7.
27 *RLP*, p. 52, *RLC*, i, pp. 26, 37b–38, 48; *PR7John*, pp. 12–13; *PR8John*, p. 155; Vincent, 'The origins of the Winchester Pipe Rolls', *Archives* 21 (1994), pp. 25–42.
28 *Chronicon Abbatiae de Evesham*, ed. W. D. Macray (RS 1863), pp. 232–3. For Poer's reforming activities as dean of Salisbury, see *Fasti*, ed. Greenway, iv, pp. xxvi–xxxviii.
29 C. Duggan, 'Richard of Ilchester', *TRHS* (1966), p. 3 and notes; T. Madox, *Formulare Anglicanum* (London 1702), no. lxxxvi.

been detached from the patrimony of Winchester with dubious legality.[30] The archdeacons who in 1204 procured Poer's election were both of them associated with Richard's family. Amicius, archdeacon of Surrey, served with Herbert Poer as a papal judge.[31] Archdeacon Roger of Winchester had been appointed to his office by Richard of Ilchester and on 6 February 1205, in the midst of the Winchester election dispute, is to be found witnessing a charter of bishop Herbert Poer at Abingdon.[32] The archdeacons' claim to participate in the election of 1205 seems to have had no twelfth-century precedent. Rather, in order to the promote their own man, Richard Poer, the archdeacons attempted to muscle in on what had previously been considered a purely monastic prerogative.

According to the pope's account of events, issued on 21 June 1205, an enquiry was held into the circumstances of the two elections, as a result of which both were quashed: Poer's because it had been conducted *per inordinatam presumptionem*, perhaps because of the archdeacons' intervention or because the elect was illegitimate; des Roches' because it had been made *per violentam impressionem*, under duress from the royal court. Des Roches' supporters were required to proceed to a new election in company with the archdeacons' proctors, but this settlement came to nothing, with the monks asserting that the archdeacons had disqualified themselves by choosing a known illegitimate. Only when Innocent reminded both parties of the dangers further delay posed to the church of Winchester could a communal election be effected. Des Roches proved the unanimous choice of both sides. The pope was clearly concerned that undue pressure had been brought to bear, and extracted oaths from the electors that they

[30] Ilchester gave Herbert Poer land near Fleet Street, London, at West Tisted, Hants. and in Winchester; *Charters and Documents illustrating the history of the Cathedral . . . of Salisbury*, ed. W. H. Rich Jones and W. D. Macray (RS 1891), pp. 71–2; *Reg. St Osmund*, i, pp. 329–30; Westminster Abbey ms. Domesday, f. 473v; *VCH: Hampshire*, iii, pp. 58–62; *PR4DR*, p. 77; *PR6DR*, p. 159, wrongly given as Henry, archdeacon of Canterbury. The land at Tisted was later recovered by des Roches; CP25(1)203/6/8; *Calendar of Charters and Documents relating to Selborne and its Priory*, ed. W. D. Macray, i, p. 2. Richard of Ilchester may well have been incapacitated during his last years since many plots of land in Winchester are said to have been granted away during his 'infirmity': *PR4DR*, pp. 76–7; Vincent, 'The origins of the Winchester Pipe Rolls', pp. 28–9.

[31] *Acta*, appendix 4 no. 11.

[32] *Acta*, appendix 4 no. 5; St John's College Oxford, Muniments ms. III. 1 (Cartulary of St Nicholas' Wallingford), f. 27v. Another of the witnesses on this occasion, Master Hugh of Gayhurst, had witnessed regularly under Richard of Ilchester, even before the latter's promotion to Winchester; *Documents preserved in France, illustrative of the history of Great Britain and Ireland*, ed. J. H. Round (London 1899), p. 277; BL ms. Harley 3650 (Kenilworth cartulary), f. 24r; *English Episcopal Acta VIII: Winchester 1070–1204*, ed. M. J. Franklin (Oxford 1993), *passim*.

were bound by no obligations or compulsion. In addition he received letters testifying to the elect's suitability from the archbishop of Tours and King John.[33] Bishop Savaric of Bath gave des Roches support at the Curia.[34] The new bishop of Winchester was duly consecrated by the pope at St Peter's on 25 September 1205.[35] On 25 October he rewarded the loyalty of the monks of St Swithun's by confirming them in tithes they held at Barton. The language of the charter issued on this occasion seems almost deliberately high-flown, repeating phrases regularly employed in the papal chancery, and describing the mutual obligation between bishop and monks, the head and members of the church of Winchester, in language that deliberately echoes the Epistles of St Paul. A similar resort to scriptural quotation in others of des Roches' charters suggests a self-conscious display of learned piety. Derided as a curialist by his critics, the bishop was yet determined to flaunt his knowledge of scripture.[36]

As a courtier, more familiar with the battlefield than the pulpit, des Roches might well appear an unsuitable candidate for the role of pastor and bishop. Later commentators have regarded him as a churchman in little more than name. Yet the pope clearly believed that he possessed some redeeming features. Perhaps above all, Innocent hoped that he would serve as a channel of communication with King John. For the remainder of 1205 des Roches stayed in Rome. Whether in an honest desire to speed reforms within his diocese, or merely to ingratiate himself with Innocent, he solicited several papal mandates designed to assist him in correcting irregularities in monasteries and churches, in revoking the alienation of episcopal property, and in enforcing discipline and residence upon the parish clergy.[37] Innocent's confidence in des Roches is shown in a mandate of December, exempting the bishop and his subjects from excommunication or suspension save by papal mandate.[38] At the same time des Roches was appointed to oversee the payment of Peter's Pence.[39] The bishop was a man of

---

[33] Migne, *PL*, ccxv, cols. 671–3; Cheney, *Innocent III*, pp. 144–7, and see *ibid.* , pp. 62, 64–5 for the Poers and dispensation for bastardy.

[34] *Coggeshall*, p. 162; *Rot. Ob.* , p. 333. Des Roches had also employed the services of a Bolognese lawyer, Merandus the Spaniard; *Chronicon Abbatiae de Evesham*, p. 153.

[35] *Flores Hist.* , ii, p. 129; *AM*, ii (Winchester), p. 79.

[36] *Acta*, no. 81, and for other quotations, see *Ibid.* , pp. lxvii–lxviii.

[37] See the pope's comments on his willingness to accommodate King John in confirming des Roches' election, Migne, *PL*, ccxv, col. 672c; Cheney, *Innocent III*, p. 146. For the reforming mandates, see *Letters of Innocent III*, nos. 643–9; Cheney, *Innocent III*, p. 33.

[38] *Letters of Innocent III*, no. 664.

[39] *Letters of Innocent III*, no. 673 (31 Dec. 1205); *AM*, ii (Waverley), p. 257, and below p. 410.

many parts. His career stands witness to a remarkable talent for appeasing the demands of both church and state. For all his entanglement in secular affairs, he was to retain the confidence of the papacy for almost the whole of his time at Winchester.

Quitting Rome early in 1206, des Roches reached England by mid-March. The temporalities of his see were restored to him from 24 March, and two days later, on Palm Sunday, he was enthroned at Winchester.[40] According to Roger of Wendover, the bishop had incurred heavy expenses at the Curia, but these must be offset against the favours showered upon him by the king.[41] Superficially, John had made a substantial profit from the Winchester vacancy: in practice much of this was sacrificed in settling the legacies made by bishop de Lucy, and in financing des Roches' election.[42] Bishop Peter appears to have received over 1,500 marks in outright gifts in 1205–6, added to which he was advanced considerable sums of money still unpaid by 1216.[43] John allowed him to levy an aid from the free tenantry of the see, advanced him loans towards restocking the episcopal manors, and apparently acted illegally in giving des Roches a valuable collection of chapel furnishings, precious vestments and ornaments of gold and crystal, that had been willed by the late archbishop Hubert Walter to the church of Canterbury.[44] To judge from later vacancies, des Roches would also have been able to extract considerable sums from his tenantry as their new lord; in the 1240s his successor, William de Raleigh, received over £550 in *recognitiones* during the first year of his episcopate. Raleigh also held a splendid feast to mark his installation. Similar junketings may well have attended des Roches' arrival in Winchester.[45]

---

[40] *RLP*, pp. 60b, 62; *RLC*, i, p. 52; *AM*, ii (Winchester), p. 79.

[41] Wendover, *Flores*, iii, p. 181.

[42] For the vacancy receipts see the account in *PR 7 John*, pp. 11–13, which covers the period 11 Sept. 1204– 24 June 1205, whereafter it is unclear whether the see's income continued to be appropriated by the crown or was diverted to the needs of the newly elected bishop, whose election occurred *c.* June 25. For the destination of this money, see Vincent, 'The origins of the Winchester Pipe Rolls', pp. 35–7, 40–1.

[43] *PR 8 John*, pp. 54, 155; *Rot. Ob.* , p. 358; *RLC*, i, p. 71. Des Roches was pardoned 1,200m of these advances in Dec. 1207, and although he continued to be accounted £1,280 of debts at the Exchequer, the debt seems never to have been repaid; *RLC*, i, p. 101; *PR 8 John*, p. 155; *9 John*, p. 144; *10 John*, pp. 121, 171; *11 John*, p. 167; *12 John*, p. 185; *13 John*, p. 180; *14 John*, p. 93.

[44] *RLP*, pp. 61b–62 (April 1206); *RLC*, i, p. 73. For the chapel furniture, see the complaints of *Gervase of Canterbury*, ii, p. 98. The furniture is listed in *RLP*, pp. 58b, 60b. Gervase states that it was valued at 300m.

[45] HRO ms. Eccles. II 159287 (Pipe Roll of the bishopric of Winchester, Bishop William de Raleigh year 2), *passim*.

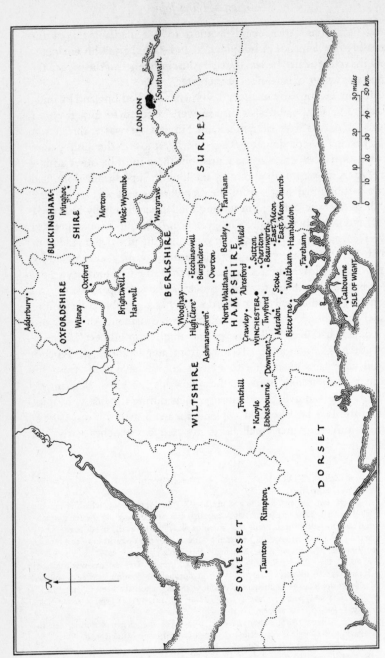

Map 2 The estates of the bishopric of Winchester

Des Roches owed his election to Winchester, one of the greatest prizes to which any churchman could aspire, directly to the favour of King John. In return he was expected to remain in the king's service, devoting his vast new resources at least in part to the needs of the court. From 1206 until the 1220s, his career is largely subsumed within the wider history of royal administration.[46] He is found at court on an average of five days a month throughout the final decade of John's reign and this, we may assume, represents only a fraction of his actual attendance. Shortly after his consecration in 1206 he spent nearly six months with the king in Poitou. He went abroad as an ambassador in January 1208 and the spring of 1216. At least four times between 1208 and 1213 he accompanied the court north of the Trent, and he followed it to the Welsh Marches in 1208, 1209, 1210 and 1213. Although he is most frequently to be found in Westminster or at sites within his own diocese or manorial jurisdiction, it is evident that he regarded curial service as an equal, possibly even as a higher, priority to his pastoral duties as bishop. Only after 1223, when his political career was interrupted and he found himself excluded from court, only then do the gaps in his itinerary suggest that he had sufficient time to devote himself whole-heartedly to the administration of his diocese.[47] Des Roches was not a 'bad' bishop, but an enthusiastic promoter of reform. Had we only his charters to go upon, without the mass of evidence linking him to the court, he would probably be regarded as one of the most enthusiastic religious patrons of his day. Nonetheless, it was in politics rather than in episcopal administration that he was to make his greatest impression upon English history.

THE BISHOP IN ROYAL GOVERNMENT 1206–1213

To speak of royal 'policy' under King John is in many ways an anachronism. The king possessed a demesne and an administration. He exercised justice over his subjects and, like every other king, he sought to push the various rights, jurisdictions and territorial claims that he had inherited, to their utmost extent. Whereas his ancestors had spent much of their time in France, after 1204 John was confined, for the most part, to his lands in England. England saw more of its king than it had done at any stage since the reign of

---

[46] Barefield, 'The king's bishop', provides an exhaustive survey of des Roches' role in government to 1216.

[47] For a comprehensive itinerary, see *Acta*, appendix 3.

King Stephen. To this extent, the country was over-governed.
Certainly it claimed to be over-taxed. After 1204 the king desired,
perhaps above all else, to reconquer the lands he had lost in France.
Enormous sums of money were collected to pay for this. But we
should be wary of elevating reconquest to the status of a conscious
or a consistent royal policy. Government was more improvisational
than planned: a matter of the king's personal will and self-interest. It
was at court and in the king's service that men made or lost their
fortunes, competing for royal favour in an atmosphere of intrigue,
bribery and ruthless sycophancy. Since King John was a suspicious
and a devious ruler, capable of acts of great cruelty, scarred by his
upbringing, his was a more ruthless court than most. It tells us much
of Peter des Roches that he was able to survive there for nearly
fifteen years, without once facing any real diminution of the king's
favour. But cruel though he may have been, John was also a king of
very great ability. Saintliness was not a quality that flourished at
court, but then neither was incompetence or feeble-mindedness. To
survive, the bishop must have been a courtier of almost superhuman
tact and efficiency.

Unlike the majority of John's alien servants, who earned their
unpopularity in the shires, des Roches was not dependent for his
authority upon the custody of royal franchises.[48] From 1206 until his
death, he enjoyed a manorial income which alone exceeded that of
the average barony by a factor of ten. Although this great wealth in
itself may have excited popular hostility, it left the bishop free from
the need to earn his living in the exploitation of the crown's estates.
In contrast to men such as Robert de Vieuxpont, Peter de Maulay
and Girard d'Atheé, deputed to provincial commands, des Roches'
activities centred upon the court itself, the Exchequer, the itinerant
household and, above all, the office of the *camera regis*.

The bishop sat as a baron of the Exchequer from at least 1208,
though even earlier he is found alongside the treasurer auditing the
accounts of the vacant Chancery and witnessing an order prior to a
general recoinage.[49] It is at the Exchequer that we find him
overseeing accounts, reminding his colleagues of earlier transactions,
recording a settlement between the earl of Salisbury and the king,
and witnessing confirmations to the monks of Reading and Mont

---

[48] For the problems caused by alien custodies in the provinces, see Holt, *The Northerners*, ch. xii, esp. pp. 228–30.

[49] *RLP*, pp. 70, 76. In 1207 he was sent to the Exchequer to consult over the accounts of sheriffs: *RLC*, i, p. 89.

St Michel.[50] His involvement in financial affairs throughout the Interdict is singled out in verses critical of the king's clerical adherents: 'The warrior of Winchester presides at the Exchequer, sharp at accountancy, slack at the Gospels, turning the king's roll.'[51]

It is probably an exaggeration to say that he 'presided' over the Exchequer; more correctly he served to link the Exchequer to the itinerant household. His earliest promotion came via the *camera regis*, and before 1204 he may have acted as semi-autonomous 'treasurer of Poitou'. One authority on the chamber describes him erroneously as *de facto* chamberlain.[52] In reality, the chamber's internal organization was flexible enough to allow the bishop an important role, without usurping the positions of the titular chamber clerks, Hubert de Burgh, Geoffrey de Neville and Richard Marsh.

Our chief evidence for the activities of the court is provided by the many thousands of writs, copied into the rolls of the royal Chancery. Although almost invariably issued in the king's name, relatively few of these letters were dictated by the king in person. Rather, they were the work of individual courtiers, acting on the king's behalf. To assess the work of a courtier such as des Roches we must pay close attention to the final clauses to such letters, most of which provide the name of a witness, who oversaw the issue of any particular writ, and a warrantor, at whose request or command the writ was first drawn up. Such evidence is far from ideal, since it remains extremely difficult to distinguish between a courtier's personal initiative and those actions undertaken at the king's behest. Nonetheless, both before and after his appointment to Winchester, des Roches supervised the issue of a bewildering variety of writs from the chamber, either as witness or warrantor, and occasionally in both capacities, exercising the broadest of delegated authority, almost certainly independent of direct supervision from the king.[53] Since the chamber stood at the very heart of

---

50   *Memoranda Roll 10 John*, pp. 35, 44, 64; *PR 11 John*, pp. 143, 198; *12 John*, p. 168; *14 John*, p. 151; *Reading Abbey Cartularies*, ed. B. R. Kemp, 2 vols., Camden Society 4th series xxxi–xxxii (1986–7), i, p. 77; *RLC*, i, p. 127b.

51   *Political Songs*, ed. Wright, pp. 10–11.

52   J. E. A. Jolliffe, 'The Camera Regis under Henry II', *EHR*, 68 (1953), p. 19 n. 1, and the same author's *Angevin Kingship* (London 1955), p. 243, award des Roches the (?spurious) title of scribe without citing any authority. See also Painter, *King John*, pp. 62, 86 for the mistaken suggestion that des Roches was chamberlain under Richard I. For the chamber in general see Jolliffe, *Angevin Kingship*, chs. xi, xii, and H. G. Richardson's criticisms of Jolliffe in 'The chamber under Henry II', *EHR* (1954), pp. 596–611.

53   For the terms *Teste* and *per* used in royal letters, see Painter, *King John*, pp. 103–4; *Acta*, introduction to appendix 3.

John's personal government, des Roches' administrative concerns necessarily mirror those of the court as a whole. The writs he authorized cover every manner of account, from the auditing of vast sums in ministers' expenses, to the provision of wine, oats, baskets and crossbows for the king and his stables. Steering our way through this frantic endeavour, it is possible to isolate three areas in which des Roches showed particular concern or expertise: finance in its broadest sense; diplomacy; and military operations.

FINANCE

Unfortunately it is not possible to determine the extent of des Roches' personal initiative in the various fiscal experiments of John's reign: the appointment of custodial sheriffs, the essays in direct taxation and customs duties.[54] Nevertheless, there is one financial experiment in which we can assign him a role with some confidence: the decision to free the chamber from the dilatory procedures of the Exchequer by establishing a series of castle treasures at Corfe, Bristol and elsewhere.[55]

This move was heralded in 1207 by the assumption of greater personal supervision by des Roches at the chamber, and the issue of several writs, witnessed by the bishop, governing the dispersal of coin from the central treasury.[56] In turn this dispersal greatly augmented the importance of those alien castellans, including Girard d'Athée, Engelard de Cigogné, Peter de Chanceaux and Peter de Maulay, who had recently been introduced to England, whose relations with des Roches have already been established, and who henceforth received custody of several of the new provincial treasures.[57] The experiment itself may have been modelled upon wartime expedients, well known to des Roches, adopted in John's continental dominion before 1204. Henceforth large sums of money by-passed the Exchequer in the charge of constables and of men such as the royal forester, Hugh de

---

[54] For which in general, see Painter, *King John*, pp. 113–48.

[55] J. E. A. Jolliffe, 'The chamber and the castle treasures under King John', *Studies in Medieval History presented to F. M. Powicke*, ed. R. W. Hunt and others (Oxford 1948), pp. 117–42; Jolliffe, *Angevin Kingship*, pp. 247–52; intro. to *PR 12 John*, p. xxxi.

[56] *RLC*, i, pp. 86b–87, 88, 95, 99b, 100b. R. A. Brown, 'The treasury of the later twelfth century', *Studies presented to Sir Hilary Jenkinson*, ed. J. Conway Davies (London 1957), pp. 35–49, esp. pp. 46–9 argues that Henry II employed provincial treasuries, although the scale of such operations under John and their control by the chamber were unprecedented.

[57] Jolliffe, 'The chamber and the castle treasures', pp. 131–4. Des Roches witnessed the orders for 3,000m to be sent to Girard d'Athée at Gloucester: *RLC*, i, pp. 99b, 100b.

Neville. In turn, such quasi-military proceedings may be linked to the need to appoint loyal courtiers to the shires and hence to the resumption of several counties from custodial to farming sheriffs in 1207. In this context it is worth noting that in August 1207, des Roches and the justiciar Geoffrey fitz Peter were sent to the Exchequer, to explain the king's wishes over the accounts of sheriffs.[58]

It is no accident that financial records modelled in part on those of the royal Exchequer were introduced to the see of Winchester shortly after des Roches' election, nor that the rolls which survive give clear indications of the bishop's personal oversight of accounts.[59] They also reveal that des Roches controlled a secondary financial office, known as the *camera*, possessing its own clerks and functions independent of the bishop's Exchequer at Wolvesey. Like the *camera regis*, the bishop's chamber was to come into its own during the period of civil war after 1215, when it superseded the more routine procedures of account to provide the bishop with day-to-day supplies of cash.[60]

Although it may be impossible to assign responsibility to des Roches for many of the fiscal experiments attempted after 1207, there can be no doubt that between 1207 and 1214 the king's financial operations were increasingly centred upon the chamber, and hence upon a department over which des Roches exerted considerable, if unquantifiable, authority. This shift towards household government was accompanied by a marked increase in the fiscal pressures placed upon the country at large: a strict rescheduling of old debts, a direct supervision of *debita Judeorum*, and a series of judicial and forest eyres geared more towards financial profit than the imposition of sound law.[61] The same period witnessed the systematic milking of the lands of the church, a process with which des Roches was to be closely associated. Moreover, the appointment of aliens to the shires caused

[58] For des Roches' mission to the Exchequer, see *RLC*, i, p. 89. In 1208 he witnessed the appointment of curial sheriffs to five counties, including the appointment of his fellow Tourangeau, Philip Mark, to Nottinghamshire and Derby; *RLP*, pp. 83b, 84, 86b. For the general change in policy towards the shires after 1207, see Holt, *The Northerners*, pp. 152–74, 222–5; D. A. Carpenter, 'The decline of the curial sheriff in England 1194–1258', *EHR* (1976), pp. 6–10; B. E. Harris, 'King John and the sheriffs' farms', *EHR* (1964), pp. 532–42, which emphasizes that the custodial system was not entirely abandoned in 1207.

[59] Vincent, 'The origins of the Winchester Pipe Rolls', 25–42, esp. pp. 37–8.

[60] The bishop's clerks Denis de Bourgueil and Robert de Clinchamps were active in the episcopal chamber from 1209; *PR4DR*, p. 18; Ms. 9DR, mm. 7d, 8d, 9d, 10. For the chamber's operations between 1214 and 1218, see below pp. 147, 169.

[61] Holt, *The Northerners*, pp. 152–74; intro. to *PR 12 John*, pp. xxii; *13 John*, pp. xxx–xxxi; *14 John*, pp. xxiii–xxvi.

considerable resentment. In particular, the appointment of Girard d'Athée to Gloucestershire seems to have been planned as part of the king's campaign against his former lieutenant, William de Briouze, who was subjected to one of the most vicious campaigns of persecution in a notoriously vicious reign. In September 1208, des Roches witnessed letters patent confirming d'Athée's pact with the men of Briouze against their erstwhile lord.[62] This affair stirred up considerable tension between crown and barons, whilst the king's explanation, that in moving against Briouze he was acting *secundum consuetudinem regni et per legem scaccarii* rather than by judgement of his court, points up the association between the Exchequer, the new financial measures implemented after 1207 and the increasingly arbitrary, increasingly resented nature of royal administration.[63]

John's vendetta against William de Briouze may well have been inspired by the knowledge that Briouze had disclosed one of the more terrible secrets of the reign: the true fate of Arthur of Brittany, in all probability murdered at Rouen in 1203. In turn, this was to involve the king in further acts of cruelty against Briouze's wife and his eldest son, who vanished into captivity at Windsor. The chroniclers state that they were starved to death. Certainly they were never seen again.[64] The murder of prisoners, above all of noble prisoners barely out of boyhood; the imprisonment of women and children; both of these were crimes associated in men's minds with barbarian peoples such as the Welsh and the Irish, beyond the civilizing influence of European codes of chivalry.[65] In effect, it is of barbarism that John was to be accused by the chroniclers, in terms that would have brought a blush to the cheeks even of his far from squeamish Plantagenet ancestors. For all its administrative efficiency, and for all that it may have drawn upon the service of churchmen such as des Roches, the court of King John was a brutal place. Between 1209 and 1213, with the king excommunicated for his failure to accept the pope's candidate for the archbishopric of Canterbury, and with the whole of England placed under papal Interdict, the civilizing influence of the church was even less in evidence. Yet des Roches chose to remain at court throughout these years. As a close counsellor of the king and as a moving spirit in financial affairs, the bishop of

---

[62] *RLP*, p. 86b, and see Painter, *King John*, pp. 240–50, esp. p. 243; Holt, *The Northerners*, pp. 184–6.

[63] *Foedera*, p. 107; Holt, *The Northerners*, pp. 184–5.

[64] Warren, *King John*, pp. 185–8; Powicke, *The Loss of Normandy*, pp. 319–22.

[65] J. Gillingham, 'Conquering the barbarians: war and chivalry in twelfth-century Britain', *The Haskins Society Journal IV*, ed. R. B. Patterson (Woodbridge 1993), pp. 67–84.

Winchester must take considerable responsibility for the trend of events. One of the principal spurs to the imposition of heavier fiscal burdens, which in turn was to do so much to poison relations between king and barons, was the king's desire to mount a reconquest of his continental possessions, a desire in which he could count upon the enthusiastic support of des Roches and his fellow aliens, but which inspired far less sympathy amongst the English baronage at large. This in turn points up the link between des Roches' financial expertise and his interests in matters military and diplomatic.

MILITARY AFFAIRS

An involvement in military affairs fits well with what we know of des Roches' early years, his service under King Richard, and his later participation in the battle of Lincoln and the crusade of Frederick II. At the chamber after 1206 he was inevitably involved in the payment of mercenaries and in the accounting of naval and castle expenses.[66] As early as 1203, he is found supplying money for the castles of Radepont and Moulineaux in Normandy, overseeing the garrisoning of Salisbury and the payment of the wages of crossbowmen and knights.[67] As bishop he supervised numerous writs which touch upon military affairs; for example, the appointment of castellans or the expense of fortifying Dover, Exeter, Sherborne and Portchester in 1208.[68] In 1212, he is to be found paying galleymen at Portsmouth and arranging for the construction of petraries on the Channel coast.[69] Besides witnessing a large number of instructions on the ransoming and detention of military prisoners, both in Poitou before 1204 and later as bishop, he himself guarded a variety of hostages; in 1214 his knights took charge of the son of John de Lacy, constable of Chester.[70] Hostage-taking, though less barbaric than the treatment meted out to Arthur or William de Briouze, was nonetheless unlikely to endear either the king or des Roches to the English baronage. Hostages were taken, in time of crisis or warfare, as a means of

---

[66] See for example *RLP*, pp. 67, 68, 71, 71b; *RLC*, i, pp. 73, 73b, 74b, 75b, 76, 87b, 91, 95, 119b, 137, 147, 153.

[67] *Rot. Norm.* , pp. 69, 87–9; *Rot. Lib.* , pp. 71–2, 100, 106; *RLC*, i, pp. 3, 10, 12.

[68] *RLC*, i, pp. 99b, 106, 106b, 108, 111, 112; *PR 14 John*, pp. xix–xx, 7.

[69] *Misae Roll 14 John*, pp. 233, 235, 261.

[70] For des Roches himself guarding hostages, see *RLP*, p. 12; *RLC*, i, pp. 134b, 137b, and as witness to ransom arrangements etc., see *RLP*, pp. 66–66b, 67b, 68, 87 (*Teste* and *per*), 89b; *RLC*, i, pp. 16b, 18, 99 (*Teste* and *per*); *Rot. Chart.*, p. 189. For the son of de Lacy, see Ms. 9DR, m. 5d; *In expensis militum episcopi quando duxerunt filium Constabularii de Cestr'*.

guaranteeing the loyalty of the hostage's family, with the clear understanding that unless the family co-operated, a hostage faced prolonged
confinement or, in extreme circumstances, physical injury and death.
Once again, King John's administration was never far removed from
brutality.

As a leading ecclesiastical tenant-in-chief, des Roches was under an
obligation to supply knights to John's armies. He himself participated
in the continental campaign of 1206, and in 1211 commanded part
of an expedition sent against the Welsh.[71] Some of his knights
served in Scotland in 1209, Ireland in 1210 and Wales in 1212.[72] In
1210 four of them helped to carry the king's jewels to Northampton.[73] The Winchester pipe rolls supply the names of more than
twenty of the bishop's knights, and of crossbowmen and mercenaries
entertained occasionally on the episcopal manors.[74] Routine gifts of
grain were made to the royal constables of Wallingford, Portchester
and Freemantle.[75] Amongst des Roches' military tenants, several
make sufficiently frequent appearances to suggest that they were
members of his household. Of these Eustace de Greinville and
Maurice de Turville occur in 1214–15 as constables of the Tower of
London and of Winchester during the bishop's period as Justiciar.[76]
His castle at Taunton was held by the Englishmen, William of
Shorwell and William de Swapham, although a garrison of foreign
mercenaries was imported for its defence in 1216.[77] Amongst his
other knights, Robert de Hotot acted as des Roches' go-between
with the royal Exchequer.[78] Geoffrey de Moneta held Farnham
castle from *c.*1208–*c.*1215.[79] Several of these men bear names

---

[71] *AM*, iii (Dunstable), p. 32.

[72] For Scotland see *PR4DR*, pp. 15, 18, suggesting that the bishop's men may also have
served on the Marches, since arms and provisions were sent to Tewkesbury. For Ireland
see the prests totalling £70 paid to the bishop's men via his steward, Roger Wacelin,
and via Stephen the clerk: *Rot. Lib.* , pp. 175, 179, 188, 197, 203. For Wales see Ms.
7DR, m. 8d.

[73] *Rot. Lib.* , p. 246.

[74] For example, see the entertainment of such men as Theobald *balistarius* with Geoffrey
de Caux carrying arms to Witney; *PR4DR*, p. 17. Ferandus *arbalistarius* given grain at
Hambledon; *PR6DR*, p. 131. Master Henry *arbalistarius* overseeing repairs to a pond at
Southwark in 1213; Ms 7DR, mm. 4d, 10.

[75] *PR 6DR*, pp. 50, 59; Mss. 7DR, mm. 2d, 7d; 9DR, m. 5d.

[76] *RLC*, i, p. 211b; *RLP*, p. 136, and below pp. 72n. , 135, 110, 115, 117, 129. For Greinville
and Turville, see *Acta*, appendix 4 nos. 38, 40. Greinville was an Anglo-Norman newly
introduced to Hampshire, Turville a hereditary tenant of the see of Winchester.

[77] *PR4DR*, p. 63; *PR6DR*, p. 162; Mss. 7DR, m. 10; 9DR, mm. 9, 9d; 11DR, m. 7d. For
the events of 1216 see below pp. 130–1.

[78] *PR6DR*, pp. 155–7; Ms. 7DR, mm. 8, 10.

[79] *PR4DR*, p. 37; *PR6DR*, p. 38; Mss. 7DR, mm. 7d-8; 9DR, m. 6.

implying Norman or Angevin descent. Here it is worth noting a letter of *c*.1220, in which the bishop apologized for the participation of various of his kinsmen and knights in tournaments, agreeing to send some of them back to his homeland to remedy the disruption they had caused.[80] There is evidence to suggest that des Roches' household enjoyed a reputation more for its martial exploits than for its aura of piety.

Two further conclusions can be drawn from a study of the bishop's knights. In the first place, those who were most active in the bishop's household were only rarely drawn from the upper levels of the landed knight service of the bishopric of Winchester. For the most part, des Roches, like other great landholders of the time, looked to new men, bound to him by ties of loyalty and personal attachment, by money fees, or by newly created tenancies. The hereditary knight service of the Winchester estates played little part in the bishop's administration, save to act as a source of feudal incidents, scutages and other fiscal obligations. Many of the aspects of retained service, traditionally associated with 'Bastard Feudalism' and assigned to the late thirteenth and fourteenth centuries, were actually in operation at Winchester in the time of des Roches.[81] Secondly, it is intriguing that, despite his close contacts with the court, none of the bishop's knights appears to have served in the king's military household. As Stephen Church has demonstrated, King John maintained a large and expensive establishment of household knights, whose strength does much to explain the king's ability to resist baronial rebellion after 1215.[82] There was little overlap between this group and that which congregated around the loyalist des Roches. Hence, when assessing the military capacity of the king's household, we should add to it the formidable resources that could be mustered in the household of des Roches or in the service of other loyalist magnates such as William Marshal. The king and his supporters may have been an even more formidable force after 1215 than their numbers might initially suggest.

Despite his liability to supply some seventy knights to the royal army there is no record of the bishop paying any scutage before

---

[80] *Foedera*, p. 163.
[81] In general, see *Acta*, p. xl.
[82] S. D. Church, 'The knights of the household of King John: a question of numbers', in *Thirteenth Century England IV*, ed. P. R. Coss and S. D. Lloyd (Woodbridge 1992), pp. 151–65. Of the knights listed by Church, only Joldewin de Doué and Walter de Verdun make any impression upon the records of the see of Winchester, and then not as personal retainers of des Roches but as royalists, entertained on the bishop's manors.

1216.[83] He was specifically excused payment in 1206, 1211 and 1214 and, as noted above, various of his men seem to have participated in the campaigns of 1206, 1209, 1210, 1211 and 1212.[84] Nevertheless, whilst respiting specific individuals, des Roches demanded scutage from his tenants at 2 marks per fee in 1209, and £2 per fee in 1214.[85] None of the £200 or more collected seems to have been passed on to the crown. Although it is conceivable that the money was used to pay mercenaries to make up the bishop's contingent in the royal army, it seems just as likely that des Roches treated scutage as a source of private income, one of the perquisites of his friendship with the king.

DIPLOMACY

John valued aliens not only for their dependence upon royal favour and hence their loyalty, but also as links to a continental lordship that might one day be recovered. Des Roches was actively involved both in diplomatic exchanges at court, and from an early date in promoting aliens within his episcopal household. His see enjoyed long-standing connections to the continent. The Winchester fairs attracted merchants from across northern Europe and the bishop was regularly granted licences to export hides and grain overseas.[86] The episcopal pipe rolls show des Roches' bailiffs importing wine from Bordeaux and conducting transactions with the merchants of Boulogne.[87] In

---

[83] In general, see H. M. Chew, *The English Ecclesiastical Tenants in Chief and Knight Service* (Oxford 1932), pp. 4, 19, 32, 86–7. The exact number of fees for which the bishop was liable is uncertain. The bishop's *carta* of 1166 acknowledges 72 fees, but in 1171–2 the vacant see was charged for its customary 60 fees plus 24 and a half of the new assessment; *The Red Book of the Exchequer*, ed. H. Hall, 3 vols. (RS 1896), i, pp. 55, 204–7. In 1211 and 1214 the royal Exchequer calculated des Roches' liability as 74 and a half fees in Hampshire: *PR 13 John*, p. 185; *16 John*, p. 134. However, the bishop's marshal, who accounts for scutage in 1210/11 and 1213/14, appears to have worked to totals of just under 65 fees, including those for Taunton.

[84] *PR 8 John*, p. 169; *13 John*, p. 134; *16 John*, p. 165.

[85] *PR6DR*, pp. 184–5; Ms. 9DR, m. 10d. See also the separate £8 and 10 shillings scutage paid from Taunton in *PR4DR*, p. 66, which at the £1 rate levied by the king in 1209 would argue 8 and a half fees. John's scutages are conveniently listed by Painter, *King John*, pp. 126–8.

[86] For export licences to des Roches, see *RLP*, pp. 62b, 78b, 158b. See also *RLP*, p. 194b, for his ship and man arrested at Bamburgh. The king apologized to merchants whose goods had been seized at the Winchester fairs during the bishop's absence on the Poitevin expedition of 1206: *RLP*, p. 74. In 1212 the fairs were extended by a week at des Roches' petition; *RLC*, i, p. 123b; Ms. 7DR, m. 9d, which notes £9 spent *in reparatione ferie*.

[87] *PR6DR*, p. 154. For an indication of the volume of foreign trade passing through Southampton see the returns to the tax of a fifteenth of 1202–4 given in the intro. to *PR 6 John*, pp. xliii–xlv.

addition, there were nearly a dozen alien priories established in the diocese besides estates and churches held by French religious houses. As such corporations became keen to shed their troublesome estates in England, so des Roches intervened to buy out the former French tenants on behalf of the new monastic houses he established in Hampshire, at Selborne, Titchfield and Netley. At least two of his nephews were promoted to English churches whose advowsons lay with alien corporations.[88] After 1205 it can hardly be accounted surprising that Frenchmen, both clerks and curialists, congregated around des Roches, who rapidly emerged as the most powerful, and increasingly the most isolated and mistrusted alien amongst a predominantly English episcopate.[89] By the same token, des Roches with his network of contacts and his earlier experience serving the Plantagenets in France, rapidly came to play a leading role in John's diplomatic initiatives.

John's chief diplomatic objective after 1204 lay in the reconquest of Normandy and Anjou via the preservation of influence in Aquitaine and the establishment of alliances with the principalities of Flanders and north-eastern France. That this initiative ended in defeat at Bouvines in 1214 should obscure neither the consistency with which the objective was pursued, nor the fundamental soundness of John's strategic thinking.[90] Even so, in monetary terms, and hence in terms of its impact upon the relations between the king and his subjects, the strategy was a costly one. Large sums were required, to maintain the king's military household, to retain mercenaries and garrisons, and to pay the enormous sums shipped across the Channel in subsidies to the king's allies in Poitou, Flanders and the Empire. By 1214, through heavy taxation, through the near annual taking of scutages and, above all, through his custody of most of the wealth of the church during the years of papal Interdict, King John had amassed a vast fortune in cash. At the same time he had placed a grievous strain upon his relations with the English church and baronage. It is hardly surprising that when most of the money was swallowed by the campaign of 1214, ended by the disaster of Bouvines, the king returned to England to face an angry reckoning.

As in the fields of financial and military affairs, although des Roches witnesses a large number of writs concerned with diplomacy, it is

---

[88] *Acta*, no. 29, appendix 4 no. 7.
[89] Above ch. 1.
[90] For an excellent overview, see R. C. Stacey, *Politics, Policy and Finance under Henry III 1216–1245* (Oxford 1987), pp. 160–4.

generally impossible to determine his precise degree of influence in such matters. On the mundane level, these letters include safe conducts to those approaching the court,[91] licences to merchants,[92] and writs touching upon operations in Ireland and Wales.[93] Given the bishop's service there before 1204, it is not surprising that des Roches is to be found witnessing a large number of instructions and appointments concerning Gascony and Poitou.[94] In 1206 he accompanied the king's expedition to France, and played a prominent part in the issue of orders for the custody of castles and the strengthening of John's relations with the Poitevin nobility.[95] Perhaps the clearest indication of his part in diplomatic affairs comes in the *Misae* rolls for 1208–9 and 1212–13. Here he is found at the chamber supervising innumerable small payments to foreigners, the majority of them Poitevins: the prior of La Grâce-Dieu, burgesses of Bayonne, clerks of Savaric de Mauléon and of his mother, of the seneschal of Gascony and of the viscounts of Angoulême and Thouars, including des Roches' successor as treasurer of Poitiers, Geoffrey de Thouars.[96] On the Winchester estates the bishop played host to a variety of Poitevin envoys, including clerks of Mauléon and Thouars.[97] The archdeacon of Poitiers was his guest on at least two occasions, besides maintaining contacts with the court. During the civil war he was to assume a political role, with des Roches as his sponsor.[98] The bishop's clerks, Geoffrey de Caux and Walter de Montmorillon, crossed to France on several occasions.[99] Walter may have served jointly under des Roches and the Poitevin magnate Hugh de Lusignan.[100] William de Saint-Maixent, besides his activities in the bishop's household and as des Roches' deputy in the royal chamber, retired after 1214 as dean of St

---

[91] *RLP*, pp. 66, 68, 79, 85, 87b, 89b–90, 99, 99b.

[92] *RLP*, pp. 65b, 90, 92b, 104b; *Rot. Chart.*, pp. 182b, 185b.

[93] *RLP*, pp. 38, 67, 72b, 87b, 88b–89; *RLC*, i, p. 81; *Rot. Chart.*, p. 194b; *Foedera*, pp. 101–2; *Misae Roll 14 John*, p. 233. The Winchester pipe rolls record regular contacts with Wales from where horses were purchased for the bishop's stables: *PR4DR*, pp. 17, 68; *PR6DR*, pp. 21, 96, 171; Ms. 7DR, m. 9d.

[94] *RLP*, pp. 63, 66, 66b, 67b, 69b, 73b, 90b–91, 91b; *RLC*, i, pp. 75, 82, 89b, 92b, 94b, 95, 118b, 119, 120b, 129, 155.

[95] *RLP*, pp. 66–68b; *RLC*, i, pp. 72b–75; *Foedera*, p. 95.

[96] *Misae Roll 11 John*, pp. 115–22, 134, 156, 169; *Misae Roll 14 John*, pp. 232, 233, 244, 258. See also *RLC*, i, p. 119; *RLP*, p. 103; *Rot. Chart.*, p. 192b.

[97] *PR4DR*, p. 39; Ms. 7DR, m. 4d.

[98] *PR6DR*, p. 42; Ms. 13DR, m. 3d; *Misae Roll 11 John*, pp. 153, 169; *Misae Roll 14 John*, p. 247, and below pp. 115, 126–7 and nn. 68–9.

[99] *RLP*, pp. 95b, 155; *Misae Roll 14 John*, p. 242.

[100] *RLC*, i, pp. 204b, 208b; SC1/1/127, where Hugh de Lusignan solicits a rent for him, formerly held by the archdeacon of Poitiers, yet another associate of des Roches.

Martin's, Angers, a position des Roches himself had once held.[101]
Another of his clerks, Master Peter Russinol may be identified with a
namesake, dean of Limoges c.1212.[102] John's seneschal in Poitou,
Robert of Thurnham, was a close associate of the bishop to whom he
made gifts of wine and who stood as his surety in fines with the
crown.[103]

Further afield, des Roches had witnessed a treaty with Navarre as
early as 1202.[104] He later witnessed letters to the king of Leon and, in
1212, paid pensions to nuncios from the count of Toulouse and the
king of Aragon, the latter mission shrouded in some secrecy but
probably aimed at recruiting support against Philip Augustus in the
build-up to Aragon's intervention in the Albigensian Crusade.[105]
Again in 1212 des Roches was instructed to entertain a Spanish knight
and to force him to promise that he would release French prisoners
on his return to Spain.[106] The bishop was also to play a leading role in
negotiations over the dower of Richard I's widow, Berengaria of
Navarre.[107]

The pensions of Breton, Norman and Flemish knights were paid
via the bishop, as were the expenses of the brother of the pirate
Eustace the monk, and of Henry, son of the duke of Saxony, who
had been sent to the English court in 1209.[108] The bishop was kept
abreast of news concerning the German emperor Otto IV.[109] Danish
nuncios were entertained at his manor of Fareham in 1214.[110] In

[101] *RLC*, i, p. 168b; *RLP*, pp. 67, 103b; *Rot. Chart.*, p. 199b.

[102] *Acta*, appendix 4 no. 18.

[103] Robert and des Roches appear together as witnesses as early as 1197; Landon, *Itinerary of Richard I*, pp. 117, 132. For Robert coming from Poitou to the bishop's manor of Taunton, see *PR4DR*, pp. 68, 70, and for his gift of two tuns of wine, half of which was drunk by Thurnham and his men, see, ibid., pp. 2, 28. See also *Rot. Ob.*, p. 419; *PR 10 John*, p. 154; *RLP*, pp. 68, 77b, 79b; *Rot. Chart.*, pp. 171b, 173b, 185, 195; *Pleas Before the King or his Justices*, ed. D. M. Stenton, 4 vols., Selden Society lxvii–lxviii, lxxxiii–lxxxiv (1952–67), iii, no. 973. Thurnham's widow and her inheritance later passed to des Roches' ally Peter de Maulay.

[104] *RLP*, p. 6; *Foedera*, p. 86.

[105] *Foedera*, p. 96; *Misae Roll 14 John*, pp. 249, 258–60, and see also *Foedera*, p. 113. For the background to Aragon's relations with France and Toulouse, see W. L. Wakefield, *Heresy, Crusade and Inquisition in Southern France 1100–1250* (London 1974), pp. 106–12.

[106] *RLC*, i, p. 121. In 1208–9 Spanish knights were entertained at the bishop's manor of Southwark; *PR4DR*, p. 60.

[107] *RLP*, pp. 154b, 181b–182; *RLC*, i, p. 141b; *Rot. Chart.*, p. 219b; *Foedera*, p. 137; SC1/1/23 and below pp. 95, 124, 164, 172, 183 n. 25.

[108] *Misae Roll 11 John*, pp. 109–12, 119–20, 129, 134;. *Misae Roll 14 John*, pp. 232–3, 260. For Henry of Saxony's dispatch to England, see intro. to *PR 11 John*, pp. xvii–xviii. In 1212 one of his men was taken ill at the bishop's manor of Downton: Ms. 7DR, m. 5.

[109] *Misae Roll 11 John*, p. 142.

[110] Ms. 9DR, m. 2d.

addition he witnessed or warranted instructions and settlements dealing with the counts of Flanders, Boulogne, St Pol and Holland, the appointment of an embassy to Germany and other matters touching upon the northern extension of John's diplomatic initiative.[111]

Perhaps the most remarkable ambassador found on the bishop's manors is the seneschal of the king of Hungary who had arrived in England in 1214, probably to discuss arrangements for Andrew II's participation in the forthcoming crusade.[112] In 1211 the bishop entertained a man named *Gavrinus de Glapino*. If we are correct in identifying him as Guerin de Glapion, John's former seneschal in Normandy, this would provide us with a further indication of des Roches' involvement in Norman affairs. Guerin is traditionally supposed to have died in the Holy Land at some time after 1208, having fallen under suspicion that he was conspiring against Philip Augustus, for whom he had deserted the Plantagenets in 1203.[113]

These then would appear to have been des Roches' chief administrative concerns before 1214: royal finance, particularly at the chamber; military affairs and diplomatic relations with the continent. By contrast he appears only twice as a justice prior to his appointment as Justiciar.[114] Between August 1213 and February 1214, various royal charters were issued by the bishop under the clause *per manum* generally reserved for the chancellor and his principal clerks.[115] Walter de Gray, the titular chancellor, was preoccupied for much of this period with missions to Flanders, whilst Richard Marsh, the senior Chancery clerk, was absent in Rome defending his part in the Interdict.[116] Des Roches presumably took charge of the Great Seal, which in December 1213 was released under his custody to Ralph de Neville.[117] Neville, later royal chancellor and one of the most

---

111 *Foedera*, pp. 103, 105, 113; *Rot. Chart.*, pp. 166b, 186, 189; *RLP*, pp. 91b–92, 98b; *RLC*, i, pp. 82b (*Teste* and *per*), 98 (*ibid.*), 100, 116, 134b.

112 Ms. 9DR, m. 4, and see also *RLC*, i, p. 153b; *Misae Roll 14 John*, p. 253.

113 *PR6DR*, p. 116; Powicke, *The Loss of Normandy*, pp. 173–4; Jouet, *Et la Normandie devint Française*, pp. 78–9. Des Roches had served alongside Guerin before 1204: *Rot. Norm.*, pp. 47, 64. See also *RLP*, pp. 70, 70b; *RLC*, i, p. 127b, for the bishop witnessing royal charters in favour of St Etienne's Caen, Mont St Michel and Marmoutier.

114 *Pleas before the King*, ed. Stenton, iii, p. cclxxi; *CRR*, vi, pp. 23, 189.

115 *Rot. Chart.*, pp. 194b–196b, 200; *Foedera*, p. 118; *Norwich Cathedral Charters* (PRS), i, p. 25 no. 39; Painter, *King John*, p. 80; West, *The Justiciarship*, p. 190.

116 *RLP*, pp. 103, 105; *Foedera*, p. 113; Cheney, *Innocent III*, pp. 69, 347.

117 *RLC*, i, p. 158b; *RLP*, p. 107. Although charters continued to be issued under des Roches' supervision until February 1214, implying that Neville served under the bishop rather than directly from the Chancery.

powerful men at the court of Henry III, thus owed his first promotion
in the Chancery to des Roches, who may have employed him at
much the same time as a steward on the Winchester estates.[118]

Throughout the reign, des Roches served prominently amongst the
inner circle of John's confidants. In this respect his career differs little
from those of a dozen or more of his colleagues. Yet des Roches was
also a bishop, spiritual head of the richest see in England. His loyalty
to the excommunicate king between 1209 and 1213 is therefore all
the more remarkable. With the appointment of John de Gray, bishop
of Norwich, as Justiciar of Ireland, and the excommunication of the
king, des Roches remained the sole diocesan active in England. This
alone must have served to isolate him from the rest of the episcopate
after 1213. While exiled churchmen bewailed the liberties of the
church, the bishop of Winchester was busy at the Exchequer or in
leading a royal army into Wales.

His allies and familiars during these years constitute an identifiable
group of secular administrators and alien constables at the heart of
King John's court; the so-called 'evil councillors' listed by Roger of
Wendover, a group of 'Southerners' to be set against the baronial
opposition, 'The Northerners', so brilliantly portrayed by J. C. Holt.
William Brewer, Richard Marsh, Walter de Gray, William of Cornhill, William of Wrotham and the forester Hugh de Neville were all
of them regularly entertained on the Winchester estates, served one
another as sureties to fines, and co-operated in matters of religious
patronage.[119] Brewer used part of his Hampshire estate to endow a
priory at Mottisfont, protected and fostered in awards by des Roches
and in turn to serve as the mother house of des Roches' own

---

[118] Neville's origins are obscure. For what little can be established, see N. C. Vincent, 'The
origins of the chancellorship of the Exchequer', *EHR* 108 (1993), pp. 110–14;
Memoranda Roll 10 John, pp. 121, 123; C47/3/46 nos. 1, 5; E401/3A, m. 4. For a
namesake, active as bishop des Roches' steward for part of the year 1213–14, see Ms.
9DR, mm. 1d, 2, 4d, 5d, 6d, 7d–9.

[119] For William Brewer, see *PR4DR*, p. 39; Ms. 9DR, mm. 2d, 4d; *Rot. Ob.*, pp. 205
(fellow sureties), 229; *Winchester Chartulary*, ed. Goodman, no. 329 (grant by Brewer to
des Roches); *RLC*, i, p. 142b (Brewer's house at Winchester); *RLP*, p. 120 (des
Roches to help Brewer's nephews); *Rot. Chart.*, p. 195b. For Marsh, see *PR4DR*,
pp. 22, 68; *PR6DR*, p. 65; Mss. 7DR, mm. 2 (Marsh's nephew Simon at Clere), 8,
11d; 9DR, m. 7d; *Letters of Innocent III*, no. 949; *RLC*, i, p. 111b; *Rot. Chart.*, pp. 196b,
197; *RLP*, p. 105. For William of Wrotham see *PR6DR*, p. 110; Ms. 7DR, m. 7d; *Rot.
Ob.*, p. 412; *RLC*, i, pp. 71, 73; *Rot. Chart.*, p. 183. For gifts to Hugh de Neville and
his huntsmen, see Mss. 7DR, mm. 2d, 6d, 7, 10d, 11, 11d; 9DR, mm. 5d, 10. For
William of Cornhill, see *PR4DR*, p. 18; *PR6DR*, pp. 42, 67; Ms. 7DR, m. 8. For
Walter de Gray, see *PR4DR*, p. 39; *RLP*, pp. 75, 95b, 102b, 103; *Rot. Chart.*,
pp. 176b, 191b (surety to des Roches), 193b, 194b.

foundation at Selborne.[120] Walter de Gray assisted another of the bishop's religious foundations, Halesowen abbey, whilst it was in co-operation with des Roches as co-founder that William of Wrotham endowed a hospital, the Domus Dei, at Portsmouth.[121] Des Roches was actively to canvass the appointment of William of Cornhill as bishop of Coventry.[122] In 1214 Richard Marsh was elected des Roches' successor as bishop of Winchester, at a time when it seemed likely that des Roches would be promoted to York.[123] To a considerable extent the future course of des Roches' career was determined by such loyalties and friendships established at the court of King John.

We lack the evidence to speak confidently of the king's personal relationships. It nonetheless seems likely that des Roches was amongst John's closest friends. The two were of much the same age. The bishop was privy to some of the darker secrets of the reign. He had been at court at the time of Arthur's disappearance in 1203, and was a close ally of Peter de Maulay who, according to one account, had actually carried out Arthur's murder.[124] For all the king's fickleness and suspicion, John was never to turn against des Roches as he did against the vast majority of even his more faithful courtiers. The king and the bishop shared a common sense of exile from their homeland in France. Both were ardent huntsmen.[125] Des Roches appears to have shared in John's coarse humour; he was fined a tun of good wine for failing to remind the king about a belt for the countess of Aumale, whilst the securities he helped to arrange for Peter de Maulay in 1212 contained several elements of the grotesque.[126] The Winchester pipe rolls record gifts of birds from the bishop to the queen and to John's daughters.[127] Both the king's legitimate

---

120   *Acta*, nos. 33–4.

121   *Ibid.*, no. 13, appendix 2 no. 4.

122   Sir William Dugdale, *Monasticon Anglicanum*, ed. J. Caley, H. Ellis and B. Bandinel, 6 vols. (London 1846), viii, p. 1243.

123   Below pp. 96–7.

124   *The Chronicle of Walter of Guisborough*, ed. H. Rothwell, Camden Society, 3rd series, lxxxix (1957), p. 144, repeated by Knighton and various later chroniclers. Des Roches was at court at the start of April 1203; *Rot. Norm.*, p. 85; *RLP*, p. 27. For the murder, see Powicke, *Loss of Normandy*, pp. 309–28; M. Dominica Legge, 'William the Marshal and Arthur of Brittany', *BIHR* 55 (1982), pp. 18–24, neither of whom mentions de Maulay's involvement.

125   Above pp. 2–3. For the king's fondness for hunting, see *Political Songs*, ed. Wright, p. 4.

126   *PR 11 John*, p. 172; *Acta*, no. 94.

127   *PR4DR*, p. 17; *PR6DR*, p. 65.

sons were born at Winchester, and perhaps the clearest sign of John's confidence in des Roches comes in 1211/12, when the bishop was entrusted with the care of the future Henry III.[128] In 1216 Henry was restored to the bishop's household where, it was stated, he had been brought up carefully and well.[129] Richard, the king's younger son, was committed to the care of des Roches' ally, Peter de Maulay, who also guarded the king's niece, Eleanor of Brittany, and during the civil war, the queen and Prince Henry.[130] John's illegitimate son, Oliver, defended Wolvesey castle for the bishop in 1216.[131]

Royal favour conferred many incidental advantages upon des Roches. In the eyes of his contemporaries it invested him with that aura of power and reflected majesty, which was in some senses the chief ambition of any man who had made his career at court. As the king's friend, des Roches was a man whose recommendation or disfavour could make or break many lesser men. Royal administration was still very much a private affair, a matter of *vis* and *voluntas*, governed by the king's personal likes and dislikes. Patronage and the pursuit of private interest took pride of place, ahead of any idea of abstract justice. To obtain justice in the king's courts, a petitioner had first to purchase a royal writ, initiating the action. Since relatively few writs could be purchased as a matter of course, petitioners had to engage in the payment of special fines, to the king and to those who had influence with the king.[132] Bribery and

---

[128] In 1210/11 the bishop sent game to Henry and in 1211/12 paid the expense of his journey from Northampton to Winchester, and a proportion of his Christmas expenses at Farnham; *PR6DR*, p. 65; Ms. 7DR, mm. 8d, 10. William, messenger of Henry, travelled to the earl of Salisbury from Winchester in 1212; *Misae Roll 14 John*, p. 243. In 1213/14 the prince's expenses were met at Merdon, Winchester, Clere and Bishop's Waltham on his going into Wiltshire. The king's daughter was also entertained at Marwell; Ms. 9DR, mm. 1, 2d, 3, 4d, 5d, 7. In 1214 Henry may have been kept with a hostage of John de Lacy, probably to be identified with de Lacy's son who was in the bishop's custody; Ms. 9DR, m. 5d, although *RLC*, i, p. 169 refers to de Lacy's brother. In the same year the bishop was refunded 15 shillings and twopence paid to Philete 'who keeps Henry the king's son', presumably the prince's nurse; *RLC*, i, p. 175b. Also in 1214 wood was sent to the queen and her family at Winchester; *RLC*, i, p. 199b. With the outbreak of civil war des Roches' knights were ordered to release Winchester castle, along with the queen and Henry, who was probably sent to Marlborough; *RLP*, p. 136.

[129] *Hist. de Maréchal*, lines 15604–6.

[130] *Hist. des Ducs*, pp. 152, 180; N. Denholm-Young, *Richard of Cornwall* (Oxford 1947), pp. 3–4. For Eleanor, see *Foedera*, p. 101; Warren, *King John*, pp. 83, 218, 221–2. In 1221 des Roches and de Maulay were jointly accused of plotting to surrender her to the French; below pp. 200–1.

[131] *Hist. des Ducs*, p. 173; *RLP*, p. 188b.

[132] In general, see P. R. Hyams' review of S. F. C. Milsom, *The Legal Framework of English*

backstairs intrigue were everyday features of life at court; a means by which courtiers such as des Roches exercised their authority, and probably too a source of considerable financial profit. Although it is impossible at this distance to fathom the precise sums that might be made, or the extent to which des Roches was capable of softening the king's notorious temper, it is clear that churchmen approaching the court chose to consult des Roches on the best means of presenting their cases before the king, a service for which the bishop was reputed to charge a heavy fee.[133]

Beyond this, des Roches' position as king's friend brought him many other tokens of favour. In 1205–6 he was advanced large sums of money, subsequently transformed into gifts.[134] He received several wardships and feudal incidents, the most valuable of which was custody of the lands and heir of Roger de Vautorte.[135] In 1206–7 des Roches agreed to pay the 600 marks owed by Vautorte to Henry de Nonant for half of the honour of Totnes.[136] However, Nonant was heavily in debt to William de Briouze, who in 1205 had obtained the reversion of the remainder of Totnes by extremely dubious means. With Nonant's death in 1207 and the subsequent fall of Briouze, the bishop escaped any payment of his fine of 600 marks, subsequently transferred to the Vautorte heir who in 1227 compounded for it with a new fine of £100.[137] Meanwhile des Roches continued to hold the

---

Feudalism in *EHR* 93 (1978), p. 861. For specific examples of bribery, see P. M. Barnes, 'The Anstey case', in *A Medieval Miscellany for Doris Mary Stenton*, ed. P. M. Barnes and C. F. Slade (PRS 1962), pp. 1–23, esp. p. 16; J. Boussard, 'Ralph Neville évêque de Chichester d'après sa correspondance', *Revue Historique*, 170 (1935), pp. 231–2; Wendover, *Flores*, iii, pp. 202–3.

[133] See Dugdale, *Monasticon*, vii, p. 1243; *Letters of Innocent III*, no. 892; *The Chronicle of the Election of Hugh abbot of Bury St Edmunds and later bishop of Ely*, ed. R. M. Thomson (Oxford 1974), pp. 38–9 (which infers a bribe), 40–1, 50–1, 116–17, 164–5. In 1213 des Roches and Geoffrey fitz Peter received 20 lampreys for the release of a prisoner: *Rot. Ob.*, p. 470.

[134] Above p. 53.

[135] In 1213 he was granted the heir of William, the bastard in Yorkshire: *Rot. Ob.*, p. 494. For his previous connection with William see *PR 6 John*, p. 188; *Rot. Ob.*, p. 205; *PR4DR*, pp. 6, 7; *PR6DR*, pp. 65, 70, 95, 179. William's widow was later married to des Roches' household knight, Eustace de Greinville, to whom she brought a claim to the Paynel inheritance; I. J. Sanders, *English Baronies: A Study of their Origin and Descent 1086–1327* (Oxford 1960), p. 55. In 1208 des Roches was granted land at Bentworth, Hants, seized from the canons of Rouen as *terra Normanorum*, in due course passed on to his household clerk Geoffrey de Caux; *RLC*, i, p. 100; *Rot. Ob.*, p. 512. For the Vautorte wardship see *RLC*, i, p. 74b; *BF*, pp. 98–9.

[136] *PR 9 John*, pp. 77, 144.

[137] *E. Rot. Fin.*, i, p. 154. In general, see Painter, *King John*, pp. 45–6; Powicke, *Loss of Normandy*, p. 349. In 1208 Nonant's widow was distrained for non-payment of her husband's fines; *Memoranda Roll 10 John*, p. 23.

Vautorte lands in Cornwall and Devon, upon which, as upon his episcopal estates, he was quit scutage in 1211 and 1214. Various debts for the Vautorte lands continued to be summoned against him until 1226 when they were pardoned as part of a general amnesty.[138] All in all the Vautorte wardship was a rich prize, acquired at the minimum of expense.

Most fines recorded against des Roches at the Exchequer went unanswered and unenforced throughout the reign.[139] During the period of papal Interdict, John authorized several regards of the forest leading to the imposition of heavy fines. In 1212 he also initiated a searching enquiry into franchises.[140] Evidence survives of this assessment at the episcopal manor of Downton and at Winchester itself, whilst the bishop's pipe roll records the visit of forest regarders in 1211/12.[141] However, as early as 1208, the bishop had received a new royal charter of liberties, exempting his own episcopal estates and those of his cathedral priory from liability for a whole series of forest offences; an immensely valuable privilege, given that much of the bishopric lay within the bounds of the royal forest.[142] In 1210 des Roches offered 2 palfreys to be quit of regard on an assart he had made at Witney, though the fine went unpaid.[143] Likewise, apart from gifts to royal foresters, the bishop seems to have incurred no injury from the enquiries of 1209–1212. In 1210 he escaped punish-

---

[138] Below pp. 191–2; *PR 13 John*, pp. 160, 259–60; *14 John*, p. 69; *16 John*, pp. 61, 63, 142; *2 Henry III*, p. 87. For the ward, Reginald de Vautorte, as a guest on the bishop's manors, see *PR4DR*, p. 39; *PR6DR*, pp. 116, 143 (the cost of feeding his hawks); Mss. 7DR, m. 8; 9DR, m. 8d, and also Exeter, Devon County Record Office ms. Courtenay of Powderham 1508M/TD51 (Courtenay cartulary), pp. 155–6; *HMC 9th Report*, pt. ii (1884), p. 404b, an agreement drawn up between Reginald de Vautorte and Thomas Basset, witnessed by *dominus Petrus Wintoniensis episcopus per cuius manum hec facta sunt.*

[139] For example, 25m des Roches owed for 10 tuns of wine was subsumed within his larger debts and apparently never repaid; *RLC*, i, p. 1b; *PR 7 John*, p. 130. The tun of wine for failing to remind the king of a belt, and the two coverings of *genettre* compounded for scutage in 1211, went uncollected; *PR 11 John*, p. 172; *12 John*, p. 189; *13 John*, pp. 181, 185; *14 John*, pp. 94, 97; *16 John*, pp. 130–1. Des Roches' position at the Exchequer also provided him with some immunity from the collection of fines; see intro. to *PR 14 John*, pp. xxx–xxxi; *Dialogus de Scaccario*, ed. C. Johnson, 2nd edn (Oxford 1983), pp. 48, 56.

[140] *AM*, ii (Waverley), p. 267; J. C. Holt, *Magna Carta and Medieval Government*, 2nd edn (Cambridge 1992), pp. 211–12; Painter, *King John*, pp. 207–11; intro. to *PR 14 John*, pp. xxiii–xxv; Holt, *The Northerners*, pp. 157–64.

[141] *PR6DR*, p. 45; Ms. 7DR, mm. 5, 8, 8d, 11, which include gifts and entertainment to the royal foresters, Hugh de Neville and Robert de Venuz. For the returns to the enquiry of 1212, see *Red Book of the Exchequer*, ii, p. 489; *BF*, pp. 52–228, esp. pp. 72–8 for Hampshire.

[142] *Rot. Chart.*, pp. 183–183b.

[143] *PR 11 John*, p. 155; *12 John*, p. 176; *13 John*, p. 10; *14 John*, p. 20; *16 John*, p. 117.

ment for enclosing a park at Taunton. Hugh de Neville, the king's chief forester, was fined 1,000 marks for permitting the enclosure, but the king actually helped des Roches to stock it with game.[144] No pleas are recorded against the bishop in the *curia regis* rolls before 1216, and the one action brought by des Roches and completed in the courts before the outbreak of civil war, was decided in his favour.[145] The rewards of loyal service were considerable and appear all the more extraordinary when compared to John's attitude towards those outside the charmed circle of royal benevolence. Des Roches himself had witnessed the brutal harrying of the erstwhile royal favourite, William de Briouze, and was present in 1213 when John imposed his notorious fine of 20,000 marks against Geoffrey de Mandeville.[146] As a leading financial officer and courtier, des Roches could hardly escape the envy of his contemporaries nor a considerable degree of responsibility for the grossly inequitable treatment of favourites and outsiders by the king and his courts prior to 1215.

Here then we have the portrait of a Tourangeau, perhaps once a soldier, later turned financier, diplomat and bishop: the central figure in a circle of French exiles increasingly isolated from the sympathies of his adopted realm, yet wielding enormous power under a king who was both his sovereign and a personal friend. It remains to assess his fortunes in combining this secular career with his duties as a churchman: his uncanny ability to retain the confidence of both the papacy and the royal court throughout John's reign.

DES ROCHES AND THE PAPAL INTERDICT 1206–1213

We have seen that in 1205–6 des Roches had gained papal assent to his election and been granted various privileges, the most valuable exempting him from excommunication or suspension save with the agreement of Rome. The Winchester election may have caused the pope considerable unease: despite allowing a 'free' election in Rome, Innocent had failed to prevent the monks of St Swithun's from bowing before pressures placed upon their convent at home. It has been suggested that this experience encouraged him to adopt a different approach in the following year. When the Canterbury

---

144 N. C. Vincent, 'Hugh de Neville and his prisoners', *Archives* 88 (1992), pp. 192–3.
145 *CRR*, v, p. 219, vi, pp. 30, 91, 171, 269, 298–9; *Pleas Before the King*, ed. Stenton, iv, no. 3104, and see *ibid.*, no. 4489; *CRR*, vii, pp. 1, 181, 275 for uncompleted actions.
146 *RLP*, p. 86b; *Rot. Ob.*, pp. 520–1, and in general Holt, *The Northerners*, pp. 72–8 and ch. x, pp. 175–93.

monks seemed certain to elect the royalist candidate, John de Gray, Innocent intervened to force them to accept his own man, Stephen Langton.[147] To this extent, des Roches' election may have had a crucial part to play in determining the future course of relations between England and the papacy. Nevertheless, curialist bishops had their uses as far as the pope was concerned, above all as a channel of communications with King John. In December 1205 des Roches was appointed collector of Peter's Pence in England, the proceeds of which had previously been diverted into episcopal and possibly royal coffers.[148] The privileges granted him at the same time may have been designed to protect him in this enquiry, though he was later to use them in defying the authority of Canterbury over quite separate issues.[149]

Nothing came of the bishop's commission on Peter's Pence, which according to the Waverley annalist was recognized by neither church nor laity.[150] The king only softened his attitude after 1213 when, anxious to curry favour at Rome, he included the tax amongst his acknowledged obligations to the papacy.[151] In addition to abandoning his commission on Peter's Pence, on his return to England in 1206, des Roches was apparently made to swear that he had procured nothing in the Curia that might affect royal policy towards the church in Ireland, currently disturbed by election disputes at Cashel and Armagh.[152]

Two further questions had arisen during his time in Rome. The first concerned the bid by bishop Savaric of Bath, a Burgundian, to retain control over the revenues of Glastonbury Abbey, extorted from the captive Richard I in 1193. Des Roches and Savaric combined to support one another. Des Roches loaned his ally money, and in March 1206 was appointed to a papal enquiry into Savaric's claims.[153] The latter had meanwhile died. Des Roches joined other bishops in

---

[147] Cheney, *Innocent III*, pp. 147–54, esp. p. 153.

[148] *Ibid.*, p. 30; *Letters of Innocent III*, no. 673.

[149] Wendover, *Flores*, iv, pp. 276–7.

[150] *AM*, ii, p. 257; *Foedera*, p. 94; Cheney, *Innocent III*, pp. 38–9; C. R. Cheney, 'The papal legate and the English monasteries in 1206', *EHR* 46 (1931), pp. 443–52; 'Cardinal John of Ferentino, papal legate in England in 1206', *EHR* 76 (1961), pp. 654–60.

[151] *Foedera*, p. 118; *RLC*, i, p. 229b; *RLP*, p. 156; *Interdict Documents*, ed. P. M. Barnes and W. R. Powell (PRS 1958), p. 40 n. 7; Wendover, *Flores*, iii, p. 254 states that Peter's Pence was specifically included in the settlement of 1213.

[152] *RLP*, p. 61.

[153] Coggeshall, p. 162; *Rot. Ob.*, p. 333; *RLC*, i, p. 61; *Letters of Innocent III*, no. 703; *Adami de Domerham Historia de Rebus Glastoniensibus*, ed. T. Hearne, 2 vols. (Oxford 1727), ii, p. 439. For the general background, see Cheney, *Innocent III*, pp. 220–5.

petitioning the pope and the legate for the election of the royal clerk, Jocelin of Wells, duly consecrated as Savaric's successor.[154] In addition, before leaving Rome, he was a participant in the opening stages of the election dispute over Canterbury. The suffragan bishops had written to appeal against their exclusion from the monastic election held after the death of archbishop Hubert Walter, but their proctors had been arrested on the way to Rome. Des Roches was able to vouch for the credentials of Master Peter of Inglesham, a member of the embassy who had escaped detention.[155]

The vacancy at Canterbury and the subsequent exile of the bishops ensured that from the moment of his return to England, des Roches was promoted to a position of great importance within the ecclesiastical hierarchy. To some extent he assumed the mantle of Hubert Walter, but in very different circumstances from those that had faced the late archbishop. From 1209 to 1213, following the flight of the clergy and the excommunication of John, des Roches remained the only bishop at court, in regular and forbidden contact with the king. His attitude was noted by several of the chroniclers and pilloried in verses critical of the curialist clergy.[156] He cannot be acquitted of involvement in the attack upon the lands of the church which accompanied John's struggle with Langton and with Rome.

In 1207 the clergy had resisted the king's demand for a thirteenth to assist the reconquest of Normandy, though in all probability they were forced to compromise by compounding for the tax as if it were a gracious aid.[157] There is no evidence of any payment being made by the see of Winchester. On the contrary, des Roches seems to have benefited from the discomfort of his colleagues, receiving 450 marks, described as being 'from the gifts of prelates'.[158] In the same year he was advanced 750 marks from the regalian receipts at Canterbury, and

---

[154] *Acta*, nos. 86–7.

[155] Migne, *PL*, ccxv, cols. 740–2, and in general see Cheney, *Innocent III*, pp. 148–9; M. D. Knowles, 'The Canterbury election of 1205–6', *EHR* 53 (1938), pp. 211–20. Peter of Inglesham had succeeded des Roches as rector of Halesowen; *RLP*, p. 49.

[156] Des Roches is noted as the sole bishop to remain in England by the continuator of Florence of Worcester, *Chronicon ex Chronicis*, ed. B. Thorpe, 2 vols. (London 1849), ii, p. 168; *The Historical Works of Gervase of Canterbury*, ed. W. Stubbs, ii (London 1879–80), p. 100; *Memoriale Fratris Walteri de Coventria*, ed. W. Stubbs, 2 vols. (London 1872–3), ii, p. 202, and see *Political Songs*, ed. Wright, pp. 10–11, quoted above p. 57

[157] Cheney, *Innocent III*, pp. 296–7; Painter, *King John*, pp. 131–6; intro. to *PR 9 John*, pp. xix–xx.

[158] *PR 8 John*, p. 155, *Rot. Ob.*, p. 358, and Painter, *King John*, p. 183.

a further £100 from the vacancy at Exeter.[159] Beyond these windfalls, he witnessed the king's demand that the Canterbury monks contribute towards the cost of a campaign in France, and in June 1207 acknowledged receipt at the chamber of lay goods seized on church property in Lincolnshire, where they had been lodged to escape assessment towards the thirteenth.[160]

Following the imposition of the papal Interdict in March 1208, des Roches' position at the *camera regis* inevitably involved him in royal reprisals against the church. Large sums seized from exiled clergy appear to have been processed at the chamber, which in the spring of 1210 spent 20 pence on parchment 'to make rolls ... for the account of bishoprics and abbeys held in the king's hands'.[161] Moreover, des Roches numbered amongst his closest colleagues the very men whose activities were singled out by the chroniclers as most damaging to the estates of the church. Both Robert of Thurnham and Guy de Chanceaux were involved in exploiting the Canterbury lands after 1208.[162] Another of the king's custodians at Canterbury, John fitz Hugh, was a guest on the bishop's manors and was also responsible for reprisals against the clergy of Sussex.[163] Girard d'Athée was granted custody of the see of Bath, where he and his associates appear to have intruded their own men, including a clerk of des Roches, into vacant livings.[164] Richard Marsh, the most notorious of John's agents in dealing with the church, was amongst

---

[159] *Rot. Ob.*, p. 358; *PR 8 John*, p. 54; *RLC*, i, p. 71; *PR 9 John*, pp. 144, 223. Previously des Roches had been given the chapel furniture of Hubert Walter, despite the protests of the Canterbury monks that it had been willed to them by the late archbishop; above p. 53.

[160] *RLP*, pp. 71, 71b; *RLC*, i, p. 86; intro. to *PR 9 John*, p. xx; Holt, *The Northerners*, p. 207.

[161] *Misae Roll 11 John*, p. 164, and in general see C. R. Cheney, 'King John and the papal Interdict', *Bulletin of the John Rylands Library* 31 (1948), pp. 295–317; 'King John's reaction to the papal Interdict in England', *TRHS*, 4th series 21 (1949), pp. 129–50; *Innocent III*, pp. 308–10; *PR 10 John*, pp. xi–xv, esp. p. xii; *11 John*, p. xxi; *13 John*, pp. xv, xviii; *14 John*, p. xxix, showing that quitclaims demanded from the clergy in 1211/12 were kept at the chamber.

[162] *Interdict Documents*, pp. 37–56, esp. pp. 41, 45, 48–9.

[163] *AM*, ii (Waverley), p. 264; *Interdict Documents*, pp. 12–14, 45, 52; *PR 12 John*, p. xxvii; *13 John*, pp. xix–xxiv; *PR6DR*, p. 65; Ms. 7DR, m. 8d, on which occasion he was taking forest pleas. In 1210/11 he was the recipient of letters from des Roches, and for much of this period he was active in the see of Winchester as sheriff of Surrey and keeper of Odiham castle. In addition he was entrusted with custody of the lands of the bishopric of Salisbury after 1209; *PR6DR*, p. 155; *Interdict Documents*, pp. 12–14.

[164] *RLP*, p. 80; *Two Cartularies of the Priory of St Peter at Bath*, ed. W. Hunt, Somerset Record Society vii (1893), pt. ii, pp. 16–18, nos. 72, 75, 78, 80; *Acta*, appendix 2 no. 3.

des Roches' closest associates.[165] The Winchester pipe rolls record that throughout the Interdict, des Roches continued to profit from the collection of Peter's Pence.[166] Fulk de Cantiloupe, placed under anathema for his treatment of the Canterbury monks, was afforded privileged treatment as a tenant of the bishop's manor of Meon, where his rents went unpaid from 1212 to 1216.[167] In 1212 des Roches' cathedral city of Winchester was chosen as the site of a meeting between the king and various Cistercian abbots, who were forced to seal letters surrendering any right to compensation for extortions made from them since 1199.[168] Given all these facts, and the undeniable evidence of des Roches' complicity in reprisals against the clergy, we can only conclude that the bishop ignored the appeals of both Innocent III and Langton that the suffragan bishops protect the liberties of the see of Canterbury.[169]

Even so, des Roches did participate in several sets of negotiations between the church and King John. As early as 1206, in company with four other bishops, he had been persuaded to write to the pope 'on the royal dignity and its preservation'.[170] In January 1208 he crossed to France, presumably to parley with Langton, and it was at Winchester, on 14 March of that year, that the archbishop's brother broke off negotiations with the king.[171] The seizure of clerical property which followed was accompanied in the case of favoured churchmen by almost immediate restoration of their temporalities. Des Roches was restored to limited jurisdiction in April and subsequently granted his full patronal powers over the religious houses of his see.[172] As recently

---

[165] Cheney, 'King John's reaction', pp. 132–4. According to the continuator of William of Newburgh John considered Marsh his God in everything to do with attacks upon the church; *Chronicles of the Reigns of Stephen, Henry II and Richard I*, ed. R. Howlett, 4 vols. (RS 1884–90), ii, p. 512.

[166] *PR4DR*, pp. 16, 32; *PR6DR*, pp. 30–1, 63, 180, 181; Ms. 7DR, m. 5d and *passim*. All these small sums were for the excess of payments (*residua*) of Peter's Pence over and above the assessed liability of each manor. Nevertheless, the principal levies may well have been counted towards the bishop's income. See intro. to *PR 14 John*, p. xxx; *Interdict Documents*, p. 40 n. 7; *Gervase of Canterbury*, ii, p. 101.

[167] *RLC*, i, p. 48; *PR6DR*, p. 120; Mss. 7DR, mm. 7, 7d; 9DR, m. 4d; 11DR, m. 6. For Fulk's attacks on Canterbury, see *Gervase of Canterbury*, ii, pp. lxxxix–xc; *Interdict Documents*, pp. 44–5, 48–50.

[168] *AM*, ii (Waverley), pp. 266–8.

[169] *Gervase of Canterbury*, ii, pp. lxxvii–lxxxvii.

[170] *Acta*, no. 88.

[171] *RLC*, i, p. 101; *Foedera*, p. 100; *RLP*, p. 80. Des Roches witnessed the safe conduct for Master Simon Langton to come to England, and its extension; *RLP*, pp. 79, 85; *RLC*, i, p. 102.

[172] *RLC*, i, pp. 108b, 111. The lands of Hyde, Newark, Wherwell and Merton were also restored to their heads by the end of April: *RLC*, i, pp. 110b–112.

as 23 March, the king had issued a lengthy charter of liberties in the bishop's favour, including major privileges in respect to the royal forest.[173] In turn des Roches himself oversaw the issue of royal writs restoring the possessions of favoured clerks, including Richard Marsh and Peter de Blois.[174]

The imposition of the Interdict served more to confuse than to compel the English clergy. Several bishops remained *in situ*, and in the spring of 1209 elections were held to fill three vacant sees.[175] In January 1209 Innocent III had written to des Roches, commanding his obedience to the bishops of London, Worcester and Ely, the executors of the Interdict.[176] Des Roches subsequently played a leading role in negotiations with the exiles, at London around Easter and at Dover in late July, at which time the conditions for a settlement were drawn up under the seals of both parties, recommending restitution of confiscated lands and a schedule of clerical damages to be made good by 31 August.[177] Des Roches apparently assured the exiles that this deadline could be met.[178] However, although the king was reluctant to risk a sentence of personal excommunication, he was even less willing to admit his liability to pay compensation, and as a result sacrificed the opportunity for a reconciliation with the church. Des Roches was amongst those sent to meet Langton when the latter crossed to Dover that October, but John failed to comply with the exiles' demands, and a solemn sentence of excommunication was passed against him on 8 November 1209.[179] Henceforth those who had intercourse with the king were themselves liable to minor excommunication, a threat which propelled the bishops of Salisbury, Rochester, Bath and Lincoln into exile, and effectively left des Roches as the sole diocesan in England from November 1209 to May 1213.[180]

---

[173] *Rot. Chart.* , pp. 183–183b, dated at Clarendon. Possibly to be related to *PR4DR*, p. 17, *In acquietencia hospicii horderii Winton', G. de Aucl(ent) euntis apud Northamptonam pro libertate novae cartae, iiis, ob.* In March the king presented des Roches' nephew, Peter de Rivallis, to a prebend at Lincoln; *RLP*, p. 80.

[174] *RLC*, i, pp. 109b, 111b, 112, including restorations to Richard Marsh and Peter de Blois *Teste* and *per* des Roches.

[175] Cheney, *Innocent III*, pp. 130–1, 156–9, 312–15; 'King John and the papal Interdict', pp. 295–300, 309, 311.

[176] *Letters of Innocent III*, no. 834.

[177] *RLP*, pp. 89b–90; *AM*, ii (Waverley), p. 262; *Gervase of Canterbury*, ii, pp. c–cvi, 103–4; *Misae Roll 11 John*, p. 123; Cheney, *Innocent III*, pp. 315–19.

[178] *Acta*, nos. 91–2; *Gervase of Canterbury*, ii, p. civ, a letter from the executors of the Interdict to des Roches.

[179] *AM*, ii (Waverley), pp. 262–3; *Gervase of Canterbury*, ii, pp. civ–cvi, cx–cxii, 104–5; Cheney, *Innocent III*, pp. 319–22.

[180] *Ibid.*, pp. 314–15.

The bishop's position during these years is not easy to assess. On the one hand he lacked any dispensation for his attendance upon the king, and whilst his recorded appearances at court, averaging six days a month before 1209, are extremely rare until May 1212, this is due more to the absence of evidence, the loss of the close and patent rolls, than to any voluntary self-exile by des Roches.[181] He undoubtedly sat as a baron of the Exchequer and supported the king's military expeditions of 1210–12. There can be little doubt that the tensions in his later relationship with Langton owed much to his failure to support the archbishop during the Interdict, although by the same token his refusal to break faith with John can only have heightened his prestige at court.

At the same time, his participation in negotiations both before and after 1209 seems to represent an honest endeavour to reconcile John to the exiles. Des Roches can hardly have relished the situation in which he found himself. If he fled, he risked sacrificing his position at court, yet by remaining at court he risked suspension from his ecclesiastical office, the bishopric of Winchester, which was in itself his chief reward for service to the king. In 1210 Langton was told that des Roches was the only one of John's familiars to counsel an immediate solution to the Interdict, without demanding unacceptable conditions from the church.[182] According to one version of events, it was des Roches who was entrusted with administering John's excommunication. No such papal mandate survives, but if true, this account might explain why no attempt was made to suspend the bishop from office, nor after 1213 to force penance from him, as enjoined upon all clergy who had remained at court.[183] In April 1211 Innocent instructed his nuncios, Pandulph and Durandus, to consult with des Roches before approaching John, and we find their entertainment at Southwark amongst the episcopal accounts for 1211. In the same year, Master Elias (of Dereham), clerk of the archbishop,

---

[181] *Acta*, appendix 3.

[182] *Gervase of Canterbury*, ii, p. cx.

[183] BL ms. Royal 13 A xii (Continuation of Ralph Niger), f. 88r; *Wintoniensis, Bathoniensis, Rovensis episcopi ex precepto domini pape regem frustra de satisfactione cohortant* (c. 1208); *AM*, i (Burton), p. 215, ii (Waverley), pp. 268–70 state that after Pandulph's meeting with the king in 1211 he absolved all John's subjects from their loyalty and entrusted publication of the sentence to the bishops of Norwich and Winchester in England, and of Salisbury and Rochester in Scotland. For a more realistic assessment of the sentence delivered by Pandulph, see C. R. Cheney, 'The alleged deposition of King John', in *Studies in Medieval History presented to F. M. Powicke*, ed. R. W. Hunt et al. (Oxford 1948), pp. 100–16. It is just possible that a hostile bull directed against des Roches (below pp. 97–8) was issued before 1213.

was a guest on the episcopal manor of Bishop's Sutton, demonstrating further contact between des Roches and the exiles.[184] On the whole it seems that the bishop trod a careful line, preserving his relations with the church without compromising his loyalty to John. This was an impressive feat. After 1213, the pope was probably too concerned with maintaining his newly established *rapprochement* with the king, to risk supporting reprisals against John's leading clerical supporters, the likes of des Roches, John de Gray and Richard Marsh.[185]

As to the practical impact of the Interdict upon the see of Winchester, the episcopal pipe rolls afford a unique and previously unexploited insight into the activities of the clergy. Superficially, the bishop's administration appears to have continued much as before. Des Roches made regular gifts of alms, to the religious of the diocese, to anchoresses at Crondall and Wargrave, to converted Jews and to the lepers of Farnham.[186] The episcopal palace at Marwell was refurbished and decorated with pictures, and glass windows were installed at Farnham castle.[187] Building work may well have continued on the Lady Chapel of Winchester cathedral, and repairs were undoubtedly effected at Romsey Abbey following a fire in 1211.[188] On 11 July 1212 another fire, possibly begun during the celebration of a scotale, engulfed Southwark and London bridge.[189] In the aftermath, besides providing alms to the monks of St Mary Overy, des

---

[184] *Letters of Innocent III*, no. 892 (14 April 1211); *PR6DR*, pp. 142, 154; Cheney, 'The alleged deposition', pp. 100–16; *Innocent III*, pp. 323–5. In 1210/11 Elias appears alongside des Roches' official, Master John of London. This visit is probably to be distinguished from a second mission in 1212, for which see *RLP*, p. 92; Cheney, *Innocent III*, p. 323 n. 92.

[185] For Marsh, see Cheney, *Innocent III*, p. 347.

[186] *PR4DR*, pp. 5, 19, 38, 43, 60; *PR6DR*, pp. 14, 41; Mss. 7DR, mm. 1d, 8, 9; 9DR, mm. 3, 3d, 6, 8d, 9, 10. In addition a regular gift of a quarter of grain was made each year to the *passori de Babileia*, presumably the keeper of the ferry at Bablock near Witney: *PR4DR*, p. 18; *PR6DR*, p. 66, and see *The Feet of Fines for Oxfordshire 1195–1291*, ed. H. E. Salter, Oxford Record Society xii (1930), p. 49.

[187] *PR4DR*, pp. 48, 53–4; *PR6DR*, pp. 13, 16, 30; Ms. 9DR, m. 6.

[188] For Romsey, see *Misae Roll 14 John*, p. 257. A Richard *cementarius* was employed at Winchester and at ?Wintney nunnery *c.* 1208–1212; *PR4DR*, p. 38; Ms. 7DR, m. 8, whose activities are unnoticed by Peter Draper, 'The retrochoir of Winchester Cathedral', *Journal of the Society of Architectural Historians of Great Britain*, 21 (1978), pp. 1–16. Draper assumes that work was discontinued during the Interdict.

[189] For the date of the fire, see Paris, *CM*, ii, p. 536; *Flores Hist.*, ii, pp. 141–2. For the circumstances, see a London ordinance of 14 July 1212, designed to protect the city from fire and to restrict the building of houses in thatch or reed, scotales henceforth to be licensed; M. Bateson, 'A London municipal collection of the reign of John', *EHR* (1902), pp. 729–30. It would appear that London bridge was already out of service in May 1212, since the royal wardrobe had to be transported by water between Lambeth and Westminster, 'when the bridge was broken'; *Misae Roll 14 John*, p. 232.

Roches presided over the refoundation of St Thomas' hospital, which was apparently well under way by 1215.[190] Throughout this period he appears to have assisted in building work at the king's new foundation at Beaulieu.[191] The Domus Dei at Portsmouth was apparently established under his supervision, before the final lifting of the Interdict in 1214.[192] In March 1209 des Roches confirmed a donation of wax to Hyde Abbey, and on 23 June 1210, was present in Winchester cathedral alongside the abbots of Beaulieu and Reading, when the Justiciar, Geoffrey fitz Peter, confirmed grants to the monks of St Swithun's.[193] From 1208 to 1213 there are regular mentions of the robes of the bishop and of the archdeacon of Winchester being carried to religious houses within the diocese.[194] At court, des Roches witnessed numerous charters confirming the privileges of more distant convents.[195]

Such evidence confirms that religious activity continued, despite but not necessarily in contravention of the Interdict, the terms of which were ambiguous and variously interpreted across the country, but which did not prohibit the sort of patronage and alms-giving which can be observed at Winchester.[196] Even such undertakings as the lighting of candles before chests of relics when the court was at Winchester did not fall under a ban directed principally against the celebration of Mass.[197] One indication that des Roches' subjects observed the Interdict, at least in respect to its prohibition of burial in consecrated ground, is provided by the existence of graveyards at Waverley and Basingstoke, used during the Interdict and only blessed after 1214.[198]

The bishop may have remained in the service of an excommunicate

---

[190] For gifts or prests occasioned by the fire, see Mss. 7DR, m. 10; 9DR, m. 9. For St Thomas' see *Acta*, nos. 56–62.

[191] *RLC*, i, pp. 136–136b; *PR 13 John*, p. 178; *Misae Roll 14 John*, p. 257.

[192] *CAR*, no. 362.

[193] *Acta*, no. 21, and see no. 34; BL ms. Add. 29436 (Winchester cartulary), f. 31v, noticed by Cheney, *Innocent III*, p. 312.

[194] The archdeacon was at Reading, and Newark in 1210/11; *PR6DR*, pp. 42, 155. The bishop's robes were carried to Newark in 1211/12, wine was sent to Reading and his cooks were sent to Waverley, possibly to prepare for his arrival; Ms. 7DR, mm. 7, 10.

[195] *Rot. Chart.*, pp. 176b, 184, 188, 188b, 189b; *CAR*, nos. 212, 227.

[196] Cheney, *Innocent III*, pp. 311–15; 'King John and the papal Interdict', pp. 295–301, 307–10.

[197] *Misae Roll 14 John*, p. 237, and see Cheney, 'King John and the papal Interdict', p. 307; 'A recent view of the general Interdict on England 1208–1214', in *Studies in Church History*, iii, ed. G. J. Cuming (Leiden 1966), pp. 159–68.

[198] *AM*, ii (Waverley), p. 282, and see *VCH: Hampshire*, ii, pp. 214–15, for the chapel of the Holy Ghost, Basingstoke, supposedly founded on an extra-mural burial site employed during the Interdict.

king, but there is no evidence that he connived at direct infringements of the papal sentence. He did his best to mediate between John and the church. In 1207 he may have benefited financially from the king's reprisals against the clergy, but this should be offset against his actions later; in 1210/11, when the king turned against the Cistercian monks of Waverley and forced their abbot to flee, des Roches awarded the convent considerable quantities of grain in charity.[199] Likewise, whilst the chroniclers state that John expelled and persecuted all Roman clergy, in 1211 des Roches is to be found making a gift of 100 lambs to a namesake and kinsman of the papal chamberlain, cardinal Stephen of Fossanova.[200] We might also note the bishop's entertainment of two well-known scholars in 1211/12, Master Robert of Bingham at Marwell, and Master John of Garland at Knoyle, which suggests a possible connection between des Roches and the schools of Oxford, supposedly dispersed in 1209.[201] It seems clear that *magistri* continued to teach at Oxford throughout the Interdict, since in 1214 their activities were specifically censured by the legate, Nicholas of Tusculum.[202] Master Robert of Bingham was subsequently to earn renown as an Oxford theologian, elected bishop of Salisbury in 1228.[203] Master John of Garland is known to have studied at Oxford under a teacher named Master John of London.[204] This latter is credited with using a tag from Averroes and has excited the attention of scholars interested in the introduction of the new Aristotle to England. He can now be identified with some confidence as des

---

[199] *AM*, ii, p. 265; *PR6DR*, p. 43. Abbot John of Waverley may be the brother John of Waverley entertained at the Wiltshire manor of Knoyle (*ibid.* , p. 90). The abbot had earlier written to Cîteaux to request instructions on the terms of the Interdict; *Gervase of Canterbury*, ii, pp. cix–cx. For the persecution of the Cistercians in 1210, see C. J. Holdsworth, 'John of Ford and the Interdict', *EHR* 78 (1963), pp. 705–8.

[200] *PR6DR*, p. 36, before shearing, so presumably spring 1211. For attacks on Roman clergy, see Cheney, *Innocent III*, pp. 309–10, and for the two Fossanovas *ibid.* , p. 93 n. 62; V. J. Koudelka, 'Notes pour servir à l'histoire de S. Dominique', *Archivum Fratrum Praedicatorum* 35 (1965), pp. 1–15, esp. pp. 12–13; *York Minster Fasti*, ed. C. T. Clay, 2 vols. , Yorkshire Archaeological Society Record Series, cxxiii–cxxiv (1958–9), ii, pp. 57–8; *RLP*, pp. 107–107b. For the cardinal's interest in English affairs see also *Acta Guala*, no. 140.

[201] Ms. 7DR, mm. 1d, 4.

[202] *Medieval Archives of the University of Oxford*, ed. H. E. Salter, Oxford Historical Record Society lxxx (1920), p. 4.

[203] A. B. Emden, *A Biographical Register of the University of Oxford to AD 1500*, 3 vols. (Oxford 1957–9), i, p. 189. Bingham was in the service of bishop John de Gray of Norwich at about this time.

[204] *Johannis de Garlandia, De Triumphis Ecclesiae*, ed. T. Wright, Roxburghe Club (London 1856), pp. v, 53–4, and in general see *Two Medieval Satires on the University of Paris*, ed. L. J. Paetow (Berkeley, California 1927), pp. 77–106, esp. pp. 82–7; W. C. Waite, 'Johannes de Garlandia, poet and musician', *Speculum* 35 (1960), pp. 179–90.

Roches' familiar, John of London, bishop's official *c.*1206–12, master of St Cross Winchester, and canon of St Paul's, in which capacity he appears to have accompanied des Roches to Rome during the latter's bid for the see of Winchester.[205] Before the lifting of the Interdict, Master John also seems to have been in correspondence with Master Thomas of Chobham, official of the bishop of Salisbury and author of a well-known treatise on confession.[206] The fact that his Oxford pupil, John of Garland, appears as des Roches' guest in 1212, suggests that John of London may have been one of those *magistri* who continued to teach after the dispersal of the schools in 1209. Garland appears at Knoyle alongside the bishop's kinsman Peter de Rivallis, who may well be identified as the *nepos episcopi* resident at Oxford in 1208/9.[207]

One final and somewhat mysterious incident throws light upon des Roches' diocese during the Interdict. The Waverley annals for 1211 note the 'martyrdom' of a man named St Simon on the Isle of Wight, 'at whose tomb many miracles have taken place'.[208] In the same year the bishop's pipe roll records that over £7 was collected on the Isle of Wight from oblations at the tomb of Simon of Atherfield.[209] Later entries show that Simon's lands had at one time been taken into royal custody, and that 'the men of Simon of Atherfield' were capable of being fined communally in 1212.[210] The evidence suggests that des Roches did his best to confiscate the offerings to Simon's tomb and to suppress the nascent cult. Was this because Simon was some sort of heterodox religious leader who flourished during the Interdict, at a time when the ordinary, sacramental functions of the church were in abeyance? Several

---

[205] *Acta*, appendix 4 no. 1.

[206] Avranches, Bibliothèque de la Ville ms. 149, f. 109v, printed in Thomas of Chobham, *Summa Confessorum*, ed. F. Broomfield, Analecta Medievalia Namurcensis, xxv (1968), p. xl, where it is dated 1214 X 17 by the editor who assumes (p. xxxvi), that Chobham can only have been appointed official after the lifting of the Interdict. In fact he was active at Salisbury for at least part of the period 1208–14; *The Canonization of St Osmund*, ed. A. R. Malden, Wiltshire Record Society (1901), pp. 37–8, 40, noticed by Cheney, 'King John and the papal Interdict', p. 312, and see *ibid.*, p. 311 for officials appointed to Worcester 1208–13.

[207] *PR4DR*, pp. 17, 19, gifts of firewood and cheeses to the bishop's kinsman from Witney, where de Rivallis was a regular guest.

[208] *AM*, ii (Waverley), p. 266, noted by Cheney, *Innocent III*, p. 59; Cambridge, Gonville and Caius College ms. 205/111, f. 249r, *Sanctus Simon martirizatus est in Insula Vecte aput Arefeld et xii Kal' Apl'* (21 March 1211), and in general, see N. Vincent, 'Simon of Atherfield (d. 1211): a martyr to his wife', *Analecta Bollandiana* (1996).

[209] *PR6DR*, p. 77.

[210] Mss. 7DR, m. 5; 9DR, m. 6d.

chronicle sources report the activities and punishment of 'Albigensians' during the Interdict, whilst the king himself was in regular contact with the Moslem rulers of Spain and with the heretic count of Toulouse.[211] The hermit Peter of Wakefield was executed for his prophecies against the king, whilst his teachings, more treasonable than heretical, are reflected in the *Invectivum contra regem Johannem*, a tract composed in the 1250s, but drawing upon memories and prejudices stretching back to the early years of the reign of John.[212] In 1212 it is no coincidence that the rebel barons are said to have considered sending for the ultra-orthodox Simon de Montfort, hero of the Albigensian Crusade, to replace King John on the throne of England.[213] However, tempting as it may be to regard St Simon and his men as part of a heretical sect, it seems more likely that Simon's martyrdom was the result of domestic violence; his wife was to be burned for his murder, a sentence meted out not for heresy or sorcery, but as the standard punishment for a woman who had killed her lord and husband.[214] St Simon was in all probability a victim of the age-old problems of an unhappy marriage. Nonetheless, the immediate success of his cult suggests yet another way in which the Interdict may have distorted the normal, smooth running of the church in England.

The air of normality exuded by the Winchester pipe rolls may mask a state of affairs by no means healthy. Between 1208 and 1212, the king had rejected every opportunity for a settlement with the church. Meanwhile a new harshness had entered his relations with the English baronage. The clergy were no longer in a position to smooth relations between barons and king. Loyalist clerks such as des Roches were amongst the most active of John's agents in the pursuit of the crown's profits, whilst the predicament of the exiled bishops can only have fuelled baronial discontent. With the breakdown of negotiations between the king and the papal nuncio, Pandulph, in 1211 rumours began to circulate that John had been deposed. Over the next twelve

---

[211] BL ms. Royal 13 A xii (Continuation of Ralph Niger), f. 89r; *Albigenses heretici Angliam veniunt et quidem intercepti comburuntur*, and see Cheney, *Innocent III*, pp. 23–4, esp. p. 23 n. 39; Paris, *CM*, ii, pp. 559–64; Cole, *Documents*, pp. 246, 249–50, 256–9. The Waverley notice of St Simon is immediately followed by an account of the Albigensian crusade.

[212] For Peter see Cheney, *Innocent III*, p. 327. For the *Invectivum*, preserved in a Burton ms. see BL ms. Cotton Vespasian E iii, ff. 168r–175v. My forthcoming paper, 'Master Simon Langton, King John and the court of France', attempts to prove a link between the tract and the circle of Master Simon Langton, brother of archbishop Stephen.

[213] *AM*, iii (Dunstable), p. 33.

[214] See *Cal. Inq. Misc.*, i, no. 568; *CRR*, vi, p. 306; Vincent, 'Simon of Atherfield'.

months the fire of London and the prophecies of Peter of Wakefield were widely reported as portents of divine disquiet.[215] Above all, the year 1212 witnessed the collapse of John's plans to mount a continental expedition. Despite the construction of a fleet and of a network of foreign alliances, the cost of which placed extraordinary burdens upon the country, the king was forced to cancel his preparations, at first temporarily, to meet the threat of a Welsh rebellion early in the summer of 1212, and then indefinitely, having, so it was said, learned of a baronial plot against his life led by Eustace de Vescy and Robert fitz Walter.[216]

Des Roches had been present in May when John reached agreement with the count of Boulogne, and he subsequently witnessed several writs preparatory to the planned expedition to Poitou.[217] On 6 July he was at Nottingham, where he witnessed instructions to the Norman mercenary, Fawkes de Bréauté, on the defence of Glamorgan.[218] Thereafter he appears to have left the court, perhaps to oversee military operations at Portsmouth and Dover.[219] Several of his colleagues at the Exchequer were implicated in the baronial plot revealed in August: Geoffrey of Norwich, William of Necton, Stephen Ridel and William of Cornhill.[220] John's immediate reaction was to lead a punitive expedition against the north, apparently accompanied by des Roches.[221] However, soon afterwards, the king turned from compulsion to compromise. Whether from a realization that he could more easily disarm his opponents by making peace with the church, or from a simple loss of nerve, in November he dispatched an embassy, headed by the abbot of Beaulieu, empowered to accept the terms for the lifting of the Interdict offered by Pandulph in 1211.[222] On 4 November he made oblations before the relics of Reading Abbey. Three weeks later des Roches witnessed orders restoring lands seized from the abbey of Mont St Michel, a conciliatory gesture in response to a request from the papal legate to

---

[215] *AM*, i (Burton), pp. 209–17, ii (Waverley), pp. 268–71; Cheney, *Innocent III*, pp. 324–8; 'The alleged deposition of King John', pp. 100–16.

[216] Holt, *The Northerners*, pp. 79–84; Painter, *King John*, pp. 264–69; intro. to *PR 14 John*, pp. xiii–xvii, xxiv–xxvii.

[217] *RLC*, i, pp. 116, 118b, 119, 119b; *Rot. Chart.*, p. 186; *Foedera*, pp. 104–5; BL ms. Add. Ch. 11235/9.

[218] *RLC*, i, p. 119b.

[219] *RLC*, i, p. 119b; *Misae Roll 14 John*, pp. 235, 237.

[220] Painter, *King John*, pp. 269–71; Cheney, *Innocent III*, p. 326.

[221] Holt, *The Northerners*, pp. 83–7; *The Charters of Finchale*, ed. J. Raine, Surtees Society vi (1837), pp. 47–8, where des Roches witnesses a charter at Durham in September 1212.

[222] Cheney, *Innocent III*, pp. 326–9.

France.[223] On the same day letters of protection were issued for the bishop's clerk, Geoffrey of Caux, going overseas, perhaps on the business of Mont St Michel, or possibly to the exiled bishops who were themselves the recipients of various conciliatory gestures.[224]

At the same time, to forestall the threat of an invasion from France, the king turned to negotiations with Toulouse and Aragon. A secret embassy from King Pedro II of Aragon was entertained at Winchester, and between December 1212 and the following April, des Roches made payments to various ambassadors, clearly hoping to enlist English support for Aragonese intervention in the Albigensian Crusade, a movement which culminated in September 1213 with the deaths of both Pedro II and Raymond VI count of Toulouse at the battle of Muret.[225]

In February 1213 the pope concluded his negotiations with representatives of the king and the exiled clergy, by demanding that John come to terms with the church by 1 June. News of this settlement reached England in April, at a time of great tension and uncertainty. Although an army had been mustered at Portsmouth, prepared for yet another expedition to the continent, these plans had to be cancelled for fear of a French invasion, announced by Philip Augustus on 8 April.[226] Des Roches was at court in March when John reached agreement with the count of Holland. He is found authorizing payments to Flemish mercenaries and the king's galleymen and, following the king's itinerary, he accompanied the court through Sussex and along the south coast.[227] It may be significant that he appears to have played no part in John's surrender of the kingdom to the papacy, which was transacted at Ewell outside Dover on 15 May. Subsequently he witnessed letters of safe conduct to the returning exiles and to Robert fitz Walter and Eustace de Vescy, the leaders of the rebellion of 1212.[228] In company with the archbishop of Dublin, the bishop of Norwich and a dozen lay magnates, des Roches issued letters to each of the exiled bishops and to the monks of Canterbury, guaranteeing that the king would honour his promises

---

[223] *Misae Roll 14 John*, p. 249; *RLC*, i, p. 127b; *DD*, no. 10; Cheney, *Innocent III*, p. 329.

[224] *RLP*, p. 95b.

[225] N. C. Vincent, 'A roll of knights summoned to campaign in 1213', *Historical Research* 66 (1993), pp. 89–90, 92–3.

[226] Cheney, *Innocent III*, pp. 329–31, and for the king's plans for an expedition in 1213, see Vincent, 'A roll of knights', pp. 89–95.

[227] *Misae Roll 14 John*, pp. 258–61; *Rot. Chart.*, pp. 190b–191; *RLP*, p. 98b; *Foedera*, p. 110.

[228] *RLP*, pp. 99, 99b.

towards the church, or forfeit his right to the regalian revenues of bishoprics and monasteries.[229] Langton landed in England on 9 July 1213, and on 20 July celebrated Mass in the presence of the king in Winchester cathedral, after which archbishop and king were entertained at des Roches' table.[230]

With the return of the exiled bishops, and in an attempt to appease the church, the king might well have sacrificed those clerical familiars who had remained loyal to him throughout the Interdict. Twice on subsequent occasions, in 1223, and again in 1234, a resurgence of ecclesiastical influence at court was to herald des Roches' disgrace. In 1213, the bishop of Winchester can have had few allies amongst the returning clergy, whose exile he had refused to share, whose lands had been despoiled with his tacit co-operation, and whose adherents had poured scorn upon des Roches as the Warrior of Winchester, too busy at the Exchequer to concern himself with the liberties of the church.

It seems likely that des Roches and Langton had only met face-to-face once before, briefly during the negotiations of 1208–9. The new archbishop had neither experience of the court nor sympathy for those engaged in its service. He arrived in England with power to suspend all clerics who had infringed the Interdict or had intercourse with the king.[231] The name of the bishop of Winchester must have been high on his list, indelibly linked to the excommunicate court and to attempts to frustrate Langton's election from 1205 onwards. The aftermath of the Interdict could have proved disastrous for des Roches, yet in the event it was not to be Langton who deposed a disobedient suffragan, but des Roches who with papal approval deposed his archbishop. This improbable *volte face* may be put down to two principal causes: Langton's inexperience and intransigence, which made any permanent reconciliation with John impossible and rapidly lost the archbishop the sympathy of both the pope and the papal mission to England: and secondly, the mutual dependence of des Roches and King John, signified by the bishop's appointment as regent and Justiciar within a few months of the exiles' return.

[229] *Acta*, no. 95.
[230] *AM*, ii (Winchester), p. 82, (Waverley), p. 276; *Walter of Coventry*, ii, p. 213; Wendover, *Flores*, iii, p. 260; Cheney, *Innocent III*, p. 343.
[231] Cheney, *Innocent III*, p. 69.

Chapter 3

THE JUSTICIARSHIP

Geoffrey fitz Peter, Justiciar since 1198, died on 14 October 1213.[1] It is possible that his position at court had become strained over the years, in which case his death occurred at a convenient moment. John was about to embark on his long-planned bid for the reconquest of Normandy, and it was essential that he should entrust the government of England to an utterly reliable regent.[2] Despite the return of the exiled clergy, the Interdict remained in force pending the agreement of compensation due to the church. Should the king's expedition end in failure, it was inevitable that the baronial grievances, which had already threatened to bring about rebellion in 1212, would boil over into open revolt.

Des Roches' commission as Justiciar is first implied in letters of 12 January 1214, and was explicitly announced to the country on 1 February.[3] According to the Waverley annalist, John appointed the bishop to subject the magnates and to subdue the contumacious; by using his power unwisely, des Roches stirred up opposition to the king.[4] The only other contemporary comment on his Justiciarship states that he was appointed 'amidst murmurings from the magnates of the entire realm that an alien had been advanced over them'.[5] Both of

---

[1]   Wendover, *Flores*, iii, p. 271.

[2]   West, *The Justiciarship*, pp. 168–72, 178–9, and for fitz Peter's relations with the king, see also J. C. Holt, 'The 'Casus Regis': the law and politics of succession in the Plantagenet dominions 1185–1247', *Law in Mediaeval Life and Thought*, ed. E. B. King and S. J. Ridyard (Sewanee 1990), pp. 21–42, esp. pp. 24–30; R. V. Turner, *The King and his Courts: The Role of John and Henry III in the Administration of Justice, 1199–1240* (New York 1968), pp. 22–3; D. M. Stenton, 'King John and the courts of justice', *PBA* 49 (1958), pp. 103–27, esp. pp. 115–18.

[3]   *RLC*, i, p. 160; *RLP*, p. 110; *Foedera*, p. 118, and see West, *The Justiciarship*, pp. 188–91, which argues for an appointment almost immediately after fitz Peter's death. West devotes a valuable chapter (pp. 178–211) to des Roches' regime as Justiciar.

[4]   *AM*, ii, p. 281.

[5]   *Coggeshall*, p. 168. Des Roches' status as Justiciar is noted but not commented upon by *The Chronicle of the Election of Hugh*, pp. 80, 88, 92, 96, and the continuation of William of Newburgh in *Chronicles of Stephen, Henry II and Richard I*, ii, p. 516.

these accounts were written with hindsight, in light of the events of 1215. It would be wrong to accept untested the contention that des Roches abused his powers, or that from the outset his appointment was unpopular.

Whatever the barons may have thought of him, des Roches possessed many qualifications to act as regent. His talents as diplomat and military strategist made him competent to continue negotiations with Flanders and the Empire, and to supply the military needs of the king in Poitou. His financial skills suited him to the presidency of the Exchequer, whilst, as a churchman, he was in a position to negotiate with Langton and the bishops for the raising of the Interdict. Above all, he had shown himself to be steadfastly loyal to the king. In the longer term, his lack of judicial experience meant that he was less well qualified for the presidency of the Bench than his legally trained predecessors, Hubert Walter and Geoffrey fitz Peter. But in the circumstances of 1214, legal training was of less significance than the trust of the king. One threat posed by his appointment was that it might disturb John's relations with the papacy: in 1198 Innocent III had forced Hubert Walter to resign the Justiciarship as an office unbecoming a bishop. However, no such objection appears to have been raised against des Roches' commission, nor for that matter, against the service of the bishop of Norwich as Justiciar in Ireland.[6]

The records of des Roches' Justiciarship are extensive: pipe, close, scutage and plea rolls survive, as do parts of an originalia roll and references to lost memoranda and other rolls. However, they are by no means comprehensive. Des Roches' administrative writs survive only for the period May–October 1214 and we lack all but a few isolated examples of his political correspondence: only one letter to Archbishop Langton, none to either the legate or the king in Poitou. Nevertheless, it is still possible to trace the history of his regency in some detail.[7] His administration can be considered under two basic headings: the church, and secular affairs.

THE CHURCH

It has become customary for historians to write of King John's surrender of the realm of England to the papacy in 1213 as a matter of relatively little significance. John, it has been supposed, did homage to the pope merely as a matter of political expediency, with no real

[6] Cheney, *Hubert Walter* (London 1967), pp. 99–100; *Innocent III*, pp. 19, 357–8.
[7] The records of des Roches' Justiciarship are discussed in detail in *Acta*, appendix 1.

intention of bringing England under direct papal rule. But this may well be to misinterpret not only the king's motives but the seriousness of his intent. The surrender of England, like the surrender of the realm of Aragon later that same year, was a carefully calculated manoeuvre which in effect brought England under direct papal protection. In the immediate term, John may have hoped to attract the pope's support against the threat of a French invasion. By doing homage to Innocent III, John provided himself with a second feudal overlord, to be played off against the Capetian king Philip Augustus and his claims to act as John's overlord in respect to the Plantagenet lands in France. In the longer term, the surrender ensured that in the decade or so after 1213, the papacy and a series of papal legates enjoyed unprecedented influence in English politics, comparable in many ways to the influence that Innocent III already commanded within the Norman kingdom of Sicily. John's homage to the pope, and the question of how this action would affect relations between England and the papal Curia, were therefore issues that baulked large at the time of des Roches' appointment as Justiciar.

In addition to this, des Roches had to do his best to patch over relations between the royal court and the English church, strained to breaking point over the previous six years. The return of the exiled bishops led neither to the lifting of the Interdict nor to the successful resolution of John's relations with Archbishop Langton. Langton demanded that financial settlement precede any relaxation of the Interdict, and rapidly came into conflict with John's attempt to promote courtiers to the many vacant offices in the church.[8] The papacy was far readier than the archbishop to accommodate the king. In May 1213 John requested the dispatch of a legate, the cardinal bishop Nicholas of Tusculum, who arrived with explicit instructions from Innocent III to support sympathetic royal candidates in the forthcoming elections. Des Roches was already familiar with the papal nuncio Pandulph, and rapidly established friendly relations with the legate.[9] Henceforth Nicholas and des Roches were to co-operate, often successfully, in by-passing Langton's objections, both in the election of royalists to vacant abbeys and bishoprics, and in the speedy solution of the Interdict.

John had promised to satisfy the financial demands of the exiled

8 For what follows see Cheney, *Innocent III*, pp. 341–9.

9 A. Mercati, 'La Prima Relazione del Cardinale Nicolo de Romanis sulla sua legazione in Inghilterra (1213)', in *Essays in History presented to Reginald Lane Poole*, ed. H. W. C. Davies (Oxford 1927), pp. 274–89, records the legate's meeting with des Roches.

clergy by Easter 1214, but by Christmas 1213 he had paid only 27,000 marks in damages. An enquiry had been ordered into compensation due to the clergy. In the diocese of Winchester, two knights were appointed to assess damages, presumably far less severe than the systematic felling of timber and depletion of livestock which had taken place in those dioceses removed from episcopal control after 1208.[10] However, when successive conferences failed to achieve a settlement, the legate began to lose patience with the archbishop and his supporters. Early in 1214 the royal embassy at Rome reached agreement with the pope. The Interdict was to be lifted as soon as the king had paid 100,000 marks, to be kept as security until individual claims were assessed. John received details of this arrangement in Poitou, and on 8 March communicated the scheme to des Roches, simultaneously instructing him to levy a tallage towards the raising of the Interdict.[11] This tallage is duly recorded amongst des Roches' writs as regent. Des Roches ordered the restoration of money taken outside the royal demesne and himself made use of some of the funds that were collected. For example, £100 was put towards building operations at Dover castle, and a further £40 from the tallage of Southampton was diverted to des Roches' own use.[12] In May 1214 he wrote to the archbishop of Dublin, asking him to collect a subsidy for the satisfaction of the church.[13] In all, it seems unlikely that much was paid to the clergy from these sources. The king's continental campaigns were too costly for the Justiciar to hold back 100,000 marks. In Rome the king's representatives solicited more lenient terms and the pope obliged them, making the lifting of the Interdict effective once 40,000 marks had been handed over. The remaining 60,000 marks were to be paid in five annual instalments of 12,000 marks, with the pope requesting that the bishop of Norwich and four lay magnates act with des Roches as guarantors of this arrangement. Even then, the legate and des Roches reduced the force of this more lenient settlement. At a council at St Paul's, the bishop of Winchester in company with his fellow guarantors gave pledges not only for the 60,000 marks which were to be paid over in five annual instalments, but for a further 13,000 marks, the sum needed to make up the 27,000 marks already paid by the king, to the required 40,000

---

10   *RLC*, i, p. 164b.
11   *RLP*, p. 111b; *Foedera*, p. 118.
12   *RLC*, i, pp. 208–9, 213; *PR 16 John*, pp. 127, 131.
13   *RLC*, i, p. 205.

marks.[14] As a result, the same council, with the bishop of Ely acting as spokesman, declared the Interdict at an end, late in June 1214.

Des Roches was never to be called upon to answer his pledges. Between June and November a mere 6,000 marks, half of the annual instalment agreed for the year, appears to have been paid.[15] In November an enquiry into the damages due to a clerk was delayed pending the outcome of the wider enquiry into compensation which must be presumed to have been still in progress.[16] However, within the next few months the clergy appear to have abandoned any hope of a financial settlement and to have accepted material substitutes, grants of privileges to archbishop Langton, and the bishops of Lincoln, Bath, London and Ely, several of which were witnessed by des Roches.[17] Even then, des Roches must have been aware that Richard Marsh was simultaneously forcing monastic convents to seal letters, prepared in the royal Chancery, surrendering any claim to money extorted from them between 1208 and 1213.[18] In speeding the end of the Interdict, and bearing in mind that his own see had suffered little injury after 1208, des Roches was prepared to sidestep the legitimate demands of his fellow bishops, to issue promises on behalf of the king which he can have had little hope would be honoured, and at the same time, to divert part of the tallage levied on behalf of the clergy to the uses of the court.

Just as Langton was thwarted over the question of compensation, so too he was outmanoeuvred by des Roches and the legate in the elections to church offices that had fallen vacant during the Interdict.[19] In effect, Langton's adherents were passed over in favour of clerks who had remained at court after 1208. On the king's departure for Poitou in February 1214, des Roches was entrusted with authority to give assent to such elections, to be supervised by a committee of five men: the lay curialists William Brewer and William de Cantiloupe, and the

---

[14] For the council see *AM*, iii (Bermondsey), p. 453; 'The annals of Southwark and Merton', ed. M. Tyson, *Surrey Archaeological Collections* xxxvi (1926), p. 49. For the pledges, see *Rot. Chart.*, p. 199; *Foedera*, p. 122; *Letters of Innocent III*, no. 976. The bishops' letters have not survived, but those of William earl Ferrers are printed in *RLP*, p. 139; *Foedera*, p. 123.

[15] *RLC*, i, p. 175b, and in general see Cheney, *Innocent III*, pp. 348–55.

[16] *RLC*, i, p. 174b. The Canterbury monks received £1,000 in compensation by Michaelmas 1214; C. Everleigh Woodruff, 'The financial aspect of the cult of St Thomas of Canterbury', *Archaeologia Cantiana* 44 (1932), p. 16.

[17] See below pp. 114–15.

[18] *RLP*, pp. 140b–141; *Chronicle of the Election of Hugh*, pp. 134–46; *Two Cartularies of Bath*, ed. Hunt, part ii, p. 18 no. 82.

[19] For the elections of 1213–14, see Cheney, *Innocent III*, pp. 155–67.

abbots of Beaulieu, Selby and St Mary's York.[20] There can be little doubt that this committee was deliberately designed to exclude Langton's influence. Beaulieu was a royal foundation and its abbot both a curialist and a Cistercian, exempt from the archbishop's jurisdiction. Selby and St Mary's were northern houses, whose abbots lay beyond the disciplinary authority of the province of Canterbury.

Over a dozen of des Roches' writs as Justiciar touch upon the elections of 1214. At Coventry he actively counselled the monks to elect William of Cornhill, his close colleague in royal administration.[21] At Cirencester he presided over the restoration of temporalities to Master Alexander Nequam, the scholar who had remained in England throughout the Interdict and whose contacts with the royal household dated back to his upbringing by the nurse of Richard I.[22] The royalist abbot of Selby was translated to Ramsey under des Roches' supervision.[23] At Barking the Justiciar was instructed to secure the election of a suitable abbess and, above all, to exclude the sister of Robert fitz Walter, only recently pardoned his outlawry for the rebellion of 1212.[24] At St Albans the king ordered des Roches to promote the brother of Walter Mauclerk and, when that failed, to delay the election until John's return from Poitou.[25] There is some evidence that des Roches encouraged the election of his fellow aliens and men from within his own diocese. The prior of Winchester was elected abbot of Burton, but prevented either by death or appeal from assuming office. In his place, des Roches oversaw the election of a Norman, formerly prior of Sherborne.[26] A canon of Merton was elected prior of Carlisle, and two members of des Roches' household, his nephew Bartholomew and Master Peter Russinol, promoted to positions within the chapter at York.[27] Besides the Norman elected

---

[20] *RLP*, p. 110b, although the same committee was already operating in January 1214; *RLP*, pp. 109–109b; *RLC*, i, pp. 160, 162.

[21] Dugdale, *Monasticon*, vii, p. 1243, and see *The Great Register of Lichfield Cathedral known as Magnum Registrum Album*, ed. H. E. Savage, William Salt Archaeological Society (1926 for 1924), no. 367; Cheney, *Innocent III*, pp. 131–2.

[22] *RLC*, i, p. 204b. For Nequam's contacts with the court, see R. W. Hunt, *The Schools and the Cloister* (Oxford 1984), pp. 1–2, 13–14; *Misae Roll 14 John*, pp. 242, 266.

[23] *RLC*, i, p. 207b.

[24] *Ibid.*, pp. 202–202b.

[25] *RLP*, p. 140; *RLC*, i, p. 202b.

[26] *RLC*, i, pp. 161b, 207; *RLP*, pp. 108b–109; *The Heads of Religious Houses, England and Wales 940–1216*, ed. D. Knowles, C. N. L. Brooke and V. C. M. London (Cambridge 1972), p. 31.

[27] For Carlisle, see *RLC*, i, pp. 162, 207b, 211, 211b; *RLP*, p. 118. For the promotions at York see below p. 96. Bartholomew was also promoted to a benefice during the vacancy at St Benet of Hulme in 1213–14; *RLP*, p. 99b.

abbot of Burton, des Roches presided over the restoration of temporalities to the newly elected Norman abbot of Westminster, who was subsequently to assist in negotiating peace with France in the autumn of 1214.[28] On royal instructions, he restored land to the Breton abbey of Villeneuve, and made gifts to a number of French clerks, including his own household familiar, the Poitevin Walter de Montmorillon, and, rather unexpectedly, to a clerk of Philip Augustus.[29] He arranged crossings to France for the precentor of Rouen and for a monk of La Couture at Le Mans, whose convent he appears to have supported in a suit before the legate.[30] Simon, a monk of St Bertin's, was provided with maintenance at Keynsham Abbey on the Justiciar's orders.[31]

Besides these contacts with French churchmen, des Roches maintained a close relationship with the papal mission headed by Pandulph and the legate Nicholas. Pandulph was entertained at Farnham and with his nephew at Southwark.[32] The legate was entertained and supplied with geese and other gifts from several of the bishop's manors.[33] The bishop's writs provided for his reception across the country and for the passage of his envoys to the continent. There is clear evidence of a correspondence between legate and Justiciar.[34] In March 1214 they are found together with Langton, in council at Northampton, consulting on an election at Bury St Edmunds. When a letter arrived for Nicholas from Robert Courcon, the papal legate in France, des Roches was called to be present when the seal was broken, and was immediately made privy to its contents.[35] Legate and Justiciar were jointly entrusted with two papal commissions, to protect Richard Marsh from ecclesiastical censure, and to head an enquiry into the dower of Richard I's widow Berengaria.[36] In addition, des Roches supervised the payment of pensions to a large number of Italian clerks, adherents of the papal mission or royal envoys to Rome.[37]

Perhaps the clearest sign of the harmony established between

---

[28] For Westminster, see *RLC*, i, p. 204b; *Heads of Religious Houses*, p. 77.

[29] *RLC*, i, pp. 204b, 206, 215; *RLP*, pp. 120, 122; and see *Rot. Chart.*, p. 196b for a grant to another Breton convent.

[30] *RLC*, i, pp. 207b, 209, and above p. 20.

[31] *RLC*, i, pp. 211–211b, 213.

[32] Ms. 9DR, mm. 6, 8d, 9.

[33] Ms. 9DR, mm. 1, 2d, 3, 4d–5d, 7d, 8d–9d.

[34] *RLC*, i, pp. 205b, 206b, 210, 211, 211b, 212b.

[35] *Chronicle of the Election of Hugh*, pp. 48–50; *C & S*, i, p. 21 n. 6.

[36] *Letters of Innocent III*, no. 949; *RLC*, i, p. 141b; Cheney, *Innocent III*, p. 101 and notes.

[37] *RLC*, i, p. 211b; *PR 16 John*, p. 28; *RLP*, pp. 118, 120, 120b.

Justiciar and legate comes in the latter's attempt to secure des Roches' translation to the archbishopric of York. This was heralded by the appointment of the bishop's nephew, Bartholomew des Roches, as dean of York, and the promotion of the bishop's seal-keeper, Master Peter Russinol, as precentor.[38] In order to effect these changes, des Roches supervised the election of the previous dean of York, Simon of Apulia, to the vacant see of Exeter.[39] The Winchester pipe rolls show that the dean, probably Bartholomew rather than Simon, was a regular guest on the bishop's estates in 1214 as were the abbots of York and Selby who, as early as January, had been sent to effect an election to the northern archdiocese.[40] This had been accomplished, with the legate's co-operation, by mid-February. Thereafter the Justiciar's writs suggest a personal interest in the see of York, with des Roches ordering repairs to the archiepiscopal, mills and forbidding a case involving the see to come before the Bench *sede vacante*.[41] Had the election been approved, there can be little doubt that the king would deliberately have exalted the new metropolitan over Langton at Canterbury, using des Roches as a bastion of royal influence in the north, just as in March 1214, des Roches' fellow alien, Peter de Maulay, was allowed to fine for the Yorkshire inheritance of Robert of Thurnham. In the same way, the king promoted curialists such as Philip of Oldcotes, Robert de Vieuxpont and Brian de Lisle to northern captaincies – to serve as outposts of royal authority in a hostile region.[42] That it was hoped des Roches might perform a similar function is suggested by a letter of 1215 in which, following his rejection by York, the bishop is said to have been offered the see of Durham.[43]

The election to York left the see of Winchester open for another curialist, Richard Marsh. The election committee was sent to St Swithun's on 6 April 1214, and in late May, the king confirmed his

38 *RLP*, pp. 101, 113b; *York Minster Fasti*, ed. Clay, i, pp. 2, 13.
39 *PR 16 John*, p. 83 and in general see Cheney, *Innocent III*, pp. 162–5.
40 *RLP*, p. 109; Ms. 9DR, mm. 5, 5d, 8d.
41 *RLC*, i, p. 208; *CRR*, vii, p. 115. The only chronicler to mention des Roches' election states that it was intended to please the king; Geoffrey of Coldingham in *Historiae Dunelmensis Scriptores Tres*, ed. J. Raine, Surtees Society, ix (1839), pp. 28–9.
42 *RLC*, i, p. 205b; *RLP*, p. 113b; *PR 16 John*, p. 94 and in general see Holt, *The Northerners*, ch. xii. Des Roches stood as the principal pledge to de Maulay's fine; C60/5d, m. 3.
43 SC1/1/6, printed by V. H. Galbraith, *Studies in the Public Records* (London 1948), pp. 136–7, 161–2, unnoticed by Cheney in his account of the Durham election, *Innocent III*, pp. 165–7.

desire that the monks elect Marsh.[44] On 28 June the legate was asked to confirm this choice. John's letters state that he had avoided asking Langton who would maliciously delay consecrating the elect.[45] This is hardly surprising, since Marsh had been responsible for some of the more outrageous extortions of the Interdict, and had only escaped suspension in 1213 by travelling to Rome to seek papal absolution. Innocent III had ignored Langton's complaints and provided Marsh with letters to des Roches, the legate and the bishop of Norwich protecting him from ecclesiastical censure.[46]

In the event, the elections to York and Winchester failed to receive confirmation. Early in January 1214, Langton held a council at Dunstable, where he forbade the legate to fill vacancies before the outcome of an appeal to the pope.[47] Feelings were running high, exacerbated by the legate's over-indulgent attitude towards royalist candidates. Langton seems deliberately to have delayed consecrating William of Cornhill as bishop of Coventry. At Bury St Edmunds, in a dispute over the abbatial election, des Roches and the legate were ranged against the canonist prior of Dunstable and Master Richard Poer who, acting as judges delegate, had already complained to Rome of the Justiciar's unwarranted interference.[48]

Complaints against the legate were to lead to his recall in November 1214. In the meantime, des Roches' candidature for York collapsed in the face of the opposition of the local clergy and the lack of support shown for his cause by the pope. The chapter of York also rejected the promotion of Bartholomew des Roches as dean.[49] A bull of Innocent III, probably to be dated to 1214, accuses des Roches of denying the liberties of the church and of effecting oppressions detestable to both God and man: 'You have said in your heart, "There is no God", since you presume to act against his church … not fearing to displease God in order to satisfy the demands of man'. The bishop should mend his ways and take heed of a series of

---

[44] *RLP*, pp. 113, 139b
[45] *RLP*, p. 139b; Cheney, *Innocent III*, p. 77.
[46] For Marsh's previous relations with des Roches, see above pp. 33 n. 78, 57, 68–70, 77–9, 81, 93; *Letters of Innocent III*, no. 949. In 1214 Marsh is found alongside des Roches at the Winchester manor of Downton; Ms. 9DR, m. 7d.
[47] Wendover, *Flores*, iii, pp. 278–9.
[48] *RLP*, pp. 117b–118, 120; *RLC*, i, p. 169b, 213; *Acta*, appendix 1 no. 1; *Chronicle of the Election of Hugh*, pp. 80–2, 92–9, 108–12, 154.
[49] *RLC*, i, p. 202b. At the same time John reopened the question of the election of an archbishop. Des Roches' clerk Peter Russinol was amongst the delegation sent from York to Rome that autumn; *RLC*, i, p. 180. He is to be found as a regular guest on the Winchester estates in 1213–14: Ms. 9DR, mm. 4, 7d, 8.

complaints, enclosed together with the pope's letters. Unless he did so, he would face such a punishment as would serve as an example to all others. This could be regarded both as a warning to proceed no further with the election at York, and as a rebuke for des Roches' conduct as Justiciar, perhaps in reply to the appeal launched by the judges delegate over the election at Bury St Edmunds.[50]

Nonetheless, it would be wrong to assume that the relations between des Roches and the adherents of Langton were wholly antagonistic. The Winchester pipe rolls record the entertainment of the legate and the archbishop together at Wolvesey, and a visit to Farnham by the bishop of Ely.[51] Quantities of game were sent from the Justiciar's park at Taunton to Canterbury, and des Roches was present, alongside Langton and four of the former exiles, at the consecration of Simon of Apulia as bishop of Exeter at Canterbury in September 1214.[52] He appears to have released a merchant from prison at Langton's bidding.[53] One of des Roches' chief lieutenants in 1214, Reginald of Cornhill, sheriff of Surrey and Kent, made over land in London to the archbishop to atone for his excesses as custodian of Canterbury during the Interdict, whilst des Roches himself oversaw the restoration of rights denied to the bishop of Ely after 1208.[54] Even in the election at Bury St Edmunds, the Justiciar's interventions were comparatively discreet. Des Roches counselled supporters of the royalist candidate that they had little chance of success against the forces of Langton, bishop Eustace of Ely and the French legate.[55] Whilst implying that the Justiciar was open to

---

50 BL ms. Add. 34254, f. 97v, printed in *The Letters of Innocent III*, no. 967, also, inaccurately in *VCH: Hampshire*, ii, p. 14. The ms., which contains a miscellaneous collection of English material, including part of the letter collection of Peter of Blois, was purchased by the British Library in 1892 from a J. Halle of Munich. The letters against des Roches are probably genuine. The Cheneys date them Feb. X April 1214, whilst allowing that they may be associated with a bull of January 1215 criticizing des Roches' conduct in the election at Bury; *Letters of Innocent III*, no. 990; *Chronicle of the Election of Hugh*, p. 154. I am grateful to Jane Sayers and to Mr Julian Conway of the British Library for their assistance with the ms.

51 Ms. 9DR, mm. 6, 7d.

52 Ms. 9DR, m. 9d; Canterbury Cathedral, D. & C. Library ms. Cart. Antiq. C115/142.

53 *RLC*, i, p. 211b; *Acta*, appendix 1 no. 1. The Justiciar appointed a monk of St Bertin's, where Langton had spent his exile, to supervise a vacancy at Keynsham. During the vacancy Langton was able to secure privileges in one of Keynsham's churches; *RLC*, i, p. 211; Lambeth Palace ms. 1212, f. 42r; *Acta Stephani Langton Cantuariensis Archiepiscopi AD 1207–1228*, ed. K. Major, Canterbury and York Society L (Oxford 1950), no. 25.

54 *Acta Langton*, ed. Major, no. 28; C60/5d, m. 3.

55 Cheney, *Innocent III*, pp. 172–3; *Chronicle of the Election of Hugh*, pp. xxi–xlvii, 50, 80–2, 112.

bribery, the chronicler of the election states that des Roches elo-
quently pleaded Bury's privileges at court.[56]

Despite his close association with the Justiciar, Engelard de
Cigogné, sheriff of Gloucester, was ordered to restore lands to Abbey
Dore which he had seized unjustly.[57] It is also possible that des
Roches spearheaded a movement, in line with the renewed Sabbatar-
ianism of church reformers, to prohibit the holding of Sunday markets
on the king's demesne manors.[58] The same year witnessed the
activities of papal commissioners sent to preach the Crusade in
England. In February 1214 over three hundred people are said to have
taken the cross at Northampton. At least one of des Roches' writs
touches upon privileges for a crusader.[59]

On 26 May 1214 the king had commanded des Roches to levy a
scutage of 3 marks from all tenants-in-chief. However, the bishop
appears to have trod warily in imposing this tax upon the church.
Early in August, he ordered the sheriffs whose bailiwicks included
lands of the archbishop and of the bishops of London, Ely, Bath and
Salisbury, to collect scutage only if the bishops were willing to pay. In
the meantime no distraint was to be made, and the sheriffs were to
notify the Justiciar of the bishops' response.[60] The absence of any
account on the pipe roll, and an explicit statement in *The Red Book of
the Exchequer*, make it clear that the returned exiles refused to pay
scutage, although a number of their under-tenants served with the
king in Poitou.[61] In only one case, that of bishop Giles de Briouze of
Hereford, does des Roches appear to have refused to respite an
episcopal scutage. De Briouze's exile after 1208 had been as much the
result of his family's quarrel with the crown as of the Interdict. Even
after the Interdict's solution he remained in hostile retirement from
court. In August 1213 the king issued safe conducts for Giles' creditors
to come to England, and was apparently pressing him for a relief of
9,000 marks for the lands of his father.[62] Des Roches dealt more
warily with Giles and his relations. In July 1214 he allowed Giles'

---

[56] *Ibid.*, pp. 38, 112, 116, 164.
[57] *RLC*, i, p. 213.
[58] *RLC*, i, p. 207; J. L. Cate, 'The church and market reform in England during the reign
of Henry III', *Medieval and Historiographical Essays in Honor of James Westfall Thompson*,
ed. J. L. Cate and E. N. Anderson (Chicago 1938), pp. 27–65, esp. p. 51.
[59] *Coggeshall*, p. 168; H. M. Cam and E. F. Jacobs, 'Notes on an English Cluniac
chronicle', *EHR* (1929), p. 96; Cheney, *Innocent III*, pp. 263–4.
[60] *RLC*, i, pp. 166b, 210.
[61] *RLC*, i, p. 201; *Red Book of the Exchequer*, i, p. 12; Holt, *The Northerners*, p. 13.
[62] The intro. to *PR 16 John*, p. xvi states incorrectly that Hereford was vacant in 1214. See
also *RLP*, p. 103; *Walter of Coventry*, ii, p. 225.

brother-in-law, Hugh de Mortimer, to succeed to his estates, whilst at the same time keeping Hugh's wife, Giles' sister Annora, hostage. In October she was released from the custody of Engelard de Cigogné to that of the legate.[63] In December des Roches witnessed alongside bishop Giles an agreement whereby another of Giles' sisters, Loretta, widow of the earl of Leicester, promised not to remarry without royal consent.[64] But, without openly attacking the Briouze family, des Roches excepted the see of Hereford from his generally conciliatory strategy towards the exiled bishops. His actions here can be compared with his far more lenient dealings with Langton and the temporal claims of the see of Canterbury. Following the death of bishop Glanville of Rochester, he made no attempt to challenge Langton's claim to custody of the vacant see. In August 1214 the king set up an enquiry into Canterbury's right to the patronage of Rochester, and ordered the archbishop to show his warrants to des Roches, William Brewer and Richard Marsh. However, a note on the Justiciar's scutage roll forbade the collection of scutage from the vacant sees of Rochester and Coventry pending further instructions.[65]

In short, as Justiciar, des Roches trod a perilous line; fulfilling his obligations as John's regent, justifying the trust reposed in him by the king, yet showing himself by no means insensitive to the attitudes of churchmen. Rather than abuse his powers, as claimed by the Waverley annalist, des Roches used them to the utmost in serving the royal interest without forcing a breach between church and state. In the process he was constrained to abandon his own designs upon the archbishopric at York. If he was by no means a moderate in his unswerving loyalty to the king, he nevertheless showed moderation in his dealings with the clergy and won the respect and co-operation of the papal mission headed by Pandulph and the legate Nicholas. It remains to be seen whether he demonstrated a similar moderation in dealing with the English baronage.

THE LAITY

As Justiciar, des Roches automatically assumed presidency of the Exchequer and the law courts. Eminently qualified to discharge his duties at the Exchequer, he lacked the training to justify his high

---

[63]   *RLC*, i, pp. 168, 168b, 170, 208, 209b; *RLP*, p. 122; *Rot. Ob.*, p. 530.
[64]   *Rot. Chart.*, p. 202b; F. M. Powicke, 'Loretta Countess of Leicester', in *The Christian Life in the Middle Ages* (Oxford 1935), esp. p. 159.
[65]   *RLC*, i, pp. 201b–202; *PR 17 John*, p. 108.

position in the courts. With the king's departure in 1214, it became necessary to revive the Bench, dormant since 1206. Here the Justiciar must have relied heavily on the experience of judges such as Simon of Pattishall, or the Norman, Henry de Pont-Audemer.[66] The plea and fine rolls for 1214 show that he presided over the issue of a large number of routine legal writs, whilst his name appears at the head of the lists of justices witnessing final concords from the spring of 1214 to May 1215. However, this by no means proves that he was in regular attendance in the courts. A long-standing legal fiction added the authority of the king's or the Justiciar's name to fines drawn up in their absence.[67] The plea rolls for the Hilary term of 1214 suggest that des Roches was absent, several cases being delayed to the Easter and Trinity sessions in order to receive his personal attention.[68] At the same time, the pipe roll lists a large number of amercements imposed by the bishop in Staffordshire, Shropshire, Hampshire and Sussex, which were almost certainly the outcome of local hearings conducted by des Roches between February and May 1214, designed to relieve the accumulation of novel disseisin, trespass and other pleas which had built up since the last general eyre in 1210.[69] The fines imposed rarely amounted to more than one or two marks. Indeed, these hearings appear to have been ameliorative rather than mercenary in intention. No associate is mentioned with des Roches, but from May 1214 onwards, the Justiciar's writs are witnessed by Master Eustace de Fauconberg, a member of the households of both Godfrey de Lucy and des Roches at Winchester. Eustace was almost certainly recruited into the Justiciar's administration in 1214 because of his experience as a royal justice. In this way, he provided a link between the legally

---

66 For the identity of des Roches' fellow judges, see *Pleas Before The King*, ed. Stenton, iii, pp. ccxc–ccxciv. For short biographies, see R. V. Turner, 'The judges of King John: their background and training', *Speculum* 51 (1976), pp. 446–61. Only one new judge was added to the Bench in 1214: Jocelin of Stukeley, steward of the abbot of Selby/Ramsey, the Justiciar's colleague on the election committee.

67 For the legal fiction, see Stenton, 'King John and the courts of justice', p. 125; H. G. Richardson, intro. to *Memoranda Roll 1 John*, p. lxxxviii n. 2; West, *The Justiciarship*, pp. 151–2, which at pp. 191–7 contributes a valuable assessment of des Roches' work in the law courts. That he was absent from the settlement of at least one case is argued by the fact that although he witnesses alongside several judges the official record of a settlement between Luffield and Eynsham, he is the only judge not also to witness the private concords drawn up between the two parties on the same occasion; *Luffield Priory Charters*, ed. G. R. Elvey, 2 vols., Northamptonshire Record Society, xxii, xxvi (1968–75), i, nos. 14, 14a; *Cartulary of the Abbey of Eynsham*, ed. H. E. Salter, 2 vols., Oxford Historical Society xlix, li (1907–8), i, nos. 230–1.

68 *CRR*, vii, pp. 58, 83, 117.

69 Intro. to *PR 16 John*, pp. xxv–xxvi, 47, 121, 133–4, 165–6; Stenton, 'King John and the courts of justice', p. 126.

inexperienced bishop of Winchester and the tradition of legal learning represented by Godfrey de Lucy and his mentors Richard de Lucy and Ranulph de Glanville, Henry II's Justiciars.[70]

Apart from his itinerant hearings of the spring, des Roches frequently intervened in the work of the courts. He ordered assizes and enquiries and wrote to the Bench to suspend or delay particular pleas.[71] However, the bulk of his work lay elsewhere, in the government of England during the king's absence. Here we can follow his progress from May to October 1214 in the two hundred or so writs preserved in the Justiciar's close roll. During this period his time was divided between London, Westminster and the Home Counties. His itinerary took him to St Albans, Bury St Edmunds, Kent, and on several occasions into his own diocese where he is found for much of September, in a position to watch over the harvest on his episcopal estates. At no time during the year did he travel further north than Staffordshire or further west than Exeter. In October he returned to London in time for the Michaelmas audit at the Exchequer.[72]

Chronologically his regency may be divided into two basic periods. During the first, from February to July 1214, his chief preoccupations were the supply of the royal armies in Flanders and Poitou, the raising of the Interdict and the assessment of scutage. A large treasure was dispatched to the earl of Salisbury and Hugh de Boves, the leaders of the English expedition to Flanders.[73] Crossbow bolts, knights, horses, hunting dogs and a party of engineers were sent to the king in Poitou.[74] Des Roches remained in regular contact with John via messengers. The Winchester pipe rolls record their entertainment at the bishop's manor of Fareham near Portsmouth, and also the regular gifts of meat and grain made by des Roches to the royal armies.[75] The bishop entertained ambassadors from Denmark and the steward of the king of Hungary, who may have been sent to negotiate over the

---

[70] For Eustace as witness to the Justiciar's writs see *RLC*, i, pp. 207–13. For his career, see *Acta*, appendix 4 no. 30.

[71] See the letters to the Bench, cited in *CRR*, vii, pp. 115, 125, 132–3, 161, 195–6, 268, 299–300, and the mention of over 100 routine legal writs initiated by des Roches following small payments from litigants recorded on the Fine/Originalia Rolls; *Rot. Ob.*, pp. 533–50. See also *RLC*, i, p. 201b, an order to des Roches from the king in Poitou instructing him to issue a writ of *mort d'ancestor*.

[72] *Acta*, appendix 3.

[73] *RLC*, i, pp. 206, 206b, 209; *PR 16 John*, pp. xxiii, 27, 79, 84.

[74] *RLC*, i, pp. 205–208b; *PR 16 John*, pp. 67, 126–7, 135, 145.

[75] Ms. 9DR, mm. 2d, 3, 5, 5d, 6d, 7d, 9, which include chickens, pigs and over 400 quarters of grain sent to the king.

forthcoming crusade.[76] On royal instructions he sent gifts to the king of Norway and subsidies for the support of the emperor.[77]

John's whole future depended upon the success of his campaign. Over the past seven years he had amassed an enormous fortune, through taxes, extortion and his seizure of the lands of the church. Now, at last, he was in a position to use this money to launch a reconquest of the Plantagenet lands in France. Two armies, one headed by the emperor Otto IV in Flanders, the other commanded by John himself and directed against Poitou, were to launch a pincer movement against Philip Augustus, to force the Capetians to abandon Normandy, Anjou and Maine. Until the early summer this strategy appeared to be progressing well, despite an evident anxiety to assemble troops and money. In May des Roches sent an optimistic report to Ireland soliciting funds for the support of the army in Flanders and for the raising of the Interdict.[78] In July the king repeated his summons for all men to serve in Poitou, save those whose presence in England was deemed essential by des Roches, the bishop of Norwich, Richard Marsh and William Brewer.[79] In anticipation of future unrest, the Justiciar continued the munitioning of English castles, but this was no more than an insurance measure. As yet, it was assumed that the king's campaign of reconquest would succeed.[80]

However, this situation was transformed after 27 July and the defeat of John's allies, the northern element of his expeditionary force, at the battle of Bouvines. The second period of des Roches' regency, from late summer to the return of the humiliated king in October, was overshadowed by preparations for the gathering storm. John appears to have learned of the defeat at Bouvines in mid-August. On 26 August he sent Thomas of Erdington to England with instructions to des Roches on the munitioning of Dover castle and the safety of the king's person.[81] News of the battle had probably already reached the Justiciar, who was forced to issue instructions for the defence of the Marches where the Welsh had seized the opportunity to reopen

[76] Ms. 9DR, mm. 2d, 4, and above p. 68.
[77] *RLP*, p. 121; *RLC*, i, p. 168 and see *PR 16 John*, p. 79, a tent for the count of Boulogne.
[78] *RLC*, i, p. 205.
[79] *RLP*, p. 118b.
[80] *RLC*, i, pp. 204–204b, 206, 207, 208–209b; *PR 16 John*, pp. xiv, 2, 27–8. In May Richard Marsh was sent to instruct des Roches on the munitioning of castles; *RLP*, pp. 139–139b. Painter, *King John*, p. 281, probably mistakenly, sees this promotion of Marsh as a safeguard against the suspect discretion of des Roches and William Brewer.
[81] *RLC*, i, p. 202.

hostilities.[82] There was a genuine fear that Philip Augustus might invade England in the absence of John and his army. On 5 September, des Roches set men secretly to watch the coasts of East Anglia.[83] His fear appears to have been that the French would use Flanders as their embarkation point, employing the local merchant fleet to provide transport across the North Sea. This would explain the Justiciar's arrest of vessels capable of carrying men and horses and his subsequent seizure of the merchants of Flanders, their ships and chattels. These latter might also serve as bargaining counters in negotiations for the release of English prisoners taken at Bouvines, including the earl of Salisbury whose ransom the Justiciar was instructed to obtain.[84]

At the same time des Roches set about the repair and garrisoning of the king's castles and houses. In August he recruited men to keep the peace in Nottinghamshire and Derbyshire.[85] In the north, Philip of Oldcotes was ordered to munition his castles following any news he might hear.[86] Dover, Corfe, Winchester and Scarborough were prepared to meet the coming storm.[87] The Exchequer session at Michaelmas must have been overshadowed by the threat of civil war, presaged by widespread resistance to scutage. On 10 October, the king landed at Dartmouth and made swiftly for the security of Corfe. Des Roches seems to have met him there around 17 October, at which time his commission as regent lapsed.[88] However, since his name continued at the head of justices witnessing feet of fines until May 1215, and since no successor was appointed until June 1215, it appears that the bishop retained the Justiciarship for a further nine months after John's return.[89]

This, then, was the basic framework of des Roches' regency. It remains to assess the extent to which his relations with the English

---

[82] *RLC*, i, pp. 212b–213; *PR 16 John*, p. 109.

[83] *RLC*, i, p. 211b.

[84] *RLP*, pp. 140–140b; *RLC*, i, pp. 209b, 210b; and see intro. to *PR 16 John*, p. xxv. The merchants were eventually released, having promised not to put in to any hostile ports or to carry cargoes to the detriment of King John; *RLC*, i, pp. 211, 212b, 213.

[85] *RLC*, i, p. 210b; *PR 16 John*, p. 68.

[86] *RLC*, i, p. 212.

[87] *RLC*, i, pp. 210–210b, 211b–213.

[88] For the date of John's return, see *The Chronicle of the Election of Hugh*, p. 112, which suggests that des Roches joined him almost immediately at Corfe: he warrants a writ there on 17 October; *RLC*, i, p. 173. Due to mistranscription *RLC*, i, p. 213 gives two writs of des Roches as at Westminster on 20 October (xx) when 9 October (ix) is clearly the date given in the original; C54/11, m. 1.

[89] *Pleas Before the King*, ed. Stenton, iii, pp. ccxciii–ccxciv; West, *The Justiciarship*, pp. 210–11. According to his testimony in 1239, Hubert de Burgh was created Justiciar at the field of Runnymede in June 1215; Paris, *CM*, vi, p. 65.

baronage and his handling of the country made rebellion more or less likely on the king's return. Is the Waverley annalist correct in stating that the Justiciar abused his authority? Here the most natural starting-point is Magna Carta and its criticisms of previous administrative practice. To what extent were these criticisms a reaction to des Roches' regime? Many of the demands made by Magna Carta were in circulation before des Roches assumed the regency in 1214. According to Wendover, in the summer of 1213 des Roches and Geoffrey fitz Peter had met at St Albans with Langton and various bishops and magnates, and there promised that the laws of Henry I would be restored and all evil customs abolished.[90] Although there is reason to suspect that this meeting was invented by Wendover, to complement his equally improbable account of Langton's rediscovery and presentation of Henry I's coronation charter in August 1213, it is clear that in 1213 the king made some form of promise to his magnates, in order to rescue his plans for a continental campaign.[91] From the moment of his appointment, des Roches would have realized the need to tread warily in his dealings with the baronage. Magna Carta clause 25 demanded that all increments be abolished and counties restored to their ancient farms. The pipe roll for 1213–14, drawn up under des Roches' authority, shows that this reform had already been implemented and that increments had been dropped.[92] Clause 17 of the Charter demanded that common pleas no longer follow the court but be held in a set location, a condition to some extent fulfilled in 1214 with the revival of the Bench under des Roches' presidency.[93] Clause 18, demanding regular local assizes, to deal with cases of novel disseisin and other pleas, is in some ways reminiscent of the local hearings conducted by des Roches in the spring of 1214.

As to the more controversial actions undertaken by des Roches, many of these were dictated by the king in Poitou. Magna Carta clause 2 laid down that on the death of a tenant-in-chief, his heir, providing he was of age, might inherit on the payment of a £100

[90] Wendover, *Flores,* iii, p. 262.

[91] Holt, *The Northerners,* pp. 92–3, 95–9; Cheney, *Innocent III,* pp. 360–2.

[92] Intro. to *PR 16 John,* pp. xx–xxiii, which places the change between Easter and Michaelmas 1214, that is to say during the period of des Roches' regency. Harris, 'King John and the sheriffs' farms', pp. 540–1 attempts to redate it to between Christmas 1212 and Easter 1213.

[93] For the fact that Magna Carta clause 17 was not aimed specifically at the revival of the Westminster Bench, see M. T. Clanchy, 'Magna Carta and the common pleas', in *Studies in Medieval History presented to R. H. C. Davis,* ed. H. Mayr-Harting and R. I. Moore (London 1985), pp. 219–32.

relief for a barony and £5 for a knight's fee. This was to outlaw several of the transactions presided over by des Roches in the previous year. For example, the Justiciar accepted a relief of 1,000 marks from Robert de Vere for the lands of his brother, Aubrey earl of Oxford.[94] In the Welsh Marches, the heir to the fitz Alan barony was first persuaded to offer a relief of 10,000 marks, and when he was unable to pay this, found himself and his lands entrusted to Thomas of Erdington, a courtier who paid a heavy fine for custody of the barony, despite the fact that the lawful heir was of age.[95] In both these instances des Roches was merely following the orders of the king.

In an even more notorious case, des Roches witnessed the exorbitant fine of 20,000 marks offered by Geoffrey de Mandeville for the marriage of Isabella, countess of Gloucester. The instalments on this fine were already overdue when John sailed for Poitou. The Gloucester lands and Geoffrey's own inherited estates were seized by the crown. Thereafter John toyed with the idea of accepting a 15,000 mark fine for the Mandeville lands from Geoffrey de Say: the latest twist in a long-standing dispute between the Says and the family of Geoffrey fitz Peter.[96] But the Gloucester estates were restored to Geoffrey de Mandeville in August 1214 and his debts were rescheduled. At the same time, des Roches sought to appease Geoffrey de Say by standing as pledge in his fine for the lands of his father. Both Geoffrey de Mandeville and Geoffrey de Say were to be amongst the 25 of Magna Carta.[97] The blame for their rebellion rests as much with the king as with des Roches. Nonetheless, de Mandeville may have harboured a more personal grievance against des Roches, over custody of the Tower of London, which Geoffrey claimed by inherited right, and over the honour of Berkhamsted, granted in fee to Geoffrey's father but whose profits were withheld after 1213 and

---

94   C60/5c, m. 3; *PR 16 John*, p. 11; *RLC*, i, p. 211.

95   *Rot. Ob.*, pp. 531–2; *PR 16 John*, pp. xxiii–xxiv; *RLC*, i, pp. 170, 212.

96   Holt, 'The "Casus Regis"', pp. 35–6.

97   *Rot. Ob.*, pp. 520–1, 523–4; *RLP*, p. 109b; *RLC*, i, pp. 163b, 209b; *CRR*, vii, p. 226; Holt, *Magna Carta*, pp. 206–11; Painter, *King John*, pp. 262–3, 282–4. The king had deliberately withheld Bristol, the most important of the Gloucester estates, from his settlement with Geoffrey. This may explain why, in August 1214, even after the restoration of the remainder of the honour of Gloucester to Geoffrey, des Roches was able to interfere in the appointment of a custodian to Keynsham Abbey, a house under the patronage of the earls of Gloucester, presumably regarded as appurtenant to the honour of Bristol; *RLC*, i, pp. 211–211b, and for Keynsham, see N. Vincent, 'The early years of Keynsham Abbey', *Transactions of the Bristol and Gloucestershire Archaeological Society* 111 (1993), pp. 95–113. The bishop's intervention at Keynsham may nonetheless have been unwelcome to Geoffrey de Mandeville.

diverted to des Roches as Justiciar.[98] Here, at least, there is clear evidence of personal resentment against des Roches as regent. Yet once again, it is hard to believe that des Roches was acting except under direct orders from the king. In a dispute between the earls of Salisbury and Hereford over the honour of Trowbridge, the Justiciar preferred to shelve any decision on the title to the honour until the king's return. It was the action taken by the king that forced the earl of Hereford into rebellion.[99]

John de Lacy was forced on royal instructions to deliver hostages to des Roches. However, the bishop allowed him partial quittance of scutage.[100] Robert de Ros failed to appear in a case before the Bench in the Trinity term of 1214. Des Roches ordered that the case be respited since Robert was in the king's service. Only when he still failed to appear, at midsummer, did the Bench order distraint against him.[101] William Malet, later amongst the 25 of Magna Carta, was granted a respite from his Jewish debts.[102] On the death of the earl of Oxford, des Roches granted his castles to Saher, earl of Winchester. In October it was the king who ordered Saher to relinquish them. Saher, too, was to figure amongst the baronial 25.[103]

As Justiciar, des Roches was responsible for the imposition of two general fiscal levies. The first, an aid for the relaxation of the Interdict, appears to have been a relatively light tallage upon the royal demesne. Its most controversial feature was not its severity, but the fact that little of the money was put towards compensation for the church, being siphoned off for other royal projects.[104] The Poitevin scutage was a different matter altogether; the heaviest scutage of the reign and the eleventh to be collected in the previous sixteen years, it was regarded by at least one contemporary as a major *causus belli* and was undoubtedly a factor in the final breakdown in relations between king

---

[98] For Geoffrey fitz Peter and Berkhamsted see *Rot. Chart.*, p. 223; *Foedera*, p. 93; C52/25, nos. 21–2. The keeper of the honour of Berkhamsted accounted more than £347 diverted to des Roches, who was also liable for scutage on part of the honour; *PR 16 John*, pp. 10, 12; *2 Henry III*, p. 73; *3 Henry III*, p. 110; *4 Henry III*, pp. 112, 126. For the Tower see Holt, *Magna Carta*, p. 208 and below pp. 115–17, 122–3.

[99] *RLC*, i, pp. 194b, 210, 212; *PR 17 John*, pp. 83–4; Holt, *Magna Carta*, pp. 206–7; Turner, *The King and his Courts*, pp. 163–4.

[100] *PR 17 John*, p. 58; *RLC*, i, p. 169; Ms. 9DR, m. 5d records the expenses of the bishop's knights *quando ducunt filium constabularii de Cestr'*. For the background to de Lacy's revolt see Holt, *The Northerners*, pp. 106, 207–8.

[101] *CRR*, vii, pp. 125, 185–6, and for Ros, see Holt, *The Northerners*, pp. 24–6, 105–6.

[102] C60/5d, m. 3; *RLC*, i, p. 204b; Holt, *The Northerners*, pp. 106–7.

[103] *RLC*, i, p. 211; *RLP*, p. 122b.

[104] See intro. to *PR 16 John*, pp. xvi–xvii , and above p. 92.

and barons.[105] Magna Carta clauses 12 and 14 reflect widespread opposition to the scutage, which was not only extremely heavy but exacted for service outside England. It was not the Justiciar but the king who had originally ordered its imposition. Nonetheless, des Roches exceeded the bounds of strict necessity, by ensuring that scutage was collected directly from several baronies before they were restored to their rightful heirs or to the men who had fined for custody. This occurred in at least five instances, and whilst by no means an outright abuse of power, was certainly to stretch royal rights to the limit.[106]

As Holt has shown, only in the aftermath of Bouvines did general resistance to the scutage emerge. Previously there had been no great refusal of service overseas, with the majority of magnates serving in Poitou or sending proxies.[107] As with the whole trend of events in 1214, it was the collapse of the king's campaign which transformed a general sense of grievance into open rebellion. Most of the accounts for the scutage, ordered by des Roches for 9 September, went by default. The Justiciar himself was pardoned any scutage owing from the diocese of Winchester, but in the majority of cases recorded in the pipe roll, barons neither paid scutage nor received quittance.[108] The administration of the account simply collapsed in the face of a widespread refusal to pay. Rather than set terms which he knew would be disobeyed, des Roches shelved the summonses against the more prominent recusants, Robert fitz Walter, Roger de Montbegon, Eustace de Vescy and Robert de Grelley. Fitz Walter was given a respite until at least 16 September, the others until 15 October, the date of the king's landing at Dartmouth.[109] Des Roches had encountered Robert fitz Walter and two other baronial leaders, the earls of Norfolk and Winchester, during the election hearings at Bury St Edmunds on 28 June, at which time their complaints may well have

---

105 *Red Book of the Exchequer*, i, p. 12; Holt, *The Northerners*, pp. 13, 98–103; *PR 17 John*, pp. 80–4.

106 *PR 17 John*, pp. 83–4; and see *RLC*, i, pp. 168–9, 208 (Beauchamp); *PR 17 John*, pp. 84, 106; *RLC*, i, pp. 170, 209b (Mortimer); *RLC*, i, p. 209b; *PR 17 John*, p. 107 (Mandeville); *RLC*, i, pp. 194b, 210, 212 (Trowbridge); *PR 17 John*, pp. 107–8 (bishoprics of Rochester and Coventry, the scutage from which may have gone to archbishop Langton).

107 Holt, *The Northerners*, pp. 98–100. Hence the large number of licences for the collection of scutage issued by the king in France; *RLC*, i, pp. 200b–201b, and by des Roches, *RLC*, i, pp. 211b, 212; *PR 17 John*, pp. 105–8.

108 Holt, *The Northerners*, pp. 101–2; *PR 16 John*, pp. 63, 134, overlooked by Holt who implies that des Roches was amongst those who refused or simply failed to pay.

109 *RLC*, i, p. 213b; *PR 17 John*, p. 106; Holt, *The Northerners*, p. 100.

been discussed.[110] Later in the summer he was in contact with David earl of Huntingdon, another magnate whose loyalty had been suspected during the rebellion of 1212. Addressing earl David in somewhat menacing tones, hinting at the harm that otherwise might come to his hostages, des Roches instructed him to come to London around 22 August for discussions.[111]

Elsewhere as regent he enthusiastically adopted the traditional procedures of Angevin government. Thus it is clear that, contrary to Magna Carta clause 40, he accepted fines and payments for assizes and judicial proceedings.[112] In a notorious case in the Devon county court, he intervened to support the oppressions of the local sheriff against the men of the county.[113] Likewise he was naturally prone to favour courtiers and to protect the rights of his colleagues in royal service. His writs as Justiciar include grants of privileges or relaxations of fiscal impositions, in favour of two royal justices, of William Brewer, of his household knight Eustace de Greinville and possibly of the former royal chamberlain, William de Harcourt.[114] He did not always support the personal ambitions of courtiers and sheriffs. For example, the sheriff of Essex, Matthew Mantel, offered 200 marks and two palfreys for the lands of William de Tregoz. Having been ordered to investigate this offer, des Roches rejected it in favour of a fine, exactly double that proposed by the sheriff, and the lands passed to Stephen de Haringot.[115] Likewise, despite his close association with Engelard de Cigogné, sheriff of Gloucester, the Justiciar refused to sanction his attacks upon the privileges of Abbey Dore.[116] Several years earlier, another of des Roches' alien familiars, Girard d'Athée, had seized control of liberties claimed by Cirencester Abbey. In 1215 the king restored these to the canons, a move furthered by des Roches' decision that Cirencester should

---

[110] *Chronicle of the Election of Hugh*, pp. 82–90. Des Roches and Robert fitz Walter appear alongside William bishop of St Andrews as witnesses to an undated charter of Saher earl of Winchester; Oxford, Magdalen College Muniments ms. Brackley Deed D116.

[111] *RLC*, i, p. 213; J. C. Holt, *King John*, Historical Association Pamphlet liii (1963), p. 9; *The Northerners*, pp. 63, 83.

[112] See *Rot. Ob.*, pp. 533–50, and for specific instances see *RLC*, i, pp. 206, 207; *PR 16 John*, pp. 24, 175.

[113] Holt, *Magna Carta*, pp. 66–7.

[114] *RLC*, i, pp. 204b, 205b, 206b, 208, 213. De Greinville held the lands of William the Bastard and was respited Jewish debt by des Roches.

[115] *RLC*, i, pp. 167b, 169, 207; *Rot. Ob.*, p. 529; C60/5d, m. 3; *PR 16 John*, p. 7. Haringot was pardoned the entire fine almost immediately.

[116] *RLC*, i, p. 213.

be quit of tallage taken by the king's justices.[117] Once again we should be wary of assuming that des Roches' dealings with church and baronage were invariably hostile.

Several of des Roches' closest colleagues in 1214 were later to join the rebellion. William of Wrotham, Keeper of the King's Ships, may already have been at odds with des Roches over various preferments in Hampshire, yet in 1214 he was to found a hospital at Portsmouth with the bishop's help.[118] Hugh de Neville had been removed as sheriff of Hampshire in 1212 but continued to receive entertainment on the Winchester estates.[119] The treasurer, William of Ely, and Reginald of Cornhill, sheriff of Kent and Surrey, were undoubtedly des Roches' most regular correspondents in 1214, yet like Wrotham and Neville they were to join the rebels after 1215.[120] Their defection can hardly be blamed upon the Justiciar's actions as regent.

In only two respects can des Roches' actions be linked directly to discontent, generated by his personal intervention rather than by his blind obedience to royal instructions or by his pursuit of traditional methods of government. In 1215 the commune of London was to demand freedom in the election of its mayor and the right for alien merchants to trade freely in the city, complaints which may reflect the circumstances of des Roches' regency.[121] Des Roches' claim to control the Tower of London by virtue of his office as Justiciar was disputed by Geoffrey de Mandeville, who demanded it as part of his family inheritance. The Tower itself was entrusted first to William of Cornhill and then to des Roches' household knight Eustace de Greinville who received supplies from the bishop's estates.[122] The Justiciar may also have interfered in the internal affairs of the city. It is suggestive that the city's sheriff and his deputy in 1214, Solomon

---

117 RLP, p. 149; *The Cartulary of Cirencester Abbey*, ed. C. D. Ross, 3 vols. (London 1964), i, nos. 83, 89 and see no. 266 for intervention there by Engelard de Cigogné in 1209.

118 For William's rebellion, see F. W. Brooks, 'William de Wrotham and the office of Keeper of the King's Ports and Galleys', *EHR* 40 (1925), p. 579. For possible signs of tension with the bishop, see *RLC*, i, pp. 123b–124; *RLP*, p. 105b; *CRR*, vii, p. 113. For letters from des Roches to Wrotham in 1214, see *RLC*, i, pp. 205b–212b *passim*.

119 Intro. to *PR 16 John*, p. xx; Ms. 9DR, mm. 5, 10. For a possible explanation of Hugh's rebellion see Painter, *King John*, pp. 231–2; Vincent, 'Hugh de Neville and his prisoners', pp. 190–6.

120 For William's rebellion see intro. to *PR 13 John*, p. xix, and H. G. Richardson, 'William of Ely, the king's treasurer (?1195–1215)', *TRHS*, 4th series 15 (1932), pp. 55–9.

121 M. Bateson, 'A London municipal collection of the reign of King John', p. 726.

122 *RLC*, i, pp. 211–211b; Ms. 9DR, mm. 4 (pigs sent to the constable from Witney), 5, 5d, 6d, 8, 9 (20 quarters of grain from Southwark).

and Hugh of Basing, should bear names associated with the diocese of Winchester.[123] It is possible too that the bishop had intervened in municipal elections. The mayor of London was entertained at the Winchester manor of Farnham in 1213–14, and des Roches was instructed by the king to implement a settlement over the heiress of a previous mayor, Henry fitz Ailwin.[124] Above all, his seizure of alien merchants and the vessels trading in the port of London appears directly linked to the Londoners' demand that foreign merchants should have freedom to come and go as they pleased.[125] London was a potential hotbed of revolt. The local landowner Robert fitz Walter and various canons of St Paul's had been implicated in the abortive rebellion of 1212.[126] Any intervention in the city's affairs by des Roches was bound to increase tensions between commune and court.

Finally, there can be little doubt that the appointment of des Roches, an alien, as regent and Justiciar, was in itself a provocative gesture by the king. Magna Carta clauses 50 and 51 were to demand the dismissal of all alien constables and the banishment of des Roches' closest allies, the associates of his fellow Tourangeau, Girard d'Athée. Clause 6, in demanding that no heiress be married to her disparagement, may have been directed, at least in part, against marriages to John's foreign favourites.[127] There can be no doubt that, as regent, des Roches was in regular contact with fellow aliens or royal officers long associated with service in Normandy and Poitou; Philip of Oldcotes was invaluable as a royal agent in the north; Philip Mark and Engelard de Cigogné were amongst the Justiciar's most trusted officers, yet both were to be prohibited by name in Magna Carta.[128] In 1213, another of the associates of Girard d'Athée, Andrew de Chanceaux, purchased the marriage of a west country heir for his

---

[123] S. Reynolds, 'The rulers of London in the twelfth century', *History* 57 (1972), p. 356 shows that they held property in the city.

[124] Ms. 9DR, m. 6, noticed by A. E. Levett, *Studies in Manorial History*, ed. H. Cam (Oxford 1938), p. 48. The mayor was presumably Roger fitz Alan; C. N. L. Brooke and G. Keir, *London 800–1216: The Shaping of a City* (London 1975), p. 376. For the heiress, see *RLC*, i, p. 171b.

[125] *RLC*, i, pp. 210b, 211.

[126] See Brooke, and Keir, *London 800–1216*, pp. 53–6; Reynolds, 'The rulers of London', p. 346; Richardson, 'William of Ely', p. 56; Richardson, 'Letters of the legate Guala', *EHR* 48 (1933), pp. 252–3; Painter, *King John*, pp. 109, 269–70.

[127] This was undoubtedly the gloss put on the term 'disparagement' by the baronial reformers of 1258; *Documents of the Baronial Movement of Reform and Rebellion 1258–1267*, ed. R. E. Treharne and I. J. Sanders (Oxford 1973), pp. 80–1; *quod non maritentur ubi disparagentur, videlicet hominibus qui non sunt de natione regni Anglie.*

[128] Holt, *The Northerners*, pp. 221–2.

sister, with des Roches standing witness to the transaction.[129] As Justiciar, the bishop presided over the award of pensions and land to a number of French and Flemish mercenaries and petitioned the king for the restoration of Thomas de St Valery to his English estates.[130] We have already seen that he enjoyed contacts with a number of alien clergy, several of whom were promoted to English benefices under his authority. Perhaps most significantly, he carried out the institution of his familiar, Peter de Maulay, to the lands and marriage of Isabella, daughter of Robert of Thurnham, acting as de Maulay's principal guarantor in his fine of 7,000 marks with the king. In effect, de Maulay was installed as a formidable bastion of royalist support in Yorkshire.[131] In the same year, the Poitevin William de Fors was allowed to succeed to the midland barony of Aumale.[132] Under des Roches' regency such men emerged as the most trustworthy servants of the court, in a land increasingly wracked by the threat of rebellion. Although the 7,000 marks offered by Peter de Maulay for Isabella of Thurnham was in its way just as extortionate as the fines exacted by John from his English barons, in the event the fine was to go entirely unpaid.

In the circumstances of 1214 des Roches' alien birth was in itself a considerable provocation. According to the Bury annalist, John had promised to eject all aliens in the aftermath of the rebellion of 1212. Coggeshall and the continuator of William of Newburgh both imply that des Roches and the aliens around him were seen as an incitement to revolt by the native baronage.[133] Ironically, in the 1190s, before he became king, John had himself used the alien birth of the regent Justiciar, William Longchamps, as a means of discrediting the administration of Richard I.[134] The king had little right to complain when in 1214 his enemies employed precisely this same tactic against the alien bishop of Winchester.

Des Roches' regency coincided with the collapse of the king's continental ambitions. Thereafter, it would have required genius,

---

[129] *Rot. Ob.*, pp. 512–13. The marriage between Sussanah de Chanceaux and Walter de Baskerville took place in January 1214, at which time Sussanah was in the custody of Philip Mark and Philip de Glori; *RLC*, i, p. 162.

[130] *RLC*, i, pp. 205b, 208, 208b, 211, 211b. For St Valery, see *RLP*, p. 115; intro. to *PR 13 John*, pp. xxxvi–xxxvii. Thomas was William de Briouze's brother-in-law.

[131] C60/5d, m. 3; *RLC*, i, p. 205b; Holt, *The Northerners*, p. 77.

[132] *RLP*, p. 122b; Holt, *The Northerners*, pp. 65–6, 105; *CP*, i, pp. 353–5. See also *RLP*, p. 116 for grants to the count of Eu to be administered by des Roches.

[133] *Memorials of St Edmund's Abbey*, ed. T. Arnold, 3 vols. (RS 1890–6), ii, p. 24; *Coggeshall*, p. 168; *Chronicles of Stephen, Henry II and Richard I*, ii, pp. 517–18.

[134] J. C. Holt, 'King John', in Holt, *Magna Carta and Medieval Government*, pp. 106–8.

greater than that of any courtier, to prevent baronial discontent from boiling over into rebellion. What evidence we have suggests that des Roches' methods were no harsher than those of the general run of John's administration. His handling of the church, his patronage of aliens and his general conduct of affairs marked no great departure from the policies adopted over the previous decade. Nonetheless, given that des Roches was the chief representative of royal government, and an alien to boot, it is only natural that his regime of 1214 should have been regarded with suspicion and dislike, and that, with the outbreak of civil war, he should have been made to shoulder much of the blame for the collapse of royal authority. During his year as regent, he had obeyed royal orders, and followed the standard practices of royal administration. But this does not exonerate him from responsibility for the storm that was about to break. The standard practices of John's reign were arbitrary and brutal. Obedience to orders has never been considered an entirely satisfactory excuse, be it in the thirteenth century, or in more recent times.

Chapter 4

MAGNA CARTA AND CIVIL WAR

The king returned to England in October 1214 to find the country close to civil war and the breaches with both the church and baronage unhealed. The legate had already felt constrained to issue letters against unnamed conspirators.[1] Des Roches himself was to spend the remainder of the year with the king, supervising the defence of the realm and the importation of foreign mercenaries. In reward for his services as regent he was granted the manor of Halesowen on which to found a Premonstratensian abbey. The king also confirmed the endowment of the Domus Dei at Portsmouth, founded by William of Wrotham with des Roches' co-operation.[2] The collapse of John's campaign in Poitou and the subsequent resistance to scutage had left royal government perilously short of funds. An attempt was made to recover subsidies paid to Ghent and Ypres.[3] Des Roches himself may have advanced the money owing from Ypres, since the town's merchants were urged on several occasions over the following eighteen months to repay the money he had pledged on their behalf.[4] Master Robert Passelewe, subsequently to earn notoriety as a member of des Roches' regime of the 1230s, was engaged on this mission to Flanders, making his earliest appearance in royal administration under the bishop's sponsorship.[5]

The bishop's expenses as regent were accounted at the Exchequer, and later in the autumn he appears to have taken some responsibility for the government of the Channel Islands.[6] In addition, he stood witness to various concessions to clergy dissatisfied with the compensation paid them in 1214. Between October 1214 and the spring of 1215, he oversaw the payment of 6,000 marks of the promised annual

---

[1] RLC, i, p. 175b; Cheney, *Innocent III*, pp. 366–7.
[2] *Rot. Chart.*, pp. 201b, 202; RLC, i, p. 174b.
[3] RLC, i, p. 175; RLP, pp. 122b, 123b–124.
[4] RLP, pp. 155, 177, 184b.
[5] RLP, p. 122b; RLC, i, p. 17b.
[6] For the Channel Islands, see *RLP*, pp. 122b, 125; *RLC*, i, pp. 175b, 177. For the regent's account, see *RLC*, i, pp. 175b–176, 176b, 179b–180.

indemnity, and witnessed various grants to Langton, and the bishops of London, Ely and Lincoln, specifically made in lieu of monetary compensation for damages suffered during the Interdict.[7] On 21 November he witnessed the charter of Free Elections, whereby the king promised to cease any unwarranted interference in church affairs, a promise he was swift to ignore. This was amongst the last acts witnessed by the legate Nicholas, whose excessively lenient attitude to royal policy and too close co-operation with des Roches had raised complaints that led to his recall to Rome.[8]

With the king's return, the military preparations initiated by des Roches in the aftermath of Bouvines continued apace. Repairs were carried out to Winchester castle and to the Tower of London, still held by the bishop's household knight, Eustace de Greinville. Des Roches himself witnessed the restoration of castles to the earl of Oxford and the appointment of a new constable to Wallingford.[9] In January 1215 the king summoned the baronial opposition to London, with the bishop serving amongst the pledges for their safe conduct. The meeting was a failure. According to one account John attempted to force the barons to issue charters relinquishing all claims to ancient liberties which the king condemned. Only des Roches, William Brewer and the earl of Chester were willing to comply with this demand, and the meeting dissolved in rancour.[10]

Throughout the spring John was preparing for war, drawing in mercenaries from across the Channel. Prominent amongst these was the Poitevin Savaric de Mauléon, news of whose landing in Ireland reached the king around 10 February. Savaric was known to des Roches. His clerks had previously been entertained on the Winchester estates.[11] Another of the bishop's former guests, William archdeacon of Poitiers, was sent to Ireland, quite possibly to serve as messenger to the arriving mercenaries.[12] Increasingly the king was dependent upon

[7] *RLC*, i, p. 175b; *Rot. Chart.*, pp. 202b, 203b, 204–204b; *Reg. Antiq. Lincoln*, i, pp. 131, 133; Lambeth ms. 1212, ff. 27r, 30v, 105v–106r; Adam of Domerham, *Historia de Rebus Gestis Glastoniensibus*, ed. Hearne, ii, pp. 447–9; *HMC Wells I*, p. 310; *The Great Chartulary of Glastonbury*, ed. A. Watkin, 3 vols., Somerset Record Society lix, lxiii–lxiv (1944–56), pp. 89–90; Strood, Medway Area Archive Office ms. D. & C. Rochester, Register Temporalium, f. 113v and in general see Cheney, *Innocent III*, pp. 353, 362–3.

[8] *C. & S.*, i, pp. 38–41; Cheney, *Innocent III*, pp. 363–4.

[9] *RLP*, pp. 122b, 123; *RLC*, i, pp. 175b, 184b, 185b, 213b; *PR 16 John*, p. 127; *17 John*, pp. 14, 33; Holt, *The Northerners*, pp. 103–4.

[10] *Foedera*, p. 120; *DD*, no. 19; Paris, *CM*, ii, p. 584; *Walter of Coventry*, ii, p. 218; *RLP*, p. 126b; Cheney, *Innocent III*, pp. 367–8; Painter, *King John*, pp. 299–300.

[11] *RLC*, i, pp. 185, 187b; Painter, *King John*, pp. 299–300, and above p. 66.

[12] *RLC*, i, p. 185b.

his circle of alien familiars: Engelard de Cigogné, Peter, Andrew and Guy de Chanceaux in the west country, Philip Mark at Nottingham, and Peter de Maulay north of the Trent. In London, the Bench and Exchequer continued to function under des Roches' presidency, although the dwindling financial resources of the crown appear to have been removed to the Tower from whose treasure the bishop supplied the needs of the itinerant court.[13] A mud wall was thrown up to divide the Tower from the city.[14] In April des Roches was present at a second and equally fruitless meeting with the baronial leaders at Oxford,[15] and at the end of the month various northern castellans were instructed to follow his orders, presumably dealing with the munitioning and garrisoning of their castles.[16] Having formally defied the king at Brackley, the rebel army marched on Northampton, where the castle was entrusted to yet another alien constable, Geoffrey de Martigny.[17]

The formal outbreak of civil war had one advantage for the king: it enabled him to reward his followers with lands seized from the rebels. In this way des Roches' former ward, Reginald de Vautorte, was granted the Devon lands of the earl of Oxford and was later given custody of Totnes castle.[18] John was especially anxious to retain the uncertain loyalty of London, and on 9 May granted the commune the right to elect their own mayor, with des Roches standing witness.[19] By this time the Bench had removed from Westminster to the Temple, perhaps for greater security.[20] On 10 May the king met with another group of baronial representatives, including the bishop of Hereford.[21]

The failure of these negotiations led to further seizures of rebel land. Meanwhile des Roches was ordered to instruct his knights, William de Falaise and Maurice de Turville, then guarding Wolvesey castle, to receive Savaric de Mauléon and the king's Poitevin mercenaries. On 16 May another of the bishop's knights was ordered

---

[13] *PR 17 John*, p. 33; *RLC*, i, p. 192b; *RLP*, p. 134.

[14] *PR 17 John*, p. 33.

[15] *RLC*, i, p. 193; *RLP*, p. 132; Painter, *King John*, p. 301.

[16] *Acta*, no. 96a.

[17] Painter, *King John*, p. 302; C. R. Cheney, 'The eve of Magna Carta', *Bulletin of the John Rylands Library*, xxxviii (1955–6), pp. 318–21.

[18] *RLC*, i, p. 200.

[19] *Rot. Chart.*, p. 207 and see p. 206 for a concession to the men of Cornwall, also witnessed by des Roches.

[20] *Pleas Before the King*, ed. Stenton, iii, p. ccxciv.

[21] *Foedera*, p. 128; Painter, *King John*, pp. 306–7; Cheney, 'The eve of Magna Carta', pp. 320–1.

to release the king's castle at Winchester to Savaric. Arrangements were made to evacuate the queen and Prince Henry from Winchester to Marlborough.[22] On the following morning, Sunday 17 May, whilst the king was in the west country and des Roches apparently seeing to the defence of his diocese, various malcontents seized the opportunity to open the gates of London to the rebel army recently decamped from Bedford, striking a mortal blow to the king's cause.[23] Henceforth London was to serve as the cornerstone of baronial resistance. John was deprived not only of his capital but of the central offices of state, above all of the treasury, which for practical purposes ceased to function from May 1215 until the autumn of 1217.[24]

Royal finances were already strained to the limit before this disaster. On 9 May John had been forced to deposit securities with the Templars who were lending money for the payment of mercenaries.[25] After the fall of London the king had no alternative but to fall back upon hand-to-mouth financing. The treasure which des Roches had supervised was presumably seized by the rebels as were the Exchequer records at Westminster.[26] Des Roches had previously removed various monies to the Tower, which after 17 May held out under the captaincy of Eustace de Greinville. From there it may have been possible to evacuate a proportion of the king's treasure. At some stage an *archa*, perhaps containing the records of the Exchequer of the Jews, had been carried from London to Winchester.[27] The provincial treasure at Corfe contained sacks of coin sealed with des Roches' seal

---

[22] *RLP*, pp. 135, 136, 136b. Here and on subsequent occasions confusion arises between the two castles of Wolvesey and Winchester.

[23] Cheney, 'The eve of Magna Carta', pp. 321–2; Painter, *King John*, p. 308; Brooke and Keir, *London 800–1216*, p. 54.

[24] Intro. to *PR 17 John*, pp. 3–4.

[25] *RLP*, p. 141.

[26] In 1217 Louis was forced to restore the Exchequer rolls, the charters of the Jews, the charters of liberties made at Runnymede and all other documents of the Exchequer in his possession: J. Beverley Smith, 'The Treaty of Lambeth, 1217', *EHR* 94 (1979), pp. 569–70. The 'Runnymede charters' are almost certainly the exemplification of Magna Carta issued by the bishops; A. J. Collins, 'The documents of the Great Charter of 1215', *PBA* 34 (1948), pp. 251–2; Holt, *Magna Carta*, pp. 260–1, 443. That these were apparently stored at the treasury implies that the rebels continued to use the latter as a working archive. It is possible but unlikely that the treasury at Westminster had escaped the attacks of May 1215. In October 1215 the king forbade any attacks upon Westminster Abbey (*RLP*, pp. 157b–158), and one chronicler reports that in 1216 Louis faced resistance from Westminster and that his men were forced to batter down the doors to the royal treasury: *Chronicles of Stephen, Henry II and Richard I*, ii, p. 523.

[27] For 'the treasure lodged at the Tower' see *RLC*, i, p. 192b; *RLP*, p. 134. For records removed to Winchester see *RLP*, p. 152 (4 Aug. 1215), probably to be identified with the charters of the Jews referred to in *PR 17 John*, p. 32 which also mentions the removal of royal treasure to Worcester.

which had presumably been removed from London.[28] Reading Abbey, previously used as a repository of royal jewels, books and valuables, was ordered to restore the king's seal and various financial records, whilst jewels deposited in a large number of religious houses were called in.[29] Such objects could be pawned. The records salvaged from the Exchequer could serve as some alternative to those captured by the rebels. Without such documents it was impossible to keep a check upon debts owed to the crown or to set about the collection of fines and farms in the counties. The king was fortunate to possess the provincial treasures established under des Roches' supervision in 1209, guarded by the bishop's alien familiars. The most important of these was at Corfe, from which Peter de Maulay was to oversee the payment of considerable sums throughout the civil war. Even so, these treasures had been severely depleted by 1215. To stave off bankruptcy it was necessary to impose heavy new fines and to resort to plunder. Mercenaries could be paid from the confiscated land of rebels. In Hampshire William Brewer set about collecting a special *impôt*. The farms of various of the county's royal manors were applied directly to the defence of Winchester castle.[30]

The loss of London set the king on the road to Runnymede. It also deprived des Roches of his role as president of the Bench and the Exchequer. From May 1215 it becomes increasingly difficult to trace his itinerary or the precise nature of his responsibilities.[31] He had apparently joined the king at Odiham by 30 May, at which time John received messengers from Rome and himself wrote to the pope, requesting assistance against the rebellion, and complaining of Stephen Langton's failure to comply with the arrangements made between royal and baronial negotiators earlier in the spring.[32] On 4 March the king had taken the cross and henceforth could expect the protections afforded a crusader. The move has generally been interpreted as an

---

[28]   *RLP*, p. 148.

[29]   *RLP*, p. 145, which acknowledges the receipt of *rotulos de camera nostra et sigillum nostrum et rotulos nostros de scaccario nostro* at Odiham on 26 June 1215. See also *RLP*, pp. 144b–150b; J. C. Holt, 'King John's disaster in the Wash', in Holt, *Magna Carta and Medieval Government*, pp. 120–2. For wardrobe accounts of John's reign consulted at Corfe castle in 1227, see C60/25, m. 10.

[30]   *PR 17 John*, pp. 34–6; *RLC*, i, pp. 226, 227. See also *PR 17 John*, pp. 45, 55; *RLP*, pp. 165b, 167, 168 for *tensuriis* and fines imposed in the Midlands in the spring of 1216. The Barnwell annalist states that in the aftermath of Runnymede John appointed provincial officials named 'sheriffs of the peace' to restore order and pursue his fiscal interests; *Walter de Coventry*, ii, p. 222.

[31]   See *Acta*, appendix 3.

[32]   *Rot. Chart.*, p. 209b; Cheney, 'The eve of Magna Carta', pp. 321–4; Cheney, *Innocent III*, pp. 373–5.

entirely cynical one, intended merely to assist John at a moment of domestic crisis. However, the clerks of the royal Chancery henceforth wrote as if the king had a genuine intention of setting out for the East. A ship was prepared for his sailing, and various fines and financial arrangements were made provisional upon the king's departure for crusade.[33]

In early June des Roches accompanied the king to Windsor and was present during the negotiation of Magna Carta, being named alongside twenty-six prelates and magnates by whose counsel the charter was granted.[34] The charter was as unwelcome to des Roches as it was to his royal master. Besides outlawing administrative methods that the bishop had adopted as the very staple of royal government, in clauses 50 and 51 it launched an attack upon des Roches' fellow aliens. All foreign soldiers (*alienigenas milites*), sergeants and cross-bowmen were to be sent home, and the king was to deprive ten named aliens of their custodies and castles in perpetuity. The men named – Engelard and Guy de Cigogné, Peter, Guy and Andrew de Chanceaux, Geoffrey de Martigny and his brothers, Philip Mark and his brothers – were amongst the kinsmen and adherents of Girard d'Athée, who had been brought to England and maintained under des Roches' patronage since 1204. The prominence assigned to them in Magna Carta reflects their record of administration in the shires, a general bias against aliens and, perhaps above all, the strategic significance of these ten men in 1215, as royal constables vital in the defence of the midlands and the west. It is also likely that negotiations at Runnymede led to the removal of des Roches from the Justiciar-ship and the appointment of Hubert de Burgh, a staunch royalist but an Englishman.[35] And yet, no attempt was made by the charter to banish des Roches himself, the most powerful alien of them all. The church would never have accepted such a sentence. However much his colleagues may have disapproved of des Roches personally, he was still a bishop, deserving the protection of the church.

By encouraging an attack against 'the aliens', the barons sought to deprive the king of his most trusted lieutenants and to tap widespread

---

[33] Cheney, *Innocent III*, pp. 261–3, and for evidence of genuine preparations for a crusade, see *RLP*, p. 183b; *Rot. Ob.*, pp. 562–3, 489; *DD*, no. 54, drawn to my attention by Simon Lloyd, and summarized in S. D. Lloyd, *English Society and the Crusade 1216–1307* (Oxford 1988), p. 209 n. 45.

[34] For the chronology of negotiations, see Cheney, 'The eve of Magna Carta', pp. 324–41 and J. C. Holt, 'The making of Magna Carta', *EHR* 72 (1957), pp. 401–22.

[35] Paris, *CM*, vi, p. 65. Hubert is first styled Justiciar on 25 June 1215; *RLP*, p. 144b. See also Painter, *King John*, p. 324.

resentment against royal administration. It is arguable that England had been more isolated from the continent in the decade to 1215 than at any other time since the eleventh century. The loss of Normandy and the Interdict had encouraged insularity at the same time as John's attempts to restore links to Europe, by the reconquest of Normandy and Anjou, by fostering alliances with Poitou and Flanders, and by maintaining aliens at court, had proved immensely expensive, and led to no appreciable result save the humiliating campaign of 1214. In general, John's policies encouraged an understandable equation between continental warfare, profligate expenditure and oppressive financial burdens.

Yet, ironically, it was just such magnates as the rebels of 1214 who had most to gain from a reconquest of Normandy. It was the likes of Robert de Ros and Humphrey de Bohun, William de Mowbray and Roger Bigod, who in 1204 had forfeited valuable estates across the Channel.[36] The ambiguities of the situation are well illustrated in 1216 when the rebel magnates, having sought to banish John's alien favourites, were themselves to invite the invasion of England by a French army. According to rumour, as early as 1212 the barons had turned to the Frenchman, Simon de Montfort, as a possible replacement for King John.[37] After 1216 a victory for Louis might have led to the restoration of their continental lands to the baronial leaders. Others were encouraged in enthusiasm for the invaders by an appreciation of the cultural and intellectual superiority of France; the likes of Gerald of Wales, who had been trained in the schools of Paris and who looked upon France as the very fount of learning and good taste.[38] Cosmopolitanism, or at least a sense of inferiority to French culture, was still endemic amongst the higher aristocracy and clergy, however much the rebel leaders might play upon native xenophobia. The annals of Waverley unconsciously summarize the irony of this situation, stating that in 1216 the barons invited Louis to invade England to prevent the realm being pillaged by aliens.[39]

The xenophobia of Magna Carta clauses 50 and 51 was very much

[36] See in general, R. C. Stacey, *Politics, Policy and Finance under Henry III 1216–1245*, pp. 167–70; Musset, 'Quelques problèmes', in *La France de Philippe-Auguste*, ed. Bautier, pp. 295–7; Holt, *The Northerners*, pp. 89–92.

[37] *AM*, iii (Dunstable), p. 33.

[38] In general see R. W. Southern, 'England's first entry into Europe', in *Medieval Humanism and Other Studies* (Oxford 1970), pp. 135–57.

[39] *AM*, ii, pp. 283–4. The continuator of William de Newburgh implies that the revolt was directly inspired by the crimes of aliens, and in writing of Magna Carta cites only the clause on the church and the anti-alien clauses 50 and 51: *Chronicles of Stephen, Henry II and Richard I*, ii, pp. 517–21.

a two-edged weapon in the hand of the rebel barons. Many of their supporters felt even less sympathy for the cause of Louis than they did for that of John and his alien favourites. The French troops imported in 1216 were no more welcome than the French courtiers of the preceding decade. The Londoners, living in one of the most cosmopolitan cities in Europe, centre of a major international trading community, nonetheless treated the surrender of their supposed French allies at Colchester with the same suspicion and contempt previously lavished on the followers of Girard d'Athée. In 1216 Geoffrey de Mandeville was to receive a fatal injury in Paris, sent there as a hostage to the tensions and mutual distrust infecting relations between the rebels and the French.[40]

Des Roches and his fellow aliens had nothing to gain and much to lose from the settlement reached at Runnymede. Magna Carta outlawed administrative methods which they had considered routine. It struck at practices in respect to wardships and heiresses which had proved most useful in advancing the careers of alien courtiers. It sought to banish many of them from England, to confiscate the rewards of their loyalty to John and to leave them stranded, despised as aliens on one side of the Channel, and as turncoats, cut off from their roots in France. It is almost certain that, by nature, des Roches was a supporter of strong royal government or, at least, that he lacked sympathy for the claims of the community against those of crown and court. His own experience of promotion would undoubtedly have conditioned him to trust more to the bounty of a grateful sovereign than to the xenophobic and envious subjects of his adopted realm. It was in the atmosphere of the court and its intrigues that he had flourished. It was the court, and his place in the king's affections that had so far shielded him from the hostility of the English baronage. In the 1230s he was to be accused of exalting the king above his subjects, and of dismissing the worst excesses of royal government as the inevitable consequences of a quite proper plenitude of royal power. The king, so he was to argue, had the right to promote or to dismiss his courtiers as and when he saw fit. There should be no restriction upon the legitimate exercise of royal patronage.[41]

In short, des Roches can have had little sympathy for Magna Carta or its proponents. In this he was joined, not only by the king and his fellow aliens, but by a majority of the bishops and higher clergy

---

[40] *Coggeshall*, pp. 179–80; Painter, *King John*, pp. 371–2.

[41] For the exact nature of the remarks attributed to des Roches in the 1230s, see below pp. 336–7.

whose support for the rebels' cause fell short of endorsing the Runnymede settlement. In particular, the sanctions clause of Magna Carta, clause 61, by forbidding any appeal to Rome while at the same time reserving the right to armed rebellion, forfeited the backing of the church.[42] Instead of endorsing the charter, the bishops, des Roches included, were willing merely to issue an exemplification, establishing an accurate record of the charter's terms but passing no further judgement upon its intrinsic legal merits.[43] King and barons waited anxiously to see which side would be the first to comply with the terms of a peace which meanwhile failed through default by both parties.

In July, negotiations were reopened at Oxford. The Tower of London was surrendered to Langton, acting as a supposedly neutral arbiter, to be returned to the king provided that peace was established by 15 August.[44] It was probably during this Oxford meeting that des Roches, in company with the archbishop and various of his suffragans, issued two letters. The first sought to clarify the meaning of clause 48 of Magna Carta, to ensure that customs necessary to the preservation of the royal forest were not outlawed. The second registered the barons' refusal to make a written acknowledgement of their legal obligations to the crown.[45]

In mid-July the king had at last complied, if only partially, with clause 50 of Magna Carta, removing four of the alien constables prohibited by name at Runnymede.[46] However, Philip Mark remained *in situ* at Nottingham, and there is no evidence that John forced any of his aliens to leave the country, as the barons had demanded. On the contrary, Andrew de Chanceaux, removed from Hereford, and Engelard de Cigogné, removed from Worcester, jointly defended Windsor during the civil war.[47] Guy de Chanceaux assisted in the defence of Dover, and Peter de Chanceaux, deposed as constable of Bristol, apparently acted as an agent of des Roches, who

---

[42] C. R. Cheney, 'The twenty-five barons of Magna Carta', *Bulletin of the John Rylands Library*, 50 (1967–8), pp. 306–7; 'The church and Magna Carta', *Theology* 68 (1965), pp. 266–72; *Innocent III*, pp. 377–8; and on appeal to Rome compare the articles with the charter, Holt, *Magna Carta*, pp. 440, 472–3.

[43] *Acta*, no. 97, and see Collins, 'The documents of the Great Charter of 1215', pp. 241, 248–55.

[44] Cheney, 'The twenty-five barons of Magna Carta', pp. 280–307; H. G. Richardson, 'The morrow of the Great Charter' and 'An addendum', *Bulletin of the John Rylands Library*, 28 (1944), pp. 422–43; 29 (1945), pp. 184–200.

[45] *Acta*, nos. 98–9.

[46] Holt, *The Northerners*, pp. 123–4.

[47] *Hist. des Ducs*, p. 181.

paid his expenses in 1216 in going from Brightwell to nearby Wallingford, seat of an important royal garrison.[48] Another member of the clan, Aimery de Chanceaux, assisted in the wartime defence of the bishop's castle at Farnham.[49] On 9 August John took the provocative step of asking Langton to surrender Rochester castle to des Roches. The archbishop refused. A week later the deadline of 15 August passed without his making any attempt to secure the restoration to the king of the Tower or the city of London.[50]

Abroad, a royal embassy had secured papal letters dated 18 June, issued without knowledge of Magna Carta, ordering the rebels to come to terms with the king, or face excommunication from Langton and his suffragans.[51] On 7 July, still ignorant of Magna Carta, Innocent issued further orders, apparently in response to royal letters of 29 May. Addressing himself to des Roches, Pandulph and the royalist abbot of Reading, the pope praised John's decision to take the cross and castigated those who disturbed the realm as worse than Saracens, ordering that they be excommunicated and that an Interdict be imposed on their lands. Should any clergy refuse to move against the rebellion, the pope empowered des Roches and his colleagues to suspend them.[52] It was a command that could only serve to inflame an already tense situation. Believing that the malcontents were still at war with their sovereign, and moved by John's complaints against the clergy, Innocent in effect empowered the royalists to overturn the peace settlement reached at Runnymede. Magna Carta could be consigned to oblivion.

The pope's letters appear to have arrived in England in mid-August, by which time the contacts between Pandulph and des Roches, initiated during the former's mission to England in 1212, had blossomed into a firm alliance. In July 1215 Pandulph was elected to the see of Norwich following representations to the chapter by

48 *RLP*, p. 179b; Ms. 11DR, m. 12d.
49 Ms. 13DR, mm. 13d–14d.
50 *RLP*, p. 181b. Already in May 1215 John had asked that Rochester be surrendered to his agents; *Foedera*, p. 121; *RLP*, p. 138b. The castle was held on Langton's behalf by Reginald of Cornhill from August 1213. See *Coggeshall*, pp. 173–4; I. Rowlands, 'King John, Stephen Langton and Rochester Castle, 1213–15', *Studies in Medieval History presented to R. Allen Brown*, ed. C. Harper-Bill, C. J. Holdsworth and J. L. Nelson (Woodbridge 1989), pp. 267–79.
51 Cheney, *Innocent III*, p. 374; *Letters of Innocent III*, no. 1013.
52 *Letters of Innocent III*, no. 1016, also printed in *Acta*, no. 100. Wendover, *Flores*, iii, pp. 336–8 records an inaccurate version of the bull. For the background see Cheney, *Innocent III*, pp. 374–5, 379.

various parties including des Roches' household clerk, Master Peter Russinol.[53] Des Roches and Pandulph served together as royal messengers to the baronial meeting at Oxford around 15 July, whilst supplies to the new bishop-elect were passed on via a servant of des Roches.[54] In early August, in company with the bishops of Exeter, Worcester and Coventry, Pandulph witnessed des Roches' foundation charter for Halesowen Abbey.[55] In pursuit of their papal commission, it seems likely that des Roches, Pandulph and the abbot of Reading convened a clerical council around 20 August, at which Innocent's letter was publicized.[56]

Between 20 August and the first week of September the king made a final effort to win Langton over, releasing 2,000 marks, presumably part of the settlement agreed in 1214 for the satisfaction of the Interdict.[57] At the same time, des Roches and Pandulph helped to settle an issue which had long soured John's relations with the papacy. Despite a chronic shortage of funds, they set aside money towards a settlement with the king's sister-in-law, Berengaria, responding to her long-standing claim for dower as the widow of Richard I: an illustration of the sacrifices that the king was willing to make in order to retain the support of the pope.[58]

The court remained at Dover for the first two weeks in September, partly to receive messages more speedily from the continent, partly to oversee the embarkation of clergy travelling to the Lateran Council.[59] It was at Dover on 5 September that the three papal commissioners, des Roches, Pandulph and the abbot of Reading, issued letters, addressed to Langton and his suffragans, publishing the papal bull of July and pronouncing excommunication in accordance with its terms against all rebels, amongst whom the citizens of London and nine rebel barons, were cited by name. Again, in accordance with the pope's commission, des Roches and his colleagues suspended all clergy who had lent support to the

---

[53] See N. C. Vincent, 'The election of Pandulph Verracclo as bishop of Norwich (1215)', *Historical Research*, 68 (1995), pp. 143–63, esp. pp. 151–2.

[54] *RLP*, pp. 149, 149b; *PR 17 John*, p. 100; Cheney, *Innocent III*, pp. 173–4.

[55] Printed in H. M. Colvin, *The White Canons in England* (Oxford 1951), p. 351.

[56] See the references in H. G. Richardson, 'The morrow of the Great Charter', pp. 192–5.

[57] *RLP*, p. 153b.

[58] *RLP*, pp. 154b, 181b, 182; *Rot. Chart.*, p. 219b; *Foedera*, p. 137. See also above pp. 44 n.6, 67, 95 and below pp. 164, 172, 188n., 251. John was unable to honour his promises to Berengaria for the next instalment of money due in 1216; *RLP*, p. 200.

[59] According to *Coggeshall*, pp. 173–4, John refused church leaders permission to attend the Lateran Council, but this was most probably a restriction limited to baronial supporters.

rebels, including bishop Giles of Hereford and five named clerks.[60] Des Roches' letters of 5 September mark the final collapse of peace negotiations between John and the barons, and herald a return to confiscations and the resurgence of civil war. At the same time they are disingenuous in the extreme, since they nowhere refer to the settlement reached at Runnymede. Instead des Roches and his colleagues mention a *triplex forma pacis*, apparently rejected by the rebels before the seizure of London in May. This *forma* was almost certainly a lost papal proposal communicated to England in the spring. Des Roches' letters, written no doubt in the expectation that they would be read by the pope, deliberately avoid any mention of Magna Carta, which the king and his supporters clearly hoped to stifle at birth.[61]

In the following week, des Roches and Pandulph added the archbishop's name to their list of suspended clergy. According to the Barnwell annalist, they issued their sentence on board ship as Langton prepared to set sail for the Lateran Council. The arch-bishop was accused of failing to move against the rebels in compliance with the pope's instructions, and of remaining in communication with the king's enemies. He had detracted from the royal dignity by refusing to surrender Rochester castle, and by granting safe conducts to baronial representatives travelling to Philip Augustus in France.[62]

Des Roches' itinerary for 1215–16 is extremely sketchy.[63] His actions of September may have won the approval of pope and king, but they undoubtedly hardened the resolve of the rebels who turned to Philip Augustus for support. Reginald of Cornhill, who had formerly held Rochester castle for the archbishop, now surrendered it to the baronial army. Des Roches was present for much of the ensuing siege. Around 19 November, he was deputed to conduct further fruitless negotiations with the barons at Erith near Dartford.[64] With the capture of Rochester he oversaw the

---

60   *Acta*, no. 100.
61   Cheney, *Innocent III*, pp. 379–80; Holt, *Magna Carta*, pp. 413–17, and for the *triplex forma*, see *Acta*, no. 100n. The copy of Magna Carta sent to Hampshire in 1215 has been preserved in a French translation in the cartulary of the hospital of St Giles, Pont-Audemer, Normandy, copied before 1219: J. C. Holt, 'A vernacular French text of Magna Carta 1215', *EHR* 89 (1974), pp. 346–64.
62   *Walter of Coventry*, ii, pp. 224–5, and see also *Coggeshall*, p. 174; Cheney, *Innocent III*, pp. 380–1.
63   *Acta*, appendix 3.
64   *RLC*, i, pp. 234b, 235; *RLP*, p. 158; Painter, *King John*, pp. 362–5.

payment of royal troops and was given disposal of Guildford castle.[65]

The advanced guard of the French invasion force sailed to join the rebels in London in December 1215.[66] In the same month, the pope appointed the abbot of Abingdon, William archdeacon of Poitiers and Ranulph of Warham to support the excommunications issued in September by des Roches and his fellow commissioners.[67] Ranulph of Warham, prior of Norwich, was almost certainly chosen as Pandulph's deputy, the archdeacon of Poitiers, as a familiar and proxy of des Roches.[68] In the New Year these delegates set about pronouncing Interdict on the lands of over thirty named individuals and on the chapter of St Paul's, whose dean was an enthusiastic supporter of rebellion.[69]

In May 1216 des Roches witnessed letters offering a safe conduct to William of Wrotham who had fled abroad and in doing so may have caused considerable disruption to the Channel defences.[70] The court spent much of the spring on the Kent coast. At some stage des Roches accompanied the earl Marshal overseas on an embassy to France, hoping to delay the French attack.[71] However, Louis landed unopposed at Thanet on 21 May. The king and des Roches retired to Winchester where they met the new papal legate Guala. On the following day, 29 May, as Louis set siege to Rochester, Guala caused des Roches to excommunicate the invaders.[72] John's dragon standard was raised, but at the news that the French were marching westwards, the king fled from Winchester. The city's mayor and the archdeacon

---

[65]   *RLC*, i, pp. 240b, 241, 242; *RLP*, p. 159. At the same time the bishop was set to oversee an election at St Denis' Southampton, he was given licence to export hides, and the Sunday market at his manor of Farnham was moved to Thursdays; *RLC*, i, pp. 239, 242; *RLP*, p. 158b.

[66]   Painter, *King John*, pp. 366–8.

[67]   *Letters of Innocent III*, no. 1029; Wendover, *Flores*, iii, p. 354; *Foedera*, p. 139. At the same time, Master Henry of Cerne was sent to the bishops of Coventry, Worcester and three Welsh dioceses with letters confirming Langton's suspension; *RLC*, i, p. 269.

[68]   For Ranulph of Warham see *RLP*, pp. 152, 171b. The abbot of Abingdon may have been chosen as deputy to the abbot of Reading. For the archdeacon of Poitiers see above pp. 17 n.9, 98, 115.

[69]   *RLP*, pp. 168, 170. For rewards to the archdeacon of Poitiers see *RLP*, pp. 173b; *RLC*, i, p. 268b. For London see above p. 111; *Coggeshall*, p. 179, and see Painter, *King John*, p. 373; Cheney, *Innocent III*, pp. 390–1.

[70]   *RLP*, p. 180.

[71]   *Coggeshall*, pp. 180–1. Ralph of Coggeshall, the chronicler, may have had personal experience of one of these embassies; *RLP*, p. 172.

[72]   *C. & S.*, i, p. 50; *Walter of Coventry*, ii, p. 230; *AM*, ii (Winchester), p. 82. On 28 May des Roches and Bishop William of Coventry witnessed a charter at Winchester; *Rot. Chart.*, p. 222. For Louis' whereabouts, see *AM*, ii (Waverley), p. 285.

of Poitiers were both dispatched overseas, presumably to recruit mercenaries, and to encourage the archbishop of Bordeaux to set sail for England to oppose the rebels.[73] On 5 June Louis left London, and in quick succession captured the castles of Reigate, Guildford and the keep of des Roches' castle at Farnham.[74] Odiham was besieged but valiantly defended by Engelard de Cigogné until 9 July.[75] Winchester had been left under the command of Savaric de Mauléon who, at the approach of the French, put the city's suburbs to the torch. However, the citizens rushed to extinguish the fire and to admit the king's enemies. Both Wolvesey and the royal castle were surrendered on Savaric's advice around 25 June. Louis entrusted Hampshire to the count of Nevers who set out to besiege Windsor, now held by Engelard who had recently abandoned Odiham in the face of over-whelming odds.[76] The king retired to Corfe where he was joined by des Roches. In late July, Louis moved to Dover. Previously he had encountered the legate at Winchester, where Guala no doubt repeated his earlier sentence of excommunication.[77] In a matter of less than a month, most of south-east England had fallen into the hands of the rebels, now openly in league with the French and determined to remove John from the throne. The king himself had made no attempt to resist the French invasion, and had retired before any pitched battle could be fought. Here, he acted not as a coward, as some of the chroniclers suggest, but as a sound tactician: pitched battles were very dangerous affairs in which a single wrong move could transform victory into defeat. For the next two years, the war was to remain an affair of skirmishes, sieges and tactical withdrawals. The king's position was an unenviable one. Much of the country was in enemy hands. But as yet, John was not so desperate as to risk everything on a single engagement.

In the meantime the Winchester pipe rolls record the havoc wrought on the bishop's estates. At the approach of the French an attempt was made to evacuate livestock to neighbouring religious houses to escape depredation. Thus stock was driven from Bishop's Sutton, Ecchinswell and Woodhay to the abbeys of Durford and Waverley, and from at least four other manors to Beaulieu, which

---

[73] *RLP*, pp. 185b, 188.
[74] Contradictory chronologies can be established from *Hist. des Ducs*, pp. 170–5; *AM*, ii (Winchester), p. 82, (Waverley), p. 285.
[75] *AM*, ii (Waverley), p. 285; Paris, *CM*, ii, p. 655; *VCH Hampshire*, iv, p. 88.
[76] *RLP*, p. 188b; *Hist. des Ducs*, pp. 173–4; *AM*, ii (Winchester), p. 83, (Waverley), p. 285; *Coggeshall*, p. 182; Painter, *King John*, p. 374.
[77] *Hist. des Ducs*, p. 177.

also gave haven to goods evacuated from the Isle of Wight. Grain and animals entrusted from Wield and Alresford to Sherborne priory were subsequently seized by the French.[78] The Charterhouse at Witham in Somerset was abandoned, the monks and goods found there being received at the bishop's manor of Knoyle.[79] The episcopal estates outside Hampshire suffered far less damage. Knoyle in Wiltshire was overrun by the earl of Salisbury between the summer and autumn of 1216.[80] Nearby, the earl Marshal directed the evacuation of stock from Downton, whilst at Ebbesbourne damage was inflicted both by the royalist count of Eu and the rebel earl of Salisbury.[81] In Oxfordshire however, the manors of Witney and Adderbury escaped unscathed, as did Brightwell and Harwell in Berkshire, close to the royalist garrison of Wallingford, whose commander, the king's bastard son Richard, accepted supplies from des Roches.[82] North of the Thames, Wargrave was guarded at Easter 1216 by the bishop's knights. Seizures of grain were effected by royalists, the mercenary captains William de Béthune, Fawkes de Bréauté and the garrison of Windsor Castle.[83] Rents from Ivinghoe were appropriated by the royalist garrison of nearby Berkhamsted.[84]

However, it is in Hampshire that the pipe rolls record the most severe depredations, the seizure of rents, livestock and grain. At Merdon, for example, the French made off with 14 of the manor's 20 plough horses, 4 of its 12 horses, 21 cows and a bull out of a total of 29 cattle, 225 ewes out of a flock of 253, many of which had been brought to Merdon for safe keeping, evacuated from manors further east. 154 of the manor's wethers had been sent to Wolvesey after shearing. The remaining 62 were all stolen, as were 26 out of 29 hogs.[85] At Bishop's Waltham, despite the provision of a guard for four weeks, Geoffrey de Lucy and the French carried off 54 quarters

---

[78] Ms. 11DR, mm. 1, 1d, 2, 3, 4d, 5, 6d, 7. These and the following details are taken from the roll covering the year of account 1215–16, but apparently drawn up c.Michaelmas 1217; see below pp. 146–7.

[79] Ms. 11DR, m. 3.

[80] *Ibid.*, m. 3.

[81] Ms. 11DR, mm. 4, 4d, including 24 shillings *in donis Francig' pro rebus domini episcopi servand'*.

[82] Ms. 11DR, m. 2d, where 24 chickens and 2 quarters of grain were sent to Wallingford. For Richard fitz Regis, see *RLP*, pp. 186b, 194.

[83] Ms. 11DR, m. 5d, Wargrave; 27 quarters of grain, 43 oxen, 7 plough horses, 21 cows and a bull, all the manor's bullocks, 6 calves, 36 sheep, 23 lambs dead or taken by the Flemings.

[84] Ms. 13DR, m. 13d, Ivinghoe farmers' account which covers the period of civil war.

[85] Ms. 11DR, m. 1d.

of grain and 53 of oats, 12 oxen, 8 plough horses, 408 out of 460 ewes, and all but 16 of the manor's 215 hogs.[86] Geoffrey de Lucy was also active at Bitterne near Southampton, where with *castellanis Hantoncestria* he seized money and stock. Bitterne, in company with a further half-dozen of the bishop's Hampshire manors, paid its rents for both summer and Michaelmas terms to the count of Nevers, Louis' lieutenant, who also sent representatives to the Isle of Wight.[87]

The overrunning of Hampshire had much the same effect upon the bishop's finances that the surrender of London had earlier upon the king's. The orderly collection of rents and profits gave place to *ad hoc* payments, frequently made via the religious or the bishop's chamber clerks. The prior of Beaulieu and the sacrist of St Swithun's received money from Waltham, Wight, Merdon and Hambledon. Brother William of Taunton, possibly a canon of Taunton priory, received at Knoyle. Profits from Brightwell and Harwell were sent to the Templars at Cowley, whilst elsewhere Templars, including the master of the order, ensured the safe conduct of money received from the bishop's manors in the Thames valley. Robert de Clinchamps, the bishop's chamberlain, received *in camera* from at least seven manors, whilst Denis de Bourgueil, another of the bishop's chamber clerks, accepted money from Tichborne. In Wiltshire, Ebbesbourne answered to the bishop's Poitevin familiar, Walter de Montmorillon. Downton paid its rents to John, formerly keeper of the episcopal estates at Southwark, which in all probability had been overrun with the fall of London in May 1215. Irregular receipts of coin are also recorded at Crawley, Alresford and at Wycombe, via Eustace de Greinville, one-time keeper of the Tower of London before its surrender to the rebels.[88]

This evidence highlights the relatively fluid nature of the war in southern England. The French advance was typified by neither

---

[86] Ms. 11DR, m. 2.

[87] Ms. 11DR, mm. 3 (where payment is recorded on the Isle of Wight *In cored' i servient' comitis de Navers.[et] cuiusdem hominis comitis de Navers morant' cum Mattheo serviente*), 7–7d, and see also the collection of rents by the count of Nevers recorded at Beauworth, Meon, Hambledon, Alresford, Wield and Bishop's Sutton. Similarly at Farnham (Ms. 13DR, m. 13d) £66 in issues was taken by the viscount of Melun, whilst the French burned one entire grange. At Bentley (Ms. 13DR, m. 14d) all the grain was seized.

[88] Mss. 13DR, m.13d; 11DR *passim* in the *liberatio* section of each account. No account for Southwark is rendered on the roll for 1215–16, although in November 1215, six months after the surrender of London, the bishop's bailiff, John of Southwark, was granted permission to export hides: *RLP*, p. 158b.

bloodshed nor any ordered annexation of lands and castles. Rather, as fortresses were overrun, so the manors in their vicinity suffered a chaotic seizure of rents, livestock and grain. Communication remained open between areas of royalist and rebel jurisdiction. In the summer of 1216, des Roches was able to exchange various prisoners he had taken, including four knights of William Marshal the younger, for members of his garrison captured at Farnham.[89] Just as the Templars were employed to collect rents from his estates, so they also served to maintain links between the king and the outposts of royalist resistance in the Thames valley.[90] Likewise, the religious enjoyed privileged access. Monasteries provided protection for evacuated chattels. The monks themselves served as go-betweens. Foreign merchants continued to visit England, although the king attempted to restrict their landings to counties west of the Isle of Wight.[91] The only members of society to suffer wholesale plunder were the Jews. The measures taken for their protection and re-establishment after the recapture of Winchester in 1217 suggest that the rebels had undertaken general reprisals against the city's Jewry.[92]

Meanwhile, with the capture of the episcopal Exchequer at Wolvesey, des Roches established a new headquarters at Taunton. Sheds were built there to accommodate livestock evacuated from further east.[93] An aid of £100 was extracted from the manor's tenantry to pay for the closure of the town with barricades of masonry and wood, and miners dug a ditch around both town and castle. In all some £400 was spent on military preparations, on robes for the bishop's knights, on a cloth and towels for their table, on 15 longbows and 5 crossbows purchased in Bristol, and on the wages and entertainment of mercenaries for an entire year, during which time they drank 41 tuns of wine. The bishop and his household were resident there on a regular basis, and from their new headquarters communicated with Bristol, Sherborne, Exeter and the royal

---

[89] *RLP*, pp. 188, 189.

[90] See *RLP*, pp. 190b, 192b; Jolliffe, 'The chamber and the castle treasures', p. 140. The Templar Alan Martel was sent in September 1216 to the garrisons at Bristol, Sherborne, Corfe, Exeter, Lydford, Bridgwater, Taunton, and to des Roches' former ward, Reginald de Vautorte at Totnes; *RLP*, p. 195b. His presence at Taunton *en route* to Exeter is recorded in Ms. 11DR, m. 8d.

[91] *RLP*, p. 195, those coming from Poitou to land between Wight and Bristol.

[92] *Pat. R. 1216–25*, pp. 59–60, and for further evidence of attacks by the rebels against the Jews of London, see *The London Eyre of 1244*, ed. H. M. Chew and M. Weinbaum, London Record Society vi (1970), no. 296.

[93] Ms. 11DR, m. 8d, and for what follows see the Taunton account, mm. 7d–9, which includes a roll of arms.

castle of Corfe, where des Roches joined the king on several occasions in June and July 1216.[94] Corfe also housed the bulk of the king's treasure, besides the queen and the royal children under the custody of Peter de Maulay. De Maulay made at least one journey to Taunton, and crossbowmen from his garrison accompanied des Roches when he travelled from Corfe to Taunton. Apparently these preparations proved a sufficient deterrent. Taunton was not attacked, although a little further north at the episcopal estate of Rimpton, Welshmen carried off fourteen of the manor's chickens.[95]

Des Roches' activities during the summer and autumn of 1216 are obscure. Apart from attending the court at Bere Regis and Corfe, and seeing to the defence of Taunton, in July 1216 he was empowered to receive back any rebels who came to him to seek reconciliation with the king.[96] This would suggest that he was not in constant attendance at court. However, when John travelled north in the autumn, des Roches seems to have followed him, or at least to have been in sufficiently close contact to receive news of the king's illness and to hurry to join the court at Newark. According to the *Histoire de Guillaume le Maréchal*, the bishop was amongst those few faithful attendants who gathered at John's deathbed in October.[97] Originally the king had intended to be buried at Beaulieu, but in the circumstances of 1216, with Beaulieu overrun by the French, he willed his body to Worcester.[98] As his corpse was prepared for its final journey, his personal effects were pilfered by his servants.[99] It seems likely that in accordance with popular practice, the king's body was disembowelled, since the abbot of Croxton who had attended him as physician was able to claim the royal viscera for burial nearby.[100] According to

[94] *Rot. Chart.*, pp. 223, 223b; *RLP*, pp. 188b, 191. Des Roches also visited Bindon in Dorset (Ms. 11DR, mm. 3, 4), and was with the king at Bere Regis on 19 June; *Rot. Chart.*, p. 223. In July he was empowered to make an exchange of prisoners from Sherborne: *RLP*, p. 189.

[95] Ms. 11DR, m. 9d.

[96] *RLP*, pp. 191, 197b.

[97] *Hist. de Maréchal*, line 15154.

[98] *Foedera*, p. 144 , translated Warren, *King John*, pp. 254–5. In 1228 Henry III considered translating the body to Beaulieu, to which it had been promised at the time of the latter's foundation; *Foedera*, p. 192; *Coggeshall*, p. 109. The effects of the civil war on John's decision to be buried at Worcester are overlooked by P. Draper, 'King John and St Wulfstan', *Journal of Medieval History* 10 (1984), p. 43. The fact that John had contemplated destroying Worcester in 1215–16, and was only dissuaded by the payment of a heavy fine, hardly argues a burning devotion to the city or its shrine; *Pat. R. 1216–25*, p. 10, and see *Acta Guala*, no. 138.

[99] *Coggeshall*, p. 184.

[100] *Walter of Coventry*, ii, p. 232. For customary practice, see R. C. Finucane, *Miracles and Pilgrims* (London 1977), pp. 28–9.

the terms of John's will, des Roches and his fellow executors were set to distribute alms to the poor and to religious houses. There is evidence that these requests were obeyed. Des Roches' foundation at Halesowen had already been jointly dedicated to the king, but in the eighteen months after John's death, the bishop supervised grants of land in Hampshire and Northampton to Croxton Abbey to commemorate the king, and came to an arrangement whereby the church of Finedon was to be appropriated to Newnham Priory on the resignation of Geoffrey de Thouars, des Roches' successor as treasurer of Poitiers, to atone for John's burning of the church of SS Peter and Paul in Bedford.[101] In 1218 des Roches was present at the dedication of John's resting place in the new cathedral church of Worcester.[102] The monks of Worcester celebrated an annual feast in the late king's memory, whilst their disappointed rivals at Beaulieu were granted a royal stud farm in the New Forest, again in return for prayers.[103] The minority council granted timber to the monks of Bruern, a pension of threepence a day to the Hospitallers in John's memory, and provided the order of Grandmont with the manor of Bulwell in Nottinghamshire to found a house of religion in his honour.[104] There were to be individual gifts in John's memory from a wide range of courtiers including the queen, Hubert de Burgh, Ralph de Neville and Brian de Lisle. The Justices of the Yorkshire Eyre of 1218–19 pardoned various amercements in return for thirty masses for John's soul. It was to King John that des Roches' foundation at Titchfield was to be jointly dedicated after 1231.[105] And yet, for all that des Roches might look back to the reign of King John with unalloyed nostalgia, teaching his royal ward, Henry III, to honour the memory of his father; in the country at large the memory of the late king was held in less respect, even in downright execration.

With John's death des Roches lost his staunchest patron and

---

[101] *Pat. R. 1216–25*, pp. 29, 41; *RLC*, i, pp. 296, 300, 331b.
[102] *AM*, iv, p. 409.
[103] *RLC*, i, p. 299b; *Pat. R. 1216–25*, p. 28. For Worcester see *Early Compotus Rolls of the Priory of Worcester*, ed. J. M. Wilson and C. Gordon, Worcestershire Historical Society (1908), p. 60.
[104] *RLC*, i, pp. 298, 342b; *Pat. R 1216–25*, p. 123.
[105] BL mss. Cotton Vitelius D ix (Cartulary of St Nicholas' Exeter), f. 65r; Stowe 955 (misc. transcripts), f. 86v; Harley 3640 (Welbeck cartulary), f. 131r; Blaauw, 'Letters to Ralph Neville', *Sussex Arch. Collections*, ii (1850), p. 36; *Acta*, nos. 67a, 69; *Rolls of the Justices in Eyre for Yorkshire 1218–19*, ed. D. M. Stenton, Selden Soc. lvi (1937), p. li, noted in Turner, *The King and his Courts*, p. 155; and see PRO 31/8/140B, pt. ii, pp. 322–4 (Philip de Aubigné); Bodl. ms. Lyell 15 (Abingdon cartulary), f. 105r (Hugh de Malo Alneto); Southwell Minster ms. 1 (Liber Albus), pp. 325–6 (Robert de Lexington the justice); CUL ms. Doc. 126 (Charter of Eustace, bishop of London).

supporter, and arguably too, his closest personal friend. In the immediate term, despite the passing of its chief character, John's reign can almost be said to have continued for several years after his death. The same men remained in positions of authority. The new king, Henry III, was influenced and his policy decided by the councillors of his late father. The end of the civil war was to bring des Roches and his fellow aliens rich rewards. However, with the death of their patron and the rapid transformation of his memory into one of extortion, bitterness and loathing, so John's servants were to become hopelessly tarnished by the legacy of his reign. As the principal surviving member of John's council, Peter des Roches was to find himself barred from office and cut off from the sympathies of the country at large, not just because of his alien birth, but because of his all too close association with the policies of his late master. Not even his position as tutor and mentor to John's heir was to save him. Indeed, within twenty years, the chief accusation levelled against the bishop was to be his friendship with John. In 1234 he was to find himself charged with every crime that could be laid against his late sovereign. Unable to vent their anger against John himself, his subjects were to accuse des Roches, as the king's surrogate, of extortion, profligacy, the loss of Normandy, the Interdict, and the deterioration of relations with the native baronage, heaping upon him responsibility for every hated incident in a thoroughly detested reign.[106]

[106] Paris, *CM*, iii, pp. 269–71, and see below pp. 213, 429.

Chapter 5

THE KING'S GUARDIAN 1216–1219

On 28 October 1216, assisted by des Roches and at least four other bishops, the papal legate supervised the coronation of Henry III in the abbey church at Gloucester. The late king's regalia had been lost, or pawned to pay mercenaries, so that it was a chaplet or makeshift crown that des Roches placed on the head of the nine-year-old boy.[1] Altogether the ceremony was something of a shambles, interrupted by protests from the abbot of Westminster and the prior of Christ Church Canterbury, and overshadowed by the news that only a few miles away the Welsh had set siege to Goodrich castle.[2] Nonetheless, the coronation provides a remarkable illustration of des Roches' reconciliation with both church and baronage. Previously reviled by native and ecclesiastical opinion as an alien and secularist, he now found himself at the centre of resistance to a French invasion, a leading ally of the papal legate, personally investing his king with the attributes of sovereignty. Civil war had forged improbable alliances between native barons, alien courtiers and the representatives of the pope.

Prior to the death of King John, des Roches had been only one of several prominent courtiers whose obedience and loyalty to the crown had brought them status and wealth. After 1216, all of this changed. For the first time since the eleventh century, the king was a minor, incapable of governing in his own right. John's courtiers found themselves, in effect, no longer the servants but the masters of the court. At Gloucester the regency was entrusted to William Marshal, but since the king was still a child in need of education, not to be subjected to the rigours of campaigning, des Roches was appointed his personal guardian, resuming in an official capacity a role that he

---

[1]   For an attempt to disentangle the various accounts of the Gloucester coronation, see *Acta Guala*, no. 36.

[2]   *Chronicle of Melrose*, ed. A. O. and M. O. Anderson (London 1936), p. 64; *Hist. de Maréchal*, lines 15347–72, and see *AM*, iv (Wykes), p. 60; J. Sayers, *Papal Government and England during the Pontificate of Honorius III (1216–1227)* (Cambridge 1984), p. 168.

had performed unofficially for several years.[3] At Bristol, on 13 November Magna Carta was reissued, transformed from an unsuccessful peace settlement forced upon an unwilling king, into a manifesto of the king's future good government.[4] The preamble to the new charter claimed the assent not only of the Tourangeau bishop of Winchester, but of his former ward, the Anglo-Norman Reginald de Vautorte, and of William de Fors and Fawkes de Bréauté: a Poitevin and a Norman adventurer. In the process, the anti-alien clauses 50 and 51 of the 1215 charter were discarded. The bishop's familiars, Engelard de Cigogné, Peter de Chanceaux and their like, had played too significant a role in the defence of the realm to be dismissed as mere alien predators.[5]

WAR AND PEACE

In the immediate term, des Roches had been appointed to save the king from unnecessary travel. However, this responsibility was not to keep the bishop from the thick of the campaign. He appears to have followed the royalist army throughout the winter of 1216–17, and at Nottingham, on 7 January, served for the first time as chief witness to letters of Henry III; a prophetic appearance since the letters granted £80 of land to des Roches' fellow Tourangeau, Philip Mark, the first of many such promotions the bishop was to obtain for the alien veterans of John's reign.[6] The precise extent of des Roches' control over the royalist campaign is uncertain, but it was the diocese of Winchester that was to serve as the principal theatre of military activity in the spring of 1217. Taking advantage of Louis' absence overseas, around 7 March the royalists set siege to the bishop's castle at Farnham. Within a week the French garrison capitulated. Des Roches imprisoned the French commander, although the garrison itself was allowed safe-conducts to rejoin the rebels in London.[7] The royalists

---

[3]   *Hist. de Maréchal*, lines 15373–610; Norgate, *The Minority of Henry III*, pp. 6–8, 120 and above p. 71 and n.128.

[4]   Holt, *Magna Carta*, pp. 378–82.

[5]   Stubbs, *Select Charters* (9th edn 1922), pp. 335–9. Clause 6 of the 1215 charter, regarded as an attack upon marriage settlements with aliens, was amended to exclude the need for assent from a minor's kin.

[6]   *Pat. R. 1216–25*, pp. 20–1.

[7]   *Hist. des Ducs*, pp. 187–8; *Hist. de Maréchal*, lines 15901–2; *Pat. R. 1216–25*, p. 37. The castle was entrusted to Hugh de Berneville (? dep. Pas-de-Calais), a knight, possibly a Fleming, associated with des Roches in 1213–14. The garrison was to include Pontius of Castile, John de Caux and Aimery de Chanceaux, all of whom are recorded taking substantial cash receipts from the manor; Mss 9DR, m. 3; 13DR, mm. 2, 5d, 6, 13d,

then moved on to Winchester, where a siege had already been opened by the earl of Salisbury and William Marshal the younger, both of them recent defectors from the rebel cause.[8] As in 1216, the citizens of Winchester within the walls supported the king, but the suburbs sided with the rebels and inflicted considerable damage on the royalist camp established at Hyde Abbey.[9] The bishop's castle, Wolvesey Palace, fell after a few days, but to the west, away from the river Itchen, the royal castle held out until late April when its French defenders were forced to sue for conducts to London.[10]

Meanwhile Portchester and Southampton had been recaptured and their defences razed.[11] Various of the royalist commanders were granted land seized from local rebels.[12] But these gains were short-lived. Louis returned from France and, marching south out of London, repeated his progress of 1216, capturing the outer bailey of Farnham and reinvesting Winchester. In a matter of only a week, the royalist achievements of the spring were wiped clean away. At Winchester, however, Louis made a decision that was to cost him the war. He divided his army in two. Whilst one force was sent to relieve Mountsorrel castle, besieged by the earls of Chester and Derby, Louis himself set out to complete his year-long assault on the royalist stronghold at Dover.[13]

News of this decision reached the royalists gathered at Northampton on 13 May. The earls of Chester and Derby had fled at the approach of the French who had turned their attention against Lincoln. Over the past half-century William Marshal, the regent, had acquired an earldom, a fortune and a formidable reputation through feats of arms. His instinctive reaction in May 1217 was to seek a pitched battle at Lincoln. Yet the Marshal's experience of tournaments and skirmishes hardly prepared him for the full-scale engagement now contemplated. Such an engagement was at odds with every principle

---

14; 14DR, mm. 1d, 9; 15DR, mm. 4d, 8d, 9. For the royalist garrison see also *RLC*, i, p. 305 and *Pat. R. 1216–25*, p. 40 which records an apparently ineffective order to Henry (*sic*) de Berneville to release the manor to Thomas Basset.

[8] D. A. Carpenter, *The Minority of Henry III* (London 1990), pp. 27–31.

[9] *Hist. de Maréchal*, iii, pp. 223–4.

[10] *Ibid.*, iii, pp. 223–5; *Pat. R. 1216–25*, pp. 60–1, which gives the name of the French commander of Winchester as Peter Letart, presumably deputy to the count of Nevers.

[11] *Hist. de Maréchal*, lines 15986, 16003–10, and see Norgate, *The Minority*, p. 26n; *Pat. R. 1216–25*, p. 62.

[12] *Pat. R. 1216–25*, pp. 28, 35, 37, 44, 52, 69; *RLC*, i, pp. 299b, 304b, 305b, 307. Beneficiaries included Beaulieu Abbey, Roger de la Zouche, Terric Teutonicus, Aimery de Sacy, Bartholomew Peche and John Marshal.

[13] *Hist. des Ducs*, pp. 190–2.

of medieval warfare, which urged the avoidance of set-piece battles. In 1214 the earl of Salisbury had received a bitter schooling in such strategy, sacrificing a decade of patient preparation by his reckless actions at Bouvines. Two years later it was the Marshal himself who had cautioned John against an attack on the French as they disembarked at Thanet. If Wendover is to be believed, the bishop of Winchester had been trained in the army of Richard I, a king who owed his reputation for military genius directly to a refusal to engage in pitched combat either in France or on crusade.[14] In this context, the Marshal's decision to seek battle at Lincoln might well be regarded as foolhardy. It was largely to the credit of des Roches that the combat developed along far different, far more advantageous lines than those envisaged by the army's veteran commander.

Des Roches was both a churchman and the king's personal guardian. Duty to his clerical office and to his ward dictated that he refrain from fighting. Yet in May 1217, leaving Henry to the care of the legate, he reverted to type as the warrior of Winchester, leading soldiers into battle. There are few parallels to the enthusiasm or the skill with which he resorted to arms. Hubert Walter had fought on crusade although bishop of Salisbury. In theory bishops might bear arms, though canon law restricted their choice of weapons and forbade the spilling of blood.[15] The criticism levelled against Hubert's activities in the 1190s was as nothing compared to the odium attached to Philip count of Dreux, bishop of Beauvais, who, between 1175 and 1217, led knights against the English and the infidel. Philip was imprisoned for his blood lust and only released after taking an oath to refrain from martial exploits. In 1214, at the height of the battle of Bouvines, he broke this resolve, charged into the fray and aimed a mostly un-bishoplike blow at the head of the earl of Salisbury. Even so, he took no prisoners for fear of papal retribution.[16] Both Hubert Walter and Philip of Dreux fought as scions of knightly families and as such they may have shared des Roches' social origins. However, in

---

[14] In general, see J. Gillingham, 'Richard I and the science of war in the middle ages', in *War and Government in the Middle Ages, Essays in Honour of J. O. Prestwich*, ed. J. Gillingham and J. C. Holt (Woodbridge 1984), pp. 78–91, and see the same author's 'War and chivalry in the "History of William the Marshal"', in *Thirteenth Century England II*, ed. P. R. Coss and S. D. Lloyd (Woodbridge 1988), pp. 1–13, esp. p. 10, which emphasizes the exceptional nature of the Marshal's decision to fight at Lincoln, the first occasion on which he had charged into battle since 1167.

[15] Cheney, *Hubert Walter*, pp. 5, 98; F. Poggiaspella, 'La chiesa e la partecipazione dei chierici alla guerra nella legislazione conciliare fino alle Decretali di Gregorio IX', *Ephemerides Iuris Canonice*, xv (1959), pp. 140–53.

[16] H. Geraud, 'Le comte évêque', *Bibliothèque de l'Ecole des Chartes*, v (1843–4), pp. 8–36.

1217 des Roches led no respectable company of knights but the highly disreputable body of the king's mercenary crossbowmen. Specifically prohibited in the councils of the twelfth-century church and portrayed, both in England and in France, as an alien southern intruder, the crossbow was very much the brutal professional amongst the gentleman-amateurs of the medieval arsenal. As recently as the Fourth Lateran Council of 1215, clerks had been specifically forbidden to accept command over crossbowmen or mercenaries.[17] Yet in 1217 we are told that des Roches was well-versed in the command of crossbowmen.[18] From his earliest years at Winchester *balistarii* had regularly been maintained on his episcopal estates. His closest alien *familiares* were sprung not from the Anglo-French nobility, but from the ranks of John's mercenary constables and captains. It would appear that the bishop's military skills had been acquired amongst the seamier, professional element of Richard I's army. Elsewhere in Europe, des Roches' military expertise might have been considered the norm rather than the exception; Caesarius of Heisterbach claimed to know of a Paris clerk who would believe anything rather than that German bishops could go to heaven, since they spent so much more of their time arranging payments to soldiers than in promoting the salvation of souls.[19] But, in England, warrior bishops were a rarity, and as such regarded with a mixture of awe and suspicion.

On 17 May, having once more pronounced excommunication against Louis and the rebels, the legate Guala took the king off towards the safety of Nottingham.[20] The campaign had acquired all the attributes of a crusade, so that the host now wore white crosses over their armour.[21] At Torksey, des Roches with his 317 cross-

---

17 See constitution 18 of the Council of 1215, and in general, sèe Powicke, *The Loss of Normandy*, pp. 224–9; P. Contamine, *War in the Middle Ages*, trans. M. Jones (Oxford 1984), pp. 71–2 and references there cited. The Paris theologians had allowed that crossbows might be used against infidels, in the defence of Christian lands; J. W. Baldwin, *Masters, Princes and Merchants: the social views of Peter the Chanter and his circle*, 2 vols. (Princeton 1970), i, pp. 220–4, esp. pp. 223–4.

18 *Hist. de Maréchal*, lines 16313–8.

19 Caesarius of Heisterbach, *The Dialogue on Miracles*, trans. H. von E. Scott and C. C. Swinton Bland, 2 vols. (London 1929), i, pp. 110–11, drawn to my attention by Taavi Davies and Michael Holmes.

20 *Hist. de Maréchal.*, lines 16225–37; Wendover, *Flores*, iv, pp. 19–20.

21 See *AM*, ii (Waverley), p. 287; Wright, *Political Songs*, p. 23 for the crosses. *Walter of Coventry*, ii, p. 235 suggests that Guala preached the war against Louis as a crusade, for which see also S. D. Lloyd, 'Political crusades in England *c.*1215–17 and *c.*1264–5', in *Crusade and Settlement*, ed. P. W. Edbury (Cardiff 1985), pp. 113–20, summarized in Lloyd, *English Society and the Crusade*, pp. 208–9, and see Carpenter, *The Minority*, p. 28n; *Acta Guala*, nos. 56, 83.

bowmen took command of the third line in the army, instructed to bring down the horses of the French knights in what was still envisaged as the set-piece battle to come.[22] However, as the host approached Lincoln, the Marshal met with his first major set-back: even after a herald had been sent into the city to invite them to fight, the rebels simply declined to offer battle.[23]

Accompanied by a lone serjeant, des Roches set out on a reconnaissance. Entering the outer bailey of Lincoln castle he saw the damage done by the rebels' siege engines and, with missiles falling around him, was invited to speak with Nicola de Haye, the castle's hereditary constable. From here, he set out once more on foot into the hostile town where he made a vital discovery, a disused gate, blocked with rubble, but communicating between town and bailey. He ordered that the gate be cleared and returned to his troops, announcing with great glee that his reconnaissance would win them the day, and that as a result he deserved to be awarded the bishop of Lincoln's palace as a prize. In des Roches' absence, Fawkes de Bréauté had attempted to lead crossbowmen into the town. Entering through another gate he had been savagely repulsed. Alarmed that Fawkes had betrayed the element of surprise, des Roches berated his men for their impatience and, curbing the Marshal's enthusiasm for an immediate attack, selected ten soldiers to accompany him on a second tour of inspection. But the Marshal was not to be held back. Forgetting even his helmet, he made off towards the gate which des Roches had discovered. The bishop shouted after him that he should wait, that the host should enter together, but finding himself ignored, he was left with no alternative but to follow the hot-headed old man. Shouting 'Now God help the Marshal!', the old man's battle cry, he spurred his horse into the rebel-infested streets.[24]

Des Roches was very much the hero of the day. In the narrow city streets, pouring down upon an unsuspecting enemy, the royalists were placed in a far more advantageous position than they would have been, tired out by their march and seriously outnumbered in the open combat planned by the Marshal. It is no coincidence that two of the chroniclers generally most hostile to des Roches, Wendover and the

[22] *Hist. de Maréchal*, lines 16267–8, 16311–34.

[23] For the battle, see Carpenter, *The Minority*, pp. 35–40 and references there cited, an account which differs in various minor respects from that presented here. For the sending of a herald and the Marshal's comments, see Wright, *Political Songs*, p. 25; *Hist. de Maréchal*, lines 16381–97.

[24] *Hist. de Maréchal*, lines 16467–42, iii, pp. 232–5.

author of the *Histoire de Guillaume le Maréchal*, bury their enmity to marvel at his martial prowess. By the same token, it is significant that the most detailed description of the bishop's actions at any stage in his career should be the account of the battle of Lincoln in the *Histoire*, commemorating des Roches the warrior, a reputation more vivid than anything he was to earn as politician or pastor.[25]

The battle of Lincoln delivered a mortal blow to the rebel cause but it did not end the civil war. Louis' resistance was shattered only after a naval battle off Sandwich in August.[26] Matthew Paris states that des Roches was present on shore during this engagement. But his account is suspect. It was composed long after the event and mentions the bishop only to contrast his reluctance to put to sea with the valour shown by Hubert de Burgh.[27] In fact des Roches' movements in the aftermath of Lincoln are difficult to trace. Early in the summer Hampshire was once more wrested from rebel control, and on 29 June des Roches was granted custody of the county as sheriff.[28] The battle of Lincoln had brought the bishop several valuable prisoners. During the succeeding months his clerk, Master Humphrey de Millières, oversaw an exchange of hostages with the count of Nevers. Des Roches himself paid the count a further £62 via the earl of Salisbury.[29] At Devizes he paid 400 marks of his own money to discharge the wages of the garrison, a shrewd deal since the mercenaries had originally demanded 1,500 marks in arrears.[30]

Des Roches appears to have played no direct part in negotiating the Treaty of Lambeth that ended the war. It is possible that the English bishops joined the legate Guala in opposing the admission of Louis' clerical adherents within the peace, a proposal rejected in an

---

[25] *Hist. de Maréchal*, lines 16259–61, 16313–18; Wendover, *Flores*, iv, p. 327, and see Gillingham's verdict, 'War and chivalry', p. 10. Des Roches' protégé, Henry of Avranches, wrote a lost poem, *Certamen inter Regem Iohannem et Barones*, which might suggest that the bishop himself was active in promoting literature on the war; *Henry of Avranches*, ed. J. Cox Russell, pp. xix, no. 98, p. 30.

[26] See Carpenter, *The Minority*, pp. 42–4; H. L. Cannon, 'The battle of Sandwich and Eustace the Monk', *EHR* 27 (1912), pp. 649–70.

[27] Paris, *CM*, iii, p. 28. The incident is unmentioned by Wendover. R. Vaughan, *Matthew Paris*, 2nd edn (Cambridge 1979), p. 13, suggests that Paris took his story from information supplied by de Burgh, who had a vested interest in playing down the valour of des Roches.

[28] *Pat. R. 1216–25*, pp. 69, 75.

[29] *Pat. R. 1216–25*, pp. 75, 79; *RLC*, i, p. 450; *PR 4 Henry III*, p. 122.

[30] *RLC*, i, pp. 317b, 467; *PR 4 Henry III*, p. 122. He also paid money to Louis' knights besieged in Winchester castle, apparently to obtain a truce, and 60m to Welsh mercenaries who had participated in the siege, probably in March–April 1217: *RLC*, i, p. 450.

earlier draft of the Treaty.[31] Possibly des Roches was too closely associated with John's regime to prove an acceptable envoy to the defeated rebels. There is evidence that he was uneasy about the Treaty's terms in respect to Normandy and to the ransoming of prisoners.[32] Only in the aftermath of negotiations did he undertake what might well be regarded as both a brave and a provocative mission. Following penance from the legate at Merton on 22 September, Louis rode with des Roches into the city of London and there surrendered custody of the Tower.[33] The bishop was the first royalist leader to enter London since the spring of 1215, a hazardous move given that his previous relations with the city had been far from cordial.[34] For the rebels to return the Tower to des Roches, who had held it as Justiciar in 1214, represented an especially humiliating restoration of the *status quo ante bellum*. A fortnight later Louis sailed for France. The minority regime issued its first recorded letter to a reconstituted Exchequer early in October, and in the following month Magna Carta was reissued accompanied by a newly drafted charter of the forests.[35]

THE RESTORATION OF ORDER

Superficially the scars of war healed quickly, and from 1217 to 1224, des Roches' career follows much the same pattern as that of the previous decade: a commanding presence at the Exchequer and in the royal household, a leading diplomat in negotiations with France and the papacy, centre of a network of alien *curiales*. Albeit that this pattern is traced against the background of a new reign, the cast of subsidiary characters and colleagues remains little changed from that of the reign of King John. Indeed, the late king's shadow loomed large for many years to come. The clerks who compiled the Winchester pipe roll for 1218 wrote as if John were still alive, referring to Henry III's sister as 'daughter of the king'. As late as 1220, all tin mined in the Cornish stannaries continued to be stamped with the insignia of King John.[36]

---

[31] Smith, 'The Treaty of Lambeth 1217', pp. 566–7.
[32] Below pp. 151–2.
[33] 'The annals of Southwark and Merton', ed. Tyson, p. 50.
[34] Above pp. 110–11.
[35] For the reconstruction of the Exchequer, see Carpenter, *The Minority*, pp. 64–6. For the charter, *ibid.*, pp. 60–4; Holt, *Magna Carta*, pp. 382–6.
[36] Ms. 13DR, mm. 12, 12d; *Pat. R. 1216–25*, p. 256. Henry III's minority forms the subject of a definitive study by David Carpenter. In what follows I have attempted to

It is as well to open a study of des Roches' career after 1217 with a consideration of the effects of the civil war on both the national and local level. The bishop's sub-tenants had mostly followed his own lead in adhering to the king. J. C. Holt has stressed the significance of tenurial relations in determining the loyalties of knights. In this respect the principal agent of rebellion within Hampshire had been William de St John, a sub-tenant of des Roches but also a baron in his own right, lord of Basing, closely related to William de Briouze whose family had been suspect for more than a decade before the outbreak of war.[37] Several of St John's tenants defected to the rebel cause in 1216, amongst them William de Falaise who, despite having served as des Roches' constable at Winchester, followed the lead of his feudal lords, the rebels St John and the earl of Hereford.[38] A similarly divided loyalty may have influenced William de Pont-de-l'Arche, a Hampshire knight holding from the rebel St John but related by marriage to William Marshal. In March 1217, Pont-de-l'Arche and John fitz Hugh, a former royal servant and associate of des Roches, abandoned the rebel cause to return to their estates. The *Histoire de Guillaume le Maréchal* heaps scorn upon their disloyalty to both the rebel and the royalist camps, for which 'even now they are despised for their conduct'.[39] Pont-de-l'Arche was one of several knights taken prisoner by des Roches. It is difficult to determine the extent of ransoms taken by the bishop, but if they followed the general pattern they may have been extremely severe. Des Roches' associate, Peter de Maulay, received several thousand pounds in ransoms, including at least £1,200 from Reginald of Cornhill, formerly des Roches' colleague as sheriff of Kent and Surrey.[40] Cornhill had been

supplement rather than merely to duplicate his study, placing des Roches' career within the framework of political activity newly established by Carpenter. At the same time my debt to Carpenter's work is such that little of the following could have been written without his criticism and advice.

[37] Sanders, *English Baronies*, p. 9; Painter, *King John*, pp. 46, 242–3, and in general see Holt, *The Northerners*, ch. v.

[38] *Pat. R. 1216–25*, p. 37.

[39] *Hist. de Maréchal*, lines 15828–33. For Pont-de-l'Arche's rebellion, see *Gervase of Canterbury*, ii, pp. 111–12; *RLC*, i, pp. 283, 318; *Pat. R. 1216–25*, p. 47. For his holding from St John, see *BF*, p. 94, and for his relation to the Marshal family, *CP*, ii, p. 126; *Hist. de Maréchal*, line 7265. For fitz Hugh, see *Interdict Documents*, pp. 12–14, and above p. 77 and n.163.

[40] *RLC*, i, pp. 481b–482, and see *Pat.R.1216–25*, pp. 6, 12, 56, 95 for de Maulay's apparent refusal to deliver Cornhill in 1217. Thorne's Chronicle in *Historiae Anglicanae Scriptores X*, ed. R. Twysden (London 1652), col. 1878, states that Cornhill owed a total of £2,116 for his transgressions.

a major force in London politics, but after 1217 his family was forced to sell much of its property in the city. Des Roches himself stood witness to a sale of £200 worth of Cornhill property to the bishop of Bath, and as late as 1221, the monks of St Augustine's Canterbury were purchasing Cornhill's land in Canterbury and Southwark to assist with his release.[41]

Another of de Maulay's prisoners, William of Lancaster, was made to pay more than £1,800, his father begging that the ransom be payable in instalments. In May 1220 the bishop of Durham reported that he had met William, destitute of either arms or horses, quite incapable of coming to London to do homage.[42] Both Reginald of Cornhill and William of Lancaster became seriously embroiled in Jewish debt.[43] As with Nicholas de Stuteville, taken at Lincoln and forced to pay 1,000 marks to his captor, William Marshal, ransom payments threatened to push such men over the threshold of bankruptcy, serving as a largely invisible force to poison relations within the baronage.[44] The animosity shown later to Peter de Maulay, may well reflect these tensions. The severity of ransoms taken by Fawkes de Bréauté was to lead after 1224 to his kidnapping by a disgruntled Burgundian who had once been his prisoner.[45] Nor were the aliens the only royalists to take ransoms. Both Hubert de Burgh and John Marshal appear to have forced harsh terms on their captives.[46]

We know little of des Roches' French captives, save that they included the commander of the garrison at Farnham.[47] Of the English rebels who owed him ransoms, the names of at least five are recorded. In the spring of 1218 the bishop's agreements with three of them were enrolled in Chancery. The entries claim that it was the debtors themselves who had requested this arrangement, but it seems more

---

[41] Twysden, *Scriptores X*, cols. 1878–9; *HMC Wells I*, p. 16 no. xl; *PR 2 Henry III*, pp. xxiii, 47–8; *The Register of St Augustine's Abbey commonly called the Black Book*, ed. G. J. Turner and H. E. Salter, 2 vols. (London 1915–24), i, pp. 607–8, ii, pp. 381–2, 607–8. There is a possibility that religious corporations were particularly astute at picking up land in return for assistance with ransom payment. See, for example, *The Cartulary of Worcester Cathedral Priory*, ed. R. R. Darlington (1968), no. 276.

[42] *RLC*, i, p. 481b; SC1/1/92, 135; Carpenter, *The Minority*, p. 197.

[43] See the Rolls of the Justices of the Jews, in Cole, *Documents*, pp. 288, 290, 293, 304, 309, 311, 319, 322–3, 325, 328.

[44] *RLC*, i, p. 600b. Stuteville also owed money to the Jews; Cole, *Documents*, p. 297.

[45] *DD*, no. 182.

[46] 'Plea Rolls of the reign of Henry III', ed. G. Wrottesley, *William Salt Arch. Soc.*, iv (1883), p. 56; S. H. F. Johnston, 'The lands of Hubert de Burgh', *EHR* 50 (1935), p. 429.

[47] *Hist. des Ducs*, p. 188 and see *Hist. de Maréchal*, lines 16997–17013 for the suggestion that he took several captives at Lincoln.

likely that it was des Roches who used his position at court to enforce terms on his former captives.[48] The Treaty of Lambeth had decreed that ransoms should only be paid up to the instalments which fell due by 12 September 1217. Louis was to nominate three of Henry III's counsellors to decide upon cases where the dating of instalments was disputed.[49] In practice, however, there is no evidence that such arbitration occurred. There must have been considerable reluctance on the part of men such as des Roches and de Maulay to abandon claims to sums which fell due after the established deadline. Indeed, this very charge was levelled against de Maulay, who ignored not only the terms of the treaty, but several mandates to deliver up Reginald of Cornhill and the hostages of William of Avranches, both of whose ransoms should have gone to the crown rather than to de Maulay personally. Admittedly, de Maulay was to claim that the ransom money had been spent in the crown's service, but the official acceptance of this account reflects the court's anxiety to placate de Maulay, and should not be taken as a sign that his claims were actually believed.[50] The safest means of ensuring payment of disputed ransoms was to hold on to a prisoner until his debts were cleared, and this appears to have been the policy adopted by both de Maulay and Philip Mark, who retained wartime captives or their hostages long into the 1220s.[51] In April 1218, the regime agreed to listen to former prisoners wishing to lodge complaints against captors who had demanded ransoms in contravention of the terms of the truce. But this undertaking specifically excluded those such as de Maulay's hostages, William of Lancaster, Reginald of Cornhill and William de Avranches, who had been captured at Rochester in 1215.[52]

Des Roches was arguably less draconian than de Maulay in the terms he imposed upon his captives. Nevertheless, disputes over the monies due to him dragged on for more than a decade. In March 1218 he obtained distraints against Brian fitz Ralph, William Dacy and Robert le Hou for non-payment of ransom. Ralph le Moine, who owed the bishop 72 marks, agreed to pay up by Christmas

48 *Pat.R.1216–25*, pp. 148, 175.
49 Smith, 'The Treaty of Lambeth 1217', p. 576 clauses 4–5.
50 *RLC*, i, pp. 481b–482; below pp. 204–5.
51 *Pat. R. 1216–25*, p. 95. Above pp. 142–3, for Cornhill. For William de Avranches' daughter, who was held as late as 1221, see *RLC*, i, p. 455b; *Pat. R. 1216–25*, p. 158. During the war, William of Lancaster had attempted to secure his release from Philip Mark by sending for the sons of three northern knights to act in his place as hostages. Mark refused to accept the arrangement, but nonetheless imprisoned the three men he had rejected as hostages, holding them as late as 1222; *RLC*, i, p. 497b.
52 *RLC*, i, p. 358b; *Gervase of Canterbury*, ii, p. 110.

1218.[53] However, William de Pont-de-l'Arche's ransom was still in dispute in 1227. Having obtained powerful securities from his kinsmen, William Marshal and William Marshal the younger, and from his overlord, William de St John, Pont-de-l'Arche was sued for a debt of £11 owing to St John and des Roches, and in August 1227 his lands were distrained.[54] William Dacy, another of the bishop's hostages, died before 1223, by which time des Roches had reassigned his ransom to the bishop of Salisbury. Dacy's son claimed that the debt had been discharged, so that des Roches was forced to resort to further action in the courts to obtain distraint of Dacy's lands.[55] None of these men was particularly wealthy, although Pont-de-l'Arche enjoyed kinship with several powerful barons. He, Dacy and Le Moine held land in Hampshire but they were not amongst the county's leading knights.[56] Nevertheless, des Roches' ability and readiness to seek support from the crown in harassing his debtors for disputed ransoms can have done little to foster affection for him in the hearts of the county community.[57]

The Hampshire gentry may have been spared any permanent upheaval after 1216, but Hampshire itself had been transformed into a battlefield. Elsewhere, few parts of the country had escaped devastation. In London the rebels had attacked the houses of royal servants, broken into Westminster Abbey and intimidated the canons of Holy Trinity. On 22 October 1217 des Roches was present when the legate granted the canons compensation for the damage they had sustained.[58] Earlier in the year, des Roches had approved compensation for King John's destruction of a church in Bedford, whilst as late

---

[53] *Pat.R.1216–25*, pp. 148, 175; *RLC*, i, p. 356. Ralph le Moine enjoyed some contact with the rebel commander Robert fitz Walter: *RLC*, i, p. 271.

[54] *Pat.R.1216–25*, pp. 175–6; *RLC*, ii, pp. 196–199b; *CRR*,xiii, no. 357, and see below p. 162 for the possibility that des Roches assisted an attempt to deprive Pont-de-l'Arche of the advowson of Swanwick, Hants.

[55] *RLC*, i, pp. 505, 536b, 541; ii, p. 188.

[56] For Pont-de-l'Arche, see *VCH Hants.*, iii, p. 23; iv, p. 387; *BF*, p. 418; E. Mason, 'The king, the chamberlain and Southwick priory', *BIHR* 53 (1980), pp. 1, 4–6. For le Moine, see *BF*, pp. 74, 77, 257. For Dacy, *RLC*, ii, p. 188 which implies that he possessed land in Hampshire although the only fee he is known to have held was at Ilchester, Somerset; *BF*, p. 79.

[57] In general, ransom settlements have attracted little attention, largely because of an understandable reluctance on behalf of the victors to record their gains. For arrangements touching the earl of Chester in January 1220, see C60/12, m. 7. For the ransom of Robert Mauduit and an arrangement involving Philip Mark and the archbishop of York, see *RLC*, i, pp. 346–346b.

[58] *Acta Guala*, no. 52. For the burning of the house of a chancery clerk, see *RLC*, i, p. 452b; for attacks on Westminster, *Chronicles of Stephen, Henry II and Richard I*, ii, p. 523; *RLC*, i, p. 340b.

as 1223, one of his clerks was carrying out repairs to a chapel in Oxford, damaged during the war.[59] The monks of Bury, Coggeshall, Tilty and St Albans had all been robbed of jewels and treasures. Carlisle had been burned by the Scots, and at Worcester the monks had been forced to melt down the shrine of St Wulfstan to meet the demands of Fawkes de Bréauté. Fawkes had also extracted a fine of 100 marks from the monks of Thorney before restoring their lands. For all the crusading piety of the royalist army at Lincoln, their victory had been followed by the violation of cathedral property and a general pillage of the city. One of the earliest pilgrims to the shrine of St Hugh of Lincoln was a local man, driven mad by the loss of his possessions during the war.[60] In the Weald of Kent, armed bands had preyed upon the French, and a Dover cartulary records the activities of William de Avranches who had despoiled his tenants of tithes and with his armed supporters had carried off the bodies of the dead.[61] From the canons of Southwick to the monks of St Augustine's Canterbury, religious communities railed against the ravages of war.[62] In Winchester itself, the suburbs had twice been put to the torch, the city walls and the royal castle undermined and Hyde Abbey used as a barracks.

Given this widespread destruction, the Winchester pipe rolls provide striking proof of the speed with which the manorial economy was restored to normality. The war had severely disrupted the accounting process on the Winchester estates. As at the royal Exchequer, the first task which faced the bishop's clerks was to assess the period from Michaelmas 1215, the date of the last full account, to Michaelmas 1217, the date of the peace.[63] The king's clerks approached this problem by auditing the first war year, 17 John (Michaelmas 1215–16), largely writing off the year 1 Henry III (1216–17), and transferring what accounts existed for it, to the first full pipe roll of the new reign, that for 2 Henry III (1217–18). Des

[59] *RLC*, i, pp. 529b, 559b; *Pat.R.1216–25*, p. 29, and see Paris, *Hist. Angl. Min.*, ii, pp. 265–6.

[60] Wendover, *Flores*, iv, pp. 6, 10–11, 24–5; *Hist. des Ducs*, p. 198; *Coggeshall*, pp. 177–8; *AM*, iii (Dunstable), p. 50; iv (Worcester), pp. 406–7; *Chronicle of Melrose*, p. 63; H. Farmer, 'The canonization of St Hugh of Lincoln', *Lincs. Architectural and Archaeological Soc. Reports and Papers*, vi, pt. ii (1956), pp. 95, 102; *Acta Guala*, no. 158.

[61] Bodl. ms. Rawlinson B461 (St Radegund's Bradsole cartulary excerpts), f. 16r no. 67; Lambeth ms. TT1 (*ibid.*), pp. 162–3. For William's mother, forced to sell land at Seaford, Sussex, to raise her son's ransom of 600m to King John, see BL ms. Harley 4757 (Robertsbridge charters), ff. 68r–v; Bodl. ms. Dugdale 18 (*ibid.*), f. 66v.

[62] Sayers, *Honorius III*, p. 256 no. 52; Twysden, *Scriptores X*, col. 1870.

[63] For the practice of the royal Exchequer see intro. to *PR 17 John*, pp. i–viii.

Roches' episcopal Exchequer followed a very similar procedure. Just as no attempt was made to draw up a pipe roll 1 Henry III, so it seems that the equivalent roll for the Winchester estates was swiftly abandoned. Instead, whatever accounts could be audited for the war years were incorporated either into the roll for 1215–16 (11 des Roches) or enrolled with those for the year 1217–18 (13 des Roches). The matching rolls 11 des Roches and 17 John were both drawn up long after the year for which they purported to account, although it is indicative of the greater success of the bishop's clerks in effecting a rapid return to order, and also, of course, of the greater ease with which they could bring officers to account, that the roll 11 des Roches was completed by *c.*Michaelmas 1218 whereas its royal counterpart was still being added to as late as 1221 and was never fully completed.[64]

Admittedly the first episcopal pipe roll of the new reign, covering the period Michaelmas 1217–18, shows signs of strain; few accounts were paid in full. Most were discharged, not at the bishop's Exchequer, but in *ad hoc* payments to the bishop's itinerant officers.[65] With the coming of peace the episcopal estates required an immediate input of cash, to purchase seed and stock, and to pay for repairs before income could be generated. The episcopal *camera* disbursed over £210 in this way to the worst-hit of des Roches' Hampshire manors.[66] The source of these chamber loans may well have been the honour of Taunton, relatively unaffected by the war, where an aid of £100 was raised and an equivalent sum released to the bishop's chamber clerks.[67] Tallage was also taken at Downton, Meon and on the Isle of

---

[64] See *ibid.*, pp. ii–iii. The account roll 11 des Roches was undoubtedly drawn up after Michaelmas 1217, since it incorporates in the same hand memoranda relating to the year 12 des Roches (1216–17). However, the bishop's clerks chose to enrol at least three accounts for 11 des Roches on the roll 13 des Roches, which would suggest that by the time this latter roll was drawn up it was already too late to enrol accounts for 11 des Roches in their proper place, namely the Pipe Roll 11 des Roches, which must therefore have been completed *c.*Michaelmas 1217 X Michaelmas 1218. For references to a lost roll 12 des Roches, apparently fragmentary and quickly abandoned, see Ms. 11DR, *passim* in the *liberatio* section of each account. For displaced accounts see Ms. 13DR, mm. 9d (Fonthill yrs. 12, 13), 13d (Farnham and Bentley yr.?11, Ivinghoe yrs. 11 and 12), 14–14d (Farnham and Bentley yrs. 12 and 13).

[65] See Ms. 13DR *passim* in the *liberatio* section of each account.

[66] Ms. 13DR, mm. 2 (Cheriton), 2d (Meon, Meon Church), 4 (Crawley), 4d (Brightwell), 5 (Harwell, Calbourne), 5d (Highclere), 6 (Burghclere), 6d (Woodhay, Ecchinswell), 7 (Ashmansworth, Wargrave), 8 (Merdon), 8d (Alresford), 9 (Wield), 9d (Morton), 10 (Bishopstoke), 13 (Beauworth).

[67] Ms.13DR, m. 11d; £33 to Robert de Clinchamps and £70 to Master John of Dartford *in camera*.

Wight.[68] Considerable funds were invested in livestock and two men, probably cattle-dealers, were supplied with over £20, to purchase stock for various of the bishop's manors.[69] Granges were built anew at Highclere, Meon, and at Taunton repairs were carried out to the castle.[70] Considerable quantities of stock had been entrusted to the safe keeping of religious houses. With the return of peace, some of these animals were recovered; cattle were driven from Beaulieu and from Bindon Abbey to Cheriton, Downton and Twyford.[71] At Knoyle, 69 sheep pillaged during the war were recovered for a payment of 10 shillings and four pence.[72] Repairs to a hall were carried out at Portsmouth and 30 quarters of grain were given to the *Tribune*, probably the constable, of nearby Portchester, which had suffered considerable damage during the war.[73] £9 was spent at Bristol in the purchase of lead, and under the supervision of a Master Philip, this was used to reline the turrets of Taunton castle. Money was also spent at Taunton in the repair of crossbows.[74] Already, before the end of the war, des Roches had been given deer with which to restock his parks and in 1217–18, his huntsmen were as active as ever, providing game for the bishop and for the legate Guala.[75]

Unfortunately many entries on the roll 13 des Roches are illegible or torn and it is impossible to calculate the bishop's manorial income until the following year 1218–19. This year produced a gross total of £3,513, of which £775 was spent locally, with over £2,700 released in cash at the episcopal Exchequer.[76] This is a remarkable sum by any standard, larger than any raised before 1216, and this despite the fact that local expenses had more than doubled since the war. In the following decade episcopal income continued to rise steadily, grossing £3,755 in 1223–4 and £4,917 in 1226–27. Dr Titow suggests that to a large extent, these rises represent the effect of inflation rather than any fundamental change in the manorial economy. Nevertheless, to compare the pipe roll 11 des Roches and its lists of livestock slain or driven off, granges burned and grain pillaged, with the roll 13 des

---

[68] Ms. 13DR, mm.1, 2d.
[69] Ms. 13DR, mm. 1d, 2, 4, 5d, 10, 10d.
[70] Ms. 13DR, mm. 2d, 5d, 11d.
[71] *Ibid.*, mm. 1, 2.
[72] *Ibid.*, mm.3, 3d; *pro redempcione xli matr' ovium xxviii multon' pro guerra x s. iiii d.*
[73] *Ibid.*, m. 8d.
[74] *Ibid.*, mm. 11d, 12.
[75] *RLC*, i, p. 316; *Acta*, nos. 187, 191; Ms. 13DR, mm. 3d, 12 (where the bishop's dogkeepers were paid 2 shillings and fourpence for 10 days *cum canibus domini episcopi ad currendis ad porcos in parco*).
[76] Titow, 'Land and population on the Bishop of Winchester's estates 1209–1350', p. 68a.

Roches, is to appreciate the resilience of the bishop's resources and the speed with which peace was matched to prosperity. In 1217–18, not content merely with the restoration of order, des Roches' clerks introduced innovations to their accounting procedure, dividing the manor of Clere into separate accounts for Burghclere and Highclere, and in the following year introducing a flexible allowance by which each bailiff was permitted leniency in his grain account, reducing petty liabilities against the cost of seed that may have been sown.[77] The bishop had always enjoyed great wealth, but the speed with which that wealth was restored to him after 1217, combined with his newly acquired stranglehold over local government, made des Roches all the more formidable a figure in the political history of the minority. It is to his political career that we must turn next.

KING AND BISHOP

At the start of Henry III's reign des Roches was in the prime of life. Possessed of twenty years experience in the technical operations of government, he had served as the new king's guardian since Henry's infancy, time in which to acquire unparalleled influence. By contrast, William Marshal, the regent, was nearing eighty years old, a warrior of international renown, but relatively inexperienced in the technicalities of the Exchequer or the chamber. In the past, his relations with des Roches had been soured by the attack against William de Briouze, whom the Marshal had sheltered from the vindictiveness of King John.[78] Even during the war, bishop and regent co-operated fitfully. At Lincoln they had worked together in less than perfect harmony. Des Roches' wartime prisoners had included the Marshal's brother-in-law, and servants of William Marshal the younger.[79] It is possible that des Roches would have preferred to see the earl of Chester promoted regent; certainly there were voices raised in favour of substituting Chester in the Marshal's place.[80]

With the coming of peace, the common causes of civil war began to break down into a more natural pattern of self-interest. The king was a mere cypher. His courtiers enjoyed a taste of personal freedom unknown in John's reign, whilst, as head of the new regime, the

---

[77] Ms. 13DR, mm. 5d, 6. Burghclere is to be distinguished from the New Burgh at Clere founded c.1218, for which see below p. 190. For the allowance see Ms. 14DR, *passim*, before the grain account of each manor.

[78] Above pp. 60, 74 and see Painter, *William Marshal*, pp. 144–8.

[79] Above pp. 139, 145.

[80] *RL*, i, p. 532; Carpenter, *The Minority*, p. 36.

Marshal presided over an executive crippled by the effects of war. It has been estimated that cash receipts from the *adventus vicecomitum* produced a mere £32 at Michaelmas 1217, nothing at the following Hilary term and thereafter less than £300 before the Marshal's death in 1219. In the same way, cash revenues from the royal demesne reached only a fraction of their pre-war totals.[81] The king's income was not necessarily squandered, but spent locally by royal agents whose strength in the shires made it difficult for the central executive to extract accounts from them. The Exchequer was starved of power and resources. For nearly eighteen months, the king's cash income was exceeded by that of magnates such as des Roches, who found it far easier to bring their private bailiffs to heel and who, as a result, became ever more deeply entrenched in the localities.

In these circumstances, personal tensions within the minority council could have a profound effect upon the national scene. The succession of a new king was always a period of great danger and instability, made all the more dangerous and unstable if the king were a minor. Henry III was the first king since the Norman conquest to have come to his throne a mere child, incapable of personal rule. Elsewhere in Europe, within the past twenty years, the Empire and the kingdom of Sicily had been plunged into anarchy during the minority of the boy-king Frederick II. Frederick's minority had been marked by dramatic events: kidnappings, foreign invasions and murder. As such it must have provided an alarming precedent to the councillors of Henry III – that of a boy-king, placed under the direct protection of the papacy, forced to contend with the rivalries and hatreds that had built up during the reign of his father and mother. It is some indication of the success of Henry's minority council, that England failed to follow the dismal example set by Sicily and the Empire. And yet, in 1218, Henry's councillors might be excused for looking into the future with great misgiving. The council was comprised of men of very different backgrounds, each with his own personal axe to grind. There was very little love lost amongst them. Instead, anxiety and mutual mistrust were the predominant emotions.

Within the council, on the surface at least, des Roches played an important role in repairing the ravages of war. In 1217–18 he was present at the Exchequer for the hearing of accounts, authorized numerous orders to the financial executive, rescheduled debts and

---

[81] Carpenter, *The Minority*, pp. 413–17.

enforced the payment of a scutage.[82] However, beneath this veneer of public service, his private interests as a magnate had already begun to intrude. The most significant indication of this lies in the bishop's attitude to the scutage of 1217. Content as a royal servant to see it imposed upon the country at large, and assisted by the crown's officers in collecting over £70 from his own sub-tenants, he nevertheless refused to pay any of the money he collected to the Exchequer.[83] The scutage was intended to meet an indemnity of 10,000 marks granted to Louis in September 1217. Des Roches' refusal to pay argues both a serious breach with the Marshal and a fundamental dissatisfaction with the handling of the French withdrawal.

To a large extent, the civil war had originated in King John's ambitions to regain his continental inheritance, ambitions that had placed unsupportable strains upon the relationship between king and baronage, but which had nonetheless been shared by John's alien courtiers and by magnates, such as the earl of Chester, whose Norman estates had been seized by the French. The royalist victory of 1217 provided an opportunity to fulfil the dream of reconquest, but it was an opportunity which the Marshal let slip. It is possible that Louis issued a vague undertaking that he would restore Normandy after the death of his father, Philip Augustus, but if such a promise was made it was never included in any official treaty and there could be little expectation that it would be honoured.[84] In return the royalists were forced to disgorge lands taken during the war, to scale down their claims to ransoms, a demand which both des Roches and de Maulay appear to have found unacceptable, and to pay a crippling indemnity before the French would leave England. The Marshal himself had little to gain by pressing the question of Normandy or by inflaming relations with France. He, more or less alone amongst the Anglo-Norman baronage, had contrived to preserve both his English and his French estates after 1204. To the Marshal, war with France threatened

---

82 RLC, i, pp. 319, 349b, 361, 364, 364b, 381b, 382, 382b; PR 2 Henry III, pp. 10, 42; E368/1, m. 4. For a useful survey of des Roches' activities at the Exchequer after 1217, see West, The Justiciarship, pp. 238–41.

83 For his refusal to pay, see E372/65, m. 2, widely known via T. Madox, The History and Antiquities of the Exchequer of England 1066–1327, 2 vols., 2nd edn (London 1769), i, p. 675n., and commented upon by Holt, Magna Carta, p. 399; Powicke, Henry III, p. 33; S. K. Mitchell, Studies in Taxation under John and Henry III (New Haven 1914), pp. 125–8. See PR 2 Henry III, p. 10; E368/1, m. 1d; E159/2, m. 8d, for des Roches enforcing the scutage as a baron of the Exchequer. For his own collection, see RLC, i, p. 373; Ms. 13DR, m. 15.

84 AM, iii (Dunstable), p. 81; Wendover, Flores, iv, p. 31; Smith, 'The Treaty of Lambeth', p. 570; Painter, William Marshal, pp. 224–5.

only the dismemberment of his private, cross-Channel lordship. However, to many others, including des Roches, the treaty of 1217 appeared to sacrifice a unique opportunity to crown the labours of more than a decade by reasserting Plantagenet claims over Normandy and Anjou.

Hence, when a general tax was imposed to fund Louis' indemnity, the bishop publicly refused to pay, not only from his own lands but from the fees he held in custody from the crown.[85] The tax was levied as a scutage, whereas des Roches had already spent heavily in waging war. Moreover it went to enrich a defeated enemy which had ravaged the bishop's estates. As a private land-owner des Roches had good cause to object to the tax. In 1217 he had won relaxation for the hard-pressed Hampshire religious from an earlier levy, a hidage, intended to fund the royalist campaign.[86] But as a leading figure in the minority council he was surely obliged to set an example by paying scutage, particularly since he showed no hesitation in enforcing payment on others, including his own sub-tenants.

This conflict between private and public interests dogged all aspects of royal government after 1217. The Marshal himself, whilst pledging his own Norman lands as security for the payment of Louis' indemnity, was never slow to obtain rewards for himself and his family, including an annual pension for his eldest son from the proceeds of the royal exchange.[87] Relations between regent and bishop were not irreparably damaged; the Marshal awarded the monks of Winchester privileges in one of his private hundreds. Another of his private charters, in favour of the Templars, was witnessed by des Roches, whilst the bishop authorized and in one case sealed royal letters in the Marshal's favour.[88] In negotiations with the Welsh, des Roches, Chester and Llywelyn attempted to appeal to the king against the Marshal's retention of Caerleon, but for the most part des Roches had little to gain by seeking confronta-

---

[85] For non-payment on fees held in custody by des Roches, see *PR 3 Henry III*, p. 101; *4 Henry III*, p. 154; E368/3, m. 3(2)d.

[86] *RLC*, i, p. 336, and see Norgate, *The Minority*, p. 82 for the hidage.

[87] For his pledges for the scutage, see *Pat.R.1216–25*, pp. 114–15; C47/13/1 no. 24. For William Marshal the younger, *Pat.R.1216–25*, pp. 138–9; *RL*, i, no. lviii, and in general see Painter, *William Marshal*, pp. 267–72.

[88] BL Add. ms. 29436 (St Swithun's cartulary), f. 39; Cotton ms. Nero E vi (Hospitallers' cartulary), f. 135v, which was also witnessed by the rebel Robert fitz Walter (printed Dugdale, *Monasticon*, vii, p. 820 no. 15; *Records of the Templars in England in the Twelfth Century*, ed. B. A. Lees (Oxford 1935), p. cxxxvii no. 3). See also *Pat.R.1216–25*, pp. 9, 148–9; *RLC*, i, p. 361, and Painter, *William Marshal*, p. 268.

tion.[89] Between them, bishop and regent effectively monopolized the issue of royal letters. The Marshal's age and declining health promised an imminent realignment of power. In the meantime, rather than prolong his squabble with the ageing regent, it was more prudent for des Roches to concentrate upon building up a clientele amongst the regime's lesser office-holders.

At the Exchequer his position had already been strengthened by the appointment of his familiar and household clerk, Master Eustace de Fauconberg, as royal treasurer.[90] Another figure who had first risen to prominence in 1214 during des Roches' time as Justiciar, Ralph de Neville, took up residence at the Chancery, where from November 1218 he had control of the newly issued royal seal.[91] Within the royal household the bishop's position was even more secure. Until 1221 the king was his personal charge. Henry is found on the Winchester estates on numerous occasions and in June 1218, he accompanied the bishop to Worcester, for the dedication of St Wulfstan's shrine, close to the tomb of King John.[92] Until 1219 Henry's sister, Eleanor, and her nurses were maintained, at considerable expense, at des Roches' castle of Taunton.[93] Henry's brother Richard was nearby at Corfe under the protection of Peter de Maulay, whilst another of the royal children, Isabella, was apparently in the custody of the bishop's fellow Tourangeau, Philip Mark.[94] In

---

[89] *Hist. de Maréchal*, lines 17788–17872; Carpenter, *The Minority*, p. 77; D. Crouch, *William Marshal* (London 1990), pp. 127–8.

[90] For Eustace see above pp. 101–2, 132n., 105.

[91] F. M. Powicke, 'The Chancery during the minority of Henry III', *EHR* 23 (1908), pp. 227–9; above pp. 68–9, and see Vincent, 'The origins of the Chancellorship of the Exchequer', *EHR* 108(1993), pp. 114–17.

[92] *AM*, iv (Worcester), p. 409; Ms. 14DR, mm. 1, 1d (king, Peter de Rivallis and bp.'s knights at Waltham), 4d (grain for king at Highclere), 5d (king's hounds at Witney), 6d (cheeses at Brightwell), 7, 7d (king at Downton), 9 (£5 expenses of king at Farnham); Ms. 15DR, mm. 1d (king's servants at Merdon), 2d (gifts to the king with his hounds at ?Bishop's Waltham), 5d (geese to the king at Brightwell), 7d (king at Downton, 14 Nov. 1219), 9 (king at Farnham), 10 (£8 and 15 shillings expenses, king at Taunton 5 days); Ms. 16DR, mm. 2 (king's expenses £3 at Highclere), 2d (Bp.'s *familia* going to visit the king at Wallingford), 5 (king at Farnham), 5d (gift of a colt and food to the king from Bishop's Sutton), 7 (wine for the king at Bishop's Waltham), 11 (provisions to king at Gillingham).

[93] Ms. 13DR, mm. 12, 12d (king's daughter, her nurses, *familia* and knights 25 Dec.1217–28 Sept. 1219, soap, cloth, candles, oil, robes, over £20 expenses including a nurse taken to Bristol); Ms. 14DR, m. 10d (at Taunton with nurses, 26 weeks 3 days, cloth for caps and robes, grain, oil, writs to London, oblations, over £6 cash expenses), 11 (at Rimpton travelling to Winchester); Ms. 16DR, m. 5 (wine and fowls to king's sister at *Kingest'* near Farnham).

[94] For Richard, see *Hist. des Ducs*, p. 180; N. Denholm-Young, *Richard of Cornwall* (Oxford, 1947), pp. 3–4. For Isabella see *Pat.R.1216–25*, p. 234.

effect, the entire royal family was placed in the personal custody of des Roches and his alien satellites.

Richard had a tutor named Master Robert of Acaster.[95] However, we know very little of the king's education. Des Roches' protégé, the poet Henry of Avranches, dedicated a metrical grammar to Henry and Richard, but it was not the sort of work to have been of any practical use as a textbook.[96] Des Roches continued to maintain contacts with scholars, the most prominent being Master William Scot, the Oxford theologian who received two substantial payments at the bishop's manor of Witney.[97] But there is nothing to link Scot to the king's household. The Exchequer and its affairs kept the bishop at Westminster for several months of each year; large quantities of provisions were sent up to London from his estates, and it was during these years that the episcopal palace at Southwark underwent substantial rebuilding.[98] It is possible that King Henry began his long attachment to Westminster Abbey under the bishop's supervision. In 1220, at the age of only thirteen, Henry laid the foundation stone of the abbey's lady chapel and in the next few years des Roches not only supervised construction work in the vicinity of Westminster, but installed a new abbot and helped ordain wide-sweeping liberties for the Westminster monks.[99]

Henry spent long periods at Wallingford castle, held by his illegitimate half-brother Richard fitz Regis. The cost of these stays

[95] E159/2, m. 2; E368/5, m. 12(1)d. For Master Robert, see *RL*, i, no. clvi; SC1/2/11; *RLC*, i, pp. 325b, 495. In 1225 a Roger and a Robert of Acaster accompanied Richard's Gascon expedition; *Pat. R. 1216–25*, p. 574. Roger subsequently held land of the earldom of Cornwall at Winnianton and *Tybista* in Cornwall; E36/57 (Earldom of Cornwall cartulary), f. 42r. Acaster near York suggests a connection with de Maulay's Yorkshire honour.

[96] *Henry of Avranches*, ed. Cox Russell, pp. 18–19, 57–8, 123.

[97] Ms. 11DR, m. 6 (gift of 66 shillings and eightpence at Witney), Ms. 16DR, m. 3 (ditto.), not noticed by Emden, *Biographical Register of the University of Oxford*, pp. 1657–8.

[98] For supplies to London, see especially Ms. 14DR, mm. 7, 8, 10, 12d; Ms. 15DR, mm. 1, 1d, 2, 2d, 3d, 4d, 5, 5d. In general the Thames was used to transport provisions from the bishop's outlying manors, Brightwell, Harwell, Wycombe and Wargrave, down river to Southwark, often with Marlow as the point of embarkation; Ms. 15DR, m. 5 (large quantity of wood from Wycombe to Marlow to await a ship); Ms. 16DR, m. 4 (£4 spent on four ship journeys carrying grain and firewood from Wargrave to Southwark). For Southwark, see M. Carlin, 'The reconstruction of Winchester House, Southwark', *London Topographical Record* 25 (1989), pp. 33–57, esp. pp. 37, 47.

[99] *RLC*, i, pp. 389b, 402, 416, 432, 439b, 540, 578; *The History of the King's Works Volume 1: the Middle Ages*, ed. R. A. Brown, H. M. Colvin and A. J. Taylor, (London 1963), p. 131, and see M. T. Clanchy, 'Did Henry III have a policy?', *History* 53 (1968), p. 214n. Henry of Avranches, des Roches' protégé, wrote a metrical life of Edward the Confessor, patron saint of Westminster, before 1245: *Henry of Avranches*, ed. Cox Russell, pp. 137–42, and see below p. 208 for des Roches and Westminster 1222–3.

was met by des Roches. At Wallingford Henry was supervised by Philip de Aubigné, a knight of Breton descent related to the Aubigné family of Belvoir, who probably served not so much as an academic tutor but to instruct the king in the arts of riding and fighting, the prerequisites of a noble education.[100] Aubigné's appointment was almost certainly subject to the approval of des Roches. As for the bishop himself, we can only guess at the lessons which he sought to instil in the king. Des Roches was a Frenchman, a witness to the collapse of the Plantagenet dominion in France. As a loyal servant of John, he had connived in the arbitrary and brutal practices of the late king's government. He had little sympathy or respect for the native English baronage, and perhaps even less for the charters of liberties which threatened to restrict the sovereign exercise of royal will. But at the same time, des Roches was a pious man, the founder of monasteries, lavish in his almsgiving, a patron of scholars and poets, a connoisseur of the arts and a lover of luxury. In later life King Henry III was to share many of these traits: a respect for the memory of his father, King John; an attachment to the Plantagenet lands in France; a taste for extravagant religious patronage; and perhaps, too, a conviction that kings should rule as kings, whatever the theoretical restrictions placed on their sovereignty by charters and councils. As a boy, Henry spent nearly ten years in the household of the bishop of Winchester, ample time in which to learn many lessons. Above all, he was raised in the shadow of older men: King John; des Roches; the Marshal; Hubert de Burgh. At the age of nine he bade farewell to his mother, who was to spend the remainder of her life in Poitou, remarrying and raising another family, apparently oblivious to the well-being of her eldest son. It is hardly surprising that for many years to come Henry was to show a dependence upon des Roches and the other veterans at court: a dependence that would have been unthinkable during the reigns of the first three Plantagenet kings.

Between 1216 and 1221, indeed from the time that he had first

---

[100] Ms. 16DR, m. 2d. For des Roches taking responsibility for payments on the king's behalf at Wallingford and personally paying the king's servants see *RLC*, i, pp. 370, 384, 391, 393, 394, 397, 403, 412, 450, 530b, 534b, 561b; *PR 3 Henry III*, pp. 8, 78, 158; *4 Henry III*, p. 122; E368/3, m. 13. For de Aubigné as the king's tutor, see *Hist. de Maréchal*, lines 15336–43, where the king is said to have clung to him particularly closely as early as 1216; *Hist. des Ducs*, p. 207; *Regesta Honorii Papae III*, ed. P. Pressutti, 2 vols. (Rome 1888–95), i, no. 3313; and see *RLC*, i, pp. 396b, 397b, 412, 443; Carpenter, *The Minority*, pp. 243, 258.

been entrusted to the bishop's care, from 1212 onwards, the king grew up under the tutelage of des Roches. Des Roches enjoyed unrivalled influence over the royal household and over the king himself. Henry's expenses were met largely from the bishop's own purse or via the wardrobe headed by des Roches' nephew, Peter de Rivallis. The provisioning of the household lay with the titular steward, William de Cantiloupe, but on a day-to-day basis Cantiloupe's duties devolved upon Eustace de Greinville, a former servant of des Roches.[101] In addition, the bishop played an important part in authorizing the expenses of the small body of mercenaries attached to the king. The majority of these men were aliens, including des Roches' namesake and kinsman Peter de Rupibus.[102]

ALIENS NEW AND OLD

The most obvious constituency of support for des Roches lay amongst the alien loyalists of the civil war. Here he commanded a following which he could not hope to obtain amongst the native baronage. But at the same time he ran the risk of hostaging his fortunes to those of an increasingly volatile and isolated group of men. Save at times of crisis, the aliens were never to constitute a coherent faction, still less an organized party at court. By no means every exiled Frenchman enjoyed close relations with des Roches, and even those who were in regular contact with the bishop did not necessarily respond to his political lead. The court of Henry III, like the court of King John, was too unstable an environment, too much dominated by competition between courtiers and by mutual distrust ever to produce stable political parties. The courtiers' motto, in the thirteenth century as at all times in history, was 'Every man for himself'. After 1224, and again during the 1230s, by no means every alien at court was to suffer as a result of des Roches' fall from power. Even some of his closest associates, most notably Philip Mark and Engelard de Cigogné, were to survive in office, despite the bishop's disgrace. Nonetheless, given his vast personal wealth, his longevity, and his prolonged enjoyment of royal favour, des Roches undoubtedly

---

[101] Greinville's appointment may have been agreed jointly by des Roches and the Marshal, since the Greinvilles were tenants of the Marshals in Normandy; *Acta*, appendix 4, no. 38.

[102] For Peter de Rupibus, see *Acta*, appendix 4, no. 44. For payments to knights, see also *RLC*, i, pp. 382b, 390, 421, 422b, 433–433b, 442, 444, 450b–451, 482b.

commanded a following, however loose, that was more coherent than those attached to virtually any other courtier. Alien birth was an important factor in this coherence, since it was their status as aliens that made des Roches and his fellow Frenchmen most vulnerable to attack from their rivals at court. At times of crisis, in 1215, during the minority of Henry III, and again between 1232 and 1234, the aliens did indeed work closely together, if only in reaction against a hostile political climate. We should be wary of overestimating their solidarity or coherence, but it is by no means anachronistic to regard the aliens as an identifiable body of men, capable of concerted action when need arose.

In the aftermath of civil war several aliens refused to disgorge wartime custodies. Peter de Maulay, for example, had come under attack for his retention of hostages. He was also engaged against the earl of Salisbury in a major dispute over the custody of Sherborne castle and the county of Somerset.[103] At des Roches' manor of Downton in January 1218, a compromise was reached whereby de Maulay retained Sherborne and the shrievalty of Somerset and Dorset. Salisbury was bought off with a promise of £1,000 from the court, a further £500 from de Maulay and a valuable wardship.[104] In the coming year, des Roches supervised the payment of most of the farm of Southampton as compensation to Salisbury.[105]

Another of the bishop's alien familiars, Engelard de Cigogné, had quarrelled with the earl of Warenne over custody of Surrey. Here again des Roches acted as mediator. Engelard was bought off, following a provisional settlement sealed by several magnates, des Roches included. He was effectively offered the choice between pressing his claim to Surrey or accepting two manors in Oxfordshire, an annual pension of £50 and the possibility of a further £100 per annum in the first escheats to fall vacant in the bailiwicks of des Roches, the Marshal, and of Fawkes de Bréauté.[106] In 1218 the

---

[103] *Pat. R. 1216–25*, pp. 38, 86–7; *RLC*, i, pp. 481b–482; *Hist. des Ducs*, p. 180; Carpenter, *The Minority*, p. 71.

[104] Ms. 13DR, m. 1; *In expensa domini Wintoniensis episcopi die mercurii ante Epiph' quando fuit ad concordiam faciend' inter Comitem Sar' et Petrum de Mallei*. For the payment of Salisbury's money from the crown see *RLC*, i, pp. 360, 370b, 381 (*coram* des Roches), 384 (*Teste* des Roches), 387b (*ibid.*), 388–388b (*ibid.*), 391b (*ibid.*), 406b, 408b. For de Maulay's offer of £500, see *RLC*, i, pp. 481b–482; Carpenter, *The Minority*, p. 71.

[105] *PR 3 Henry III*, p. 25. In 1218–19 des Roches granted the earl a dozen fowls at St Denis' Southampton, provisions in Wiltshire and at Seale near Farnham and a respite of 63/4d he owed in scutage: Mss. 13DR, mm. 3, 14d; 14DR, mm. 7d, 8, 9, 12d.

[106] Engelard had been granted Surrey by John; *RLP*, p. 178b. For the settlement and

bishop also initiated an enquiry into property which Engelard claimed to have lost in Southampton during the war.[107]

Perhaps the most significant of des Roches' actions as broker between alien constables and the regime concerned the castle of Newark-on-Trent. In 1219 the regime ordered that the castle be restored to the bishop of Lincoln, but its wartime keeper, the Flemish mercenary Robert de Gaugy, persistently refused orders to admit the bishop's officers. A settlement was only obtained by the threat of a siege and after the regent had received 100 marks from bishop Hugh of Lincoln to speed proceedings. In July 1218 des Roches served as go-between, accepting Gaugy's surrender of Newark and releasing it into the hands of bishop Hugh.[108] Tensions between aliens and native magnates were nothing new. They had existed since at least 1204, and played an important part in the outbreak of civil war. However, after 1217 the position of the aliens had changed. The death of King John removed their chief protection against native hostility. Many of John's familiars found themselves in positions of unprecedented authority in local administration. They were no longer the tools of the king but semi-independent magnates in their own right. Most of these men were of humble birth and held their lands only during pleasure. Yet Fawkes de Bréauté had risen to the command of half-a-dozen counties; Peter de Maulay felt sufficiently well-placed to challenge the earl of Salisbury, Engelard the earl of Warenne.[109] A common insecurity bound them one to another. Although as yet they could not be said to constitute a faction, they might easily become such if the hostility against them gathered momentum. Only Peter de Maulay had obtained a firm footing in England, promoted to the Fossard barony under des Roches' sponsorship. And yet, even here, de Maulay met resistance in pressing his wife's claims to her family estates.[110] After 1216 Fawkes de Bréauté attempted to follow suit, marrying the

---

dispute see *Pat. R. 1216–25*, pp. 135, 181; *RLC*, i, pp. 403–403b. Between 1213 and 1218/19 des Roches had custody of a manor called Henley, which may or may not be that in Oxfordshire awarded to Cigogné; Mss. 9DR, m. 6; 11DR, m. 5; 13DR, m. 7; 14DR, m. 12d. See C60/11, m. 10 for its award to Engelard, and in general see *Acta Guala*, no. 26.

[107] *RL*, i, no. viii, and see *RLC*, i, pp. 384b, 385, 387, 387b, 391b for grants of a wardship and Engelard's pension of £50 in 1218/19 authorized by des Roches.

[108] *Pat. R. 1216–25*, p. 164; *RLC*, i, p. 602; *Acta Guala*, nos. 70–1.

[109] See for example *Coggeshall*, p. 204 on Fawkes' origins, and for de Maulay, see *Hist. des Ducs*, p. 180: *Ot esté huissiers le roi mais puis crut tant ses afaires que il fu chevaliers et connestables dou castiel et si poissans que il guerroia al conte de Salesbieres.*

[110] Above p. 112, and see *CRR*, viii–xi *passim*, for actions against the barony's under-tenants.

countess of Devon and obtaining custody of Plympton castle. But Fawkes served only as guardian to his wife's heir, and his custody of Plympton was challenged by a local magnate, Robert de Courtenay.[111] Hugh de Vivonne, the Poitevin constable of Bristol, was married to the daughter of William Malet only to find himself saddled with the debts of his late father-in-law.[112] With des Roches' assent, Vivonne also sought to obtain Malet's widow for one of his nephews, a transaction which involved him in a network of bitter jealousies amongst the west country gentry.[113] In a letter to the king, Vivonne summed up the predicament of many aliens: in coming to England, he and his kind had forfeited all their continental possessions and prospects of promotion; the king might well cast them aside but would this be fair, given the sacrifices which they had made for the Plantagenet cause?[114]

In these circumstances it is not surprising that des Roches came to assume something of the role of protector and mediator between aliens and natives formerly played by King John. He alone of the alien courtiers possessed the territorial resources and security of tenure to serve as a refuge, once John's men came under attack. More than that, as the king's guardian he enjoyed access to royal patronage to bestow upon whomever he chose. With the king unable to govern for himself, there was an obvious risk that his courtiers would seek to alienate the crown's resources for their own enrichment. Already, by the summer of 1218, des Roches had witnessed grants in perpetuity, to the legate Guala and to various religious corporations for the soul of King John.[115] In November 1218, the issue of a new royal seal was made the occasion for a self-denying ordinance by the king's counsellors. Henceforth the demesne was to remain inviolate and no alienations in perpetuity were to be made until the king came of age.[116] Even minor awards such as markets and fairs, already granted by mutual consent to des Roches and William Marshal, were to

---

[111] *Pat. R. 1216–25*, pp. 144–5; *CP*, iv, pp. 316–18; *Walter of Coventry*, ii, p. 253; *RLC*, i, p. 393.

[112] C60/20, m. 8; Sanders, *Baronies*, p. 39.

[113] SC1/1/211 and see below p. 202.

[114] *RL*, i, no. lxxv.

[115] See *Pat. R. 1216–25*, pp. 41, 173. The only original territorial grant in perpetuity to survive from the minority is described by P. Libico, *Gualae Bicherii Presbiteri Cardinalis S. Martini in Montibus Vita et Gesta* (Milan 1767), p. 100n. Sealed with the Marshal's seal in coloured wax and issued in November 1217, these letters patent are now Vercelli, Archivio di Stato ms. Pergamene 149.

[116] *Pat. R. 1216–25*, p. 177. For the issue of the seal, whose cost was accounted by des Roches, see *RLC*, i, pp. 381b, 383.

become subject to this qualification.[117] But the ordinance created almost as many problems as it solved. In the short term, it denied the regime access to patronage which might have bound men more closely to the court or made it easier to challenge the power of local magnates. In the longer term, it left an unanswered and potentially explosive question of timing. Whoever held the initiative when the king came of age, at a date as yet undetermined, would inherit the right to influence grants in perpetuity. Jockeying for position at court was intensified rather than diminished.

Besides maintaining his contacts with men such as de Maulay and Engelard, des Roches extended his network of patronage to include several prominent alien courtiers. The Tourangeaux, Peter and Andrew de Chanceaux, proscribed by name in Magna Carta, were brought firmly within des Roches' episcopal household. Peter de Chanceaux henceforth combined service as des Roches' larderer with a role under Engelard de Cigogné at Windsor castle.[118] The Flemish (or possibly Norman) knight, Aimery de St Amand, had first appeared in England as a member of the bishop's wartime garrison at Taunton.[119] After 1217 he was promoted to various estates including escheats in Sussex and Berkshire held from the crown via des Roches.[120] Aimery's father-in-law, Walter de Verdun, was appointed deputy-sheriff of Essex under the Marshal, and served as constable of the Tower of London, either in his own right or as the representative of some magnate such as des Roches. In 1217 the Tower had been surrendered to des Roches, who appears to have supervised repairs there during the early years of the minority.[121] In Oxfordshire Walter held half of the

---

[117] Compare, for example, *Pat. R. 1216–25*, p. 166; *RLC*, i, pp. 363, 363b, 366b, 389 and C60/12, m. 6, William Brewer's fine for a market at Deeping, Lincs. , where the words *usque ad etatem domini regis* have been carefully inserted after the award. The change would appear to have been introduced in 1219/20, considerably after the ordinance of Nov. 1218.

[118] Mss 13DR, mm. 4d, 5d, 12; 14DR, mm. 1d, 4d, 5d, 6, 6d, 7d, 9, 10. For Chanceaux as Engelard's deputy, see C60/14, m. 2.

[119] Ms. 11DR, m. 9. This is apparently the earliest reference to Aimery and his brother R(alph) in an English source. For a general account, see *CP*, xi, pp. 295–6. Aimery's name is most likely derived from St Amand (dep. Pas-de-Calais), but there is an outside possibility that he should be accounted a Norman, from either St Amand (Manche) or St Amand-des-Hautes-Terres (dep. Eure).

[120] See *BF*, p. 272 for 'Dum' (?Eastbourne) in Sussex. The bp held Ilsley, Berks. as an escheat c.1218–20 (Ms. 14DR, m. 6d; 15DR, m. 5d; 16DR, m. 2d), possibly as part of the Leicester inheritance (*VCH: Berks.* , iv, pp. 26, 33). In 1220 Savill de Oseville had acquired some interest via des Roches (*BF*, p. 298), and in 1222 Aimery de St Amand warranted a grant of a market at Ilsley to Oseville (C60/17, m. 6), besides receiving oxen there (Ms. 16DR, m. 2d), prior to his own acquisition of the manor.

[121] For des Roches and the Tower see *RLC*, i, p. 450; *PR 4 Henry III*, p. 122 which may

manor of Bloxham, close to the bishop's manor of Adderbury, where in 1218–19 he was paid £7 by des Roches' bailiffs.[122] Aimery de St Amand was himself regularly entertained on the episcopal estates, and in 1223 is found amongst the bishop's military following at Montgomery.[123] In the same year he served alongside Peter de Maulay as a pledge for the count of Guînes, and in 1221 stood as guarantor for Philip de Aubigné's custody of the Channel Islands.[124] Another pledge on this occasion was provided by the Breton knight, Roger de la Zouche. Established in England before the civil war, Roger had flirted with the rebel cause, but in 1217 was granted custody of lands in Hampshire in return for estates he had forfeited in Brittany. Des Roches attested several royal awards to him and granted Roger and his wife wine at the episcopal manors of Taunton and Farnham.[125]

Aimery and Roger were both linked to another Anglo-Breton, Philip de Aubigné.[126] De Aubigné had enjoyed contacts with the see of Winchester as long ago as 1211–12. Related to William de Aubigné, lord of Belvoir, and possibly to the bishop's ward Robert de Aubigny, Philip played an active role in the royalist conquest of Hampshire. In January 1219 he received joint custody with des Roches of the lands of the widowed countess of Leicester, possibly to defray their joint expenses as guardians of the king. In June of the same year, he deputed his custody of the Channel Islands to his nephew and namesake by letters issued under des Roches' authority.[127] He received numerous

relate to 1214–15. For Walter at the Tower April 1218–? April 1219, see *RLC*, i, pp. 358, 525b, *PR 4 Henry III*, p. 106. For his relation to Aimery, see *The Cartulary of Cirencester Abbey*, ii, pp. 539–43; *E. Rot. Fin.*, i, p. 204. Stacey, *Politics, Policy and Finance*, p. 13 describes him as 'another of the Marshal's marcher connections', but in fact there is nothing to link him to the Marshal beyond his service as under-sheriff, transformed after 1218 to personal custody of Essex and Herts. His only contact with the Marches had been in 1215 when he had spent a week or so strengthening the garrison of Bridgnorth. He seems to have spent the rest of the war at Bristol, Devizes and ?Wallingford; *RLP*, pp. 136b, 137b, 147, 191, 195; *RLC*, i, p. 290b.

122 *RLC*, i, pp. 381b, 503b, 504; *RLC*, ii, pp. 6, 10; *Cirencester Cartulary*, ii, pp. 539–43; Ms. 14DR, m. 6.

123 Mss. 13DR, m. 1; 14DR, mm. 6, 7; 15DR, m. 6 (with his brother R[alph] at Highclere); 16DR, m. 2d; 19DR, m. 8; 22DR, m. 10d; C72/3, this last transcribed in R. F. Walker, 'The Anglo-Welsh wars 1217–1267; with special reference to English military developments', Oxford D. Phil. thesis (1954), chapter iii, appendix p. ii.

124 *RLC*, i, p. 515b; C60/18, m. 5.

125 *CP*, xii, pp. 931–2; *CRR*, xi, no. 524; Paris, *CM*, ii, p. 605, Mss. 13DR, m. 12d; 19DR, m. 4d; 20DR, m. 10; *RLC*, i, pp. 385, 386; *Pat. R. 1216–25*, pp. 37, 68. Before 1237 Roger surrendered his estates in Brittany to Alan, viscount of Rohan, in return for Alan's interest in the manors of Swavesey and Fulbourn, Cambs. ; Nantes, Bibliothèque Municipale ms. 1701 no. 1; *BF*, p. 616.

126 *RLC*, i, pp. 404b, 429, and see C60/11, m. 9; *RLC*, i, p. 385.

127 N. Vincent, 'Philip de Aubigné', *New Dictionary of National Biography* (Oxford,

royal grants witnessed by des Roches, and in 1223 is to be found at the episcopal manor of Bishop's Waltham hunting there 'on many occasions'.[128]

By 1214 des Roches' episcopal household had already come to include a large number of Norman clerks. During the minority this Norman influx continued. After 1216 des Roches recruited two men with strong links to the diocese of Avranches, Master Humphrey de Millières and Master Nicholas de Vienne. In 1219–20 the bishop of Avranches was himself entertained at the episcopal manor of Bitterne in the course of litigation against William de Pont-de-l'Arche over the church of Swanwick. Master Nicholas served as the Norman bishop's attorney, whilst the advowson of Swanwick passed via Master Humphrey to des Roches' foundation of Titchfield Abbey.[129] Significantly, des Roches played a leading role in an exchange involving the Norman family of Marmion. Robert Marmion the elder had come to England in 1204, leaving a son and namesake in charge of his estates near Caen. On his father's death in 1218, another son and namesake by a previous marriage made an elaborate fine at the Exchequer, by which for £500 he acquired Tamworth castle and his father's English estates, 'until such time as the lands of the English and the Normans are re-united', at which stage his possessions across the Channel would be restored to him and his Norman half-brother would come to England. Des Roches was granted an interest in this fine, receiving 100 marks of it to reimburse his expenses in the royal household.[130] In April 1219 the whole fine of £500 was transferred to him, and in the following year the Norman half-brother crossed to England and swapped places with his elder namesake. Henceforth des Roches held the

forthcoming); *CP*, iv, pp. 93–4; C. Clermont-Ganneau, 'L'origine de Philippe d'Aubigny', *Revue Critique d'Histoire et de Littérature*, new series 1 (1876), pt. ii, pp. 206–7, and see *ibid.*, pp. 173–4, 398–9; J. Havet, 'Des gardiens et seigneurs des Iles Normandes (1198–1461)', *Bibliothèque de l'Ecole des Chartes*, xxxvii (1876), pp. 190–1, 221–2; *Pat. R. 1216–25*, pp. 6, 184–5, 188, 194. Together with his brothers, named Oliver and Marchis(ius) de Aubigné, Philip had witnessed various charters of Robert IV earl of Leicester (d. 1204); Evreux, Archives Départementales de l'Eure H438; *Documents Preserved in France*, ed. Round, nos. 408, 555, 653. For Robert de Aubigny see below pp. 193–4.

[128] *RLC*, i, pp. 385, 387b, 393b, 395, 413, Mss. 19DR, mm. 2, 2d, 7d, 10; 22DR, mm. 5, 8; *Hist des Ducs*, p. 207.

[129] Ms. 15DR, m. 2; *RLC*, i, pp. 431, 437b; *Acta*, no. 67a.

[130] *PR 2 Henry III*, pp. 54–5; C60/9, mm. 5, 6. Des Roches had authorized the letters inviting Robert Marmion to peace in 1217; *Pat. R. 1216–25*, p. 84 and see *ibid.* pp. 68, 153; *RLC*, i, pp. 361–2. In general see Powicke, *The Loss of Normandy*, p. 339.

Norman Robert Marmion in custody, eventually selling his marriage to the earl of Chester for £400.[131]

The ties which bound these men one to another and to the bishop are matched by only meagre links between des Roches and the native baronage. This is not to imply that all aliens were members of an identifiable clique or that native opinion failed to distinguish between various different sorts of alien.[132] However, should an air of mistrust and factionalism develop, it was all too easy for contemporaries to point to des Roches as the central figure in a circle of alien familiars.

DIPLOMACY

In the meantime the bishop's network of alien contacts was not without its uses for the regime. Des Roches continued to command privileged channels of communication with his homeland in France. Between 1216 and 1224 at least three of the bishop's nephews, the clerks Hugh and Aimery des Roches and their brother, the knight Geoffrey, crossed to England.[133] Another kinsman, Peter de Rivallis, was accused of poaching a clerk from the Poitevin magnate Hugh de Lusignan who had meanwhile granted employment to des Roches' former associate, Walter de Montmorillon.[134] Such a network of contacts afforded the bishop a central position in English diplomacy. There were few embassies sent to either Rome or France over which he failed to exert considerable influence. Many of the envoys engaged in such missions were members of the bishop's household, or appear as guests upon his estates.[135]

His involvement in diplomacy was to arouse grave suspicions over his attitude to the French, but it is important to stress that the bishop was, if anything, more a hawk than a dove in his dealings with France. In 1217 he had refused to pay scutage, dissatisfied with the lenient terms allowed to Louis in respect to Normandy. In 1220 he

---

[131] *RLC*, i, pp. 391, 442b; *Pat. R. 1216–25*, pp. 273, 306, 307, 319; Cole, *Documents*, p. 305.

[132] See Ridgeway, 'King Henry III and the "aliens"', pp. 81–92, for the subsequent distinctions drawn between Savoyards and Poitevins.

[133] *Acta*, appendix 4, nos. 10, 42–3. Hugh and Aimery first appear in England in 1219, Geoffrey in 1221.

[134] *DD*, no. 128; SC1/1/127.

[135] See, for example, Humphrey de Millières, Geoffrey de Caux and William de Batilly, all of them familiars of des Roches engaged in missions to Poitou or Rome; *Acta*, appendix 4, nos. 4, 22, 29, and see also the Fleming, Master Robert de Airaines, involved in negotiations with Scotland; *ibid.*, appendix 4, no. 27.

resorted to gamesmanship in negotiating an extension of the truce with Philip Augustus.[136] In letters to William Marshal the younger, inviting him to attend negotiations, the bishop recommended that he come as quickly as possible, since the longer the council could meet without reaching any conclusion, the more wearisome it would be for the French.[137] Later in the same year French envoys were entertained at the bishop's manor of Farnham.[138] There is nothing to suggest that des Roches' feelings towards the French were anything other than hostile, tempered by the realization that the minority council lacked the financial resources or the political will to contemplate a bid for Plantagenet reconquest. A policy of containment depended heavily upon establishing stability in Poitou, and here des Roches maintained contacts with both the dean and the archdeacon of Poitiers, with his own successor as treasurer of St Hilaire, and with the bishop of Saintes.[139] When his episcopal steward, William de Batilly, failed to secure the release of one of the king's sisters, held as a ward by the Poitevin magnate Hugh de Lusignan, des Roches himself offered to meet with Hugh, either in the Channel Islands or Poitou.[140]

At court the bishop witnessed orders affecting missions from Saxony, Savoy and Denmark and personally presented a gold ring and a belt to a Norwegian envoy.[141] It was to des Roches that the dowager queen Berengaria appealed over the settlement of her dower.[142] Above all, the bishop's household served as the natural reception point for reports from across the Channel. Even after his fall from power, in 1225 des Roches is to be found transmitting the latest news from Normandy.[143] Not all of the information which reached him in this way was accurate. Probably in 1219/20 he received a report that the archbishop of Bordeaux had died. Des Roches wrote immediately to Hubert de Burgh, enclosing a letter to

---

[136] For 1220, see *DD*, no. 80; *Foedera*, pp. 158–9; *RL*, no. lxii; *Layettes du Trésor des Chartes*, ed. A. Teulet, H. -F. Delaborde and E. Berger, 5 vols. (Paris 1863–1909), i, p. 497a. Des Roches had also assisted in the extension of the truce in 1219; *RLC*, i, p. 391b; *Pat. R. 1216–25*, pp. 188, 196; *DD*, nos. 22, 41, 71.

[137] Carpenter, *The Minority*, p. 177; *DD*, no. 71 and see William's reply, SC1/4/74.

[138] Ms. 16DR, m. 5.

[139] For the archdeacon, see Ms. 13DR, m. 3d. For the treasurer see *RLC*, i, pp. 494, 496b, 545; Ms. 22DR, m. 13. For the bishop, *DD*, no. 95.

[140] *Foedera*, pp. 167–8. For des Roches' general involvement with Poitevin affairs, see *RLC*, i, pp. 389, 389b, 395b, 402b, 408, 414, 432, 439, 439b, 441b, 442b, 486, 496, 520, 524b, 525b, 578.

[141] *RLC*, i, pp. 343, 382, 387, 396, 465b, 522b, 578.

[142] SC1/1/23, and see *RLC*, i, pp. 381b, 388, 389b, 408, 441b, 442, 498b; *Cal.Pap.Reg.*, i, p. 54; above pp. 67, 95, 124.

[143] *Acta*, no. 127.

be forwarded to the chapter of Bordeaux, cautioning them to elect a successor loyal to the king. In the event des Roches' instructions were filed away unused. Archbishop William had merely prolonged his stay on crusade where he remained from 1218 until after October 1221.[144]

THE CHURCH

Des Roches' political influence was matched by a corresponding strength within the hierarchy of the English church. Here the most crucial factor was the weakness of archbishop Langton, discredited by his stance over the baronial rebellion, and eclipsed until 1221 by the papal legates Guala and Pandulph. Even before suspending Langton in 1215, des Roches had played an important role, co-operating with Guala's predecessor in the promotion of the courtiers, William of Cornhill and Walter de Gray, to the sees of Coventry and York, in keeping Durham vacant prior to the election of the royal chancellor, Richard Marsh, and in promoting sympathetic candidates to Exeter and Norwich.[145] The first two years of the minority witnessed the election of new bishops to Hereford, Worcester, Chichester and Carlisle, all of whom enjoyed government support. In all of these elections, the papal legates played an important role. It may well be that it was the legates who sought to restrict the crown's exploitation of the revenues of vacant bishoprics, already a bone of contention under King John.[146] No receipts from regalian right were recorded on the royal pipe rolls between 1216 and the account for the vacancy at Exeter in 1224.[147] At Ely, where Robert the bishop-elect may have been one of the few English diocesans openly to support the rebels, custody of the see was granted to the legate Pandulph, who paid a small amount of his receipts into the Exchequer and accounted for the remainder in expenses on the king's behalf.[148] Apart from Ely,

---

[144] *Acta*, nos. 113–14.

[145] Above pp. 94–6 Bishop Cornhill of Coventry was one of the few bishops to make provisions for the soul of King John, appropriating the church of West Bromwich to the monks of Worcester for the celebration of the king's obit; *Worcester Cartulary*, ed. Darlington, no. 196.

[146] In 1213 John had been made to promise to relinquish his claim to regalian receipts should he be unable to meet the demands of the church for compensation in the aftermath of the Interdict. There is evidence to suggest that, at least to begin with, he failed to exploit the vacancy receipts at Norwich, prior to the election of Pandulph as bishop in 1215; Vincent, 'The election of Pandulph Verracclo'.

[147] *Foreign Accounts*, p. 43; E372/69, m. 3d.

[148] *Foreign Accounts*, p. 46; *RLC*, ii, pp. 7b, 8b, and see *Acta Guala*, no. 25, which casts doubt on the claim that Robert supported the rebels.

however, there is no record of any money from vacancies going to support the impoverished finances of the crown.[149] The vacancy at Chichester in 1217–18 was administered by Guala and was followed by the promotion of Pandulph's official Ralph of Warham, a monk of Norwich, imprisoned by the barons during the civil war.[150] At Worcester, Guala obtained the promotion of William of Blois, following a clerical council at Winchester and the entertainment of William at des Roches' manor of Wycombe.[151] Guala was also instrumental in the translation of Richard Poer to Salisbury in 1217, and with des Roches and the loyalist bishops, secured the deposition of a rebel Scotsman, elected bishop of Carlisle, replacing him with the Burgundian abbot Hugh of Beaulieu, King John's former ambassador and a long-standing ally of the bishop of Winchester. This was a fortunate move for Hugh, who had recently been deposed at Beaulieu for a series of abuses which included eating his meals off precious plate and keeping a watch-dog tethered to his bed on a silver chain.[152]

At Hereford the death of bishop Hugh de Mapenore in April 1219 was followed by immediate consent for an election. No receipts from the vacancy reached the treasury and the new bishop, Hugh Foliot, was installed only a few months later. Mapenore's election had been supervised by the legate Guala; Foliot's was followed by gifts of game authorized by the bishop of Winchester. Foliot and des Roches were to go on pilgrimage together in 1221.[153] At Ely, following the deposition of the bishop-elect, the legate Pandulph obtained the promotion of the more tractable abbot of Fountains.[154]

Similarly, in monastic elections the legates appear to have wielded considerable influence. At Guisborough the prior resigned his office into Guala's hands.[155] Pandulph was the recipient of petitions from the convents of Cerne and of St Augustine's Canterbury, requesting

---

[149] The apparent vacancy at Norwich in 1218/19 is in fact an account for arrears owed for the period 18 Oct. 1214–22 March 1215; *PR 3 Henry III*, p. 51; *PR 4 Henry III*, p. 62, and E210/3480.

[150] *Fasti*, ii, p. 60; E210/3480 (which mentions his imprisonment); *Acta Guala*, nos. 18–20. Des Roches visited Chichester in 1218/19; Ms. 14DR, m. 2.

[151] *Acta Guala*, no. 139; *C. & S.*, i, p. 51; *AM*, iv (Worcester), p. 410, and Ms. 13DR, m. 10d for William's entertainment as archdeacon of Buckingham.

[152] *Acta Guala*, nos. 12–14, 17, 18n. , 110; *Acta*, no. 104.

[153] *AM*, iv (Worcester), p. 406; Cheney, *Innocent III*, p. 175; *Cal. Pap. Reg.*, i, pp. 40–1; *Pat. R. 1216–25*, pp. 191, 195; *RLC*, i, pp. 401b, 406b.

[154] *Foedera*, p. 155; Prynne, *Records*, iii, p. 44. Abbot John had in the previous year been appointed to the enquiry into the canonization of Hugh of Lincoln, arguing favour in important quarters; Farmer, 'The canonization of St Hugh', pp. 90–1.

[155] *Acta Guala*, no. 34, and see Sayers, *Honorius III*, pp. 180–1, which notes legatine interference at Guisborough, Shaftesbury, Penwortham and Cowick.

his help both to speed elections and to protect their churches during vacancies.[156] Once again there is no evidence that any regalian receipts were taken from royal abbeys. In 1219 des Roches was instrumental in promoting Pandulph as custodian of the vacancy at Wilton. At St Augustine's Canterbury, the legate appointed his penitentiary to guard the convent's property against the encroachments of royal bailiffs, and conducted a meticulous enquiry into the freedom of the election.[157] In the summer of 1221 Shrewsbury was given in custody to Pandulph's clerk, John Bacon.[158] It is interesting to note that between 1214 and 1219, the papal mission to England encouraged the election of monk bishops at Ely, Chichester, Worcester and Carlisle, the last great crop of such appointments. Church leaders from Langton onwards were to oppose the promotion of monks as unworldly men, unsuited to the responsibilities of diocesan government.[159]

Just as the bishops promoted under legatine influence were generally men known to des Roches or, as with Hugh of Beaulieu, appointed with his active co-operation, so des Roches was able to re-establish relations with the bishops of Lincoln, Bath, London and Salisbury who had endured exile during the Interdict. William of London and Richard of Salisbury served alongside the legate Guala in an important settlement between des Roches and William Brewer in 1218.[160] Following bishop William's resignation of the see of London des Roches was to award him pensions from three London manors.[161] Richard Poer had been des Roches' rival in the Winchester election of 1204–5 and had subsequently been disappointed in a bid for Durham. As bishop of Salisbury he set out to remove his cathedral from the royal manor of Sarum, seen traditionally as a gesture of resistance to royal control.[162] Yet in 1219 it was Poer who was appointed to assist des Roches in reforming the nunnery of St Mary's Winchester. At the Exchequer des Roches respited an account on

[156] Twysden, *Scriptores X*, cols. 1871–5; B. F. Lock, 'The Cartulary of Cerne Abbey', ed. B. F. Lock, *Proceedings of the Dorset Natural History and Antiquarian Field Club*, 29 (1908), pp. 200–1.
[157] Twysden, *Scriptores X*, cols. 1871–5; *RLC*, i, p. 408.
[158] C60/14, m. 3.
[159] M. Gibbs and J. Lang, *Bishops and Reform 1215–1272 with special reference to the Lateran Council of 1215* (Oxford 1934), pp. 5–6, although in 1219 Guala forbade the monks of Worcester from electing one of their own convent to the see; *AM*, iv (Worcester), p. 410.
[160] *Acta*, no. 82.
[161] *Acta*, no. 30.
[162] *Reg. St Osmund*, ii, pp. cii–cvi.

Poer's behalf, and between 1220 and 1225 he actively contributed to the building fund at Salisbury with an annual award of £2 from his manor of Downton.[163] Like another of Langton's pupils, bishop Benedict of Rochester, Poer served as a royal justice during the eyre of 1219, being followed in this example by his fellow exiles from the time of the Interdict, the brothers Hugh of Lincoln and Jocelin of Bath.[164] The latter was entertained in most years at des Roches' manor of Taunton, made purchases of property from the imprisoned rebel Reginald of Cornhill, witnessed by des Roches, and was assisted in building work at Wells by a small donation from des Roches in 1221.[165] None of these men could be considered des Roches' close allies. Four of them were to co-operate in his removal from court. But, for the moment, deprived of the leadership of archbishop Langton, none of them posed any serious threat to des Roches' political ambitions.

That des Roches had enemies amongst the clergy is not to be doubted, but at least in the first few years of the minority it was relatively easy for him to keep these enemies at bay. Above all he was treated by the pope and by the legates as a valuable ally, hardly surprisingly, since his own clerks provided one of the Curia's chief sources of information on England. Besides dealing with the question of papal census, a mission of 1219 headed by his familiar Geoffrey de Caux obtained papal approval for action taken by des Roches in respect to the religious of his diocese, and a privilege by which three of his principal household clerks, previously vexed by summonses to ecclesiastical courts, were to appear before no papal judge save the legate.[166]

Des Roches enjoyed close relations with both the papal legates, Guala and Pandulph. In 1216 Guala had caused him to excommuni-

---

[163] *Cal. Pap. Reg.*, p. 66; E159/2, m. 8; Mss. 15DR, m. 7d; 16DR, m. 9; 19DR, m. 5; 20DR, m. 1. The contribution is given as 43 shillings and fourpence in 1221. It followed the dispatch in 1219/20 of Master Hugh of Gayhurst, chancellor of Salisbury and a familiar of des Roches' predecessors Godfrey de Lucy and Richard of Ilchester, to solicit alms in the diocese of Winchester; *Reg. St Osmund*, ii, pp. 11–12, and see above p. 51 n.32.

[164] D. Crook, *Records of the General Eyre* (London 1982), pp. 71–5; *RLC*, i, pp. 387b, 405.

[165] Mss. 13DR, m. 12d; 14DR, m. 11; 16DR, mm. 10, 10d (1m to the subdean of Wells for building); 21DR, m. 5 (9 deer at Farnham); above p. 143. Other bishops entertained on the Winchester estates before 1225 were William of Cornhill, bishop of Coventry, at Wargrave in 1218/19 (Ms. 14DR, m. 10), Simon of Exeter and the bishop of Llandaff at Taunton in 1220/1 (Ms. 16DR, m. 10d), and the archbishop of Dublin at Witney in 1224/5 (Ms. 20DR, m. 14). See also *Acta*, no. 24 for complimentary indulgences issued by Langton, des Roches and seven other bishops.

[166] *Cal. Pap. Reg.*, i, p. 66.

cate Louis, and had entrusted him with a leading role in the coronation of Henry III. Before the battle of Lincoln the bishop was deputed to absolve the sins of the royal army, and in October 1217 accompanied Guala into the city of London when the legate began a purge of the chapter of St Paul's.[167] As early as August 1217 Guala had begun to depose rebel clergy in the west country, and for much of the remainder of his legation he was to be preoccupied with reprisals against Louis' clerical supporters.[168] At Carlisle he issued letters in company with des Roches, condemning the activities of the rebellious canons. In November 1217, together with other bishops and barons, des Roches sealed letters supporting the award of the church of Chesterton to Guala's foundation at S. Andrea Vercelli.[169] Guala helped devise a private settlement between des Roches and William Brewer, whilst the Winchester pipe rolls record gifts of fish to the legate at Wargrave on 24 October 1218.[170] They also detail wine and provisions given to him at Reading, probably in November 1218, and throw an interesting sidelight on the legate's profits from procurations, recording the expense of five crossbowmen who accompanied des Roches' chamber clerk in carrying the legate's money from Winchester to Farnham.[171] Guala was also entertained at Taunton, lodged with des Roches at Bishop's Waltham, and in 1217–18 received further presents at Wargrave.[172] It was to des Roches that he appealed over the misfortunes of one of his clerks, imprisoned by the constable of Stamford.[173]

As the Marshal's health declined and des Roches came forward to assume a more prominent role, he could already boast a firm foothold in the household and the Exchequer. By virtue of his close relations

---

[167] Above pp. 134, 138, 141. *Acta Guala*, no. 54 suggests a full-scale purge of the London chapter. For Guala's activities in general, see also Sayers, *Honorius III*, pp. 167–85; Richardson, 'Letters of the legate Guala', pp. 250–9; F. A. Cazel, 'The legates Guala and Pandulf', in *Thirteenth Century England II*, ed. P. R. Coss and S. D. Lloyd (Woodbridge 1988), pp. 15–19. My own, much fuller study of the charters and activities of the legate Guala (*Acta Guala*) is shortly to be published by the Canterbury and York Society.

[168] *Acta Guala*, no. 90, taken from BL ms. Add. 50121 (Lilleshall cartulary), f. 29r, Guala's deposition of a rebel clerk at Poulton Wilts. in favour of the nephew of the cardinal of S. Pudenziana, dated 1 Aug. 1217.

[169] *Acta*, no. 107.

[170] *Acta*, no. 82; Ms. 14DR, m. 10.

[171] Ms. 14DR, mm. 9, 10. For Guala's procurations, see Paris, *CM*, ii, p. 663; W. E. Lunt, *Financial Relations of the Papacy with England to 1327* (Cambridge Mass. 1939), pp. 538–9; Sayers, *Honorius III*, pp. 181–2. For Guala's presence at Reading, 17–18 Nov. 1218, see *Acta Guala*, nos. 16, 96.

[172] Ms. 13DR, mm. 3d, 8, 8d, 12d, 13.

[173] *Acta Guala*, no. 117.

with the papal legates, the church appeared to pose no real threat to his political ambitions. Yet, whatever the loyalty he commanded amongst aliens at court, he failed to inspire affection amongst his wartime colleagues such as the Marshal, let alone amongst former rebels, who can only have viewed his promotion with alarm. The reasons for this are not difficult to discern. He was hopelessly tarnished by association with John's arbitrary methods of government. He was hardly best suited to heal the scars of war; the man who had suspended archbishop Langton, worked to obliterate the Runnymede settlement of 1215, as a politician spearheaded the church's reprisals against the rebels, and as a churchman led a band of mercenaries into battle; a man who harried his captives for ransoms long after the ending of hostilities, who high-handedly refused to contribute to the cost of the peace settlement whilst enforcing contributions upon those less able to resist, and who consented to keep the royal patrimony intact only after he had secured valuable privileges for himself and his growing circle of alien followers. No wonder that the Waverley annalist, writing *c.*1219, singles out des Roches as the principal agent of discord, that persists 'even to this day'.[174]

The Marshal's retirement from government was a gradual affair, provoked by illness but coinciding with the issue of the royal seal in November 1218. The bishop, who had previously played only a negligible role in the issue of royal letters, rapidly assumed a leading position as witness or warranting authority. Over the next six months several hundred letters were issued *Teste, per* or *coram* des Roches.[175] This development was accompanied by the rise of two other men at court, long known to the bishop. The first of these, Hubert de Burgh, a native of Burgh near Aylsham in Norfolk, had begun his career, like des Roches, in the royal chamber. A faithful servant of King John, his service had differed from that of the bishop in that from 1204, he had remained in France, at first as a member of Girard d'Athée's garrison at Chinon and subsequently as a prisoner. Whereas d'Athée was quickly released through the good offices of des Roches, de Burgh was not to return to England for almost a decade. As a result, he escaped much of the odium which attached to John's later years and in June 1215 was considered a suitable candidate to replace des Roches as Justiciar; a concession to baronial opinion but a mark more

---

[174] *AM*, ii, p. 281; A. Gransden, *Historical Writing in England 550–1307* (London 1974), p. 412 which suggests that the annals were compiled *c.*1219, a reference I owe to David Carpenter.

[175] Carpenter, *The Minority*, pp. 103–4.

of the bishop's unpopularity than of any sympathy between the new Justiciar and the rebels. It has been suggested that Hubert and des Roches were rivals of long-standing, and that des Roches' promotion in the chamber took place at Hubert's expense in much the same way that Hubert later supplanted des Roches as Justiciar.[176] However, there is little to substantiate such a claim. Both before and immediately after the Marshal's death in 1219, the two men appear to have co-operated closely. Neither commanded the same degree of popularity as the Marshal. Hubert was a *parvenu*, lacking wealth or a close personal following; the bishop possessed vast resources and a considerable network of followers but was deeply mistrusted in the country at large.[177]

The other man who came to the fore in 1218 was Pandulph, Guala's replacement as papal legate, already long familiar with des Roches. He and the bishop had co-operated in the suspension of Stephen Langton, and hence shared a mutual interest in denying Langton any opportunity for revenge. Des Roches had been instrumental in Pandulph's promotion to the see of Norwich, where Pandulph remained bishop-elect to avoid the disciplinary jurisdiction of Canterbury.[178] In September 1218 des Roches received papal instructions to revoke letters obtained surreptitiously to Pandulph's disadvantage. Pandulph himself was ordered to assist des Roches in his schemes for the religious of Winchester and at some time, after December 1218, counselled him on a dispute between the canons of Newark and the convent of Stoke by Clare.[179]

With the bishop's rise to prominence after November 1218 there came clear signs of an attempt to win reconciliation with both church and baronage. The next few months saw the dispatch of the first general eyre of the reign, in whose direction des Roches was able to re-establish relations with archbishop Langton. In self-imposed exile, and clearly expecting resistance, Langton had obtained papal letters to his suffragans enjoining obedience.[180] In the event his return to England passed off smoothly. He and des Roches served jointly in the

---

[176] M. Weiss, 'The castellan: the early career of Hubert de Burgh', *Viator* 5 (1974), pp. 235–52, esp. p. 237; Painter, *King John*, pp. 84–6; F. A. Cazel, 'Intertwined careers: Hubert de Burgh and Peter des Roches', *The Haskins Society Journal I* (1989), pp. 173–6.

[177] See Johnston, 'The lands of Hubert de Burgh', pp. 418–32.

[178] For Guala's retirement, see *C. & S.*, i, p. 47; Sayers, *Honorius III*, p. 174. *AM*, ii (Waverley), p. 291 states that he left England *c*.Nov. 23. For Pandulph, a native of Monte Cassino, see Vincent, 'The election of Pandulph Verracclo'.

[179] *Cal. Pap. Reg.*, i, pp. 58, 65–6; *Acta*, no. 35.

[180] *Cal. Pap. Reg.*, i, p. 52.

appointment of justices for the eyre circuits and, as the visitation proceeded, des Roches intervened to protect the archbishop's liberties. Controversial cases involving the see of Canterbury were postponed under des Roches' authority, for discussion by the council.[181] Another potential rival, Richard Poer, served on the eyre, and with des Roches' assent was granted market privileges and gifts of venison.[182]

At the same time the bishop continued to foster relations with the Roman mission.[183] Papal instructions concerning the dower of Queen Berengaria were implemented under des Roches' authority, and the bishop was active in promoting the interests of Pandulph, moving to safeguard the liberties of the see of Norwich and responding to the legate's call for the release of a clerk held prisoner for several years. This last case provides an insight into Pandulph's attitude to the secular authorities. Despite his clerical status, the man was only to be released if he could find securities and if the king's officers considered it expedient to let him go.[184] Des Roches also issued letters promoting Pandulph as custodian of a vacancy at Wilton, and in the same year acted to support the legate over a fraudulent episcopal election in Ireland.[185]

MORAL REFORM

As a close colleague of the two papal legates, des Roches must be credited with at least some of the responsibility for a concerted campaign of moral reform, spearheaded by the legates and intended to bring the English church into line with various of the reforms promulgated at the Lateran Council of 1215. As we have seen, the king's council appears, if only temporarily, to have relinquished its claims to the revenues of vacant royal cathedrals and abbeys. As early as 1214 it appears that des Roches assisted in a campaign to transfer markets from Sundays to weekdays, in line with a wider Sabbatarian movement preached across much of Christian Europe.[186] In the

---

[181] *Pat. R. 1216–25*, pp. 186–7, 206–7, 210; *RLC*, i, pp. 380b, 383b, 384.

[182] *RLC*, i, p. 387; C60/11, m. 9.

[183] *Cal. Pap. Reg.*, i, p. 49; *RLC*, i, pp. 384b, 389b, 394b; Cheney, *Innocent III*, p. 95.

[184] *Cal. Pap. Reg.*, i, p. 54; *Pat. R. 1216–25*, pp. 179, 185, 189; *RLC*, i, pp. 381b, 383, 388, 388b, and see *AM*, iii (Dunstable), pp. 52–3 for Pandulph's release of clerks imprisoned at the orders of Guala.

[185] *RLC*, i, p. 408; *Acta*, no. 110. See also *RLC*, i, p. 387b for des Roches warranting a grant of a pension to Pandulph's clerk.

[186] See above p. 99; Cate, 'The church and market reform', pp. 51–65.

winter of 1218–19 these measures were accelerated, with des Roches taking personal responsibility for several such transfers.[187] At the same time, it is worth speculating upon the bishop's own observance of the Sabbath. At the royal Exchequer there is no evidence to suggest that business came to a halt on Sundays. Elsewhere, des Roches was actively involved in witnessing and authorizing writs on several Sundays each year, throughout the period 1217–23.[188] Nevertheless in his own diocese, where the manorial accounts for the years 1221–7 are individually dated, it appears that his officers took considerable pains to avoid hearing accounts on a Sunday. There were no Sunday hearings at the episcopal Exchequer in 1221 or 1224, despite the fact that this involved a break in business between Saturday and Monday hearings.

There is also evidence of a campaign against scotales on the Winchester estates. Prior to 1215, such revelries had provided a valuable supplement to episcopal finances; in the year 1213–14 for example, scotales took place on at least nine manors and generated some £20 in gross receipts.[189] By contrast, after 1217 isolated scotales took place at Bishop's Waltham and Wargrave. At Twyford, in 1218, 22 shillings and 11 pence were received 'from cider drunk in place of a scotale'.[190] In 1219–20 the bishop's men on the Isle of Wight were fined 2 shillings for holding the last such feast recorded on the Winchester pipe rolls, and at much the same time the ban on scotales was extended to the royal demesne.[191] Scotales had been specifically outlawed in Langton's synodal statutes; a point taken up and expanded upon in des Roches' own diocesan legislation of c.1224, which enjoined strict sobriety for clergy and laity alike, both in public places and in their own homes.[192]

A leading churchman accompanied each circuit of the general eyre of 1218–19, and it is possible that their leniency in imposing amercements owed something to the reformers' desire to foster the peace and mercy of God.[193] In January 1219 des Roches witnessed instructions sent to every justice in eyre, forbidding them to conduct ordeals by

[187] *RLC*, i, pp. 381b, 368b, 387. The moves affected several manors with strong links to des Roches, including Wallingford, Kingsclere, Portchester and Faringdon, this last belonging to Beaulieu Abbey.

[188] See for example *RLC*, i, pp. 383, 383b (2, 9 Dec. 1218).

[189] Mss. 7DR, mm. 4, 5, 7, 9, 10d; 9DR, mm. 2, 2d, 6d–7d, 9; 11DR, m. 2.

[190] Mss. 13DR, mm. 1d, 3d; 14DR, m. 9d.

[191] Ms. 15DR, m. 8d; *RLC*, i, p. 436b.

[192] *C & S*, i, pp. 135–6 nos. 63–4.

[193] See Turner, *The King and his Courts*, pp. 155–6.

fire and water, and enjoining temporary alternatives, in accordance with the Lateran statutes of 1215.[194] Already, before the end of the civil war, something of the Lateran reforms appears to have reached des Roches. In promoting a clerk to the church of Stamford, he was to claim that he had acted in accordance with the Lateran decree insisting that vacancies be filled after six months where no suitable election or exercise of advowson had taken place.[195] None of these reforms was without its cost. The relaxation of amercements, the ban upon scotales on demesne manors and above all the failure to exploit the revenues of vacant bishoprics and abbeys, made it even more difficult for the royal Exchequer to restore the crown's finances to their pre-war levels.

Less controversially, both Pandulph and archbishop Langton moved to forbid tournaments, a restriction which pleased moral reformers and politicians alike. Such gatherings were notoriously associated with political discontent. Des Roches himself vigorously refuted a charge that members of his household had participated in a tournament.[196] Besides threatening violent disorder, tournaments were a common accompaniment to preparations for the crusade, and it is the crusade that provides a key to the introduction of moral reforms after 1217. Indeed, it was the crusade and its preparations which had over-shadowed much of the business of the Lateran Council.[197] The Fifth Crusade attracted many prominent Englishmen, both rebels and loyalists, their rivalries healed in the common enterprise. Across Europe, in England as in Germany, Italy, Frisia and Hungary, the crusade was preached as an instrument of reform for the restoration of domestic peace.[198] Since 1213, the English church had been pledged to daily prayers and regular public processions for the support of the enterprise.[199] In 1217 the archbishop of Tyre was involved in peace negotiations in England whilst on a mission concerned with the

---

[194] *Pat. R. 1216–25*, p. 186, discussed in *Rolls of the Justices in Eyre for Yorkshire 1218–19*, ed. Stenton, p. xl.

[195] *CRR*, xii, no. 379.

[196] See N. Denholm-Young, 'The tournament in the thirteenth century', in *Collected Papers* (Cardiff 1969), pp. 100–1; *Acta Langton*, ed. Major, no. 46; *Foedera*, pp. 162–3.

[197] For the association between tournaments and crusade, see Lloyd, *English Society and the Crusade*, pp. 98–9.

[198] See J. M. Powell, *Anatomy of a Crusade 1213–1221* (Philadelphia 1986), pp. 19–20, 47, 67–87.

[199] *Letters of Innocent III*, no. 917. On the preaching of the Fifth Crusade see Lloyd, *English Society*, pp. 45–52; A. J. Andrea, 'Walter archdeacon of London and the "Historia Occidentalis" of Jacques de Vitry', *Church History* (1981), pp. 141–51; Powell, *Anatomy of a Crusade*, p. 24.

commuting of crusader vows.[200] Des Roches himself was closely involved with several crusaders. In 1216 he had been appointed to protect the crusader Savaric de Mauléon. His kinsman, William des Roches, had taken the cross, as had his familiar, the archdeacon of Poitiers, and Oliver the illegitimate son of King John, defender of Wolvesey castle in 1216.[201] The bishop's clerk, Geoffrey de Caux, commuted a crusading vow in favour of supplying the wages of four soldiers to travel in his place.[202] In addition, des Roches acted as guardian of the lands of William Ferrers, earl of Derby, who in 1218 wrote to thank the bishop and to supply a detailed account of the progress of the army in Egypt.[203] Des Roches himself had not yet taken the cross, but his charge, the infant Henry III, had assumed crusading vows immediately on his accession to the throne. Papal rhetoric made much of the responsibilities of a realm whose sovereign was both orphan and crusader.[204] England contributed heavily to the financing of the army in Egypt.[205] In turn, those who had taken the cross were exempt from secular taxation, an exemption whose interpretation was the subject of correspondence with des Roches and forced his intervention, in company with the legate Pandulph, to prevent illegal exactions at Bristol.[206]

In all of these areas – moral reform, relations with the legates and the promotion of the crusade – des Roches had shown himself to be in tune with a wider policy than mere self-interest; arguably better in tune than the Justiciar, de Burgh, whose crusading vows were commuted in 1219 on the grounds of commitment to affairs of state.[207] Superficially, as the Marshal's health declined, so des Roches edged ever closer to the centre of power. And yet by no means all of the bishop's actions were calculated to foster harmony. The six months to April 1219 were marked by a perceptible increase in alien patronage. Under des Roches' authority, Peter de Maulay was provided with a valuable quittance of suit of court for his men, and

[200] See the chronicle of William of Andres in *Monumenta Germaniae Historica Scriptores*, xxiv (Hanover 1879), p. 758; Smith, 'The Treaty of Lambeth', p. 506.
[201] SC1/1/127; Powell, *Anatomy of a Crusade*, pp. 224, 235, 242, and *ibid.*, pp. 207–58 for a convenient but by no means comprehensive list of crusaders.
[202] *Cal. Pap. Reg.*, i, p. 65.
[203] *RL*, i, no. xix.
[204] See for example *RL*, i, pp. 529, 536–7; Lloyd, *English Society*, pp. 208–9.
[205] Powell, *Anatomy of a Crusade*, pp. 100–1; Cheney, *Innocent III*, pp. 265–8.
[206] For Bristol, see R. Hill, *Ecclesiastical Letter Books of the Thirteenth Century* (privately printed Oxford 1936), p. 66 nos. 47–8, pp. 238–40; SC1/1/71; *PR 4 Henry III*, p. 79, which last reference I owe to David Carpenter. In general, see SC1/1/26; SC1/1/38.
[207] Pressutti, *Reg. Hon. III*, no. 1842.

respites of the Exchequer's demands for the 7,000 marks he had pledged for the Fossard barony in 1214.[208] Engelard de Cigogné received custody of escheats in Oxfordshire and Berkshire, and land in Ireland was awarded to both Roger de la Zouche and Philip Mark.[209] In 1219 des Roches sponsored the restoration of the St Valery lands to their Norman claimant.[210] The justices in eyre in Lincolnshire complained of undue influence being brought to bear on behalf of the Poitevin earl of Aumale in a suit against Gilbert de Gant, an action in which Aumale was later to be supported by des Roches. From Sussex, the sheriff wrote to report resistance to mandates from des Roches issued on behalf of his ward, the Norman Robert Marmion.[211]

Perhaps above all, des Roches' position at the Exchequer was the source of widespread uneasiness. The fines and scutages which had done so much to sour relations between John and his barons had not been wiped clean by civil war. Although the new regime was remarkably lenient in respiting debts and permitting generous terms for repayment, the reconstruction of the Exchequer's accounts was accompanied by the assessment of debts owing from the period before 1216. Robert fitz Walter was still being pursued for the Poitevin scutage of 1214 long into the 1220s, whilst the Hampshire rebel William de St John was pledged to reduce an enormous burden of debt.[212] Even the most outrageous of John's exactions, the fine of 20,000 marks made with Geoffrey de Mandeville, lived on to plague Geoffrey's heirs. The object of this fine, the Gloucester inheritance, was lost with Geoffrey's death in 1216, but the fine itself was transferred to Geoffrey's brother, William, and farmed out to archbishop Langton as compensation for damages suffered during the Interdict. Before William de Mandeville's death, des Roches was to vouch for the payment of half of this sum, 10,000 marks, to Langton; the remainder being assigned to the archbishop from the rents of various manors in Essex.[213] Des Roches' actions may have been intended to smooth relations with Langton, albeit at the expense of

---

[208] *Pat. R. 1216–25*, pp. 187, 192–3; *RLC*, i, p. 391; C60/9, m. 3; C60/11, m. 10; C60/12, m. 2.

[209] *RLC*, i, pp. 384b, 385, 386, 387, 387b; C60/11, m. 10.

[210] *RLC*, i, p. 387b; C60/11, m. 10.

[211] For Aumale see *RL*, i, no. xvi; *PR 3 Henry III*, p. 129; C60/11, m. 3; *CRR*, viii, p. 158; *Rolls of the Justices in Eyre for Lincoln 1218–19 and Worcestershire 1221*, ed. D. M. Stenton, Selden Soc. liii (1934), pp. li–lvi; Carpenter, *The Minority*, pp. 102–3, 165–6. For Marmion, see *RL*, i, no. xi, and above pp. 162–3.

[212] For fitz Walter, see C60/20, m. 3; C60/23, m. 6. For St John, see E159/7, m. 4d; E372/65, m. 7d; C60/18, m. 9; C60/20, m. 5; C60/23, m. 6.

[213] See *RLC*, ii, p. 110b; C60/11, m. 9; C60/25, m. 10; *E. Rot. Fin.*, i, p. 153; *Cal. Chart.*

the Mandeville family. But in general, any prospect of a return to the methods of John's reign, to harsh repayment terms and the threat of distraint, was calculated to spread dismay amongst a baronage shackled to the Exchequer by chains of inherited debt.

DES ROCHES AND THE JEWS

The years after 1215 witnessed a concerted clerical campaign against the Jews in England.[214] Diocesan legislation attempted to implement the anti-Jewish reforms of the Lateran Council. Langton and Pandulph appear to have co-operated to impose such measures as the wearing of the *tabula*.[215] By contrast, des Roches and the secular administration continued to regard the Jews as a prop to the hard-pressed Exchequer.[216] In November 1218, together with William Brewer, the bishop was responsible for imposing swingeing terms upon seven Yorkshire and Lincolnshire knights, farming their debts to Elias of Lincoln on pain of confiscation should they fail to meet Elias' terms.[217] Also with Brewer, he issued an order encouraging free travel to Jews wishing to enter England and on the same day the Exchequer was notified that since September 1218 des Roches had received 1 mark a day of the fine of 10,000 marks made between King John and Isaac of Norwich.[218] Isaac of Norwich and Elias of Lincoln were amongst the most prominent Jews in England. Isaac

R. *1226–57*, pp. 68–9, 196–7; and for des Roches' direct involvement E372/69, mm. 16, 16d, references that I owe to David Carpenter. In general, see Holt, *Magna Carta*, pp. 209–10; *CP*, v, pp. 131, 134n.

[214] In general, see J. A. Watt, 'The English episcopate, the state and the Jews: the evidence of the thirteenth century conciliar decrees', in *Thirteenth Century England II*, ed. Coss and Lloyd, pp. 137–47; H. G. Richardson, *The English Jews under Angevin Kings* (London 1960), pp. 178–88.

[215] N. C. Vincent, 'Jews, Poitevins, and the bishop of Winchester, 1231–1234', *Studies in Church History* 29, ed. D. Wood (Oxford 1992), p. 120, and see N. C. Vincent, 'Two papal letters on the wearing of the Jewish badge, 1221 and 1229', *Transactions of the Jewish Historical Society* (forthcoming, 1996), for an edition of the letters in Lambeth ms. 1212 ff. 128r, 129v.

[216] See Richardson, *The English Jews*, pp. 178–80 for licences issued to avoid the *tabula*; ibid., p. 182 for protections issued by the regime in 1218 against attacks and episcopal attempts to draw Jewish debts before ecclesiastical courts. For later measures see *ibid.*, pp. 185–6; *RLC*, i, pp. 567, 603b.

[217] Pat. R. *1216–25*, pp. 179–80, discussed by Holt, *Magna Carta*, pp. 387–8.

[218] Pat. R. *1216–25*, pp. 179–81. For the question of free travel, see Richardson, *The English Jews*, pp. 178–9. For Isaac's fine for release from prison following the tallage of 1210–11, see Richardson, *The English Jews*, p. 170; V. D. Lipman, *The Jews of Medieval Norwich* (Jewish Historical Society 1967), p. 104. For the expenditure of Isaac's fine at Dover see *RLC*, i, p. 459; *PR 4 Henry III*, p. 59, which includes the period of the fine originally paid to des Roches.

was made responsible for the administration of the Jewish tallage of 1224, and is the subject of a well-known portrait on the Jewish receipt roll, which shows him presiding over the work of seven horned demons.[219] By sponsoring their activities, des Roches and Brewer hardly courted popular sympathy, resorting to methods all too reminiscent of John's exploitation of Jewish debt, and doing so in the midst of a crusade, a period traditionally associated with heightened anti-semitism.[220]

The activities of Isaac of Norwich were the subject of specific criticisms from the legate Pandulph, hardly surprisingly given that Isaac's business activities were centred upon Pandulph's cathedral city. The Norwich monks had only recently cleared their debts to Isaac, who owned an imposing stone house in the city centre, built by the same masons who had constructed the nearby cathedral priory, possibly as a *quid pro quo* in return for loans to the monks.[221] Reckoned the outstanding Jewish money-lender of his generation, Isaac was also a patron of Hebrew scholarship, and this in a city notorious for its anti-semitism, focal point of the cult of St William and the scene of numerous pogroms, culminating in the 1230s with the indictment and execution of Isaac's principal lieutenant, Moses Moike.[222] In July 1219 Pandulph wrote to des Roches and the Justiciar, complaining against Isaac's usurious activities in respect to the convent of Westminster, conducted, as des Roches was reminded, in direct contravention of the Lateran decrees.[223]

---

[219] *Pat. R. 1216–25*, p. 496. For the drawing see E401/1565, m. 1, reproduced by J. Gillingham, *The Life and Times of Richard I* (London 1973), pp. 54–5, discussed by Lipman, *Jews of Medieval Norwich*, p. 33 whose interpretation is not altogether convincing.

[220] Richardson, *The English Jews*, p. 182; Powell, *Anatomy of a Crusade 1213–21*, pp. 21, 45.

[221] Lipman, *Jews of Medieval Norwich*, pp. 111–12; *Norwich Cathedral Charters I*, ed. B. Dodwell (PRS), p. 241 no. 381 and see *RLC*, i, p. 323b where in Sept. 1217 the prior was set to guard Isaac's starrs and cyrographs.

[222] For Isaac, see Lipman, *Jews of Medieval Norwich*, pp. 40–1, 96, 103–7. For the Norwich pogroms, see *ibid.*, pp. 59–64; *The Life and Miracles of St William of Norwich by Thomas of Monmouth*, ed. A. Jessop and M. R. James (Cambridge 1896); Finucane, *Miracles and Pilgrims*, pp. 118–21, 161–2.

[223] *RL*, i, no. xxviii. Richardson, *The English Jews*, pp. 183–4, suggests that Pandulph was lenient in his dealings with the Jews, but the evidence cited is entirely negative and Richardson himself (p. 186) recognizes that anti-Jewish measures proposed by Hugh of Wells and Langton were vigorously adopted only in the dioceses of Lincoln and Norwich. It is nonetheless intriguing that Pandulph's brother, Giles Verracclo, one-time archdeacon of Ely, appears to have intended introducing a colony of Jews to San Germano nr. Monte Cassino, Pandulph and Giles' native town; E. Gattola, *Historia Abbatiae Cassinensis per saeculorum seriem distributa*, 2 vols. (Venice 1733–4), ii, p. 454, and see Vincent, 'The election of Pandulph Verracclo', pp. 153–4.

Association with the Jews, and with Isaac in particular, can hardly have eased relations between bishop and legate, yet as late as December 1221, des Roches was still supervising the collection of Isaac's fine at the Exchequer. Subsequently, he was to authorize the first of several writs by which Isaac's liabilities were reduced from 365 marks a year to 250 marks, 200 marks and eventually by 1226 to £100.[224] There is even a suggestion that a more personal relation existed between Isaac and des Roches. In 1223 Isaac delivered 58,000 herrings to the bishop's manor of Southwark, later distributed amongst the religious of the diocese.[225] In 1218–19 his close associate and attorney, Benedict Crispin, Jew of London, was also engaged in provisioning Southwark, whilst another prominent Jew, Chera Pinche of Winchester, paid a fine of £20 via des Roches.[226] Isaac, Benedict and Chera made regular appearances before the justices of the Jews.[227] Chera was ordered to bring a charter to London with the assistance of des Roches' clerk John of Herriard.[228] Her creditors included the prior of Southwick and several Hampshire men, later to be bought out by des Roches in his foundation of monastic houses at Titchfield and Selborne.[229] Chera's inheritance passed in part to Benedict Crispin whose terms for Chera's debts at the Exchequer were reduced under the authority of des Roches.[230] The creditors of Isaac of Norwich included both William de Mandeville and William of Avranches, a wartime hostage of Peter de Maulay.[231] Peter of Narford, a Norfolk landowner, accused Isaac of sending an armed band against him to devastate his lands, and in 1219 Isaac was the subject of a letter from the justices in eyre in Lincolnshire, voicing suspicions over the ease with which he had acquired a royal writ of distraint.[232]

This is not to suggest that des Roches was necessarily an ally of the

---

[224] E368/4, m. 3d; C60/17, m. 7; E368/6, m. 5; C60/23, m. 4.

[225] Ms. 19DR, m. 12. For an earlier connection, see *RLC*, i, p. 181b; *Norwich Cathedral Charters I* (PRS), p. 25 no. 39.

[226] Ms. 14DR, m. 12d, where Benedict delivered 5 loads of herrings; *RLC*, i, p. 387. For Benedict and Isaac as mutual attorneys, see Cole, *Documents*, pp. 311–12, 314, 325–6; *CRR*, ix, pp. 153–4.

[227] Cole, *Documents*, pp. 285–332 *passim*.

[228] *Ibid.*, p. 287.

[229] *ibid.*, p. 289. Chera's creditors included Henry de Brébeuf (*ibid.*, p. 306) who denied borrowing £300 at interest, having previously been in des Roches' service *c*.1210–12; *PR6DR*, pp. 57, 65, 123, 141; Ms. 7DR, mm. 2, 3, 8d.

[230] C60/17, m. 7.

[231] For Avranches, see Cole, *Documents*, pp. 286, 317; *Pat. R. 1216–25*, p. 158; *RLC*, i, p. 455b. For Mandeville see Cole, *Documents*, pp. 311, 325.

[232] Cole, *Documents*, p. 300; *RL*, i, no. xiv, misdated, see *CRR*, ix, pp. 153–4.

Jews. The Winchester pipe rolls record his alms-giving to converted Jews at Southwark, Marwell and Twyford over several years. Nonetheless, in 1220–1 he paid for the entertainment of Jews, not specified as converts, at Fareham, and in 1225–6 he received 4 shillings *de ferme Iudei hoc anno* at Taunton, suggesting that he may actively have encouraged the Jews to settle on his estates.[233] His diocesan statutes contain none of the anti-Jewish restrictions found in those of other sees, merely enjoining a boycott against Jews who purchased church lands, books or plate to last until the goods were restored.[234] There can be little doubt that des Roches was uncomfortably associated with several prominent Jews, one of them a particular *bête noire* of Pandulph. His involvement in ransom-taking and his association with the Jews who benefited from such debts; a hint, transformed by the 1230s into a certainty, that he was exploiting the predicament of landholders mortgaged to the Jews; none of this was likely to endear him to the country at large.

THE MARSHAL'S DEATH

For those who already regarded the activities of des Roches with a jaundiced eye, his conduct between November 1218 and April 1219 provided ample evidence that he remained wedded to various of the more controversial administrative methods of John's reign. On 9 April 1219, des Roches brought King Henry from London to Reading. The Marshal lay dying at nearby Caversham. From day to day the court travelled to and from his deathbed.[235] According to his biographer, the Marshal agreed that the time had come for the barons to select a new regent and guardian for the king. At this, the bishop of Winchester rose to claim that in 1216 the regency had been given to the Marshal but that he, des Roches, had been entrusted with care of the king's person.[236] In effect, he staked a claim to be considered the Marshal's successor as regent, by virtue of his office as personal guardian of the king. But the Marshal dismissed the bishop's suggestion: it had been he, William Marshal, and not the council that had placed the king in des Roches' keeping, and by implication, he or his successor as regent was at liberty to dismiss des Roches whenever he

---

[233] Mss. 7DR, m. 1d; 9DR, m. 3; 14DR, m. 3d; 16DR, mm. 6d, 7d; 19DR, m. 12; 20DR, m. 3.

[234] *C. & S.*, i, p. 131 no. 32.

[235] This council is discussed by Carpenter, *The Minority*, pp. 103–8; Painter, *William Marshal*, pp. 276–9.

[236] *Hist. de Maréchal*, lines 17949–18018.

saw fit. When the court reassembled the following morning, the Marshal committed Henry to the care of the pope and the legate Pandulph. Uncertain, even then, that his instructions had been understood, he sent his son and John Marshal in pursuit of the king, who in front of the assembled magnates was presented to Pandulph. Des Roches stepped forwards to take the boy by the head, only to be rebuked by the young Marshal and by the legate who, once more, in the sight of all, received the king.[237]

These details come to us from only one source, the *Histoire de Guillaume le Maréchal*, which tells us that only a few days later des Roches was appointed one of the Marshal's executors and appended his seal to the Marshal's will.[238] In the same year, the *Histoire's* chief informant, John of Earley, was permitted to hunt the bishop's manor of Taunton.[239] The conference at Caversham had effected no drastic reversal in des Roches' fortunes. But if he had entertained hopes of assuming the Marshal's role at the head of the administration, such hopes were effectively dashed in the spring of 1219. Superficially, his position remained unchanged. He retained custody of the king and continued to play a prominent role in the issue of royal letters. However, whereas formerly it had been des Roches who witnessed and de Burgh who warranted the Chancery's correspondence, from May 1219 these roles were reversed.[240] Over the succeeding month a triumvirate was established, with Pandulph insisting upon control of the seal and possibly also taking command of the Tower of London.[241] It has been suggested that des Roches acted as a go-between, resolving the tensions between Pandulph and de Burgh, so that by early June 1219 the legate was able to order Ralph Neville to follow the joint commands of bishop and Justiciar.[242] Certainly, des Roches had his uses to the regime, heading negotiations with France in both 1219 and 1220.[243] However, he was never to re-establish entirely satisfactory relations with either Pandulph or de Burgh. Even

---

[237] *Ibid.*, lines 18031–18118.
[238] *Ibid.*, lines 18334–42, but see Painter, *William Marshal*, p. 282, who recognizes that des Roches, Langton, Pandulph and Richard Poer were merely honorary executors and that the will itself was administered by others.
[239] Ms. 15DR, m. 10.
[240] Carpenter, *The Minority*, pp. 132, 135.
[241] See *RL*, i, nos. xciii–xciv, xcviii, c–ciii, and the redating proposed by Powicke, 'The Chancery during the minority of Henry III', pp. 220–35. For the Tower, see the expenses accounted from Pandulph's custody of Ely; *RLC*, ii, p. 7b; *Foreign Accounts* (PRS), p. 46.
[242] SC1/6/37, and see Cazel, 'The legates Guala and Pandulf', pp. 19–21.
[243] See above pp. 163–4.

within the royal household, one chronicler implies that des Roches' custody of the king was supplemented by the promotion of Philip de Aubigné as Henry's personal guardian.[244]

Pandulph continued to be entertained as the bishop's guest and to receive gifts from des Roches' manors.[245] At Christmas 1219, des Roches once again took responsibility for the court festivities and in de Burgh's absence, king, legate and bishop stayed at the Winchester manor of Downton for the new year. There and at Salisbury they transacted negotiations over the promotion of the king's falconers, the timing of a conference with Llywelyn and the acquisition of a wardship by William Brewer.[246] Nevertheless, the evidence of the Chancery enrolments and of the correspondence between the three men, legate, bishop and Justiciar, demonstrates a growing shift in emphasis towards co-operation between Pandulph and de Burgh at the expense of des Roches. Presumably Pandulph found de Burgh an easier man to work with, less rigid, better able to deal with the native English baronage. The Chancery clerks preserved several hundred letters of the years 1219–21 directed to de Burgh, many of them from the legate. By contrast we know of only three letters from des Roches to de Burgh, of which one merely transmitted instructions from Pandulph and another, concerning the see of Bordeaux, was filed away as redundant.[247] Of the bishop's two surviving letters to Pandulph, one is largely taken up with a response to the legate's criticism over the participation of des Roches' men in a tournament and the excessive number of foreigners maintained in his episcopal household.[248] Of incoming correspondence, there are nine letters from Pandulph addressed jointly to des Roches and de Burgh, all but one of them dated before January 1220, and six of them belonging to July 1219, the first month of the triumvirate. This latter group includes the writ, already mentioned, censuring des Roches' association with Isaac of Norwich.[249] Only four of Pandulph's letters are

---

[244] *Hist. des Ducs*, p. 207.

[245] Ms. 15DR, mm. 2d (legate at Waltham), 5d (given 18 chickens at Brightwell), 8 (Christmas expenses at Downton 1219/20), 9 (grain at Farnham), 10 (fish for legate, des Roches and king at Taunton); Ms. 16DR, m. 6 (fish for legate at Southampton).

[246] Ms. 15DR, mm. 7d, 8; SC1/1/73, 184, 198; J. G. Edwards, *Calendar of Ancient Correspondence Concerning Wales*, Board of Celtic Studies (Cardiff 1935), p. 2.

[247] SC1/1/198–200, printed Prynne, *Records*, iii, p. 45; *Foedera*, p. 164; *DD*, no. 68 and see above pp. 164–5.

[248] *Acta*, nos. 118–19.

[249] SC1/1/39, 41–3, 45–9, and see SC1/1/40 addressed to des Roches and William Brewer jointly. The only joint letter from Pandulph to des Roches after January 1220 is SC1/1/49 (*RL*, i, no. cxix).

directed to des Roches alone, none of them dated after June 1220, one of them being a complaint ordering the bishop to curb the activities of outlaws near Winchester.[250] We must treat this evidence with caution. The surviving archive contains only a small number of the letters that were originally sent. Even so, it would appear that after January 1220 and the negotiation of the truce with France, des Roches' role in government went into decline. The shift of power from the bishop to other members of the council was recognized in the country at large. Henceforth there were to be remarkably few letters from petitioners directed to des Roches, either alone or as a member of the triumvirate.[251]

From May 1219 de Burgh replaced des Roches as the principal witness to royal letters, but the bishop continued prominent in the issuing of writs concerning the royal household.[252] His authority continued to be recognized under the formulae *per* or *coram*, and at times when the Justiciar was absent from the seal, many letters were issued *Teste* des Roches.[253] Nonetheless, as David Carpenter suggests, whereas de Burgh came increasingly to employ the formula *per concilium* as the warranting authority to letters he witnesses, no such letters were issued *Teste* des Roches *per concilium*, an indication perhaps of de Burgh's desire to claim general conciliar co-operation, set against des Roches' unwillingness or inability to appeal to government by consent.[254]

---

250 SC1/1/37 (*RL*, i, no. cxliii, undated); SC1/1/38 (June 1220); SC1/1/44 (*DD*, no. 61; *RL*, i, no. lxii, Jan. 1220); SC1/1/50 (*Foedera*, p. 157, Aug. 1219).

251 Of twelve such letters, one was from des Roches' own sheriff of Hampshire (SC1/2/70), eight more were from aliens or foreign correspondents: Hugh de Lusignan (*DD*, no. 36), Louis of France (*DD*, no. 22), cardinal Stephen of Fossanova (*DD*, no. 99), Hugh de Vivonne (*RL*, i, no. lxxxiii), Fawkes de Bréauté (*RL*, i, no. xl; SC1/1/26), the bishop of Saintes (*DD*, no. 95), and Queen Berengaria (SC1/1/23); the other three were from the English archbishops Langton (*Acta Langton*, ed. Major, nos. 46, 52), and Walter de Gray (*RL*, i, no. xxxii).

252 *RLC*, i, pp. 391b, 396b, 397b, 399b, 401, 401b, 402, 408–409b, 410b, 411b, 412, 414–15, 416, 416b, 422b, 433, 433b, 439, 439b, 441b, 442, 443, 444, 448.

253 For references, see *Acta*, appendix 3, itinerary after August 1219.

254 Carpenter, *The Minority*, pp. 182–3.

Chapter 6

DECLINE AND DISGRACE 1219–1227

Des Roches' alien connections, his taking of ransoms, his high-handed attitude in negotiations with France, his suspicious activities at the Exchequer in respect to Jewish debt and his outbursts at Caversham in April 1219, had already given cause for concern both in the country at large and in the mind of the legate Pandulph. Nonetheless, the bishop commanded considerable influence in the highest circles of both church and state. From 1217 onwards, he had served as virtual vice-regent of Hampshire and he was supported by the massive financial resources of the see of Winchester. It would prove extremely difficult and even dangerous to dislodge him from his position within the regime. And yet the very power and wealth that des Roches commanded made him vulnerable to accusations of self-interest and increasingly isolated him from the wider concerns which motivated Pandulph and the king's council. Between 1219 and 1221, the legate was preoccupied with the recovery of the crown's resources usurped by local magnates. Superficially at least, des Roches co-operated in attempts to bring local officers to heel. He was active, for example, in the removal of Philip of Oldcotes from the north.[1] In 1220, he was consulted over the regime's attempt to clip the wings of the Justiciar in Ireland Geoffrey de Marsh, the Poitevin Hugh de Vivonne and the king's cousin Henry fitz Count, who had threatened to establish a virtual palatinate in Cornwall.[2] As a central figure at the Exchequer he was involved in re-channelling the crown's finances through the proper offices of account, in auditing the tangled web of accounts for the war years and in enforcing scutage and other taxes.[3]

---

[1] *Pat.R.1216–25*, pp. 189–92, 224, 246–7, 269; *RLC*, i, pp. 400b, 426b, 439; C60/12, m. 8.

[2] For Marsh, see *PR 1216–25*, pp. 191, 263–4, and for Vivonne, see *RLC*, i, p. 405b. Carpenter, *The Minority*, pp. 211–17 suggests that des Roches was kept informed but played no direct part in the disciplining of Henry fitz Count, although see *Acta*, no. 116.

[3] For a general summary of des Roches' work at the Exchequer, see West, *The Justiciarship*, pp. 238–41.

The Forest Charter of 1217 had raised fundamental questions over the crown's privileges, and here des Roches worked alongside the administration in resisting the inevitable pressures for disafforestation, assessing fines for assarts and purprestures, and ordering the suspension of regards which threatened to remove entire counties from the jurisdiction of the king's foresters.[4] In all these fields des Roches was as active as any of his colleagues in agitating for the restoration and preservation of the crown's resources. Yet as this process gathered momentum, not only did it meet with strongest resistance from amongst the very circle of King John's alien familiars most closely associated with des Roches, but it threw into relief the degree to which the bishop himself, the greatest of John's servants, was amongst the principal obstacles to any genuine reassertion of central control.

HAMPSHIRE AND THE FORESTS

With the end of the civil war in Hampshire, the sheriffdom of the county had passed first to John Marshal, and then on 29 July 1217 to des Roches. With it went custody of Winchester castle, to which was added jurisdiction over the castles at Portchester, Carisbrooke and Southampton.[5] For many years bishop-sheriffs had been frowned upon by the church, and in practice Hampshire was administered by des Roches indirectly, via a deputy, William of Shorwell, episcopal constable at Taunton from 1208 to 1216. As sheriff after 1217, Shorwell combined his responsibilities to the royal Exchequer with a role analogous to that of steward of the episcopal liberties, collecting the bishop's tallage, holding the bishop's hundred courts and described on at least one occasion specifically as des Roches' steward.[6] Beneath

---

[4] For the background, see D. Crook, 'The struggle over forest boundaries in Nottinghamshire 1218–1227', *Trans. Thoroton Soc. of Nottinghamshire* 83 (1979), pp. 35–45. For des Roches' personal involvement, see *Pat. R. 1216–25*, pp. 178–9, 190–1, 197, 211–12, 238; *RLC*, i, pp. 394b, 395, 417b, 430, 436; *RL*, i, no. cxix; SC1/1/76; E159/2, m. 16; C60/11, mm. 5, 7.

[5] *Pat. R. 1216–25*, pp. 44, 69, 75, 78. For Carisbrooke see *ibid.*, pp. 90–1. For des Roches' surrender of Portchester, Winchester and Southampton castles in 1224 see *ibid.*, p. 420. The constable of Portchester had received regular grants of grain and victuals from des Roches' manor of Fareham between 1217 and 1224; Mss. 13DR, m. 8 (30 quarters to the 'Tribune' of Portchester); 15DR, m. 3 (20 quarters to the constable); 16DR, mm. 6d, 7 (20 bacon pigs to the constable and entertainment in the castle for des Roches' kinsman, Peter de Rupibus, a knight of the royal household); 19DR, m. 9d (5 quarters to the constable). Portchester forest was in des Roches' hands *c.* 1220; E32/253.

[6] For Shorwell and his activities on the bishop's estates 1217–24, see *Acta*, appendix 4, no. 23.

him, another local man, John of Herriard, served both as sheriff's clerk and as des Roches' private attorney in the royal courts.[7] Crown offices within the county were henceforth filled predominantly from within the bishop's own household. In November 1217 it was the bishop's knights, Roger d'Escures and Maurice de Turville, who headed an enquiry into the Hampshire demesne and were set to impose the king's tallage.[8] Maurice de Turville, steward of des Roches' predecessor bishop de Lucy and keeper of Winchester castle 1214–15, was appointed to both the Hampshire circuit of the 1218 general eyre, and to the Hampshire forest eyre, serving on the latter alongside William of Shorwell and the bishop's clerk and former deputy in the royal chamber, William de St Maixent.[9] Turville and Shorwell also headed an enquiry into demesne, escheats and *terra Normannorum* in 1221. In 1219, in company with William Brewer and John fitz Hugh, des Roches was set to preside over a revision of the earlier forest regard, and this despite the fact that all three men owned private interests in the Hampshire forests and that fitz Hugh's assarts were currently subject to a special enquiry in Berkshire.[10]

In theory the bishop's stranglehold over local government should have enabled him to offer a lead, ensuring that Hampshire was the first county to be brought back under the control of the Exchequer. In practice, the Exchequer receipts from the county, never large given the traditionally high level of local expenditure on the king's frequent visits to the county, dried up completely under des Roches, who paid a recorded total of 10 marks, cash down, at the Exchequer during the six and a half years that he served as sheriff.[11] By 1218, the fixed outgoings of the county more than exceeded the basic county farm and, since increments beyond the farm had been abandoned as a matter of policy, the sheriff began each year with a credit or *superplus* of more than £20.[12] The remaining income of Hampshire, from demesne, tallages, taxes and scutages collected locally, was not squandered. Des Roches spent heavily from the crown's resources, on building work at Winchester and Portchester, in paying off the earl of

[7] For Herriard, kinsman of a former royal justice, see E368/1, m. 4; Cole, *Documents*, p. 287; *CRR*, viii, p. 234, xi, no. 2384.

[8] *Pat. R. 1216–25*, pp. 147, 172.

[9] *Pat. R. 1216–25*, pp. 207, 212, 217.

[10] C60/14, m. 2d; *RLC*, i, p. 434; *Pat. R. 1216–25*, pp. 199–200. William Brewer sought to excuse himself from a forest enquiry to which he had been invited by des Roches at Hilary 1220; SC1/1/76.

[11] See E159/7, m. 4d (Sept. 1222) for the only direct render.

[12] *PR 2 Henry III*, p. 12. For the Exchequer's concerns over the high level of fixed outgoings in several counties, see intro. to *PR 4 Henry III*, p. xiii.

Salisbury's claim to Southampton, and in the wages of the royal household. Nevertheless, whatever money was spent, was spent locally under des Roches' authority without ever passing through the central offices of the treasury and Exchequer. The bishop's control over crown income can only have boosted his own prestige within the county. For example, the £450 spent under his authority in rebuilding Winchester castle went incidentally to reinforce the role of his cathedral city as a favoured royal residence.[13] As the king's paymaster, it was the bishop rather than central government whose prestige was enhanced even in the disbursement of fixed pensions from the county farm, such as the £35 paid each year to Engelard de Cigogné for his custody of Odiham castle.

We might expect to find des Roches, as sheriff of Hampshire, spearheading the recovery of royal demesne and the preservation of forest rights from the over-zealous implementation of the Forest Charter: both policies that he espoused as a member of the central executive. However, there was little incentive for him to practise what he preached. It was from Hampshire escheats that aliens such as Engelard de Cigogné and Roger de la Zouche were promised compensation and reward.[14] It was the bishop's personal familiars who maintained a stranglehold over the county, and the bishop's men who could expect to benefit from crown perquisites, like Geoffrey de Caux, des Roches' clerk, promoted to the Norman escheats of Bentworth and the church of Ringwood.[15] In respect to the forests, it is clear that the bishop was as assiduous in profiting from the weaknesses of central government as the very men whose assarts and invasions he punished elsewhere.

Hampshire was the most heavily forested county in England with more than two-thirds of its land lying within the forest bounds.[16] Several of the bishop's manors lay within this area, where forest law threatened severely to restrict des Roches' exploitation of his

---

[13] For the building at Winchester and Portchester see, *Building Accounts of King Henry III*, ed. H. M. Colvin, (Oxford 1971), pp. 90, 92, 112–56, esp. pp. 136, 156; *The King's Works*, ed. Colvin, ii, pp. 784, 858–9.

[14] *RLC*, i, pp. 403–403b; *Pat. R. 1216–25*, pp. 37, 68.

[15] *VCH: Hampshire*, iv, p. 68.

[16] See in general, M. L. Bazeley, 'The extent of the English forest in the thirteenth century', *TRHS* 4th series, 4 (1921), pp. 140–72. The management of the New Forest is well described in *A Calendar of New Forest Documents 1244–1334*, ed. D. J. Stagg, Hampshire Rec. Soc. iii (1979), pp. 3–39 which corrects many elements of the classic study of Forest law by G. J. Turner, introduction to *Select Pleas of the Forest*, Selden Soc. xiii (1899). The records of the Hampshire forest eyre have largely perished for the years before 1250.

territorial resources. In 1208 the bishop had received a royal charter of liberties, granting him freedom from the forest regard, from the expeditation of hounds and from liability for waste. Within his own woods he was to take whatever he considered necessary for his own use, without oversight or threat of interference from the king's foresters.[17] This was a quite extraordinary array of privileges, which the bishop appears to have made use of to the full. His years as sheriff after 1217 witnessed an intense flurry of assarting and enclosure. Dr Titow has suggested that more than 2,500 acres were added to the bishop's demesne under arable in the decade 1217–27, and the episcopal pipe rolls reveal an extraordinarily high level of enclosure, ditch digging and fines for entry to newly cultivated land, suggesting that beyond the bishop's demesne an even greater number of assarts and purprestures were cleared and colonized.[18] Occasionally the evidence for this is specific, as with the thirteen oxen purchased for a new purpresture at Ashmansworth in 1219.[19] At Woodhay the total area under cultivation expanded threefold between 1217 and 1231, whilst Titow's figures suggest an exceptional degree of assarting at Bishop's Waltham, Alresford, Merdon, Burghclere, Overton, Farnham, Witney and Wargrave, the latter three all manors beyond the frontiers of Hampshire but within the bounds of the royal forest.[20] The response of central government to these activities was severely circumscribed both by the bishop's charter of 1208, and by the fact that before 1224 the regard was packed with des Roches' own men. In 1219 the regarders, including the bishop's officers Shorwell, Turville and William de Saint Maixent, wrote to des Roches and to Hubert de Burgh, explaining that they had been unable to proceed with their business because three of the knights appointed to the enquiry by the king had failed to appear through 'severe illness' (*maximum infirmitatem*); since they had no instructions to proceed without these men, and since in any case their letters of appointment failed to specify whether all assarts were to be subject to enquiry, both within and without the regard, they had suspended their activities awaiting

---

[17] *Rot. Chart.*, pp. 183–183b.
[18] Titow, 'Land and population', pp. 21a, 31, 74–5, 83, 113–14.
[19] *Ibid.*, p. 75; Ms. 14DR, m. 5.
[20] Titow, 'Land and population', pp. 83–91. For an earlier assart at Witney see above p. 73. For problems which may have arisen as a result of new cultivation at Woodhay, see *CRR*, xii, nos. 1102, 1565. Assarts provided a valuable source of revenue through the sale of timber such as the 5,350 *busca* carried to Marlow from Wycombe to await river transport in 1219/20; Ms. 15DR, m. 5.

further orders.[21] The bishop's woods, of course, lay outside the regard, although it is unlikely that King John, in granting exemption from forest law, had envisaged quite the scale of the clearances that des Roches would go on to make. In 1221 the regard within the bishop's liberties was halted pending des Roches' return from overseas, and it was suspended again at Wargrave in June 1223, presumably in response to complaints that it contravened the charter of 1208.[22] Under King John the entertainment of foresters had been a regular item of expense on the bishop's manors, but between 1216 and 1224 no such payments are recorded for Hampshire. The bishop had no need to appease a body of men, powerless to cause him injury. Only with his fall from grace after 1224 do we begin to read once again of *douceurs* paid to the king's foresters and of the bishop's officers sent 'against the regard'.[23]

In his first year as sheriff, des Roches had been given temporary custody of the New Forest pending the outcome of a dispute between its former keepers, John of Monmouth and William de Neville. At some time during the minority the bishop and William Brewer made grants of land there to Beaulieu Abbey, only confirmed by royal charter in 1236.[24] The bishop himself held the royal forests around Portchester, where he is said to have felled over a thousand oaks, at least in part to help with the building work at the royal castle of Portchester.[25] Another of the Hampshire forests, Aliceholt, was held for a time by des Roches' deputy sheriff, William of Shorwell.[26] Its hereditary forester John de Venuz, was later amongst the chief patrons of the bishop's foundation at Selborne priory. Venuz made at least one grant of land, to the canons of Southwick, which despite its apparent concern to guarantee the king's rights, looks suspiciously like an over-generous exercise of private patronage within the forest

---

21 SC1/2/70.
22 *RLC*, i, pp. 454, 550b.
23 For events after 1224, see below p. 219. Foresters had been entertained at Taunton in 1218/19 and 1220/1; Mss. 14DR, m. 11; 16DR, m. 10d. The bishop's own officers took pleas of the warren at Twyford in 1218/19 and a regard of des Roches' private woods at Merdon in 1220/1; Mss. 14DR, m. 3d; 16DR, m. 1. For entertainments before 1216 see above p. 73.
24 *The Beaulieu Cartulary*, ed. Hockey, no. 2. For the New Forest, see C60/9, m. 6, *RLC*, i, p. 405b; E159/2, m. 14; E368/3, mm. 1d, 4d; E32/253.
25 E32/253; E32/157, m. 9, which states also that he felled 19 oaks in the unidentified forest *de la Rode*. The 1,000 oaks felled in Portchester forest compares to the 1,200 felled by his successor as forester, Geoffrey de Lucy, but is nonetheless the second highest total recorded prior to the 1250s.
26 E159/7, m. 4d; E368/7, m. 10d to cover pannage 1221/2 and receipts of agistors 1222/3. The bishop's huntsmen had hunted Aliceholt in 1218/19; Ms. 14DR, m. 9.

bounds.[27] Possibly the most interesting document to link des Roches to the forests is a cyrograph drawn up at Winchester on 10 August 1218. Following representations to the legate Guala, and through the arbitration of the bishops of Salisbury, London and des Roches' familiar, the treasurer, Eustace de Fauconberg, this settlement established that William Brewer was henceforth to permit the bishop and the prior of St Swithun's the same liberties within his own forests as those extended generally by the king's Forest Charter of 1217.[28] As with Magna Carta, the Forest Charter had posed important questions over the degree to which restrictions placed upon royal government would be extended into baronial liberties. Neither des Roches nor Brewer was a natural supporter of government by charter. In 1215 they and the earl of Chester had been the only magnates at court prepared to issue letters, relinquishing any claim to liberties save those which the king himself was willing to grant. In other words, they believed that the king could not be compelled to restrict the exercise of royal prerogative.[29] In 1225 Brewer was the only baron openly to oppose the reissue of Magna Carta.[30] Des Roches, as a member of the royal executive, had sought to restrict local communities in their attempts to wring disafforestation and greater freedoms from the Forest Charter. Yet here we find him, championing the Charter and as a territorial magnate encouraging its imposition upon Brewer as a means of augmenting the privileges of the see of Winchester.

There was a double standard at work here that might well explain a cooling in relations between des Roches and William Brewer, and may have fuelled speculation as to the bishop's intentions in central government. Nor was it only in respect to the forests that des Roches' private interests clashed with his avowed policies as the king's protector. After 1216 three new towns were created on the Winchester estates, at Hindon, Overton and Clere. In 1218–19, before such grants were restricted, des Roches acquired market privileges for all three as well as for his manors of Wargrave and Adderbury.[31] Many of

27 *The Cartularies of Southwick Priory*, ed. K. A. Hanna, 2 vols., Hampshire Rec. Soc. ix–x (1988–90), ii, p. 348 no. 854.
28 *Acta*, no. 82. The agreement applies to the *foresta ballie* of Brewer, which could refer to Brewer's private forests but is more likely to apply to his bailiwick as keeper of royal liberties. The 1225 Forest Charter was accompanied by the king's insistence that its privileges be extended to all private franchises; Holt, *Magna Carta*, pp. 394–5.
29 *Acta*, appendix 2, no. 5.
30 Wendover, *Flores*, iv, p. 84.
31 See M. Beresford, 'The six new towns of the bishop of Winchester, 1200–55', *Medieval Archaeology* 3 (1959), pp. 187–215, esp. pp. 195–7 for Overton Burgh (c. 1217/18), pp. 197–200 for the New Burgh at Clere (c. 1218), pp. 200–2 for Hindon in Knoyle,

his colleagues in government received similar privileges, albeit on a smaller scale; but they at least paid for their awards. There is no evidence that des Roches paid any fine for his markets until after his fall from power.[32]

More worryingly still, the bishop had gained quittance from the hidage of 1217 and refused to pay the first scutage of the reign, a refusal which had not prevented him from levying the tax upon his own sub-tenants.[33] He clashed again with the Exchequer over the implementation of another direct tax, the carucage of 1220, and once again escaped without punishment.[34] In company with William Brewer and the earl of Gloucester he complained that amercements imposed upon his men during the eyre of 1218–19 were episcopal and not crown perquisites.[35] The basis of this claim appears to have been the privilege traditionally enjoyed by barons of the Exchequer, to receive exactions made upon their demesne that would normally have been collected by the crown.[36] Here as elsewhere, Des Roches was adept at fending off the attentions of both the eyre and the Bench by a degree of complex legal pleading.[37]

He had entered the reign with a substantial backlog of unpaid debts for which his friendship with King John had guaranteed virtual immunity.[38] Over the next ten years these debts continued to be accounted and regularly respited. They were augmented by small sums owed on behalf of wards acquired since 1214 and by the disputed first scutage and eyre amercements. The bishop maintained a careful watch over his wardships, seizing upon any opportunity to evade the fines which he had contracted to pay. For example, in the

Wilts. (*c*.1219/20). For the markets see *RLC*, i, pp. 363, 363b, 366b, 389b. In addition the market at Clere was moved from a Sunday; *RLC*, i, p. 368b. It is worth noting that three of these awards were warranted by des Roches in person.

[32] E372/71, m. 13d; C60/25, m. 7.

[33] See above p. 151.

[34] *BF*, p. 298, discussed by Holt, *Magna Carta*, pp. 399–400; Powicke, *Henry III*, pp. 33–4, and see *RLC*, i, p. 437b where in Oct. 1220 des Roches claimed that the council had extended the restrictions placed upon sheriffs collecting carucage from the abp. of York, the Cistercians and the Premonstratensians, to cover all bishops and religious, who would answer directly to the Exchequer.

[35] E368/2, m. 13; E368/3, m. 4d.

[36] See *Dialogus de Scaccario*, ed. C. Johnson (Oxford 1983), pp. 48, 57–9. Brewer's amercements were excused him in 1221 for service at the Exchequer; *RLC*, i, p. 482. For des Roches' liability of 82m, see E372/70, m. 6d.

[37] See for example *CRR*, viii, p. 158, discussed by Stenton, *Rolls of the Justices in Eyre for Yorkshire*, p. liii; *CRR*, viii, pp. 178, 233–4, x, p. 125; *Bracton's Note Book*, ed. F. W. Maitland, 3 vols. (London 1887), ii, p. 92, discussed by C. T. Flower, *Introduction to the Curia Regis Rolls 1199–1230*, Selden Soc. lxii (1943), p. 55.

[38] Above pp. 72–4.

case of Reginald de Vautorte, des Roches had originally agreed a fine of 600 marks for custody of Reginald and half of the honour of Totnes. Before 1216 he avoided paying scutage on the Totnes fees, and at the time of Reginald's majority most if not all of the 600 marks fine remained unpaid. Thereafter the bishop did his best to ensure that the debt be transferred to his former ward, engaging in a lengthy dispute with Reginald before the barons of the Exchequer. The outcome was delayed until after des Roches' fall from office, but even so the bishop appears to have paid less than £300 for a wardship that might have cost him nearer £1,000. By contrast Reginald was saddled with finding a considerable portion of the fine originally contracted by his guardian.[39]

Des Roches continued to receive exemption from scutages, albeit in return for military service, for the campaigns of Bytham, Montgomery and Bedford.[40] On leaving office as sheriff of Hampshire in 1224, far from owing arrears on his farm, he was found to have amassed credits to the tune of £700 consisting of numerous loans to the crown and payments on behalf of the royal household made over the past seven years.[41] These credits more than cancelled out his debts and went a long way towards meeting a fine of £500 forced from him in 1227 in return for charters guaranteeing his episcopal liberties. The remainder of this fine, a balance of some £312, he paid in cash, this being the first time he had paid cash down at the Exchequer in settlement of a fine since his election to Winchester twenty years before.[42]

It is true that after 1216 he advanced substantial loans to the crown, to pay off mercenaries and to settle household expenses, but his accounts were entered long after the transactions they described, often to cover payments made during the civil war.[43] John had for many years encouraged his officers to deliver money directly into the

---

[39] See above pp. 72–3; E368/7, m. 2d; C60/23, m. 2; C60/25, m. 10; *E. Rot. Fin.*, p. 154. Des Roches claimed to have paid £161 6/8d of the fine into John's wardrobe. Reginald was left to pay off just over £122 at 60m a year. Des Roches was in theory due to repay a further *c.* £122, but in 1227 he was debited only with the backlog of scutage on the Vautorte lands; E372/70, m. 6d.

[40] For the clearest summary of his liabilities, see E372/70, m. 6d. For his quittance from scutages, see E372/65, m. 2d (first scutage of 1217 and Bytham), E372/68, m. 1d (Montgomery and Bedford), and see also *RLC*, i, pp. 475, 606b.

[41] For the extent of his *superplus* which was continually readjusted, see *PR 4 Henry III*, p. 122; E159/7, m. 4d; E368/7, m. 10d; E372/68, m. 1; E372/70, m. 6d; E372/72, m. 7.

[42] E372/70, m. 6d; E372/72, m. 7.

[43] For the principal writs of *computate* issued on his behalf, see *RLC*, i, pp. 317b, 412, 412b, 450, 471, 508b, 520, 530b, 531b, 534b, 561b.

chamber, by-passing not only the dilatory procedures, but the efficient record-keeping of the Exchequer. As a result the new king's minority witnessed a flurry of claims, some of them no doubt fraudulent, for sums supposedly paid into John's itinerant court. Des Roches, as the principal survivor of John's financial administration, was frequently called upon as an unofficial remembrancer, to authorize quittances for sums which it was claimed had been paid into the chamber before 1216.[44] At the same time, the bishop's own claims, for example to have paid £160 of his fine for the Vautorte wardship into John's wardrobe, were themselves open to suspicion. The Exchequer appears to have been reluctant to accept them unchallenged. In 1227 the decision to discount them against des Roches' long-standing debts to the crown was framed as an act of grace, 'pardoned the bishop for the good and faithful service which he rendered to the King and to his father king John'.[45]

Superficially des Roches' willingness to apply his own resources to the needs of the crown might be taken to indicate a selfless commitment to the interests of the king. However, *ad hoc* loans were no substitute for a revitalized Exchequer, whose control over the crown's resources appears to have been hindered rather than assisted by the bishop's government of Hampshire. All des Roches' loans were made in full expectation of repayment. They served to enhance his personal prestige and they were disbursed from an episcopal Exchequer which for the first few years of the minority controlled a cash income greater than that of the royal Exchequer at Westminster. Significantly, des Roches' loans also involved him, much to his advantage, in the most lucrative field of crown patronage still open to exploitation. Unable to repay the bishop directly, the regime resorted to grants of wardships, escheats and other feudal incidents. Already by 1216 des Roches had acquired custody of Robert de Aubigny, David of Easby and an unidentified interest in the barony of Wahull.[46] In 1218 he gained control over the lands of Simon de Montfort and administered the dower of earl Simon's widow jointly with Philip de Aubigné for three years from January 1219.[47] His personal association with the Marmion

---

[44] See *PR 3 Henry III*, p. 36; *Foreign Accounts*, pp. 43–4; E368/1, m. 7d; E368/4, mm. 3, 5.

[45] E372/70, m. 6d, and see *RLC*, ii, pp. 189b, 190b.

[46] *RLC*, i, p. 294; *PR 2 Henry III*, pp. 13, 14, 63; E368/4, m. 2(2)d; E159/6, m. 10, and for the Wahull barony, see also Sanders, *Baronies*, pp. 68–9 and below p. 216.

[47] *RLC*, i, p. 369, *Pat. R. 1216–25*, pp. 184–5, 195; C60/9, m. 3; C60/11, m. 11. Powicke, *The Christian Life in the Middle Ages*, pp. 159, 163, suggests that des Roches' arrangement with Loretta, countess of Leicester, was intended to assist in endowing her

family was cemented by his service as guardian of the Marmion heir and his receipt of the £500 fine paid by Robert Marmion after 1219.[48] In July 1220 he was briefly made custodian of the honour of Berkeley, although William Marshal the younger stepped in almost immediately to stand pledge for the Berkeley heir.[49] Meanwhile the bishop had been granted several less significant escheats and wardships to swell his already valuable collection.[50]

There is no evidence that des Roches paid any fine for these custodies, some of which were granted to him specifically in repayment of his loans to the crown.[51] The profits of such awards could be considerable. In November 1221, the bishop sold custody of Robert de Aubigny for 500 marks and the marriage of Robert Marmion for a further £400.[52] There are indications, too, that his intervention in the trade in wardships caused resentment. His political downfall was followed by suits for the recovery of the heirs of John of Merston and Baldwin Esturmy. In another case, des Roches claimed to have been granted an heiress by John Marshal and to have brought her up with the assistance of Peter de Maulay, the earl of Chester and Roger de la Zouche. But her parents, John and Lucy of Montacute, attempted to disown the girl, largely it would appear so that their lands might pass to their brother, William of Montacute, rather than to a daughter who had become little more than a stranger.[53]

Besides wardships and escheats, des Roches received incidental gifts of timber and venison, patronage for his monastic foundation at

as an anchoress. Loretta's steward received stock at Downton in 1215–16; Ms. 11DR, m. 4. Subsequently des Roches enforced a royal tallage on the Leicester lands; C60/11, mm. 2, 10.

48 *RLC*, i, p. 391; *Pat. R. 1216–25*, p. 307.

49 C60/12, m. 3, and see *RL*, i, no. clv.

50 See also *RLC*, i, p. 299b; *BF*, pp. 256, 272–4, 298; *CRR*, xi, nos. 1857, 2384, xii, nos. 773, 1523, 2667. A prest of 20m paid to the widowed countess of Winchester at Knoyle in 1224–5 (Ms. 20DR, m. 2) may suggest some interest in the lands of the earldom of Winchester. For the administration of royal escheats incorporated within the main body of the bishop's estate accounts, see East Ilsley (?Leicester land) and Henley, above pp. 158 n.106, 160 n.120. In 1223 des Roches was given disposal of the advowson of Henley; *Pat. R. 1216–25*, p. 416. Such royal custodies should be distinguished from the bishop's acquisition of wardships within his own episcopal liberties, for which see Mss. 13DR, m. 14d; 14DR, m. 12d; 16DR, m. 12; 20DR, m. 15; 21DR, m. 14d; 22DR, m. 13d.

51 For attempts to repay and reschedule his loans, see *RLC*, i, pp. 298b, 370, 391, 393, 394, 397, 403, 522b; *Pat. R. 1216–25*, pp. 6, 197.

52 *Pat. R. 1216–25*, pp. 317–19.

53 *CRR*, xi, no. 2384, xii, nos. 773, 1523, 2667, xiii, no. 24; *Bracton's Notebook*, no. 247 and for William of Montacute, see also *CRR*, x, p. 318.

Halesowen, and royal sanctions against merchants of Ypres and Bologna who were behind-hand in settling their debts.[54] His kinsmen too were brought within the orbit of crown patronage. Peter de Rivallis as wardrobe clerk received promotion to various royal livings, timber for his houses in Hampshire and a royal wardship.[55] Peter de Rupibus was retained as a member of the royal household; Geoffrey des Roches was married to a Hampshire heiress, Hugh des Roches involved in embassies to Wales, and his brother Aimery presented to the crown living of Preston.[56] Bartholomew des Roches, the archdeacon of Winchester, was employed to assess the claims of Italian crusaders who arrived in England to demand arrears due to them from the time of the Third Crusade.[57]

THE FIRST SETBACK

Des Roches had much to gain by clinging on to the reins of power. To retire would be to open the way for reprisals against his abuses in the administration of Hampshire, his encroachments upon the royal forest, and his exploitation of the various wardships he held in custody. By the summer of 1220 Hubert de Burgh had effectively displaced him at the head of the king's administration, whilst the bishop's relations with Pandulph had perceptibly cooled. Even in the royal household, matters were running far from smoothly. In May 1220 Honorius III advised Pandulph to ensure that the king be kept 'by prudent and honest men, not distrusted either by him or his kingdom, who will instruct him in good morals and teach him to fear God and to love his vassals'.[58] It was almost certainly des Roches against whom these remarks were directed.

Again in May 1220, Honorius demanded that Pandulph re-establish the king's control over the royal demesne and curb the activities of certain bishops who 'for their own good, not that of the king, are sadly enslaved by greed and have usurped the king's castles, manors and townships'. Yet another papal letter of the same month ordered that no one be permitted to hold more than two royal castles in

---

54   *Pat. R. 1216–25*, p. 326; *RLC*, i, pp. 316, 362b, 369, 399b, 401b, 428b-429, 501b, 611b, 636. For Halesowen see *RLC*, i, pp. 477, 530b, 547b, 550, 553b; C60/12, m. 3.

55   *E. Rot. Fin.*, i, p. 91; *RLC*, i, pp. 543, 553, 561; *Pat. R. 1216–25*, p. 372; C60/17, m. 3.

56   *RLC*, i, pp. 442, 450b, 566, 575, 578; *BF*, p. 367; *Pat. R. 1216–25*, pp. 199, 415, 417. For incidental grants to des Roches' clerks 1217–24, see *RLC*, i, pp. 458b, 529b, 534b, 540, 544, 557b, 559b.

57   *Pat. R. 1216–25*, p. 260; *RLC*, i, p. 408.

58   Carpenter, *The Minority*, p. 243.

custody. Des Roches, of course, held three.[59] At much the same time
Pandulph may have written to des Roches accusing him of maintaining an excessive number of alien kinsmen and knights in his
household and of permitting them to participate in a tournament.[60]
The particular tensions of 1220 can be traced in the first place to the
counsels of archbishop Langton who returned from Rome, fully
reconciled with the pope, in the spring of 1220. On 17 May Langton
conducted a splendid ceremony in which Henry was crowned anew,
superseding the coronation in which des Roches had participated and
providing the occasion for further admonitions over the restoration of
the king's demesne.[61] Des Roches himself may have been present at
the ceremony; four days later he personally restored the crown jewels
and the coronation robes to the treasury.[62] In July Langton supervised
the translation of the relics of St Thomas Becket to a newly
constructed shrine, a further indication that the archbishop was
determined to reassert his natural authority within the church, and an
occasion which Langton used quite deliberately to emphasize the
triumph of a native-born English saint.[63] The shrine itself was
designed by Master Elias of Dereham, recently returned from his
banishment for supporting the rebels against King John.[64] Fears that
Langton would also reinstate his brother, Master Simon Langton,
the most outspoken of Louis' clerical supporters, provoked a letter
of protest from several leading courtiers.[65] Meanwhile, the politics of
both church and state were turning sour for des Roches.

In the autumn of 1220, as Langton set out once more for Rome,
determined to obtain the recall of Pandulph's legation, des Roches
continued to resist the resumption of royal rights, refusing to permit
the assessors of the carucage to enter his episcopal liberties.[66] David
Carpenter has suggested that the following month saw des Roches
seriously over-reach his authority at the Exchequer. Left in charge

---

[59]   *RL*, i, no. civ, p. 535, no. 9, and see Carpenter, *The Minority*, pp. 189–90.
[60]   *Acta*, no. 118.
[61]   Carpenter, *The Minority*, pp. 187–91.
[62]   E401/3B, m. 1.
[63]   See A. J. Duggan, 'The cult of St Thomas Becket in the thirteenth century', in *St Thomas Cantilupe Bishop of Hereford, Essays in his Honour*, ed. M. Jancey (Hereford 1982), pp. 22–41, esp. p. 39 for Langton's stress upon Becket as Englishman.
[64]   Paris, *Hist. Ang. Min.*, ii, p. 242. For Elias' support of the rebels, see *Hist. des Ducs*, p. 197; *Cal. Pap. Reg.*, i, pp. 55, 63. He had returned by *c*.1219 when he witnessed a recognizance to Langton stemming from a legal suit of 4 Henry III; Lambeth ms. 1212, ff. 49v, 107v.
[65]   *Foedera*, p. 171, and see N. Denholm-Young, 'A letter from the council to pope Honorius III 1220–1', *EHR* (1945), pp. 88–96.
[66]   *RLC*, i, pp. 437–437b; *BF*, p. 298.

whilst the Justiciar went north to conduct negotiations with the Scots, the bishop not only issued letters restricting the collection of carucage on church lands, but on his own authority inspected a royal charter which, he declared, exempted the manor of Newburn from tallage. In his own name he forbade any intervention in the matter by the sheriff of Northumberland.[67] Having played no part in the reimposition of control in Cornwall, on 13 October he announced that the king would be pleased to accept a proffer of 1,000 marks for the Cornish stannaries, despite the bishop's admission that he should by rights consult both Pandulph and de Burgh before accepting such a fine.[68] It is possible that des Roches' autocratic approach at the Exchequer in October 1220 led de Burgh to introduce a reform, whereby entries on the Exchequer memoranda rolls were precisely dated, enabling the Justiciar to tell at a glance which accounts had been heard in his absence.[69] Ironically, this procedure, probably initiated as a weapon against des Roches, was adopted almost immediately by the bishop's own Exchequer, where from Michaelmas 1221 most entries on the episcopal pipe rolls are individually dated.[70]

At Christmas 1220 the tensions at court came to a head, sparked off by the revolt of the Poitevin William de Fors, earl of Aumale.[71] Aumale was not amongst the bishop's inner circle of friends. Although brought to England during des Roches' time as Justiciar and installed as a royalist satellite in the midlands, he had twice changed sides during the civil war, earning a reputation as a trouble-maker.[72] There

---

[67] *Acta*, no. 120; Carpenter, *The Minority*, pp. 225–6.

[68] On 10 October des Roches witnessed a grant of the stannaries to William de Putot (*Pat. R. 1216–25*, p. 256), but had apparently regretted his decision by 13 October when he accepted the proffer of 1,000m from John fitz Richard (C60/12, m. 2). In November, fitz Richard's promotion was confirmed by de Burgh who at the same time appointed him sheriff, adding Stephen de Croy as joint keeper of the stannaries (C60/14, m. 7). By 28 Jan. 1221 the county had been removed from him and given to des Roches' former ward, Reginald de Vautorte, pending the election of a sheriff which duly confirmed Reginald in office; *Pat. R. 1216–25*, pp. 281–2, 290. By 1221 Vautorte was if anything an enemy rather than an ally of des Roches. It is tempting to link the bishop's acquisition of livestock from Cornwall in 1220–1 to the fall of Henry fitz Count; Ms. 15DR, m. 1. In the same year Stephen de Croy was entertained at Fareham and Meon by the bp.'s orders; Ms. 15DR, m. 3, and see also *CRR*, xi, no. 670 for a case involving des Roches which suggests that Fawkes de Bréauté also benefited from the fall of Henry fitz Count.

[69] Carpenter, *The Minority*, p. 226.

[70] Ms. 16DR, *passim*.

[71] Carpenter, *The Minority*, pp. 227–34.

[72] For his career see above pp. 112, 176; R. V. Turner, 'William de Forz, count of Aumale: an early thirteenth-century baron', *Proceedings of the American Philosophical Society* 115 (1971), pp. 221–49. Fors held some land in Hampshire from which he made an award to the canons of Southwick; *Southwick Cartularies*, ed. Hanna, ii, p. 29 no. 86.

is no evidence that in 1220 des Roches encouraged his rebellion, indeed the bishop sent men and seven cart-loads of siege equipment to assist his ejection from Bytham castle.[73] Even so, des Roches' own castle at Farnham was placed under a special armed guard during the siege of Bytham, an indication of the tensions that the siege created.[74] Although not a close ally, the bishop was uncomfortably associated with Aumale. For the past two years, despite complaints from the justices in eyre, and despite the fact that Aumale had been excommunicated for participation in a tournament, des Roches had stood as his personal surety in a suit against the former rebel Gilbert de Gant.[75] The bishop appears to have attended the siege of Bytham: he was loaned money on retiring from the castle and excused scutage for his participation in the campaign.[76] Nonetheless, the siege marked a turning point in his career and provoked him into a piqued and sullen withdrawal from court. On 19 February the Exchequer began to audit his expenses as the king's guardian.[77] The exact date of the king's removal from des Roches' personal charge is unknown; but it had undoubtedly occurred by the winter of 1221.[78]

The bishop did not altogether retire from public affairs. Simultaneously with Aumale's revolt, the bishop of London expressed a wish to resign his see. Des Roches and bishop Benedict of Rochester secured him annuities from the London estates. In the succeeding weeks, the canons of London elected as William's successor Master Eustace de Fauconberg, the royal treasurer and a former lieutenant of des Roches. There are indications that des Roches intervened personally in this election. Certainly his protégé, the poet Henry of Avranches, was present during discussions amongst the chapter and wrote verses in Eustace's favour. In describing the elect as *doctrine gemma, bonorum summa, Petri consors,* Henry may have attempted a punning allusion to Fauconberg's

---

[73] Ms. 16DR, mm. 3, 5.

[74] Mss 16DR, m. 5; 22DR, m. 13d.

[75] See references cited above p. 176.

[76] *RLC*, i, pp. 453b, 475; *Foreign Accounts*, p. 18; E372/65, m. 2d. The bishop levied the Bytham scutage on his own sub-tenants, the account appearing for some unknown reason on the episcopal pipe roll for 1218–19; Ms. 14DR, m. 12d. The account is mutilated but suggests that from a theoretical total of just over £32, the bishop collected very little in the short term, though all but £7 had been cleared by the time of the next account (Ms. 16DR, m. 12), either by quittance or settlement. Further quittances were still being issued after 1225; Mss. 16DR, m. 12; 20DR, m. 15; 21DR, m. 14d; 22DR, m. 13d.

[77] *RLC*, i, p. 450.

[78] *Walter of Coventry*, ii, p. 260 suggests that the king's pupillage was ended after des Roches' return from overseas in the autumn of 1221.

affinity to the bishop of Winchester.[79] The resignation of William de Ste Mère-Eglise left des Roches as the longest serving of the English bishops, a position he was to occupy for the next seventeen years. Yet ironically, this was also the last occasion on which he was to see the promotion of a close familiar to the episcopate. When Eustace came to be consecrated on 25 April, the ceremony was performed not by his former master but by the bishop of Rochester.[80] Des Roches had meanwhile quit the country, with the outward intention of visiting the shrine of St James at Compostela.

PILGRIMAGE AND PLOT

The true motive for des Roches' pilgrimage of 1221 may never be established, but it is quite possible that it was undertaken in response to political developments at court: the first of several occasions in des Roches' career when frustrated political ambition caused him to turn to adventures overseas.[81] There was a precedent for des Roches' journey to Santiago set by the last great alien bishop of Winchester, Henry of Blois, who had visited the shrine on his return from Rome in 1153.[82] Des Roches' associate, Roger de la Zouche, had planned to set out for Compostela at some time after September 1220, and in turn the bishop's pilgrimage may have encouraged his ward, Robert Marmion, and the archbishop of York to follow suit in 1222.[83] His departure was apparently well ordered. He was accompanied overseas by the bishop of Hereford and before sailing secured royal letters of protection both for his estates and for a will that he had drafted.[84] The Winchester pipe rolls record the provisioning of a ship for the bishop's journey at Fareham and the cost of entertainments 'when the bishop returned from St James'.[85]

---

79 *Pat. R. 1216–25*, pp. 279–80, 286; *RLC*, i, p. 447b; *Cal. Pap. Reg.*, i, p. 81; *Henry of Avranches*, ed. Cox Russell, pp. 81–7, esp. p. 85, no. 47, lines 4–5. See also Ms. 16DR, m. 5 for a messenger coming to the elect of London at des Roches' manor of Farnham.

80 BL Add. Ch. 36449; *Sarum Charters*, pp. 109–10, and see Eustace's own letters on the consecration: Canterbury Cathedral D. & C. mss. Cartae Antiq. C110(4); C115(80), and also BL ms. Harley 6956, f. 164v.

81 The bishop's clerk, Master Philip de Lucy, had made a similar pilgrimage to Compostela in 1213, following his dismissal from the royal chamber; *Acta*, appendix 4, no. 34; *RLP*, p. 104b.

82 *The 'Historia Pontificalis' of John of Salisbury*, ed. M. Chibnell, 2nd edn (Oxford 1986), pp. 80, 91–4.

83 *Pat. R. 1216–25*, pp. 246, 327–9.

84 *Ibid.*, p. 286. The pilgrimage is noticed by *AM*, ii (Winchester), p. 84; iii (Dunstable), p. 68; iv (Worcester), p. 414; *Walter of Coventry*, ii, p. 260.

85 Ms. 16DR, mm. 1, 6–7d. The provisioning was supervised by a clerk named Edmund.

Compostela was a natural destination for a Tourangeau such as des Roches, since Tours was the starting point of one of the principal pilgrimage routes across the Pyrenees.[86] Yet pilgrimage was also a common prelude to the more arduous journey to the Holy Land, and it is arguable that in 1221 des Roches' thoughts had turned not so much to Compostela as to the Fifth Crusade.[87] For many years he had been associated with moral reforms, linked to anxieties for the success of the Christian army in Egypt. Several of the bishop's associates had set out for the east, most recently Philip de Aubigné, fresh from the intrigues of the royal household.[88] Langton's departure for Rome had coincided with the dispatch of two royal envoys to the Curia, Master Humphrey de Millières and Walter de Verdun, both men with strong links to des Roches who was the principal sponsor of their mission.[89] Either at Rome or amongst Philip de Aubigné's crusading companions outside the walls of Damietta, it is clear that someone was advocating a role for des Roches. By the autumn of 1221 he had been nominated as first archbishop of Damietta, a promotion that would hardly have been made unless he himself had canvassed the honour or at least made known his intention to take the cross.[90] The bishop's family had participated in every crusade since the 1090s, and it is likely that des Roches' pilgrimage to Compostela provided an opportunity for him to revisit his homeland in France.

In the meantime his absence caused rumours to flourish in England. Speculation and unease were already rife, fired by Aumale's rebellion and by Langton's negotiations in Rome. To this was added the fear that des Roches' pilgrimage masked a more sinister intent. 'Many were unsure of his destination', wrote the Dunstable annalist, 'some saying that he had gone to St James, others that he had set out for the Curia.'[91] The events which followed can be read either as the outcome of genuine suspicion against des Roches, or as a ploy by de

---

[86] See C. M. Storrs, 'Jacobean pilgrims from England from the early twelfth to the late fifteenth century', M. A. thesis (London 1964), p. 94, which at pp. 168ff. gives a useful list of English pilgrims.

[87] See Lloyd, *English Society and the Crusade*, p. 157, for the association with preliminary pilgrimages. In 1220 both Henry fitz Count and the earl of Aumale had taken the cross in the aftermath of political disgrace: *AM*, iii (Dunstable), p. 60; Norgate, *The Minority*, pp. 123, 156, glossing *Pat. R. 1216–25*, p. 240.

[88] He arrived in time to witness the fall of Damietta; Wendover, *Flores*, iv, pp. 75–7.

[89] *Pat. R. 1216–25*, pp. 257, 267–8; *RLC*, i, p. 477b.

[90] *Coggeshall*, p. 190. There is no independent evidence of this appointment, although a German chronicle reports that a tower at Damietta was reserved for the use of the new archbishop; K. R. Giles, 'Two English bishops in the Holy Land', *Nottingham Medieval Studies* 31 (1987), p. 48n.

[91] *AM*, iii, p. 68.

Burgh and his supporters to exploit the bishop's absence. At Whitsun (30 May) 1221, two of des Roches' closest alien associates, Peter de Maulay and Engelard de Cigogné, were summoned to attend court at Winchester. On the pretext of state affairs, de Maulay was taken aside into a private chamber and there accused of treasonably plotting with des Roches. The bishop had gone abroad as part of a conspiracy; his ship would be used to take Eleanor of Brittany, de Maulay's state prisoner, to the king of France. De Maulay was humiliated before the council; his clothes were torn and for a while both he and de Cigogné were imprisoned.[92]

The author of these accusations was a minor west-country knight, Richard de Mucegros, whose hatred for de Maulay may have sprung in some way from disputes over the marriage of his kinsman Robert de Mucegros to the widow of Hugh de Poinz, contracted in the previous year without royal licence. For this transgression Robert had been fined the exceptionally large sum of 300 marks, and had been threatened with the seizure of his lands.[93] Following de Maulay's dismissal from Corfe castle, his replacement as constable, John Russell, stood amongst Mucegros' pledges for the first instalment of this fine. So did Godfrey of Crowcombe, like Russell a steward of the royal household and involved in the attack upon de Maulay.[94] That Richard de Mucegros' accusations against de Maulay were taken seriously, may have owed much to his influence with leading figures at court. He or a namesake had served as a royal justice and possessed long-standing links to the family of William Marshal. Robert de Mucegros, Richard's kinsman, held land of the see of Canterbury and served subsequently as steward to archbishop Langton.[95]

Richard de Mucegros' quarrel with de Maulay, and his eagerness to drag in the bishop of Winchester, can also be related to the role played by de Maulay and des Roches in the market in royal wardships and marriages. By marrying the widow of Hugh de Poinz, Robert de Mucegros had become embroiled in the inheritance dispute surrounding the estates of William Malet. Malet had died c.1216 leaving

---

[92] The 'plot' is recorded by the Dunstable annalist: *AM*, iii, p. 68; *Walter of Coventry*, ii, p. 260; *Coggeshall*, p. 190. For commentary see Carpenter, *The Minority*, pp. 249–52.

[93] *AM*, iii (Dunstable), p. 75; C60/14, mm. 2d, 4, 6.

[94] C60/14, m. 2d; *RLC*, i, pp. 459b, 460b. Robert de Mucegros is to be found as witness to private charters of Godfrey of Crowcombe; Somerset RO, Taunton, Wyndham Papers DD/WY Box 10, Bundle T1; Hatfield House ms. 293 (Montagu cartulary), p. 70.

[95] See K. Major, 'The "familia" of Archbishop Stephen Langton', *EHR* 48 (1933), pp. 547–8; R. V. Turner, *The English Judiciary in the Age of Glanvill and Bracton, c. 1176–1239* (Cambridge 1985), pp. 132–3, 145, 188.

a widow and three daughters, one of whom, Helewise, married first Hugh de Poinz and then Mucegros.[96] A second daughter, Mabel, was married to Nicholas de Avenel. Before 1221, as sheriff of Somerset and Dorset, Peter de Maulay had intervened to oppose Avenel's claims to a wardship once held by Hugh de Poinz. Avenel paid de Maulay a douceur of 30 marks to discourage his interference, but still faced attacks from de Maulay's bailiffs.[97] On Avenel's death, Mabel married the Poitevin, Hugh de Vivonne. He, with des Roches' assistance, had already attempted to gain a foothold in the Malet inheritance by marrying his nephew to Malet's widow Alice.[98] Despite the bishop's sponsorship, this marriage was cancelled. Even so, it suggests a further link between des Roches and Mucegros. Alice, Malet's widow, was a daughter of Thomas Basset of Headington and hence the sister-in-law of des Roches' former ward Reginald de Vautorte, in dispute with the bishop over the fine to be paid for his inheritance. Several years earlier, des Roches had drafted a division of Thomas Basset's property amongst his various daughters.[99] In October 1220, following Basset's death, the bishop complained to the sheriff of Oxford that Alice Malet had entered part of her late father's estate by fraud, without pledges for the payment of her relief; the sheriff was to force her to answer for this invasion.[100] Having married into the Malet inheritance, both Robert de Mucegros and Hugh de Vivonne found themselves burdened with nearly 2,000 marks of William Malet's debts to the crown.[101] The pattern here is far from clear. Nonetheless, the accusations made against des Roches and his associates in 1221 may well have involved a complicated interweaving of rivalries and resentments amongst the west country gentry. De Maulay and des Roches were fishing in very deep waters. Their intervention in gentry property disputes was to provoke a backlash, which in 1221 came close to bringing about their downfall.

Neither Engelard de Cigogné nor Peter de Maulay had done much to earn the confidence of the native baronage. De Maulay had quarrelled with the earl of Salisbury, continued to hold prominent

[96] In general, see Sanders, *Baronies*, pp. 38–9. In 1217 des Roches had witnessed charters of Hugh and Nicholas de Poinz promising loyalty to the king on pain of forfeiture; *Pat. R. 1216–25*, pp. 107–8.

[97] *CRR*, x, pp. 106–8, and see *CRR*, xi, nos. 800, 1371, 1815, 2472.

[98] SC1/1/211. The nephew was named H(ugh?) de Chaceporc. An Eimeric de Chaceporc was still amongst Vivonne's household in the 1230s: JUST1/775, m. 18.

[99] Exeter, Devon Record Office ms. TD51 (Courtenay cartulary), pp. 154–6.

[100] *RLC*, i, p. 438b, and in general, see Sanders, *Baronies*, pp. 51–2.

[101] E368/4, m. 13; E159/5, m. 14; E368/5, m. 3d; E368/8, mm. 2d, 6, 14; C60/20, m. 8; *RLC*, ii, pp. 67b–68.

rebels to ransom up to the time of his downfall in 1221, and despite adopting a high-handed approach as sheriff, had failed to pay anything from the farm of Somerset and Dorset into the Exchequer.[102] In November 1221 the local communities fined 200 marks to be rid of the demands of de Maulay's bailiffs and to have Roger of Lafford as their sheriff.[103] Although established as a major landowner in York-shire, de Maulay was the subject of local rumour which credited him with one of the more notorious deeds of the period, the murder of Arthur of Brittany; a stark contrast to the popular legend attached to Hubert de Burgh, de Maulay's principal accuser in 1221, who was said to have refused to carry out King John's orders to blind and castrate the boy.[104] Engelard too had many enemies in England. Proscribed by name in Magna Carta, his subsequent custody of Windsor castle had been attended by complaints from the influential abbot of Reading and the excommunication of his bailiffs by the bishop of Salisbury.[105] Both abbot and bishop appealed for justice to de Burgh, a man already prejudiced against Engelard by the latter's claim to the county of Surrey made against de Burgh's kinsman and former patron, the earl of Warenne. Engelard had clashed too with the bishop of Lincoln and the abbot of Dorchester, and in 1220 had denied access at Windsor to royal officers attempting to levy the carucage.[106]

According to the Dunstable annalist, the government's fears in 1221 extended beyond de Maulay and Engelard to encompass two equally powerful aliens, Fawkes de Bréauté and Philip Mark, the garrisons of whose castles at Nottingham, Northampton and Oxford were supple-mented by men in whom the king could trust.[107] Although there was no substance to the allegations of a plot with France, the mere fact that such allegations could have taken fire, shows the extent to which des Roches' contacts with aliens, and perhaps above all his close personal supervision of Anglo-French diplomacy over the past decade,

---

[102] Above pp. 142–4, and for specific complaints against him in 1221, see *RLC*, i, p. 455b; L. G. Cruwys (ed.), 'Abstracts from the Devon assize rolls for 1218–19', *Devon and Cornwall Notes and Queries* xx (1938–9), pp. 351–2.

[103] C60/17, m. 8, although see *Somersetshire Pleas*, ed. C. Chadwick Healey, 2 vols. , Somerset Rec. Soc. , xi, xxxvi (1897, 1923), i, pp. 61–3 for evidence that Lafford was a close associate of de Maulay.

[104] *The Chronicle of Walter of Guisborough*, ed. H. Rothwell, p. 144 and see also pp. xxvii–xxviii, 261, 369, which as David Carpenter has pointed out to me, show that Guisborough had special access to information on the Maulays whose chief seat lay nearby at Mulgrave. For de Burgh and Arthur, see *Coggeshall*, pp. 139–41.

[105] SC1/1/192–3.

[106] *RL*, i, nos. cxxxviii–cxxxix, and see above pp. 157–8.

[107] *AM*, iii, p. 69.

had linked his own fortunes to those of a wider and often more volatile alien presence at court. With the bishop's emissaries passing to and fro across the Channel, there was always the possibility that their activities would be interpreted in a sinister light, particularly if des Roches were inclined to play his cards close to his chest, initiating diplomatic exchanges without fully briefing his already suspicious colleagues. In negotiations with France, des Roches was more a hawk than a dove.[108] But in 1221 tensions in Poitou and Gascony were building to a head.[109] In the past year rumours had circulated that des Roches' kinsman, William des Roches, was planning to marry his daughter into the house of Lusignan, allying the principal family in Poitou to that of the most prominent of Philip Augustus' servants. Des Roches himself had been active in negotiating with William des Roches' son-in-law, Aimery de Craon, who at one time was invited to England as a candidate for the seneschalship of Poitou. Various of Aimery's English lands were held as escheats by the bishop.[110] In the following year, the English possessions of William Marmion, a clerk and presumably a kinsman of des Roches' Norman ward, were seized following his defection to the French.[111]

All of this may explain the background to the rumours of 1221, but it in no way reduces the humiliation to which des Roches' associates were subjected. De Burgh had publicly accused des Roches and his closest allies of treason. Although the charges were almost immediately dropped, we should not underestimate the degree of resentment to which they gave rise. The bishop's return from Compostela was followed by an attempt to patch up relations between the aliens and central government. De Maulay was excused all liability for the £6,000 or more that he had received as sheriff of Somerset, and for the fine of 7,000 marks that he had made for the Fossard barony in 1214. However, Corfe castle was not restored to him, and he was subsequently deprived both of Sherborne castle and the forests of

---

[108] See above pp. 163–4. Mucegros' accusation that the bishop was preparing a ship to take Eleanor abroad, and something of the treason charge with respect to France, may reflect the provisioning of des Roches' vessel at Fareham and his decision to take the opportunity of the pilgrimage to call in at the French coast.

[109] See H. J. Chaytor, *Savaric de Mauléon, Baron and Troubador* (Cambridge 1939), pp. 44–6.

[110] *DD*, nos. 69, 70, 72–5; *Pat. R. 1216–25*, p. 246; *BF*, p. 274; *CRR*, xi, no. 1313. Henry III's mother used the pretext of a threatened alliance between Hugh de Lusignan and a Frenchwoman, presumably William des Roches' daughter, to justify her own controversial betrothal to Hugh; *DD*, no. 84.

[111] C60/17, mm. 5, 6. He is possibly to be identified as William, son of Robert Marmion, for whom see *The Boarstall Cartulary*, ed. H. E. Salter, Oxford Historical Soc. lxxxviii (1930), pp. 13–15.

Dorset and Somerset.[112] Des Roches himself was at last pardoned the demand of 159 marks made against him for the disputed scutage of 1217–18.[113] For the moment, Engelard retained control of Windsor castle and was granted custody of a royal ward.[114] But in October 1221 he was dispatched abroad to assist the defence of Poitou, with des Roches standing as guarantor for his future good conduct.[115]

This was not to restore the *status quo* but merely to provide some compensation to a faction whose position at court had been fundamentally weakened. Under de Burgh's guidance, the regime continued to insist upon the restoration of the crown demesne. In 1221 a reseizure of *terra Normanorum* was entrusted to des Roches' agents in Hampshire, and Norman land taken from the bishop's clerk Geoffrey de Caux was restored.[116] But in June 1222 a second enquiry led to Geoffrey's permanent deprivation, and the removal of custodies on a temporary basis from Engelard de Cigogné, John d'Athée and Walter de Verdun.[117] Engelard was only restored to the keepership of Odiham on the understanding that he would pay an annual rent of £50, effectively cancelling out the £50 pension which he had been paid from the time of his settlement with the earl of Warenne in 1218.[118] Those who had profited most during the early years of the minority had most to lose, as successive resumptions of demesne, forest enquiries and assertions of central authority began to whittle away at their privileges.

From his return to England in the summer of 1221 des Roches was deprived of personal control over the royal household, supervising the issue of less than a dozen household writs and attesting only two over the next three years.[119] His protégés, Peter de Rivallis and Eustace de Greinville, remained in place as wardrobe clerk and steward, but Eustace at least had become more than merely the bishop's placeman. After 1220 he served in tandem with two new stewards, John Russell and Godfrey of Crowcombe, both of whom had played a leading role in the attack upon de Maulay. In 1224 Eustace was to survive the downfall of his former master. No longer was des Roches in a position to shower patronage upon his adherents. His closest supporters had been humbled and his own prestige seriously eroded.

---

[112] *RLC*, i, pp. 466b, 481b–482; *Pat. R. 1216–25*, pp. 321, 324–5.
[113] *PR 5 Henry III*, p. 21.
[114] *RLC*, i, pp. 467b, 470b, and see pp. 494, 497.
[115] *Pat. R. 1216–25*, pp. 303, 313; *RLC*, i, pp. 470b, 471b.
[116] C60/14, m. 2d; *Pat. R. 1216–25*, p. 329.
[117] C60/17, mm. 3, 4; *RLC*, i, p. 499b.
[118] C60/18, m. 10; *RLC*, i, pp. 521b–522.
[119] *RLC*, i, pp. 482b, 500, 526b, 540, 578.

Between July and November 1221 he continued to look to the crusade as an honourable means of escape. Having assumed the cross on 19 September, he undertook a hurried search for funds and retainers.[120] In November he sold his two most valuable wardships to raise cash, secured royal letters exhorting his free tenantry to support his venture, licence to export grain and assistance from the crown in pressuring his debtors.[121] A tallage was imposed by the bishop upon various of his manors, his accounts were audited by the Exchequer, and diplomatic channels were opened up with Germany, perhaps to co-ordinate des Roches' departure with that of the emperor Frederick II.[122] He apparently intended travelling to Damietta in the company of Fawkes de Bréauté and of Peter de Maulay. De Maulay had been pledged to the crusade since at least 1220, and in November 1221 had mortgaged his estates.[123] Yet before they could set sail, news reached England of the collapse of the crusader army in Egypt. Any dreams that des Roches might have had of becoming archbishop of Damietta were dashed.[124]

Henceforth he was forced to reconcile himself to a rapidly deteriorating domestic situation. For the next three years he continued to sit as a baron of the Exchequer and as yet no outright attack was made upon his position in local government.[125] Patronage was still extended to the bishop and his household: custody of a vacancy at Hyde Abbey, benefices and gifts to various of his clerks. But this was patronage over which des Roches possessed no control, crumbs thrown to him from the rich store now controlled by Hubert de Burgh.[126] Of the dozen or so royal writs which des Roches witnessed after 1221, the only regular series was that which sanctioned the Justiciar's pension and perquisites for keeping Dover castle, a telling indication of the bishop's loss of power.[127] Des Roches continued to play some part in diplomacy, particularly in relation to France,

---

[120] *AM*, ii (Winchester, Waverley), pp. 84, 295; *Walter of Coventry*, ii, p. 250, who notes that many of des Roches' *familiares* followed their master's example in taking the cross.

[121] *Pat. R. 1216–25*, pp. 317–19, 326.

[122] *RLC*, i, pp. 465b, 467, 471, and see pp. 522, 522b for further contacts with Germany in 1222. For the tallage, see Ms. 16DR, mm. 4d (aid at Overton), 5d, 11 (tallage at Bishop's Sutton and Knoyle). The rolls for Michaelmas 1221–3 are missing.

[123] *Pat. R. 1216–25*, p. 321; *AM*, iii (Dunstable), p. 75 and see *CRR*, viii, p. 303 for de Maulay's claim to crusading privileges, Easter 1220.

[124] *Coggeshall*, p. 190.

[125] For his work at the Exchequer after 1221, see E368/4, mm. 2(2)d, 3, 3d, 5; E368/5, mm. 12(1)d, 13(1)d.

[126] For Hyde, see C60/17, m. 4; *Pat. R. 1216–25*, p. 333.

[127] *RLC*, i, pp. 495b, 515b, 526b, 573.

where he oversaw the payment of subsidies to the viscount of Thouars, and in June 1222 warranted letters supporting the royal justice, Henry de Pont-Audemer, in a bid to recover family estates in Normandy.[128] As a means of keeping his hand in at court, he continued to advance considerable sums on loan to the crown. But for a man who had formerly controlled the reins of power, his position after 1221 must have seemed peculiarly humiliating.[129]

Within the hierarchy of the church des Roches found himself little better off than in secular government. Gone were the days when he had co-operated with a friendly Roman mission to control elections and to curb the power of his own metropolitan. On his return from pilgrimage in 1221 he carried thirteen Dominican friars into England and encouraged them to seek out archbishop Langton who was impressed by their preaching.[130] By 1224 des Roches had himself established the Dominicans within the city of Winchester.[131] However, such gestures did little to ease his relations with the archbishop. On 19 July 1221 des Roches was present when Pandulph resigned his legation. According to the Dunstable annalist, Langton had secured papal letters guaranteeing that England would be subject to no further legate during his own lifetime, a prospect that can hardly have appealed to des Roches, who had enjoyed far more success in securing papal support than in reconciling himself to Langton.[132] At the Council of Oxford in 1222, Langton asserted his control over the episcopate and the English church.[133] Death also took its toll upon des Roches' clerical allies. William of Cornhill, bishop of Coventry, was paralysed by a stroke in the same month that des Roches took the cross. Hugh of Carlisle and Simon of Exeter died within the next two years, and Richard Marsh was discredited by a bitter dispute with the monks of Durham.[134] Even the younger men, whose promotion in royal service des Roches had encouraged, Ralph de Neville, elected to Chichester, and Eustace de Fauconberg, bishop of London, began to drift away from their former patron. Eustace in particular may have been alienated by des

---

[128] *Pat. R. 1216–25*, p. 333; *RLC*, i, pp. 520, 524b, 525b, 546, 578.

[129] *RLC*, i, pp. 508b, 520, 530b, 531b, 534b, 561b.

[130] *Annales F. Nicholai de Triveti*, ed. T. Hog, English Hist. Soc. (London 1845), p. 209.

[131] Below p. 234.

[132] *Flores Hist.*, ii, pp. 172–3; *AM*, iii (Dunstable), p. 74.

[133] *C. &S.*, i, pp. 100–25.

[134] For Cornhill, see *AM*, ii (Waverley), p. 295; *Cal. Pap. Reg.*, i, p. 91; *Pat. R. 1216–25*, p. 346. Richard Marsh appears to have supported Langton and the clergy against des Roches in 1224; *Foedera*, p. 171.

Roches' new found interest in the monks of Westminster. In the spring of 1222 des Roches served alongside Langton and Richard Poer, confirming Westminster in widespread exemption from the diocesan authority of London.[135] Later that same year, as if to demonstrate the independence of the Westminster monks, he rather than bishop Eustace was chosen to install Westminster's new abbot.[136] Thereafter a serious dispute arose between the abbot's men and the citizens of London. Westminster was stormed by an armed mob, and the abbot was attacked in attempting to seek refuge with Philip de Aubigné. Order was restored only after the leading trouble-makers had been hung and a heavy indemnity imposed upon the commune of London.[137] It is perhaps not surprising that in 1224 Eustace de Fauconberg, bishop of London, was to co-operate freely with Langton and others of his suffragans in excluding des Roches from court.

THE PAPAL LETTERS OF 1223

It is in this context that we must view des Roches' career after 1221. He faced a stark choice: either to sit by as his associates and eventually he himself were swept aside by a hostile church and baronage, or to attempt to arrest the process by some bold new initiative. Here there was one course of action which may have appeared particularly attractive. From the very start of the reign, the question of the king's minority and above all the timing of its end, had stood as a source of potential future discord. Whoever held the initiative when the king came of age would inherit not only the limited powers of patronage exercised during the minority, but the potential to control permanent grants of land and favours, denied since November 1218. There was no certain date at which the king was to come of age. Frederick II, for example, had been declared of age as king of Sicily in 1208 at the age of fourteen – a settlement which had been achieved through the favour of the pope. Like Sicily before 1208, England was considered a papal feoff and its king, a papal ward. Hence, it may have been the Sicilian precedent which persuaded the minority council of Henry III to limit its awards, pending the king's fourteenth birthday. But Henry had reached the age of fourteen in 1221 and still he remained a

---

[135] *Acta*, no. 73.
[136] *Acta*, appendix 3, no. 23.
[137] *AM*, iii (Dunstable), pp. 78–9; *RLC*, i, p. 569; Carpenter, *The Minority*, pp. 290–1, and for the fine see also *CRR*, xv, no. 481; C60/32, m. 4.

minor.[138] He would not reach twenty-one, the most widely accepted definition of adulthood, for another six years. If des Roches could advance the date of the king's majority he might well seize the initiative from de Burgh, and so come to dominate the king's accession to personal sovereignty.

Previous commentators have recognized that just such an attempt was made in April 1223, when the pope was prevailed upon to issue letters releasing Henry from the control of his guardians – similar in many respects to the papal intervention which had speeded the end of Frederick II's minority in 1208.[139] Traditionally the letters of 1223 are considered to have been the work of Langton and the bishops, since in the event it was under Langton's guidance, in close co-operation with de Burgh, that the pope's instructions were implemented.[140] However, David Carpenter has recently offered a far more plausible explanation of events. He has pointed out that in April 1223 there was no real motive for either Langton or de Burgh to seek such a fundamental disruption to the *status quo*; de Burgh was already the king's guardian and Langton was firmly established at the head of the church. Responsibility for any disruption was more likely to rest with a figure who felt his influence declining rather than gaining. In 1239, amongst various charges brought against Hubert de Burgh, was one that he had sent envoys to Rome to have the king declared of age: 'To which he replied that it was not he who sent nuncios to Rome but the bishop of Winchester who sent W(illiam) de St Aubin on that business, more to injure Hubert than for his comfort, so that he and others would deliver up their custodies.'[141] In short, as Carpenter has shown, it was des Roches who procured the papal letters of April 1223, even though, in the event, it was to be de Burgh and the bishops who gained the advantage in their implementation.

There is an anomaly here. At the time when de Burgh's statement suggests that William de St Aubin was busy at the Curia, he was

---

[138] See Carpenter, *The Minority*, pp. 123–4, 241–2.

[139] For the papal letters, see *DD*, no. 243 (*RL*, i, no. ccclviii); Norgate, *The Minority*, pp. 286–90. As yet no satisfactory explanation has been advanced for their peculiar state of preservation in the *Red Book of the Exchequer*.

[140] Carpenter, *The Minority*, pp. 301–6.

[141] Paris, *CM*, vi, p. 69, which gives *W. de Sancto Albano* when the original (BL ms. Cotton Nero D i, f. 168v) clearly reads *Sancto Albino*. It is worth noting that in October 1220, in the lead-up to the king's fourteenth birthday, des Roches' familiars, Humphrey de Millières and Walter de Verdun, had carried letters to Rome, issued under the bishop's authority, which seem to anticipate the king's coming of age; 'Made stronger and advancing in age day by day … we are brought from the ruin of our realm to the happy issue'; *Pat. R. 1216–25*, pp. 267–8.

actually engaged in diplomatic activity in Poitou.[142] St Aubin was a figure who had worked closely with des Roches, and in 1220 received a letter of recommendation to the bishop from cardinal Stephen de Fossanova.[143] Rather than suggest, as David Carpenter has done, that Hubert's memory had failed him over such an important detail, it is possible that St Aubin carried des Roches' petition to the Curia, not in the winter of 1222–23 but several months earlier, in February–March 1222. This particular embassy of St Aubin's was ostensibly managed by de Burgh, who paid the envoys' expenses and witnessed their letters of credence.[144] Nevertheless, St Aubin was accompanied by at least one and possibly two other men with strong ties to des Roches. The first of these, John de Pavilly, had been a guest on the Winchester manors from at least 1219–20. In 1221 he was paid over £2 and given a towel and a cloth during a stay of at least eighty-four days at Taunton castle, being found also at the bishop's manors of Rimpton, Downton, Knoyle and Ivinghoe.[145] Another clerk who may well have travelled with the mission was Robert Passelewe, whose earliest appearance in royal service had been under the auspices of des Roches as an ambassador to Flanders in 1214.[146] Later, he had attracted the attention of the legate Guala who had granted him dispensation, probably to hold two churches with cure of souls.[147] After 1218, he was engaged in near constant travel between England and Rome, delivering Guala's English pension.[148] He was undoubtedly abroad in February 1223, at which time des Roches had temporary charge of the Exchequer, and a note was entered on the memoranda roll stating that Robert Passelewe, whom the sheriff of Suffolk believed dead, was actually alive and in pursuit of the king's business at Rome.[149] Des Roches may well have used the embassy of William de St Aubin and John de Pavilly to communicate his initial proposals to the pope that the king be declared of age. The business then hung fire for the next few months, possibly pursued via Passelewe. In the spring of 1223, it was almost certainly Passelewe

---

[142] *RLC*, i, pp. 518, 541, 541b.
[143] *RLC*, i, pp. 384b, 387, 422b; *Pat. R. 1216–25*, pp. 184, 275; *DD*, no. 99.
[144] *RLC*, i, p. 514; *Pat. R. 1216–25*, p. 328.
[145] Mss. 15DR, mm. 4, 9; 16DR, mm. 9, 10–11, 12.
[146] *RLC*, i, p. 176, and above p. 114.
[147] *Acta Guala*, no. 107; *Rot. Hugh Welles*, i, p. 92, ii, p. 154; *Cal. Pap. Reg.*, i, p. 65. At some time he served as keeper of the vacant see of Ely, perhaps as a deputy for the legate; C60/23, m. 3, and see *RLC*, i, p. 253b.
[148] *RLC*, i, pp. 488, 497, 512b, 546b. For his influence with Guala, see also *DD*, no. 203.
[149] E368/5, m. 13(1)d.

who returned to England bearing the letters requested from pope Honorius.[150]

Unfortunately for des Roches, Passelewe's return coincided with two events which made it impossible to implement the letters against de Burgh. The death of Philip Augustus raised hopes that the new king, Louis VIII, might honour the promise that he had made at the end of the civil war and restore Normandy to the Plantagenets.[151] Secondly, the outbreak of war on the Marches ensured that the English baronage united behind de Burgh to oppose the Welsh.[152] Des Roches himself led a significant contingent of the army against Llywelyn: twenty knights including the alien Aimery de St Amand and William de St John, a rebel during the civil war, whose presence indicates that many of the scars of war had begun to heal. Engelard de Cigogné likewise led a force of twenty-one men, the majority of them recruited from the fees of Wallingford.[153] The bishop's kinsman Hugh des Roches was employed to carry supplies to the new fortifications at Montgomery, and in October des Roches himself stood amongst the witnesses to the Anglo-Welsh truce.[154]

It was only at this late stage that an attempt could be made to activate the papal letters of April 1223. Superficially des Roches continued to enjoy favour at court. At some time after November 1222, he had witnessed a private conveyance granting Hubert de Burgh property in Westminster.[155] In August 1223 he was given custody of the vacant see of Coventry.[156] But even here there are signs of tension, with Langton demanding an increasing say in the administration of the vacancy, anxious to avoid the circumstances of

---

[150] It is possible that a poem by des Roches' protégé, Henry of Avranches (*Henry of Avranches*, ed. Cox Russell, p. 96, no. 77), relates to these events. Passelewe is said to have braved many dangers in negotiating a triple benefit at Rome (*triplicem . . . indultum* or *triplex negotium*, lines 7–8, 15). By doing so he restored the privilege of the clergy that had been expiring miserably, but returned to England a pauper, met by ingratitude from both king and clergy. The poem is allusive but I am inclined to relate it to Passelewe's mission of 1224 for which see below pp. 213–14, 222.

[151] Carpenter, *The Minority*, pp. 309–11.

[152] *Ibid.*, pp. 311–14; R. F. Walker, 'Hubert de Burgh and Wales 1218–1232', *EHR* 87 (1972), pp. 468–76.

[153] C72/3, transcribed by Walker, 'The Anglo-Welsh wars', ch. iii, appendix pp. ii, iii, and see also *RLC*, i, p. 478 for a prest to St John authorized by des Roches.

[154] *Pat. R. 1216–25*, pp. 411, 415, 417; *RLC*, i, pp. 575, 578; MS. 19DR, m. 7d (Hugh des Roches at Highclere and Witney returning from Montgomery).

[155] Westminster Abbey Muniments ms. Westminster Domesday, ff. 347r–v; C52/34, no. 2, in the time of Ralph de Neville as elect of Chichester, Nov. 1222 X April 1224.

[156] C60/18, m. 3; *Pat. R. 1216–25*, p. 382; *RLC*, i, p. 560b. Promotions to the prebends of the vacant see included des Roches' nephew Bartholomew, and Luke, a clerk of de Burgh; *Pat. R. 1216–25*, pp. 383, 386.

the previous election, in which des Roches had assisted the promotion of the courtier, William of Cornhill, as bishop.[157] De Burgh and Langton must already have learned of the papal letters of 13 April and of des Roches' role in their issue. In August 1223 de Burgh sent William de St Aubin and John de Pavilly back to Rome, ostensibly to act over a vacancy at Carlisle, but probably also to undo the work of their previous mission, by obtaining the withdrawal of the letters declaring Henry of age.[158] This they accomplished by 20 November, although pope Honorius admitted his reluctance to withdraw his earlier letters which he had believed to be in line with the king's own wishes.[159] Meanwhile, although the Welsh expedition had boosted the Justiciar's prestige, both in the country at large, and with the king who had been permitted to accompany his guardian on campaign, de Burgh's rise to personal power in the Marches threatened an open revolt by the earl of Chester and his supporters.[160]

It now became apparent to de Burgh and Langton that, far from needing to suppress the papal letters obtained by des Roches, they could in fact use them to annul the king's minority, not in favour of the bishop of Winchester, but to revoke the stranglehold which des Roches and his associates still exercised over local government. By early November the court was in turmoil. On 8 November des Roches secured a writ from de Burgh protesting at Langton's interference in the vacant see of Coventry.[161] But on the following day the Justiciar fled from London taking the king with him into the west. According to the account later given by Fawkes de Bréauté, de Burgh persuaded Henry that there was a plot afoot to seize the realm.[162] Des Roches and his supporters mustered in London and, under the leadership of the earls of Chester and Aumale, Brian de Lisle and Fawkes de Bréauté, an assault was planned on the Tower.[163] But the opposition baulked at the prospect of armed rebellion; Aumale apart, it consisted of men whose loyalty to the

---

157 *Acta Langton*, ed. Major, pp. 78–83, no. 61. Cornhill had been paralysed since 1221. He died in August 1223, but had been made to resign his see into the hands of the archbishop two months earlier; *Regesta Honorii III*, ed. Pressutti, no. 4317; C60/18, m. 5 where in June 1223 the bishopric is said to be *in manu* corrected to *sub regimine* of the archbishop.

158 *Pat. R. 1216–25*, p. 408; *RLC*, i, pp. 558b, 583.

159 *RL*, i, p. 539, no. 14; *Cal. Pap. Reg.*, i, pp. 93–4.

160 Carpenter, *The Minority*, pp. 314–19.

161 *RLC*, i, p. 629.

162 *Walter of Coventry*, ii, p. 261, and see Carpenter, *The Minority*, pp. 318–19.

163 *AM*, iii (Dunstable), p. 83 and for independent evidence of an attack on the Tower, see the accounts for rebuilding the surrounding palisade; *RLC*, i, p. 579.

Plantagenets had carried them safely through the storms of the past two decades. Whatever their common hatred for de Burgh, they were united far more by a shared tradition of service to the crown. Summoned to attend the king on 4 December, the ringleaders, including the earl of Chester, John de Lacy, Robert de Vieuxpont and Engelard de Cigogné shied away from the prospect of civil war.[164] Already two men upon whom des Roches might have counted for support, William Brewer and Eustace de Fauconberg, had openly sided with de Burgh. Brewer's nephew had been promoted to the see of Exeter late in November 1223, whilst Eustace was entrusted by the Justiciar with the defence of Colchester castle.[165]

The meeting of 4 December appears to have passed off without incident. Des Roches was granted the living of Henley to confer upon whomever he wished. Over the next few days his nephew, Hugh, continued to receive safe conducts in carrying supplies to Montgomery.[166] However, if the Dunstable annalist is to be trusted, the following week witnessed a prophetic outburst of temper between des Roches and the Justiciar. In the midst of a council, de Burgh charged the bishop with being a traitor to the king and his realm, asserting that whatever evil had been brought about over the past twenty years was directly attributable to the malice of des Roches. Responding in kind, des Roches swore that if he had to spend everything he possessed, he would make sure that de Burgh was toppled from power. Rising up with his supporters, he stormed out of the chamber amidst the hushed whispers of those assembled.[167] The chronicler's account may be exaggerated, but it nevertheless reveals the stigma still attached to des Roches' service under King John and suggests, too, the depth of personal hatred that was to envenom relations between des Roches and de Burgh for the remainder of their lives.

The immediate cause of de Burgh's outburst may have been the opposition's decision, in the teeth of protests from Langton and the church, to send Robert Passelewe and Robert of Kent to Rome, almost certainly to secure direct papal intervention and the appoint-

---

[164] *Pat. R. 1216–25*, pp. 481–2. The council was to meet at the London Temple, but the enrolment is wrongly given as a summons to Gloucester.

[165] *Pat. R. 1216–25*, pp. 415–17. Brewer joined de Burgh's court at Gloucester; *RLC*, i, p. 575b. In July 1223 his men were accused of killing a parker at des Roches' manor of Merdon; *RLC*, i, p. 555b, and see above p. 190 for pre-existing tensions with the bishop.

[166] *Pat. R. 1216–25*, pp. 416–17; *RLC*, i, p. 578.

[167] *AM*, iii, p. 84.

ment of a legate over the head of the archbishop.[168] In addition, des Roches sent a personal spokesman, Master John of Limoges, who on 18 January obtained papal letters admonishing the king to bear in mind des Roches' many years of faithful service, to cease infringements of the liberties of the see of Winchester which was placed under the pope's protection, and to permit des Roches or his representatives to travel freely to Rome to discuss the forthcoming crusade.[169] Like King John before him, anxious to bolster his own, weakening position in English politics, des Roches was adept at playing upon the pope's anxieties for the future of the crusade.

Meanwhile an attempt by the bishop and his associates to stage a rival Christmas court at Leicester had been followed by reluctant surrender.[170] In the first week of January 1224, des Roches followed the example of Fawkes, Chester and the rest of the opposition in relinquishing his royal custodies, the county of Hampshire and the castles of Winchester, Portchester and Southampton.[171] A fortnight later he was deprived of custody of the see of Coventry, which passed to a clerk associated with the bishops of Lincoln, Salisbury and London.[172] It was these same bishops, together with bishop Jocelin of Bath, who now came forwards to assume custody of royal castles and demesne. Des Roches' old rival, Richard Poer, was given control of Hampshire.[173] De Burgh emerged victorious. His own supporters were rapidly installed in the localities, replacing the supposedly neutral bishops. At the same time, the opposition was subject to considerable realignment and defection. By no means all of the aliens were cast into outer darkness. Des Roches' fellow Tourangeau, Philip Mark, was left in place for a further year as sheriff of Nottingham; Philip de Aubigné and Hugh de Vivonne appear to have sided with de Burgh.[174] There is more than a little

---

[168] *Walter of Coventry*, ii, pp. 262–3.

[169] *Ibid.*, p. 263; *RL*, i, no. cxciv; Ms 19DR, m. 12, where Master John was received at Southwark either going to or returning from Rome.

[170] Carpenter, *The Minority*, pp. 319–25.

[171] *Pat. R. 1216–25*, p. 420.

[172] C60/20, m. 7; *RLC*, i, pp. 578, 583, 585b. For Master Michael Belet, see also Emden, *Biographical Register*, i, p. 159; *Reg. St Osmund*, ii, p. 30; *Sarum Charters*, p. 123; *Records of Merton Priory*, ed. A. Heales (Oxford 1898), p. 85. He was the brother-in-law of des Roches' familiar, Walter of Verdun, and hence related to Aimery de St Amand; BL ms. Add. 47784 (Coxford cartulary), f. 10v.

[173] E372/68, m. 1. No account for Hampshire was possible at Michaelmas 1224 or on the roll 7 Henry III. For the final date of account, see E159/7, m. 8. For Bartholomew de Kemsey, the new sheriff, bishop Poer's steward, see *Reg. St Osmund*, i, p. 318; Salisbury Cathedral D. & C. ms. Press IV Ramsbury C3/2.

[174] Holt, 'Philip Mark', pp. 23–4; *Foedera*, p. 171.

irony to the fact that it was the Paris educated bishops, Langton, Poer and their companions in foreign exile between 1209 and 1213, who spearheaded the removal of aliens from office. According to Fawkes de Bréauté, in the summer of 1224 Langton preached a sermon in which he described the aliens as 'the scourge of all native men, to whom the whole people of England was given as booty ... Take care that the aliens (*extranei*) no longer act against you.' Yet, ironically, at the very moment of his triumph, the archbishop had secured permission to seek the return to England of his brother Simon, the most avid supporter of Louis' and the French invasion force of 1216.[175]

There are signs that des Roches faced defections even closer to home. Amongst his closest associates, Eustace de Greinville remained as steward of the royal household and the bishop's deputy sheriff, William of Shorwell, transferred for a while to the service of Jocelin of Bath as under-sheriff of Wiltshire and Somerset.[176] Nor was the seizure of demesne followed by permanent deprivation for Engelard de Cigogné, whose pension was restored in January 1224.[177] Yet, however much the new regime might seek to calm fears of factional reprisal, it was inevitable that des Roches would be excluded from the higher counsels of state. The bishop had cause to suspect that his removal from local government would lead to wide-ranging erosions of his episcopal liberties. The Winchester pipe rolls show that, probably before Christmas 1223, the bishop had dispatched knights and 3,000 crossbow bolts to Winchester castle; Farnham castle was munitioned and a professional garrison installed there for sixteen days, whilst a roll of arms for Taunton suggests that military preparations extended throughout the bishop's lands.[178] In the event, however, it was not des Roches but the Norman adventurer Fawkes de Bréauté whose suspicions of the new regime forced a resort to arms.

THE SIEGE OF BEDFORD

Like the rebellious earl of Aumale, Fawkes de Bréauté had never been amongst the inner circle of des Roches' familiars. He had last appeared

---

[175] *Walter of Coventry*, ii, pp. 268–9; *RLC*, i, p. 630b; F. A. Gasquet, *Henry the Third and the Church* (London 1910), pp. 112–13.

[176] *RLC*, ii, pp. 13, 22b, 25b, 86b, 87b; E159/8, m. 3; E368/8, m. 6; E368/9, m. 5d.

[177] *RLC*, i, pp. 581, 582, 585b, 595b; ii, pp. 6b, 15, 18, 87, and see *Pat. R. 1216–25*, p. 496. In 1225 he accompanied Richard of Cornwall to Gascony; *Pat. R. 1216–25*, p. 513.

[178] Ms. 19DR, mm. 4d, 11.

as a guest on the Winchester manors during the civil war.[179] Only with the change of atmosphere at court after 1221 had he been brought closer to the bishop, as a mutual opponent of de Burgh. In the aftermath of des Roches' dismissal as the king's guardian, Fawkes had planned to accompany the bishop on crusade, and in 1222–3 it had been Fawkes' clerk, Robert Passelewe, who seems to have acted as the bishop's go-between with Rome. Exactly a month after issuing his controversial letters of April 1223, pope Honorius appointed des Roches, the abbot and the prior of Dorchester to hear the complaints of Fawkes' brother, William de Bréauté, who objected to the handling of a matrimonial suit by the bishop of Lincoln and other judges delegate.[180] William had been granted the widow of John de Wahull in marriage, and had successfully recovered her dower lands from the barony of Wahull, in which des Roches too had acquired some unspecified interest. Thereafter William was harassed by William de Talbot, who claimed a previous betrothal to John's widow, and encouraged attacks upon one of her kinsmen, a Hampshire knight named Roger de Merlay.[181] The case is inadequately documented, but it nevertheless suggests friendly relations between des Roches and Fawkes' kin: relations that must have proved particularly embarrassing in 1224, when William de Bréauté kidnapped a royal justice, barricaded himself inside Bedford castle and forced the regime to cancel a proposed expedition to Poitou, in order to effect his removal.[182]

There is no evidence that des Roches encouraged Bréauté's rebellion. As during Aumale's revolt of 1221, des Roches actively participated in the siege of Bedford and in the south-west sent men and siege engines from Taunton to further the attack upon Fawkes' garrison at Stogursey.[183] Once again, however, as in 1221 during the attack upon Aumale, he found himself excluded from royal counsels. Piqued by his rejection he withdrew from Bedford, as did Peter de

---

[179] Ms. 13DR, mm. 12, 12d, and see *The Manuscripts of the Duke of Rutland at Belvoir Castle*, iv (Historical Manuscripts Commission 1905), pp. 55–6, where *c.* 1218 des Roches witnessed a settlement between Fawkes and his parents-in-law, Warin fitz Gerald and Alice de Courcy.

[180] SC7/50/7, printed Prynne, *Records*, iii, pp. 53–4, and see Sayers, *Honorius III*, pp. 238–9, no. 31.

[181] See *CRR*, x, p. 99, xi, nos. 702, 1362; *A Calender of the Feet of Fines for Bedfordshire*, ed. G. H. Fowler, Bedfordshire Historical Record Society vi (1919), p. 61, no. 252, and above p. 193. For Merlay, see *Acta*, no. 64.

[182] Carpenter, *The Minority*, pp. 351–5, where Carpenter finds no substance to Fawkes' claims of a deliberate plot to summon an army against Bedford on the pretext of an expedition to Poitou.

[183] Ms. 19DR, mm. 8d, 9, 11. Des Roches was granted quittance from the Bedford scutage; E372/68, m. 1d.

Maulay and the earl of Chester.[184] During the siege the papal letters of December 1223 arrived in England, solicited by de Burgh before he had realized the potential advantages of ending the king's minority, rescinding the letters of April and demanding that their custodies be restored to de Burgh, des Roches and Chester. Langton dismissed these new letters as no longer appropriate to the king's circumstances and, in writing to the pope, the king was made to declare that des Roches and Chester had voluntarily withdrawn from court.[185] Although this was a less than candid account of events, des Roches had good cause to be thankful that Langton stood as a moderating influence between himself and de Burgh. Fearing that the papal letters guaranteeing his liberties would be ignored, des Roches issued an excommunication in full synod against all who disturbed the rights of the church.[186] At some time in 1224, archbishop Langton issued a general confirmation of the possessions and liberties of the priory of St Swithun's Winchester, des Roches' cathedral chapter. So far as can be established, this is the first time that the Winchester monks had sought such letters from Canterbury. Des Roches, like earlier bishops of Winchester, would have regarded the protection of his cathedral and its monks as very much his own, private responsibility, and hence may well have resented any intrusion by Langton.[187] To this extent, however well-intentioned, Langton's actions are unlikely to have been welcomed by des Roches. It was to another of the archbishop's allies, Eustace de Fauconberg bishop of London, that the council gave charge of the captive Fawkes de Bréauté. Eustace's appointment may well reflect his former close relationship with des Roches, although he is said to have scorned Fawkes' self-pitying protestations of repentance. Nonetheless, Fawkes escaped lightly compared to the fate of his garrison at Bedford, most of whom were hanged following the castle's surrender.[188] These summary executions help us to appreciate

---

[184] *AM*, iii (Dunstable), p. 87. De Maulay, Chester, Robert de Vieuxpont and Engelard de Cigogné were all granted writs *de scutagio habendo* after attending at Bedford; C72/4, mm. 1–2d. According to a Peterborough cartulary, it was at the siege that des Roches and de Burgh were consulted over the military service owing from Peterborough Abbey; CUL ms. Peterborough D. & C. 1, f. 270r.

[185] *RL*, i, no. cxcix.

[186] *AM*, ii (Winchester), p. 84. *C. & S.*, i, p. 125 attempts to link this excommunication to the issue of des Roches' diocesan statutes, but it seems far more likely to have been politically motivated.

[187] Winchester Cathedral Library ms. , The Book of John Chase (List of the Winchester muniments *c.* 1640) f. 4v; *1224 Nota carta confirmationis archiepiscopi Cant' priori Winton' edit. cum munibus* (sic). The charter itself no longer survives.

[188] Paris, *CM*, iii, p. 87; *Hist. Ang. Min.*, ii, pp. 265–6.

the depth of the hatred engendered over the previous eighteen months, and reflect a widespread conviction that the siege had led directly to the loss of Poitou. Side-tracked from their planned continental expedition, Henry and de Burgh had been powerless to prevent Louis VIII from accepting the homage of the lords of Thouars and La Marche.[189] In 1224, perhaps in an attempt to arrest such defections, des Roches himself received representatives of the arch-bishop of Bordeaux and the master of the Paris Temple. But like his political rivals, the bishop was in no position to influence events in Poitou.[190] Once again, the Capetians took advantage of a domestic political crisis in England to stamp their authority ever more firmly upon the former Plantagenet lands in France. Ironically, it was the aliens such as Fawkes de Bréauté and Peter des Roches, the men most keenly committed to the reconquest of the Plantagenet dominion, who, by stirring up political trouble in England, allowed the Capetians free rein in Poitou.

The defection of the count of Thouars may have come as a particularly bitter blow to des Roches, who had worked for several years to cement the count's loyalty. It was another, even closer associate of the bishop, Savaric de Mauléon, who was blamed most widely for the collapse of 1224. As seneschal it was he who abandoned La Rochelle to the French, apparently because he despaired of obtaining support from across the Channel.[191] In the aftermath, des Roches may have offered him sanctuary in England; the Winchester pipe roll for 1224-5 records the presence of Savaric's men at Waltham and Fareham, and of des Roches' servants sent to greet the arrival of Savaric himself.[192] A French chronicler claims that Savaric did indeed cross to England, but that he found so many enemies there that he was forced to flee.[193]

DISGRACE 1224-1227

Like his erstwhile allies in France, des Roches could expect no easy reconciliation with the court. The loosening of his stranglehold over local government meant that for the first time since his election, the

[189] Carpenter, *The Minority*, pp. 370-5.
[190] Ms. 19DR, m. 12, and see *DD*, no. 139.
[191] See Chaytor, *Savaric de Mauléon*, pp. 49-53; *AM*, iii (Dunstable), p. 91, and for Thouars see above p. 207.
[192] Mss. 19DR, mm. 2, 4d, 9d; 20DR, mm. 7d, 8.
[193] The Chronicle of William de Nangis, in Bouquet, *Recueil*, xx, pp. 762-3, and see *RLC*, i, p. 627b.

bishop was subject to the full authority of the law. Over the past ten years des Roches had made widespread incursions upon the royal forest, claiming the support of the charter of liberties that he had been granted by King John in 1208. After 1224 the new regime threatened to revoke this earlier charter, by reimposing the forest regard upon the episcopal estates. In September 1224 a special enquiry was appointed to investigate des Roches' alienations and assarts, distinct from the circuit of the forest eyre dispatched to Hampshire.[194] The records of these enquiries are lost, whilst the plea rolls of the Bench note only one action touching the bishop's administration of the forests, against an unspecified assart in Hampshire.[195] However, between 1224 and 1227 the Winchester pipe rolls record a stream of entertainments for royal foresters, suggesting an attempt to reduce the impact of hostile enquiries. Before Michaelmas 1224 the bishop's officers were sent against the regard at Overton, Farnham and Wargrave, and des Roches' clerk, Robert de Clinchamps, was dispatched to prohibit the regard altogether at Downton (*pro regardo prohibendo*). Foresters were regaled with gifts at Taunton and six quarters of grain were presented to Hugh de Neville, the king's chief forester, at Sandleford near Burghclere, where the extension of the episcopal demesne at Woodhay had threatened an invasion of the county boundary into the neighbouring Berkshire manor of Kintbury, held by the prioress of Nuneaton.[196] Neville subsequently received gifts from the bishop's officers at three or four manors, taking the regard or pleas of the forest.[197] In 1224–5 des Roches' steward attended forest pleas at Wilton, and the dean of Winchester oversaw perambulations of the forest at Overton and Highclere.[198]

Beyond his forest offences, the bishop was undoubtedly subject to a barrage of complaints from civil litigants. The records of the eyre of 1227–8 tell us nothing of des Roches beyond the names and amercements of various of his tenants, but meanwhile the plea rolls of the Bench, the Winchester pipe rolls and the records of various assizes headed by Martin of Pattishall, show something of the extent to which des Roches' abuses of power were subject to correction.[199] In

---

[194] *RLC*, i, pp. 633, 655b.
[195] *CRR*, xii, no. 12.
[196] Ms. 19DR, mm. 4d, 5, 6, 7, 9, 11. For the case at Woodhay, see *CRR*, xii, nos. 1102, 1565; Ms. 20DR, mm. 11d, 15; JUST1/36, m. 9, and see *RLC*, i, p. 615b, for reports of an attack made by des Roches' men upon a royal servant.
[197] Ms. 20DR, mm. 1d, 2, 8, 14, and see Mss. 21DR, m. 5; 22DR, m. 2.
[198] Ms. 20DR, mm. 1, 2, 11, 11d.
[199] For the eyre amercements, see E372/72, m. 7d.

1225 the bishop's principal attorney, John of Herriard, attended justices sitting at Wilton, Reading, Ilchester and Oxford as well as the county court at Bedford.[200] Subsequently members of the bishop's household travelled to hearings at Chichester and Dunstable.[201] In 1225 Herriard was present 'when Martin of Pattishall took pleas of gaol delivery and novel disseisin' at Ilchester.[202] The surviving records of this assize contain serious accusations against des Roches and his men. One member of his household at Taunton was said to have harboured thieves.[203] Furthermore, the constable of Taunton, Ralph de Meriet, and des Roches' reeve, William Bullock, had imprisoned a pair of reputed criminals without releasing them to the sheriff of Somerset. When one of the men escaped, des Roches' constable kidnapped the wife and son of a kinsman suspected of harbouring the fugitive, broke open the kinsman's deed box and carried off his charters. The woman and child were then kept in chains for a month. Despite many offers to stand bail, des Roches would only release them if John de Briwes would give him a charter surrendering all his lands to the bishop should the hostages fail to attend the bishop's summons.[204] Unfortunately this Somerset roll is unmatched by evidence for hearings within des Roches' former jurisdiction as sheriff of Hampshire.[205] The bishop clearly attached considerable importance to the assizes of 1225 since their principal agent, Martin of Pattishall, was treated to a stream of gifts and entertainments.[206] In 1224–5, at Pattishall's orders, des Roches sent a prisoner in fetters from the episcopal gaol at Farnham to London.[207] The bishop himself sought Pattishall's advice over a complicated question relating to the law of

---

[200] Ms. 20DR, mm. 2, 4, 10d, 11d, 13–14d.

[201] Ms. 22DR, mm. 5d, 7, 13d.

[202] Ms. 20DR, m. 4.

[203] *Somerset Pleas*, ed. Chadwyck-Healey, xi (1897), p. 85, no. 371.

[204] *Ibid.* , pp. 33–6, esp. nos. 122, 132.

[205] Besides the roll for Somerset, the assize records survive for Berkshire (JUST1/36) and Surrey (JUST1/863). In 1225 special justices were appointed under the presidency of Martin of Pattishall to hear cases of novel disseisin in the localities. One such panel was assigned to Hampshire, although it appears, from the absence of final concords, that this assize never actually met; *CRR*, xii, pp. xi–xiii; *RLC*, ii, p. 76b. A settlement preserved as Winchester Cathedral Library ms. Allchin Scrapbook II, f. 2 no. 6 (*Acta*, appendix 2, no. 26), claims to have been drawn up at Winchester in 1225, in the presence of Eustace de Fauconberg, Henry de Greinville and Martin of Pattishall *tunc iusticiarii domini regis*. However, as it stands, the text is a blatant forgery.

[206] Mss. 20DR, mm. 1d, 13, 14; 21DR, m. 8d; 22DR, mm. 6d,11d.

[207] Ms. 19DR, m. 4d; JUST1/863, m. 5d, and see Ms. 20DR, m. 15 for one of the bishop's officers consulting Pattishall at Southwark.

dower.[208] As chief justice, Pattishall presided over a large number of suits against des Roches; demands for restoration of wards, accusations of disseisin and pleas which touched upon the bishop's diocesan administration.

In one such case des Roches was accused of sending his official to St Thomas' hospital, Southwark. Obtaining the keys to the hospital treasury under threat of excommunication, the official had carried off whatever charters he cared to lay hands on, including bonds which, according to the London husting court, entitled the crown merchant Henry of St Albans to £52, owed for grain sold to the hospital. Des Roches had played a major role in the refoundation of St Thomas' after 1213, yet here he would appear to have over-reached his role as patron.[209] Equally instructive is a plea entered in 1224, by which Geoffrey de Lisle sought the return of an heiress he declared illegally detained by the bishop. The girl, daughter of Baldwin Esturmy, was maintained at Farnham castle for more than fifty weeks in 1224–5, despite royal orders that she be released to de Lisle.[210] In answering this charge, it is remarkable to find des Roches, once the opponent of Magna Carta and government by consent, claiming that he had been deprived of the heiress illegally, against the terms of the Charter, *per voluntatem*.[211] As with the forest concessions wrung from Brewer in 1218, it would appear that des Roches was prepared to make use of the charters of liberties whenever it suited his private interest. Ironically it was to be his own connivance in just such disseisins *per voluntatem* that was to be one of the principal accusations brought against des Roches and his regime of 1232–4.

In the immediate term, des Roches' fall was accompanied by an upsurge of litigation against him. Few if any of the escheats and wardships he held from the crown remained to him after 1224.[212] Nevertheless, of the actions brought against him, only a handful were decided in favour of the plaintiff. No lasting damage was inflicted

---

[208] *Henrici de Bracton de Legibus et Consuetudinibus Angliae*, ed. T. Twiss, 6 vols. (RS 1879–83), iv, p. 499. Perhaps related to *CRR*, xi, no. 1037 (*Bracton's Note Book*, no. 533), a case of 1223. Cannot relate to a dower case involving des Roches' official; *CRR*, xiii, no. 1609 (*Bracton's Note Book*, no. 324), considered by C. A. F. Meekings, 'Martin Pateshull and William de Raleigh', *BIHR* 26 (1953), p. 170, which fails to take into account des Roches' absence on crusade 1227–31.

[209] *CRR*, xi, nos. 2122, 2499.

[210] Mss. 19DR, m. 4d; 20DR, m. 9d; *RLC*, ii, p. 6.

[211] *CRR*, xi, no. 2384.

[212] See for example the Craon lands which des Roches had held since at least 1219 (above p. 204), which in 1224 passed to Ralph de Neville; *RLC*, ii, p. 6b (which also details losses by Peter de Maulay).

upon the liberties of his see. Des Roches himself continued to command vast territorial resources. He seems at first to have pinned his hopes upon the papacy. Before the siege of Bedford, he had considered visiting Rome in person. Thereafter his agent, Master John of Limoges, was active alongside Robert Passelewe in pressing the cause of Fawkes de Bréauté and in petitioning for the dispatch of a papal legate.[213] Both Passelewe and Master John had been banished from England in 1224; Passelewe's benefices were seized on the pretext of a debt of 10,000 marks which he was said to owe for the vacancy receipts of the see of Ely.[214] Des Roches was ordered to cease association with Master John of Limoges, who nevertheless continued his activities at the Curia, and by the summer of 1225 had secured letters favourable to de Bréauté, which he carried to the papal legate in France.[215] At home, des Roches remained in close contact with the principal lay opponent of de Burgh, the earl of Chester, who in 1224–5 was entertained on half a dozen of the bishop's manors.[216]

At the same time des Roches appears to have done his best to ingratiate himself with the new regime. Loyalty to the crown had long been one of the guiding principles behind the bishop's political career; loyalty that was unaffected by his removal from court. Responding to events in France, the king had dispatched his brother Richard, hastily created count of Poitou, together with the earl of Salisbury, to salvage what they could from the *débâcle* in Poitou and Gascony. The bishop of Winchester advanced a loan of 1,000 marks towards their expedition, more than twice the sum contributed by bishop Jocelin of Bath, one of the closest adherents of the new order at court.[217] Des Roches' manors supplied timber and over 300 quarters of grain to the army, albeit in expectation of payment, and in August 1225 the bishop himself oversaw the dispatch of treasure ships from Portsmouth. Reporting his actions in obsequious terms, he declared his intention to remain by the coast, so that he might transmit to the court whatever news reached him from overseas.[218]

The principal source of finance for this expedition was the grant of a tax of a fifteenth, made in the first months of 1225, in return for a

---

[213] *DD*, no. 182 and see above pp. 213–14.
[214] *RLC*, ii, pp. 55b–56; C60/23, m. 3, and see also *RLC*, ii, pp. 6, 17b.
[215] *RLC*, i, p. 632b; *DD*, no. 182.
[216] Ms. 20DR, mm. 1, 7, 7d, 8d.
[217] *Foreign Accounts*, p. 52; *RLC*, ii, p. 26b, and see *Pat. R. 1216–25*, p. 543.
[218] *DD*, no. 180; *RL*, i, no. ccxix. For grain, see Ms. 20DR, mm. 2, 8–9. For timber, see *RLC*, ii, p. 19.

reissue of the charters of liberties to which both des Roches and Peter de Maulay stood witness.[219] In the previous year the bishop had already been persuaded to contribute to a clerical aid voted towards the siege of Bedford.[220] Nevertheless, the fifteenth of 1225 remains the first direct taxation for which we have incontrovertible evidence of payment by des Roches. Collection on the Winchester estates was under way before Easter, headed by the bishop's attorney John of Herriard and the Hampshire knight, Hugh of Wingham.[221] In general, the assessment of the fifteenth was lenient. Taken in the spring rather than at harvest time, it failed to take account of the true value of many estates.[222] The payments recorded, manor by manor, on the Winchester pipe rolls, suggest that rather than a fifteenth, the tax produced between a twentieth and a thirtieth of the net manorial profits released to the bishop's Exchequer at Michaelmas 1225. At Taunton, for example, the tax levied was £12 and seven pence, against a net release to the bishop's treasury of £656. The total of just over £130 recorded on the Winchester rolls fails to take into account manors where no tax is recorded or where the relevant entries are illegible. Nevertheless, it can amount to little more than a thirtieth of gross manorial income which by the late 1220s was approaching £4,000 a year.[223] This figure of £130 must be treated with caution. It is, for example, far lower than the £710 accounted to the diocese of Winchester by the central collectors of the tax, who lumped together episcopal and monastic contributions.[224] At the same time, des Roches was hardly the man to offer a higher contribution than was strictly necessary. It is suggestive that, even after the payment of £710 from the bishop and the religious combined, his see ranked only sixth in the list of contributing bishoprics, although leaving aside monastic wealth, the manorial income of Winchester was far higher than that

---

[219] Stubbs, *Select Charters*, pp. 350–1. For the tax in general, see Mitchell, *Studies in Taxation*, pp. 159–69; F. A. Cazel, 'The fifteenth of 1225', *BIHR* 34 (1961), pp. 67–81.

[220] *Pat. R. 1216–25*, pp. 464–5; *RLC*, i, p. 612b, but note that no precise contribution is listed for des Roches, unlike those for other clerics; *Pat. R. 1216–25*, pp. 465–512.

[221] *Pat. R. 1216–25*, p. 571; Ms 20DR *passim*. Hugh of Wingham held land of the bishopric of Winchester, although he was not amongst des Roches' inner circle of *familiares; Reg. Pontissara*, p. 388, and see Ms. 14DR, m. 12d, where in 1218/19 he was respited 10 shillings of scutage. He witnesses at least one charter of bishop Jocelin of Bath, which might suggest that he was appointed as assessor of the tax within the see of Winchester, at Jocelin's insistence; Oxford, Corpus Christi College muniments ms. C5 Cap. 11(1) 1–13 (1 August 1226).

[222] Cazel, 'The fifteenth of 1225', pp. 69–70.

[223] Titow, 'Land and population', p. 68a which calculates the receipts for 1224 as £3,755 gross, £3,066 net, and for 1227 at £4,917 gross, £3,585 net.

[224] *Foreign Accounts*, pp. 56, 61.

of several bishops whose sees paid more in tax.[225] The case is unproven. Des Roches' contributions may have erred on the side of parsimony but at least he imposed the fifteenth, by contrast to the earl of Chester for whom no payments are recorded.[226] At one time, des Roches' house in Southwark was appointed collecting-house for the tax, although this order was subsequently cancelled in favour of the London Temple.[227]

The collection of the fifteenth coincided with the arrival in England of the papal nuncio Otto, dispatched from Rome in response to lobbying by Robert Passelewe and Master John of Limoges.[228] The pope baulked at appointing a fully fledged legate over the head of archbishop Langton. Otto came merely as a nuncio, empowered to press the cause of Fawkes de Bréauté. Des Roches entertained him and his men at Twyford and at Farnham, in the company of Langton and various unnamed earls and clerics.[229] According to one source, in the autumn of 1225, it was Otto who effected a reconciliation between des Roches and the king, suggesting that despite his domestic, political disgrace, the bishop continued to command the confidence and support of the papacy.[230] In January 1226 des Roches sent representatives to a council convened by Otto, intended to discuss a proposal that the papal Curia be financed by the allocation of benefices in perpetuity in every diocese across Europe.[231] But like Otto's recommendations in respect to Fawkes de Bréauté, these discussions came to nothing. Beyond reconciling des Roches to the court, Otto accomplished little save the enforcement of procurations.[232]

Des Roches' rehabilitation was less than dramatic. He may have

---

[225] Cazel, 'The fifteenth of 1225', p. 72.

[226] *Ibid.* , p. 71, which fails to note the extortions recorded in lieu of the fifteenth by Wendover, *Flores*, iv, pp. 138–9, which explain the absence of the city of London from the account of 1225.

[227] *RLC*, ii, pp. 73b–76.

[228] In general, see *C & S*, i, pp. 155–8. For attempts to prevent him from crossing to England, see *DD*, no. 185; *RL*, i, nos. ccxxi–ccxxiii, and note too the caution shown by the regime in granting away Fawkes' former custodies, returnable to Fawkes should the pope demand it; *RLC*, ii, p. 27.

[229] Ms. 20DR, mm. 6d, 9d, 10. A Roman clerk, possibly to be identified with Otto, was presented with food at Bishop's Sutton, and in 1225/6 a payment of one mark was made to a 'J. the Roman clerk' at Farnham; Mss. 20DR, m. 6; 21DR, m. 5.

[230] *Reg. St Osmund*, ii, p. 40.

[231] Ms. 21DR, m. 14, and see *C & S*, i, p. 155; Powicke, *Henry III*, pp. 346–9.

[232] Paris, *CM*, ii, pp. 105–10, confirmed by *Reg. St Osmund*, i, pp. 371–3, which also gives an enquiry by Otto into proofs of dispensation for pluralism. Otto did manage to win minor concessions on behalf of the exiled Robert Passelewe; *RLC*, ii, p. 97b; *Pat. R. 1216–25*, p. 553. He also brought information on the crusade; below pp. 233–4.

been spared a full-scale attack upon his liberties, but from December 1223 until his return from crusade in 1231, he witnessed no executive orders on behalf of the crown. On occasion he was called upon to vouch for past financial transactions, but the position he had held for roughly twenty years as a baron of the Exchequer appears to have been forfeit, together with his influence over both central and local government.[233] Despite his attempts to assist with the Gascon expedition of 1225, his interventions in diplomatic affairs were relatively muted. In 1225–6 he entertained Godfrey of Crowcombe and Henry of Cornhill, chancellor of St Paul's, both of them active in supplying funds to the English army across the Channel.[234] In 1226–7 the archbishop of York and Walter Mauclerk, bishop of Carlisle, were entertained at Fareham, almost certainly in the course of a mission to France.[235] The death of Louis VIII in 1226 was once again to hold out the promise of a Plantagenet reconquest overseas. Together with nine other bishops, in December 1226, des Roches issued letters guaranteeing new alliances with the Poitevin houses of Thouars and Lusignan, and in the same year resumed his contacts with Geoffrey de Thouars, treasurer of Poitiers.[236] In the final few days before des Roches set out on crusade in the summer of 1227, a reconciliation was effected between Henry III and Savaric de Mauléon.[237] Savaric appears as the bishop's guest at Farnham in 1226–7, and is said to have accompanied des Roches on the first stages of his journey to the Holy Land.[238] The bishop's familiar, Master Humphrey de Millières, was shortly afterwards sent to ensure the restoration of Savaric's lands in France.[239] Meanwhile, des Roches kept up his contacts with the Norman baronage. In December 1226 he stood pledge for the restoration of the lands of Richard de Harcourt, like Robert de Marmion a Norman who sought to preserve his territorial interests on both sides of the Channel.[240]

On occasion des Roches was called upon to witness settlements

---

[233] *RLC*, ii, pp. 4b–5, 110b; *Foreign Accounts*, pp. 43–5. He does not appear as a baron of the Exchequer after 1223 in the Memoranda Rolls or in the valuable lists printed by Heales, *Records of Merton Priory*, pp. 85, 87.

[234] Ms. 21DR, m. 13, and see *Pat. R. 1225–32*, pp. 35, 63, 90–1.

[235] Ms. 22DR, m. 8, and see *Pat. R. 1225–32*, pp. 107, 135; *AM*, iii (Dunstable), p. 103.

[236] *Acta*, no. 128; Ms. 22DR, m. 13 (messenger from the treasurer of Poitiers at Southwark).

[237] *Pat. R. 1225–32*, p. 128, and see Chaytor, *Savaric de Mauléon*, pp. 54–6.

[238] Ms. 22DR, m. 5; BL ms. Cotton Faustina Bi (Winchcombe annals), f. 27v; *AM*, i (Tewesbury), p. 70.

[239] *RLC*, ii, pp. 215–215b.

[240] *RLC*, ii, pp. 141, 142b, 160–160b, 162b, and see Powicke, *Loss of Normandy*, pp. 342–3; Jouet, *Et la Normandie devint Française*, pp. 81, 83.

between the crown and leading magnates.[241] The king himself was several times entertained on the Winchester estates.[242] With the final lifting of Henry's minority, during the first six months of 1227, des Roches made numerous appearances as a witness to royal charters. However, these appearances in themselves reveal a significant challenge to the bishop's status, and in particular to the precedence traditionally accorded to Winchester in relation to the other suffragans of the province of Canterbury. In accordance with precedents established following heated argument in the late twelfth century, des Roches had previously ranked and witnessed second only to the bishop of London, immediately after the metropolitans.[243] Yet in the rubric to the 1225 Magna Carta, and on several occasions in 1227, his name as witness appears after those of the bishops of London, Bath and Salisbury. Bath and Salisbury were in theory junior sees to Winchester, but they were held by men with greater influence within the regime headed by Hubert de Burgh.[244] The change may appear a trivial one, but it was probably much resented by des Roches.

In 1226 the king began to issue charters and grants in perpetuity for the first time since 1218. As at the start of the reigns of Richard I and John, or as in Sicily after 1220, when the emperor Frederick II demanded the renewal of all privileges granted since the death of King William in 1189, the reissue of royal charters provided an opportunity to extract fines for renewal and, in some cases, the reversion to the crown of lands and rights that had been alienated

---

[241] *Pat. R. 1225–32*, pp. 76–8. His service in this capacity to an agreement with the Irish baron, Walter de Lacy, may explain the generous gifts bestowed upon the archbishop of Dublin at Witney in 1225/6; Ms 21DR, mm. 6, 6d (archbishop given £6 to make presents, and a considerable quantity of foodstuffs). See also Ms. 20DR, m. 14 (archbishop of Dublin at Witney 1224/5).

[242] *Foreign Accounts*, p. 94 (king at Bishop's Waltham, des Roches paying for his entertainment, 21 Dec. 1225); Mss. 20DR, m. 6d (king at Wolvesey 1224/5), m. 14 (gifts to king at Woodstock); 21DR, m. 6 (gifts to king at Witney).

[243] For the debate over precedence in the 1190s and its aftermath, see J. Thorpe, *Registrum Roffense* (London 1769), p. 51; *Sarum Charters*, pp. 109–10. In 1203 Godfrey de Lucy, bishop of Winchester, had refused to attend a consecration conducted by the bishop of London as proxy to the archbishop of Canterbury, claiming that Winchester, not London, had the right to consecrate in the archbishop's absence; *Canterbury Professions*, ed. M. Richter, Canterbury and York Society lxvii (1973), no. 143.

[244] Stubbs, *Select Charters*, p. 350 (where the order is Bath, Winchester, Salisbury); C53/18, mm. 16, 19; Spalding, Gentlemen's Society ms. Crowland Cartulary, ff. 113v–114r (20 March 1227); BL ms. Cotton Vitelius D ix (Cartulary of St Nicholas' Exeter), f. 26v (22 March 1227). It is unlikely that the anomaly is due to simple scribal error. Certainly, after the spring of 1227 des Roches is almost invariably accorded his traditional precedence.

without proper warrant.[245] In England after 1226, boroughs and religious corporations fined on average between 20 and 100 marks for confirmation of their liberties.[246] Amongst the bishops, Richard Poer offered 300 marks to have the amercements of his men and those of the dean and chapter of Salisbury.[247] Jocelin, bishop of Bath, fined 500 marks and five palfreys for confirmation of the privileges of his own see and that of his brother, bishop Hugh of Lincoln. The fine was a large one but Jocelin was allowed to tallage his tenantry in order to meet the Exchequer's demands.[248] No such assistance was extended to des Roches, whose own proffer of £500, to have confirmations of the charter of liberties issued to Winchester in 1208 and of all markets and fairs he had established since the end of the civil war, was by far and away the largest single fine extracted by the Exchequer for the reissue of privileges.[249] Even the Templars, the second highest contributors, paid only £490 for a guarantee of the rights of their order throughout England.[250] Since 1223 des Roches had extended loans to the crown and had co-operated in the collection of at least three taxes: a clerical carucage after the siege of Bedford, the fifteenth of 1225, and a clerical sixteenth in 1226.[251] He was now called upon to pay more than any of his colleagues for the confirmation of his liberties. It is difficult to resist the inference that this latest fine of £500 was intended as a punitive measure, reflecting the bishop's relatively meagre contribution to the fifteenth, his avoidance of levies and fines during the previous twenty years, and perhaps above all his profiteering as sheriff of Hampshire. In practice, relatively little of the £500 was ever paid; £188 of it was simply discounted against des Roches' surplus at the Exchequer, the sum that he claimed in expenses and outgoings over and above the farm of Hampshire during his time as sheriff. Des Roches emerged shorn of at least some of the perquisites of office but still, one suspects, very much in profit.

[245] In general, see D. Abulafia, *Frederick II, A Medieval Emperor* (London 1988), pp. 140–1.

[246] For the fines, see C60/25 *passim*.

[247] C60/25, m. 7.

[248] C60/25, mm. 8, 9; *RLC*, ii, p. 177b. A similar privilege was extended to the abbot of Faversham to cover a fine of only 15m; C60/25, m. 8; *Pat. R. 1225–32*, p. 113.

[249] C60/25, m. 7 and for the charter see *Cal. Chart. R. 1226–57*, pp. 29–30; *RLC*, ii, p. 179b.

[250] C60/25, mm. 7, 9.

[251] For the sixteenth, see *C & S*, i, pp. 158–9; *Reg. St Osmund*, ii, pp. 57–76, esp. pp. 75–6; *RLC*, ii, p. 174. The tax excited a degree of combined resistance amongst the conventual clergy, for which see also *Reg. Antiq. Lincoln*, vii, pp. 133–4. The interests of Salisbury were deputed to two canons, Master Elias of Dereham and Master Luke of Winchester, who is probably to be identified with the bishop's nephew, Luke des Roches.

Certainly the Exchequer appears to have looked upon him as a net beneficiary in his financial dealings with the crown. The acceptance of his accounts, the process of auditing carried out in the spring of 1227, the decision to write off his long-standing debts and the discounting of his credits against the £500 fine, all were framed as a deliberate favour to the bishop, in recompense for his faithful service to King John and Henry III, 'and because the bishop has set out for the Holy Land'.[252] Overall, the process left des Roches at peace with the Exchequer, in possession of his liberties and of nearly a dozen markets acquired since 1216, at least one of which, at Wargrave, appears to have been retained despite firm demands for its suppression.[253] In 1231 he was to be granted the royal manor of Titchfield on which to found a religious house. The grant is said to have been made specifically to compensate the bishop for the £500 fine extracted from him in 1227, confirming the impression that both des Roches and the king regarded the fine as a punitive gesture, meriting compensation in the form of the manor of Titchfield once des Roches had been restored to favour.[254]

The bishop's decision to clear his debts at the Exchequer was merely one aspect of a wider series of preparations, undertaken on the eve of his departure for crusade. Des Roches was to spend the next four years, from 1227 to 1231, overseas, first in the Holy Land, later in Italy and France. It is to the history of these years and of the bishop's crusade, that we must turn next.

[252] E372/71, m. 13d; E372/72, m. 7.
[253] For Wargrave, see *RLC*, ii, p. 185; *Cal.Lib.R.1226–40*, p. 31.
[254] C60/30, m. 1.

Chapter 7

DES ROCHES AND THE CRUSADE 1227–1231

Frustrated in his political ambitions, des Roches had little choice but to seek employment in the affairs of his see and in preparation for the crusade to which he had been pledged since 1221. His family in France had been involved in every general passage to the east since the 1090s. He himself had attempted to join the crusade to Damietta in its final months, at the very moment when his political fortunes in England began to turn sour.[1] But Damietta fell too soon. From 1221 all crusading plans were dependent upon those of the emperor Frederick II, who had already several times delayed his sailing. In March 1223 at a conference in northern Italy he agreed to depart by June 1225.[2] Since this deadline fell in the midst of the English political crisis, it was perhaps fortunate for des Roches that the emperor was again forced to seek postponement. Under the treaty of San Germano of July 1225, the terms of which were negotiated by the former legate Guala and carried to England by the papal nuncio Otto, Frederick committed himself, on pain of the most dire papal censure, to equip an army and to sail for the east in August 1227.[3] Des Roches thus had several years in which to prepare for the crusade, rather than the few months of hasty mobilization he had allowed himself in 1221. In the meantime his crusading vows may have eased his own domestic difficulties; certainly they help to explain the indulgent attitude shown him by the papacy, and are specifically mentioned in Honorius III's letters of December 1223, guaranteeing des Roches' liberties and

---

[1] Above pp. 22–3, 25, 200. For the crusade in general see T. C. Van Cleve, 'The crusade of Frederick II', in *A History of the Crusades*, ed. K. M. Setton, vol. ii, *The Later Crusades 1189–1311*, ed. R. L. Wolff and H. W. Hazard (Wisconsin 1969), chapter 12; Abulafia, *Frederick II*, chapter 5; H. E. Mayer, *The Crusades* (Oxford 1972), chapter 11. The English involvement has recently been considered by C. Tyerman, *England and the Crusades 1095–1588* (Chicago 1988), pp. 99–101, and in greater detail by Giles, 'Two English bishops in the Holy Land', pp. 46–57. I am particularly grateful to Simon Lloyd, who read a draft of this chapter and offered much valuable advice.

[2] Van Cleve, 'The Crusade of Frederick II', pp. 429–38.

[3] *Ibid.*, pp. 439–42; *Reg. St Osmund*, i, pp. 192–5.

ordering the king to permit him to visit Rome to discuss the forthcoming expedition.[4]

Traditionally, it had been magnate and baronial families that formed the nucleus of English crusading armies, as witnessed by the role of such men as Chester, Ferrers and Robert fitz Walter in the expedition to Damietta.[5] In 1221 des Roches was to have sailed in the company of Fawkes de Bréauté and Peter de Maulay, aliens but nonetheless men of considerable standing. However, de Maulay chose not to accompany the army which finally set out in 1227, by which time, too, Fawkes had died in disgrace and exile. If des Roches sought alternative companions amongst the baronage he appears to have met with scant success. No Englishman of lay magnate status accompanied the crusade of 1227. The king had taken vows as early as 1216 but was in no position to abandon his realm. The baronage may have been discouraged by the political uncertainties surrounding the termination of Henry's minority, or by the widespread antipathy to des Roches. In any event, the bishop was joined by only a mixed force of clerics, members of his own household and minor county landholders.

Amongst the episcopate, Pandulph bishop of Norwich had taken crusading vows before 1224.[6] It is not improbable that he contemplated accompanying des Roches. Neither man had emerged unscathed from the anti-alien rhetoric of the new regime. As a papal agent, Pandulph was suspect to Langton and the English bishops, anxious to pre-empt the appointment of another legate. In 1223–4 he received £20 and his chamberlain three shillings at des Roches' manor of Southwark, perhaps as part of a mutual arrangement between the two bishops and the merchants of Bologna.[7] However, he died in September 1226. The only man of comparable status to come forward was William Brewer, bishop of Exeter. Brewer's decision to take the cross was apparently made only a few months before his departure in June 1227.[8] Three years earlier, his promotion to Exeter had been encouraged by Hubert de Burgh and the

---

[4]   Above p. 214.
[5]   In general, see Lloyd, *English Society and the Crusade*, chapter 3, pp. 71–112.
[6]   *Bracton's Note Book*, no. 942, noticed by Lloyd, *English Society and the Crusade*, p. 75n.
[7]   Ms. 19DR, m. 12, and see below p. 237. See also Ms. 22DR, m. 13, where in 1226/7 des Roches entertained a Master Elias of Gloucester, come to Southwark for the pleas of the bishop of Norwich. During des Roches' absence on crusade Master Elias was promoted to the Winchester peculiar of Witney by the archdeacons of Surrey and Winchester; *Rot. Hugonis de Welles*, ii, p. 29.
[8]   Giles, 'Two English bishops', pp. 49–50.

enemies of des Roches as a means of winning over his uncle and namesake, the veteran courtier, William Brewer.[9] Brewer senior died before the crusade sailed. Having assumed the cross some thirty years earlier, he appears to have been anxious to redeem his vows, persuading his nephew to travel in his stead. To this end he deposited 4,000 marks at the Temple church in Acre. In November 1226 the master of the Templars was instructed to release this money to the forthcoming expedition in which the bishop of Exeter would serve as Brewer's proxy; the first certain evidence we have of the bishop's decision to take the cross.[10] Beyond the long-standing relations, by no means always friendly, between the elder Brewer and des Roches, there is further evidence to link the bishops of Exeter and Winchester before their sailing. Together after 1224 they witnessed various charters of William Brewer.[11] Des Roches stood witness to a confirmation of an ordinance by bishop William concerning the deanery of Exeter.[12] They appear to have joined company in their voyage to the east and to have acted in concert on crusade, but bishop William returned to England some two years before des Roches. If not altogether a stranger before the expedition set out, he was certainly not amongst the bishop of Winchester's closest political allies. His last-minute assumption of the cross meant that he can have played little part in preaching the crusade, or in des Roches' calculations as to the likely military effectiveness of the English force.

The bishop needed to attract a body of competent knights to his cause. Wendover tells us that over 40,000 Englishmen assumed crusading vows, and although this is wild exaggeration, at least one foreign source comments on the large number of English crusaders assembled at Brindisi in August 1227.[13] Of these it has proved possible to identify less than twenty, traced via the issue of royal letters of protection, or mentioned in actions before the courts. Nearly half of

---

[9] Above p. 213, although see Ms. 19DR, m. 4d, where in 1223/4 the archdeacon of Winchester gave 5 shillings and 10 pence to a servant of the bishop of Exeter at Farnham.

[10] *Pat. R. 1225–32*, pp. 89–90; Giles, 'Two English bishops', p. 50, n. 19 and references. Wendover, *Flores*, iv, p. 145 is misinterpreted by Lloyd, *English Societies and the Crusade*, p. 83n as implying that both des Roches and the bishop of Exeter had been pledged to the crusade for five years before 1227.

[11] *HMC Wells*, p. 489; *Acta Langton*, ed. Major, no. 86; HRO ms. 13 M63/1 (Mottisfont cartulary I), ff. 49, 50 also witnessed by Martin of Pattishall, probably in 1224/5 when des Roches is known to have been at Mottisfont; Ms. 20DR, m. 6d. See also E164/19 (Torre Abbey cartulary), f. 14v for a confirmation of land by William given in the Devon county court. *anno quo venerabilis pater W. Briewer Dei gratia Exonien' Episcopus cruce signatus transfretavit.*

[12] *Acta Langton*, ed. Major, no. 98.

[13] Giles, 'Two English bishops', pp. 50–1.

these men appear to have enjoyed links to des Roches before 1227, none of them to the bishop of Exeter, suggesting perhaps that des Roches stood at the centre of the crusade's recruitment, and also that his adherents had a better chance of winning recognition from the courts. The Dover annals state specifically that des Roches served as commander (*dux*) of the English contingent by authority of the pope.[14]

Of the seven men with links to des Roches, three were clerks: the bishop's Tourangeau familiar, Peter de Chanceaux, an unidentified member of the bishop's household, perhaps named Roger, appointed archdeacon of Winchester overseas, and Nicholas de Bréauté, brother of Fawkes and hence linked to des Roches' abortive attempt to join the crusade in 1221. Nicholas was rector of several midland churches including Medbourne, Leics., to which he had been presented by the legate Guala, and Wilden Beds., which he owed to the patronage of Peter de Maulay.[15] After the siege of Bedford he had escaped the fate of the rest of his family, but had nonetheless been forced to issue letters promising to make no journey overseas without royal approval. In August 1227 the bishop of Lincoln was instructed to release him from this vow, but beyond the fact that he intended to join the crusade, perhaps as Fawkes' proxy, nothing more is heard of him until his death *c.*1238.[16]

Of the lay contingent, Reginald de Berneville was a knight, possibly of Flemish extraction, with lands in both England and Ireland. The brother and heir of Hugh de Berneville who had served as des Roches' bailiff at Taunton during the civil war, in 1225–6, Reginald is found delivering wine to the bishop's manor of Fareham, at which time he had charge of Channel shipping during Richard of Cornwall's expedition to Gascony.[17] Nicholas de Haringot was a

---

14 BL ms. Cotton Julius D v, f. 26v, and see *AM*, iii (Dunstable), p. 112.

15 See *Acta Guala*, no. 66; *RLC*, i, p. 196b; *RLP*, pp. 155, 183b; *Pat. R. 1216–25*, p. 359. Probably to be identified with the Colin de Bréauté, who in July 1224 fined 80m for the king's grace, Pandulph and the bishop of Lincoln standing as his pledges; C60/20, m. 3.

16 *RLC*, ii, p. 196b. For an altar endowed by his executors at Newnham priory see *Rotuli Roberti Grosseteste Episcopi Lincolniensis AD MCCXXXV – MCCLIII*, ed. F. N. Davis, Canterbury and York Soc. x (1913), pp. 314–15. See also *AM*, iii (Dunstable), p. 88 for service in the Holy Land imposed as penance on three of Fawkes' men after the siege of Bedford.

17 Ms. 21DR, m. 12; *Pat. R. 1216–25*, p. 539; *RL*, i, no. ccxx; *Pat. R. 1225–32*, pp. 33, 44–5; *RLC*, ii, pp. 51, 62b, 63, 110b, 112b–116, 120b. In 1220 amongst the *familia* of Philip of Oldcotes; *RLC*, i, pp. 442, 444. Granted land in Hampshire 1226; *RLC*, ii, p. 95. For Hugh de Berneville, see above pp. 135–6 n. 7. For Reginald as Hugh's heir, see *RLC*, i, pp. 446b, 479, 532b; *Cl. R. 1234–7*, p. 226.

minor Sussex knight holding land of the see of Winchester. Between 1210 and 1214 he had carried out various commissions on the Winchester estates, and in 1215 is found amongst the bishop's knights guarding Wargrave, prior to the arrival of the rebel army. In 1223 he served in des Roches' contingent on the Montgomery campaign.[18] The Marcher baron Hugh de Mortimer, who on his deathbed in 1226 was permitted to equip a proxy to discharge his obligations on crusade, was not amongst des Roches' regular allies. Nonetheless, in 1223–4 he had purchased over £10 worth of grain at des Roches' manor of North Waltham. Correspondence passed between the two men and the debt went unsummoned and uncollected long after Mortimer's death.[19] The evidence here is very scanty. Even so, the chroniclers were in no doubt that the bishop's following in the east contained many able warriors, one foreign source describing des Roches as *hominem discretum, tam armis et divitis quam bellatorum copia redimitum.*[20] Our knowledge of these *bellatores* is hopelessly inadequate; perhaps they were mercenaries hired for the expedition, perhaps alien *familiares* without land in England and therefore unrecorded in the customary sources. The fact that chroniclers such as Wendover and the Waverley annalist are amongst the best informed in Europe on the progress of the crusade would certainly suggest a considerable English presence amongst the army after 1227.

Just as we know little of the identity of the English crusaders, we know hardly any more of their recruitment. Several of the men identified above must surely have been enlisted via des Roches' own household. In January 1227 des Roches received papal letters reminding him of his long-standing commission to preach the cross, and asking him to ensure that all who had vowed themselves to the enterprise should prepare to travel in the August passage to Palestine. He appears to have discharged his duties in this respect; certainly he forwarded the pope's instructions to Richard Poer, ordering him to enforce them within the diocese of Salisbury.[21] Presumably a similar pattern was followed in other sees, with des Roches serving to co-ordinate the activities of the local diocesans.[22] Amongst others to preach the crusade were the papal nuncio Otto who arrived in England in 1225, with a bull reciting Frederick II's promises under the

---

[18] *PR6DR*, p. 70; Mss. 7DR, mm. 3d, 6d; 9DR, mm. 5d, 6; *RLC*, ii, p. 211b; *CRR*, xiii, no. 1772, xiv, no. 1322, and see also *Hist. des Ducs*, p. 193.

[19] Mss. 19DR, m. 6; 20DR, m. 11; 21DR, m. 8; 22DR, m. 10.

[20] The Chronicle of William of Andres in *MGHS*, xxiv, p. 769.

[21] *Acta*, no. 47.

[22] See in general Lloyd, *English Society and the Crusade*, chapter 2.

Treaty of San Germano and exhorting all who had taken the cross to join the emperor's expedition. This letter too was distributed amongst the English diocesans.[23] In 1223 John de Brienne, king of Jerusalem, had visited France, England, Spain and Germany and was granted a subsidy by Henry III.[24] Also prominent amongst the crusade's propagandists were the Dominican friars whom des Roches had introduced to England in 1221.[25] The work of the English friar Master Walter was recorded by both Wendover and Matthew Paris.[26] It was in the build-up to the crusade that des Roches established the friars in Winchester. In doing so he became one of only a handful of English bishops to found Dominican houses, one other being William Brewer, his companion on crusade, who introduced the Dominicans to Exeter before his departure for the east.[27] It seems that the two crusading bishops deliberately patronized the friars in the hope of furthering their common enterprise. Des Roches' diocesan legislation, issued between 1223 and 1227, specifically licensed the Dominicans to act as penitentiaries within the see of Winchester.[28]

Mention of this legislation brings us on to consider the bishop's personal preparations for crusade. Beyond the necessity to recruit companions for his expedition, des Roches was under an obligation to ensure the smooth running of his see during his absence. Already before 1227, prolonged service to the court had forced him to delegate many of his diocesan responsibilities to subordinates; to his official, Master Alan of Stokes, to the archdeacons of Surrey and Winchester, and to a succession of Irish bishops who acted as suffragans, carrying out ordinations, confirmations and the consecration of churches and altars. The most prominent of these, bishop John of Ardfert, had been active in the diocese from at least 1222. Refused admission to his own see in Ireland and subsequently deposed, he had been granted papal dispensation to retain the episcopal dignity and function as a vicar at the invitation of other bishops. Besides his service to des Roches, in the early 1220s he had consecrated a

---

23 *Reg. St Osmund*, i, pp. 192–5.
24 Van Cleve, 'The crusade of Frederick II', p. 439; Lloyd, *English Society and the Crusade*, p. 239 and below p. 238.
25 Van Cleve, 'The crusade of Frederick II', p. 439.
26 Paris, *CM*, iii, p. 177. For the general role of the Dominicans, see Lloyd, *English Society and the Crusade*, pp. 53–6.
27 W. A. Hinnesbusch, *The Early English Friars Preachers* (Rome 1951), pp. 104–6; R. C. Easterling, *The Franciscans and Dominicans of Exeter*, History of Exeter Research Group Monograph iii (Exeter 1927), p. 31. For the Winchester house, see *Acta*, appendix 2, no. 22.
28 *C & S*, i, p. 133 no. 45.

cemetery on behalf of archbishop Langton and later, possibly as vicar of Winchester, issued an indulgence on behalf of the newly canonized saint William of York. In January 1226, in des Roches' presence, he consecrated altars at Waverley Abbey, and during his master's crusade toured the diocese, returning to Waverley in 1231 and at some time dedicating an altar at Andwell priory.[29]

Alongside bishop John, des Roches deputed the day-to-day management of his spiritualities to the two archdeacons, Bartholomew and Luke des Roches.[30] The temporalities of Winchester continued to be governed from the episcopal Exchequer at Wolvesey. The Winchester pipe rolls for the years of des Roches' crusade, from Michaelmas 1227 to Michaelmas 1231, have been lost.[31] However, the roll compiled after Michaelmas 1227, following the bishop's departure, shows that des Roches had promoted another of his kinsmen, Master Hugh des Roches, to head the episcopal Exchequer in his absence.[32] There could be no better guarantee that the see would be properly maintained than to entrust the management of both its spiritual and temporal affairs to the bishop's kin. For the rest, des Roches' official, Master Alan of Stokes, his estate steward Roger Wacelin, his attorney John of Herriard and his treasurer Denis de Bourgueil, are all found playing a role in the administration of the see in des Roches' absence.[33] To some extent the bishop's household was dispersed by the crusade. Various of his clerks accompanied des Roches to Palestine, others such as Peter de Rivallis and Master Henry of Avranches sought employment elsewhere. Master Henry is believed to have left for Rome.[34] Peter de Rivallis found promotion in an unidentified church in Poitiers, and in the meantime entrusted his affairs in England to a proctor.[35] There could be little point in the bishop burdening his see with the expense of a superfluous household. Provided that his key subordinates remained in place, manorial resources would be far better put towards the cost of the crusade.

Commentators are generally agreed that crusading was a very expensive business, sufficient on occasion to precipitate the sale of

[29] *Acta*, pp. xxxiv–xxxv.
[30] *Acta*, appendix 4, nos. 7, 13.
[31] For evidence that such pipe rolls were drawn up, see for example Mss. 27DR, mm. 1d, 4d, 8d; 28DR, m. 16.
[32] *Acta*, appendix 4, no. 10.
[33] See *CRR*, xiii, nos. 373, 551, 864; *Pat. R. 1225–32*, pp. 229, 265, 267, 426; *RLC*, ii, pp. 196, 201b, 211b.
[34] *Henry of Avranches*, ed. Cox Russell, pp. 19, 123.
[35] *Acta*, appendix 4, no. 41.

land and even to induce bankruptcy.[36] Des Roches' own expenses can be assumed to have been lavish, and yet they have left no indication of strain on the Winchester pipe rolls. Before sailing for the east, des Roches acquired papal authority to farm or mortgage his estates where appropriate, but such licences appear to have been issued as a matter of common form.[37] Although our most important proofs, the Winchester pipe rolls 1227–31, have been lost, the roll for 1231–2 gives no indication that the bishop's crusade caused any fundamental change to the management of his estates. A few of his demesne resources, mills and odd plots of land were put to farm, but these arrangements were by no means exceptional in either form or number.[38] In general, des Roches' income appears to have been sufficiently vast and his administration efficient enough to bear the expense of the crusade with impunity. Far from being forced to sell land, he continued to augment his manorial resources. New purchases of land are recorded up to the time of his departure, and even during his absence, his agents in England were able to buy out the bishop of Salisbury's claim to part of the manor of Tisted.[39] On the bishop's return he immediately set about the foundation of an abbey at Titchfield, and a year later, of an Augustinian house at Selborne, endowed with newly purchased lands.

This is not to suggest that des Roches resorted to no special measures to finance his expedition. As in 1221, he sought the crown's support in pressuring his debtors into settlement, albeit without the urgency that had attended his effort to join the expedition to Damietta.[40] In the winter of 1225–6 he obtained distraint against the goods of Robert de Punteyse, in all probability a merchant with debts to des Roches.[41] The bishop's agents continued to pursue sums outstanding from ransoms extorted during the civil war 1215–17, and once again the crown intervened to press for the solution of an even

---

36 In general see Lloyd, *English Society and the Crusade*, pp. 175–97, and the same author's 'Crusader knights and the land market in the thirteenth century', *Thirteenth Century England II*, ed. P. R. Coss and S. D. Lloyd, pp. 119–36.

37 *Reg. Honorius III*, ed. Pressutti, ii, no. 6222.

38 Mss 27DR, m. 4d (Morton farmed for £23 a year, 1230–1); 28DR, m. 16 (Fonthill farmed for £30 a year, 1228–9). One popular method of raising cash, the sale of timber, is impossible to gauge from the Winchester accounts, which exclude the majority of the bishop's resources in forest and woodland. For the practice in general see Lloyd, *English Society and the Crusade*, pp. 182–3.

39 Ms. 21DR, m. 10d: over £13 spent on land purchased from the abbot of Durford, 1225/6. For Tisted see *CRR*, xiii, nos. 720, 864, 1235; CP25(1)203/6 no. 8; *Selborne Charters*, ed. Macray, i, p. 2.

40 See above p. 206.

41 *RLC*, ii, p. 163.

older debt, owed by the merchants of Ypres in repayment of subsidies advanced to Flanders in 1214. At one time des Roches was their creditor to the tune of over £1,000. In April 1227 the authorities of London were ordered to distrain all the chattels of the merchants of Ypres and Bologna until des Roches' demands had been met.[42] The Bolognese debt to the bishop was also of long standing; des Roches had been trying to secure repayment since at least 1222, although the transactions which gave rise to it are by no means clear. The Bolognese were said to owe £800 to Pandulph's executors which des Roches had advanced on Pandulph's behalf, and which the executors were presumably called upon to repay des Roches. This may well relate to a complaint by the pope in 1220 that Pandulph had used a number of Bolognese merchants to channel crusading subsidies to the Curia only for the merchants to abscond with the money.[43] Beyond their debts to Pandulph the Italians appear to have owed a further 400 marks directly to des Roches.[44] In 1221 the bishop had raised funds by selling his most valuable wards. His subsequent political eclipse involved the dispersal and confiscation of his rich collection of wardships. Nevertheless before sailing, in June 1227 he obtained royal confirmation of an arrangement whereby the heir of John de Andely, whose lands had been administered by the episcopal Exchequer since before Michaelmas 1226, was sold to Geoffrey de Lisle.[45]

Most significantly of all, des Roches settled his accounts with the royal Exchequer, fined for the reissue of his charter of liberties and confirmation of his new markets, and obtained quittance from all outstanding debts from the previous twenty years or more.[46] This settlement was described by the Exchequer as a reward for the bishop's past services *et quia in terram sanctam peregre profectus est.*[47] The writs of *computate* which completed it were issued between 19 and 28 June 1227, probably less than a week before des Roches set sail.[48] The crown was not ungenerous in assisting the bishop's passage. Besides

---

[42] For the ransoms see *CRR*, xiii, no. 357; *RLC*, ii, pp. 188, 196, 199b, and above pp. 144–5. For Ypres see *RLC*, ii, p. 180 and above pp. 114, 195.

[43] *Cal.Pap.Reg.* , i, p. 76.

[44] *RLC*, i, pp. 611b, 636; *Pat. R. 1225–32*, p. 85; *RLC*, ii, pp. 91b, 180. This arrangement may explain the £10 paid by des Roches to Pandulph in 1223/4; Ms. 19DR, m. 12. For further evidence of Bolognese involvement in the collection of the crusading twentieth, imposed after 1216, see Vincent, 'The election of Pandulph Verracclo'.

[45] *Pat. R. 1225–32*, p. 127. For John de Andely's lands held of the bishop at Ebbesbourne, see Mss. 12DR, m. 2; 22DR, m. 1d.

[46] Above pp. 226–8.

[47] E372/70, m. 6d; *RLC*, ii, p. 189b.

[48] *RLC*, ii, pp. 189b, 190b.

enforcing settlements against his debtors, at Easter 1227 the king guaranteed des Roches' rights in a woodland claimed by the chapter of Rouen.[49] Perhaps the regime was motivated by an understandable desire to speed des Roches' sailing and to rid themselves of his presence all the sooner. Their enthusiasm for des Roches' expedition did not, however, extend to any direct financial contribution. In this respect the bishop's crusade was unique amongst those undertaken by figures close to Henry's court. Unlike the king's own projected expeditions, the crusades of Richard of Cornwall, the Lord Edward or even the campaign at Damietta after 1217, des Roches was left to finance his own passage aided by neither general levy nor personal gifts from the crown.[50] One commentator suggests that the bishop carried with him the residue of monies pledged during the king of Jerusalem's visit to England in 1223, but this rests upon a misreading of the sources. What evidence there is suggests that John de Brienne had met with a less than generous reception and that much of his aid was siphoned off by the court to projects unconnected with the crusade.[51] Des Roches' contacts with the merchants of Bologna do, however, suggest that he may have benefited from the arrears of the crusading twentieth imposed upon the English church as long ago as 1216.

In all, his financial preparations appear to have been comprehensive and well-ordered. Given the extent of his private resources, only one problem remained to him: how to transfer the funds he had assembled, and possibly too the income which would build up in his absence, from England to the east? Rather than transport bulky silver pennies, one popular method was to convert them into gold.[52] The Winchester pipe rolls record that in the two years 1225–7, at least £180 and probably £280 was spent at Taunton in the purchase of

[49]   *RLC*, ii, pp. 190, 190b, 192b, 197, 201b.

[50]   For subsidies and royal grants in general, see Lloyd, *English Society and the Crusade*, pp. 177–80, and for the extraordinary measures undertaken on behalf of Richard of Cornwall and the lord Edward, see Denholm-Young, *Richard of Cornwall*, pp. 39, 56–7, 73–4; J. R. Maddicott, 'The crusade taxation of 1268–70 and the development of parliament', in *Thirteenth Century England II*, ed. Coss and Lloyd, pp. 93–116.

[51]   Tyerman, *England and the Crusades*, pp. 101, 191, which misreads *Pat. R. 1216–25*, p. 527 as a grant to des Roches rather than as a disbursement made in his presence. For other payments from the subsidy, apparently unconnected with crusading projects, see *Pat. R. 1216–25*, p. 512; *RLC*, ii, p. 21b, and see the comments of the Dunstable annalist and the French chronicler William of Andres; *AM*, iii, p. 85; *MGHS*, xxiv, p. 763.

[52]   In general, see D. A. Carpenter, 'The gold treasure of King Henry III', in *Thirteenth Century England I*, ed. Coss and Lloyd, pp. 61–88, esp. pp. 68–71. For Frederick II's accumulation of gold in the years preceding his crusade, see Abulafia, *Frederick II*, pp. 220–3.

gold coin.[53] The pipe rolls tell us nothing of the destination of the £3,000 or so, paid in cash each year to the episcopal Exchequer. A large proportion of this could also have been converted into gold.

Crusaders might deposit money before departure with the English representatives of an international organization which would ensure payment at the crusader's destination.[54] Here our evidence is largely conjectural, but the Winchester pipe roll for 1226–7 records the presence of knights Templar at Taunton, Farnham and Southwark.[55] Some of these references relate to a man named Thomas of the Temple commissioned to control Channel shipping during the Gascon expedition of Richard of Cornwall, in which capacity he served alongside Reginald de Berneville, des Roches' companion on crusade.[56] For the rest, it is conceivable that the Templars' function was to supervise the transfer of des Roches' financial resources. Certainly William Brewer had used the Templars to transport 4,000 marks to Acre, whilst the 11,000 marks which Fawkes de Bréauté had allegedly deposited with the Templars in Paris might possibly be related to his preparations for crusade.[57]

[53] Ms. 21DR, m. 3d (£80 spent *In liberatio pro xii. marc' auri de muce per breve domini episcopi*, the 12m being released to Denis the treasurer of Wolvesey); Ms. 22DR, m. 3 (£100 received *ad aurum emendum*, and subsequently released as 1529 *denar' auri musc' inferius empt'. quod pondant xxx. marc' uno denar' aureo minus*). At the conversion rates suggested by Carpenter ('The gold treasure of Henry III', pp. 63–4, 87n.) of 10 marks of silver = 1 mark of gold = 52 *denarii* of gold, these figures fit almost exactly, save that in the second account the sum in gold, 30m, would demand that the Taunton bailiffs spent £200 of silver rather than merely the £100 specially released to them. Forgetting for a moment the Exchequer's calculation that these 1529 coins 'weigh 30 marks less 1 denarius of gold', it is noticeable that had the coins been *oboli* of musc rather than gold *denarii* they would have equalled almost precisely the £100 of silver mentioned in the first part of the account (Carpenter, *Loc. Cit.* p. 63 n. 10). Perhaps the bishop's accountants were unaware that it was *oboli* rather than *denarii* that had been purchased and therefore overestimated their value expressed as marks of gold.

[54] Templars and Hospitallers transported subsidies collected by Pandulph to the Fifth Crusade; *Cal.Pap.Reg.*, i, p. 75, which may explain the substantial payments he made from the vacancy receipts of Ely to Hospitallers staying at the Tower of London; *RLC*, ii, p. 7b; *Foreign Accounts*, p. 46. For the lord Edward's use of the Templars as credit financiers on crusade, see Lloyd, *English Society and the Crusade*, p. 194n.

[55] Ms. 22DR, mm. 1, 1d, 4d, 13. The last occasion on which Templars are recorded on the Winchester estates had been in 1215/16 when they served to carry money during the civil war; above pp. 129–30. In general, see A. Sandys, 'The financial and administrative importance of the London Temple in the thirteenth century', in *Essays in Medieval History presented to T. F. Tout*, ed. A. G. Little and F. M. Powicke (Manchester 1925), pp. 154–5, 158.

[56] Ms. 22DR, mm. 1, 1d. For his activities on behalf of the crown in 1225–6 see *Pat. R. 1225–32*, pp. 11, 14, 44.

[57] For Brewer see above p. 231. For Fawkes' money deposited abroad see *DD*, no. 204; *RLC*, ii, pp. 214–214b, and also *Pat. R. 1225–32*, p. 210 for the possibility that he had deposited further sums at Troyes. See also *Cal.Pap.Reg.*, i, p. 124; *Cl. R. 1231–4*,

The Templars may also have co-ordinated preparations for the expedition in England with those of the emperor and other foreign crusaders. The papacy too served as a clearing house for information on the development of the expedition, whilst des Roches appears to have maintained his own channels of communication with Frederick. In November 1226 Henry III had written to the emperor on the bishop's behalf, thanking him for his earlier dispatches and asking him to receive envoys from des Roches, who had been sent to Italy to prepare for their master's arrival.[58] Such contacts may well explain the presence of a German man (*hominen alemmen'*) received by des Roches at Wargrave in 1225–6, who was paid 1 shilling and five pence for his commons and a further threepence for medical attention (*ad wlneribus eius curandis*).[59] Further diplomatic exchanges probably lie behind the costly presents purchased at Southwark in 1226–7, including an emerald ring and a belt which des Roches gave to an unnamed knight.[60] Contacts with the Empire had been eased after 1225 by attempts to secure an alliance between Henry III and the German princes. Marriages had been proposed between Frederick II's son Henry, king of the Romans, and Henry III's sister Isabella, and also between Henry III himself and a daughter of the Duke of Austria. In pursuit of such alliances, the bishop of Carlisle, des Roches' guest in 1226–7, headed a series of diplomatic missions to the Rhineland.[61]

By 1227 des Roches had completed his military and financial preparations. His diocese could safely be entrusted to kinsmen and subordinates. Diplomatic channels had been opened up with the emperor, and most significantly of all, the bishop had managed to heal the breach with Henry III. Having made his peace with the king and the Exchequer it remained to him only to make his peace with God.

---

pp. 303–4, for his loans from a crusader, Peter Merlot, who after 1230 sought the church's assistance in compelling the subsequent recipients of Fawkes' lands to repay his debts, threatening the excommunication of several English magnates.

58 *RLC*, ii, p. 204. Lloyd, *English Society and the Crusade*, p. 136n. probably reads too much into this letter in suggesting that des Roches hoped for a contractual arrangement with the emperor.

59 Ms. 21DR, m. 5d.

60 Ms. 22DR, m. 13. The account is badly perished but also records a gold ring worth 15 shillings and sixpence, given to a man named Bertinus Porchet, for whom see also *Cal.Lib.R.1226–40*, p. 31.

61 Powicke, *Henry III*, p. 159; *DD*, nos. 160, 187–9 and above p. 225. Other guests with diplomatic experience in Germany included the chancellor of St Paul's; *Pat. R. 1216–25*, p. 558, and above p. 225, and the abbot of Beaulieu; *RLC*, ii, pp. 26b, 42, 71b, both of whom had joined the bishop of Carlisle's mission in 1225. In 1224/5 the abbot was entertained at Bishop's Waltham and Burghclere and in 1226/7 paid 10m at Southwark; Mss. 20DR, mm. 7d, 12; 22DR, m. 13.

By 1227 des Roches must have been approaching sixty years of age. He had made a will as long ago as 1221, and in 1227 had it confirmed once more by the king.[62] For men of des Roches' status the crusade seldom threatened death in battle, but even so the hazards of foreign travel, of disease, shipwreck, and in des Roches' case, of simple old age, meant that he was by no means certain of a safe return to England. Younger men than the bishop chose to appease their maker before setting out for the east, by alms-giving, pilgrimage or benefactions to the religious.[63] Des Roches was no exception. Over the previous twenty years the Winchester pipe rolls record small but regular gifts of grain and provisions to the poor, to converted Jews, anchoresses and the regular orders. Across the diocese such alms amount to only a tiny proportion of the bishop's resources. However, from 1223–4 until the year of the bishop's sailing there is an appreciable increase in the level of alms-giving, best indicated if we tabulate donations of grain, bacon pigs and herrings over the four years 1223–7:

Michaelmas account	Grain in quarters	Bacon pigs	Herrings
1224	38	84	1,000
1225	215	16	10,500
1226	80	21	10,000
1227	881	36	3,000

The figures for herrings and bacon pigs show considerable variation; for example 40 of the 84 bacon pigs recorded for 1224 represent animals killed by the bishop in the park at Taunton, presumably for sport, subsequently given to the poor.[64] In 1226, 1,000 herrings each were given to the religious houses, mostly nunneries, of Goring, Littlemore, Wintney and St Helen's, perhaps in return for prayers. In 1226–7 identical alms were distributed amongst the religious of Ivinghoe and St Helen's.[65] Only the grain account shows a firm link to the bishop's own concerns. The extensive distribution of alms in 1225 can be put down to a poor harvest; elsewhere the account mentions bread given *pro defectu bladi*.[66] The harvests of the next two

---

[62]   *Cal.Chart.R.1226–57*, p. 42, and see above p. 199.
[63]   Lloyd, *English Society and the Crusade*, pp. 155–63.
[64]   Ms. 19DR, m. 11.
[65]   Mss. 21DR, mm. 6d, 14; 22DR, m. 13d.
[66]   Ms. 20DR, m. 3d.

years were equally disappointing, indeed in 1227 a shortage of provisions forced postponement of the Hampshire session of the general eyre.[67] However the contrast between the alms of grain in 1226 and 1227, and the fact that those of 1227 are accounted *de dono episcopi*, implies that des Roches himself ordered the extraordinary distribution of 1227, without reference to the coming harvest. It is unlikely that his subordinates could have met the food shortages of the autumn with such munificence, without the prior approval of their master, and it is worth noting that the only account roll to cover a year in which the bishop was wholly absent from his diocese, that for 1235–6, records a bare minimum of alms-giving, much of it at the steward's orders, none of it accounted *de dono episcopi*.[68] The extraordinary level of alms distributed in 1227, an average of over 30 quarters of grain on each of the bishop's manors, may well reflect des Roches' desire to mark his departure for crusade by a gesture of pious largesse.

The bishop also made more lasting benefactions in preparation for his expedition. He had already ensured the preservation of his memory by the foundation of a Premonstratensian abbey at Halesowen, by his role in the establishment of hospitals at Portsmouth and Southwark, and more recently by his introduction of the Dominicans to Winchester. Two months before sailing for the east, he added to this list of foundations by reorganizing a college of priests at Marwell originally established by Henry of Blois. Marwell itself was the site of a favoured episcopal residence, which des Roches had rebuilt and lavishly decorated during his first few years as bishop.[69] His rule for the college issued in March 1227 sought to augment its income, to ensure strict rules of residence and to reorganize the college's finances around a common fund. Stress was laid upon the daily recital of the offices, and although des Roches' rule contains no mention of the crusade or of prayers for its success, it seems likely that its timing was conditioned by the bishop's imminent departure for Palestine.[70]

One final act of piety was popular amongst crusaders prior to embarkation: pilgrimage. To some extent des Roches had already performed this duty in 1221, when his assumption of the cross was preceded by a journey to the shrine of St James at Compostela. In 1227 there is no positive evidence of his undertaking a pilgrimage, but

---

[67]   *RLC*, ii, p. 211b, and see Titow, 'Land and population', p. 126.
[68]   Ms. 31DR, *passim*.
[69]   See pp. 71 n.128, 81, 180, 474.
[70]   *Acta*, no. 31.

had he been inclined to do so he had the opportunity to pray at one of the foremost shrines in Europe on 9 May 1227, when he attended the consecration of Henry de Sandford as bishop of Rochester in Canterbury cathedral.[71] Des Roches was not without some interest in Canterbury's saints. The hospital he had refounded at Southwark was a minor centre for the cult of St Thomas Becket, and on crusade he was to re-establish yet another hospital dedicated to St Thomas, at Acre. In 1227 his presence at Canterbury indicates a degree of reconciliation with archbishop Langton.[72] After 1224 the episcopal pipe rolls record regular contacts between the two men. Des Roches sent representatives to the archbishop's conference at St Paul's in January 1226. Langton was entertained at Farnham and Taunton, and members of des Roches' household are to be found on several occasions travelling to consult with him.[73] At some time between 1222 and 1227, des Roches issued diocesan legislation confirming the provincial statutes proclaimed by Langton at the Council of Oxford and borrowing fairly extensively from the archbishop's first set of synodalia for the diocese of Canterbury.[74] It was to Langton's pupils, Richard Poer bishop of Salisbury, and Alexander of Stainsby bishop of Coventry, that the pope entrusted protection of the see of Winchester during des Roches' absence overseas.[75]

Nevertheless it is characteristic that des Roches' dealings with the archbishop should be hedged about with ambiguity. The story here goes back to 1220 and Langton's translation of the relics of Thomas Becket. Coinciding with the canonization of St Hugh of Lincoln, Langton's actions appear to have inspired a wave of enthusiasm for the translation and rediscovery of relics of the English saints. In the immediate term, the translation of St Thomas preceded by only a few weeks the foundation of the Lady Chapel in the Confessor's church at Westminster, and led directly to the translation of the relics of St Augustine at Canterbury, the principal rival to Becket's shrine at Christ Church. The next few years witnessed successful lobbying by York for the canonization of St William, and an attempt by the canons of Salisbury to obtain official recognition for the cult of St

---

71   *Flores Hist.* , ii,p. 190, where the bp of Exeter was also present.
72   Above pp. 81–2, 221.
73   Mss. 20DR, mm. 6, 10, 15 (discussions at Southwark 16 June 1225 not noticed in Langton's itinerary as given by Major); 21DR, mm. 4, 14.
74   *C & S*, i, pp. 125–37.
75   *Reg. Honorius III*, ed. Pressutti, ii, no. 6222. The protection was conditional upon des Roches' appointment of a competent vicar, for whom see John bishop of Ardfert, above pp. 234–5.

Osmund, whose tomb formed the nucleus of their new cathedral.[76] In 1224 St Wilfrid was translated at Ripon and in the same year, Langton translated the relics of St Mildrith and St Eadburg at St Gregory's priory Canterbury.[77]

Less well known is the case of Dorchester Abbey whose canons, inspired by a vision around the year 1223, located the tomb of a bishop dressed in full pontificals which they identified as the body of St Birinus, apostle to the West Saxons and founder of the pre-Conquest see of Dorchester, subsequently transferred to Winchester. This discovery was followed by numerous miraculous cures, including that of a dumb child who found himself able to speak both English and French.[78] The canons communicated their find to Rome and on 9 March 1224, at the height of des Roches' political difficulties, the pope wrote to archbishop Langton instructing him to oversee the translation of the Dorchester relics.[79] But Langton was forced to delay these proceedings, having been alerted to a major handicap to the canons' story: the objection raised by des Roches' monastic convent in Winchester, that Bede's *Ecclesiastical History* contained unequivocal evidence that the body of Birinus had been removed from Dorchester to Winchester about the year AD 700.[80] Birinus had previously been considered a fairly minor saint, but the controversy over his relics seems to have rekindled an interest in his cult. Des Roches' diocesan legislation specifically demanded observation of his feast days and at much the same time there is evidence of an enthusiasm for him

[76] E164/27 (Cartulary of St Augustine's Canterbury), ff. 129v–131; Lambeth Palace ms. TT1 (excerpts from a lost cartulary of St Augustine's Canterbury), pp. 46–8. For the others see Sayers, *Honorius III*, pp. 180, 190; *The Canonization of St Osmund*, ed. H. E. Malden, pp. iii–iv.

[77] *Memorials of the Church of SS Peter and Wilfrid, Ripon*, ed. J. T. Fowler, 4 vols., Surtees Soc., lxxiv, lxxviii, lxxxi, cxv (1882), i, p. 50; BL ms. Cotton Julius D v (Dover annals), f. 25v.

[78] The principal account of these events is printed by Laurentius Surius, *De Probatis Sanctorum Vitis quas tam ex Mss. codicibus, quam ex editis authoribus* . . . , 12 vols. in 4 (new edition, Cologne 1617–18), iv, pp. 121–3 sub 3 December, which fails to note any source beyond the comment that it came from an 'old and trustworthy' ms. It appears to derive from the accounts in Bodl. ms. Tanner 15, ff. 65r–v, and BL ms. Cotton Tiberius E i, ff. 297r–298v, collections of English saints' lives traced via T. Duffus Hardy, *Descriptive Catalogue of Materials Relating to the History of Great Britain and Ireland*, 3 vols. (RS 1862–5), i, pp. 235–7. Duffus Hardy misleadingly suggests that Surius quotes from an independent source (no. 628), as against the mss. cited which he groups together as no. 626. Amongst the other mss. that he notices (nos. 625–33), Bodl. ms. Digby 39, ff. 52r–56r contains a short life followed by collects for the feasts of Birinus' translation and deposition.

[79] *Cal.Pap.Reg.*, i, p. 95 noticed by Powicke, *Stephen Langton* (Oxford 1928), p. 144.

[80] *Bede's Ecclesiastical History of the English People*, ed. B. Colgrave and R. A. B. Mynors (Oxford 1969), p. 232 (bk iii, ch. 7).

amongst the bishop's tenants.[81] Occasionally during the 1220s the Winchester pipe rolls record oblations to the saints; a lamb to St Frideswide at Crawley in 1220–1 *pro murain*; another there in 1225–6 to St Mary Magdalene *pro mortalit' ante peritum*.[82] Two years earlier, in 1223–4, two shillings and eight pence were spent at West Wycombe on a cup given to St Birinus *pro mortalis bovium*.[83] These gifts were almost certainly made in expectation of prayers or divine intervention on behalf of sick livestock.[84] It is interesting that it should have been the men of Wycombe who called upon Birinus; their manor lay less than twenty miles from the dubious relics at Dorchester, but far from Winchester. Much this same point was taken up by the canons, who stressed that their own relics at Dorchester could claim many miracles whilst not a single cure had been effected by those at Winchester.[85] Spurred on by an Oxford anchorite, Matthew of Holywell, they wrote to the pope suggesting that the dilemma could be resolved by a simple revision to Bede's account. Rather than describe the translation of Birinus to Winchester, Bede had meant to write of the translation of 'Bertinus', an otherwise unrecorded bishop of the West Saxons who may well have been invented by the canons of Dorchester in 1224 to suit the occasion. Honorius III forwarded this suggestion to Langton in August 1225.[86] The archbishop had so far refused to translate the relics at Dorchester. Whether he relented at this latest suggestion remains uncertain. Dorchester never abandoned its claim and the canons erected a shrine to house their supposedly saintly remains. At the same time, the Winchester monks continued to attract indulgences for their rival altar of St Birinus and a note was written into the eleventh-century copy of Bede in the monastic library, drawing attention to the account of Birinus' removal from Dorchester.[87]

---

[81] *C & S*, i, p. 127, no. 10. The feast of St Birinus' deposition, 3 December, is often used by des Roches' clerks in dating entries on the episcopal pipe rolls.

[82] Mss. 16DR, m. 8d; 21DR, m. 14d.

[83] Ms. 19DR, m. 8d.

[84] *Eynsham Cartulary*, ed. Salter, i, p. 18, supplies the form for such a service to protect sheep against the murrain. The word used here, *carmen*, to describe the special collect used on such occasions, may well explain the entry on the Winchester pipe roll for 1217–18, where a sheep was sent from Bishops Waltham to the (hospital) of Mary Magdalene (Winchester), *pro carmine*: Ms. 13DR, m. 3d.

[85] Surius, *De Probatis Sanctorum Vitis*, p. 122.

[86] *Ibid.*, pp. 122–3; *Cal.Pap.Reg.*, i, p. 103.

[87] Winchester Cathedral Library ms. Bede, f. 45r; *quod hic testatur qualiter translatus fuit Birinus a Dorcestre civitate ad Wintonam per Heddam*, noticed in *Bede's Ecclesiastical History* ed. Colgrave and Mynors, pp. l–li. For the altar, see an indulgence issued by bp. John of Llandaff, 9 Sept. 1254, offering 10 days remission of sins to all *qui altare beati Birini*

Beyond its intrinsic interest and the evidence it supplies of further contact between Langton and the see of Winchester, this controversy undoubtedly excited the personal interest of des Roches, who before leaving for the crusade, commissioned Henry of Avranches to compose a metrical life of St Birinus.[88] We have seen already that des Roches patronized hospitals dedicated to St Thomas of Canterbury. In 1218 he had accompanied his pupil Henry III to the translation of St Wulfstan's relics in Worcester cathedral. Subsequently he took a close interest in the Confessor's abbey at Westminster and in 1220, may have encouraged his royal ward to lay the foundations of the Westminster Lady Chapel, the start of Henry III's lifelong obsession with the abbey and cult of St Edward the Confessor. At Winchester des Roches completed the rebuilding of the east end of the cathedral, work which may well have been associated with the overall setting of the shrine of St Swithun.[89] The poem on St Birinus he commissioned from Henry of Avranches makes much of des Roches' position as successor to the old English saints Birinus, Swithun and Aethelwold. His foundation at Halesowen was endowed with the patronage of a pilgrim centre to St Kenelm, whilst amongst his household Master Philip de Lucy gave a tooth relic of St Aethelbert to Hereford cathedral.[90]

Throughout his career, des Roches' alien origins were the subject of execration amongst the native English chroniclers. His foreign birth made him vulnerable to xenophobia stirred up against him by his political rivals, and contributed markedly to his misfortunes in 1214, 1223–4 and again during the 1230s. Yet in his own cathedral city, des Roches was surrounded by the relics of the Saxon saints, by a tradition more truly native even than the self-proclaimed Englishness of his detractors amongst the cosmopolitan higher clergy and baronage. In

---

confessoris et aliorum sanctorum in quorum honore altare nominatim dedicatum est visitaverint, discovered November 1923 in an aumbry behind the panelling of the Langton chapel of Winchester cathedral, probably once the altar of Birinus; Winchester Cathedral Library, unsorted charters.

[88] *Henry of Avranches*, ed. Cox Russell, pp. 123–5, prints excerpts. A full edition is provided by D. Townsend, 'The Vita Sancti Birini of Henry of Avranches (BHL 1364)', *Analecta Bollandiana*, cxii (1994), pp. 309–38, noting miracles associated with Birinus' relics at Winchester at p. 336. For the evidence which this poem contains of des Roches' origins see above p. 21.

[89] The relationship between the Lady Chapel and the shrine is considered in detail, though with very different emphasis, by Draper, 'The retrochoir of Winchester Cathedral', pp. 1–16; J. Crook, 'St Swithun of Winchester', in *Winchester Cathedral, Nine Hundred Years 1093–1993*, ed. J. Crook (Chichester 1993), pp. 57–68.

[90] R. Rawlinson, *The History and Antiquities of Hereford* (London 1717), appendix p. 30; Colvin, *The White Canons*, p. 181.

dealing with the bishop's fellow alien Fawkes de Bréauté, Matthew Paris twice makes Fawkes declare his fidelity to the English saints Alban and Aetheldreda.[91] Just as the first generation of Norman bishops had encouraged veneration of the pre-Conquest saints as a means of assimilation with the English church, may not des Roches have sought to follow their example?[92] It is certainly peculiar that, of all the thirteenth-century bishops of Winchester, it should have been des Roches, an alien, whose interest in the Saxon saints was most clearly pronounced.

Des Roches' commission for a life of St Birinus throws into relief yet another of the bishop's abiding interests, his concern for money. Henry of Avranches had still to be paid for his poem at the time of des Roches' sailing for the east. We know this from the concluding lines of another poem written for des Roches: Avranches' verses on the bishop's expedition to Jerusalem.[93] These latter consist of a fairly crude series of puns based on the name Peter des Roches, who becomes the rock upon which the church is founded and the stones from which the cathedral of Winchester, of saints Swithun and Peter, is fashioned: 'Now you doubly adorn Syon, Oh Peter, and labour to raise and sustain its rocks and stones.' Presuming the poem to have been written before the bishop's sailing, it contains one surprisingly prophetic variation on this overworked conceit: 'The walls of Jerusalem rejoice that destiny prepares such a rock for them who shall be both their foundation and their crowning monument (*tholus*).' In 1229 it was indeed to be des Roches who helped rebuild the walls and defence towers of the city of Jerusalem.

Thus with all his preparations complete, having made his peace with church and king, des Roches set out for the east in the company of Savaric de Mauléon and the bishop of Exeter, around the last week in June 1227. He clearly anticipated being absent for several years since he was granted letters of protection to run until Michaelmas 1230.[94] We possess far less knowledge of his activities on crusade than we do of his preparations. Our only sources are a few papal letters, the English chroniclers and the comments of a Benedictine monk of

---

[91] Paris, *CM*, iii, pp. 12–13, 120–1, v, pp. 323–4; *Hist. Ang. Min.*, ii, pp. 265–6.
[92] For the Norman use of Saxon cults, see D. J. A. Matthew, *The Norman Conquest* (London 1966), pp. 199–205; S. J. Ridyard, '"Condigna Veneratio": post-Conquest attitudes to the saints of the Anglo-Saxons', *Anglo-Norman Studies* ix (1986), ed. R. A. Brown, pp. 179–206.
[93] *Henry of Avranches* ed. Cox Russell, pp. 125–6, no. 155.
[94] *Pat. R. 1225–32*, p. 130. For Savaric de Mauléon see above p. 225. Des Roches appears last at court on 20 June; C53/18, m. 1.

Andres (dep. Pas de Calais), whose interest in des Roches could have come either through the close connections between Andres and Canterbury, or from Poitou via Andres' links to its mother-house of St Sauveur de Charroux (dep. Vienne).[95]

The course of the crusade was determined in August 1227, when Frederick II fell ill and retired from the fleet as it sailed from Brindisi. As a result he was excommunicated by the new pope, Gregory IX, and unfairly or not, found himself liable to the full penalties detailed in the Treaty of San Germano two years earlier.[96] Des Roches himself accompanied the main body of the fleet, landing in Palestine some time in early October. Within a few weeks, in company with his fellow spiritual leaders, he wrote to Gregory IX, announcing the emperor's failure to arrive, as a result of which many pilgrims had returned immediately to Europe. The 800 knights who remained had placed themselves under the leadership of the duke of Limburg, who was determined to break the truce agreed with Damascus in 1221, and to prepare for a march on Jerusalem by fortifying Joppa and Caesarea. Des Roches and his colleagues informed pope Gregory that they would wait until the following August, presumably in hope of the emperor's arrival, before launching their assault on the Holy City. Their letter was widely disseminated from Rome; at least two copies survive in English sources, one transcribed by Roger Wendover at St Albans, another bound up with the annals of Waverley Abbey sited within des Roches' own diocese.[97]

For the next twelve months the bishop was occupied in strengthening the defences of crusader Palestine. English commentators single out his work at Sidon and Joppa. The Dunstable annalist states that it was through his efforts that Ascalon was restored to Christian control, although the evidence for this restoration has been called into question.[98] At Acre, des Roches re-established the hospital of St Thomas Becket, reputedly founded by his former master Richard I. As with St Thomas' hospital, Southwark, he transferred it to a less crowded site replete with a supply of running water.[99] The precise

---

[95] The Chronicle of William of Andres, *MGHS*, xxiv, pp. 684ff. This is a rich and under-used source for events in England, drawn to my attention by Giles, 'Two English bishops', p. 51, where it is erroneously described as Italian.

[96] Van Cleve, 'The crusade of Frederick II', pp. 446–7.

[97] *Acta*, no. 129.

[98] *AM*, iii (Dunstable), pp. 112, 126; Paris, *Hist. Ang. Min.* , ii, p. 304; *CM*, iii, p. 490, and see Giles, 'Two English bishops', pp. 52–4.

[99] In general see A. J. Forey, 'The military order of St Thomas of Acre', *EHR* 92 (1977), pp. 481–9.

details of this move are far from clear. The Dunstable annalist states that des Roches placed the hospital under the custody of the order of Santiago (*Spatae Hispaniensis*), which would fit in with our knowledge of the bishop's earlier pilgrimage to the shrine of St James at Compostela. Nevertheless, by 1236, when Gregory IX came to confirm the bishop's actions, the hospital had been transferred to the rule of the Teutonic knights.[100] News of des Roches' militarization of the hospital at Acre appears to have reached England very quickly since, by the autumn of 1228, bishop Eustace de Fauconberg witnessed the establishment or possibly the refoundation of a London sister-house of the new order of St Thomas Acre.[101] The house in Palestine had already acquired gifts from courtiers with strong links to des Roches: Geoffrey fitz Peter, his predecessor as Justiciar, and Robert of Thurnham, King John's seneschal in Gascony and Poitou.[102] Their prior involvement may help to explain the bishop's intervention after 1227. Subsequently Philip Marmion and Peter de Maulay, close associates of des Roches, figure amongst the principal benefactors of the order in England.[103]

Just as des Roches' letters to the pope and even his activities as religious patron were speedily communicated to England, so the general development of the crusade was a subject of great interest at the English court. Des Roches' departure for Jerusalem was sufficiently momentous an event to be used in the dating clause to at least one private charter.[104] As the crusade progressed, so England was bombarded with newsletters from Rome, the Empire and the Holy Land. Attempting to steer between the rival polemic of pope and emperor, Henry III wrote to Frederick urging him to fulfil his vow and depart for the east.[105] Meanwhile the pope's diatribes against the emperor are reflected in the generally hostile attitude shown to

---

[100] *Acta*, appendix 2, no. 30. Although in 1291 there is specific reference to the presence of knights of Santiago at the siege of Acre, no mention is made of either the knights of St Thomas or the Teutonic order; Forey, 'The military order of St Thomas of Acre', p. 489, n. 2.

[101] *Ibid.*, pp. 483–5.

[102] *Ibid.*, pp. 486, 490; BL ms. Cotton Tiberius C v (Register of St Thomas' Acon), ff. 255r–v.

[103] Forey, 'The military order of St Thomas of Acre', p. 490; BL Cotton ms. Tiberius C v, f. 255r and see the many charters witnessed and the one issued by de Maulay's steward, Reginald of Kettleburgh, ff. 257r, 258r, 263r–264r, 266v–269r, 270r–v.

[104] Cambridge, Gonville and Caius College, Muniments Box 23, no. 23, a convention between John the cook and Master John of Gayton over land at Westoning, Beds., dated to the feast of the purification *proximum postquam dominus P. Winton' episcopus transfretavit versus Ieresol'*.

[105] *Cl. R. 1227–31*, pp. 93–4, 109.

Frederick by the English chronicles.[106] The death of Stephen Langton
and the subsequent election dispute at Canterbury inclined both king
and clergy to seek papal favour. Gregory himself faced an insurrection
in Rome. Desperate to reassert his authority over both Rome and the
Empire, in 1229 he obtained a grant of a tenth from the English
church to assist his struggle. In effect, des Roches' colleagues at home
conspired to finance an army against the bishop's leader on crusade.[107]

Despite the mounting tensions in Europe, the army in Palestine
continued to be boosted by new recruits during the course of 1228,
amongst them several men well known to des Roches. In July 1228
Henry III granted 500 marks to Philip de Aubigné who had recently
taken the cross for a second time, being already a veteran of the
crusade to Damietta.[108] De Aubigné's relations with des Roches were
by no means clear-cut. Closely associated with the bishop during the
early years of the minority, he had managed to establish equally
friendly relations with de Burgh and others of des Roches' political
rivals. After 1223 he had retained his position at court. Nevertheless,
he remained a regular guest on the Winchester estates and in 1226–7
was presented with gifts at Fareham, possibly en route to negotiating a
truce with France.[109] The fact that he received generous assistance
from the crown before sailing for Palestine indicates the degree of
favour with which he was regarded in England, and contrasts
markedly with the lack of direct aid afforded des Roches. Another
man to set sail at much the same time was the Angevin courtier,
Joldewin de Doué. Like de Aubigné, hovering on the fringes of des
Roches' network of alien familiars during the 1220s, he too had
retained his place after the bishop's fall and in May 1228 was granted
letters of protection as a crusader.[110]

[106] See Wendover, *Flores*, iv, pp. 157–93, which records several of the papal and imperial
letters directed to England, for which see also *Cal.Pap.Reg.*, i, p. 119. For hostility to
Frederick see also *AM*, ii (Waverley), pp. 303–4.
[107] Wendover, *Flores*, iv, pp. 184–5, 200–4.
[108] *Cal.Lib.R.1226–40*, p. 93.
[109] For his entertainment after 1223 see Mss. 19DR, mm. 2, 2d, 7d, 9d; 22DR, mm. 5, 8.
For his diplomatic mission of 1227 see *Pat. R. 1225–32*, pp. 107, 135.
[110] *Pat. R. 1225–32*, p. 188; *Cal.Chart.R.1226–57*, p. 57; *Cal.Lib.R.1226–40*, p. 81. Joldewin
was a native of Doué-la-Fontaine (dep. Maine-et-Loire), sprung from a family active in
Plantagenet service since the eleventh century. His executors included the bishop of
Angers and his sister, described as *domina Argentenii* (Argenton, dep. Deux-Sèvres); SC1/
3/65. His brother, Geoffrey, was married to Joan de Valura, by whose right he acquired
rents in the Isle of Oléron; *Rôles Gascons 26–28 Henry III (1242–1254)*, ed. F. Michel (Paris
1885), nos. 18, 2627. For Joldewin's involvement in diplomatic missions to Poitou and in
King John's expeditions to the province, see *RLC*, i, pp. 84b, 418b, 424b; *Pat. R. 1216–
25*, pp. 107, 126, 233; *Rot. Chart.*, pp. 200b, 220b; *RL*, i, no. cxv. Philip de Aubigné had

Far more significant than the recruitment of these Plantagenet courtiers, was the long-awaited arrival of the emperor Frederick II who landed at Joppa on 15 November 1228 to assume his place at the head of the crusade. His position was extremely delicate. No longer the honoured ally of mother church, he was shunned by the Patriarch of Jerusalem and other papal agents as an excommunicate at war with Rome.[111] In turn, this placed des Roches in an embarrassing situation. In theory the bishop should have spurned any contact with the emperor. In practice, no doubt conscious of the parallels to his previous association with King John, des Roches showed little hesitation in serving an excommunicate prince, placing the success of the crusade above the political designs of the papacy.

Rather than press on with the proposed offensive against Jerusalem, Frederick sought to obtain the city by negotiation. The winter of 1228–9 was occupied in diplomatic exchanges between his agents and the sultan of Damascus, in which the bishop of Exeter appears to have played an important part.[112] Their outcome was spectacularly successful: a treaty which guaranteed a peaceful reoccupation of Jerusalem. In March des Roches accompanied the emperor and the bulk of the crusading army into the Holy City, lost to Christendom for the past forty years.[113] On 18 March Frederick crowned himself in the church of the Holy Sepulchre, but his triumph was short-lived. Not only did he have to contend with the enmity of the pope's supporters in the east, but the very terms of the treaty with Damascus were the subject of scandal. A negotiated settlement between an excommunicate and an infidel, it failed to win over those who counselled undying war against the forces of Islam, whilst in detail it did nothing to satisfy the specific territorial claims of the Patriarchate of Jerusalem. On the day after Frederick's coronation, the archbishop of Caesarea arrived to place Jerusalem under Interdict.[114] Back in England, contradictory and confusing reports of the treaty were circulated. The Waverley annals preserve a letter which may well be from des Roches himself, dated at Acre on 20 April 1228, presenting the settlement as a remarkable victory for the church.[115] Wendover records a newsletter

at one time served to pass on his pension from the crown and des Roches had given him money towards an embassy to Poitou; *RLC*, i, pp. 467, 550. For his contacts with the Winchester estates 1220–6, see Mss. 16DR, m. 2d; 21DR, m. 9d.

[111] Van Cleve, 'The crusade of Frederick II', pp. 451–3.
[112] *AM*, i (Margam), pp. 36–7.
[113] *Ibid.*, i, p. 37; Van Cleve, 'The crusade of Frederick II', pp. 455–8.
[114] *Ibid.*, pp. 456–8.
[115] *AM*, ii, pp. 305–6. The title to the letter is missing, but note that the author describes

sent from Frederick II describing the truce in similarly glowing terms.[116] However, at much the same time the duke of Brabant wrote to the English court with a thoroughly garbled version of events, claiming that the emperor had contracted a marriage with a daughter of the sultan of Damascus, a scandalous assertion which nevertheless appears to have been credited by the author of the Dunstable annals.[117] The Tewkesbury chronicler reports that the pope sent messages to every diocese in England, denouncing the peace that had been made with the Moslems. At court this may have been less than welcome. Henry III had himself been in contact with Damascus for several years, and in 1228 had written to the sultan urging him to release his Christian hostages.[118]

The confusion reigning in England was as nothing compared to that which now developed amongst the crusading army. The emperor was already anxious to return to Europe, where a papal force was marching south to seize Apulia. On 18 March he had opened negotiations with des Roches, Brewer and the masters of the military orders to seek their assistance in the refortification of Jerusalem. Meeting no immediate response, on the following morning he and his entourage quit the city, and amidst general consternation prepared to return to the coast.[119] This should not be taken to imply a breach of relations with des Roches. William of Andres tells us that between them, bishop and emperor were responsible for rebuilding the gate of St Stephen and the Tower of David, two of the principal fortifications of Jerusalem, the latter being the site of the royal palace before 1187. To accomplish this work des Roches must have remained in Jerusalem after the emperor's departure, working perhaps with the Teutonic knights, Frederick's firm supporters, who are known to have assisted the work of rebuilding.[120]

Richard I as *perpetuae memoriae dominum nostrum*, employs a careful dating clause and writes in the first person plural, which would hardly have been the case had he been a humble Surrey knight as suggested by Giles, 'Two English bishops', p. 51.

[116] Wendover, *Flores*, iv, pp. 189–93.

[117] *DD*, no. 214 (*RL*, i, no. cclxxxii); *AM*, iii, pp. 111–12, which claims that Frederick had taken the sultan's sister as his concubine.

[118] *AM*, i, p. 73. In 1225 Henry had sent gifts to the sultan and as in 1228 used a man named Anselm of Genoa, the mailman (*Mallonus*) of the sultan, as his go-between; *RLC*, ii, p. 13b; *Cl. R. 1227–31*, p. 94. For Anselm, who received a money fee of 30m at the Exchequer and carried on a lucrative trade supplying crossbows to the court, see also *Pat. R. 1216–25*, p. 502; *RLC*, ii, p. 12b; *Pat. R. 1225–32*, p. 180; *Cal.Chart.R. 1226–57*, p. 70; *Cal.Lib.R. 1226–40*, p. 71.

[119] Van Cleve, 'The crusade of Frederick II', pp. 458–9; J. L. A. Huillard-Bréholles (ed.), *Historia Diplomatica Frederici Secundi*, 6 vols. in 11 (Paris 1852–61), iii, p. 109.

[120] *MGHS*, xxiv, p. 769. For evidence of rebuilding, see Van Cleve, 'The crusade of

Returning to Acre, the emperor found the Patriarch equipping an army for war. Rather than risk the collapse of his settlement with Damascus, Frederick placed the Patriarch under house-arrest and attempted to prevent him from communicating with Rome.[121] By late April des Roches and Brewer had also returned to Acre, and according to Wendover were subjected to the same indignities as the Patriarch. But this statement is directly contradicted by the evidence of des Roches' close co-operation with the emperor and by the annals of Winchcombe, which state that Gregory IX subsequently suspended the bishops of Exeter and Winchester from office, presumably for their refusal to support the Patriarch.[122]

Frederick sailed from Acre on 1 May 1229, and it seems likely that des Roches sailed with him. The imperial fleet put in to Cyprus on its return voyage and we must assume that des Roches was at one time on the island since a rumour reached England that he had died there.[123] Arriving at Brindisi on 10 June, the emperor moved rapidly to secure his position against the papal army. Des Roches too landed in Europe at much the same time, since by 22 July 1229 he had arrived at the papal court.[124] Whereas his erstwhile companion, William Brewer, returned almost immediately to England, des Roches stayed on in Italy acting as a mediator between pope and emperor, retaining the confidence of Frederick and rapidly establishing favour with Gregory.[125] According to both the Tewkesbury and Dunstable annalists, he played a crucial role in reconciling emperor and pope.[126] An Italian chronicler mentions his attendance at the peace negotiations at San Germano in the spring of 1230, and states that Frederick appealed to des Roches to witness his good behaviour in the east.[127] At Ceprano on 28 August, he issued letters in

---

Frederick II', p. 459; Huillard-Bréholles (ed.), *Historia Diplomatica Frederici Secundi*, iii, p. 98; *AM*, i (Margam), p. 37, and Frederick's own claims reported by Wendover, *Flores*, iv, p. 193. For the sites themselves, see T. S. R. Boase, *Kingdoms and Strongholds of the Crusades* (London 1971), pp. 8, 20–1.

[121] Van Cleve, 'The crusade of Frederick II', pp. 459–60.

[122] Wendover, *Flores*, iv, p. 199; BL ms. Cotton Faustina B i, f. 28v, and see Giles, 'Two English bishops', p. 55.

[123] SC1/6/148, printed by J. Boussard, 'Ralph Neville évêque de Chichester d'après sa correspondance', *Revue Historique* 176 (1935), p. 228.

[124] *AM*, ii (Waverley), p. 308.

[125] Giles, 'Two English bishops', pp. 55–6.

[126] *AM*, i, p. 76, iii, p. 126.

[127] The Chronicle of Richard of San Germano, ed. C. A. Garufi, in L. A. Muratori, *Rerum Italicarum Scriptores*, new edition, ed. G. Carducci and others, vol. vii, part ii (Bologna 1937–8), p. 163.

company with nearly a dozen German, Italian and French bishops confirming the settlement between emperor and pope.[128]

From August 1230 until the spring of 1231 we know nothing of the bishop's movements, but it seems reasonable to assume that he remained with the papal Curia. Clearly he was in no hurry to return to England. The frustrations of domestic politics can have had little attraction compared to the new role he had carved for himself as international statesman. Even so, he seems not to have lost touch with England. Just as his actions on crusade and his rumoured death in Cyprus filtered north to the English court, so he seems to have been visited in Italy by members of his household left behind in 1227. Bartholomew des Roches, the bishop's kinsman and archdeacon of Winchester, appears to have died in Italy in 1229. Within a month des Roches was able to notify the bishop of Salisbury of Bartholomew's death, implying an ease of communication with his adopted homeland.[129] By the spring of 1231 the bishop himself was preparing to return. In April he received a papal commission in company with the archbishop of Sens, to negotiate peace between England and France and in the following month various clerks who had accompanied him to the east were rewarded with papal dispensation to hold benefices in plurality.[130] Having met the earl of Chester to fulfil his peace mission in France, around 15 July he landed in England and on 1 August 1231 was received with great ceremony in Winchester cathedral.[131] By 10 August he had joined the English court at Painscastle on the Welsh Marches.[132]

Des Roches had been absent for more than four years. In 1227 he had sailed for the east a disappointed man, seeking consolation for his thwarted political career. The king and the government of England had been snatched from his hands. De Burgh, Langton and their allies were in the ascendant and Henry III was on the brink of a continental expedition to reconquer the Plantagenet lands in France. Church and baronage co-operated to restrict des Roches and his associates to the provinces. But much had changed during the bishop's absence abroad; Langton had died and his principal clerical ally, Richard Poer, had

---

[128] *Acta*, no. 130 and references there cited.

[129] *Reg. St Osmund*, i, p. 388; SC1/6/96.

[130] *Les Registres de Grégoire IX (1227–41)*, ed. L. Auvray, 4 vols. (Ecole Française de Rome 1896–1955), i, nos. 621, 638–9.

[131] *AM*, i (Tewkesbury), p. 76, ii (Winchester), p. 86, (Waverley), p. 310, iii (Dunstable), p. 127; Wendover, *Flores*, iv, p. 224; BL ms. Cotton Faustina B i (Winchcombe annals), f. 29v.

[132] C53/25, m. 4.

been translated from Salisbury to the distant splendours of Durham. The king's plans for an expedition to France had been cancelled, rescheduled for 1229, cancelled again and eventually resulted in 1230 in a fruitless and mismanaged progress from Brittany to Bordeaux. De Burgh was no longer the unchallenged master of the court. His personal ambitions, his mishandling of the Breton expedition and his marriage had brought him into conflict with king, barons and church.[133]

In 1231 des Roches returned the hero of the hour, a victorious crusader who had helped win back the Holy Sepulchre, basking for the first time in a truly international reputation, the confidant of emperor and pope. His crusade had been by no means an unmitigated success; its squabbles had been noted with foreboding by the English chroniclers, who found it difficult to reconcile the reconquest of Jerusalem with the excommunication of Frederick II. Wendover sought a millennial explanation; as reported by the astronomers of Toledo, the world was entering its final age, divine portents foretold the coming apocalypse.[134] Beginning with his coronation manifesto of March 1229 Frederick himself, assisted by such Hohenstaufen apologists as Nicholas of Bari, encouraged this apocalyptic outlook, with Frederick cast in the role of last emperor, destined to sit in Christlike majesty over the earth.[135]

The reconquest of Jerusalem was a momentous event. Des Roches' involvement in it brought him great prestige but at the same time, by enhancing his cosmopolitan reputation, was to prove both boon and handicap in his domestic political career. He returned to England *fêted* as warrior and statesman but all the more conspicuously an alien, steeped in the traditions of France, Rome, the Empire and the east. The crusade and the personality of Frederick II had affected him profoundly. In one of several poems addressed to the emperor, the bishop's former protégé, Henry of Avranches, reported a conversation he had with des Roches, quite possibly at the papal court after 1229:

The bishop of Winchester, who was a pilgrim and a foreigner with you in Syria, who knows you well and who in turn is well known to me, once told me that nothing pleased you more than the very best in craftsmanship, so does your virtue shine out. Be it of beast or man, a horse as swift as Pelias or

---

[133] D. A. Carpenter, 'The fall of Hubert de Burgh', *Journal of British Studies* 19 part 2 (1980), pp. 1–6.

[134] Wendover, *Flores*, iv, pp. 180–2, 194.

[135] Mayer, *The Crusades*, p. 230, and references there cited.

weapons like the Cyclops ... these things suit you and you will accept nothing else, whatever the cost.[136]

Dynamic, placing himself above all rival authorities of church and state, surrounded by magnificence and luxury, Frederick II must have appeared to des Roches in stark contrast to the petulant, indigent Henry III. The bishop might well have been tempted to regard Frederick as a far more attractive model of kingship. He was bound to him as previously he had been bound to his sovereign and friend, King John, by common resistance to Rome and by personal admiration. Yet he was to find to his cost that the sort of remarks he had made to Henry of Avranches would be less than well received at the Plantagenet court.

In material terms des Roches did not return empty handed. To Matthew Paris he gave a book by William of Tyre, on the marvels of the east, and he sent letters to St Albans in company with William Brewer and the Patriarch of Jerusalem testifying to the authenticity of a cross brought back from the valley of Josophat.[137] Somewhere on his travels, more likely at the papal Curia than in Palestine, he had acquired a precious relic, the foot of St Philip, which he gave to the monks of St Swithun's Winchester.[138] His interest in the east was to remain with him for the rest of his life; in 1237 he was commissioned to preach a crusade for the rescue of the Latin kingdom of Constantinople.[139] His will left 500 marks to the hospital he had refounded at Acre, whose London house was patronized in the 1230s

---

[136] E. Winkelmann (ed.), 'Drei Gedichte Heinrichs von Avranches an Kaiser Friedrich II', in *Forschungen zur Deutschen Geschichte*, xviii (Gottingen 1878), pp. 487–8, lines 23ff.

[137] Paris, *Hist. Ang. Min.*, i, p. 63n.; *Gesta Abbatum Monasterii Sancti Albani*, ed. H. T. Riley, 3 vols. (RS 1867), i, p. 291, which refers to a more detailed account 'at the end of the book', no longer to be found. See also R. H. C. Davis, 'William of Tyre', in *Relations between East and West in the Middle Ages*, ed. D. Baker (Edinburgh 1973), p. 71, who identifies the book brought back by des Roches as a lost chronicle based on Arab sources.

[138] *AM*, ii (Winchester), p. 86; H. Wharton, *Anglia Sacra*, 2 vols. (London 1691), i, p. 286. The entire body of St Philip had been brought to the West following the sack of Constantinople in 1204. King John presented a head relic of the saint to Reading Abbey where it quickly attracted indulgences; D. Bethell, 'The making of a twelfth-century relic collection', *Studies in Church History* 8 (1972), ed. D. Baker, p. 64, n. 1; *Reading Abbey Cartularies*, ed. Kemp, i, pp. 166,174. The foot relic was still at Winchester at the Reformation; Cambridge, Corpus Christi College ms. 111 (Inventory of Winchester cathedral *c.* 1540), p. 356, *Item St Phillipe foote covered with plate of gold and with stones*. Subsequently, it was rescued from the sack of the other relics in the cathedral treasury and smuggled to Bruges from where, in 1592, it passed to the relic collection of King Philip II of Spain at the Escorial; P. Bogan, 'Dom Thomas Figg and the foot of St Philip', *Winchester Cathedral Record*, lxi (1992), pp. 22–6.

[139] *Cal. Pap. Reg.*, i, p. 166.

by des Roches' close associates, and whose acquisition of papal privileges in 1236 coincided with the bishop's final visit to Rome.[140]

In the immediate term des Roches had much to occupy him. It is possible that like many another crusader, he had vowed to found a religious house on his return to England. Less than a fortnight after his arrival at court, he was granted the advowson of Titchfield church to bestow upon a community of canons he proposed to establish there. Lying on the Hampshire coast, close to the episcopal harbour at Fareham, Titchfield Abbey was in the 1290s to be reminded of its ancient obligation to receive the bishop of Winchester on his return from Rome or overseas.[141] It is conceivable that des Roches had landed at Fareham on his return in 1231 and established the abbey to commemorate the fact. In any event it is astonishing that, despite the expense of his expedition, he should have found the resources to endow not only Titchfield but within the next few years monastic houses at Selborne, Netley and Clarté Dieu. The king's grant of Titchfield is also a potent symbol of des Roches' rehabilitation at court; a deliberate act of compensation, intended to cancel out the punitive fine of £500 extracted from des Roches in 1227 before his departure for the east.[142]

It was not only monastic patronage that occupied the bishop on his return. There were his manorial accounts for the past four years to be gone through, and various misdemeanours to be put right. For example, the monastic treasurer of St Swithun's was found to have concealed judicial profits from the manor of Bishop's Waltham. In addition, he had seized the opportunity of des Roches' crusade to marry off an episcopal ward without permission, for which offence the bishop fined him 25 marks.[143] Several members of des Roches' household left behind in England had died during his absence; John of Herriard, his principal attorney, William de Batilly, one of his stewards, William of Shorwell once his under-sheriff of Hampshire, and two successive archdeacons of Winchester, Bartholomew des Roches and a man named Roger. Bracton was to devote a short discussion in his *De Legibus* to the problems caused by the death of the bishop's attorneys during his absence on crusade.[144] Des Roches' return was followed by a careful extent of the episcopal estates in which the chief

[140] Paris, *CM*, iii, pp. 490–1; *Les Registres de Gregoire IX*, ed. Auvray, no. 2944.
[141] *Cal. Chart. R. 1226–57*, p. 139; *Reg. Pontoise*, pp. xxx, 267. For Titchfield in general see *Acta*, nos. 67–71.
[142] C60/30, m. 1, and see above pp. 227–8.
[143] *Reg. Pontoise*, p. 667; Ms. 27DR, m. 1d.
[144] Bracton, *De Legibus*, v, p. 196.

fields, previously measured in customary acres varying from region to region, were assessed according a standard acreage.[145] Over the next few years this survey appears to have been put to good use, since we find the episcopal Exchequer querying and referring back the accounts of bailiffs who claimed suspiciously low yields for arable crops.[146]

Yet, however much time he may have devoted to his household and domestic affairs, des Roches might well regard them as a wholly unsatisfactory alternative to the great issues that had recently occupied his attention. The confidant of pope and emperor could hardly be satisfied in rooting out petty pilfering. The crusade had provided him with a taste of glory and revived his political ambitions. Rather than vegetate in his diocese, the bishop had been offered a platform from which to relaunch his career at court. And so it was that he prepared to make his most notorious intervention in English politics.

[145] Titow, 'Land and population', pp. 14, 155–6.
[146] See for example Mss. 27DR, m. 9; 28DR, mm. 3d, 11.

Chapter 8

THE FALL OF HUBERT DE BURGH

The biography of Peter des Roches to 1231 can be written as merely one aspect of a wider history, charted in the standard accounts of the reigns of John and Henry III. But for the period after 1231 there exists no reliable narrative upon which to found an assessment of the bishop's career. What to date has been a study concentrated upon one man must be widened to comprehend the court as a whole; the factions and fortunes whose rise and fall frame the so-called 'Poitevin' regime of 1231 to 1234. The years in question are crowded with incident, including a war between king and barons, as significant in its way as the far more famous baronial wars of 1215–17 and 1264–5. To understand these events, to map their progress, motivation and consequences, we need first and foremost to establish a basic chronology. In addition, the regime of 1232–4 has been seen as bringing about two fundamental changes in English government: the importation to court of a large number of aliens, specifically Poitevins; and an attempt to overhaul royal finance leading to fundamental reforms in the administration of the Exchequer and the county farms. Both of these issues, financial 'reform' and the role played by aliens, will baulk large in what follows. Inevitably, des Roches must fade for a while from centre-stage, to take up a position in the wings. Yet, just as it would be impossible to write a biography of des Roches that excluded the all-important period during the 1230s when he once again secured power at court, so we cannot hope to understand the shifting coalitions and upheavals of the 1230s without looking back to the thirty or more years of political experience which des Roches brought with him to office. The seeds of the regime of 1232–4 were sown long before the bishop's triumphant return from crusade.

In the final months of 1223 the fragile consensus of Henry III's minority council had collapsed. Des Roches and a group of associates were forced from office by an *ad hoc* alliance of bishops and barons led by the Justiciar, Hubert de Burgh. Both factions were eager to profit from the spoils promised to whomever held power when the king came of age. Des Roches' group was the more coherent, its members united by their close association with the person and policies of King John. and by the fact that many of them were aliens. De Burgh and his allies, principally archbishop Langton, half a dozen of his suffragans and the earls of Pembroke and Salisbury, formed a much looser confederation at court. They were able nonetheless to secure a wider constituency of support in the country at large: by employing anti-alien rhetoric; by activating latent hostility against men too closely linked to the detested policies of King John; and by promising to maintain those limitations upon royal power enshrined in Magna Carta. Their opponents baulked at the prospect of civil war, resigning their custodies in the early months of 1224. Only Fawkes de Bréauté was utterly disgraced. Des Roches, the earl of Chester and their adherents were excluded from the king's inner councils, but otherwise left relatively unharmed. Castles, counties and the central offices of state were henceforth reserved to de Burgh and his supporters who, with the king's coming of age, had access to a rich bounty of escheats, wardships and privileges.

Outwardly de Burgh was triumphant. Between 1224 and 1231 he consolidated an already rich estate, obtaining grants of land in Wales which established him as one of the most powerful lords in the southern Marches. But in the meantime, the loose confederation over which he had presided since 1224 showed increasing signs of strain. His marriage to a Scottish princess originally intended for the king, and his promotion as earl of Kent in 1227, catapulted him into the ranks of the higher nobility, where as a *parvenu* he failed to obtain ready acceptance. Even the king considered it expedient to limit the descent of Hubert's earldom to issue by the high-born Margaret of Scotland.[1] The countess of Salisbury spurned a proposal of marriage from Hubert's nephew, Raymond.[2]

One means by which Hubert might have compensated for his isolation would have been for him to pack the court and counties with his own placemen. Amongst his kinsmen, Richard his nephew was promoted Justiciar of Ireland; John de Burgh, Hubert's son, was granted custody of the honour of St Pol, in succession to another kinsman, Raymond de Burgh.[3] Raymond himself had been married to the widowed countess of Essex and granted custody of Berkhamsted and the manor of Dartford. Another of the Justiciar's

---

[1]   Powicke, *Henry III*, p. 767.
[2]   Wendover, *Flores*, iv, pp. 113–14.
[3]   *Pat. R. 1225–32*, pp. 178, 348; *Cl.R.1227–31*, pp. 372–4, 418–19.

nephews, Thomas de Blundeville, was elected to the see of Norwich.[4] Several members of Hubert's household were promoted at court. Luke, his chaplain, became successively dean of St Martin's London, and in 1228 archbishop of Dublin;[5] the brothers Ranulph and William le Breton, respectively treasurer of the king's chamber and sheriff of Kent (1226–32);[6] de Burgh's steward, Robert of Cockfield, sheriff of Yorkshire (1227–9) and of Lincolnshire (1229–30);[7] Bertram de Criel, who held principally of de Burgh and witnessed many of his private charters, served as constable of Dover castle until 1230.[8]

But the party of personal satellites which emerged was too small to protect the Justiciar once his position was seriously threatened. By contrast to such households as those which attended des Roches or his principal rival after 1232, Richard Marshal earl of Pembroke, de Burgh's affinity was to prove remarkably weak, not surprisingly perhaps, given the contrast between the relatively low-born de Burgh, with his unwarlike household, and the earls of Pembroke with their conquests in Ireland, Wales and on the tournament fields of France. Little help in time of trouble, de Burgh's affinity was still large enough to exacerbate jealousy at court. Rather than govern through private clique, by filling central and local administration with his own men, de Burgh attempted a delicate balancing act, ensuring that rival interests were kept in sufficient equilibrium to safeguard his own position at the wheel's still centre. It was a policy that depended

[4] *CP*, v, p. 133; *Pat. R. 1225–32*, p. 134; *Cl.R.1227–31*, pp. 418–19; Paris, *CM*, iii, p. 121. For Thomas and his kinship to Hubert, see *AM*, i (Tewkesbury), p. 69; *Acta Guala*, no. 49. He witnesses at least one of Hubert's charters before election to Norwich; Bodl. ms. Rawlinson B336 (St Radegund's cartulary), pp. 170–1. I wish to thank Dr David Crouch for allowing me access to his unpublished collections of comital *acta*, including those of Hubert de Burgh. I am currently preparing de Burgh's charters for publication.

[5] *Pat. R. 1225–32*, p. 232; *Acta Guala*, nos. 3, 76; Paris, *CM*, v, p. 531. For Luke as Hubert's chaplain and as witness to his private charters, see *Reg. St Osmund*, ii, p. 43; BL ms. Campbell Ch. II 12; Canterbury Cathedral D. & C. Library ms. Register B, f. 404r; Bodl. ms. Rawlinson B336, pp. 170–1.

[6] For Ranulph, see Wendover, *Flores*, iv, p. 244; *Pat. R. 1225–32*, p. 435. For William, see *List of Sheriffs for England and Wales*, PRO Lists and Indexes ix (1898), p. 67. For their witnessing de Burgh's charters, see *A Descriptive Catalogue of the Charters and Documents of the Lyttelton Family at Hagley Hall*, ed. I. H. Jeayes (London 1893), no. 12; Guildhall Library London ms. 25122/668; BL ms. Stowe 955 (Anstis' transcripts), f. 86v; Bodl. ms. Rawlinson B336, pp. 170–1; Lambeth Palace Library mss.1212 (Archbishopric cartulary), f. 40r–v; Register of Archbishop Warham I, f. 134r; Lambeth Charter Misc. XI/50.

[7] *List of Sheriffs*, pp. 78, 161; *CRR*, xiv, no. 1518; *Cl.R.1231–4*, p. 289; BL Harley Ch. 47E32.

[8] *Pat. R. 1225–32*, pp. 258–9; Lambeth Palace Library ms. TT1 (Dering transcripts), p. 198, and see the de Burgh *acta* cited above.

above all upon compromise and moderation, two qualities which became increasingly difficult to guarantee after 1227 and the young king's accession to full, personal sovereignty.

THE BACKGROUND TO DES ROCHES' RETURN 1227–1231

In 1227 de Burgh still retained support with barons, church and crown. Within the next four years he was to alienate each of these constituencies in turn. By 1231 the baronial alliances he had established during the king's minority had all but collapsed. The most volatile element here was the growing influence of the king's brother, Richard. In 1225 Richard had been created count of Poitou and sent to attempt a reconquest of the Plantagenet lands lost the previous year. The attempt achieved limited success, securing Plantagenet control over Gascony and a degree of support amongst the fickle Poitevin nobility, ever keen to play off the Plantagenets against the Capetians. But a heavy price had to be paid for such success; more than £50,000, the entire proceeds of the tax of a fifteenth agreed in 1225. The emphasis the expedition laid upon Poitou, and the personal interest in matters Poitevin that it awoke in Richard as count, must take at least part of the responsibility for a decisive shift in Plantagenet ambitions on the continent. Previously these had focussed upon the reconquest of Normandy and the Angevin heartlands lost in 1204. Poitou and Gascony were treated as little more than springboards from which to mount an offensive further north. By 1229, however, the king's closest advisers appear to have become convinced that Normandy was irretrievable. Henry III's claim to the duchy was to be used merely as a bargaining counter, offered to the French in the hope of winning concessions over Poitou.[9]

This shift in emphasis undoubtedly accorded with the wishes of Hubert de Burgh. De Burgh had been seneschal of Poitou before 1215. The province's loss in 1224 during the siege of Bedford must have come as a grievous blow to him, one for which he felt a high degree of personal responsibility. Almost alone amongst the higher nobility, de Burgh possessed no residual interests in Normandy. He

[9] Stacey, *Politics, Policy and Finance*, pp. 160–73, and see *DD*, no. 215, a series of proposals for an Anglo-French settlement, probably to be dated to 1229, in which, at best, the English proposed to recover the dioceses of Avranches and Coutances in order to keep open their communications with the lands which they hoped to recover further south. Should this prove unacceptable to the French, Henry proposed that Anjou and Maine be granted to one of his sisters, who was to be married to Louis IX, with reversion of her lands to Henry should she die childless.

262

had lost no family land there in the *débâcle* of 1204. Indeed, as an Englishman who had come into possession of escheated *Terra Normannorum* after 1204, he could be said to have a strong personal interest in preventing the reunification of the old Anglo-Norman realm.[10] The precise effects of reunification were unfathomable, but one likely consequence would have been to overturn much of the territorial settlement of John's reign. In the process, *Terra Normannorum* would have returned to its rightful Norman claimants. Awards of such land in England had always been reversible in the event of reconquest, with their beneficiaries promised compensation in other escheats should England and Normandy be reunited. In practice, the most likely way for such promises to have been honoured would have been for compensation to be awarded in the form of reconquered crown estates in Normandy. In other words, de Burgh might have been forced to exchange valuable and easily managed lands in England for some distant prize across the Channel, vulnerable at any moment to a revival of French influence. In this respect he was set decisively apart from many of the English nobility. What to the earls of Chester, Warenne and the other survivors of the Anglo-Norman baronage would have meant the reunification of their rightful, cross-Channel inheritances, to de Burgh merely threatened the loss of Hatfield Peverel, North Wheatley and half a dozen of his English manors, with no very attractive prospect of compensation.

This conflict of interests does much to explain de Burgh's mounting unpopularity amongst a group of magnates, including William Marshal the younger, and the earls of Chester, Norfolk, Gloucester, Hereford and Warenne. In 1229 de Burgh was blamed for the collapse of a proposed continental expedition through the inadequacy of its supplies.[11] In 1230, when the expedition finally sailed, it was de Burgh who was considered chiefly responsible for counselling against an invasion of Normandy.[12] Instead, the king was persuaded to engage in a leisurely progress through Poitou and Gascony. Little if any good was achieved. A large number of Poitevin and Gascon barons flocked to the court pledging support. Yet it was support that had to be purchased at considerable cost. For many years the failure of Plantagenet initiatives in Poitou had been blamed on the king's

[10] Johnston, 'The lands of Hubert de Burgh', pp. 424–6, lists Hubert's principal Norman fees, to which should be added Dartford and the St Pol lands held by other members of the de Burgh family.
[11] Wendover, *Flores*, iv, pp. 204–5.
[12] *Ibid.*, pp. 214–15, 217.

unwillingness to spend money. In 1230 Henry III veered to the opposite extreme. Flushed with enthusiasm by his first encounter with his continental inheritance, he pledged something approaching 4,000 marks a year in pensions and subsidies to the notoriously fickle Poitevin baronage.[13] Whether de Burgh endorsed this extravagance it is difficult to say. The chances are that it reflects the king's growing unwillingness to recognize the restraints on his patronage powers urged by the Justiciar. The problems for de Burgh in this respect had long been apparent. Henry was now a young man, aged 23 in 1230. Government was conducted in his name, although in practice a disproportionate degree of power continued to rest with de Burgh and the other figures, for the most part survivors from the reign of King John, who had been prominent in Henry's minority council. His long minority had accustomed both the king and his courtiers to a shift away from the customary personal rule of Henry's Plantagenet ancestors, towards government by council. And yet there are indications that Henry himself had begun to demand a greater say in affairs of state, freed from the nannying influence of de Burgh. Since his coming of age, the royal household had been greatly expanded. Its principal officers, the stewards, were none of them personal protégés of de Burgh. Between 1227 and 1231 nearly seventy household knights were retained, only a tiny proportion of whom owed personal allegiance to the Justiciar.[14] This was partly because de Burgh himself maintained a distinctly unmilitary household, unsuitable recruiting ground for the king. A majority of the king's new retainers were relatively landless aliens, dependent upon money fees from the crown. In this sense, the growth of the royal household and the pensions promised to Poitou both represent a significant loosening of de Burgh's control over patronage, and a vastly increased burden on the king's revenues. Neither development was calculated to ease de Burgh's problems in curbing the growth of faction, of the king's ambitions, or of royal expenditure, which could only be met by imposing unpopular exactions on the already restless English baronage.

---

[13]   *DD*, nos. 224, 229, 232–3, and in general, see E. Berger, 'Les préparatifs d'une invasion anglaise et la descente de Henri III en Bretagne (1229–1230)', *Bibliothèque de l'Ecole des Chartes* liv (1893), pp. 5–44, esp. pp. 32–7. There is no surviving *liberate* roll between July 1230 and October 1232. For the payment of pensions agreed in 1230, see *Cal.Lib.R.1226–40*, pp. 187–8, and below pp. 322–4. In 1229, as part of the proposals for an Anglo-French settlement, the English had been prepared to pledge whatever money might be required to achieve their ends, regardless of cost; *DD*, no. 215.

[14]   Walker, 'The Anglo-Welsh wars 1217–1267', pp. 70–8.

Continental policy was not the only respect in which de Burgh began to lose the confidence of the English baronage. Equally significant, the years 1228 to 1231 witnessed a series of costly and for the most part futile campaigns in Wales, personally supervised by de Burgh and aimed principally at protecting the Justiciar's lordship in the southern Marches. It was not so much that de Burgh used the crown's resources to carve out a private estate for himself; rather, that by assuming the defence of strategic points on the Marches, he weakened the barons' resolve to assist the crown by a too close identification between the king's interests and Hubert's own.[15] Hubert's actions in Wales must have been viewed with particular suspicion by William Marshal, who had already tried unsuccessfully to oppose Richard de Burgh, Hubert's nephew, in Ireland. In 1226 William had been removed as Irish Justiciar, and Richard promoted in his place.[16] In conflict with de Burgh in Wales, Ireland and France, the Marshal was potentially Hubert's most dangerous rival, related, by marriage, to the earls of Norfolk, Gloucester, Derby and Warenne. In fact William Marshal was to die in the spring of 1231, before matters could come to a head, but not before he had recruited yet another magnate into his family network, marrying his sister, the widowed countess of Gloucester, to the king's brother, Richard earl of Cornwall.[17]

Richard of Cornwall, count of Poitou since 1225, could be expected to approve of the Poitevin focus of Henry III's continental policy. But in other respects he bore a serious grudge against the Justiciar. Raised under the tutelage of the alien, Peter de Maulay, a victim of de Burgh's rise to power after 1221, Richard had by 1230 recruited into his household at least two of the alien associates of de Maulay and des Roches: Andrew de Chanceaux and his son Giles.[18] His grievance against de Burgh stemmed from the landed settlement awarded him in England. In 1227 he had been belted as earl of Cornwall, but Cornwall itself, like his other English estates, was given to him merely during pleasure and not in fee. In July 1227 the king attempted to intervene within Richard's honour, conferring one of his manors upon a member of the royal household. In addition, Richard was ordered to surrender the honour of Berkhamsted, held as

[15] Walker, 'Hubert de Burgh and Wales, 1218–1232', esp. pp. 476–86.
[16] J. Lydon, 'The expansion and consolidation of the colony, 1215–54', in *A New History of Ireland II: Medieval Ireland 1169–1534*, ed. A. Cosgrave (Oxford 1987), pp. 159–63.
[17] For Richard's marriage, see Denholm-Young, *Richard of Cornwall*, pp. 17–19; *AM*, i (Tewkesbury), p. 78, iv (Osney), p. 72.
[18] *Cal.Lib.R.1226–40*, p. 115; *BF*, p. 1425; *E. Rot. Fin.*, i, p. 239.

part of his mother's dower, to Raymond de Burgh, Hubert's nephew. Richard rebelled. Already in league with William Marshal, he attracted the support not only of the Marshal's kinsmen, Gloucester, Warenne and Derby, but of de Burgh's long-standing enemy, the earl of Chester, and of two others, the earls of Hereford and Warwick. Together they wrote to the king threatening civil war, blaming de Burgh for their troubles, and appealing to a wider constituency amongst the baronage.[19] Des Roches had set out for crusade a month before the crisis broke but there is evidence that his bailiffs supported the rebellion. Earl Richard is found receiving provisions or met by the bishop's officers at several episcopal manors, and at Taunton together with the earl Marshal and many barons, provided with over £6 of foodstuffs.[20]

In the event, Richard was bought off by the king. Nonetheless, the earls' rebellion of 1227 had highlighted the vulnerability of de Burgh. Already unpopular with the higher nobility, Hubert was safe only so long as he could retain the confidence of the king. Forfeit that and he faced destruction at the hands of an alliance, comprising his old enemies from before 1224 and the younger generation of magnates, all united by personal hostility towards him. This younger generation consisted of more than just the earls of Pembroke and Cornwall. By 1231 there were at least four earls, Oxford, Winchester, Warwick and Norfolk, already of age or in control of their family lands, who had yet to be belted with their earldoms. A further two claimants to earldoms, Simon de Montfort and William Longespée, had so far been denied their claims.[21] Whether or not this represents a conscious decision on the king's behalf to restrict the promotion and creation of earls, it can only have contributed to the tensions between de Burgh and the baronage. As one of only half a dozen earls at court, and as guardian himself of the heirs to the earldoms of Gloucester and Arundel, Hubert was placed in an even more exposed position.

By contrast with the earls, the bishops of 1231 were a veteran bunch; five of them (Winchester, Bath, Lincoln, Durham and York), raised to the episcopate before the death of King John, and at least

---

[19] Denholm-Young, *Richard of Cornwall*, pp. 9–15, which suggests that Richard only recovered Berkhamsted in 1231. In fact he was receiving issues of the honour, albeit as a special favour from the king, in 1229; *Cl.R.1227–31*, p. 157. For his loss of the manor in 1227, see *Pat. R. 1225–32*, pp. 134, 145.

[20] Ms. 22DR, mm. 3d, 5, 6, 8, 8d.

[21] *CP*, ix, pp. 590–1, x, pp. 213–14, xi, p. 382, xii, pt. ii, pp. 365, 751. In addition, the heirs to the earldoms of Arundel, Devon and Gloucester were under age in 1231. The earldom of Essex was vacant.

four more (Ely, Rochester, Carlisle and Worcester), active as arch-deacons, abbots or royal clerks before 1216. Again, in contrast to the nobility, the bishops had co-operated closely with de Burgh's regime. At least three of them – Durham, Coventry and Rochester – were former pupils of archbishop Stephen Langton. They and various of their colleagues had played a leading role in de Burgh's rise to power. After 1223 Durham and Bath sat as barons of the Exchequer; Chichester had been promoted royal chancellor, Carlisle as treasurer. Yet even here the crown's increasing financial difficulties threatened strain.

Between 1227 and 1231 England was more heavily taxed than at any time since John's reign. To some extent this was a result of the very moderation which characterized de Burgh's regime. Rather than attempt a complete overhaul of royal finances, the county farms and demesne manors were leased at favourable terms, in many cases to courtiers whose offices as sheriff were treated as perquisites in reward for service to the crown.[22] The income generated by the counties and by moderate increments over the ancient farms was inadequate for the king's needs, even in peacetime. Instead the Exchequer was forced to depend upon a range of feudal incidents and extraordinary grants of taxation, exacted with increasing frequency after 1224: the lay fifteenth and clerical sixteenth of 1225–6; a scutage of 2 marks per fee for the Welsh campaign of 1228, and of 3 marks per fee for the continental expedition of 1230, this latter provocatively called the scutage of Poitou and set at the same high rate as John's disastrous Poitevin scutage of 1214. Over the same period tallages of 6,000 and 8,000 marks were imposed against the Jews, in 1225–6 and 1229.

In 1227 heavy fines were exacted for the renewal of royal charters on the king's coming of age. Judicial visitations, both a general and a forest eyre, brought in further income through fines and amercements.[23] Most provocatively of all, although the king's plans to lead a continental expedition had twice to be delayed, on both occasions financial levies went ahead regardless. In 1226 a stillborn proposal for Henry to cross to Gascony resulted in a tallage of the royal demesne, including a fine of 500 marks against the citizens of London, apparently intended as a punitive gesture in retaliation for the Londoners' support of Louis and the rebels during the civil war. In 1229 de Burgh failed to organize a fleet for the king's crossing to

[22] Carpenter, 'The decline of the curial sheriff in England 1194–1258', pp. 10–13.
[23] Mitchell, *Studies in Taxation*, pp. 169–80; Crook, *Records of the General Eyre*, pp. 78–86; *Cl.R.1227–31*, p. 382.

Brittany, but a scutage of 3 marks per fee was taken nonetheless, and a tallage levied upon the royal demesne, including a further 1,000 marks from London. The Poitevin scutage of 1230 was thus the second scutage in two years intended to cover the costs of only one campaign.[24] The 1230 expedition was a military failure. Its diversion from Normandy to Poitou met with general disapproval. Not only did it devour two whole scutages, but it involved the king in paying or promising to pay crippling subsidies to the duke of Brittany, to the Poitevin nobility, to a host of royal household knights, and to the garrisons left behind on the king's return to England. The scutages of 1229 and 1230 generated something approaching £7,000 over the next two years. By contrast, the king promised nearly 4,000 marks in annual subsidies to Poitou, a further 6,000 marks payable almost immediately to Peter duke of Brittany, and 1,000 marks to the earl of Chester to maintain his garrisons in France during the winter of 1230–1. This is to leave aside the costs of the army on the ground: at least 20,000 marks spent in France during the course of the 1230 campaign, or the hefty annual fees payable to members of the king's military household.[25] In 1230 the king drastically over-reached his financial resources. It was to be the clergy who were most vocal in their opposition to royal taxation thereafter. They had already been persuaded to offer a papal subsidy of a tenth, a tax whose assessment and collection proved particularly stringent. In 1229 and again in 1230 they refused to pay scutage, instead offering equivalent aids of 3 marks per fee; the first sign of more widespread resentment against de Burgh and his financial policy.

With finances hopelessly overstretched, with few achievements to show despite vast expenditure in Poitou and Wales, and with mounting protest against both the person and the policies of his chief minister, the king returned to England in October 1230, his home-coming marred by yet another squabble associated with de Burgh. Bertram de Criel, a member of the Justiciar's household, had been deputed to keep Dover castle during his master's absence abroad. He was instructed to admit no one to the fortress, a natural precaution in time of war, but one which he interpreted to include even Hubert's wife, Margaret of Scotland.[26] It may be that Criel's decision reflects some deeper tension between de Burgh's household and his high-

---

[24] Mitchell, *Studies in Taxation*, pp. 180–95, and for the Londoners' loans to Louis, see *The London Eyre of 1244*, ed. Chew and Weinbaum, nos. 195, 316.

[25] See *Cl.R.1227–31*, pp. 181, 185, 191; *Pat. R. 1225–32*, pp. 400–1.

[26] BL ms. Cotton Julius D v (Annals of Dover priory), f. 29r.

born wife. In any event, the king was forced to intervene. Criel was removed from Dover and banished. Even when that banishment was revoked in February 1231, he was refused access to court to plead his cause.[27] The king later admitted that a manor Criel held in wardship had been seized back from him arbitrarily: *pro voluntate regis.*[28] This, the first of many such arbitrary acts of disseisin, was carried out, apparently with de Burgh's connivance, to punish a member of the Justiciar's own household.

One other dispute involving de Burgh's followers merits attention. For the past few years Ranulph le Breton, the Justiciar's clerk, had been building up an estate near Duddington in Northamptonshire, mostly through the acquisition of assarts in the surrounding royal forest.[29] In December 1230, on his return from France, the king began *quo warranto* proceedings for the recovery of the manor of Duddington itself, claiming it as *Terra Normannorum*. The plea was to be presented by Ranulph's brother William, implying that it had been brought very much at Ranulph's suggestion.[30] The land was seized by the crown on 7 December. On 19 January 1231, it was granted in fee to Ranulph le Breton, even before the *quo warranto* plea had been concluded in court.[31] The case was of more than passing interest, since the manor's previous tenants, Oliver and Nicola de Aincourt, claimed to hold it of William de Longespée, son and heir of the earl of Salisbury. A jury summoned locally was in due course to uphold the Aincourts' defence. In May 1231 Ranulph was required to surrender the manor.[32] However, for those already distrustful of de Burgh and his satellites, the case provided yet another example of self-advancement, flouting even the rights of such a leading magnate as William de Longespée. Far from being rebuked for their actions, William and Ranulph le Breton continued to receive promotion at court. In May 1231 William was granted a further 50 acres of assarts in the woods around Duddington; Ranulph received the nearby manor of Apethorpe, free from regard by the king's foresters.[33] Like all medieval kings, Henry III had no choice but to attempt to manipulate the distribution of land as a means of rewarding his favourites at court.

[27] *Cl.R.1227–31*, pp. 475–6; C60/30, m. 9.
[28] *Cl.R.1231–4*, p. 29.
[29] *Cl.R.1227–31*, p. 261; *Cal.Chart.R.1226–57*, pp. 11, 106.
[30] *CRR*, xiv, no. 1155.
[31] *Cal.Chart.R.1226–57*, p. 129; *Cl.R.1227–31*, p. 472; C60/30, m. 8, a writ authorized by the privy seal.
[32] *CRR*, xiv, no. 1196; *Cl.R.1227–31*, p. 505.
[33] *Cal.Chart.R.1226–57*, p. 134; *Cl.R.1227–31*, p. 507.

Yet such manipulation was bound to be resented by landholders who found themselves supplanted by courtiers and their hangers-on. Land and its possession constituted the very foundations of power and wealth. Hence the care with which the king's lawyers, and after 1215 the barons themselves via the terms of Magna Carta, sought to regulate the king's intrusions. It was to be one of the principal causes of the political discord that enveloped England after 1232, that the king and his ministers appeared to be determined upon a wholesale redistribution of land, carried out not merely through the royal courts, but on occasion transcending accepted legal custom, through the arbitrary seizure of estates and a refusal to warrant earlier royal charters. Against this, various of the barons were prepared to rebel.

De Burgh's position at court had been seriously undermined by the failure of the continental expedition of 1230. On his return to England, the king for the first time began to make use of a privy seal, as a means of sending instructions for the issue of letters under the great seal held by the royal chancellor. Previously such warrants to the great seal had been made under the seals of the king's courtiers, most often the private seal of the Justiciar, Hubert de Burgh. The change may well provide a further indication of Henry's desire for greater personal control over affairs of state, independent of the Justiciar.[34] Nonetheless, de Burgh was too deeply entrenched in his privileges to be easily displaced. Moreover, as yet there had been no irrevocable breakdown in his relations with the king. In November 1230 he was granted significant new custodies; wardship of the heirs and lands of the earl of Gloucester and of two major tenants-in-chief, albeit in return for heavy fines; 7,000 marks, including a 2,000 marks down-payment, for Gloucester, and promises of 500 marks each for the heirs of William de Avranches and Nigel de Mowbray.[35] The Gloucester wardship was especially significant. In the first place, it brought de Burgh into conflict with Richard archbishop of Canterbury, who claimed custody of Tonbridge castle during the young earl's min-ority.[36] Personal conflict with the church came at an inconvenient time for de Burgh. The clergy had yet to approve the Poitevin scutage of 1230. In January 1231 the archbishop spoke out against the tax, saying that it had been granted by the laity abroad and that the

---

[34] T. F. Tout, *Chapters in the Administrative History of Medieval England*, 6 vols. (Manchester 1920–33), i, pp. 206–13, and for an early use of the privy seal, not noticed by Tout, see *Cirencester Cartulary*, ed. Ross, no. 90.

[35] C60/30, m. 9; *Cal.Chart.R.1226–57*, p. 126.

[36] Wendover, *Flores*, iv, pp. 218–20.

clergy were therefore not bound to pay. In addition, the archbishop appears to have launched an enquiry into the circumstances of de Burgh's marriage, alleging that Margaret of Scotland was related to Hubert's second wife within the prohibited degrees of kinship. In March or April 1231 he set out for Rome to lodge his complaints with the pope.[37]

Hubert's acquisition of the Gloucester lands was also to have significant repercussions in Wales. By adding Glamorgan to his already swollen Welsh lordship, de Burgh raised his profile on the Marches at a critical moment in Welsh affairs. Six months earlier, Llywelyn had executed the Marcher baron, William de Briouze the younger, caught in adultery with Llywelyn's wife. In the immediate aftermath neither the Welsh nor the English were keen to make this a pretext for war. The Briouze lands were entrusted to William Marshal. But the Marshal died early in April 1231, providing Llywelyn with the opportunity for an attack against Radnor and the Briouze March. The realization that a new Welsh campaign might have to be launched must have come as a bitter blow at court. The king had only just returned from France. His treasury was empty, yet he was committed to financing continued hostilities against the French and to maintaining supply to his allies in Brittany and Poitou. The last thing he wanted was to divert his attention and resources westwards, into Wales. In May 1231 he set off on a progress along the Welsh border; a show of strength intended to pre-empt any further attack by Llywelyn. All went well. By early June the court was back in London, the threat in the west much reduced.[38] But at this point yet another factional squabble erupted at court; one whose repercussions were to be felt for many years to come.

Already by 1230 the principal threat to de Burgh lay in the alliance between the king's brother, Richard of Cornwall, and the Marshal earls of Pembroke. Soon after his return from France the king had confirmed Richard in possession of their mother's dower.[39] If this was an attempt to detach him from William Marshal it failed, since on 30 March 1231 Richard was married to the Marshal's sister, the widowed countess of Gloucester. The marriage is said greatly to have angered the king, but for the moment Richard suffered no reprisals.[40] Following William Marshal's death, only a week or two after the

[37] *Ibid.*, iv, pp. 218–19, 226.
[38] Walker, 'Hubert de Burgh and Wales', pp. 483–5.
[39] *Cal. Chart. R. 1226–57*, p. 129.
[40] *AM*, i (Tewkesbury), p. 78.

marriage, Richard was granted two former Marshal custodies: the lands of William de Briouze in Wales and of Theobald Butler in Ireland.[41] In all of this there was an implicit threat to de Burgh. As husband of Isabella Marshal, Richard was almost certain to come into conflict with de Burgh over the assignment of dower in the Gloucester lands. In addition, Richard's promotion to the Briouze estate opened possibilities of conflict with Hubert's southern Welsh lordship. In the event, however, it was not Richard of Cornwall but Richard Marshal, claimant to the earldom of Pembroke, who proved the source of greatest dissension at court. Following the death of William Marshal, de Burgh attempted to intervene in the Marshal inheritance. He persuaded the king to seize William's estate and to deny Richard Marshal's claim as heir, on the pretext that William's widow might be pregnant and that Richard, as lord of the honours of Longueville and Orbec in Normandy, married to a leading member of the Breton/Angevin nobility, was a liegeman of the king of France, debarred from inheriting in England.[42] This refusal to admit Richard to the Marshal estate ran directly contrary to a promise, extracted by William Marshal from the king as recently as September, that should William die, Richard would be permitted to succeed him, despite being resident in France.[43]

De Burgh's motives here may have been sinister; to dispose of a major rival, both at court and in the Marches, and to recover one of the greatest private honours for the crown. But his plan miscarried disastrously. The Marshal tenants in Wales and Ireland refused to admit the king's men. Rumours circulated that Richard Marshal was planning an invasion. On 12 May, fearing that Richard of Cornwall had become embroiled in this conspiracy, the king seized back the honour of Wallingford, held by Richard since 1229.[44] A week later the Briouze lands were taken from him and conferred upon Hubert de Burgh.[45] The resulting confusion provided Llywelyn with the ideal opportunity for an attack on the Marches. All the king's efforts

---

[41] *Pat. R. 1225–32*, pp. 388, 428, confirming an earlier assignment to Richard of the Butler lands in Ireland, first made in July 1230.

[42] Wendover, *Flores*, iv, p. 225. For the seizure of the Marshal lands by royal bailiffs see *Pat. R. 1225–32*, pp. 427, 429–30, 435–7; *Cl.R.1227–31*, pp. 489, 503–4, 587; C60/30, mm. 5, 6.

[43] *Pat. R. 1225–32*, p. 400, drawn to my attention by Daniel Power.

[44] Wendover, *Flores*, iv, p. 225; *Cl.R.1227–31*, p. 587. For the seizure of Wallingford see *Pat. R. 1225–32*, p. 434; *Cl.R.1227–31*, p. 510. Already in April 1231 Richard had been forced to relinquish two manors he held during pleasure, restored to their rightful Breton claimant, now re-allied with the king; *Cl.R.1227–31*, p. 493.

[45] *Pat. R. 1225–32*, p. 434.

to forestall a Welsh campaign were undone. In early June the Welsh attacked in force.[46] The king now had little alternative but to seek a reconciliation with the Marshal. News of the Welsh invasion reached him around 20 June. On 22 June letters of safeconduct were issued for Richard Marshal to come to England. On the same day the town but not the honour of Wallingford was restored to Richard of Cornwall.[47] Confusion still reigned. The army summoned for Wales took far longer to muster than had been hoped. Neither the Marshal nor Richard of Cornwall had arrived at court by 1 August, on which day the king was at last able to move into Wales, establishing his headquarters at Painscastle.[48] It was into the midst of this crisis that there walked Peter des Roches, the returning hero of the crusade, accompanied by his old allies, de Burgh's old enemies, Peter de Maulay, William de Cantiloupe and the earls of Chester and Aumale. Their timing was perfect.

THE BISHOP'S RETURN AUGUST 1231–JANUARY 1232

Des Roches and his associates arrived at court at some time before 10 August.[49] On 8 August Richard Marshal was allowed to do homage for the earldom of Pembroke.[50] Two days later the king made peace with Richard of Cornwall, who for the first time was granted the county of Cornwall and the honour of Wallingford in fee rather than merely during pleasure.[51] This settlement of 10 August marked a crucial turning point in Richard's career. It was witnessed by des Roches, Chester, Aumale, Cantiloupe and by Richard's former guardian Peter de Maulay, who, like des Roches, had last witnessed a royal charter as long ago as 1227. A few days later, on 13 August, the earl of Chester obtained a settlement for yet another young magnate previously denied a hearing at court. Simon de Montfort had first come to England in 1230 as claimant to the earldom of Leicester, but it was only at Chester's prompting in August 1231 that his claim was

---

[46] Walker, 'Hubert de Burgh and Wales', pp. 485–7.
[47] *Cl.R.1227–31*, pp. 590–1; *Pat. R. 1225–32*, p. 438; C60/30, m. 4.
[48] Walker, 'Hubert de Burgh and Wales', pp. 487–8.
[49] No entry was made on the charter roll between 2 and 10 August, by which date des Roches and his associates were already at court; C53/25, mm. 4, 5.
[50] *Cl.R.1227–31*, p. 541; C60/30, m. 3. Richard appears to have escaped any payment of relief for his inheritance, perhaps in compensation for the lands' unjust retention by the crown; E372/77, m. 1; E372/78, m. 15.
[51] *Cal.Chart.R.1226–57*, p. 139; C53/25, m. 4.

recognized, and a portion of the honour, though not yet the title 'earl of Leicester', bestowed upon him.[52]

Within only five days there had been a quite astonishing change in the balance of power at court. The king had been reconciled to two young earls, Richard Marshal and Richard of Cornwall, and to an earl-to-be, Simon de Montfort, all of whom received major honours. In addition he had welcomed back a group of veteran courtiers, bitter rivals of his chief minister, Hubert de Burgh. Despite the generation gap there was much to recommend co-operation between the veterans and the tyros; all possessed close personal ties to France and a far keener interest in continental affairs than de Burgh. All, save possibly Simon de Montfort, had quarrelled bitterly with de Burgh, especially the veterans whom he had ousted from power in 1224. Chester and des Roches had just returned from France, where in July 1231 they had negotiated a truce with the Capetians, set to last for three years.[53] Outwardly this represented a major advance for Plantagenet policy on the continent. The French tacitly recognized Peter of Brittany's allegiance to Henry III, and the gains that Henry had made in Poitou. However, for this to have any effect the king would need to spend the next three years consolidating his new-found Breton and Poitevin alliances, and establishing contacts elsewhere so as to meet the French with force when the truce expired. Instead, de Burgh appeared to have dragged the court into a war against Llywelyn. The clerical aid for the 1230 Poitevin campaign, eventually agreed in April 1231, had to be diverted westwards. The Exchequers of Dublin and Westminster were ordered to send their every last penny to the Marches. The pensions due to Henry's Poitevin and Breton adherents were already in arrears. It was inconceivable that their next term, due at Michaelmas, could be met. Even to pay out sums as small as 40 marks at Westminster, the Exchequer clerks were required to break open barrels of money destined for Wales.[54]

Worse still for de Burgh, the Welsh campaign went badly from the start. Shortage of supplies made it necessary to reduce the size of the English army. Military effort was concentrated almost entirely on rebuilding Painscastle, a fortress in de Burgh's custody, but of only

---

[52]   *Cl.R.1227–31*, p. 543, and see M. Wade Labarge, *Simon de Montfort* (London 1962), pp. 27–31.

[53]   For the truce and its background, see Powicke, *Henry III*, p. 183; S. Painter, *The Scourge of the Clergy: Peter of Dreux, Duke of Brittany* (Baltimore 1937), pp. 72–7.

[54]   *Pat. R. 1225–32*, pp. 429, 442; *Cl.R.1227–31*, pp. 535–6, 593; E372/75, mm. 13d, 14, 15.

limited strategic significance.[55] 'While the king rebuilt Painscastle, Llywelyn overthrew ten other castles on the marches', comments the Dunstable annalist, who notes also the speed with which des Roches was restored to favour at court, apparently bringing the king greater aid in Wales than all the other bishops combined.[56] Des Roches' rehabilitation at court was indeed spectacular. He had left England in 1227 a thoroughly frustrated man, the king glad to be rid of him. Four years later he was welcomed back as a returning hero. Shortly before setting out for crusade, he had been forced to pay a large fine for the renewal of whatever privileges he had acquired during the king's minority. He now received compensation for this, being awarded the Hampshire manor of Titchfield upon which to found a religious house, a grant specifically made to offset the punitive fine of 1227.[57] In the following few weeks he received a gift of a falcon, was pardoned scutages taken during his absence abroad, and in October 1231 was granted a fair for his manor of Witney.[58]

Meanwhile de Burgh's problems were only further compounded. Archbishop Richard died in Italy on 3 August.[59] News of his death reached England early the next month. On 6 September the king granted custody of the vacant archbishopric to Ranulph le Breton, treasurer of the royal household and a personal satellite of de Burgh.[60] But Ranulph's promotion was short-lived. A week later he found himself banished from court. No reason is given for his disgrace, nor was it particularly long-lived; he was back at court before 9 October, having meanwhile sought haven in Scotland.[61] It may be that his disgrace relates to an wider investigation into financial affairs. On more or less the same day that Ranulph was dismissed, the king ordered the seizure of the lands of Master Alexander of Dorset, justice of the Jews for the past fifteen years.[62] Both Ranulph and Master Alexander may have been suspected of sharp practice. For the

---

[55] Walker, 'Hubert de Burgh and Wales', pp. 488–91.
[56] *AM*, iii, p. 127.
[57] C60/30, m. 1; *Cal.Chart.R.1226–57*, p. 139, and for Titchfield Abbey, see *Acta*, nos. 67–71. For the fine of 1227 see above pp. 226–8.
[58] *Cl.R.1227–31*, pp. 557, 559, 571; *Cal.Chart.R.1226–57*, p. 140.
[59] Wendover, *Flores*, iv, pp. 226–7.
[60] C60/30, m. 2.
[61] *Cl.R.1227–31*, pp. 562, 599; C53/25, m. 3. He appears to have been restored as clerk of the wardrobe, appearing as such on 10 December 1231; E372/76, m. 5d. Custody of the vacant archbishopric passed via Ranulph's brother, William le Breton, sheriff of Kent (c.11 September) to Walter of Kirkham, a clerk of the wardrobe whose account for it runs from 21 September 1231 to 1 August 1232; E372/76, m. 5d; C60/30, m. 2.
[62] C60/30, m. 2.

moment, however, their fall posed no direct threat to de Burgh. Ranulph appears to have been replaced as treasurer of the king's household, first by Philip of Eye, and then before May 1232 by Richard de St John, both of them protégés of the Justiciar.[63]

It is tempting to link Ranulph's disgrace to one of the major preoccupations of the court in the autumn of 1231: the plans for the marriage of King Henry III. It may be no coincidence that it was to Scotland that Ranulph fled. Alexander II, the Scottish king, was brother-in-law to Hubert de Burgh, whose wife Margaret, Alexander's elder sister, had originally been intended for Henry III. Another of Alexander's sisters had been married to Roger Bigod, earl of Norfolk. There remained, however, a third Scottish princess, the youngest of the three and hence the least desirable match.[64] De Burgh did his best to palm her off upon the king. The scheme may have been in the air as early as 1230. Some years earlier, Hubert is said to have sabotaged a proposal that Henry III be married to a daughter of the duke of Austria.[65] Henry spent the Christmas of 1229 together with King Alexander at York; as a gesture of goodwill Alexander contributed 2,000 marks to the cost of the following year's expedition to France.[66] Whether or not a Scottish alliance was openly discussed, the question of Henry III's marriage became even more urgent after March 1231, and the match between Richard of Cornwall and Isabella Marshal. Isabella was to give birth within the next year to a son. Should the king die, the crown would now almost certainly pass to Richard of Cornwall and his issue: a bleak prospect for de Burgh.[67] Hence perhaps, de Burgh's anxiety to marry off his Scottish sister-in-law to the king. The proposal caused uproar, not least because it was regarded as scandalous that the king should consider marrying a younger sister when de Burgh was already married to the elder.[68] Furthermore, a Scottish marriage, like the campaign in Wales, must

---

63 A roll, listing payments to knights serving in Wales between July and September, later recycled as the outer-covering of a cartulary, is endorsed *Rotul(us) Ph(ilippi) de Eya Camer(arii) ann(o) xv*; Cambridge, King's College muniments ms. GBR 289 (Great Bricett cartulary roll), m. 3. For Philip as Hubert's protégé, see *Pat. R. 1225–32*, pp. 234, 247. For Richard de St John, see Dugdale, *Monasticon*, ii, p. 81, taken from BL ms. Cotton Cleopatra A vii (Tewkesbury annals etc.), ff. 95v–96r.

64 Powicke, *Henry III*, pp. 159–60, 767–8n.

65 *Ibid.*, p. 159; Paris, *CM*, iii, pp. 618–19, where Hubert is said to have informed the kinsmen of 'a certain noble lady' that Henry was an imbecile, impotent and effeminate.

66 Wendover, *Flores*, iv, pp. 207–8; *Pat. R. 1225–32*, p. 332.

67 Denholm-Young, *Richard of Cornwall*, p. 18. Powicke, *Henry III*, pp. 159–60, is almost certainly naive in suggesting that the king's Scots engagement was a love match.

68 Wendover, *Flores*, iv, p. 227.

have appeared of supreme irrelevance to those at court whose interests were principally focussed on reconquest in France.

Tempers were running high. At some time before 21 August the earl of Chester had stormed out of court. In part this may reflect his opposition to the handling of the Welsh campaign.[69] Not only had Chester established an excellent rapport with Llywelyn on the northern Marches, but for the past two years he had played a central role in Plantagenet military efforts on the continent; both achievements threatened by the Welsh campaign of 1231 and its efforts to protect de Burgh's lordship in the south. In addition, it seems possible that Chester objected to interventions within the honour of Leicester, recently released to Simon de Montfort. The story here is a complicated one, but in essence it turns upon attempts by de Burgh to secure a Norman escheat for the abbey of North Creake, a house under de Burgh family patronage. The escheat lay within the honour of Leicester, and according to an earlier agreement between the king and Chester, should have remained at the disposal of Chester and after August 1231, of Simon de Montfort. However, almost certainly at de Burgh's prompting, the king chose to disregard this earlier promise, making a much-resented intrusion within de Montfort's new estate.[70] Chester was enticed back to Painscastle by 20 September, but although the breach was superficially healed, its longer-term effects were to set both de Montfort and Chester firmly against de Burgh.[71] The Welsh had still to be brought to any sort of settlement. On 6 September a scutage of £1 per fee was announced, the fourth scutage in as many years.[72]

Over the next few weeks the king's marriage plans were finalized. On 15 October he was intending to be in York by 9 November, and ordered various items of plate to be sent to him there, presumably towards his proposed nuptials.[73] Meanwhile he returned from the Marches to Westminster, where a council was held from c.23–6 October. The magnates in attendance included des Roches and at

---

[69] *AM*, i (Tewkesbury), p. 79; *Annales Cestrienses*, ed. R. C. Christie, Record Society of Lancashire and Cheshire, xiv (1887), pp. 56–7.

[70] See N. C. Vincent, 'The first quarrel between Simon de Montfort and King Henry III', *Thirteenth Century England IV*, ed. P. R. Coss and S. D. Lloyd (Woodbridge 1992), pp. 167–77; R. Eales, 'Henry III and the end of the Anglo-Norman earldom of Chester', in *Thirteenth Century England I*, ed. Coss and Lloyd, pp. 100–13.

[71] For the earl's return to court, see C53/25, m. 3.

[72] Mitchell, *Studies in Taxation*, pp. 195–9, misdated to 1232.

[73] *Cl.R.1227–31*, p. 570.

least eight other bishops, the earl of Chester, Simon de Montfort and William de Cantiloupe.[74] Their chief business was to welcome Peter duke of Brittany, who arrived at court with another veteran minister, Philip de Aubigné, a man with strong Breton connections who had stayed on in France following the previous year's expedition. The composition of the council already suggests a body unsympathetic towards de Burgh. De Aubigné and the duke of Brittany only went to swell the ranks of those committed to a vigorous approach to affairs on the continent, frustrated by de Burgh's concentration on Wales and Scotland. In any event the king was persuaded to cancel his journey to York. The Scottish marriage was rejected, chiefly at the prompting of the duke of Brittany and Richard Marshal, two of the magnates most keenly concerned with developments in France.[75] Instead, probably at this same meeting, Henry reverted to an earlier proposal, first mooted in 1226, by which he was to marry the duke of Brittany's daughter, Yolande.[76] Wendover claims that the duke also received subsidies of 5,000 marks from the king.[77] What is beyond doubt is that continental affairs once again dominated the king's thinking. De Burgh did not emerge from the council entirely empty-handed. Royal charters were issued confirming grants he had made to the religious. The king also granted what purported to be a royal foundation charter for the abbey of North Creake, a de Burgh family foundation, already the source of tension between de Burgh, Chester and Simon de Montfort.[78] At the same time, des Roches too received letters, confirming him in possession of Titchfield, in compensation for his fine of 1227.[79] This marks the beginning of a process, destined to escalate over the course of the next six months, in which de Burgh and des Roches both became the recipients of royal favours, being played off against one another in a flurry of rival awards and privileges.

Besides the king's marriage there were several other problems to engage the attention of the October council. A truce with Llywelyn had recently been obtained, initially to last to November 1231 but renewed thereafter, in theory for a further year.[80] Royal finances may also have come under scrutiny, although as yet there was no serious

[74] C53/25, mm. 1–3.
[75] Paris, *Hist. Ang. Min.*, ii, p. 336; *CM*, iii, p. 206.
[76] Painter, *Peter of Dreux*, pp. 38–45, 78–81.
[77] Wendover, *Flores*, iv, p. 227.
[78] *Cal. Chart. R. 1226–57*, p. 141; *VCH Kent*, ii, p. 217; Dugdale, *Monasticon*, vi, pp. 487–8.
[79] C60/30, m. 1.
[80] *Pat. R. 1225–32*, pp. 452–3, 460.

attempt at reform. The sheriffs and the county farms were left untouched. Far from censuring the performance of the treasurer, Walter Mauclerk bishop of Carlisle, the king confirmed him in various privileges and granted him custody of the manors of Hayes and Harrow, members of the vacant archbishopric of Canterbury.[81] In its way, the Canterbury vacancy had occurred at an opportune moment for de Burgh. The vacancy receipts provided a welcome boost to royal finance, forestalling the complete collapse which had threatened ever since 1230. The death of archbishop Richard removed one of the Justiciar's bitterest critics. In his place, the Canterbury monks elected the king's chancellor, Ralph de Neville.[82] De Burgh probably regarded Neville as an ally; certainly everything possible was done to smooth his path. Royal assent to the election was obtained on 24 September, and at the October council instructions went out to protect the liberties of the archbishopric.[83] It was essential to tread warily, since Neville's translation from Chichester required papal assent. The king could not do as his father had done and wrack every last penny out of the vacancy. Nonetheless, de Burgh was never blind to the possibilities of personal advancement. By September 1231 the lands of one of the archbishopric's principal sub-tenants, William of Eynsford, had been granted in custody to de Burgh's son John.[84]

The rejection of the Scottish marriage represented a major setback for the Justiciar. He had tried to curb the king's enthusiasm for continental adventures, only to be frustrated by a rival group at court growing rapidly in strength and confidence. In the previous twelve months two of the Justiciar's closest personal satellites, Bertram de Criel and Ranulph le Breton, had been dismissed from office. A group of his most bitter personal enemies had been readmitted to court, quickly allying themselves with such figures as Richard Marshal, Simon de Montfort and Richard of Cornwall, fundamentally altering the composition of the king's council, diverting patronage and influence away from de Burgh. Des Roches and de Burgh had last served together at court in 1223, when their rivalry had led to violent scenes, with de Burgh blaming the bishop for most of the political troubles of the past twenty years, and des Roches vowing that he would have his revenge upon de Burgh, whatever it might

---

[81]   *Cal. Chart. R. 1226–57*, p. 140; C60/30, m. 1.
[82]   *Fasti*, ii, p. 6.
[83]   Paris, *CM*, iii, pp. 206–7; *Cl.R.1227–31*, p. 574.
[84]   *Cl.R.1227–31*, p. 564.

cost him. Now, at long last, des Roches had the opportunity to carry out his threat.

Rather than go north to York, the king spent November in a leisurely progress across southern England, returning to London early in December before passing on to Kent and the estates of the vacant archbishopric. Besides the prolongation of the truce with Llywelyn, little of any significance was transacted. Des Roches and his allies appear to have been away from court.[85] In their absence the king bestowed favours upon de Burgh's familiar, William le Breton, and on 15 December attended the consecration of de Burgh's own religious foundation, at St Mary's Dover.[86] On the following day John de Burgh was confirmed in possession of the lands of William of Eynsford, though only after promising a fine of 700 marks.[87] It was clear that the Justiciar retained the king's confidence, however much that confidence had been shaken by recent events. That there was still tension in the air can be gauged from the prohibition of a tournament planned to take place at Allerton in late November; an unsuitable venue given the strain imposed on relations with the Scots.[88] As the various factions began to close ranks at court, so the position of those left unattached grew increasingly uncomfortable. One such was the royal steward Godfrey of Crowcombe, who in mid-December obtained confirmation for life of the sheriffdom of Oxfordshire and a grant in fee of various Norman lands.[89]

THE CHRISTMAS COURT 1231

Ever since 1224, the king's Christmas courts had been organized by de Burgh, a symbol of his ascendancy. In 1231 this pattern was broken. Instead, for the first time since 1221, the king chose to spend Christmas at Winchester as a guest of Peter des Roches. The bishop was clearly aware of the significance of this decision and went to vast expense to ensure fitting entertainment. The chroniclers note the rich array of food and gifts provided.[90] Something of this can be established from the Winchester account rolls; the quantities of fish and cheeses brought from as far afield as Taunton; the bishop's

85 C53/26, m. 19.
86 *Cal. Chart. R. 1226–57*, pp. 142–3.
87 *Pat. R. 1225–32*, p. 455; C60/31, m. 7.
88 *Pat. R. 1225–32*, p. 452.
89 *Cal. Chart. R. 1226–57*, pp. 142–3; *Pat. R. 1225–32*, p. 455.
90 Wendover, *Flores*, iv, p. 232; *AM*, iii (Dunstable), p. 127.

huntsmen sent to take game, three dozen partridges and nine wood-cock for example, carried from Farnham to Winchester.[91] At South-wark an unspecified number of jewels was purchased around 17 December and carried to Guildford, presumably to meet the court when it arrived there *en route* for Winchester a few days later.[92] This bears out the remarks of the Dunstable annalist, that des Roches provided so much gold and silver, so many robes and jewels, that it would have sufficed for a coronation.[93]

Such luxury can only have heightened the king's awareness of his own financial straits. An extravagant man by nature, Henry found himself reduced to the status of guest at another man's feast. A budding patron of the arts, the king had not even enough money to pay for his latest commissions; paintings ordered for one of the chapels at Westminster by the time of the king's return to London, could only be completed two or more years later.[94] By contrast, des Roches had spent the past four years in the company of Europe's most splendid monarch, the emperor Frederick II. According to Henry of Avranches, the bishop harped constantly upon the splendour and refinement of the emperor's taste; the fact that he would accept nothing but the best in all things.[95] Frederick was everything that Henry III was not: wealthy, imposing, forceful, surrounded by magnificence and luxury. For Henry it must have been galling in the extreme, to have his former tutor sing the praises of a king so well endowed with the riches and talents he himself so signally lacked. Wendover reports an exchange that he ascribes to the spring of 1232, but which might just as well fit the circumstances of the Christmas court. Des Roches and his associates went to the king and told him that it was scandalous that he should allow the Welsh to plunder his lands. Henry replied that he was powerless to act since his treasurers assured him he had barely enough money to live out a modest existence, let alone to engage in any more costly venture. To this des Roches retorted that the king had no one but himself to blame for his poverty; his ancestors had been noble and wealthy men, but Henry had bankrupted himself by granting away every honour, custody and

---

[91] Ms. 27DR, mm. 1d, 3, 7, 7d, 8d, 9d, 10, 11d. It may be that the king's arrival at Guildford around 20 December was timed to coincide with the entrance of the monks of nearby Waverley Abbey into their new church; *Pat. R. 1225–32*, pp. 455–6; *AM*, ii (Waverley), p. 310.

[92] Ms. 27DR, m. 12.

[93] *AM*, iii, p. 127.

[94] *Cl.R.1231–4*, pp. 9, 10, 207.

[95] Above pp. 255–6.

escheat that fell vacant.[96] It seems more than likely that something of this sort was said at Christmas 1231, and that des Roches recommended himself to the king as the man best qualified to remedy matters. Since August the bishop had been only an occasional presence at court. But from Christmas onwards, throughout January and February 1232, he was to be with the king on a near daily basis.[97] His promotion was marked above all, during the final week in January when, after an absence of nearly a decade, he was readmitted as a baron of the Exchequer.[98] The writs which he witnessed on this occasion are not in themselves remarkable, but they usher in a period of financial experiment that must surely be accounted des Roches' own personal responsibility.

Here, as always, we must tread with caution. The bishop's role remains hard to establish in any detail, since we have little to guide us save his presence or absence from the witness lists and warranty clauses to royal letters. Government was still conducted in the king's name. Nonetheless, the chroniclers are in no doubt that it was des Roches who effected a fundamental change in the atmosphere at court, and that over the next two years it was to be des Roches who shaped the basic course of events. The greatest of the chroniclers, Roger of Wendover, wrote with partisan intent. Like his successor at St Albans, Matthew Paris, whose continuation of Roger's chronicle runs from May 1234, Wendover had a loathing for foreigners that on occasion warps and distorts his account of events.[99] Yet, in essence, whenever it can be checked against the facts as set out in the records of the royal Chancery and Exchequer, Wendover's narrative appears to be extremely well informed. Apart from the occasional slip in dating, his bias emerges not in points of fact, but in the moralizing gloss that he puts upon such facts. As we shall see, he greatly exaggerates the extent to which des Roches presided over a unified party of aliens at court. His portrait of Richard Marshal and the English opposition is far from accurate. Nevertheless, his perception that it was des Roches who served as the king's chief counsellor, is contradicted neither by the official sources nor by any of the chroniclers who wrote independently of Wendover. Of course, in the aftermath of des Roches' fall, after 1234, the king and his courtiers had a natural desire to shift the

---

96 Wendover, *Flores*, iv, pp. 243–4.
97 He witnesses 18 of the 27 royal charters enrolled for Jan. /Feb. 1232; C53/26, mm. 12–18.
98 *Memoranda Rolls 1231–3*, nos. 1453, 1466.
99 For the succession of Matthew Paris as continuator of Wendover's chronicle, see R. Kay, 'Wendover's last annal', *EHR* 84 (1969), pp. 779–85.

blame for the events of the past two years from the king himself to his newly disgraced ministers. There is evidence of a deliberate campaign of propaganda against the bishop and his colleagues. We must be wary of this. It was Henry who ruled, and Henry who was personally responsible for many of the more controversial initiatives of these years. The king was no longer a mere cypher, or a puppet in the hands of his council as he had been during his minority. His anger against de Burgh, and his favouritism towards des Roches were crucial in determining the course of events. On occasion, des Roches may have found himself struggling not so much to steel the king to new and controversial actions, as attempting to reign in Henry's temper and his new-found taste for personal power. Even so, as chief counsellor, as the man prepared to encourage the king's arbitrary rule, to do the king's bidding, and to resume the instruction of his one-time pupil, des Roches did more than any other courtier to sow the wind, and hence to reap the whirlwind that ensued.

ROYAL FINANCE AND THE COUNCIL: JANUARY–APRIL 1232

Late in December 1231 the pope quashed the election of Ralph de Neville as archbishop of Canterbury, largely it was supposed at the prompting of the archdeacon of Canterbury, Master Simon Langton.[100] When the news reached England, de Burgh's reaction was hardly calculated to win clerical approval. On 28 January he had his own chaplain, Richard de St John, promoted archdeacon in Langton's place. The appointment was wholly uncanonical, since the king had no right over such offices even during a vacancy.[101] St John's promotion was never effected. In the meantime, unable to secure Neville's election, the king was in no hurry to lose control over the vacancy receipts. Despite papal admonitions to proceed to a speedy election, it was not until 7 March that the Canterbury monks were given licence to nominate an alternative to Neville. Even then they were warned to ensure that their candidate was acceptable to the crown. By 16 March they had chosen as archbishop the veteran Master John of Sittingbourne, formerly prior of Canterbury, a man

---

[100] Wendover, *Flores*, iv, pp. 227–8.

[101] *Pat. R. 1225–32*, p. 461. For the possibility that St John had a seal matrix struck incorporating his new office as archdeacon, see W. de Gray Birch, *Catalogue of Seals in the Department of Manuscripta in the British Museum*, vol. 1 (London 1887), no. 1387, although the cast described here is more likely to be that of another official of the see of Canterbury.

most unlikely to secure confirmation from the pope for whose court he now set out.[102]

During these months des Roches' elevation at court proceeded apace. On 20 January 1232 the king issued him with his most sweeping grant of liberties to date, even more extensive than the one he had received in 1208 from King John. The bishop and prior of Winchester were henceforth to receive amercements charged against their tenantry in the king's courts, the chattels of condemned felons, freedom from intervention by the king's bailiffs or their men, quittance from any liability for the escape of prisoners, from toll and from suit of shire and hundred courts.[103] In its way this was as important an award as any made to des Roches by King John; the basis of Winchester's legal privileges throughout the middle ages. Later in the spring of 1232, the bishop of Norwich was to fine 2,500 marks for what was arguably a far less impressive array of privileges.[104] The bishop of Ely was likewise to claim return of writs and the amercements of his own men. His case dragged on throughout 1232 and was settled only in July the following year, when he fined 500 marks for the liberties in question.[105] By contrast des Roches paid nothing for his own, far more sweeping award. However, the king clearly considered it expedient to offset the bishop's new charter by some sort of gesture towards de Burgh. On the same day, 20 January 1232, that the charter was granted to des Roches, the Justiciar received quittance from forest regard for his manor of Hatfield Peverel and hereditary custody of the royal mews in Winchester.[106] As with the earlier transactions over Titchfield, it is clear that bishop and Justiciar were being played off against one another in competition for royal patronage, with the bishop leading the field by several lengths. Nor was des Roches the only one of de Burgh's old enemies restored to royal favour. On 25 January, Brian de Lisle was given life custody of the castle and honour of the Peak, having a few days earlier witnessed a royal charter for the first time in eighteen months.[107]

The increasing frequency with which such life awards were being

---

[102] *Pat. R. 1225–32*, p. 465; *Fasti*, ii, pp. 6, 11.

[103] *Cal. Chart. R. 1226–57*, pp. 145–6; *Winchester Chartulary*, ed. Goodman, no. 29.

[104] C60/31, m. 5; *Cal. Chart. R. 1226–57*, pp. 152–3.

[105] C60/30, m. 7; C60/31, mm. 1, 3, 4; C60/32, m. 4; *Cl.R.1231–4*, p. 138; *Cal. Chart. R. 1226–57*, pp. 183–4.

[106] *Cal. Chart. R. 1226–57*, p. 148.

[107] *Pat. R. 1225–32*, p. 460. Brian had held the honour during the king's pleasure since November 1230; C60/30, m. 9; *Cl.R.1227–31*, p. 457. He makes no appearance as witness to royal charters between November 1230 and 20 January 1232; C53/25, m. 13; C53/26, m. 16.

made almost certainly reflects a general atmosphere of insecurity at court. Change was in the air, and courtiers were anxious to protect themselves against the coming storm. A nationwide prohibition of tournaments testifies to this same sense of unease. In the first two months of 1232, tournaments were cancelled at Blyth and Stamford.[108] That at Blyth was to have been attended by various of the king's household knights, by Richard of Cornwall and by John de Burgh. They were commanded to cancel their meeting, not only because it might interrupt negotiations on the Marches, where discussions over breaches of the truce with Llywelyn proceeded throughout February, but because the king was daily expecting the arrival of the duke of Brittany.[109] A council to discuss the duke's affairs had probably been arranged during his visit the previous October. On 16 January the king sent Philip de Aubigné and one of the royal stewards to escort the duke to court. He was assured that the entire cost of his stay would be met by the king, a reference perhaps to Henry III's embarrassment that earlier undertakings to pay subsidies for the defence of Brittany had either fallen into arrears or been abandoned altogether.[110] There could be no doubt that a demand for further financial assistance provided the duke's chief motive in coming to England. A special council was summoned to London for 1 March to consider his requests.[111]

Meanwhile something desperately needed to be done to remedy the king's financial embarrassment. The Exchequer was quite incapable of paying the pensions promised to Breton and Poitevin allies in 1230. The Welsh campaign, besides swallowing most of the revenues of Ireland and the clerical aid promised in lieu of scutage for Poitou, had required the diversion of a considerable proportion of the Exchequer's ordinary receipts. A scutage for Wales, imposed in September 1231, yielded less than £900 over the next two years.[112] At Christmas 1231 des Roches and his associates may well have urged the king to overhaul his fiscal administration, singling out the management of escheats and wardships as an area particularly ripe for reform. By late January 1232 des Roches had been readmitted as an Exchequer baron.[113]

[108] *Pat. R. 1225–32*, pp. 457, 463; *Cl.R.1231–4*, pp. 131–2.
[109] *Cl.R.1231–4*, pp. 131–3. For negotiations with the Welsh, see *Pat. R. 1225–32*, p. 460; *Cl.R.1231–4*, pp. 127–8, 139.
[110] *Cl.R.1231–4*, p. 128.
[111] *Ibid.*, pp. 132–3.
[112] Mitchell, *Studies in Taxation*, pp. 197–8.
[113] *Memoranda Rolls 1231–3*, nos. 1439–75.

Des Roches' return to the Exchequer coincides with a major change in the administration of newly vacated escheats and wardships. Previously the crown had treated such estates as a stock of patronage to be bestowed on courtiers in return for a suitable fine. Much of de Burgh's landed wealth derived from his custody of crown wardships and escheats; above all from the Avranches, Mowbray, Gloucester and Briouze estates he had acquired since the king's return from France in 1230. In many cases the fines extracted for such custodies were considerable; but it could prove virtually impossible to enforce payment, precisely because the custodians tended to be favoured courtiers. Now, an alternative scheme was proposed by des Roches, involving the retention of a considerable number of escheats and wardships under direct crown management. Already in December 1231 a change in approach had been signalled. When the honour of Aigle escheated at the death of Gilbert d'Aigle, rather than award it to the highest bidder, the king deputed its management to the sheriff of Sussex, who was to answer at the Exchequer for all the honour's receipts.[114] A far more impressive change was initiated a fortnight after des Roches' return to the Exchequer, when on 8 February 1232 pairs of knights were assigned in each county, to administer escheats as and when they fell vacant, independent of the sheriffs.[115] The appointments were clearly experimental. In the short term they achieved very little, if only because no major escheat fell vacant during the system's first few months of operation. The only estate where the scheme appears to have been applied was not strictly an escheat at all but a vacancy at Cerne Abbey in Dorset.[116] Even the honour of Aigle was left under shrieval management rather than being transferred to the local keepers of escheats.[117]

In the summer of 1232 the local teams of knights were to be disbanded in favour of a more centralized system. Nonetheless, the orders of February do at least demonstrate a determination to overhaul the king's finances. At the same time, resort was made to more traditional means of boosting revenue. Already in July 1231 an eyre had been held in Yorkshire. Late in December 1231 another was appointed for Kent, the start of the second general judicial visitation in only five years, clearly prompted by a need for

---

[114] C60/31, m. 7; *Cl.R.1231–4*, p. 12.
[115] *Cl.R.1231–4*, pp. 129–31; C60/31, m. 6.
[116] *Pat. R. 1225–32*, p. 468; C60/31, m. 6.
[117] *Cl.R.1231–4*, pp. 32–3. It was to remain in the custody of John of Gaddesden, one-time sheriff of Surrey and Sussex, who accounts for it from 19 December 1231 to 24 June 1232; E372/76, m. 5.

money.[118] On 11 March 1232 a major enquiry into assarts and purprestures within the royal forest was appointed, to begin work in April.[119] But none of these measures was sufficient to meet the king's immediate needs. As previously arranged, duke Peter of Brittany crossed to England around 20 February, spending several days in company with Philip de Aubigné and John fitz Philip, one of the king's stewards, as a guest of des Roches.[120] Once arrived at court he made his anticipated demand for subsidies to pay for the defence of Brittany. In all probability the arrangements for the king's marriage to Yolande were formalized. Unable to raise the required subsidies from ordinary receipts, on 7 March de Burgh proposed to the council that they grant the king aid. The proposal was rejected. The bishops excused themselves on the grounds that there were not enough of them present to decide such an important issue. Lay opposition was headed by the earl of Chester, who declared that the king's tenants had already served in France in 1230, and hence that they were under no obligation to pay anything further.[121] There can be little doubt that this argument was principally intended to injure de Burgh, and did not spring from disapproval of the king's ambitions on the continent. Chester was more firmly committed to a vigorous foreign policy than virtually anyone else at court. By blocking de Burgh's request for aid he hoped to deal the Justiciar a mortal blow.

De Burgh had already forfeited baronial and clerical support. By 1232 his authority rested almost entirely upon the confidence of the king. In turn this confidence derived from his ability to act as moderator between the crown and the various constituencies in the country at large. The refusal of his request for aid showed that de Burgh could no longer be trusted to perform this function as mediator. Denied general taxation, the king was forced to turn to desperate measures to meet his commitments to duke Peter. On 10 March the duke was promised 3,000 marks, to be paid in full by 25 April, a date already set for yet another meeting of the council at which de Burgh may have hoped to renew his appeal for aid. A further 3,000 marks was promised, to be paid in early July.[122] Meanwhile the king's plate and jewels were pawned with the Templars and the Hospitallers, and a loan of 2,420 marks cobbled together from

---

118 Crook, *Records of the General Eyre*, pp. 86–7.
119 *Cl.R.1231–4*, pp. 30–1, 137–8, 143–7.
120 *Ibid.*, p. 128; Ms. 27DR, mm. 1d, 8d, 9d, 10.
121 Wendover, *Flores*, iv, pp. 233–4.
122 *Ibid.*, iv, pp. 233–4; *Pat. R. 1225–32*, pp. 463, 465–6.

various Italian merchants to make good the shortfall.[123] As security the king turned to the Jews, who on 2 March were forced to undertake repayment of 2,360 marks of the Italian loans by Michaelmas 1232, provided that meanwhile they were quit of arrears owing from earlier tallages.[124] Already the previous year the king had been forced to place greater reliance upon the Jews. At the Christmas court of 1231 a leading Jewish money-lender, Ursellus son of Hamo of Hereford, had fined 5,000 marks to inherit his father's estate. Like Isaac of Norwich, another of the great Jewish plutocrats, Ursellus was henceforth exempted from tallages and impositions, which therefore fell with even greater severity upon the rest of the Jewish community, less able to pay.[125] The same months may have witnessed an attempt at reform of the Exchequer of the Jews, involving the seizure of the lands of Master Alexander of Dorset, a long-standing justice of the Jews.[126]

Des Roches was well accustomed to dealings with the Jews, and had incurred censure for his association with Isaac of Norwich before 1224. Whether or not he was personally responsible for the revival of interest in Jewish finance in 1231, the effects of his regime upon the Jewish community were to be devastating. Increased financial pressures on the Jews inevitably led to increased tension with their Christian creditors. Certainly the years after 1230 witnessed an upsurge in anti-Jewish feeling. One of Simon de Montfort's first actions on inheriting his English estate in 1231 had been to expel the Jews from Leicester.[127] There were problems too amongst the Jews of Winchester. At some time in 1232 a twelve-month-old boy named Stephen was found strangled near St Swithun's priory. According to those who found the body it had been dismembered, mutilated and its eyes and heart plucked out. The boy's mother promptly fled the city, but popular suspicion fixed on Abraham Pinche, a Jew who, it was claimed, had purchased the child from its nurse so as to carry out some sort of crucifixion ritual. The sheriff was forced to imprison the

---

[123] *Pat. R. 1225–32*, pp. 466, 490, 514–15.

[124] C60/31, m. 6. The money appears to have been repaid to the Florentine lenders; *CRR*, xv, nos. 1066, 1181. In general, see Vincent, 'Jews, Poitevins, and the bishop of Winchester, 1231–1234', pp. 119–32, esp. pp. 124–5.

[125] C60/31, m. 7. For Isaac see above pp. 177–9, 182 and C60/30, m. 4.

[126] C60/30, m. 2; C60/32, m. 6. Alexander died *c*.March 1233; *Cl.R.1231–4*, pp. 197, 201–2; E40/1915; E40/2073; C. A. F. Meekings, 'Justices of the Jews, 1218–68: a provisional list', in Meekings, *Studies in Thirteenth Century Justice and Administration*, iv, p. 179.

[127] *Roberti Grosseteste Episcopi quondam Lincolniensis Epistolae*, ed. H. R. Luard (RS 1861), no. 5.

city's entire Jewry, probably for their own protection. In June 1232, following consultations at court, they were released in return for a fine of 20 marks. Officially, guilt for Stephen's murder was placed firmly with his mother who later abjured the realm.[128] Nonetheless Abraham Pinche failed to escape the citizens' retribution. Accused of stealing two shillings from a shop in Winchester as long ago as August 1230, he was tried at the assizes in 1235 and hung as a felon.[129] At least part of his unpopularity derived from his position and that of his mother, Chera Pinche, as two of the most active usurers in Hampshire. Between 1231 and 1234 des Roches was to exploit the Pinche family enterprise, persuading their debtors to part with land for his new religious foundations at Selborne and Titchfield.[130] Nor was it only at Winchester that tensions between citizens and Jews reached fever pitch. Similar accusations of child abuse and ritual circumcision were made against the Norwich Jewry at some time between 1231 and 1234.[131]

Such popular disturbances were an inevitable outcome of tightening the screws on Jewish finance. Yet the king seems to have been content to benefit from Jewish usury whilst repudiating the Jews themselves. Already, in May 1231 he had assisted in the refoundation of a hospital in Oxford, established on land which the king had expropriated from the Jews.[132] In January 1232, with des Roches as witness, he founded a house for Jewish converts in London, on the site of a former synagogue. Des Roches' suffragan, bishop John of Ardfert, consecrated the new foundation, to which the king pledged an income of 700 marks a year, payable at the Exchequer; a lavish endowment at the best of times, and one that in the circumstances of 1232 was positively ridiculous.[133] Needless to say only a fraction of the money promised was ever forthcoming. Even so, it may be that

---

[128] *AM*, ii (Winchester), p. 86 dates the murder to 18 October which cannot be correct. For details of the case, see *Cl.R.1231–4*, p. 80; JUST1/775, m. 20.

[129] JUST1/775, m. 20d; *Cal.Chart.R.1226–57*, p. 218.

[130] Below p. 359 and n.93.

[131] *CRR*, xv, no. 1320.

[132] *A Cartulary of the Hospital of St John the Baptist*, ed. H. E. Salter, 3 vols., Oxford Historical Society lxvi, lxviii–lxix (1914–17), iii, pp. xiv–xviii.

[133] Dugdale, *Monasticon*, vi, p. 683. For the house's consecration by bishop John (of Ardfert), see E372/76, m. 8d. In general see Vincent, 'Jews, Poitevins, and the bishop of Winchester', pp. 125–6, where it is suggested that Henry III's policy towards the Jews represents a conscious imitation of the measures introduced to France by Louis IX. Further confirmation of this is to be found in the way that Henry's foundation of the *Domus Conversorum* is noticed by the French chronicler, Albert of Trois Fontaines, in M. Bouquet et al. (eds.), *Recueil des Historiens des Gaules et de la France* (Paris 1734–1904), xxi, p. 607. Before 1236, various Jewish converts dwelling in the king's house at

the king hoped to salve his conscience at profiting from usury by putting at least a proportion of those profits towards a Christian mission to the usurers.

By resorting to the Jews, Henry III could do no more than stave off the inevitable financial reckoning for a month or two. Following the failure in March to secure a grant of taxation, the court left London for the west country, spending a day at Winchester in early April, and Easter at Reading. As de Burgh's fortunes dimmed, so des Roches' rose ever higher in royal favour. On 18 March he received custody of the county of Hampshire and a week later of Winchester castle, restoring him to precisely that local power base he had forfeited in 1224.[134] The previous sheriff was allowed to retain formal possession of his office until 25 April. He had answered at the Exchequer for the county farm and for an increment of £20, from which des Roches was now excused.[135] Besides these grants of offices, des Roches received other favours: a grant of two dozen deer from the New Forest, and on 10 April the exemption of his woods from the forthcoming royal regard.[136]

A council meeting had been agreed for 25 April for which the king returned to Westminster. However, to judge from the witness lists to royal charters, there were virtually no magnates at court on the appointed date, save de Burgh and the bishops of Bath and Carlisle.[137] Instead some sort of council convened a week later, on 2 May. Again its composition is difficult to establish. The only other magnates present at court by 5 May were des Roches and the earl of Chester.[138] In any event, the council once again failed to grant aid or taxation. Chester fell ill in London and on 6 May the king undertook to respect the terms of his will. The council also prohibited a tournament planned to take place at Northampton on 9 May, advancing Chester's illness as an excuse for the tournament's cancellation.[139] On 7 May the arrangements for the forthcoming eyre were formally announced.[140] But as yet, nothing had been done to rescue royal

London served on a commission appointed by the emperor Frederick II, set to investigate the charge that the Jews were committed to the ritual crucifixion of Christian children; Abulafia, *Frederick II*, pp. 244–5.

[134] *Pat. R. 1225–32*, pp. 466–7.
[135] C60/31, m. 6; *PR 14 Henry III*, p. 185; E372/75, m. 16; E372/76, m. 2; E372/77, m. 7d; E372/78, m. 1.
[136] *Cl.R.1231–4*, pp. 41, 47–8.
[137] C53/26, m. 12 (26 April).
[138] C53/26, m. 12 (5 May).
[139] *Pat. R. 1225–32*, pp. 472–3.
[140] *Cl.R.1231–4*, pp. 136–7.

finances. The render at the Easter Exchequer was almost certainly disappointing. In April, the Memoranda roll records an *adventus vicecomitum* of only £854, compared to more than £1,840 the following year.[141]

There can be little doubt that the king held de Burgh to blame for the refusal of taxation. On 7 May he extracted a hefty fine of 2,500 marks from de Burgh's nephew, the bishop of Norwich, in return for a grant of liberties. The fine was to be paid in full by the end of the year.[142] There are also indications that a root and branch reform of royal finances was under consideration. The grant of Hampshire to des Roches had been no more than a reward to a favoured courtier. But on 14 April Berkshire was removed from its former sheriff and given in temporary custody to the Exchequer clerk, Alexander of Swerford.[143] On 10 May Swerford yielded place to the professional sheriff, John Bonet. On the same day, Cambridge and Huntingdon passed in temporary custody to a clerk of the previous sheriff, Geoffrey of Hatfield.[144] The possibility that some more general change was in the air may explain a grant to the royal steward, Ralph fitz Nicholas, who on 3 May was confirmed in life possession of the sheriffdom of Nottinghamshire and Derby, apparently at the petition of the local county communities. Ralph had been appointed sheriff on lenient terms as long ago as 1224. Having caught wind of change, Ralph and the men of his shires would have been understandably keen to limit their future liabilities.[145]

In the second week of May the king left London, proceeding by easy stages to the Marches where he was due to meet Llywelyn on 23 May.[146] *En route* he participated in a ceremony which, in the circumstances of 1232, had more than purely symbolic significance. At Worcester on 19 May the body of King John was translated to a new tomb in the presence of Henry III, his sister Eleanor, Hubert de

---

[141] *Memoranda Rolls 1231–3*, nos. 1260–80, 2775–2803. There is no record of the *adventus* for the year 1230–1. David Carpenter has pointed out to me that the *adventus* figures do not provide a certain estimate of crown revenues since they exclude all Exchequer receipts save those to come in on the one day of the *adventus* itself. Nonetheless, in the absence of a receipt roll, they are our only means of gauging day-to-day cash income from the counties.

[142] C60/31, m. 5; E372/76, m. 11d. The bishop was licensed to take an aid from his men to help pay the fine; *Pat. R. 1225–32*, pp. 476–7.

[143] *Pat. R. 1225–32*, p. 469.

[144] *Ibid.*, p. 474.

[145] *Ibid.*, p. 472. Ralph was liable to pay 50 marks p.a. in place of profits over the county farm; *PR 14 Henry III*, p. 75. A splendid 'snapshot' of the court at this time is to be found in Dugdale, *Monasticon*, ii, pp. 80–1, drawn to my attention by David Carpenter.

[146] *Pat. R. 1225–32*, pp. 471–2.

Burgh and several other courtiers.[147] Des Roches may also have been present; during the next couple of days he witnessed confirmations to Worcester priory of land granted at the time of John's funeral.[148] Henry also gave the bishop of Worcester timber towards the fabric of Worcester cathedral, and the advowson of Bromsgrove to celebrate masses for the soul of his father.[149] The memory of King John seems to have been much on the minds of those at court. Richard of Cornwall's son, Henry III's nephew, born in January 1232, had been christened John. On 5 May Henry had pardoned a fine of 500 marks his father had imposed against St Albans Abbey, admitting that it had been levied more by the late king's will (*voluntate*) than by any just cause.[150] Yet it was precisely the wilful strength of his father that Henry was now being urged to emulate. With des Roches' return to court the king had welcomed back the one man most closely associated with the person and practices of King John. From Henry's earliest youth, des Roches had assumed the role of tutor and guardian, of necessity delegated by King John and later by the regency council. Always living in the shadow of older men, by 1232 Henry had begun to lose confidence in the ageing Hubert de Burgh, but was not yet ready to break every tie with his father's generation. He chose instead, and without as yet daring openly to challenge de Burgh, to trust increasingly to his former guardian, des Roches. Des Roches claimed he could remedy the king's financial plight; he shared the king's enthusiasm for France, for extravagant patronage and splendour. He told Henry that kings should be strong and rich like John or Frederick II, and Henry believed him. Within a few days of leaving Worcester and the tomb of his father, the king at last began the difficult business of easing de Burgh from power.

THE RISE OF PETER DE RIVALLIS MAY–JULY 1232

By 1232 des Roches was approaching sixty years of age, an elderly if not an old man. He was prepared to sit at the Exchequer but seems to have coveted no official title save that of bishop. This represents no modest abstinence on his part. Throughout his career he had derived power from his influence at court rather than from any particular court office. With the exception of his brief but catastrophic period as

---

[147] *AM*, i (Tewkesbury), p. 84.
[148] *Worcester Cartulary* (PRS), no. 328; C53/26, m. 10.
[149] *Worcester Cartulary*, no. 330; *Cal. Chart. R. 1226–57*, p. 154; *Cl.R.1231–4*, p. 64.
[150] C60/31, m. 5: (*finem factam*) *tempore Iohannis regis voluntate magis quam aliqua ratione.*

Justiciar in 1214, he had held no office of state despite exercising enormous influence over those who did. Between 1232 and 1234, although undoubtedly the king's chief minister, his power can be appreciated only by tracing its effect on others. Des Roches himself remained outwardly no more than the favoured bishop of Winchester. His principal satellite during these years was his nephew, an alien clerk named Peter de Rivallis.

Like des Roches, de Rivallis is described as a Poitevin by the chroniclers. Matthew Paris claims that he was *genere et origine Pictavensem*.[151] But again, as with des Roches, there is very little to substantiate this claim. In its earliest form his name is invariably spelt *Orival'* or *Aurivall*, which might suggest that he was born not in Poitou but at Roche d'Orival near Rouen in Normandy.[152] By descent he presumably shared des Roches' Tourangeau ancestry. His precise degree of kinship to the bishop is uncertain. Wendover, who was biased against them, claims that they were father and son.[153] In the Winchester pipe rolls and in the records of the royal courts they are described as uncle and nephew.[154] Matthew Paris began by adopting Wendover's description, but later went through the *Chronica Majora* as part of a more general excision of libels, erasing the word *filius* and substituting *carus*, *consanguinem* or the ambiguous *nepotem vel filium*.[155] In Paris' later, shorter chronicles, de Rivallis becomes merely the bishop's clerk or in one telling instance *alumpnum et ut dicebatur consanguinem propinquissimum*, next to which the words *id est filii* (*sic*) were written but later erased.[156] The Osney annalist calls de Rivallis the bishop's *domesticus*, Wykes his *nepotem*.[157] Whatever the precise nature of his relationship to des Roches, de Rivallis first appears in 1204, promoted by the king to various churches in the diocese of Lincoln, where des Roches was then precentor, and subsequently to a prebend at Lincoln cathedral.[158] At some time before 1225 he was made rector of Trumpington, Cambridgeshire, and under des Roches' sponsorship granted the Hampshire living of Alton.[159] A

151 Paris, *Hist. Ang. Min.*, ii, p. 342.
152 For what follows, see the biography of Peter given in *Acta*, appendix 4, no. 41.
153 Wendover, *Flores*, iv, p. 264.
154 See for example *CRR*, xv, no. 1031; Ms. 22DR, m. 5.
155 Paris, *CM*, iii, pp. 220, 240, 245, 252, 265.
156 Paris, *Hist. Ang. Min.*, ii, pp. 342, 353, iii, p. 268.
157 *AM*, iv, pp. 73, 78.
158 *RLP*, pp. 43, 80b, 84b; *Fasti*, ii, p. 107.
159 *Cl.R.1227–31*, p. 543; *AM*, ii (Waverley), p. 353; *CRR*, iii, p. 119, xvii, no. 2013; *The Cambridgeshire Portion of the Chartulary of the Priory of St Pancras of Lewes*, ed. J. H. Bullock and W. M. Palmer, Cambridge Antiquarian Soc. (1938), nos. 42, 55.

fifteenth-century account of the foundation of Mottisfont priory
mentions a Peter de Rivallis, brother of the priory's founder William
Brewer, who was known as 'the holy man in the wall' and left jewels
and money to the priory after his death.[160] The story is pure nonsense
as it stands, although de Rivallis was indeed rector of the parish
church of Mottisfont.[161] During the minority of Henry III he was
promoted clerk of the king's wardrobe, serving as such between
November 1218 and 1223, and receiving in reward the royal living of
Claverley, Shropshire, and the deanery of the royal free college of
Bridgnorth.[162]

He fell from office together with the rest of des Roches' satellites in
December 1223 and seems to have spent much of the next few years
abroad, probably in Poitou where he already had contacts, and where
by the summer of 1232 he had acquired the dignity of *chevecier* within
one of the collegiate churches of Poitiers; hence perhaps the appre-
hension of the St Albans chroniclers that de Rivallis was himself a
Poitevin.[163] In February 1230 he was granted licence to cross
temporarily to England, and after des Roches' return from crusade in
August 1231, received grants of venison from the king. Thereafter
until May 1232 his whereabouts are a mystery.[164] Only with the
king's arrival in Shropshire in May 1232 does de Rivallis begin to
appear regularly in the Chancery records. From then on his rise was
quite phenomenal.

Given his position as dean of the collegiate church of Bridgnorth, he may well have joined the court when the king arrived
at Bridgnorth on 22 May. The next few days witnessed inconclusive negotiations with Llywelyn, postponed for further discussion
to 4 August.[165] On 27 May the king once again notified his
sheriffs of Simon de Montfort's homage for the Leicester lands,
and granted the town of Wallingford to Richard of Cornwall in

---

[160] Dugdale, *Monasticon*, vi, p. 481 no. 1, which is taken from the present Bodl. ms.
Dodsworth 97, f. 81r–v, a fifteenth-century account of the foundation apparently
excised from one of the Mottisfont cartularies now in the Hampshire Record Office.

[161] *RLC*, i, p. 543; HRO ms. 13M63/2 (Mottisfont cartulary II), ff. 148r–149r.

[162] *RLC*, i, pp. 383, 391b, 410b, 415b–574 *passim*; *Pat. R. 1225–32*, p. 372; *BF*, pp. 384,
1342.

[163] *DD*, nos. 128–9; *Cal. Chart. R. 1226–57*, pp. 156–7, which here as elsewhere mistranslates
the title *capicerius* as 'treasurer'. HRO ms. 13M63/2, f. 148r shows that in 1229 he had a
proctor for his English affairs named Master William *le Brouinum* or *le Bronum*.

[164] *Cl.R.1227–31*, pp. 543, 546; *Pat. R. 1225–32*, p. 325. He may be the Exchequer baron
noted merely as P(eter) who authorizes writs on the Memoranda Roll from April 1232,
though this is far more likely to be des Roches; *Memoranda Rolls 1231–3*, nos. 1016,
1019, 1133, 1373.

[165] *Pat. R. 1225–32*, pp. 475–6; *Cl.R.1231–4*, p. 66.

fee.[166] These awards, tidying up the settlement which had first seen the readmission of de Burgh's enemies to court, were followed on 28 May by a life grant of Kenilworth castle to Stephen of Seagrave, a staunch supporter of the earl of Chester, yet another of de Burgh's enemies.[167] The king was still balancing favours between de Burgh and the rest of the court, allowing de Burgh's kinsman, bishop Thomas of Norwich, to levy an aid to help him pay the 2,500 mark fine he had made earlier for a grant of liberties. A clerk of Ranulph le Breton received a living in the king's gift.[168] It was over the next few days that Peter de Rivallis was readmitted to court, receiving instructions which suggest that he had been granted custody of various of the king's forests in Shropshire.[169]

At the start of June the court turned southwards, reaching Gloucester by 6 June. It was there that the king at last took des Roches' advice to institute a root and branch overhaul of royal finances. The decision was provoked by acute financial shortage; on 7 June desperate letters had to be dispatched to Westminster begging that money, be it as little as £100 or 100 marks, be sent to the king and to the knights keeping Painscastle as soon as possible, since Henry was completely without funds.[170] Change was signalled with a grant of privileges to des Roches, including rights of chase for life, assistance in collecting private debts and, most significantly, quittance from all accounts and arrears from the time of King John to the present day. The bishop was thus exempted from whatever financial reckoning was about to take place.[171] On 11 June, as the court headed back towards London, Peter de Rivallis was granted life custody of the royal chamber, the wardrobe, and the office of treasurer of the king's household. The terms of the award are peculiar: Peter was to retain his offices even should he abandon his clerical status, appointing a suitable agent to serve in his place.[172] The intention appears to have been to provide Peter with absolute security of tenure. But at the same time the award implies an ambiguity in his status as layman or cleric that was to loom ever larger as the landed settlement granted him by the crown grew in extent and shifted, from custodies granted

[166] *Pat. R. 1225–32*, p. 476; *Cal. Chart. R. 1226–57*, p. 155; Vincent, 'Simon de Montfort's first quarrel', p. 173.
[167] *Cal. Chart. R. 1226–57*, p. 155.
[168] *Pat. R. 1225–32*, pp. 476–7.
[169] *Cl.R.1231–4*, p. 66.
[170] *Ibid.*, p. 70.
[171] *Pat. R. 1225–32*, p. 478; *Cl.R.1231–4*, pp. 68–9.
[172] *Cal. Chart. R. 1226–57*, p. 156.

during pleasure, to awards made in perpetual fee. In the meantime, the king was weaving a network of mutually incompatible grants for life and in fee that could only be broken by revoking supposedly irrevocable charters and patents. De Rivallis' promotion of 11 June could not but be regarded as a challenge to de Burgh, who on the same day secured a confirmation of his life custody of the Justiciarship, together with a concession that he might appoint a deputy to discharge the office, even should he himself leave the country on pilgrimage or crusade.[173] This pattern, whereby every new grant to de Rivallis had to be balanced by complementary concessions to de Burgh, was to be repeated again and again over the coming month.

On the following day, 12 June, the king took an important step towards reforming administration of the county farms, removing Herbert de Alençon and William le Breton as sheriffs of Norfolk and Kent. William was a satellite of the Justiciar. He was replaced by Bertram de Criel, once an ally of de Burgh, but estranged from his former master following their quarrel over Dover castle in 1230.[174] Criel's promotion must be regarded as a blow to the Justiciar. By contrast, the man chosen to replace Alençon in Norfolk and Suffolk was de Burgh's staunch adherent and steward, Robert of Cockfield.[175] These appointments were only part of a more wide-sweeping purge of sheriffs, already heralded by the changes in Hampshire and Berkshire, and culminating in July 1232 with the promotion of Peter de Rivallis as keeper of over twenty counties. Wendover claims that, at des Roches' insistence, the king had demanded accounts from every sheriff, those found guilty of fraud being deposed and imprisoned until they had paid heavy fines.[176] There is no other proof that such an enquiry took place. However, Herbert de Alençon is known to have fined 300 marks for the king's grace before 5 July, raising the money by borrowing from the merchants of Siena.[177] Several months later, William le Breton was also forced to fine for the king's grace, offering 1,000 marks.[178] Although in neither case is punishment

---

173 *Cal. Chart. R. 1226–57*, p. 156.
174 *Pat. R. 1225–32*, p. 480, and see above pp. 268–9.
175 A few days earlier Cockfield had obtained quittance of various debts and obligations; *Cl.R.1231–4*, p. 68.
176 Wendover, *Flores*, iv, p. 244.
177 C60/31, m. 4; E372/76, m. 11d. Alençon paid 200m, being pardoned the remaining 100m in September 1232; *Cl.R.1231–4*, p. 110. For his borrowing from the Sienese which involved a conveyance of much of his property to Thetford priory, see *Cal. Chart. R. 1226–57*, p. 169.
178 C60/31, m. 2.

specifically linked to fraudulent accounting, the fate of William le Breton and Herbert de Alençon goes some way towards substantiating Wendover's claims.

De Rivallis' promotion continued on 15 June with a grant of life custody of the king's privy seal. The significance of this award, the first occasion on which custody of a royal seal had passed from titular control by the chancellor, was only partially offset by confirmation to the chancellor Ralph de Neville of his office and his custody of the great seal for life.[179] At the same time de Burgh was appeased by promotion as Justiciar of Ireland, again for life, although this was a far lesser award than that to de Rivallis, since it involved little more than titular supremacy over the Irish office exercised since 1228 by Hubert's nephew, Richard de Burgh.[180] Over the next few days the king made what may well have been significant interventions on behalf of aliens. Two Normans, William de Talbot and Richard de Harcourt, were assisted in their bids for family lands in England.[181] Talbot was a knight of the royal household, Harcourt the claimant to wide estates held of the honour of Leicester, whose restoration may well reflect some deeper scheme by the new heir to Leicester, Simon de Montfort, to introduce his followers from France to their former English lands.[182] At the same time the king went some way towards settling the long-running dispute over custody of Norman escheats which had soured relations with de Montfort, ever since the latter's introduction to England the previous August.[183] On 15 June another of the aliens who had fallen from favour with des Roches in 1223, the Poitevin Hugh de Vivonne, secured respite from his debts to the crown.[184]

Des Roches appears to have left court after 15 June, reappearing there only in mid-July. During the intervening weeks he may well have been engaged in supervising work on the king's new hall in Winchester castle.[185] In his absence, on 30 June he was granted custody of Portchester castle.[186] From Woodstock the king moved on

---

[179] Cal. Chart. R. 1226–57, pp. 156–7.

[180] Ibid., pp. 156–7; Pat. R. 1225–32, pp. 484–5.

[181] Cl.R.1231–4, pp. 76–7.

[182] BF, pp. 1392, 1394; Pat. R. 1225–32, p. 438; Cal.Lib.R.1226–40, pp. 9, 13, 41. For Harcourt, see also F. M. Powicke, 'The archbishop of Rouen, John de Harcourt and Simon de Montfort in 1260', EHR 51 (1936), pp. 108–13.

[183] At the same time a case brought by the countess of Winchester for part of Simon's honour was transferred from a local court to hearing before the Bench; Pat. R. 1225–32, p. 481; Cl.R.1231–4, p. 79; Vincent, 'Simon de Montfort's first quarrel', p. 173.

[184] Cl.R.1231–4, p. 73.

[185] Ibid., p. 70; C53/76, mm. 3, 4, 7.

[186] Cl.R.1231–4, p. 76.

to Berkhamsted and thence across country to Ely where he arrived on 22 June, intending to make a visit to the miraculous rood of Bromholm in Norfolk, said to have been fashioned from part of the True Cross rescued after the fall of Jerusalem to the Saracens.[187] At Chippenham, on 25 June, he granted de Rivallis quittance from any account for the treasury of the royal household, from the date of his appointment to 11 June when he had secured life custody, and for a year thereafter.[188] Once again, this can only have been intended to ease de Rivallis' work in overhauling crown finance. A similar quittance to de Burgh for the issues of the Justiciarship, granted five years before, was renewed at Bury St Edmunds on 27 June.[189] In all of this, the Justiciar was barely keeping pace with de Rivallis. Signs of the weakness of de Burgh's position came on 21 June, when the manor of Apethorpe was seized back from Hubert's protégé, Ranulph le Breton. Ranulph held the manor by royal charter, free from regard by the king's foresters, but there seems little doubt that its re-seizure followed allegations brought to light in the forest enquiry launched that summer.[190] Like the earlier attack against Bertram de Criel, it is interesting to note that the king was already carrying out arbitrary re-seizures in contravention of tenure by royal charter, before the fall of Hubert de Burgh, as part of an attack upon members of de Burgh's own household.

Meanwhile de Rivallis' promotion accelerated. Besides life custody of the counties of Sussex and Surrey, he now acquired the escheated honour of Aigle, again for life and in fee, rather than as a custody to be accounted for at the Exchequer. On 28 June he received his most extensive grant to date: life custody of all escheats and wardships in the king's gift, of the king's houses in Southampton, the royal park of Guildford, the manor of Kempton, of the chamberlainship of London together with supervision of the king's prises, of the mint, of every port save Dover, and of the Jewry throughout England. Custody of the vacant see of Canterbury was added two days later.[191] Such an extraordinary concentration of offices is virtually unprecedented in the history of England or of any other medieval state. Its purpose was

---

[187] For the rood of Bromholm, see Paris, *CM*, iii, pp. 80–1.
[188] *Cal. Chart. R. 1226–57*, p. 164.
[189] *Ibid.*, p. 164.
[190] C60/31, m. 4, and see *Cl.R.1231–4*, pp. 30–1, 52–3.
[191] *Pat. R. 1225–32*, p. 486; *Cal.Chart.R.1226–57*, p. 163. The grant of the Aigle lands, originally made during pleasure and including custody of the castles of Pevensey and Hastings, dated at Norwich on 28 June, was revised at Burgh on 2 July, to become a grant in fee, but excluding the two castles.

almost certainly to establish de Rivallis as a particularly high-powered inspector of royal finances, not to grant him a permanent monopoly over English government. Life custodies had been so widely distributed over the past few months, their currency so debased, that de Rivallis' promotion should not be taken at face value as irreversible, for life. Nonetheless its impact upon an already unsettled court can easily be imagined.

THE OATHS OF BURGH JULY 1232

On 2 July, at the Justiciar's ancestral manor of Burgh next Aylsham in Norfolk, the king swore an oath which has been subjected to intense analysis by historians.[192] The oath in question came whilst the king was on a tour of East Anglian religious shrines, and involved a solemn undertaking to observe the terms of charters, confirmations and privileges granted to a specified group of courtiers: Hubert de Burgh and his wife, Peter de Rivallis, the treasurer Walter Mauclerk, the chancellor Ralph de Neville (whose name was subsequently erased from the list), the two royal stewards Ralph fitz Nicholas and Godfrey of Crowcombe, and one other whose name was later erased.[193] The oath was intended to be absolutely binding. Perhaps in emulation of the security clause to Magna Carta (1215), the king was made to relinquish his right to appeal to the papacy against the oath, on pain of excommunication by the English church, suggesting that de Burgh believed he could still count upon the support of the English bishops. At the same time, Hubert de Burgh swore an undertaking to do all in his power to prevent the king from going against the promises to the various courtiers already named. It is David Carpenter's achievement to have shown that these oaths and promises were made specifically to protect de Burgh's position and to reassure those other courtiers who felt themselves threatened by Peter de Rivallis and his meteoric rise. The settlement was drawn up in the presence of de Burgh's household, at his own ancestral manor. In addition, Carpenter has drawn attention to various peculiarities in the diplomatic of the award, which suggest that the chancellor, Ralph de Neville, although present at court had deliberately distanced

---

[192] F. M. Powicke, 'The oath of Bromholm', *EHR* 56 (1941), pp. 529–48; Carpenter, 'The fall of Hubert de Burgh', pp. 1–17; 'Chancellor Ralph de Neville and the plans of political reform 1215–1258', in *Thirteenth Century England II*, ed. Coss and Lloyd, pp. 69–80.

[193] Carpenter, 'Chancellor Ralph de Neville', p. 75; C53/26, m. 4; *Cal. Chart. R. 1226–57*, pp. 164–5.

himself from the settlement, in protest against its terms, considering them irresponsible and totally inconsistent with the king's obligation to uphold the rights of the crown.[194] This may well be so. Certainly there is evidence that Neville avoided aligning himself to either of the opposed camps in the coming crisis. Although perhaps a protégé of des Roches in his youth, he had long since detached himself from the bishop's sphere of influence. By the same token, although he had served as chancellor throughout the years of de Burgh's ascendancy, he appears to have acquired no personal allegiance to the Justiciar. His unsuccessful bid for the archbishopric of Canterbury in 1231 had probably left him dissatisfied with de Burgh's handling of affairs.

Neville had one other cause for concern in the summer of 1232, overlooked by previous commentators. The promotion of Peter de Rivallis no doubt heralded an enquiry into royal finances. To ensure that his presidency of this enquiry was secure, it was necessary to give de Rivallis unrivalled control over a wide range of offices and custodies. Traditionally, commentators have assumed that he was being advanced merely as an inspector of the work of others, and that for the most part he exercised only titular authority over the offices in his charge. Yet there was a more sinister aspect to his promotion. Whilst most of his grants were for life only, on the same day, 2 July, that de Burgh extracted his oaths from the king, de Rivallis secured what was in effect his first award in hereditary fee, covering the escheated honour of Aigle with its estates concentrated in Surrey, Sussex and Hampshire.[195] Already in June he had been appointed sheriff of Surrey and Sussex for life. Unlike most of the counties that he received, Sussex was to remain in his personal charge for the next two years. On 16 July, de Rivallis received custody of the lands and heir of John de Briouze, lord of Bramber and a substantial part of east Sussex including the castles of Bramber and Knepp, yet another custody that he was to exercise in person.[196] Already he had come to acquire a powerful concentration of offices and land in Sussex, part of which was intended to pass in perpetuity to his heirs, including apparently the lands of John de Briouze, whose son was to be married to de Rivallis' niece. Many of the grants to de Rivallis were issued under a clause guaranteeing his continued possession, whether or not he remained in holy orders, raising the possibility that he might

[194] Carpenter, 'Chancellor Ralph de Neville', pp. 72–7.
[195] *Cal. Chart. R. 1226–57*, p. 163.
[196] *Pat. R. 1225–32*, p. 491; *Cl.R.1231–4*, p. 86.

repudiate his clerical status and set himself up as a secular magnate, with a wife and heirs. Nor was it was only in Sussex that de Rivallis attempted to establish himself as a landholder. On 5 July he was granted the royal castle of Lydford, Devon, and the forest of Dartmoor, paying a quit-rent in perpetuity.[197] This was one of the awards which, on Carpenter's evidence, the chancellor refused to authorize. Like the earlier grant of the honour of Aigle, it raises questions over the basic nature of the changes being attempted by des Roches. The bishop and his allies had told the king that the granting away of escheats was a principal cause of his financial straits, yet here was de Rivallis acquiring just such escheats and what, in the case of Lydford and Dartmoor, were effectively interests in the royal demesne, not merely in custody but in perpetual fee. Combined with the threat that de Rivallis' Sussex lordship posed to the see of Chichester, this self-seeking does much to explain Neville's dissatisfaction in July 1232. Above all it demonstrates that the oaths sworn at Burgh did little or nothing either to stem the growth of de Rivallis' influence at court, or to safeguard the position of the Justiciar. On the very day that the oaths were sworn, de Rivallis received the Aigle barony in fee.

As the court progressed from East Anglia to London, between 3 July and 15 July, the king added Lydford and Dartmoor to de Rivallis' lordship in fee, besides granting him life custody of all the royal forests in England and of a further nineteen counties.[198] Since May 1232 the Justiciar had barely managed to maintain his position in the face of such competition. During July he continued to receive royal charters, but like most of his recent awards they did no more than confirm him in possession of liberties granted several years previously.[199] The court spent the week from 15 July to 23 July at Lambeth and Westminster. There the king was able to recover the crown jewels he had deposited as security for his loans of March, perhaps using 1,200 marks which arrived from Ireland to redeem his debt.[200] On 16 July Peter de Rivallis received yet another block grant

---

[197] *Cal. Chart. R. 1226–57*, p. 163; *Pat. R. 1225–32*, pp. 487–8; C53/26, m. 5. A note on the charter roll states that the grant was cancelled because de Rivallis had surrendered his charter, but this surrender is unlikely to have occurred until the spring of 1234; *CPR 1232–47*, p. 42. It is possible that by Easter 1233 Lydford was in the custody of Brian de Lisle, perhaps as de Rivallis' agent; E159/13, m. 3d. Dartmoor had previously been in the custody of William Brewer; E32/25; *Pat. R. 1225–32*, p. 106, which adds slight support to the suggestion that Peter de Rivallis was in some way related to the Brewer family.

[198] *Pat. R. 1225–32*, pp. 488–9.

[199] *Cal. Chart. R. 1226–57*, pp. 163–4.

[200] *Pat. R. 1225–32*, pp. 490–1, 493; *Cl.R.1231–4*, p. 82.

of life custodies, confirming his possession of all escheats and wardships and conferring control over the king's prises, the royal castle of Marlborough, the king's houses at Clarendon, Ludgershall and Gillingham, together with custody of the lands of John de Briouze and the marriage of John's heir.[201] This last award was particularly significant, augmenting de Rivallis' lordship in Sussex and at the same time introducing him as a force to be reckoned with on the Marches. It must have come as a bitter blow to Hubert de Burgh, who since 1230 had enjoyed the homage and service of John de Briouze for the Gower peninsula, besides holding the three castles of Grosmont, Skenfrith and Llantilio by Briouze's gift.[202] In normal circumstances de Burgh would have expected to control Gower and probably the entire Briouze estate during the minority of John's heir. Instead, Gower and its castle at Swansea passed to an alien knight of the royal household, the rest of John's estate to de Burgh's arch-rival, Peter de Rivallis.[203]

De Burgh clung on for a few more days. On 18 July, his chaplain Richard de St John received a grant of property in London, and on 21 July the king confirmed various transactions in wardships held by de Burgh's nephew, Richard.[204] It is difficult to establish the king's precise intentions in all this. His promotion of de Rivallis contained an open challenge to the Justiciar. Since 1223 des Roches had vowed an intention to have his revenge upon de Burgh. The opportunity to achieve this was now within his grasp. More than likely, the king also wanted to be rid of de Burgh but lacked any clear idea of how to go about removing him. The spate of charters and patents granting custodies for life had been intended to buttress de Rivallis' position, but in the event had to be balanced against similar awards to de Burgh. In seeking to assert his own authority and to seize back control of crown patronage, the king succeeded merely in transferring even further power away from court, to individual ministers. By July 1232, both de Rivallis and de Burgh were entrenched in theoretically inviolable but nonetheless mutually incompatible positions, hedged around by grants of life custodies, of land in fee, and by the solemn oaths sworn at Burgh on 2 July. Tension at court might have been prolonged almost indefinitely had it not been for a storm which broke around 20 July. At long last the king was able to overcome his scruples

---

[201] *Pat. R. 1225–32*, pp. 491–2.
[202] *Ibid.*, pp. 417, 421–2; *Cal. Chart. R. 1226–57*, pp. 83, 127–8, and see below pp. 372–4.
[203] *Pat. R. 1225–32*, pp. 490–1.
[204] *Cal. Chart. R. 1226–57*, pp. 166–7; *Cl.R.1231–4*, p. 86.

and to take decisive action against de Burgh. The catalyst which sparked off this reaction has been identified by David Carpenter and must carry us back briefly to the events of 1231.

THE ANTI-ROMAN RIOTS AND THE FALL OF HUBERT DE BURGH

The six months to July 1232 had witnessed widespread disturbances against alien, especially non-resident Roman and Italian clergy. The movement's roots can be traced to the early years of Henry III's minority, to the widespread provision of Italians by the legates Guala and Pandulph, to the desire of the king and others to purchase support at the papal Curia, and to unpopular papal taxes imposed on the English church.[205] Beginning in mid-December 1231 with the kidnapping of a papal chaplain, Master Cinthius of S. Eustacio, canon of St Paul's, the disturbances appear to have been widespread and well-organized, prompting suspicion that they commanded covert support in high places.[206] Late in December, in Kent, the rents and grain of Rufinus, nephew of the late legate Guala, were seized, as were those of William, son of the count of Savoy. The attackers carried letters purporting to be sealed by the king, which they used to forestall intervention by the sheriff's men. In the New Year the king ordered the arrest of anyone found guilty of removing, threshing or purchasing the victims' grain, and on 10 February an assembly of bishops followed this up by excommunicating the rioters.[207]

Thus far the main thrust of the disturbances had been restricted to the vacant archbishopric of Canterbury, where the king had recently installed at least two Roman clerks, no doubt hoping to win support in Rome for his archbishop-elect, Ralph de Neville.[208] The pope had hardly endeared himself to England during these months. In accordance with a request from the late archbishop, he forbade the appointment of clerks as justices, sheriffs or royal bailiffs without papal dispensation.[209] Shortly thereafter he quashed Neville's election to Canterbury, sending papal nuncios to notify the king of his decision.[210]

---

[205] In general, see H. Mackenzie, 'The anti-foreign movement in England, 1231–1232', in *Anniversary Essays in Mediaeval History by Students of Charles Homer Haskins*, ed. C. H. Taylor and J. L. La Monte (Boston 1929), pp. 183–203.

[206] Wendover, *Flores*, iv, p. 231; *Fasti*, i, p. 75.

[207] Wendover, *Flores*, iv, pp. 228–33; *Cl.R.1231–4*, pp. 112, 128.

[208] *Pat. R. 1225–32*, pp. 452, 462. The late archbishop had also assigned rents in Wingham to the monks of Monte d'Oro, Anagni; *Cal.Pap.Reg.*, i, pp. 128–9.

[209] *Pat. R. 1225–32*, p. 457; *Cl.R.1231–4*, p. 128.

[210] *RL*, i, p. 459; *Cal.Pap.Reg.*, i, p. 128.

There followed a second wave of attacks and disturbances which according to Wendover were headed by a Yorkshire knight named Robert of Thwing acting under the pseudonym 'William Wither', literally 'William the Angry', or 'William the Ferocious'.[211] Thwing's grievance against the Romans apparently sprang from papal provision to the church of Kirkleatham, whose advowson he and his wife had only recently recovered following legal action against the monks of Guisborough.[212] Thwing commanded useful connections amongst the Yorkshire gentry, but was probably only one of several like-minded men who in March and April 1232 led attacks against the granges and rents of alien clergy. On 20 April, the king was forced to write to the count of Savoy, apologizing for indignities inflicted on his son, and in mid-May, a second general enquiry was launched to discover who had benefited from the Romans' misfortunes.[213] News of the attacks must already have come to the attention of the pope who in June wrote to the king at great length, reminding him of his obligations to Rome, of the services rendered during his minority by papal legates, and sternly demanding correction of the attacks made against those bringing papal letters into England.[214]

Already the Justiciar seems to have been suspected of complicity in these attacks. De Burgh had good reason to feel hostile to Rome. As early as 1230, the king had threatened to send for a legate to supplant Hubert at court.[215] Archbishop Richard had sought papal support in his various suits against the Justiciar, and had persuaded the pope to make enquiries into the legality of Hubert's marriage. This enquiry was still proceeding in June 1232, indeed it may well have been the subject of the papal letters whose carriers were assaulted on their arrival in England.[216] On the same day that he notified the king of

---

[211] Wendover, *Flores*, iv, pp. 230–1, 240–2; Paris, *CM*, iii, pp. 217–18; R. Hill, *Ecclesiastical Letter Books*, pp. 82–3. For the meaning of 'wither' see the *Oxford English Dictionary*, s.v.

[212] N. Vincent, 'Robert of Thwing', in *New Dictionary of National Biography* (Oxford, forthcoming); *Early Yorkshire Charters*, ii, ed. W. Farrer (Edinburgh 1915), p. 67; *ibid.*, xi, ed. C. T. Clay (1963), pp. 203–6; *CP*, xii, pt i, pp. 737–8; *Cartularium Prioratus de Gyseburne*, ed. W. Brown, 2 vols., Surtees Soc., lxxxvi, lxxxix (1889–94), ii, pp. 96–100; *CRR*, xiii, no. 2348; JUST1/1042, m. 1; Paris, *CM*, iii, pp. 609–14.

[213] *Cl.R.1231–4*, pp. 135, 138–9, and see *Pat. R. 1225–32*, p. 471.

[214] *Foedera*, pp. 203–4; *AM*, iii (Dunstable), p. 128.

[215] *RL*, i, no. cccx. The king had sought the appointment of John of Columpna, cardinal of S. Praxed, whose nephew, Master Odo, was shown considerable favour in England; *Pat. R. 1225–32*, pp. 265, 452, 462; *Cal.Pap.Reg.*, i, p. 129.

[216] *AM*, iii (Dunstable), pp. 128–9, which implies that there may also have been an enquiry, satisfactorily dealt with by Hubert, into his dispensation from the vows he had taken as a crusader before 1216.

the carriers' grievances, the pope wrote to de Burgh promising goodwill, but warning him that there was no option but for the investigation (presumably the investigation into the circumstances of Hubert's marriage) to proceed; the Justiciar, so Gregory complained, had acted rashly and with undue hostility to the enquiry.[217] There were undoubtedly links between de Burgh, earl of Kent, and various of the Kentish rioters. Robert of Thwing subsequently witnesses a charter of the Justiciar's son, although there is no firm proof that he was already associated with de Burgh in 1232.[218] In 1224 de Burgh had been able to make considerable political capital by stirring up xenophobia against his alien rivals at court. It may well be that in the circumstances of 1231–2 he hoped to repeat this success. The Roman clergy against whom the attacks were directed were for the most part non-resident. Nor was it only Italians who suffered, but other aliens, such as the Frenchman, William of Savoy. Unable to vent their fury against such absentees, it would have been only natural if the rioters had turned against the most conspicuous group of foreigners then resident in England, the likes of des Roches, his alien associates and the various Frenchmen employed in his episcopal household. Once again, it appears that what has been taken to be a spontaneous outburst of popular xenophobia, may in fact have been a carefully orchestrated political ploy, organized from within the court. As with the ambiguities surrounding earlier attacks on aliens – the fact that the self-proclaimed xenophobes of 1215, the barons, were many of them of French birth, sponsors of a Capetian bid for the throne of England, or that de Burgh and Langton, the chief instigators of anti-alien sentiment during the 1220s, were both of them former residents in France, schooled or trained abroad – so in 1232 the apparently crude xenophobia of the anti-Roman rioters might be linked to more subtle political developments at court. Ironically, the most prominent anti-alien rioter of 1232 Robert of Thwing, was shortly afterwards to unite his family by successive marriages to that of the most notorious alien active in the north of England: Peter de Maulay, lord of Mulgrave.[219] Once again, we should beware of accepting outward appearances, or of reading back into the 1230s nationalist sentiments which are more appropriate to the nineteenth century.

---

[217] *Cal.Pap.Reg.*, i, pp. 129–30; *RL*, i, pp. 549–50; *AM*, iii (Dunstable), pp. 128–9.
[218] E40/5284.
[219] *CP*, viii, pp. 558–9, xii, pt i, pp. 737–9. Thwing's later contacts with Richard earl of Cornwall may well have come via Peter de Maulay, Richard's former guardian; Denholm-Young, *Richard of Cornwall*, pp. 42, 115, 172–3.

Meanwhile the pope had established an enquiry into the circumstances of the riots, appointing the archbishop of York, the bishop of
Durham and Master John the Roman, canon of York, in the northern
province, and in the south, bishop des Roches and the abbot of Bury
St Edmunds.[220] Given the tense circumstances of 1232, with the court
riven by the hostilities between de Burgh and des Roches' kinsman
Peter de Rivallis, it is not surprising that the bishop of Winchester lost
no time in using his papal commission for private, factional advantage.
From 20 July onwards the king ordered a series of arrests, almost
certainly related to the findings of des Roches' enquiry. The list of
those arrested or disgraced bears out Wendover's claim that the
enquiry implicated leading figures at court, above all the Justiciar,
Hubert de Burgh. On 20 July the lands of Ralph and Walter fitz
Bernard were seized in Essex and Kent, including fees Ralph held of
de Burgh.[221] Two days later the royal clerks Master Ralph of
Shardlow and Master Roger de Cantiloupe were dismissed from their
duties as justices in eyre.[222] Shardlow was almost certainly a protégé
of de Burgh; his brother Hugh was the Justiciar's steward.[223] Only a
month earlier, Shardlow had been replaced by Peter de Rivallis as
sheriff of Surrey and Sussex. He was now accused of involvement in
the anti-Roman disturbances and ordered to attend court in company
with Robert of Thwing, the pseudonymous William Wither.[224]
Both Robert and Hugh of Shardlow faced heavy fines; Hugh was
imprisoned and released only in February of the following year.[225]
Again, late in July 1232, yet another of the Justiciar's satellites faced
disgrace. Ranulph le Breton, rescued from banishment in 1231,
deprived arbitrarily since June 1232 of his manor of Apethorpe, was
now ordered to quit the realm by 15 August.[226] There can be little
doubt that his disgrace was linked to the anti-Roman riots, since he
was subsequently provided with safe-conducts to attend des Roches,

[220] Wendover, *Flores*, iv, p. 241.
[221] C60/31, m. 3; *Cl.R.1231–4*, pp. 91, 151, where complicity in the attacks at Wingham
is implied; *BF*, p. 1463; *Cal.Inq.P.M.*, i, no. 468.
[222] Crook, *Records of the General Eyre*, p. 88.
[223] *The 1235 Surrey Eyre*, ed. C. A. F. Meekings and D. Crook, 2 vols., Surrey Rec. Soc.
xxxi–xxxii (1979–83), i, pp. 240–2; *Cl.R.1231–4*, p. 12. For Hugh as steward, see St
John's College Cambridge, Muniments mss. Ospringe deeds D7.84, D7.85. Master
Robert appears elsewhere as a witness to charters of archbishop Stephen Langton and
Langton's pupil, Alexander of Stainsby, bishop of Coventry and Lichfield; Lambeth
Palace Library ms. Register of Archbishop Warham I, f. 158v; *An Edition of the Cartulary
of Burscough Priory*, ed. A. N. Webb, Chetham Soc. 3rd series, xviii (1970), no. 167.
[224] *AM*, iii (Dunstable), p. 129; *Pat. R. 1225–32*, p. 493.
[225] *The 1235 Surrey Eyre*, ed. Meekings, i, p. 241; *Cl.R.1231–4*, pp. 183, 189–90.
[226] C60/31, m. 3.

the chief inquisitor into the affair.[227] Meanwhile his lands, houses and gardens were laid waste.[228] For several years, both on his own account as a landholder at Chalfont, and as an agent of de Burgh, he had engaged in attacks against the canons of Missenden Abbey in Buckinghamshire. The canons were now compensated for these attacks with a licence to carry off Ranulph's horses from Chalfont. Hay which he had misappropriated from the Templars was to be returned.[229] Late in September 1232 he fined £1,000 for the king's grace, and was restored to his lands including Apethorpe, save for the new assarts he had made in nearby woods. At the same time his brother, William le Breton, former sheriff of Kent, where the worst of the anti-Roman attacks had taken place, fined 1,000 marks.[230] Other arrests and confiscations followed. Des Roches was still active on his enquiry into the autumn of 1232.[231]

It was to be the anti-Roman riots and the accusations of complicity in them levelled against Hubert de Burgh, that brought about the Justiciar's downfall. De Burgh himself was still at court when the confiscations and arrests began. He was still there on 28 July, on which day Peter de Rivallis received yet another block, grant of offices, this time in Ireland. Superficially the award was of no very special importance; de Rivallis was to have life custody of the treasury, the chamber, prises, Jews and escheats of Ireland together with various lands, castles and towns.[232] However, named amongst these latter were the castles of Athlone and Drogheda and the towns of Limerick and Cork, all of which seem previously to have been annexed to the office of Justiciar of Ireland, held in 1232 on behalf of Hubert de Burgh by Hubert's nephew Richard.[233] Furthermore, on 28 July, de Rivallis was granted the five best cantreds within the province of Connaught, a prize that had been deliberately withheld in 1227 when

---

[227] *Pat. R. 1225–32*, p. 497.

[228] C60/31, m. 3.

[229] *CRR*, xii, no. 372, xiv, nos. 400, 973, 1281; C60/31, m. 3; *AM*, iii (Dunstable), p. 130; *Cl.R.1231–4*, p. 92. Ranulph's complicity in the anti-Roman riots may relate to his efforts in 1229 to secure a prebend at Salisbury cathedral in opposition to a papal provisor; *Reg. St Osmund*, ii, pp. 96–100; *Fasti*, iv, pp. 93–4.

[230] C60/31, m. 2; *Cl.R.1231–4*, p. 154; *AM*, iii (Dunstable), p. 130. William was eventually pardoned all but £100 of his fine; C60/33, m. 5; E372/77, m. 5. Ranulph faced a spate of hostile actions before the Bench and the Buckinghamshire eyre of Oct./Nov. 1232; *CRR*, xiv, no. 2214; JUST1/62, mm. 7d, 16, 20d, 23d.

[231] *Pat. R. 1225–32*, p. 498; *Cal.Pap.Reg.*, i, p. 132. Des Roches' subsequent interventions in the arrest of William de Clinton and in respect to Massingham church may well relate to this same commission; *Cl.R.1231–4*, pp. 163, 382.

[232] *Cal. Chart. R. 1226–57*, pp. 166–7.

[233] *Cl.R.1227–31*, pp. 20–1, 196–7; *Pat. R. 1225–32*, p. 47.

the remainder of Connaught was granted to Richard de Burgh, and whose acquisition had since been one of Richard's chief ambitions.[234] De Rivallis' grants of 28 July therefore represent a direct challenge to de Burgh; the first occasion on which Peter's promotion necessitated the deposition of de Burgh himself from any office or custody.

The following day, as the court halted at Woodstock *en route* for the Marches, de Burgh's resistance finally collapsed. Precisely what happened is unclear. At Woodstock there were gathered several of de Burgh's bitterest enemies: des Roches, who had been at court for the past fortnight, and the earls of Cornwall, Chester and Pembroke, all of whom were newly arrived, none of them having witnessed a royal charter since the council of April/May.[235] The king was about to meet with Llywelyn. The Woodstock court may well have been summoned to offer advice on the forthcoming negotiations, de Burgh's dismissal being one obvious means of furthering an Anglo-Welsh settlement.[236] Almost certainly the Justiciar was openly accused of complicity in the anti-Roman riots. Much later, in 1239, the king was to revive various accusations against de Burgh, amongst them a charge that:

Once when the court was at Woodstock, and the king happening to be alone in a certain room, the earl made a violent rush on the king with a knife endeavouring basely and treacherously to slit his throat, and it was only with difficulty and after crying out for assistance that the king could be rescued from his hands.[237]

The possibility that some sort of attack took place should not be dismissed out of hand. For the past two years de Burgh had been forced to endure a steady and humiliating decline in his standing at court, brought about by the shifting affections of a king barely out of his teens. At Woodstock the Justiciar's patience may have snapped. Long acknowledged as the king's mentor and surrogate father, who knows but that Hubert dared box the young man's ears. Nothing so serious as attempted murder could have gone unremarked in the chronicles, or unpunished, but a brief outbreak of fury may account for the stunned silence that enveloped the court over the next few

---

[234] *Cal. Chart. R. 1226–57*, p. 42; A. J. Otway-Ruthven, *A History of Medieval Ireland*, 2nd edn (London 1980), pp. 92–6.

[235] C53/26, m. 3. Brian de Lisle was also at court from 15 July, Philip de Aubigné from 28 July.

[236] Although in the event, the negotiations held at Shrewsbury on 7 August proved inconclusive and were prorogued to be resumed in October; *Cl.R.1231–4*, p. 93.

[237] Paris, *CM*, iii, p. 619.

days. On 28 July de Burgh disappears from the king's side, but not until 8 August, nearly a fortnight later, did the process of retribution against him commence.

Within less than a year after his return from crusade, des Roches had re-established himself in a commanding position in local and central government. His threat of 1223, to have revenge upon de Burgh, had been put into practice. The Justiciar was disgraced and des Roches' nephew, Peter de Rivallis, promoted to a quite extraordinary position in command of the king's finances. Des Roches and de Rivallis promised the king that they could make him rich and powerful. They may also have offered to support Henry's bid to consolidate Plantagenet lordship in France. For the moment, in ridding the king of his Justiciar, they had worked in close co-operation with a large number of barons and courtiers, equally resentful of de Burgh. Superficially at least, des Roches was restored to much the same position that he had enjoyed under King John and during the early years of the minority of Henry III. But by 1232, he was a much older and a much more embittered man, scarred by his experiences of the 1220s. Not content with de Burgh's dismissal from court, he now sought the utter disgrace of his old enemy and the confiscation of his lands, pursuing a vendetta against de Burgh far more severe than anything that de Burgh himself had attempted against the bishop after 1224. In the process, des Roches was to sacrifice much of the spirit of co-operation that had united political society against de Burgh, in the end transforming his victory of 1232 into ignominious defeat.

Chapter 9

THE COALITION

For several months after the fall of Hubert de Burgh, the court can be divided, very loosely, into three basic groups: the veterans of John's reign headed by des Roches; a group of household officers including the stewards Ralph fitz Nicholas, Godfrey of Crowcombe and John fitz Philip; and finally, the earl Marshal, his kinsmen and allies. All three groups had shared a desire for de Burgh's dismissal, but they were united by little else. In this respect they provide an interesting comparison to the disparate alliance over which de Burgh had presided since 1224. Whereas by moderation de Burgh had maintained some sort of common front for the best part of a decade, it was to take barely six months for the coalition of 1232 to break down into civil war. For this des Roches must bear the greatest blame. Where de Burgh had proceeded with tact against those ousted from power in 1224, des Roches went all out for vengeance. In the process he reopened wounds and revived tensions that stretched far back into the reign of King John.

In the immediate term, des Roches and his associates obtained no stranglehold over the court. The fall of de Burgh was a momentous event, shattering the consensus of the past ten years, to usher in a period of uncertainty and realignment. Political groupings at the Plantagenet court had always been unstable affairs, undermined by internal rivalries and by the dependence of individual courtiers upon the personal favour of the king. Although des Roches had long stood at the head of a group made up of aliens and the veterans who had served under King John, bound together more closely than most other political groupings at court, it was to take many months before these men learned to exploit the fall of de Burgh and the bishop's new-found favour to seize the political initiative. Apart from the bishop himself, Peter de Maulay and William de Cantiloupe witness a bare four charters apiece between July 1232 and the following April; Engelard de Cigogné is unrecorded at court until February 1233, the earl of Aumale until several months later.[1] Meanwhile, it is Richard Marshal who was the most active figure at court, witness to some twenty-eight royal charters, set against des Roches' eighteen.[2] Allied to the Marshal was a group of interrelated magnates: the earls of Cornwall, Derby, Norfolk and Warenne. Had it been managed with more skill, this group might have come to monopolize power at court, possibly to the exclusion of des Roches. For the rest, the king's household officers had escaped relatively lightly from the fall of de Burgh. Apart from the steward Richard de Argentan, and the treasurer of the household Ranulph le Breton, there had been no great purge at court, precisely because de Burgh had exercised so little influence over household appointments. The tensions between the three groups, veterans, householders and supporters of the Marshal, were to dominate court politics into 1233. The first problem their ill-matched coalition was asked to surmount concerned the action to be taken against de Burgh.

THE TRIAL OF HUBERT DE BURGH AUGUST–NOVEMBER 1232

The problems associated with de Burgh's dismissal were threefold. Firstly, there was the question of how to remove him from the Justiciarship and from the many custodies he held, guaranteed to him by royal charter and by the most solemn oaths. De Burgh was by no means the first chief minister to be disgraced; Richard I and John had dismissed favourites and revoked royal charters with impunity. It was precisely the desire to combat such attacks that had given rise to clause 39 of Magna Carta and its provision that no free man was to be imprisoned, disseised or in any way gone against without judgement of his peers or the law of the land. Magna Carta had introduced new complications to the replacement or dismissal of courtiers, complications which were barely touched upon during the one major revolution to hit the court between 1215 and 1232. In 1224 the liberties and custodies reclaimed from such disgraced courtiers as Fawkes de Bréauté or des Roches had been granted, not by charter in perpetuity or for life, but merely during pleasure, the king's power to issue charters having been deliberately curtailed during his minority.

In the late 1220s des Roches, hardly the most ardent supporter of

---

[1] The charter roll witness lists for Henry III's reign are unpublished. Manuscript schedules of them by the late C. A. F. Meekings are kept at the PRO by Dr David Crook who kindly put them at my disposal.

[2] *CRR*, xv, p. xxiiin.

Magna Carta, had attempted an appeal under clause 39 of the charter, claiming that one of his custodies had been seized back by the king arbitrarily, *per voluntatem regis*.[3] But on the whole, de Burgh and the victors of 1224 were scrupulous in respecting the terms of grants made in perpetuity by royal charter. Albeit in return for a heavy fine, they allowed des Roches to retain forest liberties and markets acquired with dubious legality and without charter during the king's minority.[4] Only after 1226 and the restoration of the king's power to grant charters in perpetuity, were the implications of Magna Carta finally brought home. Henceforth it would be difficult for the king to overturn any life custody or grant in perpetuity without risking a charge that he was acting with an arbitrary disregard for the law. Although Bracton and others were to allow that the king might sit in judgement on his own charters, and in theory warrant them or reject them as he saw fit; in practice the bestowal of a charter was tantamount to a promise of perpetual warranty. To overturn such a charter would, so Bracton implies, involve the king in an arbitrary act, operating over and above the due process of law.[5] It was precisely because royal charters were so hard to challenge and appeared to offer such a clear promise of warranty, that their issue had been suspended during the minority of Henry III. When the minority came to an end, courtiers sought the guarantee of grants and custodies by royal charter all the more eagerly, precisely because they appreciated the new security that such charters entailed. Henceforth the problem of dismissing or displacing courtiers became all the more intractable. Des Roches was by no means the first person at court to recommend that the king overturn specific awards guaranteed by charter, in order to remove obnoxious or errant ministers. The problem had already arisen during the five years between the ending of Henry's minority and the fall of Hubert de Burgh. Even whilst de Burgh was still in power, the king admitted acting against Bertram de Criel arbitrarily, *per voluntatem*. In June 1232 Ranulph le Breton was deprived of the manor of Apethorpe despite royal charters supposedly guaranteeing it to him in fee.[6] However, these disputes were as nothing compared to

---

3   *CRR*, xi, no. 2384, and see above p. 221.
4   Above pp. 221–2, 226–8.
5   *Bracton on the Laws and Customs of England*, ed. G. E. Woodbine and S. E. Thorne, 4 vols., Selden Society (Cambridge Mass. 1968–77), ii, pp. 108–9. In an as yet unpublished paper, David Carpenter suggests that this passage, leading into the famous *additio de cartis*, was composed by William de Raleigh in the aftermath of the fall of des Roches in 1234, in response to the Upavon case, for which see below pp. 334–7.
6   *Cl.R.1231–4*, p. 29; and see above pp. 268–9, 298.

the enormous number of charters that would have to be repudiated if de Burgh were truly to be shorn of power.

The frantic playing-off of de Burgh against de Rivallis in the first part of 1232 had ensured that life custodies and awards in perpetuity were distributed on an unprecedented scale and in such a way that it was virtually certain that not all of them could be honoured. Even after the king had accomplished de Burgh's dismissal, the problem remained: how to overturn the late Justiciar's liberties without threatening the security of every single tenancy by royal charter? Herein lay the new regime's second great challenge. As an alternative to arbitrary disseisin *per voluntatem*, Magna Carta proposed judgement by peers or the law of the land. But how was such judgement to be obtained? In the case of de Burgh the solution proved to be a primitive form of State Trial, but in the meantime there were many, des Roches included, who advocated a more forthright, less legally scrupulous approach. Finally, there was the problem of what to do with de Burgh's vast accumulation of lands and offices now restored to the crown. How was this bounty to be divided up amongst the various rival factions? The failure to provide an adequate solution to this, as to so many other problems, was fatally to undermine the stability of the court after the summer of 1232.

On 8 August, nearly a fortnight after de Burgh's disappearance from court, the king ordered him to surrender eight royal castles including Windsor, Dover and the Tower of London. The order symbolizes the king's dilemma since it continues to accord de Burgh his title as Justiciar, like the eight castles in question theoretically guaranteed to Hubert by charter for life.[7] Clearly there was disagreement within the council as to how to proceed. According to Wendover, de Burgh was summoned to render accounts for his offices and custodies stretching back to the reign of King John. He appealed to the royal charters he held absolving him from any such account, but des Roches responded that such charters were invalid having been granted by King John and hence nullified by John's death. In fact Hubert's charters had first been granted in 1227 and renewed thereafter on several occasions, most recently in June 1232.[8] Wendover's account presumably reflects uneasiness that des Roches and his supporters were out to attack the very basis of title by royal charter. The death of a king had never before been considered to invalidate his charters, although uncertainty here had made it advisable to seek confirmations from a king's

---

[7] *Pat. R. 1225–32*, p. 496.

[8] Wendover, *Flores*, iv, pp. 245–7; *Cal. Chart. R. 1226–57*, pp. 51, 74, 82, 131, 164.

successor. Certainly des Roches is likely to have recommended that the king challenge de Burgh's immunity from account. On 25 August letters were prepared commanding de Burgh, now shorn of his title as Justiciar, to leave the realm by 10 September. But they were never sent.[9] Instead he was summoned to a meeting of the council to be held on 14 September. Rather than confront his enemies, he fled to the sanctuary of Merton priory, having a few days earlier renewed his vows as a crusader.[10] By taking the cross, de Burgh adopted a ploy used by both King John in 1215 and by des Roches during the 1220s. Yet, whereas des Roches had accepted his loss of power after 1223 with relative equanimity, in 1232 de Burgh fled to sanctuary rather than submit to the judgement of the new regime at court. Perhaps he found it impossible to believe that the king, for many years his pupil, could not still be persuaded to reverse the process instigated by des Roches. Perhaps too, he felt a genuine sense of fear for his own personal safety, an indication of the depth of the hatred that over the next two years was to envenom political life. Certainly the chroniclers imply that the new regime was intent upon violent revenge against de Burgh. Wild accusations had begun to circulate: that de Burgh was a poisoner, responsible for the murder of Fawkes de Bréauté, archbishop Richard of Canterbury and William Marshal the younger; even that he had engaged in sorcery and witchcraft.[11] In these circumstances it is perhaps not surprising that Hubert was reluctant to throw himself upon the mercies of the court.

In mid-September des Roches, five other bishops, and the earls of Cornwall, Chester, Pembroke, Derby and Warenne, duly met at Lambeth.[12] Once again there was disagreement as to how to proceed. The citizens of London had greeted the Justiciar's fall with jubilation and had mounted some sort of demonstration in arms whilst the king was away on the Marches.[13] Around 17 September, perhaps prompted by a violent outburst from the king, they decided to drag de Burgh forcibly from Merton, a move in which Matthew Paris claims they had the tacit approval of des Roches, who counselled them that in all things they should obey the king's will. They were stopped only after intervention by more moderate courtiers: the earl of Chester and the

---

9   *Pat. R. 1225–32*, p. 498. For what appears to have been a later attempt at banishment, see Wendover, *Flores*, iv, pp. 251–3.

10   *AM*, i (Tewkesbury), p. 86; Wendover, *Flores*, iv, pp. 247–8.

11   Paris, *CM*, iii, p. 223.

12   See the witness lists to royal charters; C53/26, m. 2; Dugdale, *Monasticon*, vi, p. 931.

13   Wendover, *Flores*, iv, p. 248; *De Antiquis Legibus Liber: Chronica Maiorum et Vicecomitum Londiniarum 1178–1274*, ed. T. Stapleton, Camden Soc., xxxiv (1846), pp. 6–7.

chancellor, Ralph de Neville.[14] De Burgh was now bailed to appear before the council in January 1233. Meanwhile, between 18 and 22 September, his remaining custodies, castles and lands, including those he held by private inheritance, were seized by the crown and entrusted temporarily to des Roches' henchman, Peter de Rivallis.[15] A week later de Burgh's son John was stripped of every estate held from the crown.[16] Again, at some time between 23 and 30 September, de Burgh's principal title as Justiciar was bestowed on Stephen of Seagrave, a close familiar of the earl of Chester, and for the past few years the leading justice *coram rege*. Seagrave had recently received life custody of Kenilworth castle and on 28 July, the very day of de Burgh's fall, had been confirmed for life as sheriff of five midland counties and as constable of Northampton, on very favourable terms.[17] His appointment as Justiciar was intended as a gesture of goodwill towards his sponsor, Chester, and reflects Seagrave's competence to discharge the legal and judicial functions of the office without the great position as magnate or policy-maker which had typified the Justiciarship under de Burgh and his predecessors. De Burgh himself was granted permission to join his wife at Bury St Edmunds. However, having left the safety of Merton, he fled almost immediately to sanctuary once again, in the chapel of Brentwood in Essex, close to property belonging to his kinsman, the bishop of Norwich. Probably, wild rumour had made him once again fear for his life. The king ordered that his sanctuary be violated. De Burgh was taken in chains to the Tower, but on 27 September at the insistence of the bishop of London he was restored to Brentwood, where he was to remain for a further month. Finally on 23 October he was summoned to stand trial in London on pain of outlawry.[18]

Already the treatment of de Burgh had revealed disagreement at court, between hard-liners such as des Roches willing to connive at

---

14 Paris, *CM*, iii, pp. 224–6.
15 *Pat. R. 1225–32*, pp. 550–1; C60/31, m. 3. There were to be further seizures in October 1232; C60/31, m. 2.
16 *Cl.R.1231–4*, pp. 113–14; C60/31, m. 2.
17 *Cal. Chart. R. 1226–57*, pp. 155, 166. For Seagrave in general, see R. V. Turner, *Men Raised from the Dust: Administrative Service and Upward Mobility in Angevin England* (Philadelphia 1988), pp. 120–42; *The Charters of the Anglo-Norman Earls of Chester c.1071–1237*, ed. G. Barraclough, Record Society of Lancashire and Cheshire, cxxvi (1988), *passim*. He last occurs as witness without title on 23 September, and had been appointed Justiciar before the end of the month, although the dating clause of the charter he first witnesses as Justiciar is partially illegible; C53/26, m. 1.
18 Wendover, *Flores*, iv, pp. 250–2; Powicke, *Henry III and the Lord Edward*, p. 82; *Cl.R.1231–4*, p. 161.

mob violence, the more moderate councillors such as Chester, the chancellor Neville, and the bishops who opposed the violation of Hubert's sanctuary. The king was now obliged to set about extracting himself from the oaths to de Burgh sworn earlier, in July 1232. In theory these could be annulled by no authority up to and including that of the pope. Gregory IX had merely been asked to confirm the July settlement with no power to veto or alter it.[19] Nonetheless on 26 October, three days after de Burgh's summons to stand trial, the veteran clerk, Master William de St Aubin, was brought out of retirement and dispatched to Rome together with Richard de St John, a former clerk of de Burgh who appears to have reached terms with the new regime.[20] Their mission, almost certainly of des Roches' devising, was intended to pay back de Burgh exactly in kind for the indignities inflicted upon des Roches and his allies in 1224. On that earlier occasion it had been William de St Aubin who negotiated papal letters releasing Henry III from the shackles of his minority; letters solicited by des Roches but ultimately used against him by de Burgh.[21] Now, in 1232, the same Master William was once again sent to Rome. With him he almost certainly carried copies of the papal letters of 1223–4 which had ended the king's minority. A draft *inspeximus* of one of these letters survives amongst the Chancery archives, addressed to pope Gregory IX by des Roches and the bishop of Ely.[22] The intention was that Gregory should confirm the letters of his predecessor, reactivating their demand that custodies and castles alienated from the crown be restored. Whereas in 1224 this restoration of custodies had been used to de Burgh's advantage, against des Roches, in 1232 the positions of the two men were reversed. Pope Gregory's response, issued early in January 1233, was precisely as des Roches had hoped: to release the king from all oaths sworn at Burgh the previous summer, and to demand the restoration of liberties wrongfully alienated except in so far as applied to the church and churchmen. This latter qualification had the effect of lending papal support to the obligations sworn by the king in July 1232 to Peter de Rivallis and the chancellor Ralph de Neville, whilst annulling those

---

[19] *Cal. Chart. R. 1226–57*, p. 164, which perhaps deliberately imitates the attempt by the barons of 1215 to prevent appeals to Rome against Magna Carta; Holt, *Magna Carta*, pp. 287–9, 440, 472–3. Both attempts were doomed to failure.

[20] *Pat. R. 1225–32*, p. 508. St John was provided with letters of credit to assist him in purchasing papal dispensation for illegitimacy; C60/32, m. 10d; *Cl.R.1231–4*, p. 122. In the event he appears to have continued working secretly for de Burgh; below p. 369 n.24.

[21] Carpenter, *The Minority*, pp. 303–4, 310; above pp. 209–10, 212.

[22] SC1/1/21, printed *RL*, i, no. ccclviii, pp. 430–1; *DD*, no. 243; *Acta*, no. 132.

to de Burgh and his fellow laymen such as the royal stewards. For swearing the oaths in the first place, the king was sentenced to a token papal penance, to be imposed by Richard de St John.[23]

Around 10 November 1232, long before these terms had been negotiated, de Burgh was at last forced to abandon sanctuary to stand trial in London. Where des Roches and his allies had urged arbitrary methods against him, via the London mob, through the seizure of liberties awarded by royal charter, and through banishment or out-lawry, the council now attempted to devise a more acceptable alternative; a procedure approximating to that judgement by peers and the law of the land proposed by Magna Carta. In short, the first State Trial. It was attended by the new Justiciar Seagrave, by several of his colleagues from the Bench, by representatives of the city of London and by at least eight bishops and earls not including des Roches, whose absence, like that of Peter de Rivallis, may reflect disapproval of the leniency accorded de Burgh.[24] The sentence imposed by this assembly was nonetheless a harsh one. De Burgh was to be imprisoned indefinitely at Devizes castle under the custody of the earls of Cornwall, Warenne, Pembroke and Lincoln. Lands he held from the crown were to be surrendered in accordance with the orders of September. Those he held by gift or inheritance from private individuals other than the king, were to descend to his heirs, but would meanwhile be held in custody by de Burgh's four keepers, so that any pleas relating to them could be answered, and to serve as a security, forfeit should he attempt to escape from Devizes. De Burgh's treasure, in plate, coin and jewels, valued by Wendover in excess of £8,000, was confiscated for the king's own use.[25] De Burgh was treated more harshly than he himself had treated any of the disgraced ministers of the 1220s, even including Fawkes de Bréauté. Admittedly, Fawkes' brother and various of his men had been hung after the siege of Bedford, but they had been hung for treason, after an open rebellion against the king. In 1232 de Burgh was no rebel, and yet he was sentenced to close imprisonment for what might well prove the remainder of his life. Although the sentence itself may have been draconian, it was obtained by process of law, following a hearing in court. Compared to the attack against Richard Marshal in 1233, or to the events surrounding the disgrace of royal ministers under Edward I

---

[23] *RL*, i, p. 551; *Cal.Pap. Reg.*, i, p. 131; Powicke, 'The oath of Bromholm', pp. 534–6.
[24] *CPR 1232–47*, pp. 28–30. Des Roches was at court on 12 November; C53/27, m. 15.
[25] Wendover, *Flores*, iv, p. 257. The official record mentions only £150 in cash and a large collection of plate; *CPR 1232–47*, pp. 2, 5.

or Edward II, de Burgh's trial must be accounted reasonably just. It achieved the assent of the four earls set to guard Hubert and his private estate. Yet, like Henry III's later attempts to arraign Simon de Montfort, the process against de Burgh was by no means a complete success. De Burgh himself refused to recognize the legitimacy of the court that tried him. His punishment was regarded by some as being too harsh, and by others, perhaps including des Roches, as being not harsh enough. Most seriously of all, the trial lent an air of spurious legality to what was in effect the annulment of de Burgh's charters of land and liberties. Having overturned one such set of charters, it was tempting indeed for the regime to go on to challenge the charters of others, posing a threat to the security of every property holder in the country whose title to land depended upon charters from the king.

Almost immediately, the question of how to redistribute the vast array of offices and lands surrendered by de Burgh produced yet further tension within the regime. Des Roches' *alter ego*, Peter de Rivallis, proved the chief beneficiary of de Burgh's fall. Des Roches himself continued to receive favours, including in mid-September a grant of free warren for life.[26] De Rivallis as the king's agent received temporary custody of de Burgh's entire estate. Even after parts of the estate had been more widely redistributed, he was to retain control of the bulk of it as royal keeper, besides a personal life interest in the port of Dover.[27] In addition, despite the grant of Devizes castle to the four earls, the castle's bailey and *banlieu* appear to have been delivered to de Rivallis.[28] In the process, the castle's previous keeper, Gilbert Basset, was effectively dismissed from office. At much the same time, de Rivallis also replaced Gilbert Basset as constable of St Briavels castle in Gloucestershire and keeper of the forest of Dean, a controversial move since Gilbert enjoyed close links to the royal household and to Richard Marshal, potentially des Roches' greatest rival at court. St Briavels lay provocatively close to the Marshal's lordship of Chepstow.[29] De Rivallis' appointment to Dover raised a storm at court where it was supposed he had received not just the port but the castle.[30] In fact this latter was removed from its former constable,

---

[26]   *Cal. Chart. R. 1226–57*, p. 169; *Cl.R.1231–4*, p. 109.
[27]   C60/31, m. 2; *Pat. R. 1225–32*, pp. 500–1.
[28]   *Cl.R.1231–4*, p. 115. A division between custody of the keep and the bailey is implied by *CPR 1232–47*, p. 19.
[29]   *Cal. Chart. R. 1226–57*, p. 169; C60/31, m. 2; *Pat. R. 1225–32*, p. 317; *Cl.R.1227–31*, p. 322; *Cl.R.1231–4*, p. 444.
[30]   *AM*, i (Tewkesbury), p. 86.

Hubert Hose, yet another of the king's household knights, and in September 1232 granted in custody to the sheriff of Kent, Bertram de Criel, who had served as constable of Dover prior to his quarrel with de Burgh in 1230.[31]

Old scores were being settled with a vengeance. On the same day that Criel received Dover, another of de Burgh's former custodies, Knaresborough, was restored to Brian de Lisle who had last held it before the political upheaval of 1224.[32] Elsewhere, on 3 November, even before the official legal process against de Burgh, the king overturned a charter granting Hubert the manor of Kirton, Lincs., in order to bestow it upon Stephen of Seagrave, already the recipient of de Burgh's greatest office, the Justiciarship.[33] With de Rivallis rewarding himself from the stock of land confiscated from de Burgh, and with others of his associates promoted within this same estate, it is hardly surprising that there were murmurs of discontent from the rest of the court. No comparable favours had been bestowed either upon the household officers or upon the followers of Richard Marshal. Minor privileges went to the earl of Cornwall. In return for a fine of 300 marks, the earl of Warenne was allowed the marriage of Hugh de Aubigny, heir to the earldom of Arundel and a former ward of de Burgh.[34] But these grants were as nothing compared to the bounty showered upon des Roches and de Rivallis. Of the royal household, both Gilbert Basset and Hubert Hose had been deposed from custodies so that de Rivallis might be the more richly rewarded. Godfrey of Crowcombe, holder of royal patents guaranteeing him life custody of the county and castle of Oxford and the royal manor of Woodstock, was nonetheless deposed from his shrievalty in October 1232. He was replaced by John de Ulcote, a former under-sheriff of Fawkes de Bréauté and later of Stephen of Seagrave.[35] Crowcombe

---

[31] *Cl.R.1231–4*, pp. 105, 113, 154.

[32] *Pat. R. 1225–32*, p. 504; *RLC*, i, pp. 57b, 308b; *Pat. R. 1216–25*, pp. 64, 315, 418, 425.

[33] *Cal. Chart. R. 1226–57*, p. 83; *Cl.R.1231–4*, p. 163. In March 1234 it was to be granted to Seagrave by charter in perpetuity; *ibid.*, p. 395.

[34] On 9 November Richard of Cornwall was granted the dower of his wife, Isabella of Gloucester, which may well have been retained before that date by de Burgh as guardian of the Gloucester lands. Nonetheless, on the following day, the council authorized an eyre for Cornwall to sit in January 1233, the first such visitation of the county in several years and as such an obvious challenge to Richard's independence; *Cl.R.1231–4*, pp. 164, 286–7n. For Warenne see C60/32, m. 10.

[35] *Pat. R. 1225–32*, p. 507; C60/31, m. 1; D. A. Carpenter, 'Sheriffs of Oxfordshire and their subordinates 1194–1236', D.Phil. thesis (Oxford 1974), pp. 237–44, and see Vincent, 'Simon de Montfort's first quarrel', p. 175, for the possibility that Crowcombe had already been deprived of his office as royal steward by June 1232. It is possible that John 'de Ulcote' was a kinsman of the former curialist, Philip of Oldcotes.

managed to retain control of Oxford castle and of Woodstock, but his loss of the county represents a blow, both to the power of the household establishment and to the security of tenure by royal charter, already badly undermined by the attacks against de Burgh. The threat here did not rest solely with des Roches or his supporters. For several years there had been bad blood between a knight of the royal household, Waleran the German, and various leading figures at court. In November 1232 this came to a head, when Waleran was ejected from a manor in Hampshire which he had held for the past two years as a Norman escheat, and which had been guaranteed to him by royal charter. The land was now conferred upon Richard Marshal, an act of disseisin which the king later confessed to be unlawful.[36] In the autumn of 1232 there were many at court prepared to countenance arbitrary acts of disseisin or the overturning of the king's charters for personal gain; not just des Roches but apparently the Marshal as well.

THE DEATH OF THE EARL OF CHESTER OCTOBER 1232

Following the first, abortive trial of de Burgh in September 1232, the king was interrupted in his progress to the Marches for negotiations with Llywelyn, by the news that the veteran earl of Chester lay dying. Chester possessed the greatest private estate in England but had no direct heir. A partition of his lands had probably already been agreed at the time of his death on 27 October, but was announced only several weeks later. The earldom of Lincoln was revived for Chester's son-in-law, John de Lacy, whilst the county and title of Chester passed to the old man's grandson, John 'the Scot', earl of Huntingdon. In late November a provisional settlement was made for the other principal heirs: William de Ferrers, earl of Derby, and Hugh de Aubigny, claimant to the earldom of Arundel.[37] Des Roches played a part in these negotiations, and to some extent must have benefited

---

[36] *Cal. Chart. R. 1226–57*, p. 130; *Cl.R.1231–4*, p. 170; *CPR 1232–47*, p. 452. William Marshal II had held the manor of Upper Clatford prior to his death in 1231 and had subinfeuded it to his own tenants, ejected at Waleran's appointment; *Cl.R.1227–31*, pp. 490, 501, 509, 523. For Waleran's earlier quarrel with the Marshal's brother-in-law, the earl of Cornwall, see Denholm-Young, *Richard of Cornwall*, pp. 10–11. In 1231 it had been Waleran who was deputed to hold the Marshal's Irish lands against Richard Marshal; *ibid.*, p. 20.

[37] In general see R. Eales, 'Henry III and the end of the Anglo-Norman earldom of Chester', in *Thirteenth Century England I*, ed. Coss and Lloyd, pp. 100–13; R. Stewart-Brown, 'The end of the Norman earldom of Chester', *EHR* 35 (1920), pp. 26–54, esp. pp. 27–34.

from the fact that several magnates, including Ferrers the Marshal's brother-in-law, were now given an incentive to remain on good terms at court. At the same time Chester's death removed des Roches' chief personal contact with the higher nobility, leaving the bishop dangerously isolated. Fellow veteran of every political crisis since John's reign, Chester had played a crucial role in bringing down de Burgh, and had thereafter moderated des Roches' inclination towards vengeance.[38]

Added to this, the redistribution of Chester's custodies was not accomplished without controversy. Once again des Roches and his supporters emerged with more than their fair share of the spoils. Gilbert of Seagrave, son of the Justiciar, received the castle and manor of Newcastle-under-Lyme in fee farm.[39] For many years Chester had enjoyed custody of the English estates of William de Fougères, a Breton magnate related to the wives of both Chester and Richard Marshal, earl of Pembroke. In 1232 Richard Marshal duly succeeded Chester in two of the three principal Fougères manors in England. However, the third manor passed to Engelard de Cigogné, an old associate of des Roches, but a man with no hereditary claim to the Fougères estate.[40] Engelard's appointment represented an obvious snub to the Marshal. For the rest, the bulk of Chester's custodies, like those confiscated from de Burgh, were handed over to Peter de Rivallis as the king's keeper of escheats.[41]

THE KING'S FINANCES AND BRITTANY

The greatest achievement of the coalition came at its very beginning. With de Burgh's dismissal, a short-lived sense of relief and common enterprise united des Roches and the English baronage. Around the second week in September, the king obtained assent for taxation, denied during the previous year when it had been de Burgh who had put the king's request for taxation before the council. The grant of September 1232, a fortieth to be imposed on movables, represents the

[38] For de Burgh's opinion of Chester, see Paris, *CM*, iii, pp. 229–30.

[39] *RLP*, p. 137b; *RLC*, i, p. 481; *Rot. Chart.*, p. 216b; *Cal. Chart. R. 1226–57*, p. 172.

[40] *Charters of the Earls of Chester*, ed. Barraclough, no. 318; *Cl.R.1231–4*, pp. 164, 168, 334; *BF*, p. 131; *Sir Christopher Hatton's Book of Seals*, ed. L. C. Loyd and D. M. Stenton (Oxford 1950), no. 236n. Richard Marshal's wife, Gervasia, was the daughter of Alan de Dinan, first husband of Clementia de Fougères, who in 1200 married Ranulph earl of Chester.

[41] C60/31, m. 1; *Foreign Accounts*, pp. 74, 77–8. Hugh de Aubigny's share of the Chester inheritance was to be held by de Rivallis as Hugh's guardian; C60/32, m. 9.

first general subsidy to be obtained since the fifteenth of 1225.[42] A poor harvest in 1233 was to ensure that the yield of the tax was disappointingly low compared to that of 1225. The payments recorded on the Winchester pipe roll of just over £43 must be set against the £131 of 1225–6, and this at a time in 1233 when des Roches was prepared to set aside a fiftieth of his manorial income, almost as high a grant as the king's tax, to pay for his new abbey at Titchfield.[43] The political upheavals of 1232 had forced the cancellation of a general eyre, cutting deeply into the king's judicial revenues.[44] Nonetheless, for the first time in many years Henry could almost afford to forget his financial problems. Besides the fortieth, he now could count on fines and douceurs paid by de Burgh's adherents, and above all upon the vast quantities of land which had escheated to the crown, not only from de Burgh, but from Chester, the archbishopric of Canterbury and several other important honours. In September 1232 a distraint of knighthood was ordered, probably also with financial ends in mind.[45]

For more than a year the king had been struggling to meet his obligations to Brittany and to a host of pensioners in Poitou contracted during the expedition of 1230. De Burgh's fall had stemmed in no small part from failure to obtain supply to meet these promises. Now at last the king could begin paying off the backlog. Starting on 10 November, the day of de Burgh's trial, nearly £1,000 was handed over to Poitevin pensioners, mostly via intermediaries attending the Westminster Exchequer.[46] This sum represents only the Michaelmas term of their pensions for 1232, with various back payments to 1230. At Easter and Michaelmas 1233, at least a further

[42] Mitchell, *Studies in Taxation*, pp. 199–206; *Foreign Accounts*, pp. 63–73.
[43] *Cal.Pap. Reg.*, i, p. 135; Ms 28DR *passim*. As with the returns for the fifteenth of 1226 the figures for several manors are missing and it is impossible to determine the precise nature of even those sums that are listed as payments in tax. Nonetheless, where comparisons can be made, the fortieth appears to have yielded between a quarter and half the proceeds of the fifteenth. At Taunton, for example, net cash receipts in 1225/6 stood at £656 of which £12 and 7 shillings were paid in tax; in 1232/3 the comparable figures are £429 and £4. The fortieth itself appears to have been collected by a monk named brother John of Basing, presumably a member of the convent of St Swithun's. There are references too to tax assessment by Roger Wacelin, des Roches' steward, at Farnham on 6 October 1232; Mss 28DR, m. 8.
[44] As noted by Stacey, *Politics, Policy and Finance*, p. 42, where the eyre of 1234–6 is said to have raised £19, 000 after des Roches' fall.
[45] *Cl.R.1231–4*, p. 152, noted by M. R. Powicke, 'Distraint of knighthood and military obligation under Henry III', *Speculum* 25 (1950), p. 465. For the outcome of the distraint of 1232, see below pp. 376–7.
[46] *Cal.Lib.R.1226–40*, pp. 187–8.

£1,500 was paid over in this way to Poitou. Overshadowing all this, in the autumn of 1232 the duke of Brittany was promised £4,000 above and beyond the loans raised on his behalf earlier that year. None of this £4,000 was forthcoming at Michaelmas. Instead, the duke was asked to content himself with a year's lease of three Yorkshire wapentakes withheld from his honour of Richmond since its restoration to him in the 1220s.[47] Richmond alone had brought him close on £1,200 a year.[48] But the duke held out for more, seizing the fortress of St James de Beuvron in Normandy, which after Chester's death should have reverted to the crown.[49]

In due course other foreign magnates were to be welcomed back to court, including the count of Guînes who bore a long-standing grudge against Hubert de Burgh for his retention of various lands in Kent.[50] New keepers were appointed for the king's continental lands: Philip de Aubigné for the Channel Islands and Hugh de Vivonne for Gascony, both men being veterans with strong connections to France.[51] As with the duke of Brittany, there were problems in store, especially for Vivonne who had first to dislodge his predecessor's constables, who refused to surrender their castles until their wages had been paid. Despite heavy expenditure, the king's initiatives in France were to achieve only meagre results. Henry's proposed marriage to Yolande of Brittany, due to take place at Michaelmas 1232, suffered yet further delay.[52]

Expenditure on absentee Breton and Poitevin allies, albeit in subsidies agreed long before des Roches' return; the re-establishment at court and in provincial custodies of the alien veterans of John's reign; all of this was to lead to a general groundswell of resentment against des Roches and his regime, especially against the so-called Poitevins whom he was said to have introduced to every office and custody in England. The generation of Anglo-Norman landowners

---

47   *Pat. R. 1225–32*, pp. 451, 501; C60/31, m. 3; *Cl.R.1227–31*, p. 158.
48   Painter, *Peter of Dreux*, p. 82.
49   *Ibid.*, p. 81; *CPR 1232–47*, pp. 1, 5; *Cl.R.1231–4*, p. 181; *Cal.Lib.R.1226–40*, p. 210.
50   *CPR 1232–47*, p. 2. De Burgh had held the manor of Newington nr. Hythe since at least 1216; *RLP*, p. 199; *Cal. Chart. R. 1226–57*, p. 60. In November 1232 it was treated as part of de Burgh's family estate but subsequently restored briefly to the count in 1233; *Cl.R.1231–4*, pp. 166, 443; *CPR 1232–47*, pp. 289, 322; C60/32, m. 2.
51   *Pat. R. 1225–32*, pp. 502–3, and see above pp. 159, 161–2.
52   In general see Stacey, *Politics, Policy and Finance*, p. 174. The garrison of Roquefort held out against Vivonne until at least August 1233; *CPR 1232–47*, pp. 9, 22; *Cl.R.1231–4*, pp. 313, 547–8. Trubleville himself made his peace with the court several months earlier; *CPR 1232–47*, pp. 9, 11. Aubigné's appointment to sole keepership of the Channel Islands followed several alternative appointments by the council in September/October 1232; *Pat. R. 1225–32*, pp. 502, 507–8.

ejected from France in 1204 had mostly died out. Others had been turned against the very idea of reconquest by the extravagant inanity of the expeditions of 1225 and 1230. Apart from des Roches, there was not a single alien bishop in England in 1232 compared to at least nine at the time of his election to Winchester in 1205.[53] But for the moment, there seems little doubt that the king's decision to spend lavishly on Brittany and Poitou was greeted with general approval from the new council, not only from des Roches but from Richard of Cornwall, titular count of Poitou, and from Richard Marshal, lord of Longueville and Orbec, raised in Normandy, married into the Breton nobility and a staunch supporter of the duke of Brittany at court.[54] The charge that Henry III showed undue favouritism towards aliens was symptomatic, but to begin with, purely incidental to a far deeper crisis at court. When the break between des Roches and Richard Marshal came, it was to spring from political issues, above all from the king's inequitable exercise of patronage, rather than from any other cause, racial or nationalistic.

Richard Marshal has been presented in the past as a true English hero, yet he was hardly the most typical of Englishmen. Above all, he was peculiar amongst the Anglo-Norman baronage in having preserved his lands on both sides of the Channel. In 1220 he had been permitted to do homage for his father's lands in Normandy, whilst at the same time coming into possession of the English honour of Long Crendon.[55] In theory, he had nothing to gain from a reassertion of Plantagenet lordship in Normandy. Warfare between Henry III and the Capetians threatened only to dismember Richard's cross-Channel

[53] Above pp. 34–5. The birthplace of Walter Mauclerk, bishop of Carlisle (1223–46) is unknown. His family may have been Norman, native to Rouen, although Walter himself appears to have enjoyed a close personal connection to the north Midlands and the county of Nottingham: Rouen, Bibliothèque Municipale ms. Y44 (Rouen chapter cartulary), ff. 109v–113r; N. Vincent, 'Walter Mauclerk', in *New Dictionary of National Biography* (Oxford, forthcoming). Despite his name, William de Blois, bishop of Worcester (1218–36), was probably a Lincolnshire man, related to William bishop of Lincoln (1203–6), for whom see G. V. Scammell, *Hugh de Puiset Bishop of Durham* (Cambridge 1956), p. 235.

[54] For the Marshal and Brittany see Painter, *Peter of Dreux*, p. 80.

[55] For the settlement agreed by Philip Augustus in 1220, see *Recueil des Actes de Philippe-Auguste, Roi de France*, ed. H.-F. Delaborde, M. Nortier et al., 4 vols. (Paris 1916–79), iv, no. 1642. The provision for a relief payment in this settlement may explain the large sum owing by Richard Marshal to the French king, recorded in the French accounts for 1221; M. Nortier and J. W. Baldwin, 'Contributions à l'étude des finances de Philippe Auguste', *Bibliothèque de l'Ecole des Chartes* cxxxviii (1980), pp. 11, 18. For these, and for various of the references which follow, I am indebted to Daniel Power who allowed me to consult his undergraduate dissertation on the French lordship of the Marshals.

lordship. During the 1220s it was argued that William Marshal the younger should be prevented from marrying a Frenchwoman, the sister of the count of Dreux, for fear that this would provide the aliens with easier entry to England. It was hinted that Richard Marshal, William's brother, was already to be accounted a foreigner, through his possession of his family's lands in Normandy.[56] During the Breton campaign of 1230 Richard failed to come to the service of Henry III, although he and his Norman tenants were afforded special protection.[57] Thereafter, having succeeded to the earldom of Pembroke, it may be that Richard continued to do his best to smooth over the relations between England and France. In all of this, it would be quite wrong to regard the Marshal, as the chroniclers appear on occasion to have regarded him, as the very quintessence of English virtue set against des Roches, the scheming alien. The Marshal acted not as some xenophobic little-Englander, but from private motives determined by his position as one of the more cosmopolitan figures at the English court. Before 1230 Richard had enjoyed far closer contact with the Capetians and with Louis IX than des Roches had ever done. Furthermore, there is a splendid irony to the fact that Richard Marshal, reputed the guardian of England and the defender of the rights of the English baronage against des Roches and the aliens, was himself of largely French upbringing, married to Gervasia de Dinan, previously the wife of Juhel de Mayenne, a cousin and close ally of William des Roches, seneschal of Anjou, the bishop of Winchester's presumed kinsman.[58] Peter des Roches and the Marshal may well

---

[56] *DD*, no. 140.

[57] *Pat. R. 1225–32*, p. 375, and see Bouquet, *Recueil*, xxiv, part 1, introduction pp. 293–4 no. 88.

[58] For Richard's French background see *CP*, x, pp. 368–71, esp. p. 370n. Various charters he issued as lord of Longueville survive, relating both to his Norman and his English estate; Antony co. Cornwall, Carew-Pole mss., Poles Charters no. 304 (reference courtesy of David Crouch); BL, ms. Stowe 665, f. 109v; Bodl. ms. Dugdale 39 (Notley priory transcripts), f. 68r; Paris, Archives Nationales L969/357 (for Savigny); Paris, Bibliothèque Nationale mss. Latin 5424 (transcripts for Jumièges), p. 93; Latin 5430A (extracts from Mont St Michel cartularies), pp. 43–5, 226–7; Latin 5476 (transcripts of charters for La Vieuville), pp. 42, 107; Latin 10078 (transcripts for Savigny), p. 58 no. 449; Français 22325 (transcripts for Brittany), pp. 527, 565, 605–6, 669–70; Français 22357 (*ibid.*), f. 55r–v (reference courtesy of Judith Everard and Daniel Power); Rouen, Archives Départementales de la Seine-Maritime mss. 8H254 (for Foucarmont); 9H1753 (for Jumièges); 25HP1 (for Mont des Malades, Rouen); J. Geslin de Bourgogne and A. de Barthélemy (eds.), *Anciens Evêchés de Bretagne*, 4 vols. (Paris 1864), iii, pp. 65–6; H. Morice, *Memoires pour Servir de Preuves à l'Histoire Ecclésiastique et Civile de Bretagne*, 3 vols. (Paris 1742–6), i, col. 903; L. Delisle (ed.), *Cartulaire Normand de Philippe-Auguste, Louis VIII, Saint-Louis et Philipp-le-Hardi* (Caen 1882), no. 285n.; also, two charters for the honour of Crendon, issued as Richard Marshal *filius comitis Willelmi Marescalli*: San

have been cousins by marriage. To a greater or lesser extent, both men were outsiders in England. Although modern historians have tended to oppose des Roches, the Frenchman, to the English Richard Marshal, it is arguable that des Roches, with his desire to reassert Plantagenet control over northern France, was in many ways closer to the thinking of the nineteenth-century English nationalists for all that they might deride him as a foreigner. Richard Marshal, by contrast, was anxious to preserve a private, cross-Channel lordship, that would surely have been considered anathema by those historians who picture France and England in crudely nationalistic terms.

Clearly des Roches was a supporter of Plantagenet reconquest, involved in virtually every diplomatic exchange between England and France in the thirty years after 1204. And yet even here we must tread with caution. In 1232 it is likely that he promised to support the king in a more aggressive strategy towards France than that which de Burgh had been prepared to accept. He appears to have told Henry that kings should be rich and powerful, like his Plantagenet ancestors or like the emperor Frederick II. The dismissal of de Burgh and the resulting upsurge in the king's finances enabled Henry to shower gifts upon his allies in Poitou and Brittany, redeeming the promises to them first made in 1230. But beyond this, there is little evidence that des Roches counselled anything more in the way of military intervention in France. By the time that he returned to power in 1232, he and his supporters, the likes of Peter de Maulay, Engelard de Cigogné and the various alien clergy attached to his household, were no longer the out-and-out protagonists of reconquest that they once had been. Most of the them had become reconciled to their new lives in England, and had waxed rich upon English lands and custodies. No doubt the rhetoric was still there, and a willingness to pay enormous subsidies to protect what remained of the king's French lordship, but for the rest there is little evidence of a desire for more direct intervention in France through the organization of alliances and armies, such as those that had been mustered in the time of King John. To this extent, des

Marino California, Huntington Library Stowe Grenville Evidences, STG Box 5 nos. 14, 17 (reference courtesy of David Crouch). For a charter issued as earl of Pembroke, January 1233/4 and 1232 X 1234, see Longleat House muniments no. 4317; and see also below n. 105. An eighteenth-century inventory of the muniments of Longueville (Rouen, Archives Départementales de la Seine-Maritime ms. 24HP22, p. 88) refers to a grant of Richard Marshal as lord of Longueville, dated 1231, apparently now lost. For the association between William des Roches and Juhel de Mayenne, see Dubois, 'Recherches sur la vie de Guillaume des Roches', v (1869), pp. 384, 398; *ibid.*, xxxii (1871), pp. 90, 118.

Roches and the Marshal, bitter rivals though they may have been, were both of them more interested in Anglo-French negotiations and diplomacy, than in provoking an Anglo-French war.

THE MARSHAL'S GRIEVANCE NOVEMBER 1232–JANUARY 1233

Compared to the favours showered upon des Roches and his allies, Richard Marshal had lost out badly in the autumn of 1232. He had received virtually nothing from de Burgh's vast estate, and only a token grant from Chester's. Several of his kinsmen had been bought off by their involvement in the Chester inheritance. The Marshal himself had connived in an escalating assault against liberties claimed by charter, causing mounting uneasiness at court. Added to this, ever since his brother's death Richard had harboured a sense of grievance against the king. Eleanor, the king's sister, was barely sixteen years old when she was left widowed by the death of William Marshal. Any dower assigned to her would be lost to the Marshals for the foreseeable future. In the summer of 1231 she had been given a provisional settlement of half a dozen of her late husband's manors in England together with life custody of her marriage portion.[59] This latter, consisting of a dozen or so manors, was really the property of William Marshal II by virtue of his first wife. Via a devious route it had been recovered by the crown and then restored to William with reversion to Eleanor should she outlive him.[60] Overall, these losses, in dower and marriage portion, threatened to deprive Richard Marshal of well over a third of his revenues from England, besides which there was still the need to assign dower in Leinster, Pembroke and Gwent.[61] In June 1232 Richard offered an annual cash payment of £400 as a substitute for dower land in Ireland and Wales. Eleanor later claimed that the sum was inadequate and that she had been forced to accept it by the king.[62] This suggests that Henry was still keen to appease the Marshal. But the Marshal was keener still to hold on to his assets. In the year to June 1233 he paid only £250 of the promised £400. Over the same twelve months Richard's affairs were further complicated by uncertainty about his own marriage, to Gervasia de Dinan. In January 1233 the pope was persuaded to launch an enquiry into the affinity

59 *Cl.R.1227–31*, pp. 498, 509, 518, 528, 541.
60 Carpenter, *The Minority*, pp. 164–5, 203; *Cal. Chart. R. 1226–57*, p. 102.
61 For some idea of the values of these lands, see *CPR 1232–47*, pp. 125–6; *CRR*, xv, nos. 1088, 1154, 1279. Richard's Norman estate rendered more than £300 of Tours (c.£75 sterling) to Louis IX in 1238; Bouquet, *Recueil*, xxi, pp. 255, 257.
62 *Cl.R.1231–4*, pp. 144–5, 233, 310; Labarge, *Simon de Montfort*, p. 42; *DBM*, pp. 196–8.

between husband and wife. As with the earlier enquiry into the marriage of Hubert de Burgh, it is likely that papal intervention was resented by the Marshal.[63]

Whatever the tensions lurking beneath the surface, the Marshal remained in constant attendance upon the king during late November as Henry made his way to the Marches for his long overdue peace negotiations with Llywelyn. Des Roches left the court at Northampton and does not appear there again until after Christmas.[64] Meanwhile, in the company of various Marcher bishops and earls, of the royal stewards and of Simon de Montfort, the king concluded a truce with the Welsh intended to last for three years.[65] Various favours were shown at court, in particular to William de Cantiloupe and to Richard of Cornwall, at whose behest the king appears to have postponed the controversial eyre appointed to visit Cornwall.[66] What is most remarkable is that throughout December, in a court no longer dominated by des Roches or his supporters, the king continued to annul and to challenge awards by royal charter. Around 8 December he ordered the seizure of two Hertfordshire manors held previously by Richard de Argentan as Norman land under the strict guarantee of royal charters. As in most such cases, there was a dispute here dating back many years, in this instance involving the Anglo-French courtier Pain de Sourches, who had held the manors in question until 1226 when they were seized and granted to Argentan.[67] In 1232, as a satellite of the disgraced Justiciar, Argentan fell victim to the attack upon de Burgh. Pain now brought an action before the Bench. Argentan failed to attend the hearing and, perhaps unfairly, was judged to have defaulted. On 13 December the disputed manors were granted to Pain, with provision for him to take Argentan's grain and chattels to the value of those he himself had lost in 1226.[68] Admittedly there had been some sort of legal hearing before

---

63   *Cal.Pap. Reg.*, i, p. 131.

64   On 20 December the bishop was probably at Marwell, Hants, whilst the court was at Chepstow; *Acta*, no. 75.

65   *AM*, i (Tewkesbury), p. 88. For attendance at court, see C53/27, mm. 12–14.

66   *Cl.R.1231–4*, pp. 173, 286–7; *CRR*, xv, p. xiv, where the cancellation of the eyre is perhaps rather naively attributed to the winter weather.

67   For Sourches near Le Mans, dep. Sarthe, see L. C. Loyd, *The Origins of Some Anglo-Norman Families*, Harleian Society, ciii (1961), p. 27.

68   For the manors of Lilley and Willian, Herts., see *BF*, p. 14; *RLC*, i, pp. 283b, 593, ii, p. 139b; *Cl.R.1231–4*, pp. 173, 190–1; *Cal. Chart. R. 1226–57*, p. 57; *CRR*, xv, no. 1426; C60/32, m. 9.

Argentan was disseised, but to reopen such old wounds threatened yet more score settling to come.

A few days later, whilst the court was at Ross-on-Wye, orders were issued to the treasurer, Walter Mauclerk, to render accounts for his office by 3 February. At the same time the bishops of Durham and Salisbury were called to account for the taxes over whose collection they had presided since 1225.[69] This was merely the first stage in an attack upon Mauclerk's position at the treasury, guaranteed to him for life by charter and by solemn oath, yet which the king was decisively to overturn on 6 January 1233, instructing Mauclerk to surrender his office to Peter de Rivallis. Henceforth the treasury was to be administered by de Rivallis' deputy, Robert Passelewe, the former clerk and advocate of Fawkes de Bréauté, a veteran of the years of des Roches' ascendancy before 1224.[70] The attack against Mauclerk began in des Roches' absence, as the court shuttled between St Briavels and Richard Marshal's stronghold at Chepstow. No doubt it was des Roches and de Rivallis, rather than the Marshal, who engineered the treasurer's disgrace, the most serious challenge to royal charters since the trial of de Burgh. But it was a challenge with which the Marshal appears to have concurred, just as earlier he had been willing to connive at the expulsion of Waleran the German from land supposedly guaranteed by royal charter.

Roger of Wendover puts a rather different gloss on the Marshal's position during these weeks. According to Wendover, the Christmas court of 1232 saw the dismissal of all the king's native courtiers and their replacement by Poitevins at des Roches' behest. In particular, a knight serving as the Marshal's deputy at court, William of Rowden, was dismissed, much to the Marshal's fury.[71] However, Wendover appears to be telescoping later developments into the brief period of the Christmas court. William of Rowden witnesses royal charters regularly into November 1232 and again on 8 January of the following year, making sporadic appearances thereafter until mid-April 1233.[72] It is true that there may have been tension between

[69] C60/32, m. 9.
[70] *CPR 1232–47*, pp. 7–8. For Passelewe, see above pp. 114, 210–11, 213, 216, 222, 224 and n. 232. For Mauclerk's life grant, see *Cal. Chart. R. 1226–57*, pp. 164–5.
[71] Wendover, *Flores*, iv, pp. 263–4.
[72] C53/27, mm. 10–12. For William, a native of Rowden, Wilts., joint sheriff of Cumberland in 1222 with Walter Mauclerk, and a joint tenant with Reginald Basset of the king's mill at Marlborough, see *Rot. Chart.*, p. 218; *The Cartulary of Bradenstoke Priory*, ed. V. C. M. London, Wilts. Rec. Soc., xxxv (1979), nos. 116, 619; *CRR*, ii, p. 10, xi, nos. 1490, 2227, 2675; *Pat. R. 1216–25*, pp. 326, 335, 361, 365, 420.

natives and aliens at Christmas 1232. Two minor officers of the royal household disappear from charter witness lists after 28 December.[73] The king also settled land on the first of a series of aliens to be promoted under des Roches' sponsorship: Macey Bezill, a kinsman of the Chanceaux clan outlawed in clause 50 of Magna Carta, received part of the manor of Gomshall, Surrey, as Norman land in fee.[74] Bezill's name, apparently a nickname meaning 'the false' or 'the plunderer' was hardly calculated to inspire confidence in his adopted realm.[75] Simultaneously, a number of the king's alien household knights were awarded minor custodies formerly held by de Burgh or his son, John.[76] Yet there is no question of such promotions marking a whole-sale importation of des Roches' satellites to court. On the contrary, they coincide with the first significant award to Richard Marshal in many months: the Gloucestershire hundred of Awre, accompanied by a gift of forty deer to restock his parks in Ireland.[77] At the same time, the royal steward Godfrey of Crowcombe, smarting since his dismissal as sheriff of Oxford, secured the renewal of charters guaranteeing him life custody of the manor of Woodstock.[78] Conciliation remained the king's objective.

The most significant development of the past few months had little if anything to do with the promotion of aliens; it centred instead upon the growing instability caused by the king's annulment of liberties supposedly guaranteed by royal charter. What had begun as an attack directed solely against de Burgh, had spread to encompass ministers such as Crowcombe and Mauclerk, besides threatening a whole host of lesser landholders with the reopening of property disputes stretching back to the reign of King John. Richard Marshal, the most prominent magnate at court, had been given ample opportunity to stay this process had he so wished. Instead he seems actively to have assisted the opening of the floodgates, in the process

---

[73] Carpenter, 'The fall of Hubert de Burgh', p. 13.

[74] *Cal. Chart. R. 1226–57*, p. 174; *The 1235 Surrey Eyre*, ed. Meekings, no. 399 and note p. 527; *E. Rot. Fin.*, i, p. 319.

[75] See the *Anglo-Norman Dictionary*, ed. L. W. Stone and W. Rothwell, Anglo-Norman Text Soc. (London 1977–), *sub besiller* and *besile*, whence the Latin *besillare*, to falsify or mutilate, and the English 'embezzle'.

[76] *Cl.R.1231–4*, p. 179.

[77] *Ibid.*, pp. 179–80, 182; *Cal. Chart. R. 1226–57*, p. 174. Awre manor was held from 1230 by William Marshal in compensation for the manor of Bassingbourn restored to the duke of Brittany. When Richard Marshal succeeded in 1232, Awre hundred though not the manor had been withheld by the crown; *Pat. R. 1225–32*, p. 404; *Cl.R.1227–31*, p. 561; E372/76, m. 14d.

[78] *Cal. Chart. R. 1226–57*, p. 174; C60/32, m. 8. It is probably no coincidence that the charter was issued whilst the king was staying at Woodstock as Crowcombe's guest.

hastening his own downfall. Despite his ties of kinship to the king and to so many of the higher nobility, the Marshal failed to mould any sort of alliance capable of standing up to des Roches. Ironically it was the Marshal rather than Peter des Roches who found himself cut off from the rest of the court by his foreign upbringing and lack of shared experience with his peers. Henry III had a lifelong tendency to gravitate to the most powerful personalities around him, however distrusted they might be by their fellow courtiers. In 1232 this brought him ever further under the influence of des Roches, seen as the man most responsible for the king's increasingly arbitrary approach towards government. For his own part, des Roches was now an elderly man, scarred by the events of 1224, determined to reap revenge against his enemies and to ensure that never again could he or his associates be excluded from power. Rather than build bridges to the younger generation by an equitable distribution of patronage, he remained aloof and after the death of the earl of Chester, increasingly cut off from more moderate counsels at court.

THE REVIVAL OF THE PRIVY SEAL AND THE ATTACK ON MAUCLERK JANUARY–FEBRUARY 1233

Returned from the Marches, the court passed most of January and February 1233 in or around Westminster. One indication of the coming storm lies in the witnessing of royal letters. Ever since the fall of Hubert de Burgh, the majority of letters close issued under the great seal had been provided with careful notes of warranty, naming the councillors who had authorized the writ.[79] For example, early in January the king had issued writs of *liberate* for some £860 in subsidies to Gascony and Poitou. They were warranted jointly by des Roches, Seagrave and the Marshal.[80] Some such group formula had been used many times over the past few months, but from January 1233 it disappears, to be replaced by des Roches' sole warranty for the vast majority of royal letters. At the same time the privy seal, struck in 1230 to counteract the authority of de Burgh, came into more frequent use. Until the summer of 1232 and the promotion of de Rivallis to its custody, the privy seal like all subsidiary seals was in theory kept by the chancellor, although in practice deputed on a daily

---

[79] J. and L. Stones, 'Bishop Ralph Neville, chancellor to King Henry III and his correspondence', *Archives* 16 (1984), p. 237, sugggest that the reappearance of warranty notes demonstrates that Neville was often absent from court after October 1232.

[80] *Cal.Lib.R.1226–40*, pp. 194–5.

basis to semi-autonomous keepers. De Rivallis' appointment therefore represents a serious challenge to the authority of Ralph de Neville as chancellor. In the immediate term it is unlikely that use of the privy seal, as opposed to its keepership, was in any sense controversial. De Rivallis may have employed it in the administration of estates confiscated from de Burgh.[81] Otherwise it makes no appearance until January 1233, when it emerges as part of a wider administrative upheaval.[82] On 22 January the king travelled to Reading, from where he appears to have sent a privy seal warrant to des Roches at Westminster commanding the issue of letters close under the great seal.[83] At least one of these letters was controversial. A Norman escheat, previously held by a servant of de Burgh by royal charter, was now transferred to an officer of the king's wardrobe.[84] Privy seal warrants to the great seal were nothing new. They had been used regularly by King John. But in 1233 John's practice was revived in circumstances in which the privy seal enjoyed autonomy under de Rivallis, whilst the great seal remained with the chancellor under the close supervision of des Roches. Here there was an obvious challenge to the authority of the chancellor, Ralph de Neville, and a clear indication of the growing power of des Roches and de Rivallis.

On 19 January de Rivallis' temporary appointment as treasurer was confirmed.[85] Meanwhile the attack against Mauclerk shifted from offices to lands. Despite royal charters guaranteeing life possession, he was now required to surrender the county of Cumberland and every manor he held by gift of the crown. The county and Carlisle castle passed to Thomas of Moulton, chief justice of the Bench and a major local landholder.[86] The rest of Mauclerk's estate passed to Peter de Rivallis in his capacity as keeper of escheats.[87] Beginning on 8 February, Mauclerk's account for the treasury was heard before a committee of Exchequer barons including des Roches and de Rivallis. Quite what was accounted is unclear. The pipe roll records an

---

81 *CPR 1232–47*, p. 81, although the 'secret seal' mentioned here may be yet another royal seal.
82 Thereafter see *Cl.R.1231–4*, pp. 183, 191–2, 241; *Cal.Lib.R.1226–40*, p. 200; C60/32, m. 8.
83 *Cl.R.1231–4*, p. 183.
84 *Cl.R.1227–31*, p. 273; *Cal. Chart. R. 1226–57*, p. 124; *CRR*, xv, no. 1427, for the manor of Road, Somerset.
85 *CPR 1232–47*, p. 8.
86 *Ibid.*, p. 8. For Moulton, see Turner, *Men Raised from the Dust*, pp. 107–19.
87 C60/32, mm. 7, 8, which includes orders for the release of Hayes and Harrow (manors Mauclerk had held by royal grant in the vacant see of Canterbury), of Horncastle, and of Melbourne, this latter by letters under the privy seal.

inventory of the regalia, jewels, plate and some 9,200 marks stored at the treasury, together with details of the £1,000 or so received in 1228 during the interval between the death of the previous treasurer and Mauclerk's appointment. The memoranda roll under three, weekly headings notes a total, unspecified audit of £1,075.[88] Doubtless the entire process was dressed up as a further stage in de Rivallis' overhaul of royal finance, yet it was entirely factional in motivation. Henceforth, de Rivallis held unrivalled control over every office of account, the treasury, the wardrobe and the king's chamber. Around 25 February, Mauclerk fined £1,000 to be quit of further account and to recover the king's grace. He was also to surrender the king's charters granting him life possession of Cumberland, the treasury and the royal manor of Melbourne, Derbs., acquired in 1226 following the dismissal of Philip Mark, a long-standing alien associate of des Roches. In return he was to be restored to Horncastle, Lincs., a manor which he held by private, not royal grant.[89] There is no more remarkable example of the factional self-interest now rampant at court than the aftermath of Mauclerk's surrender of Melbourne. Within a fortnight it was granted to Stephen of Seagrave, no longer merely as a life custody but in perpetual fee.[90] As with de Rivallis' acquisition of Dartmoor and Lydford castle in 1232, Seagrave was effectively granted a royal demesne manor in fee. Since the 1170s

---

[88] E372/76, m. 4a; *Memoranda Rolls 1231–3*, nos. 2690–3. At the same time the bishops of Bath and Durham were excused any account for arrears of the taxes of a fifteenth and a sixteenth, originally summoned from them in December 1232; *CPR 1232–47*, pp. 11–12. Both bishops sat as barons of the Exchequer in January 1233; *Cal.Lib.R.1226–40*, p. 197; *Memoranda Rolls 1231–3*, nos. 2695, 2710, 2713, 2729, 2995, 2997, 3000, 3002, 3043, 3046, 3073–5, 3079, 3093, 3098. On 22 January des Roches attested letters granting himself and the bishop of Durham quittance from arrears on the farm of Alton, Hants, stretching back to the early 1220s; C60/32, m. 8, and see *Memoranda Rolls 1231–3*, nos. 1014, 1057, 1125, 1359, 1421, 1475, 3032; E372/76, m. 2d.

[89] Wendover, *Flores*, iv, p. 264, where Wendover states that the fine was merely £100. The fine itself, recorded in the fine rolls, requires the surrender of charters relating to the treasury *et de quadam obligatione*, perhaps a reference to the oaths sworn at Burgh in July 1232 which had been enshrined in charter form; C60/32, m. 7; *Cal. Chart.R.1226–57*, p. 164. A continuing process of account at the treasury is implied by a fine of £100 in May 1233 against William Mauduit, one of the chamberlains *pro transgressione camerarie regis*; C60/32, m. 5.

[90] For Melbourne, see *BF*, p. 152; *RLC*, i, pp. 293b, 295b, ii, pp. 18b, 181b; *Pat. R. 1216–25*, pp. 21, 23, 107, 123; *Pat. R. 1225–32*, p. 132; *Cal. Chart. R. 1226–57*, p. 175; *CPR 1232–47*, p. 60; *CAR*, i, no. 27. As with Lydford and Dartmoor, Melbourne was technically an escheat having been tenanted briefly in the twelfth century. The original charter granting the manor to Seagrave survives at Stratford upon Avon, Shakespeare Birthplace Library ms. Gregory-Hood deed no. 1298, mistakenly identified by its former owner, Arthur Gregory, as a title deed to land at Millburn Grange in Stoneleigh, Warwicks.

there had been mounting pressure to regard the royal demesne as an inalienable resource belonging to the crown, rather than as a store of patronage placed at the disposal of individual kings.[91] For Henry III to begin alienating it to favoured ministers was rash indeed.

Melbourne was not the only subject of controversy in January 1233. Title to the honour of Bolsover and the Peak had long been contested between the crown and William Ferrers, earl of Derby. After 1216 Ferrers had fought what amounted to a private war against Brian de Lisle, installed as constable of Bolsover by the king.[92] De Lisle faced disgrace with the rest of des Roches' allies in 1224 and thereafter Bolsover had come to rest with Robert of Tattershall, a tenant of the earls of Derby and hence presumably a compromise candidate agreed between the king and Ferrers.[93] But on 27 January 1233 Tattershall was ordered to yield place to Hugh Despenser, a kinsman of Stephen of Seagrave, and subsequently to Gilbert of Seagrave, the Justiciar's son. In the event he was to surrender to neither, but to the relatively neutral William Basset.[94] Nonetheless the transfer can have done nothing to put Ferrers or the rest of the court at ease. By the same token, a few days later, John de Vieuxpont was ordered to surrender Bowes castle to the duke of Brittany. Bowes had long been separated from the duke's honour of Richmond, and after 1203 had been treated by the Vieuxponts very much as a family possession. In 1228 it had passed with the wardship of John de Vieuxpont to Hubert de Burgh, after whose fall in October 1232 the crown brought *quo warranto* proceedings for its recovery.[95] Sued against John de Vieuxpont even before he had gained full possession of his estates, and intended to appease the king's Breton allies, the case can only have provoked yet further unease.

THE UPAVON CASE FEBRUARY 1233

Although it was only one amongst many such challenges to tenure by royal charter, one particular action has been singled out by

---

[91] For the concept of inalienability, first stated explicitly only in 1257, see R. S. Hoyt, *The Royal Demesne in English Constitutional History 1066–1272* (New York 1950), pp. 146–55, 160–4.

[92] Carpenter, *The Minority*, pp. 17–18, 124, 284–5.

[93] *Pat. R. 1225–32*, p. 28; *Cal.Lib.R.1226–40*, p. 55. For Tattershall, see *BF*, pp. 946–7; *Cal.Inq.P.M.*, i, no. 145; Sanders, *English Baronies*, p. 88.

[94] *CPR 1232–47*, pp. 8, 10, 12.

[95] *Rot. Lib.*, pp. 63–4; *CRR*, xiv, no. 2319; *CPR 1232–47*, p. 10; *Pat. R. 1225–32*, p. 177; R. Allen Brown, 'A list of castles 1154–1216', *EHR* 74 (1959), p. 256n.

commentators as a principal cause of the strife about to engulf the court. Early in 1233 the king was persuaded to bring *quo warranto* proceedings against Gilbert Basset for the manor of Upavon in Wiltshire. A Norman escheat, Upavon had been held by the veteran alien Peter de Maulay until *c.*1229, when it was granted to Gilbert Basset by charter in fee.[96] According to de Maulay, he had surrendered custody only after threats to his life made by Hubert de Burgh. The king was now asked to judge between de Maulay's unwarranted claim to prior possession, and Basset's perfectly legitimate tenure by royal charter. On 4 February Upavon itself was seized into the custody of Peter de Rivallis. During a court hearing two days later, the king refused to warrant his charter to Basset. Instead Upavon was restored to Peter de Maulay following an interval of more than five years; a decision which the king later confessed to have made *per voluntatem regis*, against Basset's lawful right.[97]

It is no coincidence that the Upavon case, like so many other attacks on charters in 1232–3, involved *terra Normannorum*. Tenure in such escheats, forfeited by Norman landlords after 1204, could take any one of several forms: custody during pleasure, for life or in perpetual fee. Into the 1220s the king avoided awarding such land in fee. This was not only because Henry III was unable to grant charters until he came of age, but because it was still generally hoped that the realms of England and Normandy would be reunited. Norman land was used with especial frequency to compensate Norman magnates who kept faith with King John, or aliens such as Peter de Maulay, promising an easy transition to a landed settlement once the hoped-for reconquest in Normandy had been accomplished. However, all of this changed with the king's coming of age in 1227. Henceforth, grants of Norman land in fee became customary, reserving compensation to the grantee in the event of the rightful Norman heir arriving to reclaim his estates in England. It was a change that reflects the increasing unlikelihood of reconquest abroad and which worked greatly to the disadvantage of aliens like Peter de Maulay. Such men had received generous but unwarranted grants of Norman land during John's reign and the minority of Henry III. They had lost them amidst

---

[96] For Upavon, see *RLC*, i, pp. 4, 10, 11b, 595b; *Pat. R. 1216–25*, pp. 58–9, 61; *BF*, p. 381; *CRR*, xv, no. 131; *Cal. Chart. R. 1226–57*, p. 86. The case is noticed by Powicke, *Henry III and the Lord Edward*, p. 128n.; Denholm-Young, *Richard of Cornwall*, pp. 24–5; Turner, *The King and his Courts*, pp. 248–51; Carpenter, 'The fall of Hubert de Burgh', p. 16, and C. A. F. Meekings, intro. to *CRR*, xv, pp. xxiii–xxiv.

[97] C60/32, m. 8; *Cl.R.1231–4*, p. 187; *CRR*, xv, no. 131; *Bracton's Note Book*, ed. Maitland, ii, p. 665 no. 857.

the political upheaval of 1223, only to live on to see them transformed in the hands of de Burgh and his supporters from custodies during pleasure into grants in perpetual fee, guaranteed by royal charter. Even after the Justiciar's fall such charters, issued since the king's coming of age, threatened to deny des Roches and his supporters recovery of the tenures and custodies they had forfeited a decade earlier. Hence the importance of the Upavon case, where the king signalled his willingness to uphold the grievances of de Maulay and his fellow veterans in the face of what were theoretically permanent awards by royal charter. In effect Henry raised the threat that every victim of the territorial settlement of 1224 would follow de Maulay's example and demand redress. Moreover, by revoking royal charters on a seemingly arbitrary basis, he posed a threat to the very basis of property-holding throughout the realm.

In all of this the king was guided by des Roches. The issues raised were far-reaching and constitutional: to what extent did the king possess plenitude of power; to what extent could he over-ride customary or written law, annul his own charters and refuse to honour warrants he himself had issued? But des Roches would have been most unlikely to regard the matter in such constitutional terms. In his view, and that of contemporaries, the question appeared to turn upon a simple matter of patronage. According to Roger of Wendover, in February 1233 Richard Marshal went to the king to complain of the large number of aliens promoted under des Roches' influence. No matter that as yet this alien invasion was a figment of Wendover's imagination, the response he ascribes to des Roches is entirely plausible. The bishop is supposed to have replied that the king could summon whomsoever he liked to court and reward them as he saw fit, to subdue the pride of his native subjects.[98] Never a supporter of Magna Carta, a settlement he had tried to stifle at birth, des Roches looked back to the halcyon days of King John, when kings were kings and their authority, above all their authority in matters of patronage, stood at its proper, pristine zenith. Kings such as John or Frederick II were free to reward whom they chose and to over-ride inconvenient charters or custom. As Henry III was later to complain, he had given des Roches his full confidence, raising him to be his spiritual father and counsellor. But the bishop had led him into ways that had imperilled his soul to the neglect of his obligations as a king. Des Roches had forced the king to dismiss many of his oldest and most

---

[98]   Wendover, *Flores*, iv, pp. 264–6.

trusted advisers. Furthermore, he 'made us err from the observance of justice in respect to the faithful subjects and nobles of our realm, and although by following our own whim we could do injury to our faithful subjects, he attributed (such injury) to the plenitude of royal power'.[99] In other words, des Roches appears to have argued not only that the king possessed a plenitude of royal power, but that he was not to be blamed if, in exercising such power, he did injury to various of his subjects. All of this accords with what Wendover reports of the bishop's advice to the king: that Henry should emulate the strength and determination of his Plantagenet ancestors, and brook no challenge from his unruly subjects in England.

THE MARSHAL'S RETIREMENT FROM COURT

For the king to prefer de Maulay to Gilbert Basset was provocative in personal as well as in legal terms. De Maulay – the alleged murderer of Arthur of Brittany, the former favourite of King John who had extracted vast ransoms from his English prisoners during the civil war – stood as the very embodiment of alien guile. By contrast, Gilbert Basset, knight of the royal household, closely connected to the Marshal family, commanded wide support both at court and in the country at large.[100] As a kinsman of Thomas Basset of Headington, he was related to a baronial family at odds with des Roches and de

[99] *Treaty Rolls I: 1234–1325*, ed. P. Chaplais (London 1955), pp. 8–9: ... *circa fideles et nobiles regni nostri plerumque nos fecit ab observatione iusticie deviare, dumque fidelibus nostris pro velle nostro facere possemus iniuriam attribuerat plenitudini regie potestatis.* I am grateful to John Maddicott for his help with this passage, the translation of which is still far from clear.

[100] For the Basset family, see N. Vincent, 'Gilbert Basset', in *New Dictionary of National Biography* (Oxford, forthcoming); S. L. Waugh, *The Lordship of England* (Princeton 1988), p. 212. Gilbert occurs several times as a royal household knight, together with his father, Alan, and his brother, Thomas; see, for example, C72/3, m. 1; C72/2, m. 15d. He married, but probably not until after 1234, Isabel daughter of William Ferrers, earl of Derby, a first cousin of Richard Marshal. Isabella outlived Gilbert (d.1241), remarrying Reginald de Mohun of Dunster and dying *c*.1260; *Cal.Inq.P.M.*, i, no. 500; Sanders, *English Baronies*, p. 114. Various members of the Basset family were attached to the Marshal household; Gilbert's father, Alan, and brother, Thomas, as knights of William Marshal I, a connection probably established via Alan's maternal kin, the Dunstanvilles, native to Dénestanville within the Marshal's Norman lordship of Long-ueville. Another of Gilbert's brothers, Warin Basset, served as a knight of William Marshal II on the Breton campaign of 1230. David Basset was steward to William Marshal II. Gilbert witnesses no known charter of William Marshal I or II. However, following the death of his brother Thomas in 1230, he had succeeded to an estate held of the Marshals at Speen in Berkshire; Vincent, 'Gilbert Basset'; Crouch, *William Marshal*, pp. 137, 141, 163; Painter, *William Marshal*, pp. 111–12, 280, 285; C72/2, m. 1; *Cl.R.1234–7*, p. 233. I owe my knowledge of the Marshals and their households to a

Maulay since as long ago as 1221.[101] Even before the dispute over Upavon, he had been forced to surrender his principal royal custodies, the castles of St Briavels, Devizes, and the forest of Dean, to des Roches' henchman Peter de Rivallis. In light of his wide affinity, it would have been sensible to compensate Basset for these losses. Instead, on 6 February he was deprived of Upavon, in direct contravention of charter and custom. On the following day the king issued letters under the warranty of des Roches, Seagrave and the Marshal, ordering the reseizure of the private estate of Hubert de Burgh, which since the previous November had been held in trust by the four earls guarding de Burgh at Devizes.[102] The lands were now to be handed over to Robert Passelewe, des Roches' ally, so that he might use their revenues to compensate victims, mostly alien victims, of the previous year's anti-Roman riots. In all likelihood this was a move designed to curry favour with the pope. Nonetheless, to the four earls who had previously kept the lands, it could only be regarded as a snub, particularly since the keeper substituted in their place was so closely allied to the bishop of Winchester. Added to this, although in theory set to repair the damage of the previous year's riots, Passelewe was almost immediately allowed to fine for the lands and heir of one of the rioters, obtaining private advantage from his supposedly public office.[103]

The slight to the Marshal was obvious. It was also bitterly resented. Cold-shouldered at court and made all too aware of the foreign upbringing which set him apart from his peers, the Marshal must have been doubly keen to build up some sort of following in England. The most obvious recruiting ground lay amongst the household of his late brother. Yet since the summer of 1232, Richard had been forced first to relinquish a large proportion of his English estate, his most valuable store of patronage, as dower to the king's sister, and then to stand by as Gilbert Basset, one of his family's most loyal allies, was subjected to humiliation over Upavon. The very next day Richard himself was required to surrender custody of de Burgh's estate to yet another

---

term spent working on the Marshal knights under the direction of Professor David Crouch, as a research assistant funded by the Leverhulme project on the medieval English aristocracy.

[101] Above pp. 201–2.

[102] *Cl.R.1231–4*, pp. 187–8. Banstead, Surrey, was separated from Hubert's estate and awarded to the Templars in repayment of Hubert's debts.

[103] *CPR 1232–47*, p. 11; *Cl.R.1231–4*, p. 191; C60/32, m. 8. For Henry de Cramville and the riots of 1232, in which he had bought grain from the rioters, see *Cl.R.1231–4*, p. 112; *Cal.Inq.P.M.*, i, no. 727.

satellite of des Roches. It was all too much for him. Gilbert Basset disappears from court immediately after the Upavon hearing of 6 February.[104] Richard Marshal last appears on 9 February. He made his way first to Wales where he joined Richard of Cornwall in driving Llywelyn from Radnor. He then sailed for Ireland, landing there before 1 April.[105]

[104] C53/27, m. 11.

[105] C53/27, mm. 11, 12; *AM*, i (Tewkesbury), p. 88. At Old Ross on 1 April he issued a charter in favour of Dunbrody Abbey; *Chartularies of St Mary's Abbey, Dublin*, ed. J. T. Gilbert, 2 vols. (RS 1884–6), ii, p. 160; G. H. Orpen, *Ireland under the Normans*, 4 vols. (Oxford 1911–20), iii, p. 60. Both the Dunstable annals and the Westminster *Flores* link his withdrawal from court to the Upavon case; *AM*, iii, p. 136; *Flores Hist.*, ii, p. 208.

Chapter 10

DES ROCHES IN POWER

Richard Marshal's withdrawal marks the end of the coalition which since August 1232 had dominated the court. First the household establishment had been neutralized by the attacks against Mauclerk and Crowcombe, and then the Marshal had been edged out. This left des Roches and his men alone but dangerously isolated at the centre of power. For the moment they were able to celebrate their new-found supremacy in a flurry of awards and promotions. By the end of March 1233 Peter de Rivallis had acquired personal interests in three Kent manors formerly part of de Burgh's private estate.[1] On 28 February his life interest in Pevensey castle was transformed into a hereditary award in fee.[2] The death of William Brewer that spring brought de Rivallis even greater custodies as the king's keeper of escheats, pending settlement amongst Brewer's heirs.[3] Meanwhile the royal castle of Bridgwater, recovered from Brewer, passed to Peter de Russelis, a Somerset man and former protégé of Peter de Maulay, for whom also a Norman manor in Dorset was seized back from its former custodian in what looks suspiciously like another disseisin *per voluntatem regis*.[4] Amongst de Burgh's estates, various long-term interests were conferred upon the Domus Dei Portsmouth, a hospital under des Roches' patronage.[5] Yet another of de Burgh's former manors passed to Anketil Malory, a kinsman of Stephen of Seagrave.

---

[1] Cl.R.1231–4, pp. 192–3. For Weston and Ackholt in Swanscombe, and Honeychild, Kent, see also Cal. Chart. R. 1226–57, pp. 13, 82; Cl.R.1231–4, p. 166.

[2] Cal. Chart. R. 1226–57, p. 175. De Rivallis had received Pevensey and Hastings castles for life in June 1232. Previously they had been kept by him as sheriff of Sussex; Pat. R. 1225–32, p. 486.

[3] C60/32, m. 7.

[4] CPR 1232–47, p. 13. For Winterborne Kingston, see BF, pp. 89, 1387; Cl.R.1231–4, pp. 217, 498, 519. For Russelis see CRR, xii, no. 1145; RLP, p. 161b; Pat. R. 1216–25, pp. 479–80. In 1224 various Norman escheats held by him in Dorset had been awarded to Hubert de Burgh; RLC, i, pp. 595b, 600b. He had been associated with de Maulay from at least 1215, accompanying him on the 1230 Breton campaign and witnessing at least one of his private charters; Pat. R. 1225–32, p. 358; BL ms. Cotton Tiberius C v (Register of St Thomas Acon), f. 255r.

[5] Cl.R.1231–4, p. 202; CPR 1232–47, p. 14. For Milborne Port, see also Cal. Chart. R.

By June 1233 Malory's tenancy there had been transformed into one in perpetual fee.[6] Seagrave himself was made hereditary lord of the manor of Melbourne.[7] For Brian de Lisle there were market privileges, and in April 1233 a grant of the sheriffdom of Yorkshire for life.[8] One of des Roches' clerks received an Essex manor confiscated from de Burgh's son John.[9] Engelard de Cigogné was granted land in Gloucestershire at farm, yet another award that appears to have involved summary dismissal of the previous custodian and the rejection of a royal charter.[10] Passelewe succeeded the disgraced chamber clerk, Ranulph le Breton, as custodian of an estate in Norfolk.[11]

As several of these grants bear witness, the king persisted in his refusal to warrant liberties supposedly guaranteed by royal charter. For example, since at least 1231 a moiety of the manor of Chalgrove in Oxfordshire, a Norman escheat, had been held by William of Huntercombe. Huntercombe possessed a royal charter guaranteeing his tenancy, but was nonetheless ejected from the land in February 1233, perhaps because of his association with the disgraced Walter Mauclerk. In his place the manor was granted to two knights of the royal household, aliens who had held the other moiety since 1224.[12]

1226–57, p. 71, where in 1228 it had passed to de Burgh together with Titchfield as a Norman escheat. The Titchfield connection may well explain des Roches' interest in 1233.

[6] For Arley, see *Cl.R.1231–4*, pp. 217, 232; *Cal. Chart. R. 1226–57*, pp. 25, 182; *CRR*, xv, no. 1475. I am indebted to David Crouch for the information that Anketil Malory was the son of Richard Malory of Kirkby and of Cecilia, sister of Stephen of Seagrave. See *Pat. R. 1225–32*, p. 418; JUST1/949, m. 2; CP25(1)/121/9 no. 72, which provide hints of this connection.

[7] *Cl.R.1231–4*, p. 198; *Cal. Chart. R. 1226–57*, p. 175.

[8] *Cl.R.1231–4*, pp. 207, 214; *Cal. Chart. R. 1226–57*, p. 176; *CPR 1232–47*, p. 15; C60/32, m. 6.

[9] For des Roches' clerk William fitz Humphrey and the manor of White Roding, Essex, see *CPR 1232–47*, pp. 12–13; *CRR*, xv, no. 1090; *BF*, pp. 590, 1360; *Acta*, appendix 4, no. 32.

[10] *Cl.R.1231–4*, pp. 215, 217. Thomas le Veile had held Hailes as Norman land by royal charter since 1228, but was disgraced *c*.Oct. X Nov. 1232 when he was forced to surrender both Hailes and a wardship; *Cal. Chart. R. 1226–57*, p. 77; C60/31, m. 1; C60/32, m. 9. He appears to have been a familiar of Hubert de Burgh and by the time of his death held land of the earls Marshal; *Cal. Chart. R. 1226–57*, p. 195; E40/14377; *Cal.Inq.P.M.*, i, no. 918. De Burgh's doctor had been promoted rector of Hailes by the king in 1230; *Pat. R. 1225–32*, p. 389.

[11] For Sporle, see *Cl.R.1231–4*, pp. 197, 442.

[12] *RLC*, ii, p. 8; *Pat. R. 1225–32*, p. 313; *Cal. Chart. R. 1226–57*, pp. 108, 139; *CRR*, xv, no. 1047; *Cl.R.1231–4*, p. 195. In December 1233 Drogo de Barentin, one of the alien knights, received a moiety of the manor in perpetuity by royal charter; Oxford, Magdalen College muniments ms. Chalgrove deed 55B. For Huntercombe's contacts with Mauclerk, see *Pat. R. 1225–32*, p. 464.

One of these men, John de Plesset, probably a Norman, appears regularly at court from April 1233.[13] His promotion coincides with the return of Engelard de Cigogné and the reinstatement of yet another veteran, Ralph of Bray, once a henchman of Fawkes de Bréauté, more recently established in the household of the earl of Chester and now appointed sheriff of Warwickshire and Leicestershire in succession to Seagrave.[14] Even here there was a challenge to royal charters, since Seagrave had theoretically been granted the counties for life as recently as 1232. As this last grant implies, there may have been tensions even within des Roches' immediate circle of allies and associates. Just as Seagrave was made to relinquish two of his midland counties, so Brian de Lisle was asked to surrender Knaresborough to Peter de Rivallis.[15] Yet both Seagrave and de Lisle were compensated elsewhere, de Lisle perhaps by a straight exchange for de Rivallis' castle of Lydford and his office as sheriff of Yorkshire.[16] Seagrave consolidated an already substantial private estate and secured promotions for his numerous kin. His brother-in-law Hugh Despenser, and Richard de Gray, a relative by marriage, both now appear as regular witnesses to royal charters. De Gray received part of the estate confiscated from Walter Mauclerk.[17]

Within only a few weeks of the Marshal's withdrawal, the associates of des Roches and Seagrave had devoured a rich store of patronage. In particular, the estate of Hubert de Burgh fell prey to the acquisitiveness of precisely those men supposed to guard it on behalf of the crown. Much the same can be said of other escheats in the king's hands. In some spectacular instances, the ambitions of Henry's ministers extended even to what could be considered parts of the

---

[13] See *CP*, x, pp. 545–8; C53/27, m. 10. John first appears in the 1220s together with a (?)brother named Hugh de Plesset who like John was closely associated with men named Drogo de Barentin (?Barentin nr Rouen, Seine Maritime), and Nicholas de Bolleville in the following of the Anglo-Norman, Robert de Vieuxpont.

[14] *CPR 1232–47*, p. 15; *Cal. Chart. R. 1226–57*, p. 166. For Ralph, see Carpenter, *The Minority*, p. 117; *Charters of the Earls of Chester*, ed. Barraclough, *passim*.

[15] C60/32, mm. 1, 6; E372/77, m. 4; *Cl.R.1231–4*, pp. 213, 224, 238, 403, 438, 575; *CRR*, xv, no. 1125; *Pipe Roll 26 Henry III*, ed. H. L. Cannon (Yale 1918), p. 26, which suggest that Peter was promoted not only keeper of the castle but as rector of Knaresborough church.

[16] E372/77, m. 4. De Lisle was considered liable for Lydford from Easter 1233; E159/13, m. 3d.

[17] *Cl.R.1231–4*, pp. 178, 237, 367, 401, 416; *Cal. Chart. R. 1226–57*, p. 175; C53/27, m. 14, where Richard de Gray first witnesses 14 Dec. 1232. For the de Gray kinship, see *CP*, vi, p. 171; Turner, *Men Raised from the Dust*, p. 135, which also suggests kinship by marriage between Seagrave and des Roches' clerk, Geoffrey de Caux, for whom see *Acta*, appendix 4, no. 29.

royal demesne. Moreover the favours bestowed in the spring of 1233 were as nothing compared to those which were to follow. Clearly these facts must colour our appreciation of the financial 'reforms' supposedly set in motion by des Roches.

THE REGIME AND FINANCIAL REFORM: THE EXCHEQUER

One of the principal causes of de Burgh's fall had been fiscal mismanagement, coupled to the king's belief that des Roches and de Rivallis could reform royal finances. The view that des Roches and his regime were principally concerned with financial 'reform' has obtained the support of many later commentators, beginning in the 1920s with Miss Mabel Mills who sought to portray Peter de Rivallis as 'the great financier of the period'.[18] According to Mills' analysis, de Rivallis was appointed to over twenty-one counties and numerous custodies in June and July 1232, as the first stage in a major review of the county farms. Once this had been achieved, at Michaelmas 1232 the counties were reapportioned to sheriffs, whose accounts, according to Mills, were to be cleared with remarkable dispatch. The pipe and memoranda rolls were better and more carefully kept, revealing great activity at the Exchequer and an unusual efficiency in distraint against recalcitrant debtors.[19] In turn this heralded enquiries into baronial franchises, the composition of the county farms, and tenures in Norman escheats.[20] The baronage reacted to this efficiency in 1234 by forcing de Rivallis from office, but two years later he returned to reintroduce his financial experiments in earnest.[21]

There are glaring errors in this account. For example, des Roches and de Rivallis are credited with Exchequer reforms between 1228 and 1231, in which years neither of them so much as set foot in England. De Rivallis played no part in the reforms introduced after 1236. Nonetheless, in a lengthy but by no means lucid chapter on the Exchequer, Sir Maurice Powicke endorsed Mills' conclusions, that des Roches and his henchmen were concerned to introduce fundamental financial reform.[22] Only

---

[18] M. H. Mills, 'The reforms at the Exchequer (1232–1242)', *TRHS*, 4th series 10 (1927), pp. 111–34. The phrase quoted occurs at p. 131.

[19] *Ibid.*, pp. 111–16.

[20] *Ibid.*, pp. 117–18.

[21] *Ibid.*, pp. 129–33.

[22] Powicke, *Henry III and the Lord Edward*, chapter iii, pp. 84–122, and see also Powicke, *The Thirteenth Century*, pp. 51–2, 60–6; S. B. Chrimes, *An Introduction to the Administrative History of Mediaeval England*, 3rd edn (Oxford 1966), pp. 90–6.

recently has this approach come into question, above all in David Carpenter's study of the county farms. Carpenter's work provides us with our best starting point for a reconsideration of des Roches, the financial 'reformer'.[23]

There now seems little doubt that Peter de Rivallis' promotion to the custody of so many shires in the summer of 1232 was a political rather than a financial device, and that it made very little impact upon the account at the Michaelmas Exchequer, where the sheriffs established before de Rivallis' appointment continued to answer in their own right, not as proxies for de Rivallis. Over the previous six months the changes in personnel in Hampshire, Kent, Norfolk, Suffolk and Lincoln had all been factionally motivated, to remove de Burgh's satellites from the shires.[24] There had long been debate as to the best means of extracting revenues from the county farms. By the late twelfth century the traditional sums for which the sheriffs answered at the Exchequer, the ancient farms, represented only a fraction of the true income that the counties could produce. Whatever a sheriff could collect over and beyond the county farm, he kept as private profit. To counter this, the Exchequer began to impose increments upon the farm, extra sums for which the sheriffs were made liable, intended to reduce the gap between the ancient farms and the true value of receipts. During John's reign, a brief attempt was made to abandon the ancient farms altogether, and to make the sheriffs pay all of their receipts at the Exchequer, answering as custodians in return for fixed annual wages. The experiment was swiftly abandoned, partly because it was difficult to persuade powerful men, the sort of men who the king needed to impose order in the localities, to accept office as sheriff without offering them the prospect of substantial private profit. At the same time, increments charged over and above the county farms were abandoned, at some time before 1215, a measure enshrined in Magna Carta (1215), and undertaken in response to baronial pressure, to reduce the burdens that the sheriffs exacted from local landholders. During the minority of Henry III, Hubert de Burgh had encouraged a return to moderate surcharges, no longer described as increments but as payments in lieu of profits, as a means of boosting the king's receipts. Likewise, although there was as yet no further attempt to abolish the ancient farms or to return to

---

[23] Carpenter, 'The decline of the curial sheriff in England 1194–1258', pp. 10–16, esp. pp. 14–15, and for a summary of the debate see Stacey, *Politics, Policy and Finance*, pp. 37–9.

[24] Above pp. 296–7.

the custodial experiments of John's reign, from time to time individual counties were administered on a custodial basis, largely to enable the Exchequer to gauge the true level of profits and so charge an appropriate surcharge against future sheriffs. This was the background to shrieval administration prior to the fall of de Burgh; a system of moderate surcharges in lieu of profits charged over and above the ancient county farms. Des Roches and de Rivallis are traditionally supposed to have overturned this system in favour of a far more drastic 'reform' of royal finance, yet the evidence for such 'reform' is far from conclusive.

At Michaelmas 1232 de Rivallis nominated seven new sheriffs to fill nine county custodies. He is specifically said to have presented these men (*presentavit*), implying that he was active in setting their terms of employment.[25] In four of the nine counties the new sheriffs were required to render a higher annual surcharge over the county farm in lieu of profits, the rise varying from 15 marks in the case of Devon to some 40 marks in Berkshire, where there appears to have been an enquiry into county revenues launched several months before de Rivallis' promotion.[26] In three counties the sheriffs' liabilities were reduced: by £10 in Dorset and Somerset, and quite drastically in Lincoln where the sheriff ceased to answer for profits, calculated in 1232 at just over £250 minus an allowance for keeping Lincoln castle, and instead paid a fixed charge of £100, with £5 deducted for the keeping of the castle, a net reduction of more than £100 a year.[27] Of those sheriffs not known to have been presented by de Rivallis, the liabilities of five counties remained unchanged and rose slightly in three others.[28] De Rivallis himself retained long-term custody of Sussex where his principal lay estate was situated. He also continued as sheriff of Staffordshire and Shropshire, where

---

[25] *Memoranda Rolls 1231–3*, nos. 3140–4, 3151, 3153.

[26] Berkshire £40 surcharge to 100m; Devon no surcharge to £20, keeping Exeter castle at sheriff's own expense, previously (1230) the sheriff of Devon had answered for the entire profit over the farm as a custodian receiving an allowance of £30 (*PR 14 Henry III*, pp. 13–14); Staffs./Shrops. 40m surcharge to £40. In 1231 the entire 40m had been pardoned; E372/75, m. 9.

[27] Compare *PR 14 Henry III*, pp. 292–4; E372/75, mm. 7, 12; E372/76, m. 10; *Memoranda Rolls 1231–3*, nos. 3143, 3151. In Yorkshire there was no change in terms; likewise in Gloucester where a complicated bargain was struck over the keeping of Gloucester and Bristol castles, with no surcharge; E372/75, m. 15; *Memoranda Rolls 1231–3*, no. 3142.

[28] Terms unchanged in Essex, Herts., Hereford, Lancashire and Surrey. In Norfolk and Suffolk surcharge raised from £60 to £70; E372/75, m. 4; E372/76, m. 11; E372/77, m. 11. In Oxford the surcharge remained unchanged, although the sheriff lost custody of various rents previously awarded to Godfrey of Crowcombe as a perquisite; *PR 14 Henry III*, p. 246; E372/77, m. 9; Carpenter, 'Sheriffs of Oxfordshire', pp. 251–2.

he had previous contacts as dean of the royal free chapel of Bridgnorth, and of Yorkshire which he was to relinquish at Easter 1233 to Brian de Lisle. In Yorkshire there was to be no change to the sheriff's farm under either de Rivallis or de Lisle. For Stafford and Shropshire de Rivallis offered an annual surcharge of 60 marks, a rise of 20 marks, against which must be set the 15 mark surcharge which his predecessor had paid for Sussex but which Peter was excused.[29] On taking over as sheriff of Hampshire des Roches likewise ceased to answer for a 30 mark surcharge paid by his predecessor.[30]

Taken together, the year to October 1232 witnessed the most comprehensive redistribution of counties since de Burgh had seized power a decade earlier. At least eighteen sheriffs were replaced or transferred. Yet, as David Carpenter has pointed out, the same period witnessed no financial 'reform' comparable even to the moderate experiments with profits and surcharges introduced by de Burgh after 1224.[31] Any increase in revenue, by raising surcharges, was offset by reductions elsewhere, above all by the enormous reduction in the sum paid from Lincoln. Meanwhile, the new Justiciar, Stephen of Seagrave, was confirmed in life possession of five midland counties for which he paid no surcharge save to finance the keeping of Northampton and Kenilworth castles.[32] After Seagrave's dismissal the counties in question were to yield at least 470 marks a year above their farms, a sum which must previously have gone to Seagrave as personal profit.[33] De Rivallis offered a surcharge of 60 marks a year for Stafford and Shropshire, a slight increase on his predecessor, but nothing compared to the 160 marks or more levied against his successor after 1234.[34]

With the obvious exceptions of des Roches, de Rivallis and Seagrave, relatively few of the men appointed as sheriffs at Michaelmas 1232 were politically active. Robert of Waltham, sheriff of Essex and Hertfordshire, may have served as des Roches' steward.[35]

---

[29] *Memoranda Rolls 1231–3*, no. 3140; *Pat. R. 1225–32*, p. 489. De Rivallis accounted for Yorkshire via the professional under-sheriff, John Bonet, until April 1233; C60/32, m. 6; *CPR 1232–47*, p. 15; E372/77, m. 4.

[30] E372/76, m. 2; E372/77, m. 7d. For attempts to surcharge des Roches after his fall see below pp. 466–7.

[31] Carpenter, 'The decline of the curial sheriff', pp. 11–14.

[32] *Cl.R.1227–31*, p. 259; *Cal. Chart. R. 1226–57*, p. 166.

[33] Carpenter, 'The decline of the curial sheriff', p. 12.

[34] *Ibid.*, p. 14; E372/78, m. 11.

[35] See *Acta*, appendix 4, no. 26. The name is too common to allow any certain identification. Meekings (intro. to *CRR*, xv, p. xxvi) identifies Robert de Briwes,

Oxfordshire passed to John de Ulcote, a former under-sheriff of Fawkes de Bréauté.[36] But most of the new sheriffs were professionals with experience stretching back into the reign of King John. By contrast, in the months following Richard Marshal's withdrawal from court, this political neutrality was to vanish in the face of blatant factional self-interest. Between January and May 1233 a further six sheriffs were appointed to eight counties. Virtually all were factional adherents of des Roches or major political figures at court. Brian de Lisle and the alien Engelard de Cigogné were appointed to Yorkshire and Oxfordshire on the same favourable terms as their predecessors, Brian being granted custody for life.[37] Henry fitz Nicholas, son of one of the king's stewards, was appointed to Somerset and Dorset and excused all former surcharges over the farm.[38] Not every such appointment was so lenient. In three counties the regime was able to introduce surcharges for the first time: in Cumberland where the leading justice, Thomas of Moulton, succeeded bishop Mauclerk with a surcharge of £35;[39] and in Warwickshire and Leicestershire which Seagrave was asked to surrender to Ralph of Bray, yet another returning veteran, who now paid 100 marks a year in lieu of profits.[40] Were it not for these last two changes, des Roches' ascendancy between 1232 and 1234 would have seen a net reduction in renders over the county farms. As it was, the overall net effect, balancing increases against deductions, was to raise surcharges over the farm by a derisory 10 marks a year. In this way, despite wide swings and variations in individual counties, the overall picture remained virtually unchanged.

Financially insignificant, the changes in sheriffs were political in both motive and effect, intended to transfer still lucrative county custodies into the hands of des Roches, de Rivallis and their factional adherents. As to the myth that de Rivallis' sheriffs fulfilled their obligations at the Exchequer more speedily than their predecessors, one of the chief examples advanced by Mills in support of this argument concerns the county of Lincoln, whose sheriff after 1232

sheriff of Norfolk and Suffolk from 1232, as a factional adherent of des Roches from the time of Robert's father, 'long connected with bishop Peter'. In fact, I have been able to find John de Briwes, Robert's father, recorded only once in association with des Roches, and that in what may well be an adversarial context; *Somersetshire Pleas*, ed. Chadwick-Healey, Somerset Rec. Soc. xi (1897), pp. 35–6, no. 132.

[36] Carpenter, 'Sheriffs of Oxfordshire', pp. 241–4.
[37] *CPR 1232–47*, pp. 15–16; Carpenter, 'The decline of the curial sheriff', p. 14.
[38] *CPR 1232–47*, p. 15; E372/78, m. 13.
[39] *Cal. Chart. R. 1226–57*, p. 165; *CPR 1232–47*, p. 8; E372/77, m. 6; E372/78, m. 7d.
[40] *CPR 1232–47*, p. 15; E372/77, m. 7; E372/78, m. 3d.

was quick to clear the county farm and surcharge where previously it had taken several years to obtain payment.[41] Yet, as we have seen, Lincoln was altogether an exceptional case. Given that his surcharge had been reduced by nearly 170 marks at Michaelmas 1232, it is hardly surprising that the new sheriff found it far easier than his predecessor to meet his obligations at the Exchequer. On the other hand, de Rivallis himself and his under-sheriff for Sussex, despite being excused the small surcharge paid by previous sheriffs, had still to clear their account at the Exchequer long into the 1240s.[42] Mills' contention, that the memoranda roll was better kept under des Roches' regime, likewise lacks support. The rolls for the years 16 and 17 Henry III show no outward signs of change. The individual county accounts may be slightly fuller than before, but this reflects the need to acquaint so many new sheriffs with the debts and obligations of their shires, not any great reforming zeal. The suggestion that distraints were ordered more frequently is impossible to prove or disprove, since the memoranda roll appears to note distraint on an entirely haphazard basis.[43] Throughout des Roches' ascendancy the one hint of a general Exchequer ruling occurs amidst the Wiltshire account taken in October 1232. It notes that no sheriff was to accept the pledge of a baronial steward for his master's scutage: hardly a revolutionary, nor even a new decision.[44]

In all of this we have a splendid point of comparison in Robert Stacey's study of the financial reforms put in train at the Exchequer in 1236, less than two years after des Roches' fall from power. The Exchequer barons of 1236 were to introduce wholly new methods of assessing income from the counties and the royal demesne. They drew up detailed analyses of the county revenues and dispatched county by county inquests into the king's escheats, *terra Normannorum* and landholding in general, comparable in scale to the great enquiries of 1166. Income from every aspect of county administration was carefully scrutinized and boosted by a substantial factor.[45] As witness to all this, the Exchequer memoranda rolls, uniform in length and dimension until 1234, swell enormously from a mere twelve mem-

---

41 Mills, 'The reforms at the Exchequer', pp. 115–16.

42 *PR 26 Henry III*, p. 276; *Cl.R.1237–42*, p. 74.

43 See Mills, 'The reforms at the Exchequer', p. 115, where the evidence cited is extremely vague, as for example in the remarks at pp. 117n., 119n.

44 *Memoranda Rolls 1231–3*, no. 2238. For distraint against baronial stewards, see *The Course of the Exchequer by Richard Son of Nigel*, ed. C. Johnson (London 1950), pp. 112, 116–18, drawn to my attention by Paul Brand.

45 Stacey, *Politics, Policy and Finance*, esp. chapter 2, pp. 45–92.

branes in 1233–4 to twenty-six in 1235–6.[46] The net effect of these changes was to raise the value of the county farms by some £1,200 gross, £600 net, and of the king's demesne by a further £800 a year.[47] The contrast here with des Roches' regime is unmistakable. Indeed it requires us to jettison any idea that the regime's chief impetus lay in Exchequer 'reform'. In itself this is hardly surprising. Both des Roches and de Rivallis were principally experienced in the king's household, in the offices of the chamber and the wardrobe rather than the centralized treasury. After October 1232 the memoranda rolls show that they were virtually never at the Exchequer. Both witness only occasional Exchequer writs, none later than April 1233.[48] Various orders are said to have been delivered to the Exchequer by des Roches and Stephen of Seagrave, demanding an account or respiting scutage, but when accounts were delayed for discussion it was almost invariably for discussion with Seagrave rather than des Roches.[49] Until his disgrace in December 1232 it was the treasurer Walter Mauclerk who carried the burden of work at the Exchequer. Thereafter, the bishops of Bath and Durham took his place, disappearing in February 1233 to be replaced by de Rivallis' deputy-treasurer, Robert Passelewe.[50] It is Passelewe who authorized virtually every Exchequer writ until Christmas 1233 with only occasional appearances by the chancellor, Ralph de Neville, and the bishop of Rochester.[51] The supposed authors of Exchequer 'reform', Peter des Roches and Peter de Rivallis, were in fact hardly ever at the Exchequer.

FINANCIAL REFORM: ESCHEATS AND WARDSHIPS

There is one remaining area in which des Roches' regime has earned a reputation for reform. Contemporary chroniclers make no reference

---

46 Compare E159/13 and E159/14. There is no surviving memoranda roll to cover the terms Trinity 1234–Trinity 1235. Stacey, *Politics, Policy and Finance*, pp. 52–5, draws attention to the large number of *particule proficui*, schedules of individual county farms surviving from the enquiries launched after 1236. Only one such *particula* survives for the years of des Roches' regime; E199/42/1, which claims to be a roll for Sussex for the year from 1 January 10 Henry III (1226), although dated internally *tempore H. de Burghs' vicecomitis*, to the time of de Rivallis' under-sheriff for Sussex in 1233; E372/77, m. 10d.

47 Stacey, *Politics, Policy and Finance*, pp. 57, 91–2.

48 *Memoranda Rolls 1231–3*, nos. 2700, 2705, 2712, 2719–20, 2734, 2807, 2978, 3028–32, 3035, 3040, 3080, 3082, 3084.

49 *Memoranda Rolls 1231–3*, nos. 2746–7, 3148, 3152. De Rivallis presented a sheriff to Essex/Herts in the Trinity term of 1233; *ibid.*, no. 2609.

50 *Ibid.*, nos. 2592–3156 *passim*.

51 E159/13, mm. 7–12d, and see E371/2, mm. 1d, 2d, 3d, 4d, 6d, where Passelewe is accorded the title of treasurer when receiving *originalia* from the Chancery.

to an overhaul of the counties or the Exchequer beyond noticing that sheriffs found guilty of peculation in 1232 were heavily fined. By contrast, Roger of Wendover makes much of the regime's proposal to reform the administration of escheats. According to Wendover, at some time in the winter of 1232–3 des Roches and his supporters went to the king to complain against his squandering of resources: escheats and wardships, so they argued, should no longer be given away to enrich the king's ministers, but should be used to rebuild the finances of the crown. Only then could Henry become rich and powerful like his ancestors. Wendover's account is borne out by the appointment in February 1232 of panels of county knights to serve as keepers of escheats.[52] This in turn heralded a major administrative upheaval.

The king had several means of managing escheats and wardships. From the reign of Henry II onwards, great honours tended to be kept separate from the sheriffs' responsibilities, entrusted to special keepers who answered for all profits in return for a fixed annual wage.[53] It was in this way that King John had exploited the resources of the honours of Gloucester or Perche, their keepers answering more often to the chamber than to the centralized, dilatory Exchequer. The system was extremely profitable but it relied upon an inner circle of *curiales*, often aliens, to act as John's custodians. After 1216, anxious to purchase support and by the same process to enrich themselves, the members of Henry's minority council switched to an alternative system whereby escheats and wardships were auctioned off to the highest bidder, granted to favoured courtiers at farm or in return for a suitable fine. As a result, the Exchequer assumed control both of those minor escheats still accounted by the sheriffs on a county by county basis, and also of the farms or fines owing by private individuals for the greater honours. It was a system that was potentially no less profitable than direct management by the crown. Hubert de Burgh, for example, fined 7,000 marks for the honour of Gloucester during the heir's minority. He had paid 3,000 marks of this fine by the time of his disgrace in 1232.[54] Such farming of escheats provided a useful

---

[52] Wendover, *Flores*, iv, p. 244 and see above pp. 281–2, 285–6.

[53] *The Course of the Exchequer*, ed. Johnson, pp. 94–5, written in the 1170s, assumes that all greater escheats will be managed directly by the crown, save only for minor estates of three or less manors which might be deputed to the sheriffs or to other custodians.

[54] De Burgh made a 2, 000 mark downpayment and by the time of his disgrace owed 4, 000m, although it is difficult to know whether his payments were made in cash or written off against the various sums owed him by the crown; *Cal. Chart. R. 1226–57*, p. 126; C60/30, m. 9; E372/75, m. 4; E372/76, m. 11d.

means of rewarding courtiers, above all de Burgh himself. However, in political terms it proved very difficult to persuade such courtiers to pay the money that they had promised. Fines were spread over many years, and were frequently rescheduled, so that in practice the Exchequer extracted far less from escheats and wardships than had been the case under the system of direct management favoured by King John. Hence the call made by des Roches for the king to cease squandering his resources upon individual courtiers and instead to resume control of his own estate. It was a call inspired by des Roches' memory of the methods of King John, and directed specifically against de Burgh and his adherents, the greatest beneficiaries of escheats and wardships transferred to private hands. In the short term, it led to the appointment of local knights as keepers on a county by county basis. But these men had little to occupy them before July 1232 when the experiment was abandoned. Instead Peter de Rivallis was appointed sole keeper of wardships and escheats throughout England, answering for their issues to the king.[55] Simultaneously, de Burgh's disgrace disgorged a torrent of escheats, wardships and custodies: the honours of Gloucester, Arundel, Mowbray, St Pol, Avranches and a host of lesser estates, previously held by the Justiciar or his son. All these were entrusted to de Rivallis, who within the next few months, following the deaths of the earl of Chester and William Brewer, found his responsibilities even further augmented.

In practice, day-to-day management of these estates was entrusted by de Rivallis to at least two deputies, described as early as January 1233 as the king's escheators.[56] Both men were personally associated with the regime's great figureheads: William Ruffus as a patron of des Roches' foundation at Halesowen, Bernard of Grimsby as a prebendary in de Rivallis' collegiate church of Bridgnorth.[57] Their accounts for the escheats in their custody went principally to de Rivallis in the royal wardrobe rather than to the Exchequer.[58] Since de Rivallis was keeper of the wardrobe, keeper of escheats and treasurer of the Exchequer, this in effect meant that he served

---

[55] *Cl.R.1231–4*, pp. 129–31; C60/31, m. 6; *Pat. R. 1225–32*, p. 491; above pp. 285–6.

[56] *Cal.Lib.R.1226–40*, pp. 193, 195–6, 215; *Cl.R.1231–4*, pp. 194, 421; *Foreign Accounts*, pp. 74, 81.

[57] For Grimsby, see *CPR 1232–47*, p. 21. For Ruffus, see Dugdale, *Monasticon*, vi, p. 927, no. 3; *BF*, pp. 142, 348, 593;' *Cal. Chart. R. 1226–57*, pp. 32, 182; BL ms. Cotton Nero C xii (Walsall cartulary), ff. 127r–132r. He had been involved in forest and local administration in Shrops./Staffs. throughout the 1220s, hence perhaps his links to de Rivallis.

[58] *Cal.Lib.R.1226–40*, p. 193; *Foreign Accounts*, p. 81, suggests that £831 was paid into the wardrobe set against £600 to the treasury.

simultaneously as bailiff, accountant and auditor rolled into one. Herein lay the root of a serious problem. The sheer number of escheats de Rivallis was called upon to administer meant that the system was hopelessly overloaded from the start. De Rivallis only compounded this difficulty. Rather than impose some new stream-lined form of management, he tried to combine a variety of systems, with chaotic results. The outcome was muddle, confusion and the squandering of the king's resources.

To take some of the more important examples: most of the lands confiscated from de Burgh were combined with stray manors recov-ered from William Brewer, the earl of Chester, and various rebel lands seized during the disturbances of 1233, to be accounted on a county by county basis by the escheators Ruffus and Grimsby.[59] Yet at the same time, de Burgh's honour of Raleigh, and others of his estates scattered across Kent and Essex, were entrusted to a keeper indepen-dent of the two escheators.[60] Meanwhile, de Burgh's family inheri-tance passed via de Rivallis and a committee of four earls to end up with Robert Passelewe, used to compensate the victims of the anti-Roman riots of 1232. In the process a few individual manors became detached; Banstead, for example, granted to the Templars in repay-ment of de Burgh's debts, or the various manors acquired as private perquisites by de Rivallis and his fellow courtiers.[61] Even then, there remained various stray manors which were incorporated in none of these schemes but were restored to shrieval custody and accounted for at the Exchequer, as part of the ordinary county receipts.[62] In this way, at least five separate systems operated simultaneously to control the single estate once held by de Burgh. The potential for confusion and the difficulties in ensuring any coherent, overall accountability can hardly be exaggerated.

To take further examples: the honour of Arundel was treated as an integral unit but accounted for by de Rivallis' under-sheriff in Sussex, independent of the ordinary county receipts.[63] The sparse evidence for the honour of Gloucester suggests that, at least until the spring of 1233, it was managed by Peter de Rivallis via an Exchequer clerk named Richard de la Ladhe, although Passelewe appears to have acquired a personal interest over the subsidiary honour of Clare,

59 *Foreign Accounts*, pp. 74–81.
60 *Ibid.*, pp. 86–9.
61 Above p. 338.
62 Carpenter, 'The decline of the curial sheriff', p. 15 and n. 3.
63 *Foreign Accounts*, pp. 82–5.

whilst Tonbridge castle passed to de Rivallis' under-sheriff for Sussex.[64] The archbishopric of Canterbury was kept by William of Haverhill, but custody of its two peculiar manors of Hayes and Harrow passed via Walter Mauclerk to de Rivallis as keeper of Mauclerk's confiscated estate.[65] In some instances the evidence is sketchier still. Part of the honour of William de Avranches was held by de Rivallis and William Ruffus as escheators, although the honour's *caput* including Folkestone appears to have been delegated to the sheriff of Kent.[66]

In the short term, the sheer number of custodies restored to the crown ensured that money was brought flooding back into the king's wardrobe after many years of drought. The *liberate* roll for 1232–3 shows that at least £1,700 was paid into the wardrobe from various honours including Gloucester, Arundel, Avranches and Canterbury.[67] As escheator, William Ruffus paid in an additional £530, largely by-passing the centralized treasury and Exchequer.[68] Enormous sums, between £4,500 and £6,500, were transferred from the treasury to the wardrobe, almost always delivered to de Rivallis, to cover the king's daily expenses.[69] This was in addition to the money paid in locally by sheriffs, tax collectors and custodians as the wardrobe followed the king about the country. Whereas earlier taxes had been made the responsibility of particular, central inspectors, the fortieth of 1232 was collected by the local sheriffs according to a deliberately decentralized scheme. By the summer of 1233 the tax stored in provincial treasuries was being diverted to Gloucester and the Marches, paid into the wardrobe to finance the king's war in Wales. Although an attempt was later made to audit the tax, at least £5,400 of it had to be written off as sums paid into the wardrobe.[70]

[64] *Memoranda Rolls 1231–3*, no. 2435; *Cal.Lib.R.1226–40*, pp. 193, 195–6, 205, 208–9; *Cl.R.1231–4*, pp. 427, 442–3, 459, 471, 588; *CPR 1232–47*, p. 54.

[65] *Cal.Lib.R.1226–40*, p. 201; *Cl.R.1231–4*, pp. 365, 370, 373; *Pat. R. 1225–32*, pp. 472, 474; E372/76, m. 5d; E372/78, m. 7; *PR 26 Henry III*, p. 288.

[66] *Cl.R.1231–4*, pp. 579–80; C60/33, m. 10; *Cal.Lib.R.1226–40*, pp. 195–6, 201.

[67] *Cal.Lib.R.1226–40*, pp. 190, 193, 197, 201, 207, 225, 232.

[68] *Foreign Accounts*, p. 81, of which £300 paid in at Worcester should be included amongst the £1, 700 already noted above; *Cal.Lib.R.1226–40*, p. 193.

[69] *Cal.Lib.R.1226–40*, pp. 188–239, whence the calculations in Tout, *Chapters in Administrative History*, i, pp. 221–2. In the year to October 1233 a further £600 was disbursed from the treasury to Robert Passelewe and others, to cover building work at Westminster for which no proper account survives; *Cal.Lib.R.1226–40*, pp. 196, 199, 202, 208, 223. In general, compare the size of transfers from treasury to wardrobe under des Roches with the mere £3, 429 received in the wardrobe from the treasury during the entire period 18 May 1234–3 May 1236; E372/79, m. 11d.

[70] Mitchell, *Studies in Taxation*, pp. 202–6; *Foreign Accounts*, pp. 63–73.

Apologists have made much of the fact that de Rivallis rendered accounts for his custodies.[71] Yet this is to overlook various significant *lacunae* within those accounts. For example, the honour of Raleigh is accounted only to June 1233, the escheats held by William Ruffus only to the following September.[72] There is no surviving account for the vacancy receipts at Canterbury after 1232, probably because the king agreed to pay all of the outstanding profits of the vacancy to archbishop Edmund as a gesture of reconciliation after des Roches' fall.[73] Even more remarkable, there is no record whatsoever for receipts from the honour of Gloucester.[74] Above all, de Rivallis seems never to have rendered accounts for the wardrobe itself. This means that it is impossible to verify the discharge made against the accounts of his bailiffs or to determine the fate of most of the vast sums, at least £10,000, that passed through the wardrobe during his eighteen months as keeper. The sketchy and inadequate accounts of his bailiffs were accepted, simply because it was impossible to obtain anything better. Theoretically they left de Rivallis in debt to the crown to the tune of at least £500, a figure that excludes many of his more important custodies. In the case of the honour of Gloucester, for example, accounts were swiftly abandoned as hopeless. Elsewhere, individual debts were listed against de Rivallis in the pipe roll year after year but with the discharge left blank, pending a reckoning that never took place. De Rivallis made no attempt to clear even the £500 or so that could be charged against him. In 1261, following his death, his debts were assembled and simply written off.[75]

The failure to bring de Rivallis to account sprang from two chief causes. On taking office in July 1232 he had received specific immunity from rendering accounts for the chamber, the wardrobe and the king's household for roughly a year ahead.[76] It was an

---

71 Mills, 'The reforms at the Exchequer', p. 117. The accounts themselves are printed in *Foreign Accounts*, pp. 74–90. An account by de Rivallis via William Hardel for the exchanges of London and Canterbury is to be found in E372/81, m. 15.
72 *Foreign Accounts*, pp. 74, 86.
73 Walter of Kirkham's account for the archbishopric runs from 21 September 1231 to 1 August 1232, although de Rivallis had in theory been granted custody on 30 June 1232; E372/76, m. 5d; *Pat. R. 1225–32*, p. 486; *Cl.R.1231–4*, p. 424.
74 Gloucester disappears from account between the death of earl Gilbert in 1230 and 11 June 1234, after de Rivallis' fall; E372/80, m. 1r–d, and see below pp. 355, 361–2.
75 See *PR 26 Henry III*, pp. 26, 33, 64, 72, 75, 147, 160, 181, 250, 264, 276, 288, 297, 313, 344; E372/105, m. 9; *Foreign Accounts*, p. vi.
76 *Cal. Chart. R. 1226–57*, p. 164. The privilege was referred to by de Rivallis after his fall; *CRR*, xv, no. 1289.

immunity intended to mirror similar exemptions from account granted to Hubert de Burgh. Des Roches later attempted to have de Burgh's exemptions overturned, and in the spring of 1233 helped force accounts from the former treasurer, Walter Mauclerk.[77] There was more than a little hypocrisy in all this, given de Rivallis' own signal failure to account. At the same time, his privilege of July 1232 would not on its own have saved him. His failure to account reflects not only his limited immunity but the sheer impossibility of imposing sense upon the chaos over which he had presided. Rather than devise proper means of delegating his vast collection of custodies and escheats, de Rivallis ignored the natural distinction between shrieval and honorial jurisdiction. His own hybrid system brought more cash into the king's household than had been the case under de Burgh. The king no longer had to plead with the treasury to supply the basic upkeep of the court. But in keeping the household flush with cash, de Rivallis siphoned off taxes, treasury receipts and money received from escheats and wardships into an unaccountable, uncharted morass. At least under the old system, de Burgh had paid 3,000 marks of his massive fine towards custody of the earldom of Gloucester. By contrast, de Rivallis not only failed to account for the Gloucester lands, but seems to have wrung far less from them on the crown's behalf. The only payment recorded from Gloucester, throughout de Rivallis' period as keeper of escheats, is a paltry 100 marks paid into the wardrobe in December 1232.[78]

Only in the aftermath of the fall of Peter de Rivallis could certain aspects of his administration be adapted to serve the king more efficiently. The basic principle, that escheats should be administered apart from the sheriffs' custodies, was not of de Rivallis' devising; it had been known to Henry II and widely used by John.[79] After 1234 it survived, and was developed under the guidance of Richard de la Ladhe and a clerk named Adam fitz William, appointed escheators in the place of William Ruffus and Bernard of Grimsby. In 1236 their office was supplemented by the establishment of a separate jurisdiction for the counties north of Trent. De Rivallis' fall put an end to the problems caused by one man being bailiff, accountant and auditor combined. The escheators henceforth were carefully monitored and not so overburdened with custodies as they had been in

[77] Above pp. 313–14, 329.
[78] *Cal.Lib.R.1226–40*, p. 193.
[79] In general see E. R. Stevenson, 'The escheator', in *The English Government at Work 1327–1336*, ed. W. A. Morris et al., 3 vols. (Cambridge Mass. 1947), ii, pp. 113–20.

1232.[80] In the same way, the bitter lessons taught by de Rivallis' regime, and the problems that had arisen in extracting accounts for the wardrobe, seem to have convinced the king of the necessity of keeping a careful audit of household finance. After May 1234 wardrobe accounts were demanded from each of de Rivallis' successors, delivered at the Exchequer and entered on the pipe roll.[81]

There is one final point to be made about de Rivallis and the escheats. So far it has been assumed that his mismanagement was the result of overwork; that it occurred by accident rather than design. However, there is a more sinister interpretation that could be placed upon his activities, an interpretation that contemporary commentators were keen to promote. Just as des Roches and de Rivallis were to accuse de Burgh of squandering the king's resources for personal gain, so they themselves could not escape accusations of corrupt self-advancement. There is some justice to the charges against them. Members of their regime were far from slow to stake their own, private claims to portions of de Burgh's estate, and even on occasion to manors which might be regarded as part of the royal demesne. Many of them reaped handsome profits from appointments as sheriff. De Rivallis in particular amassed a quite phenomenal lordship in southern England. In Kent and Sussex he came to possess the honour of Aigle in fee together with the castle of Pevensey; custody of the entire honours of Arundel and Avranches, of the Briouze castles of Bramber and Knepp, the royal castle of Hastings, and of Tonbridge castle, separated from the rest of the honour of Gloucester; of the county of Sussex as sheriff, and of every port including Dover. In addition, he obtained a private interest in various of Hubert de Burgh's Kent manors. As custodian of the lands and heir of John de Briouze, he not only controlled a vast estate in Sussex and the

---

[80] *CPR 1232–47*, pp. 54–5. Richard de la Ladhe is found as marshal of the Exchequer in 1220, an office supposedly in the gift of the Marshal earls of Pembroke, which raises interesting questions over his loyalty during Richard Marshal's rebellion of 1233. Later, in the 1220s, he occurs as an official of Gilbert de Clare, earl of Gloucester, and in May 1234 is described as a clerk of the chancellor, Ralph de Neville. Such widespread contacts may help explain his survival in office at court throughout the years 1220–36; Vincent, 'The origins of the chancellorship of the Exchequer', pp. 118–19; *The Early Charters of the Cathedral Church of St Paul's London*, ed. M. Gibbs, Camden Soc., 3rd series lvii (1939), no. 182; Crouch, *William Marshal*, p. 146; *CRR*, xiii, no. 770; *Cl.R.1227–31*, p. 252. For his colleagues after 1234, see C. A. F. Meekings, 'Adam fitz William (d.1238)', *BIHR* 34 (1961), pp. 1–15. For their earliest account as escheators, see E372/80, mm. 1–2d.

[81] The first such account runs from 18 May 1234; E372/79, m. 11d. Thereafter see E372/81, m. 13; E372/83, m. 7.

Marches, but apparently intended marrying his own niece, a girl named Alice, to the Briouze heir, thereby raising the possibility that his entire estate in fee would pass by inheritance into the next generation.[82] The Justiciar, Seagrave, may long before have renounced his status as a clerk in order to inherit his family estate.[83] After 1232, most of de Rivallis' grants were either hereditary or guaranteed to him regardless of whether he remained in clerical orders. This in turn raised the possibility that Peter might establish himself as one of the greatest lay magnates in southern England, his lordship carved out over a matter of only a few months, and endowed almost exclusively from royal escheats in an even more spectacular fashion than the lordship of the *parvenu* de Burgh.

THE PERSONAL ROLE OF DES ROCHES

What previous commentators have portrayed as a brave financial experiment emerges in truth as barely disguised factionalism. A temporary bonanza caused by the grant of lay subsidy, the confiscation of de Burgh's estate and the fortuitous deaths of William Brewer and the earl of Chester, masks deep-seated chaos: a breakdown in accountability, the virtual subjection of the Exchequer to control by the wardrobe, and a sinister laxity by de Rivallis as custodian of the king's resources. In none of this does des Roches' regime look forwards to the Exchequer reforms of 1236. On the contrary, its outlook was deeply reactionary, an attempt to return to the heady days between 1208 and 1214, the years of des Roches' ascendancy over royal finance, when the court of King John had been awash with cash from escheats and confiscated church lands, when the chamber had broken free from control by the Exchequer, and when the king had enjoyed great wealth and even greater freedom in its expenditure. This harking back to John's reign is as pronounced in financial affairs as in relation to the various arbitrary acts of disseisin made *per voluntatem regis*. It did not escape contemporary comment. Wendover several times compares Henry III's

---

[82] *CPR 1232–47*, p. 504. I have been unable to find any other reference to such a niece. The most likely solution is that she was a daughter of Geoffrey des Roches, the bishop's nephew, married to a Hampshire heiress in 1225. Alternatively, bearing in mind the supposed kinship between de Rivallis and William Brewer, it is interesting to note that Brewer had a daughter named Alice, widow of Reginald de Mohun (d.1213) and of William Paynel (d.1228), a middle-aged woman but still living in 1233; Sanders, *English Baronies*, p. 123.

[83] Turner, *Men Raised from the Dust*, p. 125 dismisses the story.

policies after 1232 to those of King John.[84] The Dover annalist speaks of Henry 'cleaving more to aliens than to his own men and in various other ways treading in the footsteps of his father'.[85] Likewise, a continuation of the annals of Margam states that des Roches and Peter de Rivallis precipitated war between the king and Richard Marshal, 'on account of the aliens who they made to come into England, to oppress clergy and people alike, just as was done in the time of King John'.[86] There was abusive intent to such remarks but also much truth. By 1230 King John was well on his way to becoming the bogey-man of legend. Yet des Roches looked back on the late king's reign with undisguised nostalgia.

For all that des Roches had immense influence in reviving unpopular methods of government, his personal role in the regime he sponsored remains an enigma. The chroniclers invariably refer to him as the mastermind of royal policy, yet it is his kinsman, Peter de Rivallis, whom the records show to have been the more active member of the partnership. Ironically, whilst de Rivallis, Seagrave and the rest were gorging themselves upon royal patronage, des Roches' chief preoccupation seems to have lain in works of charity and religious benefaction. Besides the abbey of Titchfield, founded on his return from crusade, in 1233 he acquired yet another royal manor in Hampshire, Selborne, where he set about the foundation of an Augustinian priory.[87] Rents and manors diverted to him from the estate of Hubert de Burgh were put towards the endowment of a hospital at Portsmouth. The escheator, William Ruffus, was persuaded to grant the advowson of Walsall to des Roches' earlier foundation at Halesowen, a grant subsequently confirmed by the king.[88] Similarly the king confirmed des Roches in possession of estates acquired in Dorset and elsewhere from the religious of northern France, later put towards the bishop's posthumous Cistercian foundation at Netley.[89] In October 1232 the abbot of Cîteaux (*Sistaus*) appears as a guest on the Winchester estates.[90] Besides recording the work of surveyors at Titchfield and the installation

---

[84] Wendover, *Flores*, iv, pp. 243–4, 269, 295–6.

[85] BL ms. Cotton Julius D v, f. 29v.

[86] M. L. Coker, 'The 'Margam Chronicle' in a Dublin manuscript', *The Haskins Society Journal IV*, ed. R. B. Patterson (Woodbridge 1993), p. 134, taken from Dublin, Trinity College ms. 507, first drawn to my attention by Martin Brett and David Carpenter.

[87] For Selborne, see *Acta*, nos. 48–50; *Cal. Chart. R. 1226–57*, p. 177; *Cl.R.1231–4*, p. 216.

[88] Above pp. 340, 351; *Cal. Chart. R. 1226–57*, p. 182.

[89] *Ibid.*, pp. 182–3.

[90] Ms. 28DR, m. 8, dated 31 October 1232. The same Farnham account records a visit by the dean of Chartres on 10 April and the abbot *de la Peruse* there in late May 1233.

there of a pair of bells, the episcopal pipe roll for 1232–3 for the first
time includes inventories of vestments and service books at Calbourne and Farnham, where previously only lists of armour and
weaponry had been kept.[91] The bishop seems also to have maintained the high level of alms-giving first recorded prior to his
departure for crusade. In the year to Michaelmas 1232, at least 352
quarters of grain were distributed amongst the poor on his manors.
In the following year, a disastrous harvest pushed this figure up to
754 quarters, not far short of the charity distributed on the eve of his
crusade and more costly, given the soaring price of grain.[92]

Yet it would be entirely wrong to assume that des Roches had
retired from all but pious concerns. His religious foundations
continued to exhibit the canny opportunism of a professional
financier. Founded upon royal largesse, both Titchfield and Selborne
were subsequently endowed with encumbered estates, purchased
cheaply by des Roches from the monasteries of northern France,
now shedding uneconomic lands in England, or from local landholders indebted to the Jews. Jewish debt could be monitored by
Peter de Rivallis, keeper of the Winchester Jewry.[93] The consequences of endowing Selborne with encumbered land were soon to
become apparent, in a rash of law suits, brought by former tenants
and mortgage holders, who were able to exploit the contorted
process by which the bishop had purchased their leases and
mortgages, to demand additional money in return for disclaiming
their rights. In the meantime des Roches' activities as property
speculator can have done little to endear him to the local Hampshire
gentry.

The political upheaval of 1232 restored des Roches to much the
same position in county government he had enjoyed between 1216
and 1223. As on that earlier occasion, he was granted a virtual
stranglehold over county affairs, as constable of Winchester and
Portchester and sheriff of Hampshire, offices which he deputed in
March 1233 to his steward Roger Wacelin, a Norman by birth and

91 Ms. 28DR, mm. 8d, 16d.
92 Mss 27DR; 28DR *passim.*
93 In general see *Acta*, pp. liv–lvi. Abraham Pinche, the Jew arrested on charges of ritual
murder in 1232 (above pp. 288–9), was the creditor of several men from whom
Selborne priory acquired land; *Cl.R.1227–31*, p. 359; *Cl.R.1231–4*, p. 103; *Charters and
Documents Relating to Selborne and its Priory*, ed. Macray, i, pp. 4, 6, ii, pp. 46, 51. Adam
of Corhampton, a benefactor of Titchfield, was similarly indebted to Abraham's
mother; Cole, *Documents*, p. 302; Dugdale, *Monasticon*, vi, pp. 933–4. For de Rivallis as
keeper of the Winchester Jewry, see *Cl.R.1231–4*, p. 416. Engelard de Cigogné appears
also to have exploited lands mortgaged to the Winchester Jews; JUST1/775, m. 10.

for nearly twenty years a leading member of the bishop's household.[94] This too mirrors the situation after 1216, when it had been to another of his stewards, William of Shorwell, that des Roches had deputed the county. In 1232, however, the bishop's position was buttressed by yet further grants of privileges; fairs for his manors at Farnham and Witney, the right to collect the amercements of his own men, the chattels of convicted felons, quittance of suit of shire and hundred courts and a life award of free warren, particularly valuable to a bishop so keen on hunting within a county most of which lay within the king's forest.[95] He was already exploiting his newly-won right to take amercements by Michaelmas 1233, when the bishop's steward is found distraining men amerced in the county court and the courts of the city of Winchester, to pay to des Roches what had formerly gone to the crown.[96] The initial grant of 1232 had been accompanied by pardons to the Winchester citizens of arrears of their farm stretching back over many years, clearly to appease the citizens, following a grant to des Roches that was bound to raise tension between bishop and city.[97] In 1232 and again in the following year, des Roches obtained extension of the annual Winchester fairs by as much as a week.[98] He also persuaded the king to harry merchants into attending for as long as possible. Since the bishop's fairs drew business away from the city's tradesmen, the citizens of Winchester quite understandably regarded their extension as an infringement of city liberties. At the same time, des Roches appears to have appropriated to himself various pleas until then heard in the city courts, together with jurisdiction over the city suburbs outside the south and east gates, previously farmed by the city bailiffs on behalf of the crown. Complaints by the citizens were already being made at Michaelmas 1233, but it was not until a year later that the king could be persuaded to heed them, after des Roches' fall. There is evidence too that, just as during his earlier period as sheriff, des Roches resumed his clearances and intrusions in the royal forest.[99]

Besides his new-found prominence in county affairs, the bishop

---

[94]   *CPR 1232–47*, p. 13; *Memoranda Rolls 1231–3*, no. 2800. For Wacelin's background see *Acta*, appendix 4, no. 25. For complaints against his shrieval administration, none of them very serious, see JUST1/775, mm. 17d, 18d.

[95]   *Cal. Chart. R. 1226–57*, pp. 140, 145–6, 169, 176.

[96]   Ms. 28DR, m. 17.

[97]   *Cl.R.1231–4*, p. 21.

[98]   *Cl.R.1231–4*, pp. 105, 234, 253–4, 265, and see also *Cl.R.1227–31*, p. 552.

[99]   Keene, *Survey of Medieval Winchester*, pp. 72–3; *Winchester in the Early Middle Ages*, ed. D. Keene et al. (Oxford 1976), pp. 255–6; *CRR*, xv, no. 1033.

was once again promoted at court as a leading speculator in feudal incidents. To begin with, there were the various royal escheats granted him to endow his new religious foundations. In 1232 he benefited materially from the arrest of the royal justice, Master Robert of Shardlow, for complicity in the anti-Roman riots. Des Roches acquired Shardlow's lease over the lands of Thomas Testard, a long-standing creditor of the bishop, whose debts could now be called in.[100] For many years des Roches had been associated with the Anglo-Norman family of Marmion. In July 1233 he acquired a seven-year custody over the entire Marmion estate in England, including the wardship and marriage of Philip Marmion. The award was drawn up by Philip's father, Robert, and looks suspiciously as if des Roches were obtaining settlement of a debt.[101] Robert himself had been the bishop's ward between 1219 and 1221, and it may be that some sort of financial obligation still lingered. In any event, des Roches was still in control of the Marmion estate and of its chief castle, Tamworth, at the time of his death in 1238.[102]

One other wardship may have been acquired by des Roches. The annals of Tewkesbury and Hailes state that the bishop was given custody of Richard de Clare, heir to the earldom of Gloucester.[103] Unbeknown to the court and whilst he was still a ward of de Burgh, Richard de Clare had been betrothed to de Burgh's daughter Megotta.[104] His whereabouts are unrecorded between 1232 and the spring of 1234, when he appears together with his brother William, and a schoolmaster, as a long-term guest at Windsor castle.[105] We have seen that after 1232 the fate of the Gloucester lands is itself somewhat mysterious. Their keeper appears never to have accounted for them to the royal Exchequer, and no receipts from them are recorded save for one small payment into the chamber, made in December 1232. Until at least the following May they were to be treated as a royal custody under the general authority of Peter de Rivallis, but thereafter nearly a year passes without their being so

---

[100] *Cl.R.1231–4*, pp. 68, 110–11. Testard's debts represented relief on a tenth of a fee held of the bishop at Tongham, Surrey, and the arrears of his late brother, Master Robert Testard, a former episcopal bailiff; Mss. 27DR, mm. 8d, 9, 12d; 28DR, m. 17; *The 1235 Surrey Eyre*, ed. Meekings, i, pp. 245–6.

[101] *Cal. Chart. R. 1226–57*, p. 186, and see above pp. 162–3, 193–4.

[102] *CPR 1232–47*, p. 231; *Cal. Chart. R. 1226–57*, p. 248; *Cl.R.1237–42*, p. 62.

[103] *AM*, i, p. 86; BL ms. Cotton Cleopatra D iii (Hailes annals), f. 42r, and see the rather vague remarks in M. Altschul, *A Baronial Family in Medieval England: The Clares, 1217–1314* (Baltimore 1970), pp. 60–1.

[104] Powicke, *Henry III and the Lord Edward*, pp. 760–8.

[105] E372/78, m. 16.

much as mentioned.[106] It seems possible that, in the meantime, their revenues were diverted to des Roches. The Hailes annalist states specifically that the bishop's custody of Richard de Clare led to dissension amongst the English baronage, who claimed that the boy should more properly have been entrusted to his step-father, Richard of Cornwall.[107] Two years earlier, Richard of Cornwall had been married to the widowed countess of Gloucester, sister of Richard Marshal, in whose right he controlled dower in the Gloucester estates. In August 1233 des Roches was briefly to be granted custody of the heir to the earldom of Devon, together with Carisbrooke and Christchurch castles, only to resign these custodies a fortnight later in favour of Richard of Cornwall, no doubt in an attempt to balance favours at court.[108] However, sincere though this attempt may have been, there can be little doubt that des Roches was amongst the principal, material beneficiaries of royal patronage after 1232. Until his fall eighteen months later, he was to remain in near daily attendance upon the king. Although his interventions were to be less obtrusive and his self-advancement less blatant than that of colleagues such as de Rivallis or Seagrave, it is impossible to ignore the fact, trumpeted by the chroniclers, that it was des Roches who exercised the greatest single influence over the king. To this extent, the political crisis about to engulf the court was very much of the bishop's own making.

[106] *Cal.Lib.R.1226–40*, pp. 193, 208–9; *Cl.R.1231–4*, pp. 222, 442–3; *CPR 1232–47*, pp. 35, 54; *Memoranda Rolls 1231–3*, no. 2435.

[107] BL ms. Cotton Cleopatra D iii, f. 42r: (1233) *Orta est discensio inter Henricum regem et inter quamplures de magnatibus suis ut comes Ricardus Marescallus, Ricardus Siward, Gilbertus Basset et alii plures, propter Petrum de Ripariis episcopum Winton', eo quod rex tradidit ei custodiam Ricardi de Clara quin potius dictam custodiam tradisset fratri suo comiti Cornubie qui matrem dicti Ricardi de Clara duxit in uxorem, asserentes quod dictam custodiam dicto comiti Cornubie decentius convenisset quam episcopo*, a reference first drawn to my attention by David Carpenter.

[108] *CPR 1232–47*, p. 23; *Cl.R.1231–4*, pp. 252–3.

Chapter 11

THE GATHERING STORM

The king's coffers were now well supplied. Yet throughout his life, Henry III exhibited a remarkable talent for spending more than he possessed. Besides taxation and the income from escheats, in March 1233 he turned to the Jews to provide even further money. The Jews had been used the previous year to finance loans from Italian merchants. The intention in 1233, as on that earlier occasion, appears to have been to use Jewish money to fund subsidies to the king's allies in France. On 2 March, a Jewish tallage of 10,000 marks was announced, £1,000 of it to be paid by Easter 1234, the rest at £2,000 a year thereafter: a scheme witnessed by des Roches. Not only was this the heaviest single tax as yet demanded from the Jews, but it fell upon those least able to pay, the great Jewish money-lenders of Norwich and Hereford being exempt by virtue of the heavy fines they had already made with the crown.[1] The tallage appears to have been part of a wider attack. In April 1233, whilst the king was spending Easter at Canterbury, he issued legislation restricting the rate of interest on Jewish loans to twopence in the pound per week, insisting that loans be made by cyrograph not tally, prohibiting the use of church goods as security and ordering that Jews unable to find pledges for good conduct by Michaelmas be banished from the realm.[2]

Many of these restrictions appear to have been copied directly from statutes issued over the past few years by the Capetian kings of France. The means by which they were transmitted into England are uncertain; perhaps via the aliens at court such as des Roches and de Rivallis, perhaps via the Frenchman Simon de Montfort, who only the previous year had expelled the Jews from Leicester. Just as in the 1240s Henry's rebuilding of Westminster Abbey was carried out in

---

[1] CPR 1232–47, pp. 12–13. I cannot agree with Stacey, *Politics, Policy and Finance*, p. 144, and his attempt to redate the tallage to 1232. There is no mention of the new levy on the roll of the Jewry for Hilary/Easter 1233, which nonetheless refers to earlier tallages of 2, 000, 4, 000 and 6, 000m; E401/1565.

[2] H. G. Richardson, 'Glanville continued', *The Law Quarterly Review* 54 (1938), p. 393.

conscious and competitive imitation of Louis IX's work at the Sainte-Chapelle, so a decade earlier Henry may have set out deliberately to emulate the French king's policy towards the Jews. In so doing, he may have hoped to win favour from the English church, which for many years had frowned upon official exploitation of Jewish money-lending. It is no coincidence that the anti-Jewish statutes of 1233 were issued at Canterbury, in the midst of an acrimonious dispute over election to the vacant archbishopric, perhaps as part of an attempt to heal the ever-widening breach between the king and the English bishops.[3] At the same time, there is considerable irony in the prospect of an administration, dominated by alien ministers, already subject to anti-alien rhetoric in the country at large, seeking to recover popularity by an attack against the Jews. Just as the most vociferous criticism of aliens at court had long tended to come from those whose own identity as Englishmen was, to say the least, questionable, so in the 1230s the king's alien ministers, des Roches and de Rivallis, may have connived in the persecution of a social group, the Jews, which could be considered even further beyond the pale than the aliens themselves. Those who feel insecure are often the first to play upon the insecurity of others. Persecuted minorities are seldom slow to find a target upon which to practise persecution of their own. In 1233 the king's French ministers fell victim to a xenophobic attack, headed by Richard Marshal, himself very nearly a Frenchman. Thereafter, hoping to improve their popularity in England, the aliens connived in a campaign against the Jews; a campaign which itself was copied directly from the Capetian kings of France. Once again, we must be wary of picturing the political tensions of the 1230s in simple black and white, aliens versus Englishmen. In fact, the situation was rich with irony and subtle overtones.

Meanwhile the influx of cash, from the Jews and from so many other sources, at last enabled the king to honour his promises to Brittany. Duke Peter crossed to England. On 26 April he and Simon de Montfort were entertained by des Roches.[4] The king acknowledged debts of 10,000 marks to the duke to cover all arrears, 6,000

[3] In general, see Vincent, 'Jews, Poitevins, and the bishop of Winchester', pp. 129–32. The restriction of interest to twopence in the pound is possibly related to a writ found in Westminster Abbey ms. Muniments no. 6719, drawn to my attention by Robert Stacey, addressed to the sheriff and cyrographer of Nottingham and dated at Westminster, 26 May, ordering them to accept no Jewish bond in which interest exceeded twopence in the pound per week, in place of an earlier 'assize' in which interest had been restricted to threepence in the pound.
[4] Ms. 28DR, m. 8, which speaks of the earl of Leicester, more likely to be a reference to Simon than Aimery de Montfort, although Simon was only granted his title officially in 1238.

marks to be paid immediately and a further 2,500 marks at Christmas. The remainder was to be discounted. At the same time Peter's forcible occupation of St James de Beuvron received tacit recognition, with the king agreeing to reimburse 1,800 marks, calculated as Peter's expenses from the date of the death of the earl of Chester to Christmas 1233.[5] In late April the massive sum of 7,800 marks was paid over to Peter in cash. In addition, at least another 1,000 marks was distributed amongst his Breton followers. Two days later des Roches witnessed writs of *liberate* authorizing the payment of a further 1,500 marks, the Easter term owed to the king's pensioners in Poitou.[6] Within a week the treasury had disgorged over 10,000 marks, a vast sum, equivalent to the entire Jewish tallage ordered the previous month, or almost half the proceeds of the lay fortieth, all of it shipped across the Channel to Brittany and Poitou.

The implication of all this is that des Roches and the new regime were anxious to promote a more vigorous approach towards reconquering the Plantagenet lands in France. And yet, as we have seen, their real interest lay in consolidation rather than in organizing a new continental campaign. In order to secure the king's French alliances they were prepared to indulge in lavish expenditure, but no attempt was made to organize an army of reconquest. On the contrary, in July 1233 Philip de Aubigné and the bishop of Rochester were sent overseas to negotiate an extension of the Anglo-French truce agreed in 1231.[7]

THE CANTERBURY ELECTION AND THE CHURCH

Since the summer of 1232 the English church had been in turmoil. The monasteries were disturbed by a general visitation ordered by the pope. Several refused to admit their local diocesans as visitor, launching appeals in Rome. According to Wendover the visitation was entrusted particularly to members of the Premonstratensian and Cistercian orders, the principal recipients of des Roches' religious patronage.[8] Meanwhile the campaign of 1232 against Roman clergy

5   *Cal.Lib.R.1226–40*, pp. 210, 239.
6   *Ibid.*, pp. 210–12; E401/10B, m.1, shows that all the promises to Brittany and Poitou were honoured.
7   *DD*, nos. 234–5.
8   Wendover, *Flores*, iv, pp. 258–63; *AM*, i (Tewkesbury), p. 89, iii (Dunstable), p. 132; Paris, *CM*, iii, pp. 238–40; *Bartolomei de Cotton Historia Anglicana*, ed. H. R. Luard (RS 1859), p. 117; William of Andres in *MGHS*, xxiv, p. 771; *Cal.Pap.Reg.*, i, pp. 132–3. The abbots of Cîteaux (*Sistaus*) and ?Prémonté (*La Peruse*), may both have visited des Roches at Farnham in 1233; Ms. 28DR, m. 8.

had been followed by a general enquiry into damages and the restitution that should be made. Early in 1233 various of those accused of involvement in the attacks were released from gaol.[9] De Burgh's private estate was set aside, supposedly to finance compensation for the rioters' victims. In March, Ranulph and William le Breton were excused the bulk of their massive fines of the previous autumn.[10] At much the same time, the abbot of St Edmunds set out for Rome, spurred on by an appeal against the visitation of his house. He had been des Roches' fellow inquisitor into the anti-Roman riots, and it may be that he carried with him to Rome a report on the enquiry's findings. The pope's response, issued in April 1233, was to empower des Roches and others to reduce the value of English benefices held by Rufinus, a nephew of the former legate Guala and a principal target of the rioters of 1232.[11] It also appears that des Roches' enquiry had laid accusations against bishop Roger of London. Since the chroniclers speak of Roger strenuously defending Roman clerks within his own diocese, his disgrace in 1233 probably owed more to his political sympathies, above all his support for Hubert de Burgh, than to any real evidence of wrongdoing. He was nonetheless forced to seek absolution in Rome.[12] Nor was he the only bishop to fall foul of the new regime. Following bishop Mauclerk's dismissal from the treasury, the bishops of Bath and Durham had stepped into the breach, but they too vanish once Mauclerk's accounts had been rendered, thereafter witnessing only occasional royal charters.[13] Besides the chancellor Ralph de Neville, des Roches became the sole churchman in regular attendance upon the king, an isolated position he had last occupied between 1208 and 1213, the years of the papal Interdict. Wendover states that in 1233 it was des Roches who sought to persuade the king that the bishops were his enemies, but the records suggest that it was the bishops themselves who shunned

---

[9] *Cl.R.1231–4*, pp. 183, 189–90.

[10] *Ibid.*, p. 188; C60/32, mm. 2, 6.

[11] *CPR 1232–47*, p. 13; *Cal.Pap.Reg.*, i, p. 132, and for the abbot, said to have been suspended from office, see *AM*, i (Tewkesbury), p. 89.

[12] Wendover, *Flores*, iv, pp. 233, 263, and see *Cal.Pap.Reg.*, i, p. 132.

[13] They appear together on 4 May, the bishop of Bath occasionally through July–October 1233; C53/27, mm. 1–2, 5–10. The bishop of Ely witnesses a charter on 19 October, the archbishop of York and the bishop of Rochester on 11 July, the latter bishop making occasional appearances at the Exchequer in November 1233 and January 1234; C53/27, mm. 1, 2; E159/13, mm. 8, 9d, 11d; *Foedera*, p. 210. William Brewer, bishop of Exeter, makes an isolated appearance as witness to a royal charter on 13 January 1234; Stratford upon Avon, Shakespeare Birthplace Library ms. Saunders Transcripts E1/66, ff. 15v–17v no. 489.

court.[14] Vigorous attempts were made to win them back. In July 1233 charters of confirmation were issued for bishop Jocelin of Bath and his brother the bishop of Lincoln. The bishop of Ely was confirmed in various liberties and granted the amercements of his men, return of writs and forest privileges, all of which had been disputed in the eyre of 1232. In return the bishop fined 500 marks, paid almost immediately, a bargain price compared to the sum extracted for similar liberties in 1232 from the bishop of Norwich.[15] Bishop Ralph de Neville of Chichester, politically far more significant than the bishop of Ely, was charged nothing at all for a wide-ranging collection of privileges, including the right to take amercements, and return of writs.[16] In the north, the bishop of Durham and the abbot of St Mary's York offered 700 marks for the disafforestation of all land between the rivers Ouse and Derwent, where their rights had been disputed for more than a decade. Their fine was to be accepted the following year, after des Roches' fall.[17] Meanwhile, the archbishop of York was allowed to purchase the custody and marriage of a royal ward.[18] Most of these proffers and awards were made in the early summer of 1233, at a time when the king was particularly anxious to obtain support in his attack against Richard Marshal. Nonetheless, the bishops remained universally mistrustful of des Roches, ranking amongst the most outspoken critics of his regime.

The cause of their mistrust is obvious. Many of the bishops were pupils of archbishop Langton, or his fellow exiles from the time of the Interdict of John's reign. In 1224 they had co-operated with Langton in toppling des Roches from power. Their ability to take collective action had been reinforced after Langton's death by the need to cope with prolonged vacancies in the archbishopric of Canterbury. By the spring of 1233, Canterbury had been vacant for nearly two years. Bids by the cathedral's monks and by the chancellor, Neville, had come to nothing. However, in the immediate aftermath of de Burgh's fall, the king had assented to the election of Master John Blund, a scholar and canon of

---

[14] Wendover, *Flores*, iv, p. 265.
[15] *Cal. Chart. R. 1226–57*, pp. 183–5; *CPR 1232–47*, p. 21; *Cl.R.1231–4*, p. 138; C60/32, m. 4; E372/77, m. 9d. For the bishop of Norwich's fine see above pp. 284, 291.
[16] *Cal. Chart. R. 1226–57*, pp. 177–80.
[17] *RLC*, i, p. 417; *Cl.R.1227–31*, p. 225; *Cl.R.1231–4*, pp. 56, 169, 187, 232–3, 477; C60/32, m. 5d; C47/12/7 no. 75; C60/33, m. 5; Durham, Prior's Kitchen Library ms. Cartuarium III, ff. 213v–214r. The fine paid in 1234 was raised to 800m to cover the disafforestation of Langwith Hay, excluded from the proffer of 1233.
[18] C60/32, m. 4.

Chichester, recently employed as royal envoy to Rome.[19] Blund had sat at the Exchequer since 1230 and was generally regarded as a placeman of des Roches.[20] Whether or not des Roches engineered his election to Canterbury, he undoubtedly did everything in his power to ensure its confirmation. He is said to have loaned or given Blund up to 2,000 marks and to have written to the emperor Frederick II on his behalf.[21] Throughout the next eighteen months, des Roches was to vet the appointment of royal proctors to Rome. Many of the men selected were veterans of Henry III's minority: Master William de St Aubin, Master John of Caen and Master John of Limoges, des Roches' household clerk and a one-time advocate of Fawkes de Bréauté. Another diplomatic envoy, Master Simon de Etelan, alias Simon the Norman, began his career at court during the years of des Roches' ascendancy.[22] Also in Rome, the bishop's protégé Henry of Avranches, composed over 200 lines of verse in support of Blund's election. Addressed to the pope, Henry's verses vilified Blund's opponents by associating them with the anti-Roman riots of 1232. But unfortunately for des Roches, Blund was known to hold two benefices, without papal dispensation, a charge that not even Henry of Avranches could deny.[23] Moreover, it is clear that Blund's candidature aroused widespread opposition both in England and in Rome, precisely because of his close association with des Roches.

Since his crusade and his subsequent residence in Italy, des Roches had basked in the confidence of pope Gregory, a confidence that helped the bishop enormously in his campaign against de Burgh. Yet the pope's support was by no means unqualified. In February 1233 de Burgh's close confinement in chains was ended, perhaps in expectation of papal letters insisting that he be released from captivity

---

[19] *Fasti*, ii, p. 6.

[20] In general, see D. A. Callus, 'Introduction of Aristotelian learning to Oxford', *PBA* 29 (1943), pp. 241–9; Emden, *Biographical Register of the University of Oxford*, p. 206; *Cl.R.1227–31*, pp. 80, 109, 342.

[21] Wendover, *Flores*, iv, p. 267; Paris, *CM*, iii, p. 243; Paris, *Hist. Ang. Min.*, ii, p. 355; *AM*, iv (Osney), pp. 73–4.

[22] *Pat. R. 1225–32*, p. 508; *CPR 1232–47*, pp. 11–14, 33; F. M. Powicke, 'Master Simon the Norman', *EHR* 58 (1943), pp. 330–43, reprinted in *Henry III*, pp. 772–83. For Master John of Limoges, see *Acta*, appendix 4, no. 33. For Master John of Caen, see *Acta Guala*, no. 140n.

[23] *Henry of Avranches*, ed. Russell, pp. 127–36. Line 110 (p. 132) speaks of letters in Blund's support from the chancellor, possibly the chancellor of the University of Oxford, but more likely to be Ralph de Neville, in whose cathedral church of Chichester Blund was a canon, and whose nephew Blund is known to have guided in his reading; SC1/6/56, noted by J. and L. Stones, 'Bishop Ralph Neville', p. 255.

altogether.[24] Throughout the spring, as des Roches' agents pressed
the cause of John Blund, it is clear that an opposition party was just as
active against him. An alternative candidate for the archbishopric,
Master Edmund of Abingdon, was already being canvassed from
within this opposition group. Blund's unpopularity was partly political, partly scholastic in origin. As a teacher at Oxford, he is chiefly
remembered for his championing of the newly translated works of
Aristotle. His *Tractatus de Anima* follows sound Aristotelian principles
and as such represents a challenge to the Augustinian philosophy of
more conservative Oxford *magistri*.[25] It would be wrong to assume
that des Roches was unaware of such scholastic wrangles. His earliest
diocesan official, Master John of London, may have been one of the
first men to teach the new Aristotle at Oxford, a decade or more in
advance of Blund. Des Roches' nephew, Peter de Rivallis, may well
have studied at Oxford. Certainly the bishop sponsored other *alumni*
of the Oxford schools. John of Ardfert, des Roches' suffragan, was
studying there in 1229. Master Humphrey de Millières, one of the
bishop's closest familiars, owned houses in Oxford used as lodgings by
the son of Henry III's seneschal of Poitou. In 1231 alternative
accommodation had to be found for the boy so that Humphrey might
resume his studies.[26] The furore caused by Blund's election to Canterbury may well explain des Roches' clash in the summer of 1233 with
one of the more conservative Oxford *magistri*, Master Robert Bacon,
a close friend of Edmund of Abingdon, and a man whose teaching on
the soul ran directly contrary to that of Blund. At a meeting of the
king's council in June 1233, Robert is said to have preached a sermon,
employing puns on the name Peter des Roches, recommending that
the king steer between the rocks and the stones if the ship of state

[24] *AM*, i (Tewkesbury), p. 88. On 7 February de Burgh's wife was asked to speak with
the sheriff of Norfolk and Suffolk about letters obtained in Rome on her husband's
behalf; *Cl.R.1231–4*, p. 296. These may be linked to the disgrace of Richard de St
John, a former chaplain of de Burgh, sent to Rome as an envoy of the new regime in
October 1232, but in March of the following year, deprived of his lands and benefices,
perhaps because in secret he had used his mission to work on de Burgh's behalf;
Cl.R.1231–4, pp. 86, 202, 431; *Cal.Pap.Reg.*, p. 131. The papal registers for 1233 are
extremely sketchy. On 3 May the pope wrote to Henry III urging clemency towards
de Burgh; SC7/15/8.
[25] Callus, 'Introduction of Aristotelian learning', pp. 247–52; *Iohannes Blund: Tractatus de
Anima*, ed. D. A. Callus and R. W. Hunt, Auctores Britannici Medii Aevi, ii (London
1970), esp. intro. pp. vii–xii. For the opposition, see B. Smalley, 'Robert Bacon and
the early Dominican school at Oxford', *TRHS* 4th series, 30 (1948), pp. 1–19, esp.
p. 15.
[26] *Cl.R.1227–31*, pp. 265, 552; Emden, *Biographical Register of the University of Oxford*,
pp. 1496–7, and see above pp. 83–4.

were not to founder.[27] Previously regarded as entirely political in motivation, this outburst might better be seen as the outcome of des Roches' unwarranted dabbling in matters academic.

The Canterbury dispute gave rise to des Roches' first major setback. Around 1 June 1233, the pope quashed John Blund's election, outwardly as a consequence of his unlicensed pluralism, in fact, as the chroniclers recognize, because the pope was unwilling to grant des Roches control over both spiritual and temporal affairs. Instead, Canterbury's proctors were urged to nominate Edmund of Abingdon. This they refused to do without permission from their convent at home. But in due course both monastic and royal assent were forthcoming. By October 1233 Edmund's election merely awaited papal approval.[28] The king's assent to all of this may have been reluctant, but after so many years without a pastor it was essential both to Canterbury and the entire English church that the archbishopric be filled.

In 1233 it was the bishops and higher clergy that proved the first constituency openly to criticize des Roches. The same months which saw him worsted over Canterbury witnessed one other major setback for his regime. Towards the end of March there were violent rains, heralding one of the wettest summers in memory. The political disputes between des Roches and the Marshal were to be fought out against a background of rain and flood.[29] Virtually every chronicler has a particular local disaster to report: inundations at Worcester on 22 May, and at Winchester on 19 July. A few days earlier, the conventual buildings at Waverley were struck by flood, the water rising as high as eight feet. Bridges and houses were swept away. The Winchester pipe rolls bear out remarks in the annals of Osney that meadows were left unmown; whatever hay could be reaped simply rotted in the barns during a hot, humid autumn. The effects of all this, not least upon the yield of the king's tax of a fortieth, must have been severe. Des Roches' manorial profits fell sharply after twenty years of near continual growth. Grain and fodder were in short supply.[30] Added to

---

[27] Wendover, *Flores*, iv, p. 268; Paris, *CM*, iii, pp. 244–5. For Bacon and his contacts with Edmund, see Smalley, 'Robert Bacon', pp. 1–19; Emden, *Biographical Register of the University of Oxford*, p. 87.

[28] Wendover, *Flores*, iv, p. 267; *Cal.Pap.Reg.*, i, p. 135; William of Andres in *MGHS*, xxiv, pp. 772–3; C. H. Lawrence, *St Edmund of Abingdon* (Oxford 1960), pp. 124–8; *Fasti*, ii, pp. 6–7.

[29] Wendover, *Flores*, iv, p. 266; Paris, *CM*, iii, pp. 242–3.

[30] *AM*, ii (Winchester), p. 86, (Waverley), p. 312, iv (Osney), p. 74, (Worcester), p. 425; Ms. 28DR, *passim* esp. mm. 15, 15d, 16d.

the economic effects, there was a more deep-seated air of depression and unease. Some regarded the rains as a portent of divine discontent. Their arrival coincided with the first signs of a more serious crisis in des Roches' relations, not only with the church, but with the English lay baronage.

FOREIGN RELATIONS: FRANCE, SCOTLAND, WALES AND IRELAND

De Burgh's fall in 1232 had caused considerable problems in the outlying areas of Plantagenet dominion, where previously his regime had guaranteed some sort of stability. Only in Poitou and Gascony, the areas with which they were personally most familiar, did des Roches and his colleagues achieve any success, and then only after a massive injection of funds and following a period of several months, in which the new seneschal of Gascony, Hugh de Vivonne, faced armed resistance. Nonetheless, by the summer of 1233 Vivonne's predecessor, Henry de Trubleville, had been brought to heel. In July 1233 the king was able to open negotiations with the French for a renewal of the truce, due to expire in twelve months' time.[31]

Less successful were the relations between des Roches' regime and the outlying areas of the British Isles. As brother-in-law of the Scottish king Alexander II, Hubert de Burgh had done much to guarantee peace between England and Scotland. His fall raised fears that Hubert's Scottish allies would come to his rescue. Amongst the victims of 1232, both Ranulph le Breton and bishop Mauclerk sought refuge or assistance in Scotland.[32] Previously, the kings of Scotland had been denied any ceremony of crowning by a bishop, a reminder of the theoretical subjection to England of the Scottish monarchy and church. However, in May 1233 there were rumours that Alexander II was considering a new style of coronation, prompting appeals from Henry III and the archbishop of York. There were signs too of violent disturbances in the north. By the summer of 1233 these were to necessitate an expensive garrisoning of the borders.[33]

Even more alarming was the situation in Wales and Ireland. De

---

[31] Stacey, *Politics, Policy and Finance*, pp. 172–6; *Cal.Pap.Reg.*, i, p. 134; *Foedera*, p. 210; *CPR 1232–47*, pp. 11, 14–15, 22, 25; *Cl.R.1231–4*, p. 221. Trubleville had returned to court in England by 17 June 1233; C53/27, m. 4.

[32] *Cl.R.1227–31*, p. 562; *CRR*, xv, no. 1074.

[33] *CPR 1232–47*, p. 16. For the Scots coronation, see *The Acts of Malcolm IV King of Scots 1153–1165*, ed. G. W. S. Barrow, Regesta Regum Scottorum, i (Edinburgh 1960), p. 27. In 1231 the north of Scotland had come under attack from a major Norwegian force, which may add significance to Henry III's continuing good relations with

Burgh's disgrace preceded the death of the earl of Chester by only a few months and coincided with vacancies in the great Marcher lordships of Briouze and Clare. Henceforth the entire March, from the Dee to the Wye, lay open to attack. In December 1232 a truce had been agreed with the Welsh, with arbitrators appointed to establish terms. But no settlement was reached. Instead, in March 1233, in the immediate aftermath of his withdrawal from court, the earl Marshal joined his brother-in-law, Richard of Cornwall, in driving Llywelyn from Radnor.[34] Their offensive was almost certainly launched without the approval of Henry III or his ministers, since it wrecked the chances of a truce and provided Llywelyn with a convenient pretext for reopening hostilities of his own. The Marshal presumably hoped to cement an alliance with Richard of Cornwall, to re-establish control over Radnor, part of the Briouze March in Cornwall's custody, and to assert his supremacy over the lesser Marcher barons, left leaderless by the death of so many of the greater tenants-in-chief. Yet there were deeper motives at work, and older wounds being reopened on the Marches, none more painful than those of the Briouze family.

King John's favourite, William de Briouze, had at one time commanded a vast estate, comprising the Sussex rape of Bramber, the honour of Totnes, land in Munster in Ireland, and two substantial Welsh lordships: the Gower peninsula with Swansea, and the central Marches west of Hereford including the castles of Grosmont, Skenfrith, Llantilio, Hay-on-Wye, Brecon, Radnor and Abergavenny. But in 1210 William fell victim to the most vicious attack of a notoriously vicious reign. His wife and eldest son were put to death by King John. William himself was hounded into exile. His lordship was permanently dismembered.[35] By the late 1220s it had been divided between two of his grandsons. John de Briouze held Bramber and Gower; William de Briouze the younger, John's cousin, controlled Totnes and the castles west of Hereford. In the course of this partition, the Marcher castles of Grosmont, Skenfrith and Llantilio had been alienated in fee to Hubert de Burgh, who also obtained John de Briouze's homage for Gower.[36] King John's attack left deep scars, especially amongst the baronage of Ireland and the Marches, a closely

Norway in 1233–4; A. O. Anderson (ed.), *Early Sources of Scottish History AD 500 to 1286*, 2 vols. (London 1922), ii, pp. 480ff; *CPR 1232–47*, p. 21; *Cl.R.1231–4*, p. 532, and see below pp. 417–18.

[34] *AM*, i (Tewkesbury), p. 88; *Annales Cambriae*, ed. J. Williams ab Ithel (RS 1860), p. 79.

[35] Painter, *King John*, pp. 238–50.

[36] Carpenter, *The Minority*, pp. 85, 138–9, 141–2, 179, 218–19, 246–7.

interrelated group resentful of any outside interference. It was in Ireland that William de Briouze had sought refuge, with William Marshal earl of Pembroke, and with his kinsmen Walter de Lacy and Hugh, Walter's brother, earl of Ulster. There had followed an invasion of Ireland by King John, in which the Lacys were forced to abandon Ulster, prompting more than a decade of skirmishing until they could obtain redress. The Marshal honour of Leinster was also brought under closer control. Meanwhile, John's attempt to restore order in Wales led to the importation into former Briouze custodies of aliens such as Girard de Athée and Fawkes de Bréauté, heightening resentment within Marcher society and leading to the first stirrings of baronial rebellion against the king.[37]

The memory of these events was to do much to determine Marcher sympathies for many years to come, and was to play a crucial role in the downfall of des Roches' regime of 1232–4. In the course of 1230, William de Briouze the younger was caught in adultery with the wife of Llywelyn ab Iorweth and ignominiously hung. Shortly afterwards John de Briouze was fatally injured in a riding accident.[38] Both men left only minors or daughters to succeed them. Coinciding with the disgrace of Hubert de Burgh, their deaths brought the entire Briouze lordship as constituted in 1210, back under crown control. Totnes was granted as dower to the widow of William de Briouze the younger, although the king retained possession of the castle.[39] The central Marches passed in custody to Richard of Cornwall, a stranger to the region and therefore a controversial choice as keeper.[40] Most provocative of all was the distribution of John de Briouze's estate and of the Welsh lordship confiscated from Hubert de Burgh. De Burgh's honours of Carmarthen and Cardigan, with their theoretical lordship over the Briouze honour of Gower, passed to Peter de Rivallis, as did custody of Glamorgan together with the castles of Cardiff and Newport, which de Burgh had held in his capacity as guardian of Richard de Clare. In practice, de Rivallis was required to depute custody of his castles to constables chosen by the king, including the alien knight Philip le Breton, who received charge of Gower and Swansea.[41] But this did not put an end to de Rivallis' interest in south

---

[37] Painter, *King John*, pp. 243–4.
[38] Walker, 'Hubert de Burgh and Wales', p. 483; *Brut y Tywysogyon or The Chronicle of the Princes (Peniarth Ms. 20 version)*, ed. T. Jones (Cardiff 1952), p. 231.
[39] *Cl.R.1227–31*, pp. 354–5; *Cl.R.1231–4*, p. 262.
[40] Denholm-Young, *Richard of Cornwall*, pp. 19–20; *AM*, i (Tewkesbury), p. 88.
[41] *Pat. R. 1225–32*, pp. 490–1, 500–1; *Cl.R.1231–4*, p. 198; *CPR 1232–47*, pp. 6, 17; *Cal. Chart. R. 1226–57*, p. 169.

Wales. In July 1232 he received both the Sussex and Welsh lands of John de Briouze, whose heir was to be betrothed to de Rivallis' niece. He also came to control St Briavel's castle and the forest of Dean as the king's bailiff for life. A few months later he was granted the castles of Grosmont, Skenfrith and Llantilio, which in the 1220s had been wrested by de Burgh from the Briouze estate. In due course the three castles were to be confirmed to de Rivallis in perpetual fee.[42] The implications of all this were only too clear. De Rivallis, an alien associated with precisely those aliens intruded into the Briouze estate by King John, was being promoted to a private and quite possibly hereditary lordship in the Marches, carved out from the former Briouze estates. His promotion was made possible by the turmoil in Marcher society brought about by the death or disgrace of most of the greater tenants-in-chief. But in turn, this turmoil, the threat of a Welsh attack, the resentment against aliens intruded as constables or keepers, and the Marchers' long-standing suspicion of the king's intentions, all combined to raise tensions to near fever pitch.

A similar situation greeted de Rivallis in Ireland.[43] De Burgh's nephew Richard had established some sort of *modus vivendi* as Irish Justiciar prior to 1232, attempting to push royal authority westwards into Connaught. As with Hubert's promotion in Wales, so Richard's advances in Ireland were resented by a powerful local constituency, especially amongst the Marshal following. Again as in Wales, once de Burgh fell from power it was not the Marshal who benefited but Peter de Rivallis, who in July 1232 received a grant of offices and lands in Ireland, including the five best cantreds of Connaught previously withheld from Richard de Burgh. The challenge to Hubert de Burgh implicit in this award may well have precipitated his downfall.[44] In September 1232, Richard de Burgh was removed as Irish Justiciar. Instead of promoting the Marshal or one of his associates in his place, the regime appointed the relatively neutral Maurice fitz Gerald.[45] Peter de Rivallis probably had little control over the selection of constables for the various castles supposedly in his keeping.[46] Nonetheless, in May 1233, when fitz Gerald petitioned to have the five cantreds of Connaught annexed to his title as Justiciar,

---

[42] *Pat. R. 1225–32*, pp. 502, 505; *CPR 1232–47*, pp. 2, 504; *Cal. Chart. R. 1226–57*, p. 185.
[43] In general, see Otway-Ruthven, *A History of Medieval Ireland*, pp. 92–8.
[44] Above pp. 307–8.
[45] *Pat. R. 1225–32*, p. 499.
[46] This at least is the implication of *CRR*, xv, nos. 1031, 1064, and see *CPR 1232–47*, p. 9, for evidence that de Rivallis had still to take up his offices in Ireland as late as January 1233.

the king refused, almost certainly to placate de Rivallis.[47] Meanwhile, Connaught itself was plunged into turmoil. Richard de Burgh refused to answer to the new regime, ignoring repeated summonses to England, and fortifying his castle of Meelick against the crown. The native Irish rose to sweep away every vestige of Plantagenet influence from Connaught. As in Wales, the problems of an already weak administration were compounded by association with the personal ambitions of Peter de Rivallis, increasingly at odds with the Marshal and his powerful network of allies and kin.[48] In 1231 it had been to Leinster, Pembroke and his outlying tenantry that Richard Marshal had turned for support when denied his inheritance in England. In March 1233 he repeated this appeal. His withdrawal from court was followed by an assault against Radnor designed to assert his leadership on the Marches, after which the Marshal sailed for Ireland, presumably to drum up support amongst his men in Leinster.

THE KING'S COUNCIL AND BARONIAL OPPOSITION APRIL–MAY 1233

In the immediate term, Richard Marshal's withdrawal led to no great disturbance at court. The Marshal had failed to cement any real alliance amongst the higher nobility. During the spring of 1233, the king continued to bestow gifts of venison and timber on Marshal kinsmen such as the earls of Cornwall and Derby, as if nothing were amiss.[49] What problems there were appear to have been between des Roches and the established royal household. The bishop continued to reap a rich harvest of personal favours. On 14 April he was granted a fair for his manor of Farnham. On the following day, William of Rowden, the Marshal's one remaining representative at court, made his last recorded appearance as witness to a royal charter.[50] Perhaps responding to rumours of trouble in Wales, as early as 24 April it was decided that the court would spend Pentecost (22 May) at Gloucester, convenient for negotiations on the Marches.[51] Meanwhile, on 4 May, the king was persuaded to issue a positive torrent of charters. Des Roches received the royal manor of Selborne on which to establish a house of religion. Simultaneously, Seagrave the Justiciar received

[47] *Cl.R.1231–4*, p. 306.
[48] *Ibid.*, p. 306; *CPR 1232–47*, pp. 8–9, 11; Orpen, *Ireland under the Normans*, iii, pp. 180–1; Wendover, *Flores*, iv, p. 225.
[49] *Cl.R.1231–4*, pp. 208–11.
[50] *Ibid.*, pp. 208, 210; *Cal. Chart. R. 1226–57*, p. 176; C53/27, m. 10.
[51] *Cl.R.1231–4*, p. 211.

various confirmations. A further eight such charters were granted to the royal steward, Ralph fitz Nicholas, and a staggering total of thirty-two was issued in favour of Ralph de Neville, the chancellor.[52] Most of these were simply renewals of earlier awards, but in addition, Neville was guaranteed life custody of the king's great seal and of the Chanceries of England and Ireland. He was also awarded the right to collect amercements taken from his men. A fortnight later, seven confirmations were issued on behalf of another of the royal stewards, Godfrey of Crowcombe.[53] Clearly there was unease over the king's treatment of charters, hence the eagerness of courtiers to have such awards renewed. But it was to be of little avail. In the aftermath of the council meeting at Gloucester, one of the king's first actions was to appoint the alien, Engelard de Cigogné, as keeper of the manor of Woodstock, which in theory had been guaranteed to Godfrey of Crowcombe for life. At the same time, Engelard was made sheriff of Oxfordshire, yet another office guaranteed to Crowcombe but wrested from him the previous December.[54] Crowcombe himself appears to have withdrawn from court in disgust. His experience showed that no manner of solemn confirmation could guarantee the king's charters or patents against arbitrary annulment. In due course Crowcombe's place as steward was filled by Aimery de St Amand, an alien for many years associated with des Roches.[55]

Besides the dismissal of Crowcombe, the Gloucester council of late May included a ceremony of knighthood in which the king belted Hugh de Vere, Roger Bigod and Thomas of Newburgh with their earldoms of Oxford, Norfolk and Warwick.[56] As with the earlier recognition afforded Richard of Cornwall, Simon de Montfort and Richard Marshal, the intention seems to have been to purchase support amongst the younger generation of the nobility, for several years frustrated by the denial of their titles or lands.[57] But the earls in question do not appear to have greeted their promotion in the spirit intended. There remained a serious divide between des Roches and the younger generation, who were sympathetic towards, if not openly allied with the Marshal. Besides the belting of earls, the Gloucester

[52] *Cal. Chart. R. 1226–57*, pp. 177–81.
[53] *Ibid.*, p. 181. As in January, when Crowcombe had received similar confirmations, the award was made whilst the king was staying at Woodstock, a manor in Crowcombe's keeping.
[54] *CPR 1232–47*, p. 16, and see above pp. 280, 299, 319–20.
[55] *CRR*, xv, p. xxxviii, and above pp. 160–1, 211, 214 n.172.
[56] *Cl.R.1231–4*, p. 219; *AM*, i (Tewkesbury), p. 90.
[57] Above pp. 266, 272–3.

ceremony also involved the knighting of many lesser men, perhaps as an outcome of the distraint of knighthood ordered the previous October. Doubtless many answered their summons. William Long-espée, for example, was knighted at Gloucester, although he was denied his father's title as earl of Salisbury.[58] Others, however, kept away: our first certain proof that there was an identifiable constituency amongst the lay baronage, deliberately ignoring summonses to court.

From Gloucester the court set out westwards, probably to inspect the state of the Marches. At Feckenham on 1 June, the king issued instructions for the appointment of watchmen, imposing a nationwide curfew upon every town and village, to last until Michaelmas 1233.[59] The watch is known to have been enforced in des Roches' county of Hampshire, where it resulted in a case of mistaken identity at Meonstoke in mid-September.[60] The fear of armed resistance which it reveals sprang, no doubt, from the refusal of various knights and barons to attend court, and from the increasing detachment of Richard Marshal.

Having gone north along the Welsh border to Wenlock, the king heard that behind him the Marshal intended holding a tournament at Worcester. On 6 June hurried instructions were issued, summoning the would-be participants to court.[61] On the same day the king authorized his first overtly hostile move against the Marshal. Since the previous autumn the Marshal had withheld payment of a substantial part of the annual sum of £400, agreed in lieu of dower in Ireland and Wales for the king's sister, Eleanor. The king now ordered that the money be recovered by distraint against the Marshal's lands.[62] On the following morning, before leaving Wenlock to intercept the malcontents at Worcester, Henry authorized distraints against a number of individuals believed hostile to the court. In the wake of his loss of Upavon a few months earlier, Gilbert Basset was now deprived of two further Norman manors theoretically guaranteed to him by royal charter, one of which, Sutton in Surrey, he had held since at least 1216.[63] In August 1233, Sutton was restored to its original, presumably Norman or alien heirs, in return for a fine of £100

58 *AM*, i (Tewkesbury), p. 90; *Cl.R.1231–4*, pp. 210–11, and see below pp. 383–4.
59 *Cl.R.1231–4*, pp. 309–10.
60 JUST1/775, m. 19.
61 *CPR 1232–47*, p. 17.
62 *Cl.R.1231–4*, p. 310.
63 *Ibid.*, p. 235; C60/32, mm. 4, 5; *RLC*, i, pp. 294, 346b, 587b, 595b, 612; *Cal. Chart. R. 1226–57*, pp. 56, 94; *CRR*, xiii, no. 928; *BF*, pp. 67, 253, 448, 614, covering the two manors of Kirtlington and Sutton.

supported by various pledges, including those of the aliens Engelard de Cigogné, Aimery de Chanceaux and Aimery de St Amand. The same heirs were also restored to manors in Essex, held before his disgrace by Hubert de Burgh.[64] The arbitrary seizure of Sutton in June 1233, rather than the earlier attack on Upavon, may lie behind Wendover's claim that Gilbert Basset was propelled into rebellion by the loss of a manor granted to him by King John, a description that would apply to Sutton but not to the better known case of Upavon.[65]

In addition to the attack against Gilbert Basset, on 7 June William Ferrers, son of the earl of Derby, was deprived of yet another Norman escheat guaranteed by royal charter from before 1216.[66] Hugh of Kinnersley, a knight attached to the Marcher baron Walter of Clifford, faced the confiscation of land in the forest of Dean. The king claimed it as assart, although Hugh had received it by royal charter as recently as 1227.[67] On the same day distraints were ordered against three men, Roger de Somery, Gilbert son of John of Sandford and William son of Drew of Montacute, for failing to attend the king at Pentecost to be knighted.[68] The attack against all three men appears to have been politically motivated. Sandford, a close contact of the Marshal and a kinsman of Gilbert Basset, very quickly fined to be restored.[69] Somery, like the young William Ferrers, was a cousin of Richard Marshal. In August 1233 he was restored to his lands in return for surrendering hostages.[70] William of Montacute was a kinsman and former ward of Alan Basset, father of Gilbert Basset, the principal trouble-maker in the summer of 1233.[71] Basset, Montacute,

---

[64] C60/32, m. 3, and for the Essex manors of Wickford and Canewdon also granted to the heirs of Master Urric the Engineer see *BF*, pp. 276, 1463; *Cal. Chart. R. 1226–57*, pp. 12, 82; *Cl.R.1231–4*, pp. 168, 179, 275; *CRR*, xv, no. 1895.

[65] Wendover, *Flores*, iv, pp. 269–70.

[66] C60/32, m. 5; *Cal. Chart. R. 1226–57*, p. 55, for the manor of Stebbing, Essex.

[67] C60/32, m. 5; *Cal. Chart. R. 1226–57*, p. 48; *Cl.R.1231–4*, pp. 231–2, 426. For Hugh and his association with the Cliffords, see *ibid.*, p. 257; *Cal.Lib.R.1226–40*, pp. 35, 47, 125–6; *Cal.Inq.P.M.*, i, nos. 324, 356.

[68] C60/32, m. 5.

[69] For Sandford's fine see C60/32, m. 4. For the kinship between the Basset and Sandford families, see London, College of Arms ms. Glover Collection A, ff. 99r–v, 106r.

[70] *Cl.R.1231–4*, p. 247; Sanders, *English Baronies*, p. 113.

[71] *CRR*, xii, nos. 826, 2227; Waugh, *The Lordship of England*, p. 211. He was related to the Montacute barons of Chiselborough, in whose inheritance des Roches had meddled prior to 1227 via his custody of Katherine, daughter of John of Montacute. Katherine subsequently married firstly Warin Basset (d.s.p. 1233), brother of Gilbert, and secondly Michael, son of the royal steward Ralph fitz Nicholas; *CRR*, xii, nos. 2093, 2243, 2667, xiii, nos. 24, 734, 816, 1110, 1150, 1909–10, 1921, 2494, 2765, xiv, nos. 269–70; Sanders, *English Baronies*, p. 34.

Kinnersley and William Ferrers were to remain at odds with the crown for much of the coming year.

The seizures of 7 June provide us with our earliest list of malcontents. They also raise an important point of law. The men attacked had failed to attend court when summoned. They may well have been suspected of participating in the forbidden gathering at Worcester, which had gone ahead despite the king's prohibition.[72] The court reached Worcester on 9 June, too late to apprehend the participants. The king was perfectly entitled to distrain the lands of those refusing summonses or taking part in a prohibited muster, provided always that such distraint was temporary, pending proper judgement in the king's courts. But those who suffered distraint in June 1233 had good reason to fear that they would be denied a proper hearing; that, as with the attacks upon liberties held by de Burgh, Mauclerk, Basset or Crowcombe, their own privileges by royal charter would be permanently overturned. Although various of those attacked came in to make their peace, others remained aloof, their numbers swollen as opposition to the king and suspicion of his intentions mounted. The chroniclers are agreed that whatever the contempt shown by the malcontents, the court itself, inspired no doubt by des Roches, failed to act properly. Instead of obtaining judgement by peers or by the law of the land, the methods proposed by Magna Carta as alternatives to arbitrary, royal will; the king began issuing *ultimata* to his discontented subjects. When those *ultimata* expired he began arbitrary confiscation of their lands.

HOSTAGES AND CASTLES JUNE 1233

It was not only amongst the king's own subjects that trouble was brewing. On 13 June instructions were issued for the defence of Strettondale in the Shropshire Marches.[73] On the same day, hostages were taken from a number of important Marcher barons. Ever since the Marshal's unlicensed attack against Radnor, there had been a risk that breaches of the truce with Wales might provoke a counter-attack from Llywelyn. Hostage-taking was almost certainly a pre-emptive gesture intended to forestall any further private offensives against the Welsh.[74] Nonetheless, it was a policy especially associated in men's

---

[72] The citizens of Worcester were later fined 100m for allowing the Marshal's men to gather: C60/32, m. 4, subsequently pardoned in full; E372/78, m. 10d.

[73] *CPR 1232–47*, p. 18.

[74] *Cl.R.1231–4*, pp. 312–13; Walker, 'The Anglo-Welsh wars', pp. 298–9.

minds with the detested reign of King John. Various of the hostages were entrusted to des Roches' factional adherents Engelard de Cigogné and Stephen of Seagrave. They were delivered up in the presence of the aliens des Roches, Peter de Maulay, Andrew de Chanceaux and Peter de Rivallis. To many, it must have seemed as if the worst practices of John's reign were being revived. On 13 June, new arrangements were made for the keeping of Devizes castle, presumably because of fears for the security of Hubert de Burgh. Walter de Goderville, a Norman follower of Fawkes de Bréauté, married to the widow of another of King John's henchmen, Philip of Oldcotes, was now appointed constable: a controversial choice and one which suggests that the committee of four earls and their four knightly delegates, set to keep de Burgh, could no longer be trusted by the king.[75] The bailey of Devizes had already been deputed to the custody of de Rivallis, kept separate from the castle's donjon held by the earls. Now even the donjon was ordered surrendered, although it was to take Goderville more than a month to obtain possession. Meanwhile the Marches were thrown into even greater turmoil. Welsh sources speak of an attack by Llywelyn against Brecon castle, probably in late June, after which the Welsh withdrew via Clun and Oswestry, burning and pillaging as they went.[76] Already the danger of an alliance between Llywelyn and the English malcontents must have been apparent to the king and his court.

A further set of summonses had been issued for a parliament to meet at Oxford around 24 June. In the interval, on 15 June, orders went out for the arrest of Gilbert Basset and Walter of Clifford. All of their lands were to be distrained and entrusted to the keeping of Peter de Rivallis.[77] Basset had apparently been driven into rebellion by the attacks on his estate. Clifford's grievances are less clear. Unlike Basset, he was no protégé of the Marshal earls of Pembroke, nor as far as can be established had he suffered any material loss at the hands of des Roches' regime. The attack against his vassal Hugh of Kinnersley, earlier in June, may be either a cause or a symptom of Clifford's rebellion. He himself was later to marry Margaret, daughter of Llywelyn and widow of John de Briouze. It may be that a prior

---

[75] *CPR 1232–47*, p. 20; *Cl.R.1231–4*, pp. 228, 236, 312–14; *Foedera*, p. 210. For Walter, presumably a native of Goderville, 3km from Bréauté, dep. Seine-Maritime, see *RLC*, ii, p. 20; *Pat. R. 1216–25*, pp. 185, 574; *Pat. R. 1225–32*, p. 434; Paris, *CM*, ii, p. 641, iii, pp. 5, 203; *Cal.Inq.P.M.*, i, nos. 181, 201.

[76] *Brut y Tywysogyon*, ed. Jones, p. 231. For the date see *Cl.R.1231–4*, p. 314.

[77] C60/32, m. 5.

association with Margaret led Clifford to adopt the cause of his Briouze kinsmen against de Rivallis and the courtiers preying upon the Briouze estates.[78] By contrast to Gilbert Basset whose lands lay almost entirely in England, Clifford belonged to precisely that sector of Marcher society which Richard Marshal would have been most anxious to attract to his cause. His breach with the court shows that to some extent, the Marshal had succeeded in his objective.

It was now the Marshal's turn to suffer confiscation. On 20 June he was deprived of the two Norman escheats that he had obtained from Chester's inheritance the previous autumn.[79] At much the same time, orders were issued for the destruction of property at Compton Bassett in Wiltshire, probably in retaliation for some sort of attack by Gilbert Basset, the start of his notorious campaign of guerrilla warfare. Although as yet there had been no formal judgement against him, Basset was effectively being treated as an outlaw. The reprisals against Compton were to be directed by Walter de Goderville, suggesting that Gilbert's offence may have included a sortie against Devizes. This is all the more likely, given Gilbert's recent service as constable of Devizes, one of the offices he had lost to Peter de Rivallis in 1232. Gilbert knew Devizes and its region well. Already he may have realized the advantages of linking his own grievances to those of the imprisoned Hubert de Burgh.[80]

The court now settled at Woodstock to await the parliament summoned for 24 June. Patronage continued to be bestowed on a controversially factional basis. Anketil Malory, a kinsman of the Justiciar Seagrave, received the manor of Arley, Staffs. in perpetual fee, formerly part of de Burgh's private estate. Another of Seagrave's relations, Hugh Despenser, was confirmed in possession of land in Rutland long the subject of contention with the earl of Hereford, who claimed to have been unjustly deprived of it by King John.[81] Not until 27 June, three days after the appointed date, did the king move on from Woodstock to Oxford. By then it must have been apparent that the Marshal and most of his fellow malcontents would boycott the court. Various conciliatory gestures were attempted. For a fine of 40 marks Hugh of Kinnersley was restored to the lands seized

---

[78] For the marriage, first mentioned in November 1234, see Sanders, *English Baronies*, p. 36; *CP*, ii, p. 302; *Cl.R.1234–7*, p. 5.

[79] C60/32, m. 4. For the manors of Twyford and West Kington, see above p. 321 and n. 40.

[80] *Cl.R.1231–4*, pp. 311–14; *CPR 1232–47*, pp. 19–20.

[81] *Cl.R.1231–4*, pp. 231–2; *Cal. Chart. R. 1226–57*, p. 182. For Ryhall, see *ibid.*, pp. 57, 125; *RLC*, i, pp. 216b, 349b; *CRR*, xv, nos. 1087, 1190, 1293; *BF*, pp. 618, 1150.

from him in Herefordshire.[82] William Ferrers' manor of Stebbing was restored to his father, the earl of Derby. Richard Marshal himself was licensed to retain the summer term of rents paid at Twyford.[83] Yet the Marshal, Ferrers, Kinnersley and their associates were not to be bought off. The Oxford parliament for the first time saw something approaching a common front between lay and clerical opposition. It was at Oxford that Henry received news of the quashing of John Blund's election to Canterbury, and it was at Oxford too that Master Robert Bacon preached his punning sermon against des Roches.[84]

The king now made his way back to London. According to Wendover, he had agreed to summon the malcontents a further three times.[85] If they still refused to attend, they were presumably to be judged outlaws, their lands forfeit to the crown. Meanwhile distraint was renewed against the Marshal for dower payments to Eleanor. On 1 July the manor of Kirtlington, recently confiscated from Gilbert Basset, was conferred upon Henry de Trubleville, former seneschal of Gascony now restored to royal favour.[86] An alien knight of the royal household received land seized arbitrarily from Richard de St John, de Burgh's chaplain.[87] These were only the first of many such grants of rebel lands. They must have confirmed the worst fears of Basset and his associates, convinced that they were the victims of permanent confiscations, not merely of temporary distraint pending judgement in court.

THE WESTMINSTER PARLIAMENTS JULY 1233

Tensions on the March were building to a head. The king had summoned serjeants from four Marcher counties to attend him by 1 July. It was not a feudal summons. Those involved were offered wages, although the king still insisted that lists of absentees be drawn up. Special arrangements were made to recruit a defence force in the forest of Dean.[88] Custody of Montgomery and Snead on the central Marches was entrusted to William de Bouelles, an alien knight of the

[82] C60/32, m. 4 (*c.* 15 July).
[83] *Cl.R.1231–4*, pp. 231–2.
[84] Also at Oxford the bishops were persuaded to prohibit the holding of tournaments, a further sign of tension; *Cl.R.1231–4*, p. 233; Wendover, *Flores*, iv, p. 268; Paris, *CM*, iii, pp. 244–5; *CPR 1232–47*, p. 20.
[85] Wendover, *Flores*, iv, p. 268.
[86] *Cl.R.1231–4*, pp. 233, 235, 240.
[87] *Ibid.*, p. 234; *CRR*, xv, nos. 1222, 1311, for Stanstead, Essex.
[88] *Cl.R.1231–4*, p. 313; *CPR 1232–47*, p. 19.

royal household, previously active in Gascony and Poitou.[89] But it was not only on the Marches that there was trouble. At Devizes, the custody of Hubert de Burgh continued to give cause for alarm. Walter de Goderville was instructed to prevent the disobedient knights in possession of the donjon from obtaining victuals more than one day at a time. In due course, custody of both the bailey and the town of Devizes was conferred upon Ralph of Williton, a familiar of Peter de Rivallis.[90]

Fears for the safety of Devizes can only have been increased by the realization that one of the greatest Wiltshire landholders, William Longespée, was threatening to throw in his lot with the Marshal. By 30 June, Longespée had been required to surrender his daughter as hostage.[91] The girl was entrusted to the keeping of her grandmother, suggesting that the regime was anxious to tread carefully. Nonetheless, the mere fact that the king continued to take hostages must have been deeply disturbing to anyone with a memory of John's reign. Like the young William Ferrers, Longespée appears to have established good relations with his kinsman Richard Marshal.[92] In May 1233 he had attended court at the same time as the claimants to the earldoms of Oxford and Warwick. Both the latter were belted as earls, but Longespée was merely knighted, his claim to his father's earldom of Salisbury being implicitly denied.[93] The effect of this appears to have been to push Longespée close to the brink of rebellion. A charter that should probably be dated to the summer of 1233, shortly after his knighting at Gloucester, suggests that the earldom was very much in his thoughts: 'Know that we shall confirm (this present award) as soon as by divine grace we are invested with the sword of the earldom of Salisbury.' The charter is witnessed by Richard Marshal, William

---

[89] *CPR 1232–47*, pp. 18, 20. For Boeles (?Bouelles, dep. Seine-Maritime), see also *RLC*, i, p. 475b; *Pat. R. 1225–32*, pp. 389, 433, 470; *Cl.R.1231–4*, p. 196; Paris, *CM*, iv, p. 628.

[90] *Cl.R.1231–4*, p. 312; *CPR 1232–47*, p. 20. For Williton, see *ibid.*, p. 95.

[91] *Cl.R.1231–4*, p. 233.

[92] Richard witnesses several Longespée charters, and in one instance is addressed by William as his 'dearest friend': *Lacock Abbey Charters*, ed. K. H. Rogers, Wiltshire Record Society, xxxiv (1978), nos. 6, 7, 18a; *The Cartulary of Bradenstoke Priory*, ed. V. C. M. London, no. 303.

[93] The explanation traditionally advanced for the denial of William's title is that the earldom of Salisbury was held by William's father *iure uxoris*, so that William himself could not inherit until after the death of his mother. However, in 1219, no such objection appears to have been raised to the claims of the younger William Marshal to the earldom of Pembroke, despite the fact that the earldom of Pembroke, like that of Salisbury, had descended by marriage, and that in 1219 William Marshal's mother was still alive. The parallels between these two cases may have been yet another factor, inclining Longespée towards support for Richard Marshal.

Ferrers and Gilbert Basset.[94] Clearly, Longespée was mixing in dangerous company.

The king's ultimatum of late June had specified a parliament at Westminster for 11 July. According to Wendover, the malcontents once again stayed away, sending messengers to demand the dismissal of des Roches and his fellow aliens. Unless this were done, they threatened to drive Henry from the throne and to install a new king in his place. In reply, des Roches recommended the king to make war against his rebellious subjects with the aid of foreign mercenaries. A new deadline was set for the Marshal and his supporters to submit by 1 August.[95] Telescoping the events of several weeks, Wendover then describes the attack against Basset, and the taking of hostages as if they were an outcome of the parliament of 11 July. Nonetheless he is probably correct to portray the king's response as one of defiance. Henceforth there are few signs of any attempt to appease the malcontents. On the contrary, the July parliament witnessed yet further promotion for des Roches and the aliens. The manor of Dartford, a Norman escheat held until 1232 by John de Burgh, was given first to Peter de Maulay, and then a few days later to the Poitevin earl of Aumale in perpetual fee. This marks Aumale's rehabilitation at court after an absence of nearly ten years. Henceforth, he appears as a regular witness to royal charters.[96] At much the same time, the king granted land to the Poitevin household knight William de Nersac, and to Aimery de Rivallis, perhaps synonymous with the bishop's nephew Aimery des Roches.[97] The manor of Sutton in Surrey, formerly Gilbert Basset's, was conferred during pleasure upon Jordan de Montmartin, another alien knight.[98] Macey de Plesset, in all likelihood a kinsman of the alien courtier John de Plesset, received

---

[94] Lacock Abbey, Wiltshire, mss. New Cartulary, ff. 8r, 9v; Old Cartulary, f. 10v: *Noverit universitas vestra quod cum divina prestante gratia insigniti fuerimus gladio comitatus Sar', non obstante priore confirmatione nostra, confirmabimus ...*, calendared in *Lacock Abbey Charters*, no. 18a, where it is misdated. See also *ibid.* New Cartulary, f. 66r–v; Old Cartulary, f. 23r: *statim cum comes effectus fuerit Sarr', carta sua confirmabit ...*, and Old Cartulary, f. 9r: *Et cum idem comes effectus fuerit, maiori sigillo suo ... omnia predicta sepedicte domui confirmabit.* I am grateful to Simon Lloyd for his transcripts from these manuscripts. Paris, *CM*, iv, p. 630, suggests, much later, that William became reconciled to the denial of his title.

[95] Wendover, *Flores*, iv, pp. 268–70.

[96] *Cl.R.1231–4*, p. 238; *Cal. Chart. R. 1226–57*, p. 186. Aumale had witnessed an isolated charter on 25 February 1233, and appears regularly at court from 9 July onwards; C53/27, mm. 1–2, 11.

[97] *Cl.R.1231–4*, pp. 239–40. For Aimery, see *Acta*, appendix 4, no. 40. For Nersac, see *CPR 1232–47*, p. 170.

[98] *Cl.R.1231–4*, p. 241. For Montmartin, see *Cal.Lib.R.1226–40*, p. 212.

part of the manor of Exning in fee. This involved the dismissal of the previous tenant, in what the king was later to admit had been a disseisin *per voluntatem*, in direct contravention of a royal charter.[99]

These same weeks witnessed a renewal of the attack against Walter Mauclerk. His grain at Thurrock in Essex was granted to Richard de Gray, a kinsman of Stephen of Seagrave. A chapel he held in Cumberland was seized on behalf of local landowners, who claimed to have possessed it in the time of King John. As elsewhere, the king was later to admit that this had been an unlawful seizure, *per voluntatem*.[100] Mauclerk determined on exile, but at Dover he was refused permission to cross and was physically assaulted.[101] Attacks were renewed against Ranulph le Breton, one of the regime's earliest victims.[102] Des Roches and de Rivallis continued to enrich themselves, the bishop acquiring control of the Marmion estates and various minor gifts.[103] Most controversially of all, on 18 July the castles of Grosmont, Skenfrith and Llantilio were granted to de Rivallis in perpetual fee for the service of two knights.[104] There could be no more brazen advertisement of de Rivallis' intention to carve out a private empire for himself, assembled from the Marcher estates of de Burgh and the Briouze family.

On 18 July summonses were issued for an expedition to Ireland. The feudal host was to assemble at Gloucester by 29 August, ready to board an invasion fleet waiting at Ilfracombe.[105] Ostensibly the army was intended to deal with revolt by the native Irish and their reoccupation of Connaught. However, the choice of Gloucester and Ilfracombe as mustering points is significant. The king left his options open, either to fulfil his avowed intention to cross to Ireland, or to turn the host loose against Wales. Here there was an obvious threat to the Marshal, and probably also a deliberate echo of King John's campaign against William de Briouze in 1210. On that earlier occasion Briouze's men in Ireland had been routed in an expedition led by the king, whilst Briouze himself and his allies in Wales faced a second royal invasion force. The 1210 campaign was especially familiar to des Roches, who himself had led one of the contingents against the

---

[99]   *Cl.R.1231–4*, pp. 214, 223; *Cal. Chart. R. 1226–57*, pp. 30, 185, 189; *CRR*, xv, nos. 583, 1207, 1308.
[100] C60/32, mm. 3, 4; *Cl.R.1231–4*, pp. 250, 401.
[101] Wendover, *Flores*, iv, p. 272; *AM*, iii (Dunstable), p. 138.
[102] C60/32, m. 3.
[103] *Cl.R.1231–4*, p. 242; *Cal. Chart. R. 1226–57*, p. 186.
[104] *Cal. Chart. R. 1226–57*, p. 185, misdated in the printed version.
[105] *Cl.R.1231–4*, pp. 315–18.

Welsh.[106] Now, twenty years on, he appears to have revived the scheme, with Richard Marshal cast in the role once played by William de Briouze.

For the moment the threat seems to have worked. The second of the three councils mentioned in the king's May ultimatum was set to meet at Westminster on 1 August. If Wendover is to be believed, the Marshal arrived in London, ready to throw himself upon the king's mercy. He lodged with his sister, the wife of Richard of Cornwall, who on the eve of the council warned him that there was a plan afoot to have him arrested and imprisoned just as de Burgh had been the previous year. The Marshal fled to join his allies in Wales.[107] Wendover's account throws light on the perceived attitude of Richard of Cornwall towards the Marshal's cause, but it is not borne out by the Chancery records. These confirm that there may well have been a council meeting in London on 1 August.[108] But at about the same date the Marshal and his supporters assembled in arms at High Wycombe, a manor belonging to Gilbert Basset. Their meeting was not a success. To judge from the lists of those later disseised for their attendance, it attracted few supporters save the personal retinues of the Bassets and of Richard Marshal, principally the knights of his late brother William. The only magnate of any significance to attend was the young Roger Bigod, earl of Norfolk, the Marshal's nephew.[109] As soon as rumours of the Wycombe assembly reached court, levies were summoned in a swathe of counties stretching eastwards from the Marches into Buckinghamshire, the route taken by the Marshal and his men. They were to arrest any travellers bearing arms.[110] In the meantime, there was contact between Wycombe and the court. On 3 August the king left London for Windsor, the first stage of his journey to Gloucester where he was due to meet his expeditionary force, but also convenient for communication with Wycombe. At Windsor the king was persuaded to grant safe-conducts to the Marshal going into Wales and to Bigod and his men returning home.[111] Some sort of settlement had been cobbled together. An entry on the fine roll suggests that the Marshal promised that he and all those he had harboured contrary to the king's instructions, presumably a reference

[106] Warren, *King John*, pp. 195–8, and see above p. 62.
[107] Wendover, *Flores*, iv, p. 270.
[108] The bishops of Bath, Salisbury and Winchester, and the earls of Cornwall and Warenne were all present at court on 3 August; C53/27, m. 2.
[109] C60/32, m. 3
[110] *CPR 1232–47*, p. 21; *Cl.R.1231–4*, pp. 317–18.
[111] *CPR 1232–47*, p. 22.

to Basset and Clifford, would come in to throw themselves on the mercy of the king and his court.[112] For the moment Henry appears to have been satisfied with these assurances. He recalled the local levies guarding the roads, and most significantly, on 7 August ordered that the Irish fleet assemble not at Ilfracombe but at Milford Haven in Pembroke, a venue that would have been unthinkable had the Marshal's loyalty still been in doubt.[113] What might once have been an invasion force directed against either Wales or Ireland was now firmly committed to Ireland alone. The king clearly believed that his problems on the Marches were close to a solution. Yet it was not to be. Within a fortnight he was openly at war with the Marshal. Thus far, the drift to war had been very much the responsibility of des Roches and those others who counselled the king to ignore the just complaints of his barons. By contrast, the actual of outbreak of hostilities was controlled not from the court, but by the Marshal and his men, and by their persistent failure to submit to any form of settlement.

THE DRIFT TO WAR

As the court moved westwards, various of the Marshal's supporters came in to make their peace. Orders for the restoration of the lands of Roger de Somery, the Marshal's cousin, were issued on 12 August dependent upon Somery surrendering hostages.[114] At the same time, several leading malcontents including the Marshal himself, Walter of Clifford and Roger Bigod released charters or hostages to the king, pledging all their lands as security for future good conduct. The Marshal's charter is said to have been unlike the others (*non qualem alii*), but its terms are not recorded. The exchange of hostages and prisoners, and the pledging of estates as tokens of good conduct are ominously reminiscent of the practices of King John.[115] Such threats were to do nothing to halt the onset of civil war. By 13 August the king himself appears to have abandoned any hope of a peaceful settlement. Orders were issued for the confiscation of the lands of the principal malcontents: Walter of Clifford, William of Rowden, William le Gros, Gilbert Basset, his brother Warin and their kinsmen

---

[112] C60/32, m. 3, printed below n. 120.
[113] *Cl.R.1231–4*, pp. 318–19.
[114] *Cl.R.1231–4*, p. 247.
[115] *Ibid.*, pp. 320–1. For John's practice, see Holt, *Magna Carta*, pp. 191–5; Vincent, 'Hugh de Neville and his prisoners', pp. 190–7.

Thomas de Grelley and Richard Siward.[116] At first the king asked merely that their lands be seized by the sheriffs but that nothing be carried away. The attack against Clifford was justified as a distraint for Jewish debt.[117] But very quickly the confiscations altered both in form and extent. In the week or so after 14 August, at least thirty-five named individuals suffered the loss of their estates. The king's orders state specifically that confiscation was being enforced as punishment for armed attendance at the Wycombe assembly. Most controversially of all, the lands seized were no longer to be held in trust by the crown, but distributed amongst sixty or so beneficiaries.[118] Five of these men were major barons who merely received back land taken from rebel sub-tenants. A further thirty-eight, nearly three-quarters of the total, were either factional adherents of des Roches or courtiers, including des Roches himself, Engelard de Cigogné, William de Cantiloupe, Robert Passelewe and Peter de Rivallis. Particularly well represented were the knights of the royal household, at least twenty-three of whom received rebel land, a clear majority being aliens: Gascons, Normans, Poitevins and des Roches' fellow Tourangeaux.[119]

Instead of making his way to Gloucester as planned, the king now pressed on into the Marches, reaching Hereford by 19 August, where he waited for the next ten days. It was at Hereford on 23 August that he at last authorized confiscation of the Marshal's own estates and the lands of Roger Bigod, earl of Norfolk, henceforth to be held by the sheriffs rather than being distributed amongst loyalists.[120] What had

[116] C60/32, m. 3. For de Grelley and his kinship to the Bassets, see Waugh, *The Lordship of England*, pp. 211–12; Sanders, *English Baronies*, pp. 130–1.

[117] C60/32, m. 3, and for Clifford's Jewish debts, see *Cl.R.1231–4*, p. 314.

[118] C60/32, m. 3 provides the most comprehensive list of confiscations, headed *De terris diversorum diversis commissis qui fuerunt cum comite Mar' apud Wycumbe cum equis et armis*. It is enrolled between writs dated 15 and 17 August, although clearly corrected and augmented over the course of several weeks.

[119] Those who qualify as household knights or *curiales* are Hugh de Gournay, Peter de Russelis, John de Talbot, Brian de Lisle and Walter his son, Richard de St Germain, Samson Foliot, Ralph fitz Nicholas, William de Cantiloupe the elder, Robert Lupus, the bishop of Winchester, Robert and Walter Passelewe, Hugh the king's butler, Robert de Briwes, Henry de Trubleville, Hubert Hose, Robert de Pavilly, Peter de Rivallis, William de Gamaches, and the alien household knights Walter de Goderville, William de Brissac, Macey Bezill, Macey de Martigny, William de Nersac, Engelard de Cigogné, Everard de Châteauvilain, William de Dampierre, Bartholomew le Bigod, Joldewin de Doué, Walter de Fontibus, Gerard de Lamberseth, Aimery de St Amand, Matthew de Plessy, Philip le Breton, William de Commendas and Ferrand the crossbowman.

[120] C60/32, m. 3, noted in the margin as: *de terris comitis R(icardi) Marescall' capiendis in manum regis*; Rex vicecomiti Wigorn' salutem. Scias quod licet R(icardus) Marescall' comes Penbr' nuper venisset super nos cum equis et armis apud Wycumbe et nos ad petitionem quorundam magnatum nostrorum concedemus ei quod sub conductu

happened to destroy the fragile settlement agreed only a fortnight before? The writs issued on 23 August provide the only official justification for the king's actions. Used in conjunction with the remarks of Wendover and the other chroniclers, they go a long way towards explaining the sudden change of attitude in mid-August; the abandonment of the planned muster at Gloucester, and the controversial decision to confiscate rebel estates. According to the king's account, the Wycombe assembly had been followed by promises from the Marshal that he and his men would come in to court to seek mercy. Instead of this, the malcontents had seized the castle of Hay-on-Wye and fortified it against the king. Attacks had been made against Philip le Breton, one of the king's alien constables active in the March. The seizure of Hay presumably occurred at some time between the return of the malcontents from Wycombe, and 13 August, when news of it forced the king into drastic action against the rebels and sent him scurrying off to Hereford. There, according to the same account, the Marshal sent nuncios to court seeking the king's grace. But in the meantime yet another castle, Ewyas, was seized by the rebels. In these circumstances the king had no choice but to make war.[121] On 26 August he acknowledged an alliance with Morgan of Caerleon, a Welsh baron for many years bitterly resentful of the Marshal family's occupation of his ancestral lands. Henceforth, the king promised, there would be no peace with Richard Marshal without Morgan's approval.[122] The Irish expedition was cancelled.

nostro rediret ad partes suas sub tali forma quod quidam nostrorum qui cum ipso venerant contra nos armati, et quos secum contra prohibtionem nostram retinuit et adhuc retinet, subsequenter venissent ad nos posituri se in misericordiam nostram vel subituri iudicium curie nostre, et idem comes postea similiter venisset positurus se in misericordiam nostram vel iudicium curie nostre subiturus, nec tamen ipse comes nec alii supradicti ad nos postea venire curaverunt sicut predictum est, immo quod gravius est idem comes quoddam castrum, videlicet Hayam quod est cuiusdam baronisse nostre que inde nobis fidelitatem fecit et cuius heredes sunt in custodia nostra, occupavit et contra nos munivit, licet etiam post ea ad nos mitteret idem comes nuntios suos apud Hereford' ad gratiam nostram petendam, nihilominus quoddam aliud castrum scilicet castrum de Ewyas quod fuit in manu cuiusdam alterius baronisse nostre et per quod marchia nostra plurimum fuit asse(r)turata, occupavit et contra nos hostiliter munivit, necnon quod gravius nos movet, quandam domum Philippi le Bret in manu forti prostravit et inde fecit asportari; et quia in tot et in tantis excessibus contra pacem nostram temere venire presumpsit, tibi precipimus quod omnes terras et tenementa ipsius comitis quas habuit in balliva tua, cum omnibus bladis, instauris et aliis rebus et possessionibus suas, capias in manum nostram et ea salvo custodias donec aliud inde precepimus. Teste rege apud Hereford' xxiii die Augusti. Eodem modo scribitur vicecomitibus Berk', Sussex', Warewic', (Wiltes' *cancelled*), Oxon', Buk', Glouc'.

121 C60/32, m. 3.
122 *CPR 1232–47*, p. 24. For Morgan's grievance, see Crouch, *William Marshal*, pp. 127–8.

Instead the host was diverted from Gloucester to Hereford. On 31 August the king set out to besiege Hay-on-Wye, the opening move of his campaign of civil war.[123]

Why had the Marshal or his men attacked Hay and Ewyas? Hay formed part of the inheritance of William de Briouze (d.1230), Richard Marshal's brother-in-law. In 1233 the king was to claim that the castle was held, technically at least, by Briouze's widow Eve. In practice, however, after Briouze's death, it appears to have passed with the rest of his lands into the keeping of William Marshal II (d.1231), and thereafter to Richard of Cornwall.[124] Since March 1233, when Richard Marshal and Richard of Cornwall had mounted their joint attack against Radnor, their friendship had come increasingly under strain. Richard of Cornwall returned to court in June 1233 after an absence of more than six months. He was present when hostages were delivered on the Marches and attended the council in London on 3 August.[125] Wendover implies that, like the earls of Chester and Lincoln, Richard was bribed by des Roches to abandon the Marshal. There may well be some justice to this charge. Around 3 August, des Roches was granted custody of the lands and heir of the earl of Devon, including the castles of Carisbrooke and Christchurch. By 25 August he had relinquished them in favour of Richard of Cornwall, a gesture which might easily be construed as a bribe.[126] Just as in 1227 Richard had withdrawn his support from William Marshal at a crucial moment, bringing about the collapse of baronial resistance to the king, so in 1233 his desertion of Richard Marshal made him a figure of loathing amongst the rebel camp. It seems entirely plausible that the seizure of the castle of Hay-on-Wye marks the opening of this private vendetta between the Marshal's men and Richard.

The second castle referred to by the king, Ewyas Lacy, had been held until his death in 1230 by Gilbert de Lacy, eldest son of Walter de Lacy lord of Meath. On Gilbert's death, the king judged that his lands should revert to his father, sparking a dispute over dower

---

[123] *Cl.R.1231–4*, p. 322; *CPR 1232–47*, p. 24, which suggests that initially it had been proposed that the host be diverted from Gloucester to Shrewsbury.

[124] *Pat. R. 1225–32*, pp. 336, 339; *CPR 1232–47*, p. 52; D. L. C. Cathcart King, *Castellarium Anglicanum*, 2 vols. (New York 1982), p. 18. The fact that the castle was technically in the keeping of Eve is suggested by the royal letters in C60/32, m. 3 (printed above n. 120), where it is said that Hay belonged to a certain baroness who had done homage for it to the king.

[125] *Cl.R.1231–4*, p. 312; C53/27, mm. 2–3. He had last witnessed a royal charter on 9 December 1232.

[126] Wendover, *Flores*, iv, p. 271; *CPR 1232–47*, p. 23; *Cl.R.1231–4*, p. 252; C60/32, m. 3; and see *Cl.R.1231–4*, p. 252, for a grant of rebel land to Richard.

between Walter de Lacy and Gilbert's widow, Isabella, sister of the earl of Norfolk, who in 1233 joined his kinsman, the Marshal, in rebellion.[127] Like Richard of Cornwall, Walter de Lacy was a long-standing ally of the Marshal family, who in 1233 deserted Richard Marshal for the king. Again like Richard of Cornwall, he was to face bitter, personal reprisals from the knights of the Marshal during the winter of 1233–4. The seizure of Ewyas reflects yet further tensions within the Marshal's network of kin and familiars. It is no coincidence that the family interests engaged both at Hay and Ewyas involved the fortunes of the Briouze estate. Hay was a Briouze castle, the Lacys and the Marshals were Briouze kin. It was precisely in that region of the Briouze Marches where Peter de Rivallis was carving out his private empire, that the crisis of August 1233 erupted. Nonetheless, the crisis itself was not of de Rivallis' making. It began not with armed conflict between Richard Marshal and the king, but as a private vendetta between the Marshal's men and those that they regarded as deserters. Henceforth the civil war was to develop not so much as a war against the crown, as an explosion of violence within the Marshal's own affinity.

DISTRAINT, SUMMONSES AND THE ALIENS

According to Wendover, the confiscation of rebel land in mid-August had followed the malcontents' refusal to attend three successive summonses to treat with the king: at Westminster for 11 July, at Westminster again on 1 August and finally for Gloucester on 14 August. Here Wendover probably errs; the Chancery sources mention a summons to Gloucester for 29 August.[128] The confiscation of rebel lands began a fortnight ahead of this deadline, as a result of the seizure of Hay, an event unmentioned by the chroniclers. But in the aftermath of confiscation, Wendover appears to have been better informed, noting that the king seized the rebels' manors, destroyed their parks and fishponds, and gave what was left to his alien favourites. At des Roches' prompting, he then sent the bishop of St David's formally to diffidate Richard Marshal.[129] In all of this, Wendover claims the king acted without judgement of any court or of the rebels' peers, a phrase repeated on several occasions within the

---

[127] *Cl.R.1227–31*, pp. 464–5; *CPR 1232–47*, p. 42; Sanders, *English Baronies*, p. 95, and see Cathcart King, *Castellarium*, p. 208 for the castle of Ewyas Lacy, *alias* Longtown.

[128] Wendover, *Flores*, iv, p. 271, as against *Cl.R.1231–4*, pp. 315, 318.

[129] Wendover, *Flores*, iv, pp. 268–73.

subsequent narrative and which was undoubtedly inspired by clause 39 of Magna Carta, showing both how widely the language of the charter had been disseminated by the 1230s, and how in 1233 the king was believed to have acted arbitrarily, against the charter.[130] Henry himself was well aware of these complaints. The royal letters of 23 August, justifying the attack upon Richard Marshal, twice refer to a promise made by the Marshal and his men that they would place themselves in the king's mercy and submit to the judgement of his court (*ponituri se in misericordiam nostram vel subituri iudicium curie nostre*).[131] The wording here is significant. Clearly, the king wished to imply that he had offered the rebels a legal settlement in keeping with the terms of Magna Carta. Yet, whereas Magna Carta clause 39 spoke of judgement by peers or by the law of the land (*per legale iudicium parium suorum vel per legem terre*), in 1233 the king offered merely judgement 'by our court'. In 1233 the king's court was dominated by des Roches and the Marshal's enemies. It was not at all the sort of assembly likely to dispense the law of the land, the *legem terre*, as recognized by Magna Carta and demanded by the Marshal and his men.

The problems the king faced in summoning recalcitrant subjects to court were similar to those experienced in the ordinary course of litigation when one or other party defaulted. The remedy in such cases was either the dismissal of the suit with amercement against a defaulting plaintiff, or if the defendant was the defaulter, a series of three summonses followed by the attachment of goods, lands or person to ensure attendance.[132] A similar procedure appears to have been adopted against the malcontents in 1233: the issue of three summonses followed by the attachment of land. But, already in July 1233, the king had gone beyond simple attachment, ordering the destruction of Gilbert Basset's property. More controversially still, after 13 August attachment yielded place to full-scale confiscation, with the release of rebel estates from crown custody into the hands of particular courtiers. The rebels themselves had as yet issued no formal

---

[130] Wendover, *Flores*, iv, p. 271 (*absque judicio curiae suae et parium suorum*), and see p. 276 (*absque judicio parium suorum*), p. 283 (*stare juri et judicio parium meorum in curia sua*). For the dissemination of Magna Carta, specifically cited by Wendover, *Flores*, iv, p. 286, see J. R. Maddicott, 'Magna Carta and the local community 1215–1259', *Past and Present* 102 (1984), pp. 25–65.

[131] C60/32, m. 3, printed above n. 120.

[132] For the process of attachment, see S. F. C. Milsom, *The Legal Framework of English Feudalism* (Cambridge 1976), pp. 8–9; F. Pollock and F. W. Maitland, *The History of English Law*, 2 vols., 2nd edn (Cambridge 1968), ii, pp. 592–3, references courtesy of Benjamin Thompson.

renunciation of their homage. There had been no formal judgement against them, nor any process of outlawry. Nonetheless, Basset and his fellows were to all intents and purposes being treated as outlaws.

Added to this fundamental flaw in the legal process, several of the chroniclers single out the peculiar unpopularity of those insinuated into rebel lands. The annals of Tewkesbury, Osney and Dover all associate the outbreak of war with the king's decision to promote aliens within estates seized from the Marshal's men.[133] Even the chronicler of Andres, writing in northern France, notes the uproar caused by the king's favouritism towards des Roches, de Rivallis and a host of Poitevins, Flemings and Brabantines.[134] Here once again, we have an echo of the reign of King John. In August 1233 Henry III adopted practices last applied during the civil war of 1215–17. On that previous occasion, King John had summarily deprived rebels of their lands, substituting courtiers, often alien knights of the royal household, in their place. In 1233 it was not only the policies but the very personalities of 1215 that Henry revived. At least ten of the household knights granted rebel lands in 1233 had received similar grants after 1215.[135] Most were aliens, by far the largest constituency to receive rebel lands either in 1215 or 1233. Such men were well placed to defend the land in question. Moreover, the king's military retinue was vastly expensive even in peacetime. By granting rebel property to his knights in place of money wages, the king reduced the burden placed on his purse. Doubtless both of these motives, the strategic and the financial, played their part in 1233. Yet what most impressed contemporaries was the influx of aliens into the English countryside. Aliens whose lives had been passed at court, as members of the royal household, were suddenly intruded as property holders in the localities, an invasion previously experienced only at the height of civil war.

The chroniclers are virtually unanimous in associating des Roches' return to court with the promotion of aliens, especially of Poitevins. Indeed the term 'Poitevin Government' has been applied to the entire period of des Roches' ascendancy between 1232 and 1234.[136]

---

[133] *AM*, i, p. 90, iv, p. 76; BL ms. Cotton Julius D v, f. 29v.

[134] *MGHS*, xxiv, p. 772. For the chronicler's sources see above pp. 247–8.

[135] Nicholas de Lettres, Peter de Russelis, Brian de Lisle, Henry de Trubleville and the aliens Philip le Breton, Walter de Goderville, William de Bouelles, Engelard de Cigogné, Ferrand the crossbowman and Joldewin de Doué all received land both in 1215–17 and 1233.

[136] For its fullest and most recent expression, see Clanchy, *England and its Rulers*, part iii, esp. pp. 216–21. I am extremely grateful to Michael Clanchy for an extended discussion of the problems raised by the idea of 'Poitevin Government'.

Powicke was the first historian to query the exact number of Poitevins active at court, and we now know that the very authors of the so-called Poitevin regime, des Roches and de Rivallis, were not themselves natives of Poitou.[137] It is true that des Roches sponsored the return to court of the likes of Peter de Maulay, Engelard de Cigogné and the earl of Aumale, some of whom could indeed be considered Poitevins, but the alien element in government remained very small; smaller by far than it had been at any time during the reign of King John. Des Roches and de Rivallis both installed alien lieutenants in the counties under their charge: the Norman Roger Wacelin as under-sheriff for Hampshire, the Tourangeau Aimery de Chanceaux to a similar position in Sussex. Yet for the most part, they worked via English subordinates. De Rivallis' escheators, his deputies at the Exchequer, his local custodians and his constables were almost all of them Englishmen.

Why then do Wendover and the chroniclers speak of the country being swamped with Poitevins; of their intrusion into every position formerly occupied by native councillors or constables? In part the answer lies in the use of 'Poitevin', not so much as a description of geographic origin as an abusive epithet, a usage well-attested from the twelfth century onwards, and given even greater impetus by the association between Poitou and the vast waste of resources on the expeditions of 1207, 1214, 1225 and 1230. Added to this, the one hint the chroniclers had as to Peter de Rivallis' background lay in his title as *capicerius* of Poitiers, accorded him in the witness lists to royal charters and in the many privileges granted him during his ascendancy.[138] No wonder, when a self-proclaimed official of Poitou was amassing such extraordinary private gains, a virtual empire in Sussex and south Wales, that commentators tended to brand him and his associates 'Poitevins'. Looking beyond des Roches and his circle, it is apparent that two other alien groups received conspicuous patronage after 1232. The first of these, the magnates and barons resident in Brittany and Poitou, were the beneficiaries of enormous subsidies from the Westminster Exchequer. But few if any of these men were protégés of des Roches. Their fees had first been awarded in 1230, when des Roches was away in Rome. The most that the bishop did was to ensure that these obligations were met; a vast sum, perhaps in

---

[137] Powicke, *Henry III*, pp. 123–4, and see above chapter 1.
[138] See for example *Chartulary of Chichester*, ed. Peckham, nos. 134, 138–40, 148, 767, 795, where the title *capicerius* is erroneously translated as 'treasurer'.

excess of 25,000 marks, vanishing in subsidies across the Channel, mostly in the twelve months after October 1232.[139]

The second group of aliens prominent in 1232–4 was also set apart from des Roches. For many years the royal household had included a substantial body of alien knights, sprung from all parts of France and the Low Countries. After Christmas 1232, a number of these men, previously retained by money fee, began to receive territorial settlements, often in the escheats left vacant by de Burgh. Exact numbers are unimportant. Wendover undoubtedly exaggerates in speaking of the hordes of aliens to arrive at Dover in the summer of 1233, or of two thousand Poitevin knights and serjeants brought to England by des Roches.[140] It is unlikely that there were ever more than fifty aliens in the king's household at any one time.[141] Far more significant is the fact that in August 1233 a large proportion of these men, many of them last seen in the English countryside during the civil war of John's reign, were intruded into the lands of the Marshal's rebellious affinity; intruded moreover, following a process of disseisin against the lands' former occupants widely regarded as unlawful and undoubtedly reminiscent of the methods of King John, when the likes of Girard d'Athée and Fawkes de Bréauté had first been dispatched to take charge of the lands of the Marcher, William de Briouze.

For the past year the king had shown undue favouritism towards a particular, narrow faction. The security of royal charters had been undermined in order to revive quarrels stretching back to John's reign. Arbitrary methods of government; seizures of land *per voluntatem regis* without proper judgement in court; the hounding of disgraced ministers; the extortion of enormous fines; hostage-taking; the issue of promises of fealty pledging entire estates as security; the whole range of techniques known to King John had been revived with alacrity

---

[139] See the figures compiled by Painter, *Peter of Dreux*, p. 82, which lists Breton pensions alone of between £10, 000 and £16, 000, to which must be added at least £2, 500 in pensions to Poitou in the year to October 1233; *Cal.Lib.R.1226–40*, pp. 187–8, 194, 211–12, 236–7.

[140] Wendover, *Flores*, iv, pp. 264, 268, 272.

[141] For the household in general, see Walker, 'The Anglo-Welsh wars', chapter ii, pp. 66–90; Stacey, *Politics, Policy and Finance*, pp. 185–6. Walker, 'The Anglo-Welsh wars', p. 80 concludes that a list compiled in 1234 of 71 knights comprises virtually the entire royal household. Of these only 23 are definitely or more than likely aliens; C47/2/1 no. 10. By comparison, a roll of serjeants, mostly Flemings, compiled for the 1215 Rochester campaign, lists over 300 aliens active in England in the king's service; BL ms. Add. 41479, printed by S. D. Church, 'The earliest English muster roll, 18/19 December 1215', *Historical Research* 67 (1994), pp. 1–17. For the count of Guînes and the advocate of Béthune active with Flemish mercenaries on the Marches in 1233, see *CPR 1232–47*, pp. 2, 25, 27; Wendover, *Flores*, iv, pp. 280–1.

under des Roches' sponsorship. In the process the Marshal had been edged into resistance, by his personal grievances over the dower of the king's sister, by the inequitable distribution of favours at court, and by the promotion of Peter de Rivallis within the close-knit society of the Marches. Nonetheless it was not his own grievances but those of his household that finally drove the Marshal to rebellion.

Lacking a following of his own in England, Richard Marshal was naturally anxious to attract the allegiance of those men lately attached to his brother, William Marshal II. The seizure of Upavon from Gilbert Basset, although only one of many such seizures *per voluntatem*, had brought Basset's kinsmen and familiars into alignment against the crown. The household of William Marshal had been a successful and intensely self-confident organization: closely interrelated, bound together by a rich distribution of land and patronage in England, Wales and Ireland. During the 1220s the Marshals and their affinity had achieved remarkable military triumphs in Ireland and in south Wales. Significantly, it is the only secular affinity of its day known to have commissioned a biography of its founder and patron: the *Histoire de Guillaume le Maréchal*, extolling the virtues of William Marshal I and, by inference, of his successor William II.[142] It was an affinity capable of operating as a court in miniature, with its own internal loyalties and dynamic. On his accession, Richard Marshal was something of an outsider to this group. He had witnessed a bare half dozen of his elder brother's charters. Although lord of the Giffard estate in England by partition with William II, Richard appears to have spent most of his time in France.[143] It was in France that he was raised and married, his wife being unusual amongst the brides of Anglo-Norman magnates in possessing few claims to land in England.[144] Richard makes no impact on the great saga of his family. His most prominent appearance in the *Histoire* is not so much an appearance as an absence: in 1219, when Richard is to be found at the court of the French king rather than at

---

142 The remarks of Crouch, *William Marshal*, pp. 1–8, 133–49, can be extended to the household of William Marshal II.

143 *Ibid.*, pp. 68, 94, 131; *CP*, x, p. 368; *Reading Abbey Cartularies*, ed. Kemp, ii, no. 1056; *The Lyttelton Papers* (Sotheby's Sale Catalogue for 12 December 1978), pp. 12–13, no. 5; *Calendar of Ormond Deeds 1172–1350 AD*, ed. E. Curtis, Irish Manuscripts Commission (Dublin 1932), pp. 23, 36; *Layettes*, ii, no. 1826 (references courtesy of David Crouch). For the Giffard lands, see Crouch, *William Marshal*, pp. 64n., 131; *Cal. Chart. R. 1226–57*, p. 142, which shows that at least part of the honour was at farm at the time of Richard's accession to the earldom of Pembroke.

144 For Gervasia's English estate in Dorset, at Ringwood, Hants and Burton Latimer, Northants, see *RLC*, ii, p. 99; *CRR*, xiv, nos. 672, 1149–50, 1723, 2230; *Cl.R. 1227–31*, pp. 36, 542; *Cl.R.1231–4*, p. 427; *BF*, p. 937.

the deathbed of his father.[145] David Crouch detects a tinge of francophobia in the *Histoire*; a mistrust of Frenchmen and French ways imparted by the Marshal's followers who commissioned the biography, virtually all of them English by birth.[146] This was a sentiment unlikely to smooth the passage of the Frenchified Richard Marshal into his English inheritance. All the signs are that Richard experienced difficulty coming to terms with his family's friends and dependants. There were problems for example with Richard Siward, a former tenant of the Marshals, deprived at Richard Marshal's accession of the manor of Bere Regis. There were problems, too, with the Marshal's brother-in-law, William Ferrers, and above all with Eleanor, William Marshal's widow.[147]

Traditionally it has been assumed that it was Richard Marshal himself who led the rebellion of 1233; that his men merely followed his lead in supporting Gilbert Basset and in defying the king. In fact, on the contrary, it was Basset and his kinsmen – his brothers Philip and Warin, his nephew William of Montacute, his brother-in-law Richard Siward, his cousin Thomas de Grelley – who first went on to the offensive. Richard Marshal was dragged along in their wake. Anxious to assert his leadership over the Marshal affinity, he supported Basset over Upavon. As late as August 1233 he was willing to make terms with the crown, sending messengers to the king at Hereford, whilst Basset and the rest of the Marshal affinity caused havoc by their attacks on Hay and Ewyas, and their vendetta against former allies they believed guilty of desertion. Subsequently Richard Marshal was to be portrayed as the true-born Englishman, challenging des Roches and the alien intruders. Yet, as in the case of Stephen Langton a decade earlier, or as with the barons who rebelled against King John after 1215, the Marshal's avowed patriotism reflects deep insecurity as to his own status as an Anglo-Norman abroad. In many ways his outlook was to prove more French than English. In the immediate term he was edged into rebellion almost against his will, keeping faith with an affinity far more enthusiastic for resistance and far more confident of its ability to defy the king than Richard was himself. Where Siward and the Bassets openly invited war with the court, it was the king who had to make the first moves in diffidating the

[145] *Hist. de Maréchal*, lines 19, 113–22.
[146] Crouch, *William Marshal*, pp. 44, 115, 140–2.
[147] For Ferrers see *CRR*, xiv, nos. 2075, 2157. For Siward, who was forced by the terms of William Marshal II's will to yield place to William's younger brother, Walter, see *Cl.R.1227–31*, p. 552; D. Crouch, 'The last adventure of Richard Siward', *Morgannwg* 35 (1991), p. 11.

Marshal.[148] Thereafter, throughout the opening stages of civil war, it was to be the Marshal affinity, not the Marshal himself, that determined the course of events. The chroniclers speak of a curse upon the heirs of William Marshal I. In the very strength of the Marshal affinity lay the seeds of Richard Marshal's destruction.

[148] For the diffidations of 1233, see Wendover, *Flores*, iv, pp. 269, 273; *CPR 1232–47*, p. 25. The king's defiance was delivered via Anselm le Gros, bishop of St David's, Richard Marshal's cousin, for whom see Crouch, *William Marshal*, p. 166.

Chapter 12

THE MARSHAL'S WAR

Throughout the autumn and winter of 1233–4 England was plunged into turmoil; the most serious civil disturbance since the baronial rebellion of John's reign and, like that earlier war, blamed by many on the ambitions and policies of Peter des Roches. Nonetheless, it is important not to exaggerate the extent of the war of 1233–4. The rebellion against John had involved a substantial proportion of the higher aristocracy and baronage; London was lost to the king for more than two years, during which time royal authority extended over no more than a handful of garrisons and the counties of the far south-west. There was to be nothing comparable to this in 1233. In the 1230s, rebel activity concentrated on the southern Welsh Marches and led to the temporary seizure of less than half a dozen of the king's castles. England suffered a series of skirmishes at the hands of rebel raiding parties, but although these attacks were daring, and served to humiliate the various courtiers whose manors were pillaged, they in no sense constituted a campaign of military conquest and laid siege to not a single castle outside the Marches. Above all, despite the sympathy evinced for the rebels by leading barons and churchmen, rebellion itself was limited to a handful of men, never more than fifty or sixty of knightly status, most of them personal adherents of Richard Marshal, the one magnate openly to make war upon the king.

CIVIL WAR: THE FIRST CAMPAIGN AUGUST–SEPTEMBER 1233

The war itself fell into two campaigns divided by a brief truce. Having issued his diffidation of the Marshal, the king directed a brief but effective attack against the rebel castles. Between 28 August and 7 September, his forces recaptured Hay and Ewyas. Walter of Clifford was brought to heel. The king then moved south to lay siege to the Marshal's castle at Usk, which surrendered in less than three days, even before the king's siege engines had been brought to

399

bear.[1] At Usk yet another settlement was patched together. Perhaps deliberately, Wendover misconstrues its nature, claiming that the garrison's surrender was a gesture of magnanimity on behalf of a rebel force far stronger than the king's puny army. According to Wendover, the rebels surrendered merely in order to promote a more permanent peace, which they were promised would be arranged within the coming fortnight.[2] As we shall see, there may well have been a term of a fortnight agreed at Usk, but it was not for a negotiated peace. Rather, it was a deadline set by the king for the unconditional surrender of all rebel knights. In all other respects, the speed with which the rebel castles fell reflects the king's overwhelming superiority.

The Marshal's one hope had lain in attracting allies to his cause, and in this he had failed. Former friends such as Richard of Cornwall were bought off by the court. Elsewhere there had been fears of disturbance, especially in the west country, scene of much rebel activity during the civil war of 1215–17. It was from the Wiltshire and Somerset gentry that the Marshals had recruited many of their supporters. Richard Marshal's sister, the widow of William de Briouze, held the honour of Totnes in dower, in a region of Devon long associated with personal enmity towards des Roches. Of the rebels of 1233, Richard Siward was married into the Basset family of Headington, related both to Gilbert Basset and to such west country families as Vautorte and Malet, with scores to settle against des Roches stretching back more than twenty years.[3] The bishop himself appears to have caught wind of trouble in the west; on 2 August he installed a mercenary garrison at Taunton castle.[4] Meanwhile, the king fortified Bridgwater and various other western strongholds.[5] Late in August, Eve de Briouze was compelled to surrender Totnes and her dower lands in the Marches.[6] The threat of a western rebellion was averted. Elsewhere, although the Marshal continued to command the loyalty of his young kinsmen, William Ferrers heir to the earl of Derby, and Roger Bigod earl of Norfolk, there is no record of disturbances either in the Ferrers estates or in East Anglia. Above all there was as yet no stirring from the greatest of the Marshal's potential

[1] *CPR 1232–47*, p. 25; *Cl.R.1231–4*, pp. 265–8; E372/78, m. 14. The only reliable account of the war is that by Walker, 'Anglo-Welsh wars', pp. 307–68.
[2] Wendover, *Flores*, iv, pp. 273, 275–6, 284.
[3] Above, pp. 201–2.
[4] Ms. 28DR, m. 18.
[5] *Cl.R.1231–4*, p. 256; E372/78, m. 13.
[6] C60/32, m. 2.

allies, Llywelyn ab Iorweth. Since July, Llywelyn's activities had been confined to the northern March. Strenuous efforts were made by the court to ensure his neutrality. On 2 September, the day before marching on Usk, the king proposed sending representatives to Llywelyn to discuss a permanent peace.[7] Meanwhile, the southern Welsh lord, Morgan ap Hywel, was transformed into an active ally against the Marshal, being encouraged to conduct a private campaign for the recovery of Caerleon, seized by the Marshal's father in 1217. He may also have been encouraged to recapture Usk, lost by his family as long ago as the 1160s.[8]

Faced with all this, the Marshal had little choice but to sue for terms. At Usk, around 7 September, a truce was agreed. Rebels appear to have been given a fortnight in which to make their peace with the crown. Meanwhile, an attempt was made to recover their land from loyalist custodians and restore it to the sheriffs; a tacit admission of the extraordinary nature of the earlier seizures.[9] A halt was called to the devastation of Gilbert Basset's parks and enclosures.[10] Perhaps a third of the rebels surrendered immediately. In return for pledges of good conduct they were restored not only to their lands but to the grain and chattels taken in August.[11] Various strategic castles were withheld by the king: Totnes from Eve de Briouze, Framlingham from Roger Bigod, Clifford castle from Walter of Clifford, and apparently Usk itself from the Marshal.[12] It was agreed that Morgan ap Hywel and the Marshal would make good any injuries inflicted on one another since the start of hostilities; Morgan was asked to attend court so that his claims over Caerleon might be properly aired.[13] The Marshal's other grievances against the crown were to be considered by a council summoned to meet in London on 2 October.[14]

---

[7]   *Cl.R.1231–4*, p. 322. *Calendar of Ancient Correspondence Concerning Wales*, ed. Edwards, pp. 33–4, preserves a letter, dated to 1233 by the editor, suggesting that the Marshal was already in league with the Welsh in an attack against Carmarthen and Kidwelly as early as 1 August. However, the year is more likely to be 1231 than 1233. In 1231 a Welsh attack against Carmarthen coincided with the attempt to exclude Richard Marshal from his inheritance; *Brut y Tywysogyon*, p. 229.

[8]   *CPR 1232–47*, p. 24; *Cl.R.1231–4*, p. 322. For his grievances see Crouch, *William Marshal*, pp. 127–8.

[9]   C60/32, m. 2, ordering sheriffs to recover the lands of William Crassus (or le Gros), Robert Musard, Henry of Earley, and Gilbert, Philip and Warin Basset.

[10] *Cl.R.1231–4*, pp. 264–5.

[11] *Ibid.*, pp. 257–62, 266, 268–9.

[12] *Ibid.*, pp. 258, 262–3, 267; *CPR 1232–47*, p. 25.

[13] *CPR 1232–47*, p. 26; *Cl.R.1231–4*, pp. 322–3.

[14] Wendover, *Flores*, iv, p. 273.

Confident that the Marshal had been pacified, the king then made his way back to Hereford. On 12 September he authorized a formal division of the knights' fees within the lands of the late earl of Chester, expected for more than a year. Perhaps to ensure his loyalty, the earl of Derby, father of the recently rebellious William Ferrers, was denied actual possession of his share of the Chester fees between the rivers Ribble and Mersey.[15] From Hereford the king then went north along the Marches. At Kidderminster on 21 September, he received the news for which he had been waiting; the torrential rains prevented Llywelyn from coming in person to negotiate, but the Welsh nonetheless offered pledges of peace and goodwill.[16] Des Roches too appears to have been lulled into a false sense of security. On 8 September he dismissed the special garrison appointed to guard Taunton.[17]

But once again, in making peace with the Marshal, the court overlooked the original root and cause of the Marshal's disaffection: the grievances of his men. Basset, Siward and their kinsmen simply refused to recognize the settlement made at Usk. Siward in particular seems never to have been included in the peace. His lands were not restored to shrieval keeping and were still being awarded to a knight of the royal household on 17 September.[18] Set against the dozen or so rebels who surrendered to court, the majority held aloof. Many attempted forcibly to eject the loyalists installed in their estates, without any formal submission to the crown. Their reason for doing so is clear. The truce of Usk coincided with harvest time in a year of exceptional scarcity. Rebel landlords were understandably anxious to deprive intruded royalists of the grain and stock on their manors. Nonetheless, the rebels' failure to reach terms, and their forcible ejection of loyalists provided the crown with a pretext for the renewal of confiscation. A fortnight's deadline from the surrender of Usk would carry us to 21 September, and from 21 September we duly find a series of orders to the sheriffs to restore rebel land to the loyalists, the aliens and household knights who had held it in late August.[19]

In August the rebels had included a wide variety of men, not only those attached to the Marshal, but clients of Roger Bigod and Walter

---

[15] *Cl.R.1231–4*, pp. 263–4, 267.
[16] *Ibid.*, pp. 323–5.
[17] Ms. 28DR, m. 18.
[18] *Cl.R.1231–4*, pp. 267, 324.
[19] *Ibid.*, pp. 270–3, 324; C60/32, m. 2. Meanwhile the castles of Aberllynfi and Pipton, which the rebels refused to surrender, were to be seized by the king's men and either munitioned or razed; *Cl.R.1231–4*, pp. 272–3; Cathcart King, *Castellarium*, pp. 16, 564.

of Clifford. By contrast, the diehards who persisted in rebellion after the truce of Usk were almost exclusively attached to the Marshal. With the exception of a few knights of Glamorgan, tenants of the Clare earls of Gloucester, who may have resented the way in which their lands had been managed by the crown, there were to be no new defections to the Marshal. Most of Richard's followers were in middle age, in some cases senior to Richard himself. Almost without exception, they are to be found over the previous twenty years holding land of the Marshals or witnessing the charters of William Marshal II, Richard's elder brother.[20] It was the younger members of this affinity who found it easiest to defect to the crown: the likes of Richard of Cornwall, Roger de Somery, Henry of Earley and Robert Musard, whose attachment to William Marshal II had been in essence brief.[21] By the same token, a number of veterans, followers not so much of William II as of his father, the likes of John of Monmouth and Hugh of Sandford, took the opportunity to make peace with the king. After August 1233, it is no exaggeration to say that England was plunged into civil war between the king on one side, and on the other the household and affinity of a dead man, William Marshal II. It is a remarkable proof of the community of feeling engendered amongst the Marshal's followers that the bitterest of the fighting that winter should have centred upon those considered traitors to the Marshal's cause. At one time or another John of Monmouth, Walter de Lacy, Richard of Cornwall and Hugh of Sandford were to suffer vicious reprisals for their perceived treachery to the Marshal. In August 1233 the war had opened with a private vendetta against Walter de Lacy and Richard of Cornwall. After September it continued more as an internecine struggle within the Marshal affinity than as a conflict between Richard Marshal and the king.

As yet there was no attempt to re-seize the Marshal's own lands. Nonetheless, alarming moves were made in respect to Caerleon. At Worcester on 22 September, the morning of his departure for

---

[20] Information obtained from a study of the household of William Marshal II, carried out under the guidance of Dr David Crouch. For a recent study, which reached me too late for its conclusions to be properly incorporated here, see R. F. Walker, 'The supporters of Richard Marshal, earl of Pembroke, in the rebellion of 1233–1234', *Welsh Historical Review* 17 (1994), pp. 41–65. Walker (pp. 57–60) notes the defection to Richard Marshal, after the truce of Usk, of such prominent Glamorgan knights as Gilbert de Umfraville, Raymond de Sully and William de Somery.

[21] For Musard and Earley, see *Cl.R.1231–4*, p. 280; *CPR 1232–47*, pp. 59, 60; Sanders, *English Baronies*, p. 83; *Cl.R.1227–31*, p. 541. Roger de Somery had made peace with the king as early as August 1233 and actually fought alongside the royalists during the winter; *Cl.R.1231–4*, pp. 247, 547; *CPR 1232–47*, p. 60.

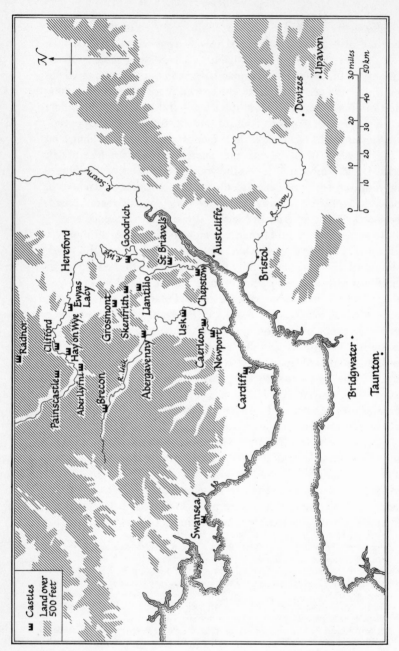

Map 3   The southern Welsh Marches during the civil war of 1233

London, the king appointed an assize of Marcher barons headed by Walter de Lacy, to hear Morgan's claims to Caerleon. The assize was set to meet at Hereford on 2 October, the same day appointed for the Marshal to attend the king in London.[22] The coincidence may well have been deliberate. Richard was required to absent himself from the Marches at a time when one of his most important Marcher interests was to be debated at Hereford; debated, moreover, by an assize headed by Walter de Lacy, a Marshal kinsman and one-time ally, but for several months past a defector to the court. The civil war of August 1233 had arisen as a result of the Marshal's connivance in an attack against Lacy's castle at Ewyas. It was unlikely, with this attack fresh in his memory, that Lacy would prove sympathetic to the Marshal claims over the castle of Caerleon. All in all, it appears that the king decided to fire a warning shot across the Marshal's bows before leaving for London. As yet, however, the Marshal remained immune from, and apparently indifferent to, the renewed disseisins and confiscations ordered against his recalcitrant affinity.

THE FAILED TRUCE SEPTEMBER–OCTOBER 1233

Hostilities both in August and September 1233 were initiated by the Marshal's men, not Richard himself. At least one chronicler suggests that Richard actively opposed the guerrilla tactics that were now to be adopted. As to the inspiration of such tactics, there can be little doubt that their principal author was Richard Siward. Sprung from a humble Yorkshire family, Siward first appears around 1215 arraigned for murder, suggesting that he was already no stranger to violence. Thereafter he entered the household of William Marshal II via service to the Marshal's kinsman, the Poitevin earl of Aumale. In 1221 he had led a successful skirmishing party in support of Aumale's occupation of Bytham castle. He was eventually pardoned and raised into the ranks of the middling baronage by virtue of his marriage *c.*1230 to Philippa Basset, sister of Gilbert and widow of the earl of Warwick. David Crouch has amassed a weight of evidence to suggest that by 1231 Siward had become detached from Richard Marshal. It was the misfortunes of his brother-in-law, Gilbert Basset, not loyalty to the Marshal, that provoked Siward's rebellion.[23] His name first appears amongst the malcontents in August 1233, whereafter he quickly rose to become the most daring of the rebel

---

[22] C66/43, m. 3d.
[23] Crouch, 'The last adventure of Richard Siward', pp. 7–12.

commanders.[24] He was the only rebel to be tacitly excluded from the terms of the truce of Usk. Following the re-seizure of rebel lands around 22 September, he returned to the offensive. The court was making its way from the Marches to London preparatory to the conference with the Marshal summoned for 2 October. Probably somewhere near Oddington in Gloucestershire, on 26 September, Siward struck, sweeping down on the royal baggage train to carry off harness belonging to the bishop of Winchester.[25]

Throughout September, des Roches and his adherents had continued to make free with royal patronage. Des Roches had obtained extension for the Winchester fairs; Peter de Rivallis was granted land at Grosmont, supposedly part of the dower of Isabella de Lacy, sister of the earl of Norfolk. Various of de Burgh's manors were awarded to Stephen of Seagrave and to the alien, Baldwin count of Guînes.[26] Nothing had been done to stem the spate of disseisins *per voluntatem*, the initial grievance that had driven Gilbert Basset and his fellows into rebellion. By singling out des Roches' property for attack, Siward sought to demonstrate that the rebels' quarrel was with the bishop and his colleagues, not with the king himself. Throughout the winter, the rebels scrupulously avoided attacks against the king or his estates, concentrating instead upon ministers such as des Roches, Seagrave and Passelewe.[27]

From Gloucestershire, Siward and his companions fled south into Wiltshire, making their way along the Ridgeway to Hampstead Marshall in Berkshire, where they took provisions and a change of horses from the Marshal's bailiffs. The king was left floundering about between Woodstock and Oddington, necessitating a delay to the London council called for October. Des Roches' clerk, Master Humphrey de Millières, took up the chase and at some point managed to recover the bishop's looted harness. The rebels themselves got clean away. In the villages they came to, they pretended to be king's men returning from the Marches to London.[28] It may be that London really was their destination; perhaps they hoped to repeat the triumphs of 1215, when a rebel seizure of the city had forced

---

[24] C60/32, m. 3.
[25] *CRR*, xv, no. 214; *CPR 1232–47*, p. 26; *Cl.R.1231–4*, p. 326. For the court's movements between Oddington and Woodstock see *Cl.R.1231–4*, pp. 273–4, 324–5. The attack may be related to the cessation of writs enrolled on the fine roll between 26 September and 17 October; C60/32, m. 2.
[26] *Cl.R.1231–4*, pp. 259, 265, 268; C60/32, m. 2.
[27] As noted by Wendover, *Flores*, iv, p. 286.
[28] *CRR*, xv, no. 214.

concessions from the crown and the grant of Magna Carta. But if so, they were to be disappointed. London in 1233 appears to have remained staunchly royalist. Its citizens had been overjoyed by the dismissal of their arch-enemy, Hubert de Burgh, and were thereafter pacified by a pardon from arrears of taxes and tallages.[29] Here was no refuge for Siward and his band who for the next month vanish into some unknown retreat.

Meanwhile the king received further alarming reports from Devizes. On the night of 28 September, Hubert de Burgh had persuaded one of his gaolers to carry him, fettered as he was, from the castle keep into the sanctuary of the parish church. It was a remarkable escape, prompted, according to Wendover, by rumours that des Roches was about to be appointed constable of Devizes, raising fears for Hubert's life.[30] Clearly some sort of trouble had been anticipated. On 1 October, still unaware of Hubert's escape, the king ordered those guarding the bailey to do all in their power to restore de Burgh to the vault in which he had first been kept and to confine him in three sets of chains.[31] But these instructions arrived too late and in any case would have been impossible to implement without the consent of the knights who controlled the keep, independent of the king's men in the bailey. It was a retainer of one of these knights, William de Millières who, in company with de Burgh's chamberlain, removed Hubert from the castle.[32] When morning came, the garrison commander had the escapees dragged back, much as de Burgh had been forcibly removed from Brentwood the year before. As on that earlier occasion, it was the church authorities that intervened to save him. The bishop of Salisbury demanded that Hubert be restored to sanctuary, and when this demand went unanswered, excommunicated the garrison man by man. He then set out for London to lodge his complaints with the king.[33]

Relations between des Roches and the higher clergy had worsened since the spring. Criticism focussed particularly upon the treatment of

---

[29] Above pp. 267–8, 314–15 and see C60/32, m. 4, where in June 1233 the citizens were pardoned arrears of a fine of £1, 000 owing since 1222. For the fine itself, see Carpenter, *The Minority*, p. 291; *CRR*, xv, no. 481.

[30] Wendover, *Flores*, iv, pp. 274–5; *AM*, iii (Dunstable), p. 138; *Flores Hist.*, ii, p. 211; Coker, 'The "Margam Chronicle" in a Dublin manuscript', p. 135.

[31] *Cl.R.1231–4*, pp. 274, 325–6.

[32] *Ibid.*, pp. 277–8, 545; *CPR 1232–47*, p. 27. William was presumably a retainer of Humphrey de Millières, knight of John earl of Lincoln, who had guarded de Burgh since 1232; *Cl.R.1231–4*, p. 180; *Cal.Lib.R.1226–40*, p. 190. Both men were related to Master Humphrey de Millières, des Roches' official; *Acta*, appendix 4, no. 4.

[33] Wendover, *Flores*, iv, pp. 274–5; Coker, ' "Margam Chronicle" ', pp. 135–6.

Walter Mauclerk, bishop of Carlisle. Disgraced at court and deprived of lands held by royal charter, Mauclerk had been physically assaulted when, in August 1233, he had attempted to go into exile in Flanders. His assailants, the garrison of Dover, were excommunicated by Roger Niger, bishop of London, himself the victim of factional in-fighting at court. Accused of complicity in the anti-alien riots of 1232, Niger had been forced to travel to Rome to plead his innocence. On his way home he was robbed, something which can have done little to improve his temper towards the court. He had landed at Dover just in time to witness Mauclerk's humiliation.[34] Bishop Roger's influence should not be underestimated. He was shortly to be appointed custodian of the spiritualities of the vacant see of Canterbury, suggesting that he may already have been in the trust of the future archbishop Edmund.[35] Beyond the personal grievances against des Roches, there was a wider groundswell of clerical opposition to his regime. The pope had responded to this movement in June by quashing John Blund's election to Canterbury. In September he wrote to the king and to three bishops, including des Roches, demanding that de Burgh be released from captivity; letters which arrived too late to have any effect upon de Burgh's escape.[36] The Franciscans and Dominicans are said to have been especially active in voicing criticism of the regime. There is irony in this, since des Roches was himself an enthusiastic patron of the Dominicans and in the summer of 1233, as papal agent, had assisted in the foundation of a Franciscan house at Reading.[37]

THE WESTMINSTER COUNCIL OCTOBER 1233

Siward's attack upon des Roches, followed by the news from Devizes, forced a week's delay to the council planned for 2 October. When it finally assembled, the meeting was to be dominated by two principal issues: clerical discontent and the Marshal's continued refusal to attend court. According to Wendover, the bishops begged the king to make peace with the nobility. Apparently they laid much emphasis upon

[34] *Ibid.*, p. 272; *AM*, iii (Dunstable), p. 134; *Cl.R.1231–4*, p. 255.
[35] *The Cartulary of Shrewsbury Abbey*, ed. U. Rees, 2 vols. (Aberystwyth 1975), ii, no. 368d.
[36] *Cal.Pap.Reg.*, i, p. 137.
[37] Paris, *CM*, iii, p. 251; *AM*, i (Tewkesbury), p. 92, iii (Dunstable), p. 134; Wendover, *Flores*, iv, p. 282; *Cal. Chart. R. 1226–57*, p. 187. In the year to Michaelmas 1233 des Roches provided the Winchester Dominicans with at least 25 quarters of grain in alms; Ms. 28DR, mm. 2d, 3, 4, 6d, 14. For further activity by the Dominicans as peacemakers in the summer of 1234, see *Cl.R.1231–4*, p. 419.

the terms of Magna Carta, referring specifically to clause 39 and its provision of judgement by peers or the law of the land. Des Roches interjected that there were no peers in England as there were in France and that the king had authority, via his appointed justices, to banish the guilty from England and to condemn them by process of law.[38] These are enigmatic remarks and have inspired contradictory interpretations amongst historians. Powicke, for example, suggested that des Roches, the Frenchman, was pouring scorn on the pretensions of the *parvenu* English nobility.[39] More convincingly, Michael Clanchy suggests that a distinction was being drawn between France, where noblemen were entitled to special consideration before the law, and England where 'In accordance with the principles of common law established by Henry II, all freemen were equal in the king's court and ... judgment by peers meant (simply) judgment by other freemen.'[40] In France, trial by peers was a privilege reserved for a dozen or so of the greatest tenants-in-chief.[41] This system, with its concentration upon a specialized court of privileges, may have had a particular allure for Richard Marshal. Richard is said to have been Marshal of the French army in 1231. His family were undoubtedly hereditary marshals of England. In both countries the marshalcy involved jurisdiction over those tribunals which would later be termed courts of chivalry, reminiscent in their specialized jurisdiction of the French court of peers.[42] Far from it being des Roches who set out to scorn the English nobility, it may well have been the Marshal who was the more ardently francophile, in 1233 demanding a French interpretation of Magna Carta to allow for a privileged trial by fellow noblemen. Certainly the Marshal appears to have harped on about trial by peers in a way that suggests it was he rather than des Roches who was anxious to put a specialized interpretation on the term *pares*.

[38] Wendover, *Flores*, iv, p. 276.
[39] Powicke, *Henry III*, p. 76 and see P. Vinogradoff, 'Magna Carta, C.39. Nullus Liber Homo etc.', in *Magna Carta Commemoration Essays*, ed. H. E. Malden (London 1917), pp. 86–7, and F. M. Powicke, 'Per Iudicium Parium vel per legem Terrae', *ibid.*, pp. 96–121.
[40] Clanchy, *England and its Rulers*, pp. 220–1.
[41] For the French system, see B. C. Keeney, *Judgment by Peers* (Cambridge Mass. 1949), pp. 13–32. French practice was undoubtedly known of in England. It is referred to by Wendover, and Matthew Paris, who preserves the earliest recorded list of the twelve peers of France; *ibid.*, pp. 129–30nn.
[42] Crouch, *William Marshal*, pp. 205–8; G. D. Squibb, *The High Court of Chivalry* (Oxford 1959), pp. 1–2; J. H. Mitchell, *The Court of the Connétable* (Yale 1947), pp. 6–8. Richard's marshalcy in France is alleged by *AM*, iv (Osney), p. 72. In 1226 William Marshal II and the king had considered referring their differences over Caerleon to a specially constituted court of peers; *Pat. R. 1225–32*, pp. 82–3.

Perhaps equally striking is the moderation of the rest of the statement Wendover attributes to des Roches. Whatever the meaning of his remarks about peerage, the bishop made no attempt to justify arbitrary royal government; barons were only to be condemned after judgement in court, albeit in courts presided over by the king's appointed officers. This is a far more moderate line than that which Wendover ascribes to des Roches a few months earlier, when the bishop is said to have claimed that the king could banish whomsoever he chose from court and install alien loyalists in their place, without recourse to any tribunal or judgement.

Another sign of moderation at the Westminster council is provided by the award of safe-conducts to Richard de St John, a former royal chaplain who had been banished and whose lands had been confiscated in March 1233, apparently because he had obtained papal letters on behalf of de Burgh.[43] At the same time, the king bowed to pressure from the bishops. By 15 October de Burgh had been restored to sanctuary in Devizes. Royal assent was at last forthcoming for the election of Edmund of Abingdon as archbishop of Canterbury.[44] But the bishops remained unimpressed, threatening to excommunicate des Roches, de Rivallis, Seagrave, Passelewe and all those who had estranged the king from his subjects. Des Roches retorted, as he was entitled to, that he was exempt from the authority of any bishop in England, since he had been consecrated in Rome by the pope and possessed letters from Innocent III freeing him from excommunication or suspension save by direct papal authority. To forestall the bishops, he then appealed directly to Rome. This explains the dispatch to the Curia of Master John of Limoges, des Roches' clerk, early in November.[45] Meanwhile the clergy withdrew from court; a situation unprecedented since the Interdict of John's reign. Between 19 October 1233 and the following April, the only bishops to witness royal charters were des Roches, the chancellor Neville, and, in one isolated instance, William Brewer bishop of Exeter, des Roches' former companion on crusade.[46]

Clerical hostility was only fanned by the second main issue to be discussed in council: the king's relations with Richard Marshal. The

---

[43] *Cl.R.1231–4*, p. 327; above p. 369 n. 24.
[44] *Ibid.*, p. 327; *CPR 1232–47*, p. 27
[45] Wendover, *Flores*, iv, pp. 276–7; *CPR 1232–47*, p. 32. For the privilege, undoubtedly genuine, granted in 1205, see *Letters of Innocent III*, ed. Cheney, no. 664.
[46] Above p. 366 n. 13.

truce of Usk had assumed surrender by the Marshal and his followers, and their attendance in court. Instead, the majority of the Marshal's men persisted in rebellion, and from 22 September were subjected to renewed confiscation of their lands. As yet the king may have hoped to divide the Marshal from his rebellious affinity. Although threatening moves were made over Caerleon, the king continued to treat Richard as a repentant but loyal subject. He was asked to assist in the capture of Richard Siward and may indeed have opposed the more outrageous exploits of Siward's band.[47] According to the Tewkesbury annalist, he fully intended honouring his promises to attend court, and had travelled as far east as Woodstock when rumours of treachery sent him scurrying back to the safety of the Marches.[48] On 12 October, three days into the Westminster council, the Marshal was licensed to remove whatever stores he had deposited at Usk. But the king's temper was wearing thin. During the following week he ordered the seizure of Caerleon castle. According to the official explanation, the Marshal had failed to appear at Hereford to defend himself against Morgan ap Hywel. By judgement of the justices of the Bench, acting in the presence of the king and the Justiciar, it was ordered that Caerleon be distrained, pending the Marshal's attendance in court.[49]

The king acted here with far greater caution and legal propriety than he had shown earlier that summer. He appears to have done his utmost to salvage the September truce, to prevent rebellion spreading from the Marshal's men to the Marshal himself. As late as 14 October, the door to reconciliation was left open. The Marshal was promised free disposal of crops from Twyford and West Kington, Norman escheats seized from him several months earlier. On the same day an attempt was made to prolong the truce with Llywelyn, whose son David was granted part of the estate confiscated the previous year from Hubert de Burgh. This was one of the few awards of de Burgh's property to be made outside the charmed circle of courtiers and aliens: a measure of the importance attached to preserving peace with the Welsh.[50]

---

[47]   Cl.R.1231–4, p. 325. For the suggestion that he opposed Siward's raids, see *The Metrical Chronicle of Robert of Gloucester*, ed. W. A. Wright, 2 vols. (RS 1887), ii, pp. 722–3, set against the claim of the Margam annals, that Siward operated on the direct instructions of the Marshal; Coker, ' "Margam Chronicle" ', p. 136.

[48]   AM, i, p. 90.

[49]   Cl.R.1231–4, p. 278; CRR, xv, no. 489.

[50]   Cl.R.1231–4, p. 280. For Purleigh, see *ibid.*, pp. 280, 356, 367; *Cal. Chart. R. 1226–57*, pp. 12, 69, 81–2, 434; CRR, xv, no. 1895, for the manor of Purleigh, Essex.

THE RENEWAL OF HOSTILITIES

It was not until 17 October that the king moved against the Marshal, authorizing the seizure of his estate *en masse*, the land being transferred to the custody of Peter de Rivallis as escheator.[51] On the following day-five of the more important Marshal manors were released to Richard of Cornwall, together with land that Gilbert Basset held of the honour of Wallingford; a further attempt to guarantee Cornwall's loyalty, and one likely to deepen even further the animosity that had developed between him and the Marshal.[52] The catalyst for these actions was the news that in company with Llywelyn, the Marshal had forcibly ejected the king's garrison from Usk.[53] The nightmare of a rebel alliance with Wales had come to pass. According to Wendover, the host was now ordered to assemble at Gloucester by 2 November, the third military summons to have been issued in the past six months.[54]

Meanwhile, freed from the restraint that had characterized his attempts to appease clergy and rebels, the king reverted to his former, lavish patronage of courtiers. Stephen of Seagrave received a grant in perpetuity of a manor once the property of de Burgh. Others of de Burgh's manors passed during pleasure to the alien Macey de Bezill.[55] Peter de Rivallis was confirmed as farmer of Knaresborough. Brian de Lisle received custody of the royal manor of Freckenham.[56] There were custodies too for Michael fitz Nicholas, son of one of the royal stewards, and for Robert Passelewe's brother Hamo, appointed constable of Windsor and Odiham.[57] Stebbing in Essex was once again confiscated from William Ferrers, and granted to Henry de Trubleville. At the same time, the earl of Derby, William's father, was appeased by receiving the administration of his share in the Chester inheritance, denied him when the fees of the late earl of Chester had been distributed in the summer of 1233. A month later he was granted Stebbing on his son's behalf.[58]

On 17 October, the very day of the confiscation of Richard

---

[51] C60/32, m. 2.

[52] *Cl.R.1231–4*, p. 281.

[53] Wendover, *Flores*, iv, pp. 275–7; *AM*, i (Tewkesbury), pp. 90–1; Walker, 'Anglo-Welsh wars', pp. 315–24.

[54] Wendover, *Flores*, iv, p. 277.

[55] *Cl.R.1231–4*, p. 281; *Cal. Chart. R. 1226–57*, p. 187.

[56] C60/32, mm. 1, 2; E159/13, m. 7.

[57] C60/32, m. 1; *Cl.R.1231–4*, pp. 281–2.

[58] *Cl.R.1231–4*, pp. 281, 283, 344; *CPR 1232–47*, p. 32.

Marshal's estates, the king authorized payments of nearly £1,000, the Michaelmas term of the pensions owed to Poitevin and other French allies.[59] He was also obliged to keep up subsidies to Brittany. Peace negotiations with France had broken off inconclusively in August 1233, with no renewal of the truce which was due to expire the following July.[60] It was therefore all the more important that the king's continental allies be prepared for the possibility of hostilities from the French. The massive subsidies paid to duke Peter of Brittany the previous spring had been intended as only the first stage of a settlement, another 2,500 marks falling due at Christmas 1233. The chances of this money becoming available were greatly reduced by the revival of civil war. Instead, on 20 October, the duke was allowed to continue farming three Yorkshire wapentakes which had been granted him a year before in lieu of cash. As Christmas approached, this award was augmented by a grant of the manors of Twyford and West Kington, Norman land previously transferred to Richard Marshal from the Chester estate.[61]

Even more provocatively, the king began to award heiresses and wardships to aliens at court. On 3 October he had granted Macey Bezill the custody and marriage of Agnes, daughter of Reginald Basset, a former associate of the Marshal family and a distant cousin of Gilbert Basset.[62] The death of another Marshal familiar in November, Hugh of Sandford, was followed by the award of his eldest daughter to the alien, John de Plesset. Sandford's younger daughter went to the king's household knight, Robert Lupus.[63] Around 19 October, the king sought to divide the inheritance of the Yorkshire baron Nicholas de Stuteville, partitioning it between the local landholder Hugh Wake and William de Mastac, an alien distantly related to the king. Mastac appears to have received a share of the Stuteville lands even before being granted Stuteville's younger daughter in marriage, proceedings whose irregularity was compounded by the king's attempts to exclude Stuteville's chosen heir from his inheritance; yet another case in which Henry was later to admit that he had acted

[59] *Cal.Lib.R.1226–40*, pp. 236–7.

[60] *Cl.R.1231–4*, p. 246; *CPR 1232–47*, p. 22; *Foedera*, p. 210.

[61] C60/32, m. 1; *Cl.R.1231–4*, p. 353.

[62] *Cl.R.1231–4*, p. 277. With the Marshal's familiar, William of Rowden, Reginald held a fulling mill at Marlborough. He witnesses at least one charter of John Marshal, nephew of William I; *Rot. Chart.*, p. 218; *The Sandford Cartulary*, ed. A. M. Leys, 2 vols., Oxford Rec. Soc., xix, xxii (1938–41), i, no. 44.

[63] *Cl.R.1231–4*, pp. 338, 399, 408; C60/33, m. 9. Lupus' origins are unclear, but it is unlikely that he was an alien.

arbitrarily, *sine summonitione et sine iudicio*.[64] The most notorious alien marriage, that planned between the niece of Peter de Rivallis and the heir of John de Briouze, had apparently been agreed several months earlier. Nonetheless, in November 1233, the king demanded that John de Briouze's widow deliver up two of her younger sons whom she had so far refused to surrender to de Rivallis.[65]

The king's control over marriages and wardships had always been a sensitive issue. Only by the careful manipulation of such feudal incidents could families build up affinities and kinship networks such as that of the Marshals or the Bassets which loomed so large in the events of 1233. The intrusion of aliens into such a system was detested, not only because it disrupted the operation of local power politics, but because the aliens themselves were often considered to be of insultingly low birth. Names such as Macey Bezill, 'the plunderer', or Robert Lupus, 'the wolf', were hardly calculated to boost their holders' appeal as husbands-to-be. Bezill in particular spent years before he was able to obtain a bride. In 1234, it was judged that his custody of the daughter of Reginald Basset, sold meanwhile to Engelard de Cigogné, was invalid, since Basset had held of the king only in socage; Magna Carta clause 37 decreed that the king had no right of wardship or marriage of widows in socage tenures.[66] Undeterred, Bezill went on during the 1240s to profit from a lucrative trade in heiresses. So unappealing was he as a potential husband that a whole succession of women appears to have been willing to pay him money rather than become his bride.[67] It was almost certainly marriages such as this that the authors of Magna Carta had in mind when they demanded that no woman be married to her disparagement. Certainly the barons of 1258 were to gloss disparagement as marriage to 'those who are not true born Englishmen (*de natione regni Anglie*)'.[68] In the spring of 1234 the bishops are said to have accused des Roches and his fellow courtiers of disparaging noble women and wards by granting them to their own alien associates. In particular, the

---

[64] *Cl.R.1231–4*, pp. 340, 342, 351, 383; C60/32, m. 2; *CRR*, xv, no. 1026. The case is considered in detail by Powicke, 'Per Iudicium Parium'; pp. 104–5; Turner, *The King and his Courts*, pp. 250–1. William de Mastac may have been a kinsman of Boso de Matha (*Mastak*') count of Bigorre *iure uxoris*, and lord of Cognac, perhaps by descent from an illegitimate son of King Richard I; Abbott, *Provinces, Pays and Seigneuries of France*, pp. 461, 468–9. Boso visited England in 1234; *Cl.R.1231–4*, p. 539; E372/79, mm. 5, 5d.

[65] *Cl.R.1231–4*, p. 330.

[66] *CRR*, xv, no. 1061; C60/33, mm. 2, 5.

[67] *CPR 1232–47*, pp. 243, 285, 375, 475, 478.

[68] *DBM*, pp. 80–1.

king's cousin, Eleanor of Brittany, and Henry's sisters, were considered to be at risk.[69] As early as 1221, it had been rumoured that des Roches and Peter de Maulay had sinister designs upon Eleanor of Brittany. In 1233 she remained at Bristol castle under the custody of des Roches' familiar Roger Aliz, a Hampshire knight promoted from episcopal into royal service.[70] The two royal princesses, Eleanor and Isabella, had been des Roches' wards prior to 1220, but seem not to have been in the bishop's keeping thereafter. Nonetheless it was clearly feared that they might be forced to accept undesirable partners. Negotiations for Isabella's marriage to the emperor Frederick II, the hero of des Roches' crusade, were almost certainly put in train during the period of the bishop's ascendancy.[71]

CIVIL WAR: THE SECOND CAMPAIGN NOVEMBER 1233

Henry III had failed to heal the breaches with Richard Marshal or the church. No permanent settlement had been reached after the siege of Usk. His household knights, many of them aliens, remained in possession of rebel lands. The rebels themselves refused to make their peace. The Westminster council of October 1233 had been followed by the renewal of civil war on the Marches, and by the withdrawal of virtually all of the higher clergy from court. The king's attempts to appease clerical opinion by restoring Hubert de Burgh to sanctuary only led to further complications. On 29 October de Burgh was snatched from Devizes in yet another raid led by Richard Siward. According to a vivid account, found in a recently rediscovered continuation of the annals of Margam, Siward and his men chose market day at Devizes to launch their attack. Whilst various of his supporters mingled with the crowds in the town, Siward and a band of Welshmen charged in on the terrified inhabitants, making such a clamour that it was feared that the Marshal and Llywelyn had come in person with their entire army. Bundling de Burgh on to horseback, the attackers made their escape, assisted by a fog that shrouded the

---

[69] Wendover, *Flores*, iv, p. 296.

[70] Above p. 201. Bristol and Eleanor are said to have been held from *c.*October 1233 to May 1234 by Peter de Rivallis via Roger Aliz; E372/77, m. 1d; E372/78, m. 15. For Aliz, see *Acta*, appendix 4, no. 37.

[71] Isabella appears to have been kept mostly at Gloucester and at Marlborough, the second of which passed into the custody of des Roches' steward Roger Wacelin in 1233; E372/78, m. 16; *Cl.R.1231–4*, pp. 65, 79, 107, 235–6, 430. Eleanor received provisions at des Roches' manor of Ivinghoe in 1231–2; Ms. 27DR, m. 4d. For contacts with the empire in 1233–4, leading to Isabella's betrothal first announced by the emperor in November 1234, see *Treaty Rolls*, i, p. 6; E372/78, m. 7; *Cl.R.1231–4*, p. 303.

town of Devizes and the countryside for several miles around. At the crossing of the Severn estuary, at Aust, they spent several anxious hours, repulsing an attack from the men of Bristol. It was feared that no ship would arrive to carry them into Wales, and that de Burgh would have to be left to fend for himself whilst his rescuers fled into hiding. All night they waited, whilst over and over again de Burgh repeated an invocation to the Virgin Mary: 'Fear not, Our Lady will save you; Fear not, Our Lady will save you.' At last, towards dawn, a ship arrived. Having fought off yet another attack launched from Bristol, they landed at Chepstow, where they were greeted in person by Richard Marshal.[72] In military terms the raid achieved little. De Burgh was in no fit state to fight alongside the Marshal. His former supporters in England showed no inclination to throw in their lot with the rebels: a telling contrast to the strength of the loyalties engendered amongst the affinity of the Marshals, great warriors who by carving out lordships for themselves in Leinster and south Wales had acquired military experience, land and patronage very different from those of the *parvenu* de Burgh. Nonetheless, Siward's rescue attempt was significant, if not in recruiting men to the Marshal's cause, then as a powerful exercise in propaganda. Wendover claims that Hubert had been plucked from certain death at the hands of des Roches.[73] The claim is probably a groundless one. Des Roches was not a murderer. Nonetheless, it may well have been believed, providing the opposition with yet further valuable propaganda. Henceforth, the bishop's two greatest rivals, the Marshal and de Burgh, were united in opposition.

Just as fury against the Marshal had prompted the king into over-lavish patronage of aliens and courtiers, so de Burgh's escape provoked reprisals, swinging popular opinion yet further behind the rebels. In mid-November the sheriff of Wiltshire was ordered to outlaw de Burgh, Siward, Basset and the two men who had escaped with Hubert from Devizes castle. Outlawry itself was to be by appeal in the county court on behalf of those set to guard de Burgh.[74] It was later agreed that this process was irregular. The king admitted as much in January 1234, when he revised his earlier instructions, allowing for summonses to three successive county courts followed by outlawry in the fourth, in accordance with law

---

[72] Coker, ' "Margam Chronicle" ', pp. 136–8, and for further details see Wendover, *Flores*, iv, p. 277; *AM*, i (Tewkesbury), p. 91; *Cl.R.1231–4*, pp. 328–9, 350; E372/78, m. 15.

[73] Wendover, *Flores*, iv, pp. 273–4.

[74] *Cl.R.1231–4*, pp. 544–5.

and custom.[75] Even then, the sentence was subsequently overturned on the grounds that outlawry could only follow formal conviction in the king's court; no such conviction had been pressed against de Burgh and his companions, who were nonetheless subject to all the penalties and hazards of outlawry, including the threat of capture dead or alive.[76] In October 1233 the king reverted to his earlier policy of ordering the destruction of rebel property, including that of Richard Marshal. Orchards and gardens were to be uprooted, houses and fishponds destroyed; arbitrary punishments which seem to have elicited nothing but sympathy for the rebels in the country at large.[77]

Twice the king believed he had brought the Marshal to settlement; twice his hopes had been dashed. The nightmare of an alliance between the rebels and Llywelyn had now come to pass. The entire border-country from Cheshire south to Bristol was open to attack. As the king wearily made his way back to the Marches, forced for the second time that year to call upon the help of the knight service of England, he can have had only one thought: to inflict such a defeat upon his enemies that they would never again dare challenge the royal will. Relations with the lesser Marcher lords were still tense. Even though Clifford and the Marshal's Marcher allies had made peace with the crown, they were still required to deliver hostages and castles as security. In November, as during the summer, it was considered expedient to guard against rebellion in the west country. This may explain why the knight service of Cornwall was excluded from the king's summons to Hereford. In the same way, the knights of the five most northerly counties including Yorkshire were not required to fight in the Marches.[78] The danger here was all too obvious. Relations with Scotland had deteriorated ever since de Burgh's disgrace. De Burgh's brother-in-law, King Alexander, now threatened to throw in his lot with the rebels, laying claim to the counties of Cumberland and Northumberland as part of the abortive marriage settlement between Henry III and the Scottish king's younger sister, proposed by de Burgh in 1231.[79] The Scots may even

---

[75]   *Ibid.*, p. 545.
[76]   Powicke, 'Per Iudicium Parium', pp. 105–7.
[77]   C60/33, m. 11; *Cl.R.1231–4*, pp. 542–3.
[78]   *Cl.R.1231–4*, pp. 544–5. For other defence measures in the west, including the garrisoning of Corfe and Sherborne, see *ibid.*, p. 546; *CPR 1232–47*, pp. 31–3; E372/78, mm. 13, 13d, 16.
[79]   That such a claim was made can be inferred from the settlement eventually reached in 1237; *Anglo-Scottish Relations 1174–1328*, ed. E. L. G. Stones, 2nd edn (Oxford 1970), pp. xxiii, 38–53.

have entered a formal alliance with the English rebels. An inventory of the Scots' royal archive compiled in the 1280s refers to 'letters of the confederation of Richard Marshal'.[80] Carlisle and Cumberland were in uproar over the attack upon bishop Mauclerk. Carlisle itself was placed under Interdict on 27 November, although the cathedral canons ignored the sentence, much as they had done after 1215 when they had supported the Scots against King John.[81] During the winter Henry III was forced to spend at least £200, preparing engines and repairing the walls of Bamburgh and Newcastle-upon-Tyne against the threat of a Scottish invasion.[82]

To begin with, the king appears to have planned a major offensive in south Wales, similar to that of August. All supplies to Wales were prohibited, and all ships by which such supplies might be carried were impounded. The feudal host was summoned to meet at Hereford by 18 November. Meanwhile, around 12 November, Henry pushed westwards.[83] His first staging post was the castle of Grosmont, now held in perpetual fee by Peter de Rivallis. Apparently the castle and its promontory were too narrow to accommodate the entire court, the king's baggage train being left overnight on the plain below. There it fell prey to ambush. Des Roches, Seagrave and de Rivallis were forced to stand by as their wagons were looted. The Marshal himself refused to take part in the attack, according to Wendover, being unwilling to raise arms against the king. Once again, it was the Marshal's men in company with the Welsh who actually did the fighting. Significantly, the only royalist known to have been killed at Grosmont was the veteran Hugh of Sandford, once a familiar of William Marshal I, now considered a turncoat by the Marshal household.[84] Confirming the impression that the war was degenerating into a vendetta amongst the Marshal affinity, from Grosmont the rebels moved on to Monmouth, where they besieged the castle of John of

---

[80] *The Acts of the Parliament of Scotland*, ed. T. Thomson and C. Innes, vol. i 1124–1423 (London 1844), p. 108: *littera confederationis Ricardi Marscalli*. The Scots archive was dispersed and large parts of it destroyed during the wars of Edward I's reign. All of Alexander II's legitimate sisters were married to allies of the Marshal: Margaret to Hubert de Burgh, Isabella to Roger Bigod earl of Norfolk, and Marjorie, after 1234, to Gilbert Marshal, Richard's successor as earl of Pembroke.

[81] *Chronicon de Lanercost*, ed. Stevenson, p. 42.

[82] E372/78, m. 12d.

[83] *Cl.R.1231–4*, pp. 338, 542–5.

[84] Wendover, *Flores*, iv, pp. 278–9; *AM*, i (Tewkesbury), p. 91. In general see Walker, 'Anglo-Welsh wars', pp. 342–6. For Sandford, see *Cl.R.1231–4*, p. 339; Crouch, *William Marshal*, pp. 199–200. His brother had acted as guardian to Richard Marshal during the latter's childhood; Painter, *William Marshal*, pp. 146, 173; Crouch, *William Marshal*, pp. 109–10.

Monmouth, yet another veteran familiar of William Marshal I. As a sign of their hatred, they set fire to John's family foundation, the abbey of Grace Dieu.[85]

The Grosmont raid effectively brought an end to the planned royal offensive. Instead the king retired to Hereford, until in mid-December he moved even further from the fighting, to the relative security of Gloucester. It was in the aftermath of his humiliation at Grosmont that Henry authorized the controversial outlawry of Siward, Basset and de Burgh. His fury and frustration are easy to understand. The Marshal and the Welsh were left to take the offensive. In October their forces had temporarily seized Abergavenny, a Briouze fortress. They also occupied much of Glamorgan including the castles of Cardiff and Newport, an indication of the weak control exercised by the king within the lands of the earldom of Gloucester, theoretically in the keeping of Peter de Rivallis, but in practice delegated to local officers by who knows what contorted chain of command. In November 1233 the Welsh went on to lay siege to Carmarthen.[86] The king was unable even to obtain ecclesiastical sanctions against his enemies. Twice during November, in church councils at Cirencester and Gloucester, the clergy met in an attempt to bring about peace, on the second occasion in direct contravention of royal orders.[87] The king is said to have considered sending for a papal legate to assist him against the bishops, yet another echo of the despondency and chaos of King John's final years.[88]

ROYAL FINANCE

One other problem confronted the court. In 1231 it had been de Burgh's inability to raise income, combined with the financial effects of war in Wales, that propelled the court into bankruptcy, persuading the king to turn to des Roches for a solution. A similar combination of events was repeated in the winter of 1233–4, the one difference being that it was now des Roches and his colleagues who were unable to meet the need for supply. The period of bonanza, in which escheats and wardships had come pouring into the crown, was at an end. The king's ministers had made deep inroads into de Burgh's estate for

---

[85] *AM*, i (Tewkesbury), p. 91, ii (Waverley), p. 312, and see Wendover, *Flores*, iv, pp. 289–90; *Cl.R.1231–4*, p. 331.
[86] *Brut y Tywysogyon*, pp. 231–3; Walker, 'Anglo-Welsh wars', pp. 332–3, 346–8, 354–6.
[87] *AM*, i (Tewkesbury), p. 91; *CPR 1232–47*, pp. 32–3.
[88] Wendover, *Flores*, iv, p. 288.

personal gain. Many of the king's more valuable wardships, the Gloucester, Chester and Devon estates, had been granted away to buy support from the likes of Richard of Cornwall or the earl of Derby. Lands confiscated from rebels and from Richard Marshal were inadequate even to pay the wages of the king's household knights. Unable to trust the local Marcher lords, after the summer of 1233 the king was forced to draft in mercenary garrisons to defend a vast collection of castles from Shropshire southwards into Somerset and Devon. Added to this, there was the cost of defence against the Scots. The greatest windfalls of all, the lay subsidy of a fortieth granted in 1232, and the tallage of 10,000 marks against the Jews, had already been depleted by the subsidies paid or promised to Brittany and Poitou. The disastrous harvest of 1233 pushed up the price of foodstuffs, further devaluing the king's cash resources. From August onwards, most of the proceeds of the fortieth stored in provincial treasuries were redirected to the Marches, siphoned off into the payment of mercenaries and the cost of maintaining the court at Hereford and Gloucester.[89] In 1232 bankruptcy had been blamed on de Burgh's failure to obtain lay subsidy, but a year later the king was bankrupt once again, even after lay subsidy, regardless of unprecedented taxation against the Jews and in spite of the richest haul of escheats and wardships assembled since John's reign. The receipt at the *adventus vicecomitum* in September 1233 was only £1,751, less than at Easter that year and nearly £1,000 down on the Michaelmas *adventus* of 1232.[90]

It had been intended to charge a scutage for the king's abortive expedition to Ireland in August 1233. When the army was diverted from Ireland to campaign against the Marshal, fines were still levied 'for the army of Ireland which remained in Wales'. Those who offered them, mostly churchmen, were promised that they might recoup the money from their tenantry as if it were a scutage. Writs to this effect were drawn up but never dispatched. Instead, the brevity of the Usk campaign and its apparent success prompted the king to waive his right to the money offered. Only 60 marks, fined by the abbot of St Augustine's Canterbury, seems to have been paid cash down.[91] But the peace did not hold. The revival of civil war led to the renewal of demands for scutage. From 29 October onwards, those

---

[89] *Cl.R.1231–4*, pp. 255, 337; *CPR 1232–47*, pp. 33, 37; E372/78, mm. 14, 15; *Foreign Accounts*, pp. 63–73.

[90] *Memoranda Rolls 1231–3*, nos. 2775–2803, 3099–138; E159/13, m. 12.

[91] C60/32, m. 2; E372/78, mm. 6, 15.

who had fined earlier for the Usk campaign were asked to pay their proffers with all dispatch. At the same time, many new fines were taken, again mostly from churchmen. They were described variously as fines in lieu of scutage or as aids for knights sent against the Marshal, and the sums offered were substantial.[92] Once again there was an understanding that the money could be recovered from subtenants, but as at Usk, no writs to this effect seem to have been issued, prompting accusations from the abbot of Peterborough that his fine of £100 had been obtained under false pretences.[93] The overall effect must have been to heighten animosity between the church and the court. Very little of the money offered could be collected. Perhaps as little as 250 marks from a total proffer of over 1,000 marks was recovered by Michaelmas 1234, wholly inadequate to meet the cost of the war.[94] Two facts stand out: the church and especially the bishops preferred to offer money rather than to send knights against the Marshal, a sign of their disaffection with royal policy. Secondly, both attempts to raise scutage, in August and again in November 1233, had to be abandoned, the first occasion since 1214 when the collection of scutage had broken down. The campaign against the Marshal was politically too sensitive to allow a general military levy. In 1214 it had been des Roches whose heavy-handedness was blamed for resistance to the notorious scutage of Poitou. In 1233, for the second time in his career, he was to be associated with the collapse of consent for military taxation.

Denied scutage, the king was forced to sell off various of his more lucrative wardships and escheats, reverting to precisely that system which had operated before de Rivallis' supposed reforms. By February 1234 three of the wards held successively by de Burgh and de Rivallis had been disposed of: the heir of Nigel de Mowbray, sold to the earl of Lincoln for 1,000 marks; the Avranches heir, sold to William Brewer bishop of Exeter for 2,000 marks; and Hugh de Aubigny, heir to the earldom of Arundel who fined 2,500 marks to have free administration of his estates during what remained of his minority.[95] The sums offered were far larger than those originally obtained from de Burgh, who had paid 500 marks each cash down for the Avranches and Mowbray wardships, and apparently nothing at all for custody of

---

[92] C60/33, mm. 10, 11.
[93] CUL ms. D. & C. Peterborough I (Peterborough cartulary), f. 270r: *Abbas tandem fecit finem .c. li(brarum), et propter finem illum promissum fuit scutagium abbati, et formata fuit breve de scutagio assisendo, et quia breve fuit besiliata abbas perdidit tunc scutagium.*
[94] E372/78 passim.
[95] C60/33, mm. 8–11.

the Arundel lands.[96] But although the new fines may look impressive, and although they were set at steep terms of repayment, virtually no money was collected. Neither the earl of Lincoln nor Hugh de Aubigny had paid in a single penny by Michaelmas 1234. The bishop of Exeter handed over 250 marks, but his ward, the Avranches boy, died before any more money was forthcoming.[97] The auction of wardships thus did nothing to solve the king's financial crisis. If anything, it only compounded the problem, yielding very little in cash terms, whilst depriving the king of whatever income might otherwise have been collected via direct management of the estates in question. Simultaneously, the overrunning of Glamorgan by the rebels and the election of archbishop Edmund cancelled out most of the benefits that had accrued from the honours of Canterbury and the earldom of Gloucester.

Some attempt was made to impose stricter terms for debts. In November 1233, instructions were issued for the bishop of Durham to pursue bishop Mauclerk for 500 marks of assorted debt.[98] But the political situation was too tense to allow distraint against the greatest of the crown's debtors, the lay baronage. On the contrary, in an effort to curry favour, the regime was obliged to relax or respite a large variety of repayments.[99] After Christmas 1233 a tallage was imposed on the royal demesne, the only remotely successful fiscal measure attempted during these months, yielding more than 2,000 marks, of which the majority was paid by the following Michaelmas.[100] Des Roches himself was prevailed upon to lend money to the crown. Already in October 1233 he had provided £100 to pay the king's mariners, and he subsequently advanced credits of 800 marks to royal ambassadors sent to Rome.[101] But des Roches had been badly hit by the recent harvest. His manorial receipts were down by as much as a third on previous years. He alone could not be expected to meet the cost of the war, and in any event, always the canny businessman, he appears to have recovered his loans almost as soon as they were made, by the simple expedient of withholding everything he owed for the fortieth on movables.[102]

[96] C60/30, m. 9; *Cal. Chart. R. 1226–57*, pp. 49, 126.
[97] E372/78, mm. 4d, 6d, 7d.
[98] C60/33, m. 11.
[99] C60/33, mm. 9, 10; E159/13, m. 8, covering respites or reschedules on behalf of William Longespée, William de Cantiloupe and the earls of Aumale and Norfolk.
[100] C60/33, m. 9; *Cl.R.1231–4*, p. 363; Mitchell, *Studies in Taxation*, pp. 207–8.
[101] *Cl.R.1231–4*, p. 329; *CPR 1232–47*, p. 33; *Cal.Lib.R.1226–40*, pp. 267–8.
[102] *Foreign Accounts*, pp. 71–2. For manorial receipts, compare Mss. 27DR; 28DR.

From the king's point of view, the most depressing aspect of this crisis must have been the squandering of vast resources to achieve an entirely negative objective. The Welsh campaign of 1233 was a war not of conquest but containment. At de Burgh's fall the king had found himself possessed of wealth which would have been unimaginable earlier in his reign; great prospects opened before him. For many years, the failure of Plantagenet initiatives abroad had been blamed on inadequate finances. Now at last it was possible to shower favour on the nobility of Brittany and Poitou in the hope of reaping even richer rewards in future. The Welsh appeared to have been pacified. There were plans for conquest in Ireland. However, all of these prospects were blighted by the Marshal's rebellion. The court settled down to a dismal waiting game, forced to spend the coldest winter months in a temporary encampment, cut off from the comforts of London. The Christmas festivities of 1233 made a sorry contrast to the magnificence with which des Roches had entertained the king at Christmas two years before. In an ice-bound landscape, short of money with barely enough food to supply his needs, it would not be surprising if the king began to grow impatient with his ministers.[103] Late in December news arrived that Richard Siward had carried out another raid into England, pillaging the Justiciar's principal manor of Seagrave in Leicestershire, Richard of Cornwall's favourite seat at Beckley and a nearby manor belonging to des Roches.[104]

THE COURT

Our view of the court during these months is obscured by the shortage of records. The charter and *liberate* rolls are missing after October 1233. Chance survivals enable us to reconstruct perhaps a third of the lost charter roll, and to learn something of the personalities around the king. Of the sixteen surviving charters issued between November 1233 and April the following year, des Roches is witness or beneficiary to every one.[105] Seagrave witnesses all but three, and

---

[103] For conditions, see Wendover, *Flores*, iv, p. 289.
[104] *AM*, iv (Osney), p. 76; Wendover, *Flores*, iv, pp. 282, 290; *Cl.R.1231–4*, p. 363.
[105] The sources are *CAR*, nos. 17, 333; *Cal. Chart. R. 1257–1300*, p. 115; *Cal. Chart. R. 1300–1326*, p. 199; *Archaeologia* 15 (1806), pp. 209–10; *Selborne Charters*, ed. Macray, i, pp. 10–14 (including one charter which should perhaps be redated to 1233); *Reg.Antiq.Lincs.*, i, pp. 177–8; *HMC Wells*, pp. 17–18; *Sarum Charters*, pp. 231–2; *Cartulary of Chichester*, ed. Peckham, no. 808; *Descriptive Catalogue of the Charters and Muniments in the Possession of Lord Fitzhardinge at Berkeley Castle*, ed. I. H. Jeayes (Bristol 1892), no. 231; *Descriptive Catalogue of Derbyshire Charters*, ed. I. H. Jeayes (London 1906), nos. 1161–2; *Cartulary of Osney Abbey*, ed. H. E. Salter, 6 vols., Oxford Hist. Soc., lxxxix–

there are regular appearances by various household knights including the alien John de Plesset. The earls of Aumale, Derby, Hereford, Chester, Lincoln and Warenne were all at court on more than one occasion. Richard of Cornwall appears only on 14 March 1234, on which day he was granted the manor of Haughley in perpetual fee, formerly part of de Burgh's estate.[106] Although he had incurred the hatred of the rebels for deserting the Marshal, Richard appears to have remained detached from court. More remarkable still is the fact that after October 1233, Peter de Rivallis witnesses not a single recorded royal charter. He was undoubtedly still at court. He received money in the wardrobe and seems still to have controlled many aspects of government. The vast majority of administrative writs continued to be issued under his warranty.[107] Since notes of warranty were included both in the enrolment and on the original writ itself, the country continued to be bombarded with letters in which de Rivallis' name appeared almost as often as that of the king.[108] No wonder the opposition complained that not a single royal writ or instruction could be issued without de Rivallis' say, or under his seal: presumably the privy seal kept in his custody.[109] It may be that the physical detachment between the wardrobe and the Chancery explains de Rivallis' absence from witness lists. At the same time, it is possible that his name was deliberately suppressed from charter witness lists, perhaps as that of the royal minister most hated in the country at large, perhaps at the insistence of the chancellor, Ralph de Neville. De Rivallis received no fresh grant of patronage after the summer of 1233. His control over wardships and escheats was loosened by the auctioning off of the de Aubigny, Avranches and Mowbray lands. It may be that his relations with the king were increasingly strained.

This is not to suggest that the king ceased to favour controversial figures at court. Although there were no new awards to des Roches,

---

xci, xcvii–xcviii, ci (1929–36), vi, pp. 80–1; C47/12/7, no. 70; E36/57 (Earldom of Cornwall cartulary), f. 69r–v; BL ms. Cotton C ix (Hospitallers' cartulary), f. 50r (misdated to 1232); Bodl. ms. Ashmole 1527 (Lichfield cartulary), f. 96r; CUL ms. Ely 3/28 (Ely Liber M), f. 111r; Durham, Prior's Kitchen Library ms. D. & C. Durham, Cartuarium III, ff. 213v–214v; Oxford, Magdalen College muniments ms. Chalgrove Deed 55B; Stratford upon Avon, Shakespeare Birthplace Library ms. E1/66 (Saunders' transcripts), ff. 15v–17v; Westminster Abbey Muniments nos. 15163, 15208.

[106] E36/57 (Earldom of Cornwall cartulary), f. 69r–v; *Cl.R.1231–4*, p. 385.

[107] *CPR 1232–47*, pp. 33–5, 37, 40; *Cl.R.1231–4*, pp. 329–405 *passim*.

[108] See, for example, Angers, Archives Départementales de Maine-et-Loire 193H1 no. 13, original letters patent of Henry III for Fontevraud, 20 October 1233, ending with the warranty clause *per P. de Ryvall'*.

[109] Wendover, *Flores*, iv, p. 296.

both Seagrave and Passelewe continued to receive lands from de Burgh's former estate, in fee. Seagrave seems also to have assembled a rich collection of gifts and douceurs from private individuals such as the earls of Chester and Derby, Simon de Montfort and Henry de Trubleville.[110] Amongst the aliens at court, Macey Bezill received the manor of Westhall.[111] Another of de Burgh's manors held of the crown, Ospringe in Kent, passed to the alien household knight Joldewin de Doué.[112] In January 1234 Peter de Maulay was appointed constable of Devizes, the first time that he had held crown office since 1221, and ominously reminiscent of the years after 1215 when, as castellan of Corfe, his influence had extended across the entire south-west.[113] On the very eve of the regime's collapse, in March 1234, Brian de Lisle was appointed life constable of Bolsover, reviving another of the more controversial appointments of John's reign, and threatening a return to the private war that had raged after 1215 between de Lisle and the earl of Derby.[114] Yet such promotions, charters and awards for life, were becoming irrelevant. The court was in turmoil. The king's actions lacked assent from the majority of churchmen or barons. The repeal and annulment of royal charters from the summer of 1232 onwards had served to undermine the whole currency of such awards. In due course, it was to prove easy to sweep away the privileges guaranteed to Seagrave, Passelewe, de Rivallis and their colleagues, precisely because these men had done so much to undermine the security of tenure by royal charter.

THE REBEL CAMP

If the prospects for the king were bleak then they were bleaker still for the Marshal. In a rebellion not of his own making, the Marshal had no clear objective other than to inflict the utmost injury on his former colleagues at court. After October 1232, allied to Llywelyn, he appears to have been regarded with some justification as a traitor by the king. Communications between the court and the rebels appear

[110] *Cl.R.1231–4*, pp. 332, 368; *Archaeologia* 15 (1806), pp. 209–10; Stratford upon Avon, Shakespeare Birthplace Library ms. E1/66 (Saunders' transcripts), ff. 15v–17v no. 489; BL ms. Harley 4748 (List of titles to Seagrave cartulary), ff. 3r, 9r, 10r, 14v, 22v, 24v, 30v; Turner, *Men Raised from the Dust*, pp. 139–40. Various of the charters merely mentioned in the list of titles to the Seagrave cartulary are preserved in fuller versions in BL ms. Egerton 3789 (Glover transcripts).

[111] *CAR*, no. 17; *Cl.R.1231–4*, p. 379; *Cal. Chart. R. 1226–57*, p. 82.

[112] *Cal. Chart. R. 1226–57*, p. 11; *Cl.R.1231–4*, pp. 396–7.

[113] *Cl.R.1231–4*, p. 361.

[114] *CPR 1232–47*, pp. 41–2; C60/33, m. 8; above p. 334.

to have been kept open by the religious, especially the friars. Wend-over reports an encounter between the Franciscan, Agnellus of Pisa, and the Marshal at Margam late in December 1233. Agnellus carried peace terms from the king and messages from the Justiciar urging Richard to throw himself on the king's mercy as a prelude to peace; he might then expect a reasonable settlement of lands in Here-fordshire, an offer that implies the confiscation of the remainder of the Marshal estate, and one which Richard could never seriously have entertained. Agnellus is also said to have transmitted the accusations being made against Richard at court: that he had rebelled for no just cause, without any threat to his property or his personal safety; that he was allied to the king's capital enemies, the French, the Scots and the Welsh; that he had openly attacked the king at Grosmont, but that his army was now hopelessly outnumbered. The king's kinsmen could easily be brought to England to put down rebellion.[115] The king enjoyed full support in Rome and could expect to detach the Marshal from his allies abroad.

In all of this Wendover was writing with partisan intent; setting up a version of the king's case that was not only repugnant in itself, with its veiled references to the king's relations in Poitou, but which could all the more easily be rebuffed in the response Wendover attributes to the Marshal. According to this latter, the Marshal denied responsibility for the war; he had always been willing to answer to the law and judgement of his peers in the king's courts, yet the king had attacked his lands without any justice. At Usk the king had been offered generous terms, but he had broken his word, renewing his diffidation of the Marshal and depriving him of his hereditary office at court. Even then, it had been the Marshal's men, not Richard himself, who attacked the king at Grosmont. Whilst prepared once again to trust the king, he could never have faith in his ministers, who had broken oaths sworn to the Marshal, to de Burgh and in respect to the liberties contained in Magna Carta. Wendover then turns the debate towards the question of alien influence. Richard is said to have argued that it was not he but the king who relied on foreign powers. The king of Scots and Llywelyn had rebelled only because of the injuries inflicted on them by the English court. The Marshal had heard it said that des Roches was in league with the emperor Frederick II and intended

[115] The only royal kinsman known to have been brought to England during this period was William de Mastac, for whom see above pp. 413–14 and n. 64. The reference here can hardly be to Hugh de Lusignan, Henry's stepfather, who had failed to support Henry against Louis IX during the Breton expedition of 1230.

subduing the entire realm to imperial control. It was des Roches and his allies who were the king's true enemies. Wendover ends his account with yet another reference to the Marshal's men without whom, in the words attributed to Richard, 'I can do nothing towards reaching a permanent settlement'; an accurate summary of the Marshal's dilemma ever since Basset, Siward and their confederates had edged him into rebellion.[116]

Overall, Wendover provides a peculiar blend of hearsay and wishful thinking. He may nonetheless paint an accurate picture of the prejudices at work in the rival camps. The references to des Roches' plot with the Empire could well have been fuelled by the glowing references the bishop is known to have made to Frederick II, by negotiations for the marriage of the king's sister Isabella, and (who knows) by some sort of residual memory of the claims to sovereignty over England put forward by Hohenstaufen propagandists from the 1150s onwards. Des Roches had spent several years on crusade and in Italy in the emperor's company, whilst the history of Frederick's minority appears to have been well known in England, referred to as an example of minority rule by the councillors of the boy-king, Henry III, after 1216.[117] Nonetheless, to brand des Roches a Hohenstaufen conspirator is as ludicrous as to portray the francophile Richard Marshal as an Englishman through and through. Anti-alien sentiments were widespread and had long proved useful in the hands of des Roches' enemies. In 1233 the distinctly un-English Richard Marshal sought to use them in a court-centred, politically motivated vendetta. His success in playing the alien card should not obscure the basic hopelessness of his cause. At best he faced a humiliating reconciliation with the king, at worst the confiscation of his entire estate. In the New Year his forces opened a new offensive against Shrewsbury, but their overall position continued to crumble.[118] Since the summer the king had been able to rally support in Ireland. The majority of the Anglo-Irish nobility, including the Lacy lords of Ulster and the once rebellious Richard de Burgh, now joined the Irish Justiciar, Maurice fitz Gerald, in a private war against Leinster. The Marshal's Irish tenantry, nearly all of them landholders in England and south Wales, were mostly engaged in the rebellion on the Welsh

---

[116] Wendover, *Flores*, iv, pp. 282–9.

[117] Above pp. 150, 208–9. For imperial claims to overlordship, see K. Leyser, 'Frederick Barbarossa, Henry II and the hand of St James', *EHR* 90 (1975), pp. 481–506, esp. pp. 504–6, reprinted in Leyser, *Medieval Germany and its Neighbours 900–1250* (London 1982), pp. 233–40, esp. pp. 238–40.

[118] Wendover, *Flores*, iv, p. 291.

Marches. In their absence the entire lordship of Leinster was threatened with dismemberment. In was in this context, towards the beginning of February 1234, that the Marshal decided to quit Wales. Left to fight on alone, Llywelyn soon opened negotiations with the king. Meanwhile the Marshal crossed to Ireland, a gesture that Wendover presents as defiant, intended to spread rebellion across the Irish Sea, but which in fact was more a sign of desperation.[119] Ireland had been involved in rebellion from the start. The Marshal crossed to Leinster, not to foment trouble but to forestall the collapse of his Irish lordship.

[119] Wendover, *Flores*, iv, p. 300. The continuation of the Margam annals claims that the Irish barons, 'by common counsel', had sent nuncios to England demanding the dismissal of des Roches, de Rivallis and Stephen of Seagrave. When this demand was refused, they issued a diffidation of the king and his supporters; Coker, 'The "Margam Chronicle"', p. 138. In general, see Orpen, *Ireland under the Normans*, iii, pp. 59–70.

Chapter 13

THE FALL OF PETER DES ROCHES

Just as the Marshal seems to have despaired of victory in Wales, so around 12 January the king abandoned the Marches where he had been confined for the past three months, returning to London by slow stages. *En route,* he made a deliberate detour to visit des Roches' cathedral city of Winchester, spending at least three nights there between 24 and 27 January.[1] The intention may have been to prepare for forthcoming negotiations in London. The threat that the English bishops would excommunicate the court was the king's chief concern. Whatever his desire to retain des Roches in power, Henry was equally anxious to avoid a breach with the church. Immediately after leaving Winchester he authorized a gift to Edmund, the archbishop-elect of Canterbury.[2]

At the council convened at Westminster on 2 February, it was Edmund who served to focus criticism against des Roches, accusing him of hating the people of England and of estranging Richard Marshal, the finest Englishman of them all. Des Roches was blamed for every disaster of the past thirty years: the loss of Normandy, the squandering of the wealth of King John, the Interdict, the siege of Bedford, and the loss of La Rochelle and Poitou. Together with de Rivallis, he had engineered the present crisis for personal gain, fortifying castles against the king's own subjects, devouring every office of state without the least intention of rendering accounts. Scarcely a writ could be issued without de Rivallis' seal or authorization, so that he and the 'Poitevins' were sovereign in England rather than the king. Eleanor of Brittany, the royal princesses and many noble heiresses were in alien hands, or disparaged by alien marriages. Overturning laws and breaking oaths, the aliens even dared to ignore the sanctions of the church. The king was offered a stark alternative: dismiss his evil councillors or face certain excommunication.[3]

---

[1] *Cl.R.1231–4*, pp. 371–2; Wendover, *Flores*, iv, p. 291.
[2] *Cl.R.1231–4*, p. 372.
[3] Wendover, *Flores*, iv, pp. 295–7; Paris, *CM*, iii, pp. 269–71. An English abstract of this

Edmund was not the only bishop to speak out. Accused of being too familiar with the Marshal, Alexander of Stainsby bishop of Coventry and Lichfield denied the charge, issuing an excommunication against those he dubbed the king's true enemies, naming no individuals but making it plain that his sentence was directed against des Roches and his associates. Alexander had long been a leading agent of the pope and it may be that the accusations levelled against him followed some attempt at negotiation with the rebels, sponsored by the pope, just as later that spring Alexander was to play an important role in negotiations with the Welsh.[4] At the same time, another of the bishops, Ralph de Neville, Henry III's chancellor, is said to have been temporarily deprived of the king's great seal. The story is unsubstantiated and forms part of a highly embroidered account by Wendover and Paris, in which des Roches and his satellites conspired to trick the king into writing to Ireland, supporting the Irish loyalists in any sort of attack against Leinster or the Marshal, who was to be treated as an outlaw, to be captured dead or alive. Undoubtedly the king sent reinforcements into Ireland, including Walter de Lacy and the royal steward Ralph fitz Nicholas.[5] The Anglo-Irish baronage may well have been encouraged to regard the Marshal as an outlaw, with Leinster the prize for his capture. But there is no evidence that any specific undertaking was committed to writing. Whether or not the chancellor lost custody of the seal, archbishop Edmund's remarks about the authorization of royal writs leave no doubt that control of the king's seals remained a politically sensitive issue, with Neville increasingly detached from des Roches and his regime.

The Westminster council was followed by the restoration of the temporalities of his archbishopric to Edmund; his consecration awaited only the arrival of the *pallium* from Rome. According to Wendover, the king promised to follow Edmund's advice as soon as it became possible to obtain accounts from de Rivallis and his other ministers. He then set off on a tour of East Anglian shrines, perhaps hoping to demonstrate his piety in the face of the criticisms voiced by

speech, taken from the printed version of Paris' chronicle, preserved as London, Inner Temple ms. Petyt 538/17, ff. 44r–45v, has been catalogued as if it were an independent source. It is not.

4   Wendover, *Flores*, iv, p. 295; Paris, *CM*, iii, p. 268. In general, see N. C. Vincent, 'Master Alexander of Stainsby, bishop of Coventry and Lichfield 1224–1238', *Journal of Ecclesiastical History* (forthcoming 1995).

5   Paris, *CM*, iii, pp. 266–7; Wendover, *Flores*, iv, pp. 292–3. For the reinforcements, see *Cl.R.1231–4*, pp. 351–2, 368, 376; *CPR 1232–47*, p. 35.

the clergy.[6] Already the previous month he had magnanimously allowed Richard Siward's wife to join her husband in Wales.[7] At Buckenham, on 14 February, he ordered the restoration to Margaret de Burgh, Hubert's wife, of eight manors previously administered by Passelewe.[8] This appears to have been part of a wider display of royal clemency. A few days earlier, the king had exempted widows from the tallage imposed on the royal demesne.[9] He also issued instructions allowing any free man owing suit to either a royal or baronial court, to appoint an attorney without the restriction, previously enforced, that such attorneys obtain letters from the king before being admitted to the courts in question. The order seems to have been agreed at the Westminster council. Significantly it is said to have been issued *per commune consilium regni nostri*, a phrase which harks back to the years 1219–20, when the inclusion of the phrase *per consilium* in the warranty clauses of royal writs had likewise hinted at the eclipse of Peter des Roches.[10] The ordinance on attorneys is significant as the first writ issued since des Roches seized power specifically to refer to Magna Carta, allowing that the terms of the Charter were to be observed in baronial as well as royal courts, in accordance with Magna Carta clause 60. In the hands of the opposition since 1232, Magna Carta had acquired a status little short of holy writ. Merely by referring to it, the king signalled his detachment from des Roches, and his conversion to the programme expounded by the bishops.

The court now moved on to Bromholm, where the king took possession of relics to be kept in his private chapel for the remainder of his life and where he ordered a silver likeness of himself to be placed, most likely a votive offering to commemorate his recovery from sickness: a sickness that in the circumstances of 1234 may have been less physical than political and intellectual.[11] As Powicke and others have noted, besides the inherent religiosity of Henry's pilgrimage, it marked a quite deliberate retracing of the steps he had taken in July 1232.[12] It had been during a visit to Bromholm in 1232

---

6   Wendover, *Flores*, iv, p. 297; *Cl.R.1231–4*, p. 375.
7   *CPR 1232–47*, p. 36, and see *ibid.*, pp. 38–9 for the restoration of castles and hostages to former rebels.
8   *Cl.R.1231–4*, pp. 378, 380; *AM*, i (Tewkesbury), p. 92; Wendover, *Flores*, iv, p. 297.
9   *Cl.R.1231–4*, p. 377.
10   *Ibid.*, p. 551, and see above p. 183; Carpenter, *The Minority*, pp. 182–4, 209. The warranty clause *per ipsum regem, coram Wintoniensi episcopo, iusticiario et aliis de consilio regis* makes an isolated appearance in June 1233; *Cl.R.1231–4*, p. 227.
11   *CPR 1232–47*, p. 39; *Cl.R.1231–4*, p. 382. The relics were lent to the king by the monks of Norwich cathedral priory.
12   Powicke, *Henry III*, p. 135.

that the king was persuaded to issue his oaths in favour of de Burgh and the court. In 1234 the king's return to Bromholm coincided with desperate pleas to the treasury to stave off bankruptcy. On 21 February 1234 Passelewe was ordered to send at least £1,000, borrowing it if necessary, to reach court at Northampton where a council had been convened.[13] Meanwhile, the king made a leisurely progress from Norfolk into the midlands. At Huntingdon on 24 February, the court suffered yet another audacious attack by Richard Siward, who looted and burned the nearby manor of Alconbury, the property of Stephen of Seagrave. The flames were clearly visible in Huntingdon, but Seagrave was too terrified to give chase. According to Wendover, the king was unable to disguise his amusement at the Justiciar's plight.[14]

The court reached Northampton on 6 March, where some sort of council was convened around Ash Wednesday (8 March).[15] Following the Westminster council, archbishop Edmund and his diocesans had sought to bring about peace on the Marches, acting without any sanction from the court but perhaps under instructions from Rome. The bishops of Coventry and Rochester were sent into Wales, and around 6 March negotiated a truce with envoys from Llywelyn, provisionally set to last until the summer. The terms were communicated to the court at Northampton, and received royal assent, pending a further council meeting at London on 9 April where the bishops' truce could be debated in full. Meanwhile instructions were issued to royal agents on the Marches to cease hostilities.[16] Recent weeks had seen a military breakthrough for the king. The Marshal had departed for Ireland. At the end of February the Welsh siege of Carmarthen had at long last been broken. A week or so later there had been further success, when a party of rebel knights was cut

---

[13] *Cl.R.1231–4*, p. 551.

[14] Wendover, *Flores*, iv, pp. 297–8. The St Albans chroniclers appear to have had special access to information on Alconbury; *ibid.*, pp. 320–2. In compensation for the attack Seagrave was licensed to assart a nearby wood, perhaps used as cover by the raiders. As with his title to the manor, obtained with dubious legality from the earls of Chester who held it together with the other estates of earl David of Huntingdon, as a royal custody during the minority of earl David's heir, Seagrave's possession of the wood later to be challenged. According to the king, what Seagrave claimed as merely a defile in nearby woodland was in fact a substantial part of the royal forest; *Archaeologia* 15 (1806), pp. 209–10; *Foedera*, p. 211; *CRR*, xv, nos. 1136, 1363; *Cl.R.1231–4*, pp. 268, 385; *Cl.R.1234–7*, p. 454; *RLC*, i, pp. 415b, 443b; *Charters of the Earls of Chester*, ed. Barraclough, no. 460.

[15] Des Roches, Seagrave, the earls of Chester, Lincoln and Aumale and Philip de Aubigné are all known to have been at court; *Cal. Chart. R. 1300–1326*, p. 199; *Selborne Charters*, ed. Macray, i, pp. 13–14.

[16] *Cl.R.1231–4*, p. 555; *CPR 1232–47*, pp. 41, 43.

off and forced to seek sanctuary in Flaxley Abbey.[17] Yet however much the king may have been tempted to press on to victory, he was forced to consider his financial situation. The £1,000 he had asked Passelewe to raise was duly forwarded to Northampton, but only after the Jews had been forced to pay it as an extraordinary tallage over and above the 10,000 marks demanded from them the previous year, prompting accusations of embezzlement against Passelewe, de Rivallis and their satellites in charge of the Jewry.[18] There was simply not enough money for the king to maintain his army in Wales. In addition, the time was rapidly approaching when he would be required to provide further aid to Brittany. Since Christmas, duke Peter had been fobbed off with promises of subsidies, none of which had been honoured. The truce agreed with France in 1231 was due to expire within a matter of months. On 12 February the pope had issued safe-conducts on behalf of des Roches and the bishop of Exeter, preparatory to negotiations to prolong the truce. Involvement in negotiations overseas may help to explain des Roches' weakening grasp over events in England.[19] In any event, a combination of factors – bankruptcy, eagerness to preserve recent military successes, and perhaps above all the prospect of renewed war in France – inclined the king to accept the bishops' truce in Wales, the clearest indication to date that it was the bishops who had seized the initiative in moulding royal policy.

The early weeks of March witnessed significant changes in personnel at court. Godfrey of Crowcombe, absent since the previous May, resumed his place witnessing royal charters from 21 February, and after 3 March, warranting numerous royal writs.[20] On 14 March, Richard of Cornwall makes his first recorded appearance at court since the outbreak of civil war.[21] Walter of Clifford, one of the original rebels of 1233, was in March 1234 restored to Clifford castle, withheld as security at the time of his submission the previous autumn.[22] The Marshal's brother-in-law, William Ferrers, had his debt repayments at the Exchequer rescheduled, and

---

[17] *Cl.R.1231–4*, pp. 384, 393, 397–8, 554, which incidentally show the royal administration at odds with yet another bishop, Hugh of Hereford. In general see Walker, 'Anglo-Welsh wars', pp. 354–6.

[18] *CRR*, xv, no. 1118; E372/78, m. 7; *CPR 1232–47*, p. 40; Vincent, 'Jews, Poitevins, and the bishop of Winchester', p. 127.

[19] *Cal.Pap.Reg.*, i, p. 139.

[20] BL ms. Cotton C ix (Hospitallers' cartulary), f. 50r, dated 21 February 16 Hen. III, but at Chippenham which would fit only 1234; *Cl.R.1231–4*, pp. 383–4.

[21] *Cal. Chart. R. 1257–1300*, p. 115.

[22] *CPR 1232–47*, p. 41.

received protection against incursions upon his share in the inheritance of the late earl of Chester.[23] None of this precluded continued patronage of des Roches and his associates. At the Northampton council, des Roches himself was confirmed in possession of the manor of Selborne.[24] But change was undoubtedly in the air. The bishops were now aligned in united opposition to the regime, their most significant political intervention since 1223 and, as on that earlier occasion, spearheaded by the protégés and pupils of archbishop Langton. They appear to have won the pope's approval. Papal support had been crucial in de Burgh's downfall, but the experience of civil war, anxiety over the captivity of de Burgh and the conduct of the Canterbury election had turned Gregory IX against des Roches. Papal initiatives may well have lain behind negotiation with the Welsh. By April 1234, Gregory was openly deploring the king's promotion of aliens, instructing archbishop Edmund and the bishop of Ely to censure such intruders and to revoke any improvident grants of lands or offices by the king.[25] Allowing for the delay between their issue and their arrival in England, it is remarkable the extent to which such letters seem to have pre-empted and to have determined the course of the attack upon des Roches.

THE DISMISSAL OF PETER DES ROCHES MARCH–APRIL 1234

From Northampton the court returned briefly to London and thence to Canterbury, where Edmund was to be installed as archbishop. On 24 March Peter de Rivallis was asked to surrender Lydford castle and the forest of Dartmoor, granted to him in fee by royal charter two years earlier, one of his more controversial promotions in what was effectively royal demesne. He appears to have surrendered his charter without a struggle, but the implications of his surrender were plain to see.[26] For the past two years, de Rivallis and his colleagues had encouraged the king in the repudiation of royal charters. Now they themselves were to fall victim to just such arbitrary attacks. On 27 March, at Westminster, the king issued charters to at least half a dozen bishops, licensing them to draw up wills disposing of stock and grain, free from interference by bailiffs appointed to keep episcopal vacan-

---

23 *Cl.R.1231–4*, p. 392; C60/33, m. 8.
24 *Selborne Charters*, ed. Macray, i, pp. 13–14.
25 *Cal.Pap.Reg.*, i, p. 140.
26 CPR 1232–47, p. 42; *Cal. Chart. R. 1226–57*, p. 163. The writ of 24 March was warranted by Stephen of Seagrave and Peter de Rivallis himself, suggesting that it marked no permanent breach between Peter and the court.

cies. The grants were extended to several of the regime's most bitter critics, including bishop Alexander of Coventry.[27] On 3 April a similar award was made to the newly consecrated archbishop Edmund, the last occasion on which des Roches appears as a witness to a royal charter for many years to come.[28] Already, on 17 March he had warranted his last royal writ. De Rivallis warrants only one set of royal letters later than 28 March.[29]

At Canterbury on 2 April, Edmund was consecrated archbishop. By great good fortune a list of some sixty-seven individuals present at the ceremony survives. It was a tense occasion indeed, since besides the king and his household, it brought together the political associates of des Roches with figures long critical of, or victimized by, his regime: William and Ranulph le Breton, and the archbishop of Dublin, all of them former associates of de Burgh; Richard of Cornwall, the chancellor Ralph Neville with nearly a dozen of his clerks; and eleven bishops including Roger bishop of London, who preached a sermon before the king. Peter de Rivallis is unmentioned and must be presumed absent. In the cathedral itself, the bishop of London occupied the central seat before the high altar, with the king to his left. Des Roches was seated next to the king, a sign of his continuing prominence. All the other bishops, save William Brewer of Exeter, preferred to seat themselves on the far side of the building, to the right of the bishop of London. There could be no better signal of des Roches' isolation.[30]

It had been agreed several weeks earlier that a council would meet on 9 April, to ratify the truce with Llywelyn. It was here at last that the king broke with des Roches. According to Wendover, Edmund and the bishops renewed their threat of excommunication. In response, the king publicly ordered des Roches to return to his diocese and to meddle no more in affairs of state.[31] In fact, the breach

---

[27] *Reg.Antiq.Lincs.*, i, p. 178; *Sarum Charters*, pp. 231–2; *HMC Wells*, pp. 17–18; *Chichester Chartulary*, ed. Peckham, no. 808; *The Great Register of Lichfield Cathedral known as Magnum Registrum Album*, ed. H. E. Savage, William Salt Arch. Soc. (1926 for 1924), no. 220, misdated to 26 March; see Bodl. ms. Ashmole 1527 (Lichfield cartulary), f. 96r. Similar grants had been made to des Roches and the bishops of Lincoln and Bath in 1227, but although these privileges were renewed in 1234, des Roches' apparently were not; *Cal. Chart. R. 1226–57*, p. 42.

[28] Lambeth ms. 1212, ff. 32v–33r.

[29] *Cl.R.1231–4*, pp. 391, 397, 405.

[30] *Early Charters of the Cathedral Church of St Paul's London*, ed. M. Gibbs, Camden Soc., 3rd series, lviii (1939), pp. 140–2, no. 182.

[31] Wendover, *Flores*, iv, pp. 298–9; *Cl.R.1231–4*, pp. 395, 555; in the event, the council met at Westminster.

may not have been so acrimonious. On 10 April, Edmund and six of his suffragans witnessed charters confirming des Roches' foundation of a priory at Selborne.[32] Des Roches himself was to continue active until late May in attempts to renew the truce with France.[33] Nonetheless, the Westminster council undoubtedly witnessed great change. The escheators, the treasury, the chamberlain of London and the keepers of the exchange were told to answer directly to the king, ignoring any further instructions from de Rivallis. The Winchester Jewry were to obey Robert Passelewe in de Rivallis' place.[34] At the same time, des Roches' protégé, Roger Aliz, relinquished his custody of Bristol castle.[35] After 23 April the court began to replace de Rivallis' appointees in the localities, nominating new sheriffs to seven counties. Wendover claims that this was accompanied by violent threats of retribution against de Rivallis himself.[36]

The problems now faced by the king were in many ways similar to those that he had encountered in dismissing Hubert de Burgh. The chief custodies held by Peter de Rivallis, his castles in Ireland, Wales and the Briouze lands, and his vast new estate in Sussex, had all been guaranteed by royal charter, either for life or in perpetual fee. At least to begin with, the king made only half-hearted attempts to overturn these awards. The bishop of Bath was allowed to assume control of the wardrobe, and de Rivallis was deposed from his other financial offices including the keepership of escheats, but elsewhere he remained in possession of a powerful concentration of castles and lands. His former colleagues, Passelewe and Seagrave, remained untouched as treasurer and Justiciar; indeed, Passelewe's influence was boosted by his promotion to various offices vacated by de Rivallis. Meanwhile a group of ministers wholly incompatible with the old guard was intruded at court. Men disgraced in 1232 were reinstated and expected to work alongside their former persecutors. Godfrey of Crowcombe was restored as royal steward.[37] Walter Mauclerk was given back the estates he had held by royal charter, and pardoned most of the £1,000 he had fined on his dismissal from the treasury.[38]

32 *Selborne Charters*, ed. Macray, i, pp. 10–13.
33 *CPR 1232–47*, p. 45; *Cl.R.1231–4*, pp. 559–60, 562.
34 C60/33, m. 8; *Cl.R.1231–4*, p. 412; *CPR 1232–47*, p. 44.
35 *CPR 1232–47*, p. 43; *Cl.R.1231–4*, p. 419.
36 *CPR 1232–47*, pp. 43–4; Wendover, *Flores*, iv, p. 299.
37 For grants of forest and other rights to Crowcombe, see C47/12/7, no. 73; Bodl. ms. Twynne 24 (Studley cartulary extracts), p. 646; *Cl.R.1231–4*, pp. 410, 413.
38 *Cl.R.1231–4*, pp. 401–2, 404; C60/33, m. 7.

There were favours too for the archbishop of Dublin, once the private chaplain and more recently the outspoken advocate of Hubert de Burgh.[39]

Meanwhile, an attempt had to be made to salvage royal policy in Wales and France. The Westminster council confirmed the truce with Llywelyn set to last until late July.[40] The duke of Brittany was promised aid. In return for a quitclaim of all outstanding subsidies and debts, he was to receive the sum of 6,572 marks, to be paid over in its entirety within a fortnight of Easter (23 April). In addition, the king agreed to equip a force of sixty knights to garrison St James de Beuvron at his own expense from 24 June to 14 September, the force to be ready to sail by 1 June. Once the truce with France expired on 24 June, the king would make good any territorial losses suffered by duke Peter by grants of land in England.[41] The determination to salvage something of the vast effort and expense put into his Breton alliance guided Henry, both in respect to the truce with Wales and to the dismissal of de Rivallis. Peace on the Marches and relative harmony at court were essential, if he were to avert disaster in France. Over the past two years whole taxes and tallages had been shipped abroad, supposedly to strengthen Henry's Poitevin and Breton allies towards the moment in 1234 when the truce with France expired. Given the fickleness and duplicity of the allies in question, it is doubtful whether the king could ever have achieved his object. Nonetheless, from Henry's standpoint it was tragic that his diplomatic initiative approached its climax at the worst possible moment, with vicious infighting at court and with neither money nor men to sustain a defence against the French. Henry can have had little hope of raising the sum, more than £4,000, promised to duke Peter. It had taken a tremendous effort to raise even the £1,000 needed for the court's immediate expenses at Northampton. Poitevin and other foreign envoys arriving in April 1234 to collect the Easter term of their pensions, were warned that the treasury was empty. They were asked to wait until Michaelmas for payment, at a moment when it was more essential than ever that the king purchase their goodwill.[42] Even the sixty knights promised for St James de Beuvron proved difficult to recruit, with all the king's men tied down by the precarious truce with the Welsh. Summonses were issued on 20 April and a fleet

[39] *Cl.R.1231–4*, pp. 404, 409.
[40] *CPR 1232–47*, p. 43.
[41] *Cl.R.1231–4*, p. 556.
[42] *CPR 1232–47*, pp. 44–5, 54; *Cl.R.1231–4*, p. 564.

prepared at Portsmouth, but the situation in Wales forced postponement of its sailing until long after the deadline insisted upon by duke Peter.[43]

THE DEATH OF RICHARD MARSHAL

It would not be surprising if the king blamed most of his troubles on Richard Marshal. It was Richard and his associates who had forced the squandering of the king's resources on the campaign in Wales, in the process wrecking the diplomatic initiative in France. Richard had persistently refused offers of a settlement. In practice, though not perhaps in precise legal terms, he was regarded as an outlaw.[44] His flight to Ireland in February 1234 had facilitated a truce with Llywelyn, but there was always the risk that Richard might return to renew the war. By April, only a handful of rebels had come in to court to make their peace, and of these none were Marshal men, but adherents of the Briouze or Clifford factions formerly allied with Richard. Away from the Marches, Richard Siward continued his campaign of guerrilla warfare against the court.

The king had been forced to operate in ignorance of the Marshal's intentions. News from Ireland was sparse. The majority of the Anglo-Irish sided against the Marshal but, in pursuing their own private vendettas, continued to ignore instructions from the king. With hindsight, the chroniclers were to allege a plot against the Marshal, hatched by des Roches and his friends, effected via secret letters and at least one royal writ surreptitiously obtained from the Chancery. But in reality the evidence points not to conspiracy but to total confusion. Peter de Rivallis was unable to control the appointment of constables to his various castles in Ireland, let alone to co-ordinate some sinister, cross-Channel plot. Wendover's allegation that Geoffrey de Marsh, a leading Anglo-Irish magnate, acted in league with the court in urging the Marshal on to battle, seems utterly unrealistic; in fact Marsh was to be severely punished for his support of the Marshal's rebellion.[45] All

---

[43] *Cl.R.1231–4*, pp. 420, 443–4, 558–9; *CPR 1232–47*, p. 44; C47/2/1, no. 10, although at least 3, 000 marks were paid to Brittany late in May; *Cl.R.1231–4*, p. 564; E372/78, m. 7.

[44] See the remarks of Wendover, *Flores*, iv, p. 291.

[45] *Ibid.*, iv, pp. 291–3, 300–2; Orpen, *Ireland under the Normans*, iii, pp. 59–70; B. Wilkinson, 'The council and the crisis of 1233–4', *Bulletin of the John Rylands Library* 27 (1942–3), pp. 387–91. For de Rivallis' inability to control appointments in Ireland, see *CRR*, xv, no. 1064. For the longer term consequences of Marsh's involvement, see Powicke, *Henry III*, pp. 740–59; C60/35, m. 15.

in all, the Marshal enjoyed scant success from the moment of his arrival in Ireland. Aware, perhaps, of the peace initiatives going on in Wales, he agreed to meet the Irish Justiciar, Maurice fitz Gerald, at the Curragh on 1 April. His forces were greatly outnumbered at the meeting, but rejecting a demand that he surrender all his remaining castles, the Marshal chose to transform what had been intended as a peace conference into an armed mêlée; a natural temptation for one whose family fortunes had been made on the tournament fields of France. But Richard was not the knight his father had been; indeed, his father would never have been fool enough to enter combat on such inequitable terms. Wendover portrays Richard, deserted first by the his supposed Irish allies, then by the fifteen faithful retainers he had brought with him from England, until alone, his horse struck down beneath him, its hooves hacked away, he was brought low by base assailants wielding pitchforks and staves. At the last moment he was dealt a treacherous wound in the back. Carried to a nearby castle belonging to fitz Gerald, he showed signs of recovery until the surgeon sent to treat his wounds, through treachery or incompetence, probed them too deeply. A fever set in and on 16 April, Palm Sunday, Richard died.[46]

There is much in Wendover's account that is fanciful, much too that may be intended to echo classical or chivalric archetypes: the hero deserted by his men, cut down by base and treacherous foes. The Osney annalist quite explicitly compares Richard's last stand to that of Roland and Oliver in the *Chanson de Roland*, and to the defeat in battle of Judas Maccabeus, the Jewish hero who rescued Jerusalem from alien, Syrian persecution.[47] But, whatever its accuracy, the accepted image of Richard Marshal's death remains a powerful one. How ironic that Richard's rebellion should end with his desertion by the selfsame knights with whom he had striven so hard and at such a cost to keep faith. A love of tourneying, of mêlées and hand to hand combat, had won great wealth for his father but were to lead Richard to his death. In life, Richard, the Frenchman, had been portrayed by the chroniclers as the very embodiment of English virtue; in death, an Englishman abroad in Ireland, he is likened to the greatest warrior of the French *Chansons de Geste*, count Roland, saviour of the Franks.

[46] Wendover, *Flores*, iv, pp. 301–8, and see Coker, ' "Margam Chronicle" ', pp. 139–40. The Dunstable annals, *AM*, iii, pp. 136–7 mention a truce made in Ireland by Gilbert Marshal, broken by Richard, and the presence at the Curragh of Richard de Burgh and of Walter and Hugh de Lacy, once Marshal allies, now bitter enemies.

[47] *AM*, iv, pp. 79–80. In the *Chanson*, Roland's horse, Veillantif, like Richard Marshal's, is killed beneath him at the height of battle.

Once again, we find ourselves caught up in a bewildering tangle of national stereotypes, in which Frenchmen are cast as the most English of the English, and where English heroes can be dressed in colours borrowed directly from France.

At the very moment the Marshal was struck down, archbishop Edmund was preparing for consecration at Canterbury. Richard's death came a whole week after the Westminster council and the dismissal of Peter de Rivallis. Had communications with Ireland been better, the Marshal might never have entered his fatal tournament at the Curragh. As it was, news of his capture and death took several weeks to cross to England. In the interval, the court remained poised between its various incompatible factions, still harassed by the threat of renewed war on the Marches.

RETRIBUTION AND RECONCILIATION

Negotiations with the Welsh were due to take place early in May. Perhaps with a view to keeping in touch with his envoys, the king left London in the final week of April. Once again his movements were dogged by Richard Siward, who on 26 April burned the manor of Swanbourne belonging to the family of Robert Passelewe. On 2 May he ambushed the royal baggage train as it passed between Reading and Wallingford, absconding with goods belonging to the Justiciar, Seagrave. From the Thames valley, Siward then made his way north to Ivinghoe, des Roches' manor, which was put to the torch on 12 May.[48] Wendover claims that these raids were made in reprisal for Richard Marshal's death, but with the exception of the burning of Ivinghoe, it seems that the attacks were made before the news from Ireland had reached either Siward or the court. Siward's raids are better regarded as an attempt to maintain the pressure against ministers such as Passelewe and Seagrave, left in power despite des Roches' fall.

Only after the court reached Woodstock, on or around 6 May, did the king learn of the Marshal's death. A display of remorse was deemed appropriate, but in reality Henry's chief feeling must have been one of relief.[49] Richard de Burgh was congratulated on his part

---

[48] Wendover, *Flores*, iv, p. 308; *Cl.R.1231–4*, pp. 414, 557. For Swanbourne, see also *Rot.Hugh Welles*, i, p. 92; *A Calendar of the Feet of Fines for the County of Buckinghamshire 7 Richard I to 44 Henry III*, ed. M. W. Hughes, Bucks. Arch. Soc. iv (1942 for 1940), pp. 58, 79. At much the same time Siward is said to have kidnapped and ransomed William de Hollewer, sheriff of Herts., Robert Passelewe's brother-in-law; Paris, *CM*, iii, p. 289.

[49] Wendover, *Flores*, iv, p. 309; *AM*, iii (Dunstable), p. 137.

in the battle at the Curragh, and asked to be patient for his reward, until the arrival of the greater Irish magnates at court.[50] The Irish themselves, in the first flush of enthusiasm, sent messengers with a schedule of proposals to be put to the king: Henry should cross immediately to Ireland, where he would find more wealth than he or his father could have dreamed possible. All the Marshal's castles and manors were well stocked and held by the king's men; together with those confiscated from other rebels they were valued at 30,000 marks. In Ireland the king might decide how to reward those who had won him his victory; in other words, how to partition the Marshal lordship of Leinster. Meanwhile Connaught should be restored to Richard de Burgh, or there would be no peace.[51]

In fact the king's principal concerns in May 1234 lay not in Ireland, but in France and with the factional disturbances at the English court. The Marshal's death cleared the way for a full-scale purge at court. On 7 May, the day the news arrived from Ireland, Peter de Rivallis was formally indicted to appear in London on 25 June to render his accounts.[52] Already the king seems to have appreciated the connections to be drawn between the death of the Marshal, peace with the rebels, and retribution against de Rivallis, disgraced in April but still to be relieved of his vast accumulation of lands, offices and wardships. On the same day, 7 May, moves were initiated to effect reconciliation with Hubert de Burgh. Various rebels, including a nephew of Richard Siward, were released from prison, and on 12 May safe-conducts were issued to the Marshal's kin to attend court, including his brother and principal heir, Gilbert Marshal.[53]

Between 16 May and 4 June the court was established at Gloucester, and it was there at last that a full settlement was effected. De Burgh, Gilbert Marshal and the remaining rebels came in to seek mercy. The outlawry of de Burgh, Siward and Basset was declared

---

[50] *Cl.R.1231–4*, p. 561.

[51] C47/10/13, no. 3, printed in *Documents on the Affairs of Ireland before the King's Council*, ed. G. O. Sayles, Irish Manuscripts Commission (Dublin 1979), pp. 2–3, no. 3. It is a measure of Ireland's isolation that this schedule continues to treat des Roches as a leading figure at court, more than a month after his fall. It also reveals the opprobrium in which Geoffrey de Marsh was held as a result of recent events. For the eventual settlement in Ireland, in which heavy ransoms were taken against the rebels, but in which the Marshals were restored to Leinster and Richard de Burgh to Connaught, see *Cl.R.1231–4*, pp. 425, 465, 525, 541; *CPR 1232–47*, pp. 52–3, 73, 82, 87–8; C60/33, m. 1.

[52] *Cl.R.1231–4*, p. 419, in which de Rivallis is accorded his formal title as *capicerius* of Poitiers.

[53] *Ibid.*, pp. 419, 422; *CPR 1232–47*, p. 45.

illegal. Rebel lands were returned. Upavon was restored to Gilbert
Basset, the king admitting that its seizure had been unlawful, *per
voluntatem regis*.[54] Archbishop Edmund and his fellow bishops took
the leading role in council.[55] It was they who effected a firm truce
with Llywelyn.[56] Likewise, it was they who promoted the air of
justice and co-operation that prevailed at court that summer. Their
administration lies beyond the scope of this study. Here it must
suffice to say that from May 1234, great stress was laid upon precisely
those principles of consent and right judgement which des Roches
and his regime had flouted. In August 1234 a general eyre was
appointed, supplemented in the following April by an eyre for the
forest.[57] Such visitations had a fiscal as well as a judicial aspect; the
general eyre, for example, was to raise nearly £20,000 in fines and
amercements.[58] However, at the same time, they helped bring law
and judgement into the provinces and provided a spur to legal
reform. The lawyers around the king, the so-called court *coram rege*
which had functioned sporadically since 1227, acquired new status.
The first *coram rege* roll of Henry's reign commences in June 1234,
and the court's chief justice, William de Raleigh, rose quickly to
become the king's most influential minister.[59] In accordance with
the spirit of legality fostered by the bishops, between April and
October 1234 there was a series of new rulings on the bailing of
prisoners and on the frequency with which sheriffs and hundred
courts should meet, referring explicitly to the liberties contained in

---

[54] *Cl.R.1231–4*, pp. 427ff., esp. p. 437; *CPR 1232–47*, p. 48, and see the excellent account
by Meekings, intro. to *CRR*, xv, pp. xxv–xxviii.
[55] For charters issued at Gloucester, witnessed by the archbishops of Canterbury and
Dublin and the bishops of Durham, Bath, Carlisle, Coventry and Rochester, see *Cal.
Chart.R.1226–57*, p. 220; *Cal. Chart. R. 1257–1300*, p. 216; C53/29, m. 4; C47/12/7,
no. 74. The bishops continue the most prominent witnesses to royal charters
throughout the summer of 1234; *Cal. Chart. R. 1257–1300*, pp. 434, 472; *Cal.
Chart.R.1300–1326*, pp. 214, 361–2; *CAR*, nos. 18, 19, 27; C47/12/7, no. 75; C52/30,
no. 16; *Cartularium Prioratus de Gyseburne*, ed. W. Brown, i, p. 132, no. 230; BL ms.
Harley Ch. 58H46; Angers, Archives Départementales de Maine-et-Loire 101H167;
193H1 no. 2 (Fontevraud cartulary), ff. 4r–6v; 193H1 nos. 14, 15, 16; Durham, Prior's
Kitchen Library ms. Cartuarium III, ff. 213v–214v.
[56] *Cl.R.1231–4*, pp. 421, 562, 564–5, 568–9. Archbishop Edmund was at Shrewsbury on
1–2 May, presumably for negotiations with the Welsh; Stafford, Staffordshire Record
Office, Duke of Sutherland's Collection ms. D593/A/1/32/5; *Shrewsbury Cartulary*, ed.
Rees, i, no. 57. On 14 May he was granted all the exits of the archbishopric and mint
of Canterbury, probably backdated to cover the entire vacancy since 1231. This would
explain the king's acknowledgement of debts to Edmund of 4, 400m early in June;
Cl.R.1231–4, p. 424; *CPR 1232–47*, p. 55.
[57] *CPR 1232–47*, pp. 76–8, 125.
[58] *The 1235 Surrey Eyre*, ed. Meekings, i, p. 135.
[59] *CRR*, xv, pp. xxi–xxiii, xxviii–xxxvii, nos. 1023ff.

Magna Carta.[60] In the hands of the opposition, Magna Carta had become the very touchstone of good government. Late in August 1234 the sheriffs were ordered to proclaim and uphold the Charter in its entirety in every county court. The text referred to was to be that of 1225. But although the text itself remained unaltered, the proclamation of 1234 can with some justification be regarded as a full reissue of the Charter, previously overlooked by historians.[61]

In tandem with this devotion to Magna Carta, the new regime adhered to a programme of what can best be described as 'moral reform'. In the six months after des Roches' fall, a prohibition of scotales, first made during the king's minority, was renewed and there were confirmations of clerical tithes throughout the royal demesne.[62] The justices in eyre were instructed to reserve cases involving advowsons of cathedral prebends or matters touching upon the law of bastardy for hearing *coram rege*.[63] An expulsion of clerical concubines from Oxford received the king's support, as did a programme of anti-Jewish measures building on those already instituted in 1233. The Jews were henceforth to be excluded from any save the largest towns. Warwick, for example, secured their expulsion and the burgesses of Newcastle upon Tyne fined 100 marks for a charter forbidding any Jew to reside there in future.[64] At Tewkesbury, in June 1234, a new and heavy fine was imposed against the Jews, over and above the tallage of 10,000 marks.[65] For his own part, the king continued to indulge in pious works. The Osney annalist portrays him at the feast of All Souls 1234, ordering his men to find and feed ten thousand paupers, a number that was considered impossibly high.[66]

It was the Gloucester parliament which saw the birth of this new order. By the same token, it was at Gloucester that the king began harrying the old regime. Here the stories from Ireland reported by archbishop Edmund, of secret letters and of plots to murder the

---

[60] *Cl.R.1231–4*, pp. 587–9, also preserved in *Eynsham Cartulary*, ed. Salter, i, pp. 169–70.
[61] *Cl.R.1231–4*, pp. 592–3.
[62] *Ibid.*, pp. 518, 566, and for scotales, see above pp. 81 and n. 189, 173.
[63] *Ibid.*, pp. 598–9.
[64] *Ibid.*, pp. 515–16, 568, 571, 592; C60/33, m. 6; Newcastle upon Tyne, Tyne and Wear Archives ms. 574/95.
[65] C60/33, m. 4, and in general see Vincent, 'Jews, Poitevins, and the bishop of Winchester', pp. 127–9.
[66] *AM*, iv, p. 77, also found in the anonymous *Brut* in BL ms. Cotton Otho B xiv, f. 211r. The king was certainly in the vicinity of Oxford at the time, making further grants to the hospital of St John there, refounded in the 1230s under the guidance of his almoner, Geoffrey; *Cl.R.1234–7*, pp. 4–5; *Cartulary of the Hospital of St John the Baptist*, ed. Salter, i, no. 75, iii, pp. xiv–xvii.

Marshal, seem to have been used to secure the disgrace of des Roches, de Rivallis and their colleagues. We must begin with des Roches. Several months earlier, the pope had appointed him to renew the truce with France. Given the tense nature of Anglo-French relations in May 1234, the king was in no hurry to revoke this commission. Anxious to avoid war, and mindful of the difficulties in raising money or men for the support of his continental alliances, the king pinned his hopes on renewing the truce. Even after the news of the Marshal's death, des Roches continued to head negotiations. Joined by the bishop of Exeter, by Master John Blund his former candidate for the archbishopric, and by the abbot of Westminster, he was still active in diplomacy on 25 May.[67] There seems to have been talk of buying him off. Letters were drawn up, acknowledging debts to him on the king's behalf, of sums ranging in units of a thousand from 2,000 to 6,000 marks.[68] Probably the king intended a form of golden hand-shake, with des Roches to be offered first the smallest sum of 2,000 marks and then, should he refuse this, the larger bonds in ascending order. In the event, he was to have nothing. Negotiations with the French collapsed, and with them des Roches' usefulness. On 29 May his proxy was dismissed as sheriff of Hampshire.[69] Two days later, the king wrote to the duke of Brittany, steeling him for war. Whatever money could be assembled, perhaps as much as 3,000 marks, was dispatched in subsidy. Knights were hastily mustered, crossing from Portsmouth early in June.[70] In these circumstances there could be no payoff for des Roches. His letters of credit were revoked. In June 1234 he suffered an amercement of £100 for defaulting in a routine case before the court *coram rege*.[71] Later that month, he was to face pleas from Gilbert Marshal and the citizens of Winchester, demanding redress of grievances inflicted by the bishop over the past two years.[72] But all in all, des Roches was to escape very lightly, even in comparison to the aftermath of his fall in 1224, when he had been forced to fine 500 marks and to defend a stream of hostile actions in the courts.

No such leniency was extended to Stephen of Seagrave or Robert

67   *Cl.R.1231–4*, p. 562.
68   *CPR 1232–47*, p. 47.
69   *Ibid.*, p. 50 and see *Cl.R.1231–4*, p. 428, where Wacelin, the under-sheriff, had already been required on 28 May to surrender Marlborough castle.
70   *Cl.R.1231–4*, pp. 443–4, 564; Wendover, *Flores*, iv, pp. 315–16. 500m promised to Hugh de Lusignan on 4 June apparently went unpaid; *CPR 1232–47*, p. 54.
71   C60/33, m. 3; *CRR*, xv, p. xxv, no. 1023.
72   *CRR*, xv, nos. 1033, 1204, 1257, 1268.

Passelewe, both of whom had weathered the storm of April 1234 only
to fall at Gloucester. As late as 21 May Seagrave continued to warrant
royal letters. His son Gilbert was awarded the manor of Burton
Latimer, confiscated from Richard Marshal's widow.[73] Stephen was
still at court on 26 May when the storm against him broke, with the
demand that he surrender Kenilworth castle.[74] Most of the lands and
custodies he or his son had acquired since 1232 were recalled. In the
process, the king overturned a large number of charters and patents
guaranteeing possession for life or in perpetuity. By contrast to the
arbitrary annulment of such privileges over the past few years, the
king pursued his actions via the courts.[75] Stephen himself offered
£500 to obtain grace, before fleeing to the sanctuary of Leicester
Abbey. He emerged in mid-July, under safe-conducts from the
bishops, and in a hearing before the king endeavoured to shift the
blame for the late regime's failings on to de Rivallis and his colleagues.
Through the influence of archbishop Edmund, he was allowed to go
free, and despite the recall of much of the estate he held by royal
grant, he was to be reconciled to court by 1236 and shortly afterwards
reintroduced to royal service.[76] A similar fate awaited Robert Passelewe. During the king's progress to Gloucester, Passelewe had
remained at the Exchequer, presiding there until at least 26 May.[77]
When news reached him of the purge effected at Gloucester, he fled
to sanctuary. Many believed he had set out for Rome, just as in 1224,
when he had sought to place the grievances of Fawkes de Bréauté
before the pope. In fact he went into hiding in the London Temple,
concealed in a cellar and feigning illness, 'like a hare', as Paris puts it.[78]
In this way, he avoided the confrontation between the king and his
disgraced ministers on 14 July. Deposed from the treasury, in due
course he was to be stripped of most of the estate he had acquired
since 1232, again following action in the courts. His management of
the Jewry was subjected to particularly close scrutiny. Like Seagrave,
he is said to have fined for the king's grace, returning to a prominent
position in English government after 1236.[79]

[73] *Cl.R.1231–4*, p. 427.
[74] *Ibid.*, p. 432.
[75] *Ibid.*, pp. 471, 475, 567; C60/33, m. 6; *CRR*, xv, nos. 1059, 1102–3, 1129, 1136–8,
1209, 1262, 1264, 1321, 1346, 1363, 1381, 1384, 1404, 1477, 1502, 1883, 1981, 2023.
Most of these references relate to the manor of Alconbury, for which see above p. 432.
[76] *CPR 1232–47*, p. 54; Wendover, *Flores*, iv, pp. 312–314; Paris, *CM*, iii, pp. 295–6;
Turner, *Men Raised from the Dust*, pp. 131–2, and see C60/35, mm. 18, 14, 9.
[77] *CRR*, xv, p. xxvn.
[78] Wendover, *Flores*, iv, pp. 312–14; Paris, *CM*, iii, p. 293; *Cl.R.1231–4*, pp. 438, 563.
[79] Wendover, *Flores*, iv, p. 325; *CPR 1232–47*, pp. 78–9; *CRR*, xv, nos. 1043, 1058,

THE PURSUIT OF PETER DE RIVALLIS

The most protracted proceedings were those that attended the fall of Peter de Rivallis. The story here is a remarkable one, worth telling in detail. Following his dismissal in April, Peter had been ordered to attend court on 19 June, in order to render accounts.[80] In the meantime, attempts were made to prevent him from exploiting the resources of the honours of Briouze and Aigle which remained in his custody, guaranteed to him by royal charter.[81] On the pretext that they posed a threat to the security of the realm, menaced by the French and the Welsh, the king ordered the surrender of the various castles that Peter held in Sussex and the Marches, together with Peter's chief ward, the heir of John de Briouze. The boy himself was to be sent to court, although Peter was told that he might retain possession of the Briouze lands and the right to marry off the boy, when the time should come. Peter wrote back, promising to attend court as required. But by 19 June he had still not appeared, nor had he surrendered the castles or the Briouze heir. Instead, he had to be summoned a second and then a third time. Richard de Argentan, a former victim of the regime, was sent to intercept de Rivallis whom he met at Canterbury. Quite what Peter was doing at Canterbury remains unclear. Perhaps he had gone there to throw himself upon the mercy of archbishop Edmund. Alternatively he may have considered fleeing to France. The Winchester annals suggest that both de Rivallis and des Roches were refused permission to cross overseas from Dover, at some time before the end of June.[82] At their meeting at Canterbury, Peter refused to recognize Argentan's credentials as a royal messenger. He claimed that the Briouze boy was too ill to be sent to court, and, furthermore, that he himself did not dare to attend until he had been issued with royal letters guaranteeing his personal safety.[83] His fears here were probably justified. According to Matthew Paris, the king had already uttered various threats against

---

80 1110–24. He offered a fine of 600m for the king's grace, of which £100 was excused him in May 1235 in return for a loan that he had earlier raised on the king's behalf. The remainder of the fine was to be repaid at 100m a year, reduced in February 1236 to 60m a year; C60/34, m. 7; C60/35, m. 13.

80 *Cl.R.1231–4*, p. 419.

81 *Ibid.*, p. 439.

82 *AM*, ii, p. 86, and for later prohibitions, see *Cl.R.1231–4*, pp. 570–1.

83 These, and many of the following details are to to be found in the records of the case against de Rivallis, recorded in the roll of the court *coram rege*; *CRR*, xv, no. 1031.

Peter, declaring, for example, that if Peter were not a clerk he would have had his eyes plucked out.[84]

The king, however, scorned Peter's request for a safe-conduct, claiming that such letters were unnecessary in time of peace; Peter would not be attacked, save through due process of the courts. On 23 June, Henry was told that de Rivallis had been sighted between Rochester and London, coming to render his accounts, accompanied by the Briouze boy riding on a large black horse. On the following morning, three Franciscans, all of them foreigners, arrived at court, again requesting safe-conducts on Peter's behalf. The king replied by letter, asking Peter to wait in London until 28 June when his accounts could be heard, but still refusing to issue safe-conducts. In the meantime, various conciliatory gestures were made. The sheriff of Kent was ordered to restore the falcons that Peter claimed to have left in Tonbridge castle, and the sheriff of Sussex was told to allow bishop des Roches to take possession of timber from the Briouze estates, which de Rivallis had bestowed upon the bishop's hospital at Portsmouth.[85] But this was not enough to allay Peter's fears. By the time that the king's councillors met on 28 June, ready to hear his accounts, Peter had fled from London to Winchester. Only his clerk, Philip of Willington, was left behind to answer the council's charges. On 30 June, spurning Philip's representations, the council commanded that Peter be distrained to attend court.[86] Letters were dispatched to Sussex and the Marches, demanding that his castles be seized, if necessary by force.[87] Most alarmingly of all, either on his own initiative or as a representative of the king, Richard Siward set out for Winchester. There, on 2 July, he appears to have entered the cathedral precinct, where he seized various horses belonging to the bishop and the prior of Winchester in an attack reminiscent of his earlier acts of banditry against des Roches and his allies. The citizens of Winchester had long been at odds with des Roches, and it may be that they too took the opportunity to mount reprisals. According to the Winchester annals, although the bishop placed the city and cathedral of Winchester under Interdict and excommunicated the raiding party, on 3 or 4 July, the wrongdoers did penance and were absolved, so that city and church were reconciled.[88]

84 Paris, *CM*, iii, p. 272.
85 *Cl.R.1231–4*, pp. 459, 461.
86 *CRR*, xv, no. 1031.
87 *Cl.R.1231–4*, pp. 462–3; *CPR 1232–47*, p. 58.
88 *AM*, ii, pp. 86–7. The citizens' complaints against the bishop's extension of his liberties within the city, were heard at court around 2 or 3 July 1234; *CRR*, xv, no. 1033.

The English bishops now intervened in an effort to bring about peace. Although the king still refused to issue safe-conducts, the English bishops took it upon themselves to guarantee Peter's safety. On 14 July both he and des Roches attended the king at Westminster. There yet another angry scene broke out. According to Matthew Paris, the king accused de Rivallis of abusing his custody of the royal seal by obtaining the letters to Ireland which had brought about the death of Richard Marshal.[89] The report entered on the plea roll says nothing of these letters which, as we have seen, may well have been an invention of the chroniclers. Instead, according to this, the official court record, Peter was asked to surrender custody of the castles he held in Ireland, to which he replied that he had already done his best to arrange this, but that his deputy in Ireland had been unable to implement his orders. As for the Briouze boy, who the king ordered returned to court, Peter claimed that he knew nothing of his whereabouts, and that he wished to await the arrival of the archbishop of Canterbury before answering further. Although urged by his councillors to allow Peter some leeway, Henry rejected Peter's promise to surrender his castles, demanding that he first obtain security for this surrender from the bishops or the baronage. This, Peter claimed, he was unable to do, begging once again that the king await the arrival of the archbishop. But the king had lost patience. Peter was committed to the Tower, pending the surrender of his castles and his ward, or until he obtained securities that such a surrender would be carried out.[90] Paris adds that Peter had arrived at court in clerical dress, bare-headed to display his tonsure, but with a dagger hanging at his waist. When he was taken to the Tower it was found that he was wearing a coat of mail beneath his outer garment.[91] Improbable as this may seem, it is to some extent substantiated by the report in the plea roll, which though mutilated towards the end, appears to suggest that Peter came armed to Westminster (*armatus fuit*).[92] Both the chroniclers and the plea roll agree that after three days in the Tower, Peter was released on bail supplied by archbishop Edmund, and allowed to return to Winchester. At the same time, from 14 July onwards, the king initiated a wide-ranging, county by county enquiry into Peter's misdeeds.[93] A damning indictment of his extortions and

---

[89]   Paris, *CM*, iii, pp. 294–5.
[90]   *CRR*, xv, no. 1064.
[91]   Paris, *CM*, iii, pp. 294–5, based upon Wendover, *Flores*, iv, pp. 313–14, although the latter makes no mention of the dagger.
[92]   *CRR*, xv, no. 1064, p. 238.
[93]   *Cl.R.1231–4*, pp. 573–83; *CPR 1232–47*, p. 78.

profiteering was delivered by the London Jewry.[94] Various disseisins that he had committed were ordered corrected.[95]

In mid-August des Roches was summoned to court, to respond to the charge that he had failed to secure Peter's surrender of the castles and the Briouze heir. The records of this hearing are difficult to interpret, but suggest a genuine breach between the bishop and de Rivallis. With his far longer experience of court intrigue, des Roches may well have tired of his nephew's refusal to bow to the inevitable. Whereas the younger man seemed to believe that even now it might be possible for him to salvage at least part of his vast lordship, des Roches saw that prevarication could do nothing to remedy a hopeless cause. With his greater personal knowledge of the king, des Roches may also have realized that Henry's threats of violence were never very serious, so that de Rivallis had less to fear than he might suppose. In any case, the bishop told Peter to attend the king when summoned, to which Peter replied that he dared not do this, for fear of his life. Des Roches then sequestered whatever benefices Peter held within the diocese of Winchester. Peter responded by appealing to archbishop Edmund, who appointed ecclesiastical judges to hear his complaints. If the king and the bishops required him to do more, des Roches declared that he was willing to comply. In October 1234, the king and the council conceded that des Roches had acted to the best of his ability. So long as de Rivallis remained within the sanctuary of Winchester cathedral, des Roches was to continue to sequester his benefices; as soon as he left church, however, the bishop was to ensure that he attend court.[96]

Not until 18 October did the king grant the safe-conducts that de Rivallis had asked for, and even then, when Peter had got as far as Oxford, only a few miles from the court at Woodstock, they were withdrawn, with Peter being ordered to return immediately to Winchester.[97] It may be that it was too late for him to turn back, or that the order was subsequently rescinded. He undoubtedly attended court at Woodstock on 31 October.[98] There he sought to bargain

---

[94] *CRR*, xv, nos. 1110–24, directed against de Rivallis and his fellow ministers, most prominently Robert Passelewe. For a summary, see M. Adler, 'The testimony of the London Jewry against the ministers of Henry III', *Transactions of the Jewish Historical Society of England* 14 (1935–9), pp. 141–56; Vincent, 'Jews, Poitevins, and the bishop of Winchester', p. 127.

[95] *Cl.R.1231–4*, pp. 485, 495–6, 542.

[96] *CRR*, xv, nos. 1091, 1126.

[97] *CPR 1232–47*, p. 74; *Cl.R.1234–7*, p. 1.

[98] *CRR*, xv, no. 1289 suggests that the safe-conducts had been issued on 18 October only after prolonged negotiations, and after Peter had written to the royal steward, Ralph

with the king. In return for surrendering the vast majority of the lands and custodies that he held by royal charter, including the office of sheriff in twenty-two counties, which he listed laboriously, one by one, he offered 1,000 marks to retain possession of the royal treasury, the honour of Aigle, Pevensey castle and the castles of Bramber and Knepp together with the marriage of the heir of John de Briouze. In many ways this was a foolhardy proposal. There was no prospect whatsoever that he would be permitted to remain as the king's treasurer, let alone retain possession of his estates in Sussex. In all, he seems hopelessly to have misread the king's mood. Perhaps he still found it impossible to believe that Henry could have turned so completely against him, when for the previous two years he had commanded the king's confidence to such an extraordinary extent. At their previous encounter in July, Wendover attributes a speech to Peter in which he is said to have thrown himself on Henry's mercy. 'Lord king', he is made to declare, 'I was raised by you and made rich in material goods. Do not destroy the man that you have made. Give me but a little time that I may render accounts for the things demanded of me.'[99] Perhaps, Peter really did believe that all could be made right by a few accounts. If so, he was mistaken. Far from accepting his offer of 1,000 marks, the king refused to treat with him, or even to discuss the matter in person. His surrender of the twenty-two counties and his other lands was refused. There was to be no question of a deal. Instead, the king sent word that he was to attend at Westminster on 17 November. Even then, Peter continued to press for more, asking that the king assist him in distraining his former lieutenants to render accounts, that he recognize Peter's privileges as a clerk, and honour the terms of the charter of immunity he had granted in 1232, save only for its promise of quittance from account. In addition he requested an extension of his safe-conduct, and the appointment of 'faithful men' to hear his accounts. The king, needless to say, refused all of these requests.[100]

On 17 November Peter duly attended at Westminster, and over the next few days attempted once again to strike a bargain. He now

---

fitz Nicholas, asking that he procure the letters that were required. These were eventually issued, on the advice of the archbishop and various others, who warned the king that to refuse would be to supply Peter with an excuse for his continued failure to render accounts.

[99] Wendover, *Flores*, iv, p. 313.
[100] *CRR*, xv, no. 1225, and for the other requests made by Peter, see *ibid.*, no. 1289. For the charter of immunity, which granted quittance from accounts for roughly a year from June 1232, see *Cal. Chart. R. 1226–57*, p. 164.

offered to surrender all the custodies he held by royal charter, and to restore land that had been given him by the king's brother, Richard of Cornwall, provided only that he was allowed to retain the heir of John de Briouze, without any of the Briouze castles.[101] For this he offered the king 700 marks. Once again, the king was unmoved, although he did at last agree to recognize Peter's clerical privileges, to prolong his safe-conducts and to appoint an impressive array of courtiers to hear his accounts.[102] Peter replied that at least three of these men – the bishop of Carlisle, Godfrey of Crowcombe and John Marshal – were his personal enemies and therefore unacceptable. Furthermore, he demanded the return of his lands that had previously been distrained, and entered a lengthy argument, much of which has been lost from the plea roll, but apparently to the effect that the king's ancestors had never before removed justices from the Bench or barons of the Exchequer merely out of love or hatred for a particular person (*odio vel amore alicuius*); arguments which refer directly to Magna Carta with its prohibition upon the exercise of arbitrary royal will, and, possibly, also to the Charter's insistence that no clerk be amerced according to the value of his benefices, but solely according to his private, lay tenement.[103] The hypocrisy of this is almost incredible, given the way that both de Rivallis and des Roches had connived in the arbitrary dismissal and persecution of their rivals at court. And yet, in the winter of 1234, so inviolable had Magna Carta become as a touchstone of good government, that the king's ministers had no choice but to give Peter's arguments serious consideration. Early in December, in the presence of the archbishop of Canterbury and various magnates, it was agreed that love and hatred were not sufficient cause for the dismissal of royal officials, but that the king nonetheless had the right to demand that officials be answerable for their misdeeds. In addition, since Peter had been unable to provide securities for rendering his accounts, it was judged that the king had acted rightly in distraining upon his lands. Peter himself was summoned to appear again in January 1235.

---

[101] *CRR*, xv, no. 1289. The king had undertaken in July 1234 that he would make no peace with Peter until the latter restored land in Cornwall that he had obtained from earl Richard; *CPR 1232–47*, p. 62; C60/33, m. 5.

[102] On 23 November Peter's safe-conduct was extended, though only for a further two days, to 25 November; *CPR 1232–47*, p. 82.

[103] *CRR*, xv, no. 1289 p. 322, where the mutilated portions can to some extent be reconstructed from those parts that survive. For clause 22 of the 1215 Magna Carta, on the amercement of clerks, modified in the reissue of 1217, see W. S. McKechnie, *Magna Carta: A Commentary on the Great Charter of King John*, 2nd edn (Glasgow 1914), pp. 298–9.

Hereafter, the case vanishes from the plea rolls. In January 1235 licence was granted for des Roches to cross overseas, although de Rivallis and his ward, the son of John de Briouze, were specifically excluded from this order, suggesting that the boy had still not been surrendered to the king.[104] A month later, the king accepted fines from nine of Peter's former bailiffs, to be pardoned the king's anger and quit from further account.[105] Between April 1235 and May 1236, Peter was regularly granted extensions to his letters of safe-conduct, at first insisting that he make no attempt to visit his rents or any sea port, but later relaxed so as to prohibit only his crossing overseas.[106] In the interval, he appears to have made various gifts to the king, of gold and silk.[107] On 4 May 1236 he was pardoned the king's anger and granted protection for himself and his men. So far as can be established, the vast majority of his debts for the years 1232–4 had not been cleared, even by the time of his death in 1262.[108] However, although this suggests that the king's attack upon him dissolved into a futile and ultimately meaningless process, there is evidence to suggest that even as late as January 1236, he was still the subject of controversy at court. On 2 January that year, letters were drawn up, demanding that Peter, and apparently also Stephen of Seagrave, go into exile on pain of outlawry.[109] The letters were withdrawn, or possibly never sent. Nonetheless, even at this late stage it would appear that the animos-

---

[104] *Cl.R.1234–7*, p. 163.

[105] *CPR 1232–47*, p. 95. For the fine of one of these men, William Ruffus, set at 80m and still unpaid in 1243, see *Cl.R.1242–7*, p. 52. Aimery de Chanceaux apparently fined £17 and 10 shillings, most of which was pardoned him in 1238; E372/81, m. 10d; E372/82, m. 12d. The accounts from various of Peter's bailiffs, entered in *Foreign Accounts*, pp. 74–90, had apparently been rendered by Michaelmas 1236, and could conceivably coincide with the pardons of February 1235; *ibid.*, pp. vi, 81 and note.

[106] *CPR 1232–47*, pp. 101, 103, 114, 131, 136. He is to be found at Bishop's Sutton and Farnham in 1235/6, and at Bitterne in the following year with the archbishop of Bordeaux and the bishop of Bazas; Mss. 31DR, mm. 8d, 10d, 12; 32DR, mm. 1, 11d.

[107] E372/79, mm. 5d, 11d which records 5 samite cloths received from the emperor, the pope and Peter de Rivallis, distributed as gifts to the king of Scotland and the bishop-elect of Valence; and 11 pence of gold, 7 (?gold) cups and 9 *paribus pelinum'* (unidentified) received from de Rivallis alone. The cups were given to the religious, to serve for the reservation of the eucharist.

[108] *CPR 1232–47*, p. 145, and for the clearance of his debts, see above p. 354. Paris, *CM*, iii, pp. 138–9 claims that shortly after his pardon, in June 1236, de Rivallis co-operated with Simon de Montfort to secure the imprisonment of Richard Siward. Siward was undoubtedly imprisoned, although there is no evidence that de Rivallis played any part in this; *Cl.R.1234–7*, pp. 363–4, 366–7.

[109] *Cl.R.1234–7*, p. 332. The enrolment is garbled, but refers both to de Rivallis and to a man named Stephen, surely Stephen of Seagrave, who was to be pursued via the sheriff of Warwick and Leicestershire. At some time before November 1235, Seagrave had been accused of concealing various of the profits he had made as sheriff of Bedfordshire

ities of the past few years were still far from healed. In April 1237, Peter received the first in an occasional series of favours from the king, granting him timber to maintain him at Banstead in Surrey.[110] Two months later he was licensed to cross to Poitou, provided that he returned to answer the king for whatever charges might be made against him, before November 1237. His pardon of May 1236 would therefore appear to have been less than absolute.[111] In 1238 he witnesses a pair of charters issued by bishop des Roches, and after the bishop's death served as one of des Roches' executors.[112] However, he was to spend most of the next decade in relative obscurity, returning to court only after 1250, being readmitted as a baron of the Exchequer in 1253 and as treasurer of the king's wardrobe for a brief few months in 1257–8.[113]

Between 1232 and 1234 Peter de Rivallis had amassed one of the most extraordinary lordships in English history: a vast swathe of land stretching across much of Sussex and the Weald, combined with castles in the Welsh Marches and the promise that he might ensure the descent of these estates to a niece who was to be married to William, son of John de Briouze. It was a lordship of very short duration, founded upon the shifting sands of royal favour, and undermined by an attack upon the whole security of tenure by royal charter: an attack in which Peter had freely co-operated. Peter's estate was to be entirely dismembered after his removal from court in 1234. And yet, this process of dismemberment tells us much about the new political climate. It shows the extent to which the archbishop of Canterbury served to mediate between the king and his former ministers, softening the impact of their fall, just as after 1224 archbishop Langton had intervened to prevent Hubert de Burgh from reaping wholesale revenge upon des Roches. It demonstrates, too, the extent to which Magna Carta had been enshrined as a manifesto of good government. Even Peter de Rivallis realized this, in his efforts to appeal to the Charter against the sentence of the court. After 1234, it was the king himself who spearheaded the attack upon Peter. A minor in 1224, and for the next ten years dominated by the ministers of the late king John, Henry had at last come of age. It was he, not his

and Buckinghamshire. He claimed that the concealment had actually been made by one of his clerks, and on 21 January 1236 the Exchequer was ordered to respite the demands made against him, pending further investigation; C60/35, mm. 14, 18.
[110] *Cl.R.1234–7*, p. 440, and see *Cl.R.1237–42*, p. 65; *Cl.R.1242–7*, p. 206.
[111] *CPR 1232–47*, p. 186; *CRR*, xvi, no. 16.
[112] *Acta*, nos. 51, 53; *CPR 1232–47*, p. 423.
[113] *Acta*, appendix 4, no. 41.

courtiers, who refused to bargain with de Rivallis. Whilst the council urged restraint, the king's anger played an important part in de Rivallis' disgrace. Peter himself appears to have been slow to appreciate this fact. He thought that it was still possible to salvage at least some of the spoils of office. He tried to strike a deal with Henry. Like Hubert de Burgh before him, he made the mistake of assuming that Henry could be won round; a king who had proved himself so tractable, could surely not have changed, almost overnight, into a wrathful enemy, set upon revenge.

Like his Plantagenet ancestors, Henry was a man of strong passions. Unlike his father, King John, he was easily led. He depended upon his ministers in a way that would have been unthinkable under John. A mere boy of nine when he came to the throne, for the first ten years of his reign, indeed arguably until the fall of Peter des Roches in 1234, Henry had been dominated by the counsels of older men. Even afterwards, he was to rely upon a series of chief ministers in a way that reveals much of the sense of dependence that his childhood and his long minority had engendered. But Henry was neither a simpleton, nor blessed with an even temper. He bore grudges, and on occasion could explode in petulant rage. Courtiers overlooked this fact at their peril. Men who, for a while at least, appeared to hold the entire government of England in their hands, who may even have fancied themselves invulnerable, were to find the king's anger very hard to bear. In 1232, Hubert de Burgh had been so outraged by Henry's swing of mood against him, in favour of des Roches, that he may even have dared box the king's ears. By continuing to treat the king as a mere boy, to be directed and led, Hubert failed to heed the warning signs. Two years later, de Rivallis made a similar mistake. Astounded by the change that had come over his relations with the king, he could not believe that it was Henry rather than his private enemies who had wrought the change. In July 1234 Peter came to court, dressed in a coat of mail, ready to negotiate with the king. It was with the king, not his ministers, that Peter sought to strike a bargain. Like Hubert before him, he presumed too much upon his own indispensability. Only one man at court avoided these mistakes: Peter des Roches, arguably a more skilful courtier than either de Burgh or de Rivallis. In 1221 and again in 1224, des Roches had learned lessons that he was to put to good account in the 1230s. He knew, only too well, how devastating the loss of the king's confidence could be. In 1234, rather than support de Rivallis in his resistance to the royal will, des Roches buckled under. He saw that it was best to co-operate with the new regime, and to trust that the king's anger would soon pass, as it had passed before. As a result, he alone of all the king's ministers emerged relatively unscathed in the aftermath of the regime's collapse.

The Italian chronicler, Salimbene, has an illuminating story to tell of a jester who so outraged King Henry by his insolence, implying that the king was a simpleton, that Henry ordered him to be hanged. The terrified man was dragged away by Henry's courtiers, to all appearances as if they intended taking him straight to the scaffold. However, the moment they were outside, the courtiers let him go, nonetheless assuring the king that his orders had been carried out.[114] The story may be an apocryphal one. Nonetheless, it suggests that Salimbene, like des Roches, appreciated that Henry's anger, though terrible, was not long lasting.

THE REGIME OF 1232–1234: AN OVERVIEW

This leads us on to one of the central questions to be raised by des Roches' regime: who governed England between 1232 and 1234, the king or his ministers? As we have seen, for much of the period it is very hard to assign des Roches any precise role in the direction of royal policy. Yet, the records of the Chancery and the Exchequer show that he was a powerful presence at court. Between 1232 and 1234, he witnessed the vast majority of royal charters. A large number of administrative letters and writs were issued under his warranty or witness. His nephew Peter de Rivallis was installed in a host of offices at court and in the localities. And yet des Roches himself held no great office of state. He remained merely the bishop of Winchester. Government was conducted in the name of the king. It was in the king's name that all of the most controversial acts of the regime were undertaken, and it is royal charters and letters that provide our principal source for the chronology of events. For this reason, it is hardly surprising that in writing the history of the regime, we are forced to speak of the king far more than we speak of des Roches.

Clearly, the events of 1232–4 would never have taken place without the king's assent. Although at least one contemporary writer continues to refer to him as *rex puer*, Henry was more than a mere child.[115] It was only because he supported the policies of his ministers that those policies could be put into practice. Once the king's

[114] Salimbene de Adam, *Cronica*, ed. F. Bernini, 2 vols., Scrittori d'Italia clxxxvii–clxxxviii (Bari 1942), i, p. 443.
[115] Coker, ' "Margam Chronicle" ', p. 138.

confidence was withdrawn, after the spring of 1234, his ministers were very soon toppled from power. Henry believed that des Roches and de Rivallis could deliver the promises that they made. They offered to rid him of Hubert de Burgh, whose domination the king had come to resent. They held up to the king an image of majesty that appealed to him, modelled in part upon King John, in part upon the emperor Frederick II. Henry was to be rich and powerful. He was to summon whom he chose to court, without necessarily heeding the advice of his over-mighty subjects. According to des Roches, inconvenient awards and promotions made by royal charter could be overturned. If his subjects rebelled, then Henry was within his rights if he made war against them. His family lands in France could be regained, if only the king had the financial resources, and could wield sufficient power to overcome the distaste for foreign adventure shown by his native English subjects. In all of these respects, des Roches and his colleagues held out a pleasing prospect to the king. But, without the king, his ministers could have achieved nothing. Ultimately, the responsibility for the events of 1232–4 rests with the king, not his ministers.

And yet, as the chroniclers were quick to point out, by listening with such rapt attention to the advice of des Roches, Henry merely replaced one set of domineering courtiers, the group headed by de Burgh, with another, led by the bishop of Winchester. Far from acceding to personal sovereignty, the king handed over the government of his realm to the adherents of des Roches. It is no coincidence that the chroniclers, chiefly Roger of Wendover, repeat speech after speech made by des Roches, or by his enemies at court, with only an occasional report of the words spoken by Henry III. After 1232, Henry's ministers spent as much time settling old scores, and reaping revenge upon their own personal enemies, as they ever did in boosting the influence or the financial stability of the crown. The new regime claimed to have obtained unparalleled wealth for the king, and yet its members went on to enrich themselves from the crown's resources; none more so than des Roches' nephew, Peter de Rivallis, with his lordship in Sussex and the Marches. The persecution of de Burgh, the overturning of royal charters, the attacks upon members of the royal household, and eventually upon the Marshal and his men, were not motivated by abstract considerations of policy or from a concern for the best interests of the king. Rather, they sprang from the desire of des Roches, Peter de Maulay, Peter de Rivallis and their other associates, many of them aliens, to be restored to the influence that they had enjoyed before de Burgh's accession to power in the 1220s. Government became embroiled in petty in-fighting. Increasingly it commanded the support of an ever more narrow clique, as those who challenged its motives and methods were excluded from court. Even within that clique, there were tensions. Des Roches' faction was stronger than many another at court, but it never constituted a political 'party' in the modern sense of the word. Too much depended upon the personal favour of the king; the court was too unstable an environment for a man such as des Roches to command anything other than a shifting coalition of support. In the end, no courtier was above the king. By the spring of 1234, the English bishops, the majority of the royal household, and, most significantly of all, the earl Marshal and his sympathizers, had been forced into opposition. Des Roches and his supporters stood exposed, claiming to represent the true interests of the king, yet faced by baronial rebellion and the threat of excommunication from the church. As long ago as 1223, des Roches had vowed to do all in his power to bring about the disgrace of Hubert de Burgh. In the 1230s he was given the opportunity to put these threats into practice. Ultimately, the blame for abusing that opportunity rests with des Roches rather than with the king.

What, if anything, did the regime achieve? After 1232 enormous sums were spent upon alliances with Brittany and Poitou, intended to consolidate Plantagenet influence on the continent. And yet, by the time that the regime fell in 1234, virtually nothing had been gained. The soldiers and money shipped across the Channel were used, not to defend Plantagenet interests, but by the duke of Brittany to conduct a private war against his own personal enemies. When this had been concluded, the duke promptly made his peace with France.[116] St James de Beuvron, and remaining outposts of Plantagenet influence north of the Loire were surrendered to the French.[117] At much the same time, Capetian power in Normandy was greatly augmented by the death of Richard Marshal. Over the previous thirty years, the Marshal family had managed to retain possession of its lands both in England and Normandy. Richard's death in 1234, and the accession of his brother Gilbert, a subject of Henry III, provided the French with a pretext for the seizure of the Marshal honours of Longueville and Orbec. By 1238 Longueville was contributing almost as much to the Capetian treasury as the entire royal demesne in the Pays de

---

[116] Painter, *The Scourge of the Clergy*, pp. 84–7.
[117] *CPR 1232–47*, p. 67; *Cl.R.1234–7*, pp. 169–70.

Caux.[118] Far from assisting the recovery of Henry's continental lordship, the regime of 1232–4 actually precipitated the collapse of the last
great cross-Channel landholding to unite England and Normandy.
The dispatch of so much wealth to allies abroad, and the ignominious
defection of these allies once the money ran short, can only have
confirmed the distaste felt by the English baronage for all continental
adventures. The goal of Plantagenet reconquest receded even further
into the mists of make-believe.

The regime's approach to Brittany and Poitou had one further,
incidental effect: a perceptible upsurge in the level of taxation levied
against the Jews. It was the English Jewry who were burdened with
much of the cost of Henry's subsidies to Brittany and Poitou. The
regime of 1232–4 marks a watershed in Anglo-Jewish relations.
Henceforth new and swingeing taxes were to be imposed against the
Jews, leading inevitably to the souring of relations with their Christian
creditors. By 1234 expulsions and restrictions upon the Jewish
community were being adopted as a matter of official policy.[119] Here,
once again, des Roches and his regime bequeathed a bitter legacy.

Thus far, we have spoken of the regime's approach to France and
the Jews as if these initiatives were the outcome of deliberate policy.
But in fact, throughout the period 1232–4, policy took second place
to personalities. For all its vaunted intention to solve the financial and
political problems of the king, the regime can hardly be credited with
abstract financial or political 'reforms'. We have seen that with regard
to the king's finances very little was achieved. The whole-sale
replacement of sheriffs, and the return to direct management of
escheats, were carried out for factional advantage, in order that des
Roches and his allies might obtain lucrative positions in local government. Des Roches and de Rivallis made little attempt to overhaul the
management of the king's Exchequer, but instead worked through
the chamber and the treasury of the king's household, departments
with which they had both been closely associated prior to 1224.
When reform came, some two years after the fall of des Roches, it
was to be along very different lines, carried out chiefly through the

---

[118] For the seizure of Longueville and Orbec by the French, see Bouquet, *Recueil*, xxi,
pp. 255, 257, xiv, part i, pp. 43–5, nos. 327, 331, 334–6, which suggest that even
before 1234, Louis had seized the castle of Léhon in Brittany, belonging to Richard's
wife, Gervasia de Dinan. For various of these references I am indebted to Daniel
Power.

[119] In general, see Vincent, 'Jews, Poitevins, and the bishop of Winchester', pp. 119–32,
extending the arguments of R. C. Stacey, '1240–60: a watershed in Anglo-Jewish
relations?', *Historical Research* 61 (1988), pp. 135–50.

Exchequer, and accompanied by a systematic enquiry into the crown's resources. At best, the chaotic methods employed by des Roches and de Rivallis, and the breakdown of accounting procedures between 1232 and 1234, may have provided the later reformers with an example of how *not* to proceed, and hence ensured the stricter regulation of accounts passing through the royal household.

Even in respect to the Plantagenet lands in France, it is questionable whether des Roches' regime pursued any very coherent policy other than to maintain the subsidies, already agreed during the Breton campaign of 1230, to the king's allies in Brittany and Poitou. Between 1232 and 1234 there was to be no attempt to launch a campaign of military conquest on the continent. The armies mustered during these years were directed against Wales and Ireland, not against the French. Had the political consensus in England not broken down, and had the king not been forced to make war against the Marshal, it is conceivable that des Roches might have planned some more ambitious strategy, ready to meet the Capetians in strength when the Anglo-French truce expired. As it was, by the summer of 1233, des Roches' chief concern appears to have been simply to contain the threat from France, through his unsuccessful efforts to negotiate an extension of the truce. For all that the chroniclers might write of it as an alien ministry, headed by Frenchmen and dedicated to the promotion of foreigners to castles, offices and lands, the regime of 1232–4 appears to have lacked anything approaching a coherent foreign policy. As we have seen, many of the aliens that it promoted were not themselves the creatures of des Roches, but knights of the royal household, granted temporary possession of rebel lands, to keep the peace and to reduce the burden that their wages had previously placed upon the king's purse. Amongst those aliens closest to des Roches – Peter de Maulay, Engelard de Cigogné and the family Chanceaux – it seems likely that by the 1230s, their enthusiasm for reconquest in France had faded in direct proportion to their acquisition of lands and favours in England. What had Peter de Maulay, baron of Mulgrave in Yorkshire, to gain from a reassertion of Plantagenet lordship overseas? What, indeed, could Peter des Roches hope for from France, after thirty years of exile as bishop of Winchester? Clearly, des Roches and his associates were more enthusiastic in their support for continental alliances than the vast majority of the English baronage. No doubt, reconquest was something for which des Roches continued to hope. Certainly, he appears to have done his best to strengthen the alliances between the English court and the disaffected barons of Brittany and Poitou. But as a priority, reconquest took second place after 1232 to the bishop's pursuit of power in England: power for himself and his associates, and vengeance upon his enemies.

If the regime was driven by personality rather than policy, then it was upon the personal level that it was to have its longest-lasting effects. To begin with, it was crucial in bringing about the downfall of Hubert de Burgh. Although the legal process employed here was far from satisfactory, and although the king had no choice but to repudiate an enormous number of awards, theoretically made in perpetuity to Hubert and his heirs, thereby opening the floodgates to the attack upon royal charters that was to follow, it is arguable that the downfall of de Burgh was an essential step upon the king's path towards personal sovereignty. In the immediate aftermath, it is true that Peter de Rivallis was promoted to a collection of offices and estates even more remakable than that previously held by de Burgh. One over-mighty minister was brought low, only to be succeeded by another. But in 1234 de Rivallis too was disgraced. Never again was Henry to lavish quite such favour upon one single man. Not even his Savoyard or Lusignan kinsmen in the 1240s or 50s could lay claim to quite the combination of offices and land that de Burgh and de Rivallis had held.

After 1234, the chief beneficiary of the lands seized from de Burgh and de Rivallis was the king's brother, Richard of Cornwall, who in the following twelve months received the honour of Knaresborough, the manors of Haughley and Kirton formerly held by de Burgh, and custody of the Briouze estates in Sussex and Wales.[120] In later years, although marred by occasional disagreements, the relations between Richard and the king were to be generally harmonious. Indeed, by the 1250s it was to be the enormous wealth of Richard, and the loans that he made to the crown, that preserved the king from bankruptcy. By granting so much land to his brother rather than to someone from outside the royal family, the king avoided at least one of the pitfalls of the past ten years. In the same way, the office of Justiciar, held in succession by the over-mighty courtiers, Hubert de Burgh and Stephen of Seagrave, was deliberately left vacant after

---

[120] Denholm-Young, *Richard of Cornwall*, pp. 164–70; *Cal. Chart. R. 1226–57*, pp. 191, 193; *CPR 1232–47*, pp. 89–90. In 1235 the king offered to restore the honour of Eye, then held by Richard, to Henry duke of Lorraine. But the duke died before this could be put into effect; *CPR 1232–47*, p. 103; *Treaty Rolls*, ed. Chaplais, no. 83; Denholm-Young, *Richard of Cornwall*, p. 166.

1234. Henceforth, although it is possible to identify a series of men who served in effect as king's chief minister, none of them was to be awarded the Justiciarship, previously the principal outward symbol of power at court. Likewise, whereas de Rivallis had been granted a wide array of official titles, as treasurer of the Exchequer and the wardrobe, chamberlain and so forth, in future such offices were to be reserved, individually, for lesser men. In 1236 the king was to attempt, for the moment unsuccessfully, to depose the last great officer of state, the chancellor Ralph de Neville.[121]

Advantageous as these changes may have been, none of them was anticipated in 1232 when des Roches and his associates seized power. To des Roches, the harrying of Hubert de Burgh was no abstract matter of policy, intended to strengthen the authority of the crown; rather it was an act of personal revenge, undertaken principally so that the bishop and his clients might seize the offices and lands that Hubert had possessed. This spirit of revenge was to underpin the entire course of the regime, with its repudiation of royal charters, and its attempt to sweep away the landed settlement established since 1224. In the process, des Roches' regime was to engender hatreds and vendettas of its own. Not until 1237, following intervention by the papal legate Otto, were two of its chief actors, des Roches and Stephen of Seagrave to be reconciled to their former victims, de Burgh, Gilbert Basset and Richard Siward. In the meantime, Richard of Cornwall is said to have procured the banishment of Siward, whose attacks upon Richard's manors had not been forgotten.[122] Even after the supposed reconciliation of 1237 there is evidence that old wounds had by no means healed. After 1239, with Stephen of Seagrave established once again as a leading minister at court, there were to be wild accusations thrown at the heads of Ranulph the Breton, Gilbert Marshal, and above all, against the aged Hubert de Burgh, who was to stand trial on a series of charges very little changed from those that had been made against him in 1232. Seagrave's part in all this is unproved, but it is undoubtedly the case that the hatreds of the early 1230s lived on to plague a future generation and to pursue Hubert de Burgh almost literally to his grave.[123]

The fall of des Roches and de Rivallis was a dramatic event, but for the moment it heralded no comprehensive change in the composition of the court. Various of the bishop's associates, Peter de Rivallis,

---

[121] Paris, *CM*, iii, pp. 363–4.
[122] *Ibid.*, iii, pp. 363, 369, 404.
[123] For the trials of 1239–40, see Stacey, *Politics, Policy and Finance*, pp. 135–6.

Robert Passelewe and Stephen of Seagrave, were disgraced following the council meeting at Gloucester in May 1234, but in every case the disgrace was to be relatively short-lived. Brian de Lisle died within a few weeks of the collapse of the bishop's regime. But for the rest, several of des Roches' colleagues survived in office, more or less unaffected. Engelard de Cigogné, for example, was actually promoted at the Gloucester council, being appointed sheriff of Berkshire and keeper of the castles of Windsor and Odiham, in succession to Robert Passelewe's brother.[124] The Poitevin, Hugh de Vivonne, although deposed as seneschal of Gascony, remained in the king's service, and in February 1235 was awarded custody of a royal escheat.[125] Likewise, Peter de Maulay had returned to court by January 1236, when he was appointed sheriff of Northamptonshire.[126] De Maulay could presumably count upon the support of his former ward, the king's brother, Richard of Cornwall. Engelard weathered the storm of 1234 in much the same way that he had managed to survive in office ten years earlier, following the attack upon des Roches and Fawkes de Bréauté in 1224.[127] Of the veterans at Henry's court, Peter de Maulay, Engelard de Cigogné, Hubert de Burgh and des Roches himself, the survivors from the administration of King John, none was permanently disgraced by their part in the events of 1232–4. Aliens, such as de Maulay, Engelard and Hugh de Vivonne, continued prominent in royal service. Even so, the survivors of John's reign were never again to occupy quite the place at court that they once had held. Age alone would have made this inevitable. By 1234, most of these men were sixty years old or more. Within another decade all of them were to be dead. Even before their deaths, they had yielded place to a younger generation, many of whom had come to maturity amidst the crisis of 1232–4. Simon de Montfort, William Longespée, Richard of Cornwall and many other young barons had observed the progress of des Roches' regime, as minor players in their own right. Such matters are hard to quantify, but it seems likely that at least some of these men had learned from the experience. At the very least, they had witnessed the effects of arbitrary royal government, and the promotion of a particular, narrow faction at court. They had seen, too, the disastrous results of civil war, both for the rebel leader Richard Marshal, and for the king's ministers, des Roches and de Rivallis.

---

[124] *CPR 1232–47*, pp. 46, 49–50, 81; *Cl.R.1231–4*, pp. 461, 533; C60/34, mm. 9, 14, 16.
[125] *Cl.R.1234–7*, pp. 42, 49.
[126] *CPR 1232–47*, p. 133; C53/29, m. 8.
[127] See above, p. 215.

After 1234, it was to be a further thirty years before another baron was to dare to declare open war upon the king. Meanwhile, des Roches' regime may have taught its successors to steer a more moderate course; to avoid narrow factionalism, and to govern wherever possible by common consent rather than arbitrary royal will. The nightmare of 1233–4, in which the whole security of tenure by royal charter had been thrown into question, leading to civil war between barons and king, and between one baronial family and another, was not an experience that either the king or the barons were anxious to repeat.

Of all the men who came of age during the regime of 1232–4, none should have learned more than the king himself. Indeed, in the words of Sir Maurice Powicke, the events of these years had offered Henry one of his most significant 'Lesson[s] in Kingship'. Yet Henry was always a slow learner. Henceforth, it is true, there was to be little question of his returning so wholeheartedly to the administrative methods of his father. On the whole, for the next twenty years of his personal rule, the king was to try to govern through consent rather than compulsion, by cajoling and appeasing his barons rather than by making war against them.[128] The *vis et voluntas*, the *ira et malevolentia* of his Plantagenet ancestors, were never again to serve as guiding principles in the government of the realm. But there had been no fundamental sea-change in royal government. When occasion demanded, Henry was still capable of reviving the administrative techniques that had served his ancestors: hostage-taking, the repudiation of royal charters, the denial of baronial and ecclesiastical grievances, government through clique, and the exercise of arbitrary royal will. After 1234 the theoretical powers of the monarchy were in no way reduced. The king continued to reign supreme, with no authority placed between him and God. Indeed, by bringing about the fall both of de Burgh and Peter des Roches, it is arguable that the events of 1232–4 raised the king to a far stronger personal role in government than he had ever played before. Only in one respect can we discern a major shift in emphasis. Magna Carta, in 1232 still untested as a manifesto of good government, came of age after 1234 in much the same way as the king. Although, as we have seen, the appeal made to the Charter by Richard Marshal was in many ways peculiar, arguing for a technical interpretation of the Charter's promise to provide judgement by peers, very different from the gloss that would later be put upon it by lawyers and historians, the reissue

---

[128] In general, see D. A. Carpenter, 'Kings, magnates and society: the personal rule of King Henry III, 1234–1258', *Speculum* 60 (1985), pp. 39–70.

of the Charter in 1234, repeated in 1237, was effectively to place permanent limitations upon the exercise of brute, royal power. To this extent, the spirit of King John was permanently laid to rest. It is no coincidence that the men who came forward in 1234 to dominate royal counsel should have been those most devoted to peace, stability and respect for legal form: the English bishops, and the lawyers, above all the chief justice *coram rege*, William de Raleigh. It was Raleigh who after 1234 supervised the legal process against the king's *disseisins per voluntatem*, who headed the negotiations with Peter de Rivallis and the restoration of royal charters, including that which granted Upavon to Gilbert Basset, whose repudiation in 1233 had been a principal cause of civil war. Through the writings of Henry de Bracton, Raleigh's pupil, we can appreciate something of Raleigh's conception of royal power. The king was still supreme, empowered to govern by direct authority from God. In theory, no one could sit in judgement upon royal charters save the king himself. But, should the king choose to overturn such charters, as he had done after 1232, or should he ignore the advice of his great men in council, then he did so at his peril. This was Raleigh's message, a direct reponse to the lessons of the 1230s, offered to king and courtiers alike.

Finally, what of Peter des Roches? Since 1232 he has loomed across the pages of this narrative, the most influential of the king's counsellors, blamed by the chroniclers and the king for the new departures in government, yet casting his great shadow from the periphery, only rarely to be found at centre-stage. It was the return of des Roches in 1232 that ushered in the events of the next two years. When he fell, in 1234, his associates and a whole style of government fell with him. It was des Roches who desired revenge upon Hubert de Burgh, who promised the king that he could make him rich and powerful, who encouraged Henry to look to the examples of King John and the emperor Frederick II. It was des Roches whose interventions, in the patronage of his fellow aliens, in counselling the repudiation of royal charters, in the Canterbury election dispute, were seized upon by the chroniclers as indications of the degree to which royal government was in fact little more than government by the bishop of Winchester. It is the words ascribed to des Roches by Roger of Wendover – that there were no peers in England as there were in France, that the king had the right to summon aliens to court to subdue his over-mighty subjects – which, for the chroniclers at least, served to typify the entire style of government attempted in England after 1232. The regime of the early 1230s was not some accidental collection of courtiers, pursuing abstract policy on behalf of the crown: it was a regime put in place and dominated by the personality of Peter des Roches. And yet, just as the bishop's influence after 1232 is veiled behind the official routine of witnessing and warranting royal writs and letters, so his fall from power in 1234 was a relatively muted affair, marked by little of the drama that accompanied the fall of Seagrave, Passelewe and de Rivallis.

After 1234 des Roches was to live for a further four years. Never again was he to dominate the political scene in England, and yet although, in the immediate aftermath of his fall, attempts were made to bring him to account for the misdeeds of the late regime, retribution very swiftly yielded place to reconciliation. Hence it is that we return from the broad canvas to the narrow, from the court as a whole to the single figure of des Roches. It is with the bishop's final years that this study must close.

Chapter 14

THE FINAL YEARS 1234–1238

In June 1234 Peter des Roches was toppled from power. His offices as sheriff and constable were taken away from him, and the bishop himself was ordered to return to his diocese, to meddle no more in affairs of state. To begin with at least, he was threatened with an onslaught from his enemies, many of whom were now reintroduced to court. In July 1234 he faced an armed attack upon the precinct of his cathedral, headed by the former rebel Richard Siward. At the Bench, he was fined the quite disproportionate sum of £100 for failing to attend the king's justices.[1] Over the past few years, as sheriff of Hampshire, he had escaped paying any surcharge or increment, beyond the ancient county farm. The Exchequer now set out to remedy this situation, decreeing that des Roches was to answer for Hampshire on the same terms as the sheriff he had replaced in 1232, paying £30 in arrears of an annual surcharge of £20. At the same time, he was made liable for £120, described as an aid for the king's Breton campaign of 1230, and presumably intended as a punitive gesture, to make up for des Roches' failure to contribute to the clerical aid extracted in 1232 from the other English bishops. By the end of 1235 he had paid £80 of this sum.[2] However, of his other obligations, all but £10 of the surcharge for Hampshire was written off against his expenditure as sheriff, whilst the remaining £10 was transferred to the account of his former deputy, Roger Wacelin, who had cleared it by 1238.[3] The £40 outstanding from the clerical aid, and the £100 amercement charged in 1234, were still unpaid at the time of des Roches' death.[4] Of the loans of 800 marks that he had made on behalf of the crown, more than 500 marks still remained unpaid at the time of his fall. However, in 1237 the king acknowledged his obligation to repay the money. The debt was eventually

---

[1] CRR, xv, no. 1023; C60/33, m. 3.
[2] E372/79, m. 5d; E372/80, m. 10d.
[3] E372/82, m. 7d.
[4] E372/83, m. 6.

discharged to the bishop's executors, whilst in the meantime des Roches withheld payment of an equivalent sum in the proceeds of the tax of a fortieth due to the crown.[5] In all, there seems to have been no financial attack upon the bishop comparable to that which had taken place during his earlier period of disgrace, in the 1220s.

At the Bench, in the summer of 1234, des Roches faced a spate of hostile pleas. In one case, he was made to surrender custody of a ward to Gilbert Marshal, newly recognized as earl of Pembroke.[6] However, when the citizens of Winchester demanded redress for the bishop's usurpation of their liberties, the king did little other than to allow that the citizens might retain their ancient privileges, without making any overt attack upon des Roches. In the same way, although des Roches was required to answer for the failure of his nephew, Peter de Rivallis, to obey his summons to court, the council accepted the bishop's claim that he had done all in his power to force de Rivallis to comply.[7] There was also trouble within des Roches' own cathedral convent, where a group of the monks obtained papal letters against des Roches, directed to the archbishop of Canterbury and the bishop of Rochester, demanding the restoration of goods which des Roches had illegally withheld.[8] The original papal mandate does not survive, although it is possible that the case was a serious one, involving an attempt by the monks to revive their long-standing grievance over the distribution of property between bishop and chapter, in which the twelfth-century bishops of Winchester had seized numerous manors claimed as the right of the convent of St Swithun's. But in 1234, the monastic proctors appear to have acted without the assent of their prior or a large part of their convent. They were made to confess this fact to the pope, and in March 1235 bishop and convent were reconciled.[9]

Between 1232 and 1234, des Roches had benefited greatly from royal favour. He had received at least two royal manors upon which to found religious houses, a major charter of liberties for the see of Winchester, a series of royal wardships, including apparently a large part of the honour of Gloucester, and an unquantifiable sum in the

---

5   *Cal.Lib.R.1226–40*, pp. 267–8, 390; *Foreign Accounts*, pp. 72–3.

6   *CRR*, xv, no. 1204.

7   *CRR*, xv, nos. 1033, 1091, 1126, and see above pp. 360, 449.

8   The case can to some extent be reconstructed from *Reg.Greg.IX*, no. 2686, which suggests that it was first brought at some time before July 1234.

9   *AM*, ii (Winchester), p. 87, where the reconciliation was effected between proxies, after des Roches' departure abroad. In the aftermath, the monks were faced with a claim for expenses from the professional proctors they had appointed in Rome, settled after July 1235 for a payment of 21m; *Reg.Greg.IX*, no. 2686.

profits of his office as sheriff of Hampshire. Most of these spoils were left untouched after 1234. His religious foundations at Selborne and Titchfield remained in possession of their lands and royal charters. Although the Gloucester estates were restored to the crown, des Roches was allowed to retain custody of the heir of Robert Marmion, together with the important honour of Tamworth, which he still held at the time of his death in 1238.[10] As after his disgrace a decade earlier, when the king's justices and foresters had been bombarded with entertainment and presents, so for the judicial eyres of 1235–6, the Winchester pipe rolls record a stream of presents to justices sitting at Reading, Taunton and elsewhere.[11] Nonetheless, the eyre made no major assault upon the bishop's liberties, which were specifically protected in letters from the king.[12] The Hampshire eyre of December 1235 witnessed only a small number of pleas against des Roches, most of which were abandoned before coming to judgement. Likewise, it saw only minor complaints against the administration of his deputy sheriff, Roger Wacelin.[13]

The leniency shown towards des Roches after 1234 may in part reflect the bishop's age. He was by now a spent volcano, an old man who could surely pose no further threat to the king or his court. In part too, it reflects the moderating influence of the English bishops, who in the summer of 1234 came forwards to supervise the peace established between court and baronage. Having toppled des Roches and his regime from power, the bishops had no desire to prolong the process of vendetta and revenge that had done so much to envenom English politics over the past two years. Nor would they have been anxious to sponsor a personal attack upon des Roches. Des Roches was, after all, a bishop. His henchmen, Robert Passelewe and Peter de Rivallis, were both clerks. As such, they merited the protection of the church. In 1237 it was to be the bishops, meeting in clerical council, who objected most strongly when the king's foresters threatened to encroach upon the liberties of the see of Winchester.[14] To a greater extent even than archbishop Langton in the 1220s, the bishops served to cushion the fall of the regime of 1232–4, softening the king's desire

---

[10] *CPR 1232–47*, p. 231, and see *Acta*, no. 3, appendix 2, no. 45.
[11] Ms. 31DR, mm. 1, 1d, 2d, 3d–4d, 5d, 11d, 12d, and for the aftermath of 1224, see above pp. 218–22.
[12] *Cl.R.1234–7*, p. 222.
[13] For pleas against des Roches, see JUST1/775, mm. 1, 2d, 5d, and for those against Wacelin, mm. 17d, 19d, the most serious being a demand that he restore 100 shillings taken from the men of Andover in punishment for their infringement of royal liberties.
[14] *AM*, i (Burton), p. 254.

for retribution. It may also be that des Roches tried hard to rebuild his personal relations with the new order at court. In 1236, huntsmen of archbishop Edmund are to be found taking live game in des Roches' park at Bishop's Waltham, no doubt to restock the Canterbury estates.[15] In 1237, shortly before his death, des Roches' old rival, Richard Poer bishop of Durham, is to be found as a guest at Taunton and Highclere, whilst in April 1237 des Roches appears to have attended Richard's obsequies, at Tarrant in Dorset.[16] Amongst Poer's executors was Master Elias of Dereham, later to perform a similar service for both des Roches and archbishop Edmund. Even as early as 1234 Master Elias is to be found witnessing charters, both at Winchester and at Canterbury, spanning the households of des Roches and archbishop Edmund in a way that suggests a close *rapprochement* between bishop and metropolitan. Many years earlier, Elias had served as executor to Stephen Langton and William Marshal, earl of Pembroke.[17] Hence, his service under des Roches symbolizes not only the rebuilding of relations between des Roches and the English bishops, but, most remarkably, the resumption of des Roches' contacts with the family of Richard Marshal.

According to Wendover, Richard Marshal was killed in 1234, some would say murdered, as a direct result of the malice and personal hatred of des Roches. Yet within a few years of his death, there are indications in plenty that Richard's family had re-established contacts with des Roches. Taken all in all, this evidence casts serious doubt upon Wendover's allegations of a plot against the Marshal's life, masterminded by the bishop of Winchester. In September 1237 for example, Gilbert Marshal, Richard's heir, is to be found as the bishop's guest at Highclere.[18] In the same year, des Roches was asked by the pope to confirm a gift that Gilbert had made, bestowing the Surrey church of Witley upon the papal foundation of S. Maria de Gloria at Anagni.[19] Most remarkable of all is the evidence linking des Roches to Richard Marshal's widow, Gervasia de Dinan. In 1234 the Marshal estates in Normandy were confiscated by Louis IX. At the

---

[15] Ms. 31DR, m. 11d.

[16] Ms. 32DR, mm. 7, 13d, 14d, and for Poer's death, see Paris, *CM*, iii, pp. 391–2. In November 1237 des Roches was present at the Exchequer to hear the accounts of Poer's executors; *Cl.1237–42*, p. 9.

[17] For Elias, see *Acta*, p. xliii, nos. 51, 53; Crouch, *William Marshal*, p. 131n.; C. H. Lawrence, *St Edmund of Abingdon* (Oxford, 1960), pp. 302, 312.

[18] Ms. 32, m. 14d, and see *Acta*, no. 343 for the Marshal knight, Henry of Earley, hunting the bishop's park at Taunton.

[19] *Reg.Greg.IX*, no. 3818, and see *Acta*, no. 85, which suggests that the grant was ineffective.

same time, Richard's widow appears to have lost possession of her family lands in England: principally the manors of Burton Latimer in Leicestershire, and Ringwood in Hampshire, once held by her father. In due course, Gervasia was to make a number of grants from her remaining Breton estate, in return for prayers for the soul of Richard Marshal.[20] She also sought to bestow the manor and church of Ringwood upon the Norman abbey of Foucarmont 'for the salvation of my husband, earl Richard of good memory'. The gift was set out in a charter of June 1235, but as early as November 1234 Gervasia had written to King Henry III, and to 'the reverend father', the bishop of Winchester, requesting that they confirm her award.[21] In the event, Foucarmont was never to obtain possession of Ringwood, which continued to be treated as a crown escheat.[22] Nonetheless, the mere fact that within six months of Richard Marshal's death, his widow could write to des Roches, asking him to confirm an award made for the salvation of Richard's soul, suggests very strongly that Gervasia herself did not credit the stories in which des Roches was made personally responsible for Richard's death. Once again, we are re-minded of the fact that Gervasia de Dinan and Peter des Roches were related to one another, if only distantly, by marriage. Once again, it would appear that even before the papal legate effected peace between des Roches and the former rebels in 1237, the bishop had gone a considerable way towards patching up relations, both with the leaders of the English church and with the family of the Marshal. Reconciliation appears to have been as much des Roches' desire as it was the desire of the archbishop and the majority of the king's counsel.

Following his disgrace in the 1220s, des Roches had looked to adventures overseas as a means of escaping his predicament in England. In much the same spirit, after his fall in 1234, he accepted an invitation from the papacy to assist in Gregory IX's campaign against

---

[20] *Anciens Evêchés de Bretagne*, ed. Bourgogne and Barthélemy, iii, pp. 79–80, iv, pp. 367–8.

[21] Rouen, Archives Départementales de la Seine-Maritime 8H10, which includes three charters relating to the grant, also copied into Rouen, Bibliothèque Municipale ms. Y13 (Foucarmont cartulary), f. 62r–v. One of these texts is partially printed in Bouquet, *Recueil*, xxiii, p. 441, which adds further details from a local chronicle. For the cartulary references I am indebted to David Crouch.

[22] *Cl.R.1231–4*, pp. 339–40, 431; *Cal. Chart. R. 1226–57*, pp. 227, 244, 253; *CRR*, xvi, no. 79. The fact that Gervasia's original letters to King Henry are today amongst the archives of Foucarmont, suggests either that they were produced in duplicate or that they were never actually sent. The letters to des Roches, however, are referred to in a charter granted to Foucarmont, suggesting that they may well have been sent as agreed.

the rebellious citizens of Rome. The English court was probably as anxious to see the back of des Roches as des Roches was glad to escape from court. In January 1235 he was granted licence to cross overseas, and according to the Winchester annals, he set out for the continent in early March.[23] Matthew Paris states that the pope had summoned him, both because of his military skills and in order to take advantage of the bishop's great wealth.[24] Perhaps too, the pope, who had long enjoyed good relations with des Roches, wished to rescue the bishop from his domestic difficulties and, by speeding his with-drawal from England, to ease the tensions at court.[25] Certainly, at the papal Curia over the next eighteen months des Roches was to obtain numerous favours: confirmations from Gregory IX for his religious foundation at Halesowen, for the hospital he had refounded at Acre, and assent to sales made to him by the chapter of Le Mans from their property in England.[26] As for his precise role in the pope's war against Rome, we know very little. Despite the claims of Matthew Paris, he arrived in Italy too late to participate in the defence of Viterbo in October 1234, although Paris may be correct in suggesting that des Roches assisted in raids against the Roman suburbs.[27] The Dunstable annals state merely that he led a force of knights and crossbowmen to the pope at Perugia, and it is in Perugia, Assisi and Viterbo that the Curia appears to have spent most of the coming year.[28]

Des Roches' time at the Curia coincided with a brief lull in the hostilities between papacy and Empire. He would have had the opportunity to renew his contacts with Frederick II, who remained in Italy until May 1235.[29] Herein lay a cause of great distress to des Roches. On 27 April, a month or so after the bishop's sailing, the king was persuaded to write Frederick a letter of warning. The bishop, so

---

[23] For the licence, dated 28 January, see *Cl.R.1234–7*, p. 163. The Tewkesbury and Winchester annals state that he set out from Winchester on 2 February, and according to the Winchester annals he crossed overseas on 4 March. Paris dates his sailing to around Easter (8 April); *AM*, i, p. 95, ii, p. 87; Paris, *CM*, iii, p. 309. He is last recorded in England at Winchester on 22 February 1235; *Acta*, no. 70.

[24] Paris, *CM*, iii, p. 309.

[25] *Treaty Rolls*, ed. Chaplais, no. 30, provides specific proof that in 1234 the pope had written to Henry III requesting that des Roches might be sent to his aid.

[26] *Reg.Greg.IX*, nos. 2686, 2944, 3109–10.

[27] Paris, *CM*, ii, pp. 303–5; *Hist. Ang. Min.*, ii, p. 373, and see Wendover, *Flores*, iv, p. 323. For the battle of Viterbo, see D. Waley, *The Papal State in the Thirteenth Century* (London 1961), pp. 142–3; *Cronache e Statuti della Città di Viterbo*, ed. I. Ciampi, Documenti di Storia Italiana v (Florence 1872), p. 19; *Cronache dei secoli xiii e xiv*, ed. C. Minutoli and others, Documenti di Storia Italiana vi (Florence 1876), p. 72.

[28] *AM*, iii, p. 142, and for the pope's itinerary, see *Reg.Greg.IX*, iv, pp. 282–5.

[29] T. C. Van Cleve, *The Emperor Frederick II of Hohenstaufen* (London 1973), pp. 372–7.

Frederick was told, had at one time served as spiritual father and counsellor to the king, but by abusing his powers had persuaded Henry to do great injury to the faithful men of the realm, leading to war between the king and his subjects. Des Roches might try to poison Frederick's mind against those whom the king had recently recalled to his council, but the emperor should put no trust in his words. Frederick should also write to the pope, warning him against des Roches, lest the bishop persuade Gregory to do injury to the king. In all of these matters, the emperor should listen to the advice of Walter Mauclerk, bishop of Carlisle, the king's special messenger. A similar warning was conveyed to the master of the Teutonic knights, requesting that he procure letters from Frederick to the pope, against des Roches.[30]

Henry's letters of April 1235 are significant, above all as an indication of the extent to which the king now blamed des Roches for the events of the past three years. They also demonstrate that des Roches still had enemies in England, determined to do him harm. Their wording may conceal a particularly sharp barb, since in describing the bishop's misdeeds, the letters claim that des Roches had referred to a plenitude of royal power (*plenitudo regie potestatis*). To Frederick II, as the writer was surely aware, the words 'plenitude of power' were calculated to serve as a red rag to a bull. It was precisely this same expression, *plenitudo potestatis*, that the papal Chancery employed in claiming supremacy for the pope over the Empire and the imperial church.[31] As to the letters' timing, they were sent in the midst of a flurry of diplomatic exchanges between England and the continent: the preparations for the marriage of Henry's sister Isabella to the emperor Frederick, which eventually took place in June 1235; the negotiation at Paris of an Anglo-French truce, and the attempts to obtain papal dispensation for a marriage between King Henry himself and the eldest daughter of the count of Ponthieu.[32] It may have been feared that des Roches would use his influence with both emperor and pope, to wreck one or all of these initiatives. There can be little doubt that the letters were delivered, and that for a time at least, they

---

[30] *Treaty Rolls*, ed. Chaplais, nos. 15, 16; *RL*, i, no. ccclxxxix. In the event it seems unlikely that the bishop of Carlisle, a confirmed enemy of des Roches, ever delivered the letters. He appears at the English court, witnessing royal letters until at least mid-June 1235; *Cl.R.1234–7*, pp. 87, 94, 99, 102.

[31] For the concept of papal plenitude of power, see I. S. Robinson, *The Papacy 1073–1198: Continuity and Innovation* (Cambridge 1990), pp. 92, 120, 182–3, 186–7.

[32] For the proposed alliance with Ponthieu and the Anglo-French truce, see *Treaty Rolls*, ed. Chaplais, nos. 60–7, 70, 75; *Cl.R.1234–7*, pp. 158, 160–1, 175; *DD*, nos. 238–9.

soured the previously good relations that had existed between des Roches and the emperor. According to Matthew Paris, in 1237, when Henry III asked des Roches to attend as his representative at a council summoned by Frederick, the bishop refused. He is said to have reminded the king of the earlier complaints made against him to the emperor. Having branded des Roches a trouble-maker, it would simply not do for the king to send him with some contradictory letter of credence; the emperor would only suppose that both Henry and des Roches were fickle and not to be trusted.[33] On crusade in the late 1220s, des Roches had shown himself an admirer and a loyal supporter of Frederick II. It must have been cruel indeed to find himself rejected by a man with whom his relations had previously been so close.

With peace established between the pope and the Roman commune, des Roches had little to keep him in Italy, save for the fear that a return to England would not be welcomed by the king. In the spring of 1236 the pope made representations to Henry, requesting licence for des Roches to return to take charge of his diocese. In his reply, sent in May to both the pope and the bishop, the king claimed that des Roches had left England of his own free will, at the specific invitation of the pope, and that he was free to return whenever he chose. If Henry had ever expressed anger towards the bishop then the bishop should fear no longer; through papal favour, all such rancour had been wiped clean.[34] At much the same time, Henry made the opening moves in a bid to have a papal legate appointed to England, to assist him in his political and financial difficulties. Clearly he was anxious to establish good relations with Gregory IX. If the pope wished des Roches to return to his diocese, then Henry was in no position to object.[35] Des Roches seized the opportunity for a reconciliation, and crossed to England in late September 1236. According to Matthew Paris, he returned an ill and broken man.[36] Certainly, one of his first actions was to secure royal assent for the drawing up of his will.[37]

During his absence, the king had several times visited Winchester and the episcopal estates. The bishop's officers had showered him with presents, including large quantities of fish for the Christmas festivities of 1235, which the king spent at Bishop's Waltham,

---

[33] Paris, *CM*, iii, pp. 393–4.
[34] *Treaty Rolls*, ed. Chaplais, nos. 30–1.
[35] *C. & S.*, p. 237.
[36] Paris, *CM*, iii, p. 378.
[37] *CPR 1232–47*, p. 166.

Marwell and at Winchester itself. This same Christmas court had witnessed various gestures of reconciliation towards the ministers disgraced in 1234: a safe conduct for Stephen of Seagrave, and the appointment of Peter de Maulay as sheriff of Northampton.[38] Again, at Pentecost 1236, the king and his new queen, Eleanor of Savoy, returned to Winchester and Marwell, spending four weeks there in May and June. Once again there were presents from the bishop's men, although at Marwell more than £10 had to be spent in repairing the wall and rails around the park which the king's men had broken, whether by accident or design remains unclear.[39] Even before the king came to Winchester, on 4 May he had issued a general pardon for Peter de Rivallis. Thereafter, the Winchester court saw the rehabilitation of Stephen of Seagrave, the issue of pardons for two of des Roches' former servants, and licence for de Rivallis to make a brief journey overseas, to Poitou.[40] Shortly afterwards, perhaps through the influence of de Rivallis and Simon de Montfort, the former rebel, Richard Siward, was placed under arrest.[41] Siward may well have objected to the pardons granted to so many of the veterans of des Roches' regime. Indeed, he may have threatened to revert to his former ways, launching armed attacks upon his enemies.[42] In September 1236 the king at last recognized the claims of the bishop and the prior of Winchester to a hearing in a long-running dispute over the ownership of a whale, washed up on the foreshore some six months previously. The case was of more than passing interest. It had prompted a sentence of excommunication from des Roches' officials against the king's bailiffs, and in due course it was to involve the king in warranting the liberties and charters of the see of Winchester.[43]

By the summer of 1236, Henry III was once again beset with difficulties, political and financial. His marriage to Eleanor of Savoy, and the promotion at court of his new wife's uncle, William of Savoy, bishop-elect of Valence, had stirred up resistance from a large part of the English baronage, including Henry's own brother, Richard of Cornwall. The cost of the Savoyard marriage, and of the

---

38   CPR 1232–47, p. 133; Ms. 31DR, mm. 7d, 11d.
39   CPR 1232–47, pp. 146–50; Ms. 31DR, mm. 11d, 12d.
40   CPR 1232–47, pp. 145, 150, 186; CRR, xvi, no. 16; Paris, CM, iii, p. 368.
41   Paris, CM, iii, p. 369; Cl.R.1234–7, pp. 363–4, 366–7.
42   See the letter to Alexander of Scotland in CPR 1232–47, p. 158.
43   CRR, xv, no. 1967; Cl.R.1234–7, pp. 378–9; AM, ii (Winchester), p. 87. The bishop's argument was to the effect that the fish was not of the sort that normally went to the king, but was of a variety known in English as 'Thurlehaved'. In addition, he objected to attachments being made by the king's officers within the episcopal liberties, contrary to his charter of 1232.

dower of £20,000 promised to Frederick II in 1235 on his marriage with Henry's sister Isabella, had stretched the king's financial resources to breaking point.[44] In theory des Roches might have stepped into this situation, much as he had stepped in, following his return from crusade in 1231, to take up his role again at the centre of English political life. In practice, by the autumn of 1236 he was too old, too tarnished by the events of the past few years, and probably too ill and exhausted to resume the reins of power. During the last eighteen months of his life he makes only occasional appearances as a witness to royal charters.[45] He continued to make gifts to the king, and in return received various confirmations of his liberties. In December 1237, he was given the right to supervise the collection within his own liberties of a tax of a thirtieth, granted in return for the confirmation of Magna Carta made the previous January.[46] Apart from des Roches, of the forty witnesses to this confirmation, only five could claim to have been mentioned, either on the royal or the baronial side, in the original version of Magna Carta issued in 1215.[47] The older generation of courtiers was rapidly yielding place to younger men.

Of his interventions after 1236, perhaps the most important were those that involved the newly appointed papal legate Otto, who arrived in England in the summer of 1237, and who is said to have been showered with gifts by des Roches. It was Otto who at last reconciled the bishop to his former enemies, Hubert de Burgh, Richard Siward and Gilbert Basset.[48] The meeting between these men must have been an extraordinary one indeed. Yet we have no eye-witness to tell us what took place. Did des Roches and de Burgh exchange the kiss of peace? If so, it must have been a remarkable sight to behold. For at least two of the participants, Stephen of Seagrave and Hubert de Burgh, the reconciliation was by no means a permanent one. Within the next few years, Seagrave appears to have persuaded the king to arraign the aged de Burgh on charges of treason.[49] But by

44 In general, see Denholm-Young, *Richard of Cornwall*, pp. 32–3; Stacey, *Politics, Policy and Finance*, pp. 42–3; E. L. Cox, *The Eagles of Savoy* (Princeton 1974), pp. 47–51.

45 C53/30, mm. 6, 7; *Cal. Chart. R. 1257–1300*, p. 227: 28, 30 Jan., 20 March 1237, 11 May 1238.

46 *Cl.R.1234–7*, p. 515; *Cl.R.1237–42*, pp. 15, 18, 22, 43; *AM*, i (Tewkesbury), pp. 103–4. For a gift from des Roches to the king, see *Cl.R.1234–7*, p. 416.

47 The five were Jocelin bishop of Bath, William earl Warenne, Hubert de Burgh, and two barons, rebels in 1215, Richard de Percy and Richard de Montfichet who had stood amongst the baronial 25 named in the original charter.

48 Paris, *CM*, iii, pp. 404, 412.

49 Stacey, *Politics, Policy and Finance*, pp. 135–6.

the time this trial took place, des Roches was dead. For the bishop, the peace of 1237 was almost certainly sincere.

The close relations now established between des Roches and the legate Otto were to involve the bishop in the final dramas of his life. In January 1238, Henry III sanctioned a marriage between his sister Eleanor, and the Frenchman, Simon de Montfort. The alliance had to be kept secret, in part because Eleanor had not yet obtained papal dispensation, releasing her from the vows of chastity that she had taken after the death of her first husband, William Marshal the younger, in part because no assent had been sought or obtained from the English baronage. When the marriage became known, it sparked a violent reaction, both from the king's brother Richard of Cornwall, and from Eleanor's brother-in-law, Gilbert Marshal. However much they might dress up their grievances in constitutional terms, both men had a strong private interest in preventing Eleanor from remarrying: Richard, in order to protect his claim to the throne, should the king die childless; Gilbert, because of his financial settlement with Eleanor as the widow of the late William Marshal. In February 1238 the two earls threatened to rebel, reviving the prospect of civil war with all the disastrous consequences that followed between 1232 and 1234.[50] On that earlier occasion it had been des Roches who had counselled the king to defy his barons, and if necessary summon Frenchmen to put down the rebel English. But des Roches had changed. In 1238, far from supporting the Frenchman de Montfort, he joined the papal legate in recommending Henry to make peace with Richard and Gilbert, and to accept the peace terms that they offered.[51] Des Roches, the former champion of the aliens against the English baronage, had by 1238 become a defender of the English barons opposed to the alien Simon de Montfort.

This was not quite the end. There were various commissions to be discharged as a papal judge delegate, and a request from Gregory IX that des Roches assist the bishop-elect of Valence in preaching a crusade for the recovery of the Latin empire of Constantinople.[52] In the spring of 1238 des Roches was granted safe-conduct to travel overseas as the king's ambassador, presumably to France.[53] Although it is uncertain whether he ever made this journey, which would have

---

[50] Denholm-Young, *Richard of Cornwall*, pp. 34–7; Labarge, *Simon de Montfort*, pp. 45–52.

[51] Paris, *CM*, iii, p. 458. Richard of Cornwall had been regularly entertained on the Winchester estates in the two years prior to September 1237; Mss. 31DR, m. 7; 32DR, mm. 9d, 11.

[52] *Reg. Greg. IX*, nos. 3541, 3944, 3946; SC7/15/34.

[53] *CPR 1232–47*, p. 217.

been his last Channel crossing, he was involved to the very end of his life in the diplomatic exchanges that had preoccupied him for the previous forty years. The last of the Winchester pipe rolls to be drawn up during his time as bishop, for the year to Michaelmas 1237, records the presence of the archbishop of Bordeaux and the Gascon bishop of Bazas at half a dozen of des Roches' manors, and of a canon of St Lô entertained at Hambledon.[54] In late April 1238 des Roches was summoned to make what was to be positively his last appearance on the public stage. A visit to Oxford by the papal legate had resulted in a violent clash between the legate's men and various clerks attending the Oxford schools. The legate was forced to take shelter in Osney Abbey, and one of his servants was killed.[55] Des Roches was appointed by the king to quell the disturbances and to punish the guilty clerks. In company with the royal chancellor, Ralph de Neville, the abbots of Eynsham and Abingdon, and the theologian, Master Robert Bacon, he imposed a sentence of Interdict upon the city of Oxford early in May.[56] Here, even at the last, various threads in his career were drawn together. Ralph de Neville had been the bishop's protégé as long ago as 1214, indeed his first promotion in the Chancery had come about through the influence of des Roches. Later the two men had quarrelled, so that Neville had stood aloof from des Roches' political interventions during the 1220s and again between 1232 and 1234. Another of his fellow commissioners in 1238, Master Robert Bacon, was the same man who in 1233 had preached a punning sermon against des Roches, warning the king to steer between the rocks and the stones, the *petrae* and the *rupes*. Now, at last, des Roches, Master Robert and Ralph Neville were brought together again, defending an Italian cardinal against the xenophobic brutality of the Oxford schools.

Thereafter there were to be no further adventures for Peter des Roches, save for the final adventure of death. During the past two years he had achieved reconciliation with the king and with many of his former enemies. Arguably, throughout this time, his mind was already fixed upon the need to atone for his sins and to make his peace both with God and man. In 1237 he had sought permission from the general chapter of Cîteaux to have a Cistercian monk and two lay brothers living permanently in his household. On his return to England, one of his chief concerns had been to make proper

---

[54] Ms. 32DR, mm. 4, 4d, 6, 9d, 11d.
[55] C. & S., p. 260 and notes.
[56] *Flores Hist.*, ii, p. 225; *CPR 1232–47*, pp. 217–18.

provision for the religious houses that he had founded, and to purchase property for a further two Cistercian abbeys, to be established by his executors after his death.[57] In the midst of these arrangements, whilst staying at his manor of Farnham in Surrey, he fell ill. There was still time for his household to gather, and for the bishop to issue a series of charters from his deathbed.[58] Amongst those who attended him during these last few days were his nephew, Peter de Rivallis, his ward, the Norman Robert Marmion, and the Englishman Master Elias of Dereham, perhaps already making plans for the bishop's tomb.[59] Des Roches died at Farnham on 9 June 1238. His body was carried to Winchester for burial, but his heart was interred separately at the nearby Cistercian abbey of Waverley. His will made lavish provision for obit celebrations, gifts to the religious, and an endowment of stock and seed corn to be held in perpetuity by his successors as bishops of Winchester. Money was distributed far and wide, to the monasteries of Hampshire, to the cathedral canons of des Roches' native city of Tours, and to the distant hospital of St Thomas at Acre, refounded by the bishop on crusade. There was also money and land bequeathed to establish two new Cistercian houses, one planted in Hampshire, the centre of des Roches' activities and the source of most of his wealth, the other founded overseas, at La Clarté Dieu, probably only a few miles from the bishop's birthplace in the Touraine.[60] Thus, even at the last, the bishop divided his attentions between his adopted realm of England and his homeland in France.

So died Peter des Roches, for nearly forty years a man of immense influence and power, the friend of kings, popes and emperors; a shepherd of souls who had ridden armed into battle; a courtier of genius, reputed a bishop in little more than name, yet a sensitive patron of the arts and the founder of nearly a dozen abbeys, priories and hospitals; a Frenchman, and a patron of his fellow aliens at court, yet a Frenchman who did more than most Englishmen to foster the cult of the Anglo-Saxon saints, and whose last intervention in politics, only a few months before his death, had come supporting the English baronage against the alien, Simon de Montfort. Reputed the friend of murderers, his letters abound in quotation from the Scriptures.

---

[57] C. A. F. Meekings, 'The early years of Netley Abbey', *Journal of Ecclesiastical History* 30 (1979), pp. 1–37, and see *Acta*, nos. 3, 25, 40, 51–2, for des Roches' charters issued in 1237–8 and for his purchase of property from the chapter of Le Mans later put towards the foundation of Netley Abbey.

[58] *Acta*, nos. 53–4, 84.

[59] *Acta*, p. xlii, no. 53.

[60] The will no longer survives, but for an attempted reconstruction, see *Acta*, no. 43.

Scholars and artists as much as crossbowmen and knights found a place in his household. The very chroniclers who worked hardest to blacken his reputation, benefited from his largesse. His had been a rich life, and one crowded with contradictions. At the last, even Matthew Paris put aside his prejudice to marvel at the bishop's career. 'By his death', Paris remarks, 'the whole council of the English realm, both of the king and the church, incurred an irreparable loss'.[61]

Personality, character, physical appearance, all are qualities hard to establish in the lives of medieval men and women, even in a life so well-documented as that of des Roches. Peter des Roches, 'Rocky Stones' or 'Stony Rocks', may well have been a 'hard' man, but ruggedness and rigidity were common characteristics at the Plantagenet court. At best, our evidence provides insights into des Roches the politician, des Roches the property owner and financier. The rest remains guess-work, colours tentatively applied long after the original had faded to a monochrome blur. Even so, certain features stand out. Des Roches was a Frenchman, dedicated to the patronage of his fellow countrymen and above all to the reconquest of the Plantagenet dominion lost in 1204. Raised in the service of kings whose authority reached from the Cheviots to the Pyrenees, in later life he was to strive for the reconquest of this lordship whose collapse had consigned him to thirty years of exile in England. From this sprang a fundamental antipathy to the ambitions and interests of the insular English baronage. To this extent, des Roches was a reactionary, devoted to methods of government and a landed settlement taken for granted in his youth; prepared to champion the memory and the administrative techniques of his friend, King John, long into the 1230s, for all the hatred that such atavism inspired at the English court. Mere nostalgia played little part in all this. At the heart of des Roches' policy lay a perception of kingship, its nature and extent, perhaps never openly articulated, but shared by the bishop with many of his fellow aliens, anathema to those of his contemporaries who preferred rule by consent to rule by the king's arbitrary will, the consolidation of a limited English realm to the pursuit of dominion over much of northern France. Des Roches' perception of kingship was to live on, even after the bishop's death, ingrained in the mind of the greatest of his pupils, King Henry III.

Such a statement cannot pass unqualified. Like many of his caste, des Roches could be driven by ruthless self-interest. After 1232, his

---

[61] Paris, *CM*, iii, pp. 489–90.

vendetta against Hubert de Burgh plunged England into two years of turmoil and civil war. Yet, ironically, by the time that des Roches returned to power, the ambition that had once been dearest to his heart, the reconquest of the Plantagenet lands in France, had already begun to fade. By 1230 des Roches was as much an Englishman in his diocese as he was a Frenchman at court. As a courtier he might champion the king's right to govern by arbitrary will, but as bishop of Winchester, lord of one of the greatest estates in England, he was quick to defend the liberties of his see, appealing where necessary to the terms of Magna Carta and the Charter of the Forests. Beginning as an alien and an exile, by 1230, like many of his closest associates, he had acquired far greater status and wealth in England than he had ever possessed in France. Active in diplomatic exchanges to the very end of his life, he nonetheless let slip the opportunity to attempt a full-scale reconquest of the Plantagenet dominion. Herein lies one explanation, albeit a subtle and a fleeting explanation, of why the breach between England and France, opened in 1204, was never entirely healed.

Fifty years or more after des Roches' death, the chronicler of Lanercost in far away Cumberland set out to record what he could of the great courtier bishop of Winchester. He was able to set down only one, peculiar story. Out hunting one day in his forests, pursuing wild beasts when he would have done better to take pleasure in the salvation of souls, des Roches encountered King Arthur, 'once lord of the whole monarchy of Britain'. When the two men had dined together, des Roches asked that the king provide him with a token of their meeting. Arthur told Peter to close and then to open his hand, whereupon a butterfly flew out. For the remainder of his life, whenever the bishop opened his hand, the same miracle was repeated. So famous did it become, that people often begged for a butterfly as a benediction, and des Roches became known by many as the bishop of the butterfly.[62] Des Roches, the French lepidopterist, meeting Arthur of the Britons – it seems hardly the most likely of encounters – and yet, in its way, with its juxtaposition of English romance, British kingship and French *savoir-faire*, the story may have more of truth in it than at first meets the eye.

[62] *Chronicon de Lanercost*, ed. Stevenson, p. 23, first drawn to my attention, many years ago, by the Rev. Peter Gallup.

BIBLIOGRAPHY

I CITED UNPRINTED PRIMARY SOURCES

Angers

Archives Départementales de Maine-et-Loire 101 H167 (Fonds Fontevraud)
193 H1 (Fonds Fontevraud)

Antony, Cornwall

Carew-Pole Ms. Poles Charters no. 304 (Charter of Richard Marshal)

Avranches

Bibliothèque Municipale Ms. 149

Cambridge

Christ's College	Muniments Mss. Creake Abbey Add.(b) (Creake cartulary)
	At.19 (Charter of Simon de Montfort)
Corpus Christi College	Ms. 111 (Inventory of Winchester cathedral)
Gonville and Caius College	Ms. 205/111 (Miscellaneous collections relating to the Isle of Wight)
	Muniments Ms. Box 23 no. 23
King's College	Muniments Ms. GBR 289 (Great Bricett cartulary roll)
St John's College	Muniments Mss. Ospringe deeds D7.84, D7.85
University Library	Mss Additional 3020–1 (Red Book of Thorney)
	D. & C. Ely G/3/28 (Ely Liber M)
	D. & C. Peterborough I (Peterborough cartulary)
	Doc. 126 (Charter of Eustace bishop of London)

481

Bibliography

Canterbury

Cathedral Library   Mss. D. & C. Cartae Antiquae C109, C110,
C115, C254
Register B

Dublin

Trinity College   Ms. 507 (Continuation of the annals of
Margam)

Durham

University Library   Archives and Special Collections Ms. D. &
C. Cartuarium III

Evreux

Archives Départementales   H438 (Charters of Lire)
de l'Eure

Exeter

Cathedral Library   Ms. 3518 (Obit list)
Devon Record Office   Ms. Courtenay of Powderham 1508M,
TD51 (Parentela Courtenayorum)

Hereford

Cathedral Library   Muniments no. 868

Lacock

Lacock Abbey   Lacock cartularies

Limoges

Archives Départementales   Ms. I Sem.8 2 (List of Benefactors of
de Haute-Vienne   Grandmont)

London

British Library   Additional Mss. 29436 (Winchester cartulary)
34254 (Papal bulls)
35296 (Spalding cartulary)
47784 (Coxford cartulary)
50121 (Lilleshall cartulary)
Arundel Mss.   17 (Newenham register)
19 (Tintern cartulary)

Cotton Mss.	Julius D v (Dover annals)
	Tiberius C v (Register of St Thomas' Acon)
	Tiberius E i (Life of St Birinus)
	Claudius B iii (York Minster cartulary)
	Nero C xii (Walsall cartulary)
	Nero D i (Liber Additamentorum of Matthew Paris)
	Nero E vi (Hospitallers' cartulary)
	Otho B xiv (Anonymous Brut)
	Vitelius D ix (Cartulary of St Nicholas' Exeter)
	Vespasian A xvi (Waverley annals)
	Vespasian E iii (Burton Abbbey tracts)
	Domitian A iii (Leominster cartulary)
	Domitian A xiv (Hyde cartulary)
	Cleopatra A vii (Tewkesbury annals etc.)
	Cleopatra C vii (Merton cartulary)
	Cleopatra D iii (Hailes annals)
	Faustina A iv (St Neot's cartulary)
	Faustina B i (Winchcombe annals)
	Charter Roll iv. 58 (Letter book of St Augustine's Bristol)
Egerton Mss.	2104A (Wherwell cartulary)
	3789 (Glover transcripts)
Harley Mss.	3640 (Welbeck cartulary)
	3650 (Kenilworth cartulary)
	4748 (Segrave cartulary)
	4757 (Robertsbridge charter transcripts)
	6956 (St Paul's London cartulary transcript)
Loans Ms.	29/55 (Rememoratorium de Tychefeld)
Royal Ms.	13 Axii (Continuation of the chronicle of Ralph Niger)

Stowe Ms. 665 (Charter transcripts)
Stowe Ms. 955 (Charter transcripts)
Additional Charter 19067
Campbell Charter II.12
Harley Charters 47E32, 58H46

College of Arms	Ms. Glover Collection A
Guildhall Library	D. & C. St Paul's Ms. 25,122/668
Inner Temple Library	Ms. Petyt 538/17 (Excerpts from Matthew Paris)
Lambeth Palace Library	Mss. 1212 (Cartulary of the archbishopric of Canterbury)
	Register of archbishop Warham I

| | | TT1 (Excerpts from Kent cartularies) |
| | | Cartae Miscellaneae XI/7, XI/50 |

Public Record Office   Mss.   C47 (Chancery Miscellania)
C52 (Cartae Antiquae Rolls)
C53 (Charter Rolls)
C54 (Close Rolls)
C60 (Fine Rolls)
C66 (Patent Rolls)
C72 (Scutage Rolls)
C145 (Miscellaneous Inquisitions)
CP25(1) (Feet of Fines)
E32 (Forest Proceedings)
E36/57 (Earldom of Cornwall cartulary)
E40 (Exchequer Ancient Deeds Series A)
E159 (Memoranda Rolls, King's Remembrancer)
E164/19 (Torre Abbey cartulary)
E210 (Exchequer Ancient Deeds Series D)
E368 (Memoranda Rolls, Lord Treasurer's Remembrancer)
E372 (Pipe Rolls)
E401 (Exchequer Receipt Rolls)
JUST1 (Justices Itinerant Plea Rolls)
PRO31/8/140 A–B (Cartulaire de la Basse Normandie)
SC1 (Ancient Correspondence)
SC7 (Papal bulls)

Westminster Abbey   Ms. Domesday
Muniments 511, 15163, 15208

Longleat

Muniments 4317 (Charter of Richard Marshal)

Nantes

Bibliothèque Municipale   Ms. 1701 no. 1 (Charter of Roger de la Zouche)

Newcastle upon Tyne

Tyne and Wear Archives   Ms. 574/95 (Liber Cartarum of Newcastle)

Bibliography

Oxford

Bodleian Library   Ashmole Ms. 1527 (Lichfield cartulary)
Digby Ms. 39 (Life of St Birinus)
Dodsworth Ms. 97 (Mottisfont transcripts)
Dugdale Mss. 18 (Robertsbridge transcripts)
        39 (Notley charter transcripts)
Lyell Ms. 15 (Abingdon cartulary)
Rawlinson Mss.   B150 (Anonymous Brut)
         B336 (Excerpts from cartulary of St Radegund's Bradsole)
         B461 (Excerpts from cartulary of St Radegund's Bradsole)
         D763 (Cartulary of St Thomas' Southwark)
Tanner Ms. 15 (Life of St Birinus)
Topographical Ms. Devon d5 (Newenham cartulary)
Twynne Ms. 24 (Excerpts from cartulary of Studley priory)

Corpus Christi College   Muniments Ms. C5 Cap.11(1) 1–3 (Charters of bishop Jocelin of Bath)

Magdalen College   Muniments Mss. Brackley Deed D116
         Chalgrove Deed 55B

Merton College   Muniments Ms. 1730 (Charter of Geoffrey des Roches)

St John's College   Muniments Ms. III.1 (Cartulary of St Nicholas' Wallingford)

Paris

Archives Nationales   Ms. L969 no. 357 (Charter of Richard Marshal)

Bibliothèque Nationale   Mss. Latin 5424 (Transcripts for Jumièges)
Latin 5430A (Extracts from Mont-St-Michel cartularies)
Latin 5476 (Transcripts for La Vieuville)
Latin 5480 part 1 (Transcripts for Fontevraud)
Latin 10078 (Transcripts for Savigny)
Latin 17129 (Transcripts for the Touraine)
Nouv. acq. Latin 1183 (Copy of the Liber Compositionum of St Maurice Tours)
Français 22325 (Transcripts for Brittany)
Français 22357 (Transcripts for Brittany)

Bibliography

Touraine-Anjou 12 part 1 (Housseau transcripts)

Poitiers

Archives Départementales de la Vienne   1H16 (Fonds Quinçay)

Rouen

Archives Départementales de la Seine-Maritime Mss.:
8H (Fonds Foucarmont)
9H (Fonds Jumièges)
24HP (Fonds Longueville)
25HP (Fonds Mont de Malades)
Bibliothéque Municipale, Mss. Y13 (Foucarmont cartulary)
Y44 (Rouen chapter cartulary)

Salisbury

Cathedral Library   Ms. D. & C. Press IV (Ramsbury) C3/2

San Marino, California

Huntington Library, Stowe Grenville Evidences STG Box 5 nos.14, 17

Southwell

Southwell Minster   Ms. 1 (Liber Albus)

Spalding

Spalding Gentlemen's Society   Ms. Crowland Cartulary

Stafford

Staffordshire Record Office   Paget Ms. D(W)1734/J/1071
Duke of Sutherland's Collection
Ms. D593/A/1/32/5

Stratford upon Avon

Shakespeare Birthplace Library   Ms. Gregory-Hood deed 1298
Saunders Transcripts E1/66

Strood

Medway Area Archives Office   Ms. D. & C. Rochester L2
Register 3 (Liber Temporalium)

Bibliography

Taunton

Somerset County Record Office   Wyndham Papers Ms. DD/WY
                                                     Box 10 Bundle T1

Tours

Archives Départementales de l'Indre-et-Loire G48, G1066
                                                              H253, H373, H480, H513
                                                              H148 (Fonds de La Clarté
                                                                 Dieu)
                                                              H710 (Fonds de Mon-
                                                                 toussan)
Bibliothèque Municipale   Ms. 1324 (Transcripts for Fontaines-les-
                                              Blanches)

Vercelli

Archivio di Stato   Ms. Pergamene 149 (Letters patent of Henry III)

Winchester

Cathedral Library   Mss.   Allchin Scrapbook II (Mounted charters)
                                       Bede's Ecclesiastical History
                                       The Book of John Chase (Muniment List *c.*1640)
                                       Unsorted charters
Hampshire Record Office   Mss. Eccl.II 159271–159285 (Pipe Rolls of
                                              the bishopric of Winchester). For further
                                              details see the list of abbreviations above
                                              pp. xvii-xix.
                                              1M63/1–2 (Mottisfont cartularies I and II)
Winchester College   Muniments 2786, 4222, 15237–8

2   PRINTED PRIMARY SOURCES

ANDRES, William of, 'Willelmi Chronica Andrensis', ed. J. Heller, *Mon-
   umenta Germaniae Historica Scriptores*, xxiv (Hanover 1879), pp. 684–773.
Annales Cambriae, ed. J. Williams ab Ithel, Rolls Series (London 1860).
Annales Monastici, ed. H. R. Luard, 5 vols., Rolls Series (London 1864–9).
AVRANCHES, Henry of, *The Shorter Latin Poems of Master Henry of Avranches
   relating to England*, ed. J. Cox Russell and J. P. Heironimus, Mediaeval
   Academy of America Studies and Documents, no. 1 (Cambridge, Mass.
   1935).
'Drei Gedichte Heinrichs von Avranches an Kaiser Friedrich II', ed.

E. Winkelmann, *Forschungen zur Deutschen Geschichte*, xviii (Gottingen 1878), pp. 484–92.

'The Vita Sancti Birini of Henry of Avranches (BHL 1364)', ed. D. Townsend, *Analecta Bollandiana*, cxii (1994), pp. 309–38.

BATH, *Two Cartularies of the Priory of St Peter at Bath*, ed. W. Hunt, Somerset Record Society, vii (1893).

BEAULIEU, *The Beaulieu Cartulary*, ed. S. F. Hockey, Southampton Record Series, xvii (1974).

BEDFORDSHIRE, *A Calendar of the Feet of Fines for Bedfordshire*, ed. G. H. Fowler, Bedfordshire Historical Record Society, vi (1919).

BERKELEY, *Descriptive Catalogue of the Charters and Muniments in the Possession of Lord Fitzhardinge at Berkeley Castle*, ed. I. H. Jeayes (Bristol 1892).

BLUND, John, *Tractatus de Anima*, ed. D. A. Callus and R. W. Hunt, Auctores Britannici Medii Aevi, ii (London 1970).

BOARSTALL, *The Boarstall Cartulary*, ed. H. E. Salter, Oxford Historical Society, lxxxviii (1930).

BOOK OF FEES, *Liber Feodorum. The Book of Fees commonly called Testa de Nevill*, 3 vols. (London 1920–31).

BRACTON, Henry de, *Bracton's Note Book*, ed. F. W. Maitland, 3 vols. (London 1887).

Henrici de Bracton de Legibus et Consuetudinibus Angliae, ed. T. Twiss, 6 vols., Rolls Series (London 1879–83).

BRADENSTOKE, *The Cartulary of Bradenstoke Priory*, ed. V. C. M. London, Wiltshire Record Society, xxxv (1979).

BRITTANY, *Mémoires pour Servir de Preuves à l'Histoire Ecclésiastique et Civile de Bretagne*, ed. H. Morice, 3 vols. (Paris 1742–6).

Anciens Évêchés de Bretagne, ed. J. Geslin de Bourgogne and A. de Barthélemy, 4 vols. (Paris 1864).

Brut y Tywysogyon or The Chronicle of the Princes (Peniarth Ms. 20 Version), ed. T. Jones (Cardiff 1952).

BUCKINGHAMSHIRE, *A Calendar of the Feet of Fines for the County of Buckinghamshire, 7 Richard I to 44 Henry III*, ed. M. W. Hughes, Buckinghamshire Record Society, iv (1942 for 1940).

Building Accounts of King Henry III, ed. H. M. Colvin (Oxford 1971).

BURSCOUGH, *An Edition of the Cartulary of Burscough Priory*, ed. A. N. Webb, Chetham Society, 3rd series, xviii (1970).

BURY ST EDMUNDS, *Memorials of St Edmund's Abbey*, ed. T. Arnold, 3 vols., Rolls Series (London 1890–96).

The Chronicle of the Election of Hugh abbot of Bury St Edmunds and later bishop of Ely, ed. R. M. Thomson (Oxford 1974).

Calendar of the Charter Rolls, 6 vols. (London 1903–27).

Calendar of Liberate Rolls, 6 vols. (London 1917–64).

Calendar of Miscellaneous Inquisitions I: Henry III and Edward I (London 1916).

Calendar of entries in the Papal Registers relating to Great Britain and Ireland 1198–1304, ed. W. H. Bliss (London 1893).

Calendar of Patent Rolls Henry III, 4 vols. (London 1906–13).

CANTERBURY, *The Register of St Augustine's Abbey commonly called the Black Book*, ed. G. J. Turner and H. E. Salter, 2 vols. (London 1915–24).

CANTERBURY, Gervase of, *The Historical Works of Gervase of Canterbury*, ed. W. Stubbs, 2 vols., Rolls Series (London 1879–80).

Canterbury Professions, ed. M. Richter, Canterbury and York Society, lxvii (1973).

CARISBROOKE, *The Cartulary of Carisbrooke Priory*, ed. S. F. Hockey, Isle of Wight Record Series, ii (1981).

Cartae Antiquae Rolls, ed. L. Landon and J. Conway Davies, 2 vols., Pipe Roll Society, New Series, xvii, xxxiii (1939–60).

CERNE, 'The Cartulary of Cerne Abbey', ed. B. F. Lock, *Proceedings of the Dorset Natural History and Antiquarian Field Club*, 29 (1908), pp. 195–204.

CHATEAU-DU-LOIR, *Cartulaire de Château-du-Loir*, ed. E. Vallée, Archives Historiques du Maine, vi (Le Mans 1905).

CHESTER, *Annales Cestrienses*, ed. R. C. Christie, Record Society of Lancashire and Cheshire, xiv (1887).

The Charters of the Anglo-Norman Earls of Chester c.1071–1237, ed. G. Barraclough, Record Society of Lancashire and Cheshire, cxxvi (1988).

CHICHESTER, *The Chartulary of the High Church of Chichester*, ed. W. D. Peckham, Sussex Record Society, xlvi (1946).

CHOBHAM, Thomas de, *Summa Confessorum*, ed. F. Broomfield, Analecta Medievalia Namurcensis, xxv (1968).

CIRENCESTER, *The Chartulary of Cirencester Abbey*, ed. C. D. Ross, 3 vols. (London 1964).

CLARTE DIEU, P. Robert, 'L'Abbaye de la Clarté Dieu', *Bulletin trimestriel de la Société Archéologique de la Touraine*, xxxviii (1976).

Close Rolls of the Reign of Henry III, 14 vols. (London 1902–38).

COGGESHALL, Ralph of, *Radulphi de Coggeshall Chronicon Anglicanum*, ed. J. Stevenson, Rolls Series (London 1875).

COTTON, Bartholomew of, *Bartolomei de Cotton Historia Anglicana*, ed. H. R. Luard, Rolls Series (London 1859).

Councils and Synods with other documents relating to the English Church II: 1205–1313, ed. F. M. Powicke and C. R. Cheney, 2 vols. (Oxford 1964).

COVENTRY, Walter of, *Memoriale Fratris Walteri de Coventria*, ed. W. Stubbs, 2 vols., Rolls Series (London 1872–3).

Curia Regis Rolls of the Reigns of Richard I, John and Henry III preserved in the Public Record Office, 17 vols. (London 1922–).

DERBYSHIRE, *Descriptive Catalogue of Derbyshire Charters*, ed. I. H. Jeayes (London 1906).

DEVON, 'Abstracts from the Devon Assize Rolls for 1218–19', ed. L. G. Cruwys, *Devon and Cornwall Notes and Queries*, xx (1938–9), pp. 338–52, 395–416.

DICETO, Ralph de, *Radulfi de Diceto Opera Historica*, ed. W. Stubbs, 2 vols., Rolls Series (London 1876).

Bibliography

Diplomatic Documents preserved in the Public Record Office 1101–1272, ed. P. Chaplais (London 1964).

Documents of the Baronial Movement of Reform and Rebellion 1258–1267, ed. R. F. Treharne and I. J. Sanders (Oxford 1973).

Documents illustrative of English History in the Thirteenth and Fourteenth Centuries, ed. H. Cole (London 1844).

Documents on the Affairs of Ireland before the King's Council, ed. G. O. Sayles, Irish Manuscripts Commission (Dublin 1979).

Documents preserved in France, illustrative of the History of Great Britain and Ireland, ed. J. H. Round (London 1899).

DOMERHAM, Adam de, *Adami de Domerham Historia de Rebus Glastoniensibus*, ed. T. Hearne, 2 vols. (Oxford 1727).

DUBLIN, *Chartularies of St Mary's Abbey, Dublin*, ed. J. T. Gilbert, 2 vols., Rolls Series (London 1884–6).

DUGDALE, Sir William, *Monasticon Anglicanum*, ed. J. Caley, H. Ellis and B. Bandinel, 6 vols. (London 1846).

DURHAM, 'A number of interesting documents ...', ed. R. Blair, *Proceedings of the Society of Antiquaries of Newcastle upon Tyne*, series 2, x (1902), pp. 302–15.

Historiae Dunelmensis Scriptores Tres, ed. J. Raine, Surtees Society, ix (1839).

Registrum Palatinum Dunelmense: The Register of Richard de Kellawe, Lord Palatine and Bishop of Durham 1311–1316, ed. T. D. Hardy, 4 vols., Rolls Series (London 1873–8).

English Episcopal Acta IV: Lincoln 1186–1206, ed. D. M. Smith (Oxford 1986).

Epistolae Saeculi XIII e Registris Pontificum Romanorum Selectae per G. H. Pertz, ed. C. Rodenberg, 3 vols., Monumenta Germaniae Historica Epistolae (Berlin 1883–94).

EVESHAM, *Chronicon Abbatiae de Evesham*, ed. W. D. Macray, Rolls Series (London 1863).

Excerpta e Rotulis Finium in Turri Londinensi Asservatis ... AD 1216–72, ed. C. Roberts, 2 vols. (London 1835–6).

EXCHEQUER, *Dialogus de Scaccario*, ed. C. Johnson (revised edition, Oxford 1983).

The Red Book of the Exchequer, ed. H. Hall, 3 vols., Rolls Series (London 1896).

EYNSHAM, *The Cartulary of the Abbey of Eynsham*, i, ed. H. E. Salter, Oxford Historical Society, xlix (1907–8).

FINCHALE, *The Charters of Finchale*, ed. J. Raine, Surtees Society, vi (1837).

FLAMBOROUGH, Robert of, *Liber Poenitentialis*, ed. J. J. Francis Firth (Toronto 1971).

Flores Historiarum, ed. H. R. Luard, 3 vols., Rolls Series (London 1890).

Foedera, Conventiones, Litterae et cujuscumque generis Acta Publica, ed. T. Rymer, new edition, vol. I part i, ed. A. Clark and F. Holbrooke (London 1816).

FONTAINE-DANIEL, *Cartulaire de l'Abbaye Cistercienne de Fontaine-Daniel*, ed. A. Grosse-Dupéron and E. Gouvrion (Mayenne 1896).

FORESTS, *Select Pleas of the Forest*, ed. G. J. Turner, Selden Society, xiii (1899).

A Calendar of New Forest Documents 1244–1334, ed. D. J. Stagg, Hampshire Record Society, iii (1970).

FREDERICK II, *Historia Diplomatica Friderici Secundi*, ed. J. L. A. Huillard-Bréholles, 6 vols. in 11 (Paris 1852–61).

Gallia Christiana in Provincias Ecclesiasticas distributa, 16 vols. (Paris 1715–1865).

GARLAND, John of, *Johannis de Garlandia De Triumphis Ecclesiae*, ed. T. Wright, Roxburghe Club (London 1856).

Two Medieval Satires on the University of Paris, ed. L. J. Paetow (Berkeley 1927).

Gesta Regis Henrici Secundi, ed. W. Stubbs, 2 vols., Rolls Series (London 1867).

GLASTONBURY, *The Great Chartulary of Glastonbury*, ed. A. Watkin, 3 vols., Somerset Record Society, lix, lxiii–lxiv (1944–56).

GLOUCESTER, Robert of, *The Metrical Chronicle of Robert of Gloucester*, ed. W. A. Wright, 2 vols., Rolls Series (London 1887).

GLOUCESTERSHIRE, *Pleas of the Crown for the County of Gloucester*, ed. F. W. Maitland (London 1884).

GODWIN, Francis, *De Praesulibus Angliae Commentarius* (London 1616).

GREGORY IX, *Les Registres de Gregoire IX (1227–41)*, ed. L. Auvray, 4 vols. (Ecole française de Rome 1955).

GROSSETESTE, Robert, *Roberti Grosseteste Episcopi quondam Lincolniensis Epistolae*, ed. H. R. Luard, Rolls Series (London 1861).

Rotuli Roberti Grosseteste, ed. F. N. Davis, Canterbury and York Society, x (London 1910–13).

GUALA, Philadelfo Libico, *Gualae Bicherii Presbiteri Cardinalis S. Martini in Montibus Vita et Gesta* (Milan 1767).

H. G. Richardson. 'Letters of the legate Guala', *English Historical Review*, 48 (1933), pp. 250–9.

The Acta of the Legate Guala 1216–1218, ed. N. Vincent, Canterbury and York Society (forthcoming 1996).

GUISBOROUGH, *Cartularium Prioratus de Gyseburne*, ed. W. Brown, 2 vols., Surtees Society, lxxxvi, lxxxix (1889–94).

GUISBOROUGH, Walter of, *The Chronicle of Walter of Guisborough*, ed. H. Rothwell, Camden Society, 3rd series, lxxxix (1957).

HATTON, *Sir Christopher Hatton's Book of Seals*, ed. L. C. Loyd and D. M. Stenton (Oxford 1950).

HEISTERBACH, Caesarius of, *The Dialogue on Miracles*, trans. H. von E. Scott and C. C. Swinton Bland, 2 vols. (London 1929).

HENRY II, *Recueil des Actes de Henri II roi d'Angleterre et duc de Normandie concernant les provinces françaises et les affaires de France*, ed. L. Delisle and E. Berger, 4 vols. (Paris 1909–27).

HEREFORD, R. Rawlinson, *The History and Antiquities of Hereford* (London 1717).

Histoire des Ducs de Normandie et des Rois d'Angleterre, ed. F. Michel, Société de l'histoire de France (Paris 1840).

Bibliography

HONORIUS III, *Regesta Honorii Papae III*, ed. P. Pressutti, 2 vols. (Rome 1888–95).

HOWDEN, Roger de, *Chronica Rogeri de Hovedene*, ed. W. Stubbs, 4 vols., Rolls Series (London 1868–71).

INNOCENT III, *Selected Letters of Innocent III*, ed. C. R. Cheney and W. H. Semple (London 1953).

The Letters of Pope Innocent III (1198–1216) concerning England and Wales, ed. C. R. Cheney and M. G. Cheney (Oxford 1967).

Interdict Documents, ed. P. M. Barnes and W. R. Powell, Pipe Roll Society, new series, xxxiv (1958).

Lacock Abbey Charters, ed. K. H. Rogers, Wiltshire Record Society, xxxiv (1978).

LA COUTURE, *Cartulaire des Abbayes de Saint-Pierre de la Couture et de Saint-Pierre de Solesmes*, ed. P. d'Albert duc de Chaulnes (Le Mans 1881).

Lambeth Charters, ed. D. Owen (London 1968).

LANERCOST, *Chronicon de Lanercost*, ed. J. Stevenson, Maitland Club (Edinburgh 1839).

LANGTON, Stephen, *Acta Stephani Langton Cantuariensis Archiepiscopi AD 1207–1228*, ed. K. Major, Canterbury and York Society, l (Oxford 1950).

LA ROCHELLE, *Cartulaire du Temple de la Rochelle (1139–1268)*, ed. M. de Richmond, Archives Historiques de la Saintonge et de l'Aunis, i (1874).

Layettes du Trésor des Chartes, ed. A. Teulet, H.-F. Delaborde and E. Berger, 5 vols. (Paris 1863–1909).

LEGATE, 'La Prima Relazione del Cardinale Nicolo de Romanis sulla sua Legazione in Inghilterra (1213)', ed. A. Mercati, *Essays in History presented to Reginald Lane Poole*, ed. H. W. C. Davies (Oxford 1927), pp. 274–89.

LE MANS, *Cartulaire du Chapitre-Royal de Saint-Pierre de la Cour du Mans*, ed. M. d'Elbenne and L. J. Denis, Archives Historiques du Maine, iv (1903–7).

Liber Controversiarum Sancti Vincentii Cenomannensis, ed. A. Chédeville, Institut de Recherches Historiques de Rennes (Paris 1968).

LEWES, *The Cambridgeshire Portion of the Chartulary of the Priory of St Pancras of Lewes*, ed. J. H. Bullock and W. M. Palmer, Cambridge Antiquarian Society (1938).

LICHFIELD, *The Great Register of Lichfield Cathedral known as Magnum Registrum Album*, ed. H. E. Savage, Collections for a History of Staffordshire, edited by the William Salt Archaeological Society (1926 for 1924).

LIMOGES, *Chroniques de Saint-Martial de Limoges*, ed. H. Duplès-Agier, Société de l'Histoire de France (Paris 1874).

LINCOLN, *The Registrum Antiquissimum of the Cathedral Church of Lincoln*, ed. C. W. Foster and K. Major, 12 vols., Lincoln Record Society, xxvii–xxix, xxxii, xxxiv, xli–xlii, xlvi, li, lxii, lxvii–lxviii (1931–73).

Rotuli Hugonis de Welles Episcopi Lincolniensis AD MCCIX–MCCXXXV, ed. W. P. W. Phillimore and F. N. Davis, 3 vols., Canterbury and York Society, i, iii, iv (London 1907–9).

'The canonization of St Hugh of Lincoln', ed. H. Farmer, *Lincolnshire Architectural and Archaeological Society Reports and Papers*, vi, part ii (1956).

LONDON, *De Antiquis Legibus Liber: Chronica Maiorum et Vicecomitum Londiniarum 1178–1274*, ed. T. Stapleton, Camden Society, xxxiv (1846).

M. Bateson, 'A London municipal collection of the reign of King John', *English Historical Review* (1902), pp. 729–30.

The Early Charters of the Cathedral Church of St Paul's London, ed. M. Gibbs, Camden Society, 3rd series, lvii (1939).

The London Eyre of 1244, ed. H. M. Chew and M. Weinbaum, London Record Society, vi (1970).

Luffield Priory Charters, ed. G. R. Elvey, 2 vols., Northamptonshire Record Society, xxii, xxvi (1968–75).

LYTTELTON, *A Descriptive Catalogue of the Charters and Documents of the Lyttelton Family at Hagley Hall*, ed. I. H. Jeayes (London 1893).

The Lyttelton Papers (Sotheby's Sale Catalogue for 12 December 1978).

MADOX, Thomas, *Formulare Anglicanum* (London 1702).

The History and Antiquities of the Exchequer of England 1066–1327, 2 vols. (London 1711).

Magni Rotuli Scaccarii Normanniae sub Regibus Anglie, ed. T. Stapleton, 2 vols. (London 1840–4).

MARGAM, M. L. Coker, 'The "Margam Chronicle" in a Dublin manuscript', *The Haskins Society Journal* iv, ed. R. B. Patterson (Woodbridge 1993), pp. 123–48.

MARSHAL, William the, *L'Histoire de Guillaume le Maréchal*, ed. P. Meyer, 3 vols., Société de l'Histoire de France (Paris 1891–1901).

MEAUX, *Chronica Monasterii de Melsa ab Anno 1150 usque ad Annum 1406*, ed. E. A. Bond, 3 vols., Rolls Series (London 1866–8).

MELROSE, *Chronicle of Melrose*, ed. A. O. and M. O. Anderson (London 1936).

Memoranda Roll 1 John, ed. H. G. Richardson, Pipe Roll Society, new series, xxi (1943).

Memoranda Roll 10 John, ed. R. Allen Brown, Pipe Roll Society, new series, xxxi (1956).

Memoranda Rolls 16–17 Henry III, ed. R. Allen Brown (London 1991).

MERTON, 'The annals of Southwark and Merton', ed. M. Tyson, *Surrey Archaeological Collections*, xxxvi (1926), pp. 24–57.

Records of Merton Priory, ed. A. Heales (Oxford 1898).

Miscellaneous Records of the Norman Exchequer 1199–1204, ed. S. R. Packard, Smith College Studies in History, xii nos. 1–4 (Northampton Mass. 1926–7).

MONTE CASSINO, E. Gattola, *Historia Abbatiae Cassinensis per saeculorum seriem distributa*, 2 vols. (Venice 1733–4).

NEVILLE, Ralph de, W. H. Blaauw, 'Letters to Ralph de Nevill bishop of Chichester (1222–24) and Chancellor to King Henry III', *Sussex Archaeological Collections*, iii (1850), pp. 35–76.

J. Boussard, 'Ralph Neville Evêque de Chichester d'après sa correspondance', *Revue Historique*, 176 (1935), pp. 217–33.

NEWBURGH, William of, *Historia Rerum Anglicarum*, in *Chronicles of the Reigns of Stephen, Henry II and Richard I*, ed. R. Howlett, 4 vols., Rolls Series (London 1884–90).

NORMANDY, *Cartulaire Normand de Philippe-Auguste, Louis VIII, Saint-Louis et Philipp-le-Hardi*, ed. L. Delisle (Caen 1882).

NORTHAMPTON Annals of, H. M. Cam and E. F. Jacobs, 'Notes on an English Cluniac chronicle', *English Historical Review*, 44 (1929), pp. 94–104.

NORWICH, *The Charters of Norwich Cathedral Priory*, ed. B. Dodwell, 2 vols., Pipe Roll Society, new series, xl, xlvi (1974–85).

The Life and Miracles of St William of Norwich by Thomas of Monmouth, ed. A. Jessop and M. R. James (Cambridge 1896).

NOYERS, *Cartulaire de l'abbaye de Noyers*, ed. C. Chevalier, Mémoires de la Société Archéologique de Touraine, xxii (1872).

ORMOND, *Calendar of Ormond Deeds 1172–1350 AD*, ed. E. Curtis, Irish Manuscripts Commission (Dublin 1932).

OSNEY, *Cartulary of Osney Abbey*, ed. H. E. Salter, 6 vols., Oxford Historical Society, lxxxix–xci, xcvii–xcviii, ci (1929–36).

OXFORD, *Medieval Archives of the University of Oxford*, ed. H. E. Salter, Oxford Historical Record Society, lxxx (1930).

A Cartulary of the Hospital of St John the Baptist, ed. H. E. Salter, 3 vols., Oxford Historical Society, lxvi, lxviii–lxix (1914–17).

OXFORDSHIRE, *The Feet of Fines for Oxfordshire 1195–1291*, ed. H. E. Salter, Oxford Record Society, xii (1930).

PARCE, *Chronique de Parcé*, ed. H. de Berranger, Archives Départementales de la Sarthe Inventaires et Documents (Le Mans 1953).

PARIS, Matthew, *Matthaei Parisiensis, Monachi Sancti Albani, Chronica Majora*, ed. H. R. Luard, 7 vols., Rolls Series (London 1872–83).

Matthaei Parisiensis Historia Anglorum, ed. F. Madden, 3 vols., Rolls Series (London 1866–9).

Patent Rolls of the Reign of Henry III, 2 vols. (London 1901–3).

Patrologiae Latinae cursus completus – Series Latina, ed. J.-P. Migne, 221 vols. (Paris 1844–64).

PHILIP AUGUSTUS, *Catalogue des Actes de Philippe-Auguste*, ed. L. Delisle (Paris 1856).

Recueil des Actes de Philippe-Auguste, Roi de France, ed. H.-F. Delaborde, M. Nortier et al., 4 vols. (Paris 1916–79).

Pipe Rolls 1 John – 5 Henry III, ed. D. M. Stenton, P. M. Barnes et al., Pipe Roll Society (London 1933–90).

Pipe Roll 26 Henry III, ed. H. L. Cannon (Yale 1918).

Pleas Before the King or his Justices, ed. D. M. Stenton, 4 vols., Selden Society, lxvii–lxviii, lxxxiii–lxxxiv (1952–67).

POITIERS, *Documents pour l'histoire de l'Eglise de St Hilaire de Poitiers*, ed. L. Rédet, 2 vols., *Mémoires de la Société des Antiquaires de l'Ouest*, Series 1, xiii, xviii (1847–52).

Recueil de Documents concernant la Commune et la Ville de Poitiers, ed. E. Audouin, Société des Archives Historiques de Poitou, xliv (1923).

Bibliography

POLITICAL SONGS, *The Political Songs of England, from the Reign of John to Edward II*, ed. J. T. Wright, Camden Society, 1st series, vi (1839).

PONTOISE, John de, *Registrum Johannis de Pontissara, episcopi Wintoniensis, AD MCCLXXXII–MCCCIV*, ed. C. Deedes, 2 vols., Canterbury and York Society, xix, xxx (London 1915–24).

POTTHAST, A. (ed.), *Regesta Pontificum Romanorum 1198–1304*, 2 vols. (Berlin 1874–5).

PRYNNE, William, *The Third Tome of an Exact Chronological Vindication . . . of the Supreme Ecclesiastical Jurisdiction of our . . . English Kings* (London 1668).

READING, *Reading Abbey Cartularies*, ed. B. R. Kemp, 2 vols., Camden Society, 4th series, xxxi–xxxii (1986–7).

Recueil des Historiens des Gaules et de la France, ed. M. Bouquet et al., 24 vols. (Paris 1734–1904).

RICHARD I, *Chronicles and Memorials of the Reign of Richard I*, ed. W. Stubbs, 2 vols., Rolls Series (London 1864–5).

The Itinerary of King Richard I, ed. L. Landon, Pipe Roll Society, new series, xiii (1935).

RIGORD, *Oeuvres de Rigord et de Guillaume le Breton*, ed. H. F. Delaborde, 2 vols., Société de l'Histoire de France (Paris 1882–5).

RIPON, *Memorials of the Church of SS Peter and Wilfrid, Ripon*, ed. J. T. Fowler, 4 vols., Surtees Society, lxxiv, lxxviii, lxxxi, cxv (1882–1908).

ROCHESTER, *Registrum Roffense*, ed. J. Thorpe (London 1769).

Rôles Gascons 26–28 Henry III (1242–1254), ed. F. Michel (Paris 1885).

Roll of Divers accounts for the early years of the Reign of Henry III, ed. F. A. Cazel Jr, Pipe Roll Society, new series, xliv. (1974–5).

Rolls of the Justices in Eyre for Lincoln 1218–19 and Worcestershire 1221, ed. D. M. Stenton, Selden Society, liii (1934).

Rotuli Chartarum in Turri Londinensi asservati, ed. T. Duffus Hardy (London 1837).

Rotuli de Liberate ac de Misis et Praestitis, ed. T. Duffus Hardy (London 1844).

Rotuli Litterarum Clausarum in Turri Londinensi asservati, ed. T. Duffus Hardy, 2 vols. (London 1833–4).

Rotuli Litterarum Patentium in Turri Londinensi asservati, ed. T. Duffus Hardy (London 1835).

Rotuli Normanniae in Turri Londinensi asservati, ed. T. Duffus Hardy (London 1835).

Rotuli de Oblatis et Finibus in Turri Londinensi asservati, ed. T. Duffus Hardy (London 1835).

ROUEN, L. de Glanville, *Histoire du Prieuré de Saint-Lô de Rouen*, 2 vols. (Rouen 1890–1).

Royal and other Historical Letters illustrative of the Reign of Henry III, ed. W. W. Shirley, 2 vols., Rolls Series (London 1862–6).

RUTLAND, *The Manuscripts of the Duke of Rutland at Belvoir Castle*, iv, Historical Manuscripts Commission (1905).

SABLÉ, G. Menage, *Histoire de Sablé*, part 1 (Paris 1683).

Bibliography

ST ALBANS, *Gesta Abbatum Monasterii Sancti Albani*, ed. H. T. Riley, 3 vols., Rolls Series (London 1867).

ST BERTIN, *Les Chartes de Saint-Bertin*, ed. D. Haigneré, 5 vols. (St Omer 1886–99).

Salimbene de Adam, *Cronica*, ed. F. Bernini, 2 vols., Scrittori d'Italia, clxxxvii–clxxxviii (Bari 1942).

SALISBURY, *Charters and Documents illustrating the history of the Cathedral ... of Salisbury*, ed. W. H. Rich Jones and W. D. Macray, Rolls Series (London 1891).

   The Canonization of St Osmund, ed. A. R. Malden, Wiltshire Record Society (1901).

   The Register of St Osmund, ed. W. H. Rich Jones, 2 vols., Rolls Series (London 1883–4).

SALISBURY, John of, *The 'Historia Pontificalis' of John of Salisbury*, ed. M. Chibnall, 2nd edn (Oxford 1986).

SANDFORD, *The Sandford Cartulary*, ed. A. M. Leys, 2 vols., Oxford Record Society, xix, xxii (1938–41).

SAN GERMANO, Richard of, 'Ryccardi di Sancto Germano Chronica', ed. C. A. Garufi, in L. A. Muratori, *Rerum Italicarum Scriptores*, new edn, ed. G. Carducci et al., vii, part ii (Bologna 1937–8).

SCOTLAND, *The Acts of the Parliament of Scotland*, ed. T. Thomson and C. Innes, vol. i, 1124–1423 (London 1844).

   Early Sources of Scottish History AD 500 to 1286, ed. A. O. Anderson, 2 vols. (London 1922).

   The Acts of Malcolm IV King of Scots 1153–1165, ed. G. W. S. Barrow, *Regesta Regum Scottorum*, i (Edinburgh 1960).

   Anglo-Scottish Relations 1174–1328, ed. E. L. G. Stones (2nd edn, Oxford 1970).

SELBORNE, *Calendar of Charters and Documents relating to Selborne and its Priory*, ed. W. D. Macray, 2 vols., Hampshire Record Society (1891–4).

SHREWSBURY, *The Cartulary of Shrewsbury Abbey*, ed. U. Rees, 2 vols. (Aberystwyth 1975).

Somersetshire Pleas, ed. C. Chadwick-Healey, 2 vols., Somerset Record Society xi, xxxvi (1897, 1923).

SOUTHWICK, *The Cartularies of Southwick Priory*, ed. K. A. Hanna, 2 vols., Hampshire Record Series, ix–x (1988–9).

STAFFORDSHIRE, 'Plea Rolls of the Reign of Henry III', ed. G. Wrottesley, *Collections for a History of Staffordshire edited by the William Salt Archaeological Society*, iv (1883), pp. 1–215.

Stoke by Clare Cartulary, ed. C. Harper-Bill and R. Mortimer, 3 vols., Suffolk Record Series, Suffolk Charters iv–vi (1982–4).

STUBBS, William, *Select Charters*, 9th edn, ed. H. W. C. Davis (Oxford 1922).

SURIUS, Laurentius, *De Probatis Sanctorum Vitis ... tam ex Mss. codicibus, quam ex editis authoribus*, 12 vols. in 4 (new edition, Cologne 1617–18).

SURREY, *The 1235 Surrey Eyre*, ed. C. A. F. Meekings and D. Crook, 2 vols., Surrey Record Society, xxxi–xxxii (1979–83).

SUSSEX, *An Abstract of Feet of Fines relating to the County of Sussex from 2 Richard I to 33 Henry III*, ed. L. F. Salzmann, Sussex Record Society, ii (1903).

Taxatio Ecclesiastica Angliae et Walliae, auctoritate Papae Nicholai IV, circa 1291, ed. S. Ayscough and J. Caley (London 1802).

TEMPLARS, *Records of the Templars in England in the Twelfth Century*, ed. B. A. Lees (Oxford 1935).

TOURS, *Martyrologe Obituaire de l'Eglise Métropolitaine de Tours*, ed. J. J. Bourassé, Mémoires de la Société Archéologique de Touraine, xviii (1865).

Recueil des Chroniques de Touraine, ed. A. Salmon (Tours 1854).

Chartes de Saint-Julien de Tours (1002–1300), ed. L.-J. Denis, Archives Historiques du Maine, xii (Le Mans 1912–13).

Treaty Rolls I: 1234–1325, ed. P. Chaplais (London 1955).

TRIVET, Nicholas de, *Annales F. Nicholai de Triveti*, ed. T. Hog, English Historical Society (London 1845).

TWYSDEN, R., *Historiae Anglicanae Scriptores X* (London 1652).

VENDOME, *Cartulaire de l'abbaye cardinale de la Trinité de Vendôme*, ed. C. Métais, 6 vols. in 5, Société Archéologique du Vendômois (Paris/Chartres 1893–1904).

WALES, *Calendar of Ancient Correspondence Concerning Wales*, ed. J. G. Edwards, Board of Celtic Studies (Cardiff 1935).

WELLS, *Calendar of the Manuscripts of the Dean and Chapter of Wells Vol. I*, Historical Manuscripts Commission (London 1907).

WENDOVER, Roger of, *Rogeri de Wendover Chronica sive Flores Historiarum*, ed. H. O. Coxe, 5 vols., English Historical Society (London 1841–4).

WHARTON, Henry, *Anglia Sacra*, 2 vols. (London 1691).

WINCHESTER, *The Chartulary of Winchester Cathedral*, ed. A. W. Goodman (Winchester 1927).

The Pipe Roll of the Bishopric of Winchester 1208–9, ed H. Hall (London 1903).

The Pipe Roll of the Bishopric of Winchester 1210–11, ed. N. R. Holt (Manchester 1964).

English Episcopal Acta VIII: Winchester 1070–1204, ed. M. J. Franklin (Oxford 1993).

English Episcopal Acta IX: Winchester 1205–1238, ed. N. Vincent (Oxford 1994).

WOODLOCK, Henry de, *Registrum Henrici Woodlock, diocesis Wintoniensis, AD 1305–1316*, ed. A. W. Goodman, 2 vols., Canterbury and York Society, xliii–xliv (1940–1).

WORCESTER, *Early Compotus Rolls of the Priory of Worcester*, ed. J. M. Wilson and C. Gordon, Worcestershire Historical Society (1908).

The Cartulary of Worcester Cathedral Priory, ed. R. R. Darlington, Pipe Roll Society, new series, xxxviii (1968).

WORCESTER, Florence of, *Chronicon ex Chronicis*, ed. B. Thorpe, 2 vols. (London 1849).

Bibliography

YORK, *The Cartulary of the Treasurer of York Minster and related documents*, ed. J. E. Burton, Borthwick Texts and Calendars, v (York 1978).

York Minster Fasti, ed. C. T. Clay, 2 vols., Yorkshire Archaeological Society Record Series cxxiii–cxxiv (1958–9).

YORKSHIRE, *Rolls of the Justices in Eyre for Yorkshire 1218–19*, ed. D. M. Stenton, Selden Society, lvi (1937).

Early Yorkshire Charters, vols. i–iii, ed. W. Farrer (Edinburgh 1914–16), vols. iv–x, ed. C. T. Clay, Yorkshire Archaeological Society Record Series, extra series (1935–55).

3 SECONDARY SOURCES

Abbott, P. D., *Provinces, Pays and Seigneuries of France* (Canberra 1981).

Abulafia, D., *Frederick II, A Medieval Emperor* (London 1988).

Adler, M., 'The testimony of the London Jewry against the ministers of Henry III', *Transactions of the Jewish Historical Society of England*, 14 (1935–9), pp. 141–85.

Altschul, M., *A Baronial Family in Medieval England: The Clares 1217–1314* (Baltimore 1970).

Andrea, A. J., 'Walter archdeacon of London and the "Historia Occidentalis" of Jacques de Vitry', *Church History* (1981), pp. 141–51.

Baldwin, J. W., *Masters, Princes and Merchants: The Social Views of Peter the Chanter and his Circle*, 2 vols. (Princeton 1970).

'La Décennie décisive: les années 1190–1203 dans la règne de Philippe Auguste', *Revue Historique*, 266 (1981), pp. 311–37.

The Government of Philip Augustus: Foundations of French Royal Power in the Middle Ages (Berkeley 1986).

Barefield, J. P., 'The king's bishop: the career of Peter des Roches in the royal administration 1197–1216', unpublished Ph.D. dissertation (Johns Hopkins University, Maryland 1967).

Barnes, P. M., 'The Anstey case', in *A Medieval Miscellany for Doris Mary Stenton*, ed. P. M. Barnes and C. F. Slade, Pipe Roll Society, new series, xxxvi (1962), pp. 1–24.

Bates, D., 'The rise and fall of Normandy, *c.*911–1204', in *England and Normandy in the Middle Ages*, ed. D. Bates and A. Curry (London 1994), pp. 19–35.

Bazeley, M. L., 'The extent of the English forest in the thirteenth century', *Transactions of the Royal Historical Society*, 4th series, iv (1921), pp. 140–63.

Bedford, W. K. Ryland, *The Blazon of Episcopacy* (Oxford 1897).

Beresford, M., 'The six new towns of the bishop of Winchester, 1200–55', *Medieval Archaeology*, 3 (1959), pp. 187–215.

Berger, E., 'Les préparatifs d'une invasion anglaise et la descente de Henri III en Bretagne (1229–1230)', *Bibliothèque de l'Ecole des Chartes*, liv (1893), pp. 5–44.

Bethell, D., 'The making of a twelfth-century relic collection', *Studies in Church History*, 8 (1972), ed. D. Baker, pp. 61–72.

Boase, T. S. R., *Kingdoms and Strongholds of the Crusades* (London 1971).

Bogan, P., 'Dom Thomas Figg and the foot of St Philip', *Winchester Cathedral Record*, lxi (1992), pp. 22–6.

Boissonnade, M. P., 'Administrateurs laïques et ecclésiastiques Anglo-Normands en Poitou à l'époque d'Henri II Plantagenêt (1152–1189)', *Bulletin de la Société des Antiquaires de l'Ouest*, 3rd series, v (1922), pp. 156–90.

Boussard, J., *Le Comté d'Anjou sous Henri Plantagenêt et ses fils (1151–1204)* (Paris 1938).

Brooke, C. N. L. and Keir, G., *London 800–1216: The Shaping of a City* (London 1975).

Brooks, F. W., 'William de Wrotham and the office of Keeper of the King's Ports and Galleys', *English Historical Review*, 40 (1925), pp. 570–9.

Broussilon, B. de, *La Maison de Craon 1050–1480*, 2 vols. (Paris 1893).

Brown, R. A., 'The treasury of the later twelfth century', in *Studies presented to Sir Hilary Jenkinson*, ed. J. Conway Davies (London 1957), pp. 35–49.

'A list of castles 1154–1216', *English Historical Review*, 74 (1959), pp. 249–80.

Burrows, Montagu, *The Family of Brocas of Beaurepaire and Roche Court* (London 1886).

Callus, D. A., 'Introduction of Aristotelian learning to Oxford', *Proceedings of the British Academy*, 29 (1943), pp. 229–81.

Cannon, H. L., 'The battle of Sandwich and Eustace the Monk', *English Historical Review*, 27 (1912), pp. 649–70.

Carlin, M., 'The reconstruction of Winchester House, Southwark', *London Topographical Record*, 25 (1989), pp. 33–57.

Carpenter, D. A., 'Sheriffs of Oxfordshire and their subordinates 1194–1236', unpublished D.Phil. thesis (Oxford 1974).

'The decline of the curial sheriff in England 1194–1258', *English Historical Review* (1976), pp. 1–32.

'The fall of Hubert de Burgh', *Journal of British Studies*, 19 (2) (1980), pp. 1–17.

'Kings, magnates and society: the personal rule of King Henry III, 1234–1258', *Speculum*, 60 (1985), pp. 39–70.

'The gold treasure of King Henry III', in *Thirteenth Century England I*, ed. P. R. Coss and S. D. Lloyd (Woodbridge 1986), pp. 61–88.

'Chancellor Ralph de Neville and the plans of political reform 1215–1258', in *Thirteenth Century England II*, ed. P. R. Coss and S. D. Lloyd (Woodbridge 1988), pp. 69–80.

The Minority of Henry III (London 1990).

'King Henry III's statute against aliens: July 1263', *English Historical Review*, 107 (1992), pp. 925–44.

Cate, J. L., 'The church and market reform in England during the reign of Henry III', in *Medieval and Historiographical Essays in Honor of James Westfall Thompson*, ed. J. L. Cate and E. N. Anderson (Chicago 1938), pp. 27–65.

Cazel, F. A. Jr, 'The fifteenth of 1225', *Bulletin of the Institute of Historical Research*, 34 (1961), pp. 67–81.

'The legates Guala and Pandulf', in *Thirteenth Century England II*, ed. P. R. Coss and S. D. Lloyd (Woodbridge 1988), pp. 15–21.

'Intertwined careers: Hubert de Burgh and Peter des Roches', *The Haskins Society Journal I*, ed. R. B. Patterson (London 1989), pp. 173–81.

Chaytor, H. J., *Savaric de Mauléon, Baron and Troubador* (Cambridge 1939).

Cheney, C. R., 'The papal legate and the English monasteries in 1206', *English Historical Review*, 46 (1931), pp. 443–52.

'The alleged deposition of King John', in *Studies in Medieval History presented to F. M. Powicke*, ed. R. W. Hunt et al. (Oxford 1948), pp. 100–16.

'King John and the papal Interdict', *Bulletin of the John Rylands Library*, 31 (1948), pp. 295–317.

'King John's reaction to the papal Interdict in England', *Transactions of the Royal Historical Society*, 4th series, 21 (1949), pp. 129–50.

English Bishops' Chanceries 1100–1250 (Manchester 1950).

'The eve of Magna Carta', *Bulletin of the John Rylands Library*, 38 (1955–6), pp. 311–41.

'Cardinal John of Ferentino, papal legate in England in 1206', *English Historical Review*, 76 (1961), pp. 654–60.

'The church and Magna Carta', *Theology*, 68 (1965), pp. 266–72.

'A recent view of the papal Interdict on England 1208–1214', in *Studies in Church History*, iii, ed. G. J. Cuming (Leiden 1966), pp. 159–68.

Hubert Walter (London 1967).

'The twenty-five barons of Magna Carta', *Bulletin of the John Rylands Library*, 50 (1967–8), pp. 280–307.

Medieval Texts and Studies (Oxford 1973).

Pope Innocent III and England (Stuttgart 1976).

Chergé, M. de, 'Mémoire historique sur l'abbaye de Montierneuf de Poitiers', *Mémoires de la Société des Antiquaires de l'Ouest*, series 1, xi (1844), pp. 147–276.

Chew, H. M., *The English Ecclesiastical Tenants in Chief and Knight Service* (Oxford 1932).

Chrimes, S. B., *An Introduction to the Administrative History of Mediaeval England*, 3rd edn (Oxford 1966).

Church, S. D., 'The knights of the household of King John: a question of numbers', in *Thirteenth Century England IV*, ed. P. R. Coss and S. D. Lloyd (Woodbridge 1992), pp. 151–65.

'The earliest English muster roll, 18/19 December 1215', *Historical Research*, 67 (1994), pp. 1–17.

Clanchy, M. T., 'Did Henry III have a policy?', *History*, 53 (1968), pp. 203–16.

England and its Rulers 1066–1272: Foreign Lordship and National Identity (Oxford 1983).

'Magna Carta and the common pleas', in *Studies in Medieval History presented to R. H. C. Davis*, ed. H. Mayr-Harting and R. I. Moore (London 1985), pp. 219–32.

Clermont-Ganneau, 'L'origine de Philippe d'Aubigny', *Revue Critique d'Histoire et de Littérature*, new series, 1 (1876), pt. ii, pp. 206–7.

Collins, A. J., 'The documents of the Great Charter of 1215', *Proceedings of the British Academy*, 34 (1948), pp. 233–79.

Colvin, H. M., *The White Canons in England* (Oxford 1951).

The History of the King's Works Volume I: The Middle Ages, ed. R. A. Brown, H. M. Colvin and A. J. Taylor (London 1963).

Conklin, G., 'Les Capetiens et l'affaire de Dol de Bretagne, 1179–1194', *Revue d'Histoire de l'Eglise de France*, 78 (1992), pp. 241–63.

Contamine, P., *War in the Middle Ages*, translated by M. Jones (Oxford 1984).

Cox, E. L., *The Eagles of Savoy* (Princeton 1974).

Crook, D., 'The struggle over forest boundaries in Nottinghamshire 1218–1227', *Transactions of the Thoroton Society of Nottinghamshire*, 83 (1979), pp. 35–45.

Records of the General Eyre (London 1982).

Crook, J., 'St Swithun of Winchester', in *Winchester Cathedral, Nine Hundred Years 1093–1993*, ed. J. Crook (Chichester 1993).

Crouch, D., *William Marshal* (London 1990).

'The last adventure of Richard Siward', *Morgannwg*, 35 (1991), pp. 7–30.

'Normans and Anglo-Normans: a divided aristocracy?', in *England and Normandy in the Middle Ages*, ed. D. Bates and A. Curry (London 1994), pp. 51–67.

Davis, R. H. C., 'William of Tyre', in *Relations between East and West in the Middle Ages*, ed. D. Baker (Edinburgh 1973), pp. 64–76.

Denholm-Young, N., 'A letter from the council to Pope Honorius III 1220–1', *English Historical Review* (1945), pp. 88–96.

Richard of Cornwall (Oxford 1947).

Collected Papers (Cardiff 1969).

Draper, P., 'The retrochoir of Winchester Cathedral', *Journal of the Society of Architectural Historians of Great Britain*, 21 (1978), pp. 1–16.

'King John and St Wulfstan', *Journal of Medieval History*, 10 (1984), pp. 41–50.

Dubois, G., 'Recherches sur la vie de Guillaume des Roches', *Bibliothèque de l'Ecole des Chartes*, xxx (1869), pp. 378–424, xxxii (1871), pp. 88–146, xxxiv (1873), pp. 503–41.

Duggan, A. J., 'The cult of St Thomas Becket in the thirteenth century', in *St Thomas Cantilupe Bishop of Hereford, Essays in his Honour*, ed. M. Jancey (Hereford 1982), pp. 21–44.

Duggan, C., 'Richard of Ilchester, royal servant and bishop', *Transactions of the Royal Historical Society*, 5th series, 16 (1966), pp. 1–21.

Eales, R., 'Henry III and the end of the Anglo-Norman earldom of Chester', in *Thirteenth Century England I*, ed. P. R. Coss and S. D. Lloyd (Woodbridge 1986), pp. 100–13.

Easterling, R. C., *The Franciscans and Dominicans of Exeter*, History of Exeter research group monograph, iii (Exeter 1927).

Bibliography

Emden, A. B., *A Biographical Register of the University of Oxford to AD 1500*, 3 vols. (Oxford 1957–9).

Finucane, R. C., *Miracles and Pilgrims* (London 1977).

Flower, C. T., *Introduction to the Curia Regis Rolls 1199–1230*, Selden Society, lxii (1943).

Forey, A. J., 'The military order of St Thomas of Acre', *English Historical Review*, 92 (1977), pp. 481–503.

Foster, J. E., 'The connection of the church of Chesterton with the abbey of Vercelli', *Proceedings of the Cambridge Antiquarian Society*, 13, new series 7 (1908–9), pp. 185–211.

Galbraith, V. H., *Studies in the Public Records* (London 1948).

Gams, P. B., *Series Episcoporum Ecclesiae Catholicae* (Ratisbon 1873).

Gasquet, F. A., *Henry the Third and the Church* (London 1910).

Geraud, H., 'Le comte Evêque', *Bibliothèque de l'Ecole des Chartes*, v (1843–4), pp. 8–36.

Gibbs, M. and Lang, J., *Bishops and Reform 1215–1272 with special reference to the Lateran Council of 1215* (Oxford 1934).

Giles, K. R., 'Two English bishops in the Holy Land', *Nottingham Medieval Studies*, 31 (1987), pp. 46–57.

Gillingham, J., *The Life and Times of Richard I* (London 1973).

'Richard I and the science of war in the Middle Ages', in *War and Government in the Middle Ages, Essays in Honour of J. O. Prestwich*, ed. J. Gillingham and J. C. Holt (Woodbridge 1984), pp. 78–91.

'War and chivalry in the "History of William the Marshal"', in *Thirteenth Century England II*, ed. P. R. Coss and S. D. Lloyd (Woodbridge 1988), pp. 1–13.

Richard the Lionheart, 2nd edn (London 1989).

'Conquering the barbarians: war and chivalry in twelfth-century Britain', *The Haskins Society Journal IV*, ed. R. B. Patterson (Woodbridge 1993), pp. 67–84.

Richard Coeur de Lion: Kingship, Chivalry and War in the Twelfth Century (London 1994).

Graham, R., 'An appeal for the church and buildings of Kingsmead Priory c.1220', *The Antiquaries Journal*, 11 (1931), pp. 51–4.

Gransden, A., *Historical Writing in England 550–1307* (London 1974).

Griffifths, Q., 'The Capetian kings and St Martin of Tours', *Studies in Medieval and Renaissance History*, 19 (1987), pp. 83–125.

Hardy, T. Duffus, *Descriptive Catalogue of Materials Relating to the History of Great Britain and Ireland*, 3 vols., Rolls Series (London 1862–5).

Harris, B. E., 'King John and the sheriffs' farms', *English Historical Review*, 79 (1964), pp. 532–42.

Havet, J., 'Des gardiens et seigneurs des Iles Normandes (1198–1461)', *Bibliothèque de l'Ecole des Chartes*, xxxvii (1876), pp. 183–237.

'Philippe d'Aubigny', *Revue Critique d'Histoire et de Litterature*, new series, i (1876), part ii, pp. 173–4, 398–9.

Heads of Religious Houses, England and Wales 940–1216, ed. D. Knowles, C. N. L. Brooke and V. C. M. London (Cambridge 1972).

Bibliography

Hill, R., *Ecclesiastical Letter Books of the Thirteenth Century* (Oxford 1936).

Hinnesbusch, W. A., *The Early English Friar Preachers* (Rome 1951).

Holdsworth, C. J., 'John of Ford and the Interdict', *English Historical Review*, 78 (1963), pp. 705–14.

Holt, J. C., 'Philip Mark and the Shrievalty of Nottinghamshire and Derbyshire in the early thirteenth century', *Transactions of the Thoroton Society of Nottinghamshire*, 56 (1952), pp. 8–24.

'The making of Magna Carta', *English Historical Review*, 72 (1957), pp. 401–22.

'A vernacular French text of Magna Carta 1215', *English Historical Review*, 89 (1974), pp. 346–64.

'The end of the Anglo-Norman realm', *Proceedings of the British Academy* (1975), pp. 223–65.

'The loss of Normandy and royal finance', in *War and Government in the Middle Ages: Essays in Honour of J. O. Prestwich*, ed. J. Gillingham and J. C. Holt (Woodbridge 1984), pp. 92–105.

Magna Carta and Medieval Government (London 1985).

'Feudal society and the family in early medieval England, iv: the heiress and the alien', *Transactions of the Royal Historical Society*, 5th series, 35 (1985), pp. 1–28.

'The "Casus Regis": the law and politics of succession in the Plantagenet dominions 1185–1247', in *Law in Mediaeval Life and Thought*, ed. E. B. King and S. J. Ridyard (Sewanee 1990), pp. 21–42.

Magna Carta, 2nd edn (Cambridge 1992).

The Northerners, 2nd edn (Oxford 1992).

Howell, M., *Regalian Right in Medieval England* (London 1963).

Hoyt, R. S., *The Royal Demesne in English Constitutional History 1066–1272* (New York 1950).

Hunt, R. W., 'English learning in the late twelfth century', *Transactions of the Royal Historical Society*, 4th series, 19 (1936), pp. 1–35.

The Schools and the Cloister (Oxford 1984).

Hyams, P. R., Review of S. F. C. Milsom, *The Legal Framework of Medieval Feudalism*, *English Historical Review*, 93 (1978), pp. 856–61.

Jaeger, C. S., 'The courtier bishop in "Vitae" from the tenth to the twelfth century', *Speculum*, 58 (1983), pp. 291–325.

Johnston, S. H. F., 'The lands of Hubert de Burgh', *English Historical Review*, 50 (1935), pp. 418–32.

Jolliffe, J. E. A., 'The chamber and the castle treasures under King John', in *Studies in Medieval History presented to F. M. Powicke*, ed. R. W. Hunt et al. (Oxford 1948), pp. 117–42.

'The Camera Regis under Henry II', *English Historical Review*, 68 (1953), pp. 1–21, 337–62.

Angevin Kingship (London 1955).

Jouet, R., *Et la Normandie devint Française* (Paris 1983).

Kay, R., 'Wendover's last annal', *English Historical Review*, 84 (1969), pp. 779–85.

Bibliography

Keene, D., *Survey of Medieval Winchester*, Winchester Studies II, 2 vols. (Oxford 1985).

Winchester in the Early Middle Ages, ed. D. Keene et al., Winchester Studies I (Oxford 1976).

Keeney, B. C., *Judgment by Peers* (Cambridge, Mass. 1949).

King, D. L. C. Cathcart, *Castellarium Anglicanum*, 2 vols. (New York 1982).

Knowles, M. D., 'The Canterbury election of 1205–6', *English Historical Review*, 53 (1938), pp. 211–20.

The Monastic Order in England (Cambridge 1940).

Koudelka, V. J., 'Notes pour servir à l'histoire de S. Dominique', *Archivum Fratrum Praedicatorum*, 35 (1965), pp. 1–15.

Labarge, M. Wade, *Simon de Montfort* (London 1962).

Lambron de Lignim, H., 'Girard d'Athée', *Touraine Mélanges Historiques* ii (Tours 1855).

Lawrence, C. H., *St Edmund of Abingdon* (Oxford 1960).

Lecointre-Dupont, M., 'Pierre des Roches, Trésorier de Saint-Hilaire de Poitiers, evêque de Winchester', *Mémoires de la Société des Antiquaires de l'Ouest*, series 1, xxxii (1868), pt. 1, pp. 3–16.

Le Faye, D., 'Selborne priory 1233–1486', *Proceedings of the Hampshire Field Club*, 30 (1973), pp. 47–71.

Legge, M. Dominica, 'William the Marshal and Arthur of Brittany', *Bulletin of the Institute of Historical Research*, 55 (1982), pp. 18–24.

Le Neve, John, *Fasti Ecclesiae Anglicanae 1066–1300*, revised edn by D. E. Greenway, 4 vols. (London 1968–).

Levett, A. E., *Studies in Manorial History*, ed. H. Cam (Oxford 1938).

Leyser, K., 'Frederick Barbarossa, Henry II and the hand of St James', in *Medieval Germany and its Neighbours 900–1250* (London 1982), pp. 215–40.

Lipman, V. D., *The Jews of Medieval Norwich*, Jewish Historical Society (1967).

Lloyd, S. D., 'Political crusades in England c.1215–17 and c.1264–5', in *Crusade and Settlement: Papers Read at the First Conference of the Society for the Study of the Crusades and the Latin East and Presented to R. C. Smail*, ed. P. W. Edbury (Cardiff 1985), pp. 113–20.

English Society and the Crusade 1216–1307 (Oxford 1988).

'Crusader knights and the land market in the thirteenth century', in *Thirteenth Century England II*, ed. P. R. Coss and S. D. Lloyd (Woodbridge 1988), pp. 119–36.

Longuemar, M. de, 'Essai historique sur l'église collegiale de Saint-Hilaire le Grand de Poitiers', *Mémoires de la Société des Antiquaires de l'Ouest*, series 1, xxiii (1857), pp. 1–381.

Loyd, L. C., *The Origins of Some Anglo-Norman Families*, Harleian Society, ciii (1961).

Lunt, W. E., *Financial Relations of the Papacy with England to 1327* (Cambridge, Mass. 1939).

Lydon, J., 'The expansion and consolidation of the colony, 1215–54', in *A New History of Ireland II: Medieval Ireland 1169–1534*, ed. A. Cosgrave (Oxford 1987), pp. 156–78.

Bibliography

Mackenzie, H., 'The anti-foreign movement in England 1231–1232', in *Anniversary Essays in Mediaeval History by Students of Charles Homer Haskins*, ed. C. H. Taylor and J. L. La Monte (Boston 1929), pp. 183–203.

Maddicott, J. R., 'Magna Carta and the local community 1215–1259', *Past and Present*, 102 (1984), pp. 25–65.

'The crusade taxation of 1268–70 and the development of Parliament', in *Thirteenth Century England II*, ed. P. R. Coss and S. D. Lloyd (Woodbridge 1988), pp. 93–117.

Maitland, F. W., *The History of English Law*, 2 vols., ed. F. Pollock and F. W. Maitland 2nd edn (Cambridge 1968).

Major, K., 'The "familia" of archbishop Stephen Langton', *English Historical Review*, 48 (1933), pp. 529–53.

Mason, E., 'The king, the chamberlain and Southwick priory', *Bulletin of the Institute of Historical Research*, 53 (1980), pp. 1–10.

Matthew, D. J. A., *The Norman Conquest* (London 1966).

Maussabré, F. de, 'Généalogie historique', *Compte Rendu des Travaux de la Société du Departement de l'Indre à Paris*, year 3 (Paris 1853–6), ch. 5, pp. 132–62.

Mayer, H. E., *The Crusades*, translated by J. Gillingham (Oxford 1972).

McKechnie, W. S., *Magna Carta: A Commentary on the Great Charter of King John*, 2nd edn (Glasgow 1914).

Meekings, C. A. F., 'Martin Pateshull and William de Raleigh', *Bulletin of the Institute of Historical Research*, 26 (1953), pp. 157–80.

'Adam fitz William (d.1238)', *Bulletin of the Institute of Historical Research*, 34 (1961), pp. 1–15.

'The early years of Netley Abbey', *Journal of Ecclesiastical History*, 30 (1979), pp. 1–37

Studies in Thirteenth Century Justice and Administration (London 1981).

Meffre, J. A., 'Tablette chronologique de l'histoire de l'abbaye de Marmoutier', *Mémoires de la Société Archéologique de la Touraine*, xvii (1865), pp. 543–97.

Mills, M. H., 'The reforms at the Exchequer 1232–42', *Transactions of the Royal Historical Society*, 4th series, 10 (1927), pp. 111–34.

Milsom, S. F. C., *The Legal Framework of English Feudalism* (Cambridge 1976).

Mitchell, J. H., *The Court of the Connétable* (Yale 1947).

Mitchell, S. K., *Studies in Taxation under John and Henry III* (New Haven 1914).

Musset, L., 'Quelques problèmes posés par l'annexation de la Normandie au Domaine Royal Français', in *La France de Philippe-Auguste: Le temps des Mutations*, ed. R. H. Bautier (Paris 1982), pp. 291–309.

Norgate, K., *The Minority of Henry III* (London 1912).

Nortier, M. and Baldwin, J. W., 'Contributions à l'étude des finances de Philippe Auguste', *Bibliothèque de l'Ecole des Chartes*, cxxxviii (1980), pp. 5–33.

Orpen, G. H., *Ireland under the Normans*, 4 vols. (Oxford 1911–20).

Otway-Ruthven, A. J., *A History of Medieval Ireland*, 2nd edn (London 1980).

Oury, G.-R. (ed.), *Histoire Religieuse de la Touraine* (Tours 1975).

Painter, S., *William Marshal* (Baltimore 1933).

The Scourge of the Clergy: Peter of Dreux, Duke of Brittany (Baltimore 1937).

Studies in the History of the English Feudal Barony (Baltimore 1943).

King John (Baltimore 1949).

Poggiaspella, F., 'La chiesa e la partecipazione dei chierici alla guerra nella legislazione conciliare fino alle Decretali di Gregorio IX', *Ephemerides Iuris Canonice*, xv (1959), pp. 140–53.

Powell, J. M., *Anatomy of a Crusade 1213–1221* (Philadelphia 1986).

Powicke, F. M., 'The Chancery during the minority of Henry III', *English Historical Review*, 23 (1908), pp. 220–35.

'Per Iudicium Parium vel per Legem Terrae', in *Magna Carta Commemoration Essays*, ed. H. E. Malden (London 1917), pp. 96–121.

'Master Alexander of St Albans – a literary muddle', in *Essays in History presented to Reginald Lane Poole*, ed. H. W. C. Davis (Oxford 1927), pp. 246–60.

Stephen Langton (Oxford 1928).

'The bull "Mirarmur Plurimum" and a letter to Archbishop Stephen Langton, 5 September 1215', *English Historical Review*, 44 (1929), pp. 86–93.

The Christian Life in the Middle Ages (Oxford 1935).

'The archbishop of Rouen, John de Harcourt and Simon de Montfort in 1260', *English Historical Review*, 51 (1936), pp. 108–13.

'The oath of Bromholm', *English Historical Review*, 56 (1941), pp. 529–48.

'Master Simon the Norman', *English Historical Review*, 58 (1943), pp. 330–43.

King Henry III and the Lord Edward, 2 vols. (Oxford 1947).

The Loss of Normandy 1189–1204, 2nd edn (Manchester 1960).

Powicke, M. R., 'Distraint of knighthood and military obligation under Henry III', *Speculum*, 25 (1950), pp. 457–70.

Rédet, L., 'Observations sur les noms de lieux dans le Département de la Vienne', *Mémoires de la Société des Antiquaires de l'Ouest*, series 1, xiii (1846), pp. 301–67.

Reynolds, S., 'The rulers of London in the twelfth century', *History*, 57 (1972), pp. 337–57.

Rhodes, W. E., 'Peter des Roches', *Dictionary of National Biography*, 60 vols. (London 1885–99), xlv, pp. 52–6 *sub* 'Peter'.

Richardson, H. G., 'William of Ely, the king's treasurer (?1195–1215)', *Transactions of the Royal Historical Society*, 4th series, 15 (1932), pp. 45–90.

'Glanville continued', *The Law Quarterly Review*, 54 (1938), pp. 383–98.

'The morrow of the Great Charter' and 'An addendum', *Bulletin of the John Rylands Library*, xxviii (1944), pp. 442–3, xxix (1945), pp. 184–200.

'The chamber under Henry II', *English Historical Review* (1954), pp. 596–611.

The English Jews under Angevin Kings (London 1960).

Bibliography

Ridgeway, H., 'King Henry III and the "aliens"', in *Thirteenth Century England II*, ed. P. R. Coss and S. D. Lloyd (Woodbridge 1988), pp. 81–92.

'Foreign favourites and Henry III's problems of patronage, 1247–1258', *English Historical Review*, 104 (1989), pp. 590–610.

'William de Valence and his "Familiares", 1247–72', *Historical Research*, 65 (1992), pp. 239–57.

Ridyard, S. J., '"Condigna Veneratio": post-Conquest attitudes to the saints of the Anglo-Saxons', in *Anglo-Norman Studies*, ed. R. A. Brown, ix (1986), pp. 179–206.

Robinson, I. S., *The Papacy 1073–1198: Continuity and Innovation* (Cambridge 1990).

Rowlands, I., 'King John, Stephen Langton and Rochester Castle, 1213–15', in *Studies in Medieval History presented to R. Allen Brown*, ed. C. Harper-Bill, C. J. Holdsworth and J. L. Nelson (Woodbridge 1989), pp. 267–79.

Salmon, A., 'Nouveaux documents sur Girard d'Athée', *Mémoires de la Société Archéologique de Touraine*, xiii (1862), pp. 193–213.

Saltman, A., *Theobald Archbishop of Canterbury* (London 1956).

Sanders, I. J., *English Baronies: A Study of their Origin and Descent 1086–1327* (Oxford 1960).

Sandys, A., 'The financial and administrative importance of the London Temple in the thirteenth century', in *Essays in Medieval History presented to T. F. Tout*, ed. A. G. Little and F. M. Powicke (Manchester 1925), pp. 147–62.

Sayers, J., *Papal Government and England during the Pontificate of Honorius III (1216–1227)* (Cambridge 1984).

Scammell, G. V., *Hugh de Puiset Bishop of Durham* (Cambridge 1956).

Smalley, B., 'Robert Bacon and the early Dominican school at Oxford', *Transactions of the Royal Historical Society*, 4th series, 30 (1948), pp. 1–19.

Smith, J. Beverley, 'The Treaty of Lambeth, 1217', *English Historical Review*, 94 (1979), pp. 562–79.

Smith, J. M. H., 'The "archbishopric" of Dol and the ecclesiastical politics of ninth-century Brittany', *Studies in Church History*, 18 (1982), pp. 59–70.

Southern, R. W., 'England's first entry into Europe', in *Medieval Humanism and other Studies* (Oxford 1970), pp. 135–57.

Robert Grosseteste: The Growth of an English Mind in Medieval Europe (Oxford 1986).

Spear, D. S., 'The Norman empire and the secular clergy 1066–1204', *Journal of British Studies*, 21 (1982), pp. 1–10.

Squibb, G. D., *The High Court of Chivalry* (Oxford 1959).

Stacey, R. C., *Politics, Policy and Finance under Henry III 1216–1245* (Oxford 1987).

'1240–60: a watershed in Anglo-Jewish relations?', *Historical Research*, 61 (1988), pp. 135–50.

Stenton, D. M., 'King John and the courts of justice', *Proceedings of the British Academy*, 49 (1958), pp. 103–27.

Bibliography

Stevenson, E. R., 'The escheator', in *The English Government at Work 1327–1336*, ed. W. H. Dunham, W. A. Morris, J. R. Strayer and J. F. Willard, 3 vols. (Cambridge, Mass. 1940–50), ii, pp. 109–67.

Stewart-Brown, R., 'The end of the Norman earldom of Chester', *English Historical Review*, 35 (1920), pp. 26–53.

Stones, J. and L., 'Bishop Ralph Neville, chancellor to King Henry III and his correspondence: a reappraisal', *Archives*, 16 (1984), pp. 227–57.

Storrs, C. M., 'Jacobean pilgrims from England from the early twelfth to the late fifteenth century', unpublished M.A. thesis (London 1964).

Titow, J. Z., 'Land and population on the Bishop of Winchester's estates 1209–1350', unpublished Ph.D. thesis (Cambridge 1962).

'The decline of the fair of St Giles Winchester in the thirteenth and fourteenth centuries', *Nottingham Medieval Studies*, 31 (1987), pp. 58–75.

Tout, T. F., *Chapters in the Administrative History of Medieval England: The Wardrobe, the Chamber and the Small Seals*, 6 vols. (Manchester 1920–33).

Turner, G. J., 'The minority of Henry III', 2 parts, *Transactions of the Royal Historical Society*, 2nd series, 18 (1904), pp. 245–95, 3rd series, 1 (1907), pp. 205–62.

Turner, R. V., *The King and his Courts: The Role of John and Henry III in the Administration of Justice, 1199–1240* (New York 1968).

'William de Forz, count of Aumale: an early thirteenth century baron', *Proceedings of the American Philosophical Society*, 115 (1971), pp. 221–49.

'The judges of King John: their background and training', *Speculum*, 51 (1976), pp. 447–61.

The English Judiciary in the Age of Glanvill and Bracton, c.1176–1239 (Cambridge 1985).

Men Raised from the Dust: Administrative Service and Upward Mobility in Angevin England (Philadelphia 1988).

Tyerman, C., *England and the Crusades 1095–1588* (Chicago 1988).

Van Cleve, T. C., 'The crusade of Frederick II', in *A History of the Crusades*, ed. K. M. Setton, vol. ii, *The Later Crusades*, ed. R. L. Wolff and H. W. Hazard (Wisconsin 1969), ch. 12.

The Emperor Frederick II of Hohenstaufen (London 1973).

Vaughan, R., *Matthew Paris*, 2nd edn (Cambridge 1979).

Vincent, N. C., 'Hugh de Neville and his prisoners', *Archives*, 88 (1992), pp. 190–7.

'Jews, Poitevins, and the bishop of Winchester, 1231–1234', in *Studies in Church History*, 29, ed. D. Wood (Oxford 1992), pp. 119–32.

'The first quarrel between Simon de Montfort and King Henry III', in *Thirteenth Century England IV*, ed. P. R. Coss and S. D. Lloyd (Woodbridge 1992), pp. 167–77.

'The origins of the chancellorship of the Exchequer', *English Historical Review*, 108 (1993), pp. 105–21.

'A roll of knights summoned to campaign in 1213', *Historical Research*, 66 (1993), pp. 89–97.

Bibliography

'The early years of Keynsham Abbey', *Transactions of the Bristol and Gloucestershire Archaeological Society*, 111 (1993), pp. 95–113.

'The origins of the Winchester Pipe Rolls', *Archives*, 21 (1994), pp. 25–42.

'Simon of Atherfield (d.1211): a martyr to his wife', *Analecta Bollandiana* (forthcoming 1996).

'Master Alexander of Stainsby, Bishop of Coventry and Lichfield 1224–1238', *Journal of Ecclesiastical History* 46 (forthcoming 1995).

'The election of Pandulph Verracclo as bishop of Norwich (1215)', *Historical Research*, 68 (1995), pp. 143–63.

'Two papal letters on the wearing of the Jewish badge, 1221 and 1229', *Transactions of the Jewish Historical Society* (forthcoming 1996).

'Philip de Aubigné', 'Gilbert Basset', 'Robert of Thwing' and 'Walter Mauclerk', *New Dictionary of National Biography* (Oxford forthcoming).

'Master Michael Belet and the foundation of Wroxton priory', *Oxfordshire Record Society* (forthcoming).

'Master Simon Langton, King John and the court of France' (forthcoming).

Vinogradoff, P., 'Magna Carta C.39, Nullus Liber Homo etc.', in *Magna Carta Commemoration Essays*, ed. H. E. Malden (London 1917), pp. 78–95.

Waite, W. C., 'Johannes de Garlandia, poet and musician', *Speculum*, 35 (1960), pp. 179–90.

Wakefield, W. L., *Heresy, Crusade and Inquisition in Southern France 1100–1250* (London 1974).

Waley, D., *The Papal State in the Thirteenth Century* (London 1961).

Walker, D., 'Crown and episcopacy under the Normans and Angevins', in *Anglo-Norman Studies*, v, ed. R. Allen Brown (Woodbridge 1983), pp. 220–33.

Walker, R. F., 'The Anglo-Welsh wars 1217–1267; with special reference to English military developments', unpublished D. Phil. thesis (Oxford 1954).

'Hubert de Burgh and Wales 1218–1232', *English Historical Review*, 87 (1972), pp. 465–94.

'The supporters of Richard Marshal, earl of Pembroke, in the rebellion of 1233–1234', *Welsh Historical Review*, 17 (1994), pp. 41–65.

Warren, W. L., *King John* (London 1961).

Watt, J. A., 'The English episcopate, the state and the Jews: the evidence of the thirteenth century conciliar decrees', in *Thirteenth Century England II*, ed. P. R. Coss and S. D. Lloyd (Woodbridge 1988), pp. 137–47.

Waugh, S. L., *The Lordship of England* (Princeton 1988).

Weiss, M., 'The castellan: the early career of Hubert de Burgh', *Viator*, 5 (1974), pp. 235–52.

West, F., *The Justiciarship in England 1066–1232* (Cambridge 1966).

Wilkinson, B., 'The council and the crisis of 1233–4', *Bulletin of the John Rylands Library*, 27 (1942–3), pp. 387–91.

Woodruff, C. Everleigh, 'The financial aspect of the cult of St Thomas of Canterbury', *Archaeologia Cantiana*, 44 (1932), pp. 13–32.

INDEX

In the spelling of personal names I have attempted to adhere to the eminently sensible guidelines laid down by John Le Patourel. Surnames derived from locations in England are preceded by the preposition 'of', with the place name spelt according to its standard modern form: thus Stephen of Seagrave, not Stephen de Segrave. French toponyms take the preposition 'de', as in the name Geoffrey de Caux, and once again, wherever possible have been spelt according to the appropriate French place name, even when an Anglicized version has gained currency: thus William de Briouze, rather than William de Braose. Toponyms which cannot be identified with any particular location in England or France retain the preposition 'de'. French Christian names have been translated (Peter rather than Pierre), and Peter's surname de Rupibus rendered throughout as des Roches. Unfortunately, established usage makes it impossible to apply these rules in every case. The earl Warenne is so familiar, that to write of the earl Varenne would be considered hopelessly eccentric; 'Hubert of Burgh', native to Burgh next Aylsham in Norfolk, must remain Hubert de Burgh. In only one case have I deliberately set out to challenge convention. The bishop's nephew, traditionally known as Peter 'de Rivaux', is referred to throughout in the Latin version Peter de Rivallis. 'Rivaux' is a meaningless name, not French, Latin or English. Rivallis, although as yet unidentified as a toponym, can at least claim to follow medieval usage.

Index

Aethelwold, St, 6, 21, 246
Aigle (dep. Orne), honour of in England,
    286, 298, 300–1, 446, 450
  Gilbert de, 286
  Master Gilbert de, 33 n. 78
Aigueblanche (dep. Savoie), Peter de,
    bishop of Hereford, 35 n. 90
Aincourt (Ancourt, dep. Seine-Maritime),
    Nicola and Oliver de, 269
Airaines (dep. Somme), Master Robert de,
    163 n. 135
Airvault (dep. Deux-Sèvres), 27
Alban, St, 247
Albigensians, 85
  crusade against, 25, 67, 85, 87
Alconbury (Cambs.), 432 and n. 14, 445 n.
    75
Alençon (dep. Orne), Herbert de, 296–7
    and n. 177
Alexander II, king of Scotland, 276, 371,
    417–18, 426, 452 n. 107
Aliceholt (Hants.), forest of, 189 and n. 26
aliens, geographical origins of, 7, 26–30, 32,
    35–6, 293, 394
  amongst the English episcopate, 34–5 and
    n. 88, 324
  assimilation into English society, 38–9,
    158, 246–7, 326–7
  attack upon in Magna Carta, 111–12,
    119–21, 135
  as mercenaries and constables, 62–3, 65,
    87, 112, 114, 115–16, 118–20, 330,
    374, 382, 384, 388, 393, 395, 402,
    415
  coherence of as a political grouping,
    39–40, 156–7, 163, 457
  criticism of by King John, 112
  ease of encouraging alien clerks to
    England, 31–2
  marriages of, 38, 111 and n. 127, 121,
    414–15
  presentation of by historians, 6–13, 14ff.
  presentation of in the Bible, 7
  promotion of during the reign of Henry
    III, 156–63, 358, 374, 388, 391,
    393–5, 425, 429, 434, 459
  relations of with Peter des Roches, 32ff,
    65ff, 119, 156–63, 175–6, 182, 196,
    336, 476–7
  'xenophobia' towards, 37, 89, 120, 215,
    246, 305, 323–6, 364, 397, 426–7,
    459
Aliz, Roger, 415, 436
Allerton (N. Yorks.), 280

Alresford (Hants.), 128–9, 188
Alton (Hants.), 293, 333 n. 88
Amboise (dep. Indre-et-Loire), 23, 27 n. 62
Amicius, archdeacon of Surrey, 51
Amiens (dep. Somme), 47
Anagni (Italy), convent of Monte d'Oro at,
    303 n. 208
  convent of S. Maria de Gloria at, 469
Andely, John de, 237
Andover (Hants.), 468 n. 13
Andres (dep. Pas-de-Calais), William of,
    chronicler, 238 n. 51, 247–8, 252,
    393
Andwell (Hants.), Benedictine priory of,
    235
Angers (dep. Maine-et-Loire), abbey of St
    Nicholas at, 20
  bishop of, 250 n. 110
  collegiate church of St Martin at, 19
  dean of, 20 n. 27, 66–7
Angevin kingship, concept of, 8, 14
Angoulême (dep. Charente), lords of, 66
  Isabella of, queen of England, 46, 70–1
    and n. 128, 117, 131–2, 155, 204 n.
    110, 266, 271
Angoumois (France), 46
Anjou (France), 19, 20, 22–4, 26, 65, 103,
    120, 152, 262
  conquest of, 42–3
  Geoffrey count of, 19 n. 25, 45
  natives of, 8, 29, 34 n. 88, 40, 63, 250 n.
    110
  Plantagenet rule in, 45–6
Apethorpe (Northants.), 269, 298, 306–7,
    312
Apulia (Italy), 252
  Simon of, bishop of Exeter, 96, 98, 124,
    165, 168 n. 165, 207
Aquitaine, 43–5, 65
  church of, 47 n. 10
  Eleanor of, queen of England, 14, 23 n.
    43, 44
Aragon (Spain), 67, 87, 91
  King Pedro II of, 87
Ardfert (Ireland), John bishop of, 234–5,
    243 n. 75, 289 and n. 133, 369
Argentan (dep. Orne), Richard de, 311,
    328, 446
Argenton (dep. Deux-Sèvres), lady of, 250
    n. 110
Aristotle, teaching of the works of, 83, 369
Arley (Staffs. / Warwicks.), 341 n. 6, 381
Armagh (Ireland), see of, 75
Arthur, King, 480, *and see* Brittany

Index

Index

Index

Index

Index

Index

Inglesham (Wilts.), Master Peter of, 76

Innocent III, pope, 20, 50–52, 74–5, 78–81, 87, 90–1, 97, 118, 123–5, 208, 410
    letters of against Peter des Roches, 97–8

Interdict, papal upon England, 9, 65, 68–9, 73, 76–94, 98–9, 102–3, 115, 124, 167–8, 176, 366–7, 410
    against rebel lands 1215, 126
    blamed upon Peter des Roches, 133, 429

Ireland, 62, 66, 90, 103, 115, 172, 176, 184, 232, 234, 260–1, 265, 272, 285, 301, 307–8, 327, 330, 371, 373–5, 377, 385–6, 420, 423, 436, 441, 443–4, 448, 459
    Chancery of, 376
    Exchequer of, 274
    Justiciarship of, 297
    Richard Marshal's rebellion in, 339, 427–8, 430, 432, 438–40

Isabella, daughter of King John, 153, 160, 415 and n. 71, 427, 472, 475

Italy, 174, 228–9, 240, 253–4, 275, 427, 471, 473
    merchants of, 288, 363
    natives of active in England, 34 n. 88, 195, 303ff

Itchen (Hants.), river, 136

Ivinghoe (Bucks.), 128, 210, 415 n. 71, 440
    Benedictine priory of, 241

Jerome, St, 6

Jerusalem (Holy Land), 4, 22, 22 n. 41, 25, 247–9, 251–3, 255, 298
    king of, see Brienne
    patriarch of, 251, 253, 256

Jews, converts to Christianity, 81, 180, 240
    attacks upon, 130 and n. 92, 177–80, 288–90, 363–4, 443, 445, 449, 458
    custody of held by Peter de Rivallis, 298, 307
    debts to, 107, 109 n. 114, 143, 177–80, 359, 388
    Exchequer of, justices of, 275, 288, records of, 117 and nn. 26–7, 178
    legislation against, 363
    taxation of, 9, 59, 178, 267, 288, 363, 420, 433, 443

Joan, daughter of King John, 164

John, King, 1, 8, 10, 11, 23, 24 n. 49, 25–7, 29, 226, 228, 251, 256, 260, 266, 291–2, 309–11, 313, 321, 326, 330, 336, 347, 350–1, 355, 373, 378, 381, 385, 393, 395, 399, 410, 418–20, 425, 429, 454, 456, 462, 464

    ambitions for reconquest in France, 43, 49, 56, 61, 65, 76, 86, 89, 151
    bishops of, 34–5, 79, 85
    chamber of, 42, 57–8, 66, 77 and n. 161, 118 n. 29, 170–1, 192–3, 199 n. 81, and see wardrobe
    Chancery of, 56–7, 68–9, 93, 119, 145 n. 58, 332
    charter of free elections of, 115
    children of, 49, 70–1, 128, 131, 141, 153–4, and see Richard of Cornwall, Eleanor, Richard fitz Regis, Henry III, Isabella, Joan, Oliver
    Christmas courts of, 280–1
    clerks of, 18
    contacts with heretics, 85
    court of, 6, 9, 14, 46–7, 51, 55, 60–1, 69–72, 80, 82, 116, 121, 124, 156
    bribery at, 71–2
    religious activities at, 82
    crusade of, proposed, 118–19, 123, 214, 314
    death of, 131–2, 134
    deposition of, proposed, 85–6, 120
    destruction of a church at Bedford, 132, 145
    diplomatic initiatives by, 65–8
    enquiries into franchises and forests, 73–4
    evil councillors of, 4, 69
    Exchequer and treasury of, 56–60, 62, 64 n. 83, 73, 80, 86, 90, 100, 102, 104–5, 114, 116, 117–18, 193
    records of, 117–18 and nn. 26, 29
    Red Book of, 99, 209 n. 139
    excommunication of, 79–80
    expedition against the north, 86
    exploitation of vacant churches, 49, 53, 165 n. 146
    expulsion of Roman clergy, 83
    financial 'policy' and taxes of, 55–6, 58–61, 65, 76–7, 117–18, 176–7
    tallage for the lifting of the Interdict, 92–3, 107
    fine with Isaac of Norwich, 177
    fondness for hunting, 70
    friendships of, 70–1, 191, 479
    harrying of William de Briouze, 60–1, 372–3, 385
    hostage-taking by, 61–2, 109, 387
    household knights of, 63
    humour of, 70
    gifts to the religious for the soul of, 132 and n. 105, 159, 165 n. 145
    interventions in episcopal elections, 49–55

Index

La Marche (dep. Vienne), counts of, 28–9, *and see* Lusignan

Lamberseth, Gerard de, 388 n. 119

Lambeth (London), 81 n. 189, 301, 314
Treaty of, 140–1, 144, 151–2

Lancashire, 345 n. 28

Lancaster (Lancs.), William of, 143–4 and n. 51

Lanercost (Cumberland), chronicle of, 3, 480

Langeais (dep. Indre-et-Loire), 21 n. 36

Langton, Master Simon, 78, 85 n. 212, 196, 215, 283

Langton, Stephen, archbishop of
Canterbury, 1, 50, 78–81, 85 n. 212, 88, 90, 105, 108 n. 106, 115, 124, 168 and n. 165, 176–7, 178 n. 223, 181 n. 238, 200, 207–8, 224, 230, 235, 250, 254, 306 n. 223, 453, 468–9
complaints against in 1215, 118, 125
custody of Rochester and the Tower of London, 122–3, 125
diocesan legislation of, 173, 243
election to Canterbury, 75–6
opposition of to the appointment of monks as bishops, 167
prohibtion of tournaments by, 174
pupils of, 267, 367, 434, *and see* Richard Poer, Henry de Sandford, Stainsby
relations with Peter des Roches, 88, 91–100, 170–2, 183 n. 251, 211–12, 217, 243–6
returns to England in 1220, 196
role in the minority of Henry III, 165, 209, 212–13, 217, 260
role in the translation of St Birinus 243–6
steward of, 201
suspension of, 125, 126 n. 67, 165, 171
use of anti-alien rhetoric by, 37, 215, 305, 397

Langwith Hay (Yorks. E.R.), 367 n. 17

La Rochelle (dep. Charente-Maritime), 26 n. 60, 218, 429

Lateran Council of 1215, 124–5, 138, 172, 174, 177–8

Lecointre-Dupont, M., 15

Léhon (dep. Côtes-du-Nord), 458 n. 118

Leicester (Leics.), 214
honour of, 160 n. 120, 194 n. 50, 273–4, 277, 294, 297
Augustinian abbey of, 445
Jews of, expelled, 288, 363
Loretta countess of, 100, 161, 193 and n. 47

Robert (IV) earl of, 162 n. 127, *and see* Simon de Montfort

Leicestershire, 342, 347, 452 n. 109

Leinster (Ireland), 327, 373, 375, 416, 427–8, 430, 441

Le Loroux (dep. Indre-et-Loire), Cistercian abbey of, 21, 25

Le Mans (dep. Sarthe), 22, 32
abbey of La Couture at, 20, monk of, 95
abbey of St Pierre-de-la-Cour at, 20
cathedral church of, 20, 471, 478 n. 57

Lenton (Notts.), Benedictine priory of, 39

Leon (Spain), 67

L'Epau (dep. Sarthe), abbey of, 21

Le Perray-Neuf (dep. Sarthe), Premonstratensian abbey of, 25

L'Etoile (dep. Vienne), abbey of, 29

Les Andelys (dep. Eure), 19

Letart, Peter, 136 n. 10

Lettres, Nicholas de, 393 n. 135

Lexington, Robert de, 132 n. 105

Lichfield (Staffs.), bishops of, *see* Stainsby
cathedral church of, 48

Lilley (Herts.), 328 n. 68

Limburg (Netherlands), duke of, 248

Limerick (Ireland), 307

Limoges (dep. Haute-Vienne), 67
Master John of, 18, 214, 222, 224, 368, 410

Limousin (France), baronage of, 44

Lincoln, battle of, 4, 61, 136–40, 143, 146, 169
bishops of, Hugh, 35, 79, 93, 115, 158, 167–8, 178 n. 223, 203, 214, 216, 227, 232 and n. 15, 266–7, 367, 435 n. 27
castle, 345
cathedral church of, 48, 79 n. 173, 293
shrine of, 146
earl of, *see* John de Lacy
Elias of, 177
St Hugh of, 146, 166 n. 154, 243, *and see* William of Blois

Lincolnshire, 77, 176–7, 179, 261, 344–8

Lisieux (dep. Calvados), archdeacon of, 34 n. 88
Arnulf bishop of, 1

Lisle (IOW), Brian de, 96, 132, 212, 284, 301 n. 197, 308 n. 235, 319, 334, 341–2, 346–7, 393 n. 135, 412, 425, 462
and Walter his son, 388 n. 119

Lisle, Geoffrey de, 221, 237

Littlemore (Oxon.), Benedictine priory of, 241

Index

Index

Stephen, the clerk, 62 n. 72
Stephen, King, 56
Stogursey (Somerset), castle of, 216
Stoke by Clare (Suff.), Benedictine priory
  of, 171
Stokes, Master Alan of, official of Peter des
  Roches, 234–5
Strettondale (Shrops.), 379
Stubbs, William, 5, 11
Stuteville (Etoutteville-sur-Mer, dep. Seine-
  Maritime), Nicholas de, 143, 413
Stukeley (Cambs.), Jocelin of, 101 n. 66
Suffolk, sheriff of, 210, 344, 345 n. 28, 347
  n. 35
Sully, Raymond de, 403 n. 20
Surrey (England), 48, 157, 203, 220 n. 205,
  298, 306, 345 n. 28
  archdeacon of, 50, 230 n. 7, 234, 300
Sussex, 8, 77, 87, 101, 160, 176, 233, 286,
  298, 300–1, 306, 340 n. 2, 345–6,
  348, 349 n. 46, 352–3, 356, 394,
  436, 447, 460
Sutton (Surrey), 377–8, 384
Swanbourne (Bucks.), 440
Swanscombe (Kent), 340 n. 1
Swansea (W. Glamorgan), 302, 372–3
Swanwick (Hants.), church of, 145 n. 54, 162
Swapham, William de, 62
Swavesey (Cambs.), 161 n. 125
Swerford (Oxon.), Alexander of, 291
Swithun, St, 6, 21, 39, 246–7

Talbot (dep. Seine-Maritime), John, 288 n.
  119
Talbot, William de, 216, 297
Tamworth (Staffs.), 162, 361, 468
Tarrant (Dorset), 469
Tattershall (Lincs.), Robert of, 334
Taunton (Somerset), 3, 32, 64 nn. 83, 85,
  67 n. 103, 74, 98, 130–1, 147–8, 153
  nn. 92–3, 161, 168 and n. 165, 169,
  181, 182 n. 245, 189 n. 23, 210,
  215–16, 219–20, 232, 238, 243, 266,
  280, 322 n. 43, 468–9 and n. 18
  castle of, 62, 130, 148, 153, 160, 185, 400,
    402
  Jews of, 180
  park at, 74, 241
  priory of, 129
  wealth of, 48
  William of, brother, 129
Templars, 22 n. 40, 117, 129–30, 152, 227,
  231, 239–40, 287, 307, 338 n. 102, 352
Temple, Thomas of the, 239

Terre Normannorum, see Normandy
Testard, Master Robert, 361 n. 100
Testard, Thomas, 361 and n. 100
Teutonic knights, 249, 252, 472
Teutonicus, Terric, 136 n. 12
Teutonicus, Waleran, 320, 329
Tewkesbury (Gloucs.). 62 n. 72, 443
  annals of, 252–3, 361, 393, 411, 471 n. 23
Thanet, Isle of (Kent), 126, 137
Thetford (Norf.), Augustinian priory of,
  296 n. 177
Thompson, Benjamin, 392 n. 132
Thorney (Cambs.), Benedictine abbey of, 146
Thouars (dep. Deux-Sèvres), lords of, 29,
  66, 207, 218, 225
Thouars, Geoffrey de, treasurer of Poitiers,
  66, 132, 164, 225
Thurnham (Kent), Robert of, seneschal of
  Poitou and Gascony, 38 n. 101, 67
  and n. 103, 77, 96, 112, 249
Thurrock (Essex), 385
Thwing (E. Yorks. / Humberside), Robert
  of, 304–6
Tichborne (Hants.), 129
Tillières-sur-Avre (dep. Eure), honour of, 30
Tilty (Essex), Cistercian abbey of, 146
Tisted (Hants.), 236
Titchfield (Hants.), Premonstratensian
  abbey of, 4, 6, 65, 132, 162, 179,
  228, 236, 257, 275, 278, 284, 289,
  322, 341 n. 5, 358–9, 468
Titow, J. Z. 148, 188
Toledo (Spain), astronomers of, 255
Tonbridge (Kent), castle of, 270, 353, 356,
  447
Tongham (Surrey), 361 n. 100
Torksey (Lincs.), 138
Totnes (Devon), castle and honour of, 72,
  116, 130 n. 90, 192, 372–3, 400
Toulouse (dep. Haute-Garonne), Raymond
  VI count of, 67, 85, 87
Touraine (France), 18–21
  conquest of, 42–3
  natives of, 8, 24, 26–9, 32–4, 40–1, 111,
    135, 160, 200, 232, 388, 394
  tournaments, 174, 182, 196, 198, 280, 285,
    290, 377, 382 n. 84
Tours (dep. Indre-et-Loire), 19, 21, 23, 24
  n. 49, 200
  abbey of St Maurice at, 33
  archbishop of, 20, 47 n. 10, 52
  cathedral church of, 20
  obituaries in, 41, 478
  collegiate church of St Martin, 47 n. 10

Index

Tracy (dep. Manche), honour of, 30
Tregoz (Troisgots, dep. Manche), William
  de, 109
Trent (England), river, 55, 355
triplex forma pacis, 125
Troarn (dep. Calvados), abbey of St Martin
  at, 20
Trois Fontaines, Albert of, 289 n. 133
Trowbridge (Wilts.), 107, 108 n. 106
Troyes (dep. Aube), 239 n. 57
Trubleville (?Trouville, dep. Seine-
  Maritime), Henry de, 323 n. 52,
  371, 382, 388 n. 119, 393 n. 135,
  412, 425
Trumpington (Cambs.), 293
Turville (Tourville, dep. Eure), Maurice de,
  62, 116, 186, 188
Tusculum (Italy), Nicholas cardinal bishop
  of, papal legate, 83, 90–1, 92–3,
  95–7, 100, 114–15
Twyford (Bucks.), 381 n. 79, 382, 411, 413
Twyford (Hants.), 148, 173, 180, 189 n. 23,
  224
Tybista (unident., Cornwall), 154
Tyre (Holy Land), archbishop of, 174–5
Tyre, William of, 256 and n. 137

Ulcote, John de, 319, 347
Ulster (Ireland), 373, earl of, *see* Hugh de
  Lacy
Umfraville (Offranville, dep. Seine-
  Maritime), Gilbert de, 403 n. 20
Upavon (Wilts.), 312 n. 5, 334–6, 338, 377–
  8, 396–7, 442, 464
Upper Clatford (Hants.), 320 and n. 36
Upton (Northants.), 39 n. 103
Urric, Master, the engineer, 378 n. 64
Usk (Gwent), 399–403, 411–12, 415, 420–
  1, 426

Valence (dep. Charente), Aymer de, bishop
  of Winchester, 35 n. 90, 48 n. 15, 49
  William de, 13, 34
Valence (dep. Drôme), William bishop-
  elect of, 49, 452 n. 107, 474, 476
Valura, Joan de, 250 n. 110
Vaucouleurs (dep. Meuse)
Vautorte (dep. Mayenne), family, 400
  Reginald de, 72–3 and n. 138, 116, 130
  n. 90, 135, 192–3, 197 n. 68, 202
  Roger de, 72
Veile, Thomas le, 341 n. 10
Venuz, John de, 189–90
  Robert de, 73 n. 141

Vercelli (Italy), Augustinian abbey of S.
  Andrea at, 169
Verdun (dep. Meuse), Walter de, 63 n. 82,
  160–1, 200, 205, 209 n. 141, 214 n.
  172
Vere, Aubrey de, earl of Oxford, 106–7
  Hugh de, earl of Oxford, 266, 376, 383
  Robert de, earl of Oxford, 106, 115–16
Vermandois (France), 47
Verracclo, Giles, archdeacon of Ely, 178 n.
  223, *and see* Pandulph
Vescy, Eustace de, 86–7, 108
Vienne (unident., France), master Nicholas
  de, 36, 162
Vieuxpont (unident., ?Normandy), John
  de, 334
  Robert de, 56, 96, 213, 217 n. 184, 342
  n. 13
Vieux-Pont (dep. Calvados), honour of, 30
Villeneuve (dep. Loire-Atlantique), abbey
  of, 95
Viterbo (Italy), 471
Vivonne (dep. Vienne), Hugh de, 159, 183
  n. 251, 184, 202, 214, 297, 323, 371,
  462

Wacelin, Roger, 36, 38, 62 n. 72, 235, 322
  n. 43, 359–60, 394, 415 n. 71, 444 n.
  69, 466, 468 and n. 13
Wahull, barony of (Beds.), 193, 216
  John de, 216
Wake, Hugh, 413
Wakefield (W.Yorks.), Peter of, 85–6
Wales, 55, 62, 66, 69, 261, 327, 339, 371–4,
  377, 431, 436, 460
  bishops of, 126 n. 67
  campaigns against, 211–12, 265, 267,
  271–5, 353, 385–7, 418–19, 423,
  429, 432–3, 438, 459
  Gerald of, 120
  Marches of, 106, 260, 277, 302, 308, 314,
  328, 331, 357, 372–5, 377, 379–80,
  382–3, 386, 388, 400–2, 405–6, 411,
  420
  rebellion in, 86, 103–4, 399ff., 412,
  415, 417–18, 427–8
  men of, 131, 134, 281, 415
  mercenaries from, 140 n. 30
  negotiations with, 152–3, 195, 328, 372,
  375, 430, 432, 434, 437, 439–40, 442
  and n. 56
Wallingford (Berks. / Oxon.), 62, 115, 123,
  128, 153 n. 92, 154–5, 161 n. 121,
  173 n. 187, 211, 440

540

Index

Cambridge Studies in Medieval Life and Thought
Fourth series

* *Also published as a paperback*